Transforming the Personal,
Political, Historical and Sacred
in Theory and Practice

Transforming the Personal, Political, Historical and Sacred in Theory and Practice

Manfred Halpern

Editor
David T. Abalos

University of Scranton Press
Scranton and London

© 2009 University of Scranton Press
All rights reserved.

Library of Congress Cataloging-in-Publication Data

Halpern, Manfred.
  Transforming the personal, political, historical and sacred in theory and practice / Manfred Halpern.
      p. cm.
  Includes bibliographical references.
  ISBN 978-1-58966-178-3 (pbk.)
  1. Political science—Philosophy.   2. Political participation.   3. Compassion—Political aspects.   I. Title.
  JA71.H266 2009
  320.01—dc22

                                                                                        2009026158

Distribution:

University of Scranton Press
Chicago Distribution Center
11030 S. Langley
Chicago, IL 60628

PRINTED IN THE UNITED STATES OF AMERICA

This book is dedicated to Manfred's family

Contents

Preface	ix
Acknowledgments	xiii
Introduction	1
Invitation to an Unfamiliar Journey	

PART ONE: THE HEART OF THE MATTER

1. The Archetypal Drama of Transformation	17
2. Questions about the Drama of Transformation	47
3. Who Are We?	79
Knowing, Interconnecting, and Fulfilling the Four Faces—and Also the Source—of Our Being	

PART TWO: THE FOUR WAYS OF LIFE

4. Enclosing Ourselves in Emanation as a Way of Life	103
5. In the Service of Incoherence	137
6. Deformation: A Way of Life Moving Us toward Destructive Death	171
7. Transformation as a Way of Life	221

PART THREE: CHOICES WITHIN EACH WAY OF LIFE: INTRODUCING ARCHETYPAL RELATIONSHIPS AND STORIES

8. Nine Archetypal Relationships	235
9. The Archetypal Drama of Being Competent	269

10. Transforming Love, Romantic Love, and Other Forms 277
    Contrasting Archetypal Dramas
11. What Archetypes Shape Culture—and Race and Ethnicity? 289
12. Archetypal Dramas of Being Masculine and Feminine 311

PART FOUR: THE THEORY AND PRACTICE OF TRANSFORMATION

13. The Nature of Archetypal Dramas 325
14. Choosing from among Four Sacred Sources 337
15. What Kind of a Theory is This? 353
16. On Justice 359

   Bibliography 393
   Index 403

Preface

Two weeks before his death, Manfred Halpern asked me to finish this book, which had become his lifelong work. He had submitted an earlier version to Princeton University Press but felt that there was much more he wanted to say in the development of the theory of transformation so that he withdrew the manuscript. Above all, he felt that he had not written enough about the deepest realm of our lives, the source of the fundamentally more loving and just, the deepest sacred source that inspires us to participate in the continuous journey of transforming the personal, political, historical, and sacred faces of our being.

Through his writing and teaching he asked the question: "In the service of what deeper sacred source am I doing what I am doing?" He was a guide who taught us to discover and nurture our own personal and creative imagination and intuition, to enact our political face of being by seeing politics as what it is that we can and need to do together to create a more loving and just society, to re-vision the historical face of our being as our participation in bringing about new turning points, and in doing so, to make history, and to acknowledge our own personal, political, and historical faces as a manifestation of the deepest transforming source. He truly touched and enhanced the lives of all those with whom he came in contact.

Manfred began his courses by saying to his students, "Don't believe what I say. Test it with your own life, with your own experiences." By so doing he proved to be a superb teacher—an escort who guided his students into a whole new way of looking at politics. He taught us in his writings and his teaching to be radical, that is, to get to the roots, to the underlying, sacred forming causes of things by asking fundamental questions that would take us to the heart of the matter—testing, and living the theory and journey of transformation within the experiences of our own life. Thus he enabled us to discover and speak with our own voices. When he taught us the theory of transformation, we knew that it was not simply a matter of listening to a new vocabulary or learning a sophisticated set of interrelated hypotheses. We ourselves discovered how to theorize—to be theorists by participating and journeying to a new way of seeing and relating to ourselves, the world around us, and the deeper underlying sacred sources that give ultimate meaning and value to our concrete reality.

Manfred introduced us to the power of archetypal dramas, the stories of our lives that we practice in the service of four fundamentally different underlying and overarching ways of life. He taught us that each of us is an experiment of the depths—that we are vessels of the sacred, within which universal archetypal dramas are being played out. The most important of these stories is the core drama of life, the journey of transformation. The core drama, which he discovered and each of us can also discover and participate in by the nature of our humanity, begins when we discern where we are in our journey. The core drama of life is a drama of three Acts, with two Scenes within each Act. This journey has as its goal to lead us to our self, the deeper self, and to enter a new world that we often glimpsed but did not really understand. Like Vic Lovell, Ken Kesey's friend, Manfred led us into a lair of dragons so that we could face our own dragons—the stories enacted in partial ways of life that at times arrested our lives and kept us as partial selves on the journey.

Manfred never sought to be the founder of a new school of thought. He said that what he had done was to rediscover a 2,000-year-old tradition that represents the best of all religious heritages: the realization that life is an unfinished struggle to discover the self, one's neighbor, the world, and the deepest sacred source of our being. Our vocation as human beings is to respond to the call that comes from the deepest depths and to complete our selves, the world, and the sacred. All are unfinished. What a marvelous task.

In one of our last conversations, Manfred said, "Don't be a scribe. Let your own voice be heard. If you disagree or don't understand something, put an asterisk there and say why you don't agree." As I took the manuscript home, I felt a great sense of love and honor that Manfred asked me to finish his book, and yet I felt inadequate. I was one of Manfred's students in the first seminar in which he taught the theory of transformation, a graduate course, The Politics of Modernization, in 1968. It was an extraordinary experience that helped me for the first time to connect the dangling aspects of my life.

At the time, he had not yet discovered the source of the fundamentally new, the underlying sacred realm of archetypes, the four archetypal ways of life, or the archetypal journey of the core drama of life. But he knew that traditional social science had failed to explain why the lives of individuals, cultures, religions, and societies were falling apart. Manfred taught us that because social scientists did not understand this breaking they concentrated on stability and, at best, the reformation of what was already present. They could not see the way to alternatives that were new and better. They were blind to the possibility of transformation.

I had the opportunity to engage the theory by testing it as I wrote my doctoral dissertation, applying the theory to *The Breakdown of Authority in the Roman Catholic Church in the United States*. Following my completion of doctoral studies, I returned to full-time teaching at Seton Hall University where I created courses in which I taught the theory for the next thirty years. During this time I also wrote several books in which I applied the theory of transformation to Latino politics in the United States. Manfred read all of my chapters and we discussed together how to see the experiences of Latina women and Latino men in a new way and, most importantly, to describe and create actual alternatives, strategies of transformation that could be practiced here and now.

As I was teaching and writing about the theory, Manfred was writing this book. Due to his bouts with cancer, the book was delayed, but he was not discouraged. He used the time to delve more deeply into the process of transformation. Above all he wanted to develop the theory as fully as possible. He felt that he was writing and teaching about politics as a participant and contributor within the counter-tradition of transformation. But he went beyond what earlier practitioners of transformation like Ibn Arabi, Carl Gustav Jung, Moses Maimonides, and Giordano Bruno had taught him.

At times he became concerned that, in his efforts to develop the language and conceptual aspect of the theory, the manuscript was becoming so philosophical and, at times, abstract that it might become inaccessible to many. Manfred was deeply concerned about this. He encouraged me to develop and test the theory by teaching and writing about archetypal dramas so that we could see in everyday life how people lived the theory that he sought to make available. He also wanted to do more to apply theory to practice and so, in the current manuscript, once he had spelled out the heart of the theory, he began to apply it to practice in order to demonstrate how this perspective helped us to see and respond to problems as opportunities— opportunities to create fundamentally new and more compassionate alternatives.

Over the last few years, Manfred sent me each chapter as he wrote it so that I could read it and then meet with him to discuss it. Following our discussions, he would revise it before it was typed. During this period we had extensive conversations about how to organize the chapters and how each chapter contributed to explaining the theory of transformation. When I took the manuscript home in January of 2001, Manfred had completed all but the last two chapters. Chapter 15—"What Kind of a Theory is This?"—was handwritten and the footnotes were missing. Chapter 16, "On Justice," remained to be written. And over the years, Manfred had several typists who assisted him with preparing the manuscript. As a result, various font sizes, formats, spacing, and software were used. It took months to untangle the technological differences and make them compatible. Almost all of the footnotes were incomplete.

Before taking on the task of finishing the final chapters, I wanted to read with great care the first fourteen chapters of the book for ideas, while keeping an eye on style. I did some rewriting and polishing of the text looking for clarity in expression but making sure that Manfred's meaning was being authentically conveyed.

By means of phone calls, emails, and Internet access to libraries, I was able to track down the sources for the footnotes for Chapter 15—a blessing due to modern technology. But Chapter 16, "On Justice," was the greatest challenge.

Manfred left behind boxes filled with manila folders, marked simply "Justice," bulging with notes written with No.-2 pencils on yellow pads. I began to go through these notes searching for a coherent outline of the main ideas that he wanted to include. Then another blessing happened; I discovered in his notes an earlier version of the chapter. So I set about taking the most recent notes, reflecting Manfred's latest thinking on justice, and constructed the chapter. I believe that as it stands it represents the heart of what he wanted to say.

I am amazed again and again by the current significance of the book. Chapter 6, "The Way of Life of Deformation," has sections that are prescient in their description of the kinds of issues that we are now facing as individuals and as a nation: terrorism, fundamentalism, and war. One of the greatest concerns for Manfred was the rise and spread of fundamentalism not only in Islam but also in Judaism and Christianity. He would have been deeply troubled by the attack of 9/11 but also by the simplistic and dangerous responses to Islam that are fueled by ignorance, the arrogance of power, and the desire for revenge.

Finally, finishing Manfred's manuscript has been for me a profoundly moving experience. It is a truly brilliant work in the best sense of brilliant, that is, it has provided light and guidance so that we can see our way. Every time I return to the book, I feel simultaneously inspired by its vision and eager to get the book published so that his message will be available to others. The theory of transformation has been for many of us both a guide and a grounding by which to teach, write, work, do scholarship, and live our lives together with others.

He guided us to recognize the connectedness of all four faces of our being as we travel through the core drama of life. As a teacher, friend, and colleague, Manfred Halpern, rediscovered and retold for our time the journey and process of transformation as set down in this book. Often under very difficult circumstances, he brilliantly kept alive for us the light and wisdom of the counter-tradition of transformation. I only hope that I have done justice to this work of my friend and colleague, Manfred Halpern.

David T. Abalos
Princeton, NJ

Acknowledgments

First of all this is Manfred's book. As my friend and colleague, Manfred was one of my first teachers when I began my graduate work and later he served as the director of my dissertation. He was a guide to me as I began my vocation as a teacher and scholar. Even before he finished this, his own book on transformation, he read all the chapters and made recommendations as I wrote my first book, in which I applied his theory of transformation to the Latino community in the US. Through the publication of this book his teaching and wisdom can continue to live on through generations of his family, his Princeton students and colleagues as well as many others all of whom he blessed with the personal, political, historical and sacred faces of his being.

I know that Manfred would have wanted to thank his many students and colleagues whom he considered as part of a transforming community at Princeton University. He was especially fond of Profs. Nancy Bermeo, Elaine Pagels, Carol Rigolot, Richard Falk, George Kateb, Fred Greenstein, Sheldon Wolin, and Doug Doig. Among the Politics Office staff he was especially close to Dorothy Dey.

For over 36 years Manfred taught undergraduate and graduate students in the Politics Department. Twice his courses were voted as one of the top 10 undergraduate courses at Princeton. Some of his students who stood out during this time were James Bill, Anna Cabrera, Find Findsen, David Snyder, Kathy Korner, Betsy Wright, Oscar Suarez, Eric King, and Areyh Botwinick,

A special recognition is owed to Profs. Carol Rigolot of Princeton and Ted Becker of Auburn who provided excellent reviews of the manuscript and then made invaluable recommendations that contributed to the acceptance of the manuscript for publication.

I was appointed as a Faculty Fellow in the Politics Department at Princeton for the academic year 2002–2003. I applied for this position specifically so that I would have a base from which to work on Manfred's manuscript I am grateful to Seton Hall University who awarded me a sabbatical during this time. When I began to edit the manuscript it was a daunting task. I was limited in my knowledge of reconciling different formats, styles and discs. Several different typists had worked on the manuscript, each with their own peculiarities. The person who stepped forward with a combination of professionalism and generosity to untangle the various threads and provide me with a coherent whole was Chris Mackie. His knowledge of information technology was invaluable as he guided me through the process and organized the manuscript into chapters so that I could begin the task of editing. During the Spring semesters from 2006–2009 I served in the Politics Department as a Visiting Professor. This was a blessing because as I worked on Manfred's book I had access to the library, parking, office space and technical assistance all of which were invaluable to finishing the book. I am deeply grateful for my friends and colleagues in the Politics Department, Chris Achen, Nancy Bermeo , Lisa Baratta, and Doug Rosso who were of great help to me each in their own way as I prepared the manuscript. It was a blessing to have Ms. Sam Roze of the Office of Information Technology at Princeton to assist me in the preparation of the Index that she discovered could be dramatically accelerated by the use of the proper software. Sam is a wonderful member of Princeton's Office of Information Technology who has been a beacon of instruction and guidance for many of us. Sam worked collaboratively with Ms. Patty Mecadon of the University of Scranton Press to save me from countless hours of manually doing the Index.

Finally, I am grateful to the people at the University of Scranton Press especially Jeff Gainey without whose timely intervention this book would not have been possible. I worked closely with John Hunckler, my copy editor, who did a first- rate job in preparing the manuscript for publication. It was clear to me as I read his comments and suggestions that John knew, really knew and understood, the theory of transformation and how it was being applied to practice. Patty Mecadon was very helpful in the final stages of the printing of the book. To all of you I say thank you.

Introduction

Invitation To An Unfamiliar Journey

From the beginning to its seeming end, this book prepares us for an unfamiliar journey of being. Being, spoken both as a noun and as a verb, is constituted of four interpenetrating faces—personal, political, historical, and sacred faces. Our personal face: always unique, even when we seek conformity under the impact of the other three; becoming more unique as we free ourselves to become consciously and critically creative in connecting with ourselves and our other three faces of being. Our political face: what we can and need to do together, not only power exercised in the public realm. Our historical face: where we come from; the connections we seek to nourish or else insist on preserving; the turning points we create—or else, that are imposed upon us. Our sacred face: living underlying patterning forces which shape the structure, dynamics, and values of the stories in which we live our lives.

This theory of transformation, unlike any other in our time, offers a way of analyzing problems in terms of the stories that now control and possess our being, and above all clarifies the persistently renewable process by which we liberate all four faces of our being so that we may help create and participate in fundamentally better stories in which we are truly and wholly ourselves—with ourselves and with others.

Why take such a journey? Perhaps the most powerful sign of optimism currently being publicized is that, for the first time in history, a significant minority in a number of countries around the world have been able to organize a relatively stable and profitable system of political and economic power accompanied by a historically unique growth in knowledge, productivity, communication, bureaucratic control and organization, and accumulation of capital and weaponry. In almost two dozen cases, for example in Germany, the United States, and Japan, this growth has also been enhanced by democratic participation in some aspects of the political realm—though life remains everywhere far from democratic in all that we can and need to do together. But increasingly and ever more rapidly, people all over the world are also experiencing the breaking of established relationships, stories, and ways of life that had provided capacity, inspiration, interconnectedness, meaning, and purpose to our lives.

That great breaking is not what theorists or practical analysts normally talk about because the lenses that shape our vision—whether liberal, conservative, traditional, scientific, pragmatic, structuralist, or postmodern—do not allow us to see it or to understand its dynamics. Yet this kind of dissolution (not only of concrete relationships but also of their underlying foundations) is not an infantile disorder of the "less developed" countries or a burden carried temporarily by those who have just freed themselves from oppressive regimes—that is, by people who have not yet become like, or caught up with, the West. This kind of breaking, as we shall look into it, has become the substance of humankind's first shared, worldwide experience.

In the face of this deep and pervasive crisis, where does the fundamentally new and better come from? How can we participate in bringing it into being? What, basically, are our alternatives? These questions constitute the heart of our inquiry. We shall show that transformation—the journey that leads us to the fundamentally new and better with respect to all four faces of our being—is a drama that always has the same underlying structure and dynamics but is always unique in its particular experience and outcomes. (It can never be pre-programmed.)

One crucial fact that gives coherence to this theory is that, as ways of life, there are only three fundamental alternatives to transformation, and each of these radically different choices constitutes a fragment of the core drama of transformation. The other three ways of life are these: *emanation*, when we constitute a web of life in the service of a mysteriously overwhelming source (a dying way of life); *incoherence*, when we compete to organize, and again and again reorganize, fragments of life (the most prevalent way in our time); and *deformation*, when our complete attachment to a single fragment of life draws us into the road to destructive death (an ever-growing menace in our time).

We all live at every moment—arrested and possessed, or else consciously, creatively, and critically moving—in the core drama of transformation, and nowhere else. But if we arrest ourselves at a crucial moment in this process of renewal and consolidate it into a way of life, then, living within a fragment of the core drama of life, we cannot solve any fundamental problems. In this summary, I can only raise claims to knowledge. But these four ways of life are not abstractions. Each of them is open to us by virtue of our being human. The text of this work explores the structure and dynamics, the justice or injustice—along with many examples—of these radically different experiences.

When I began this inquiry into the breaking of the established relationships, stories, values, and ideas of our life and the problem therefore of where the fundamentally new and better comes from, I knew nothing about this journey and the choices along its road. This theory of transformation seeks to understand and evaluate an experience of participating in such creation that we have normally been deprived of—deprived even of the consciousness of our deprivation. To reopen this discussion requires us to find connections that earlier orthodox boundaries of belief and current orthodox boundaries within and between academic disciplines have prevented us from discovering and testing.

What we shall be doing will therefore seem strange, unlikely, even preposterous. For example, we shall analyze radically different sacred forces patterning all aspects of what we now call the secular realm, and not only what some call the sacred realm. We shall inquire into the power and the limits of different sacred forces and how we can free ourselves from all sacred forces which seek to rule and control us, and to participate instead with the sacred force that cannot rule us. We would not be able to enter into such an exploration unless each of us (and not only an authorized elite) could experience what we here call the sacred. Certainly, I shall offer no absolutes and nothing to believe in.

Also, for example, I will show that every kind of relationship and story in which we live our lives inspires us to act and to be moved by dynamics and norms intrinsic to it. Hence, this theory of transformation is at once explicitly empirical and normative—for long a forbidden combination. Moreover, this theory will offer decisive grounds for choosing between the justice or injustice of different stories. This theory therefore also resorts to terms almost all contemporary philosophers shy away from—*truth*, *reality*, *love*, and *compassion*—and also employs terms hardly ever used by social scientists, such as *always* and *never*. But since this theory of transformation can only be applied (and tested) in a concrete case, a single counter-example would compel a revision or even an abandonment of this theory, for this theory offers no abstractions, no models, no ideal types, but only descriptions of different kinds of experiences.

It may be helpful to say at the outset that the fuller description, explanation, and evaluation of this theory and journey have led to highly varied responses. Students in my courses over the past twenty-five years, and others, including colleagues who have read earlier drafts of this manuscript, have so far reacted in one of the following ways: Total bafflement, then dropping out. "A valuable alternative to know about, but I am not ready to take it." There has been fierce opposition to this dissent from all governing paradigms in philosophy, social science, religion, and psychology—this challenge to so much that now inspires and governs our lives. But more than a few have been deeply attracted to trying this journey themselves in order to understand and act in fundamentally more fruitful ways with respect to problems actually facing them.

One promise can be made at the outset: Nothing in this journey involves intellectual, emotional, or physical coercion. We can help others to understand the process of transformation, and support them compassionately during the critical turning points of this drama. But no one can transform someone else. Transformation works only if we free ourselves to be filled anew and to practice it.

Then why does this perspective also encounter such fierce opposition? This theory offers so many interconnecting links for thought and practice of a kind that have not been made for centuries that it seems at first glance to be imperialist, hegemonic, and universalistic, leaving no room for questions that seem not already to have been answered within this theory's framework. At a time when feminism is just beginning to unmask age-old forms of repression and to free us to see and experience far more varieties of expressing gender than masculine dominance had hitherto permitted, and when a multicultural perspective frees us for the first time to discover the realities of our personal, political, historical, and sacred past and present and to shape our future to express the true diversity of all four faces of our being and freely link them anew, indeed what madness it would be for any theory to say yes, we already know how to understand and organize it all!

The only final truth this theory asserts with absolute certainty is that there never will be and never can be a final theory or practice of transformation. One reason why it took a quarter of a century to write and rewrite this book is that I kept seeing what I had not seen before—both past errors and new insights. Transformation is in fact an ever-renewing process.

To propose a theory that can help us to discover wholeness of being does, however, require a deliberate break with all inherited dogmas about who "we" (in opposition to "them") are and must be, and with all modern theories that by their very nature can only provide knowledge about a fragment of life, and with all theories that deconstruct, often with great insight, but then leave us deconstructed.

A concern with wholeness of being challenges not only established modes of thought but all the forces that shape our lives within us and around us. Many of us feel that all we know and cherish is being attacked when we are told that the ways of life in which most of us have lived for most of history are by their very nature fragile (however successful our controls work at the moment) and anxiety-generating (hence the emphasis on power and control and their requirements and limits) because these ways constitute only arrested fragments of the core drama of life. We feel in the first instance taken over (and do not see it as an opportunity for liberation) when we are told that people who live in emanation, incoherence, or deformation cannot from within each fragment really understand each other's way of life. We cannot yet understand the wholeness of transformation, and therefore remain especially vulnerable to the constant threat of the road to destructive death, given the intrinsic fragility of our fragment. The more we live in the service of transformation, however, the more we come to understand all four ways of life and what is missing in ourselves and in our relations with others in the other three stories—but certainly no one likes to be fundamentally challenged from a position he or she does not yet understand.

Wholeness of being also involves developing a theoretical and practical ability to discover and respond to the deepest source of our being and to the choices we have with respect to the ultimate meaning and purpose of life—ultimate in the sense of the deepest ground we can find now for what we are, and what we are thinking and doing here and now, not in some distant or transcendent future. Most theorists dropped these subjects at least a century ago. For those who still care, these subjects have become solely subjective and private matters—except for moments at select public ceremonies. This work asks us to test the reality, truth, and value of the four radically different choices we all have by virtue of being human.

To be so directly and immediately addressed in all central aspects of our being becomes even more threatening when we discover (as we will in the first chapters) that if we take this theory seriously, our first practical step will be to enter consciously, critically, and creatively into incoherence. But in this journey, we do not stay in incoherence by turning it into a way of life. Instead, it becomes part of the process of transformation. We break not only with the concrete persons, ideas, values, and norms which we now experience to be unbearable, untenable, or at least unfruitful, but also with the living underlying patterning forces that shaped the story and way of life that had until now empowered these concrete manifestations.

We empty ourselves to be filled afresh from the deepest depth of our being with an inspiration of what is fundamentally and concretely new and better, and to take courage to test it in practice. But in the face of all these warnings about what from our present perspective looks like a threat—but what, in the experience of transformation, turns into a more fruitful capacity—it may be worth repeating that this is a theory, that like any other human claim, may well be mistaken, and that every reader (and not only a specialist) has already lived long enough to be able to challenge its central assertions.

There are only four radically different ways of life? Any reader may respond, "I have lived—or read about—another, several others, or else, a way of life that cannot be described without distortion in terms of one of the four." These four overarching stories (or any of the other smaller archetypal stories to be found in this book) always manifest this structure and dynamics and never others? Any reader may say, "But look what significant aspects of the story this version leaves out or distorts." This is indeed a theory about human participation.

The first two chapters of this work try to describe, explain, and evaluate the entire journey of transformation. The remaining chapters are intended to enlarge and deepen these explanations and their implications. Since the first chapters will speak only briefly of a number of crucial matters that will be more fully explored only later, it may be useful to complete this introduction by clarifying a few of these essential matters now. But since we have not yet taken that journey, we can clarify them only in a preliminary way. If opening the door in this way is likely to raise more questions in the reader's mind than this introduction yet answers, that will indeed be in the spirit of consciously and critically moving first into incoherence.

The journey of transformation is a drama that always has the same living underlying patterning structure—a drama of three Acts, each with two Scenes. During this experience, we discover why aspects of the concreteness of our life have become unbearable, what sacred forces had previously empowered these particular manifestations of life, why and how to empty ourselves both of these manifestations and their underlying forces, and how to participate creatively anew with the deepest depth of our being and test our new inspiration with all four faces of our being. Since we have never had and can never have such an experience while we remain within incoherence as our dominant way of life, this introduction will first explain briefly the experience of such sacred or archetypal underlying forces and then, again briefly, why we have such deep trouble understanding that experience from our dominant perspective.

Archetypal analysis as used in this work takes the sensuously concrete and particular with utmost seriousness: Everyone needs bread today and each particular child needs our care today. But our archetypal analysis also sees every concreteness as the manifestation of living underlying patterning forces, not merely as contingent or accidental. And unless these archetypal forces can be shown to have real power to shape our lives, any figure of speech concerning them could be, and ought to be, deconstructed.

Most social scientists also look for patterns, but their statements about patterns tend to be hypotheses limited solely to those variables that can be isolated and experimentally controlled, or else they tend to develop abstractions, that is, ideas that separate us from the concrete, such as "social systems" or "impersonal market forces." Archetypal analysis offers no abstractions whatsoever. It respects but does not limit itself to knowledge of the precisely ascertainable. It also takes seriously and tries to understand theoretically as far as possible the experience of the genuine mysteries of life—for example, creativity, love, and hate.

Before I say more about archetypes, it may be useful to distinguish the kind of archetypal analysis presented here from that offered by Plato and C. G. Jung. I have learned a great deal of value from both, and especially from my experience with Jungian analysts. But Plato speaks at times as if archetypes were ultimate entities (the *good*, the *beautiful*, the *circle*). We shall explore archetypes instead as dramas—stories that link us here and now with the depths. Plato also speaks at times as if all archetypes were fixed and eternal. We shall examine at least one major archetypal drama dying and others coming to be born. Plato held all archetypes to be good. We shall also analyze archetypal forces that render us only partially human or lead us into destruction. Plato also saw archetypes at times as inspiring us to withdraw from the merely concrete. We shall see that every archetype necessarily requires all four faces of being. Any archetype weakens and moves toward dying if we deny it concrete expression. Jung focused on the personal and (especially the mythological expressions of) the sacred faces of archetypes. He was often naive about the political and historical face of archetypes.

By *archetypes* I mean sacred patterning forces that move through each and all of us—that are transpersonal in that sense, not merely subjective or objective—and thus constitute a ground of being we all share by virtue of our human nature. These transpersonal forces mold the underlying structure and dynamics of the dramas in which, in an infinite variety of concrete manifestations, we express our lives. Nothing concrete exists except as a manifestation of an archetype. Our most important freedom is to liberate ourselves to become aware of what dramas we now live, how much they limit our capacity as human beings, and to choose the most just and loving way of living instead. Only the experience of the archetypal drama of transformation can free us to discover and choose wholly to be ourselves.

I speak of archetypal dramas as sacred forces for several reasons. As long as we remain unconscious of any living underlying patterning force that shapes our lives, its mysteriously overwhelming power possesses and commands us. We cannot command or change it. This is the conception that for many centuries cultures all over the world have held of the sacred. I begin from this fact of life and the pervasive (if no longer universal) personal, political, and historical acknowledgment that such is the nature of the sacred. I begin from this fact in order to initiate an entirely new joining of discourse, however discomforting it may initially be to all concerned. This work will examine, within a single framework of archetypal analysis, the grounds on which we can choose between sacred forces. To analyze archetypes as the experience of sacred forces is to enable our selves to look into the sacred as freely and as deeply as possible. To explore the archetypal stories of our lives allows us to join in a critical discussion of the structure, dynamics, and norms in which these forces manifest themselves—regardless of whether we believe in one or a few of these forces as god(s); reject belief in any of them as gods; or, as believers, agnostics, or atheists, we are unaccustomed to recognizing as sacred forces the living underlying patterning forces that shape the dramas of our seemingly secular lives. We thus introduce the possibility of a new and fruitful kind of dialogue between people who in our time ignore, denounce, or cannot understand each other in a kind of fundamental experience they do not know they share.

If we fail to recognize these forces in the depths of our being, we say that we cannot know the ultimate meaning and purpose of life when we live in the service of incoherence. And we then stop ourselves, yes, because the force of the archetypal drama stops us from further inquiry into the depths of our being. If we devote our life above all to gaining and exercising competence in the service of incoherence, we recognize that we can only be competent if we become specialists. But the archetypal drama of being competent keeps us from tuning in to the fact that in this way of life, however highly we may be valued for our competence, there is no convertible currency between that value and being valued as a human being. We feel compelled to devote most of our life to being (as noun and verb) a fragment of life.

Before we have gained power to control a sufficient large chip of life, we often try to compensate for this fragmenting and competitive organization and reorganization of insecurity that constitutes incoherence as a way of life by giving ourselves to romantic love. I am referring here to a particular archetypal drama in which the rest of the world disappears for the lovers. Indeed, the two lovers also disappear: each fantasizes an image of the other; each tries to live up to this image, until one of them is no longer able or can no longer bear to live up to that fantasy, and thus betrays the other. As long as we remain possessed by this archetypal drama, we keep searching for new, concrete manifestations of just such a lover, unable as yet to realize that this drama always ends this way. When we give up in sheer disillusionment, we usually devote ourselves instead to a marriage without romantic expectations and to a competition for power and success that above all draws our energy—and perhaps to occasional affairs that express our power or our capacity to add fragments of fun to our lives. We shall systematically describe and analyze these and other archetypal dramas in the service of incoherence in the chapters to come.

All I would like to do here is to indicate in advance that archetypal stories involve no mere plots, no simple causation. Each drama always patterns the structure and dynamics—the what, how, and why—of the story in which we live: what we who enact it hold in common, the limits we must not violate, the types of relationships that are authorized or else rendered marginal, what desires and intentions are freed or else repressed, the roles that are dominant, and the tastes, purposes, conceivable means, rules, and morality. Power does not work unless we—the powerful, the less powerful, and the powerless—share the same archetypal story. Otherwise, power becomes illegitimately violent and/or impotent.

The greatest power of the powerful lies not in their capacity for physical coercion (although that matters, too), but in the force that lies behind that power and legitimizes it. The real power of the powerful of the status quo arises from their larger capacity, inspired and justified by the underlying patterning force which we currently share with them, to reinforce the concrete and unconscious conformity of our performance in this form and type of story. The real cost is that the powerful, the less powerful, and the powerless all live in stories which compel us to repress the uniqueness and the wholeness of our being—to repress what in fact, given the problems our present stories cannot overcome, we can and need to do together.

Archetypal stories are not the equivalent of what in recent scholarship has been called "narratives." At any one moment and certainly over time, the story of our life (and the history of our society) is normally constituted by a number of different archetypal dramas, some of them consciously or unconsciously in conflict with each other. In the modern age, people also live (as we shall see) in the service of radically different ways of life with regard to different problems facing them. These archetypal ways of life are the overarching dramas that profoundly affect the capacity and freedom with which we perform all dramas in their service, and also the meaning, purpose, and justice we know and experience within them. That kind of service we shall also explore in detail.

Archetypes are not eternal. New ones are coming into being in our time. Also, people now are moving into dramas and overarching ways of life that we have not experienced for centuries. A growing proportion of half the population of the world—women—are struggling for the freedom at last to discover and live in stories that enable them to express their actual being, and no longer to be contained within archetypal stories dominated and contorted by men. Not only has this past prevented, inhibited, limited, and distorted the expression of archetypal stories of being feminine, thanks to masculine domination (and so also malformed and narrowed the masculine, however powerfully men could embody and enforce their authorized stories), but it has also kept us from finding out what other stories arising from the deepest depths of our being are also us.

Women, being present in every family, in every society, may well turn into the vanguard of transformation as each one discovers what underlying patterning forces have hitherto diminished and curbed their being and take courage to struggle through the archetypal drama that brings us to the fundamentally new and better. For in its essential features, the past of women is replicated by the domination of the archetypal dramas of conquering cultures or of indigenous elites over most races and ethnic groups, and also everywhere over the exploited and the poor, shaping the stories of the lives of the great majority to make them fit into the governing stories of the powerful.

Each of us and every group can begin transformation only here and now, and that means that we all begin from concretely different historical starting points and under concretely different political conditions. And indeed, however much we begin within an inherited culture, no culture (whatever its present official doctrine) was ever constituted of only one single repertory of dramas over time. And however much we previously conformed to its dominant stories we are each of us personally unique.

But as we begin to free ourselves to experience ourselves in our actual wholeness, and therefore also truly experience our difference from our past self and from contemporary others, we could succumb to at least two temptations. One is to limit the change we seek to the legitimization of a previously suppressed or discriminated-against archetypal drama (for example, being gay or lesbian, or Black, or Jewish) by having us accepted as part of incoherence—the organization and reorganization of fragments, as a way of life. That constitutes re-formation, not yet transformation. Another temptation is to separate ourselves even from others on this same journey in order to guard and enhance our treasured new difference.

These reformations prevent us from fully emancipating ourselves—breaking out of the way of life that most oppressed and warped our being so that we may come now to discover and live all the stories that most enable us to rejoice in the fullness of our being. Even if we succeed in advancing one step and engaging in coalition politics to fight together for all separate and particular new stories in which we now seek to live freely, we would only be gaining together each of our additional fragments in the service of incoherence. The greatest need and strongest motive for coalition politics is to help each other, in an initially hostile environment, move through the drama of transformation together in all aspects of life that need to be uprooted, seeded, cared for, and harvested anew.

This is a theory about practice, and practice involves all four interconnected faces of being. We deny or repress any one of them at our peril. What this brief discussion of archetypes, I hope, has also made clear is that they are not universals. All of them are open to us by virtue of our being human, but none of them constitutes our fixed universal or eternal fate. They constitute no ahistorical foundation for our lives. They are born and they die with our partial involvement or else with our full participation, as we shall see. They are not complete without our concrete personal, political, and historical expression of them.

To speak of being fully human is therefore to refer to the archetypal and concrete experience of the freedom and capacity to fundamentally change a particular problem for the better at this moment, and to nourish that moment for as long as possible for us at this place at this time. Since this cosmos never stands still, we shall no doubt see a need for us also in this case to participate in renewed creation. That is also why we can never attain the fundamentally best or the perfect or final answer or reach any idealist or utopian solution. In the service of transformation, we do not seek salvation but work to discover and then to test in practice what is fundamentally—and not only incrementally—better than what we experienced before.

Why choose transformation? The proof that persuades us is to be found in each concrete case, but always in the context of the fact that we have only four basic choices, three of them are only fragments of the core drama of life. In this introduction, no convincing case can be made, but it may be helpful to usher in now for a first visit the four most powerful sacred forces that create the underlying structure and dynamics of the overarching dramas of our lives.

The sacred force that inspires us to move again and again through the drama of transformation is the only sacred force that cannot and does not try to command, control, or possess us. It is no Lord, King, or Master. Instead, it requires our conscious, critical, creative participation, for why would this source (but not master) of the core drama of life persist in constantly recreating this drama of transformation unless it was itself still on an unfinished journey? This source is not all-powerful or all-knowing; it is not changeless, not transcendent or supernatural, not solely spiritual, but requires being in all four of its interconnected faces so that we may enter into fruitful dialogue together. Dialogue (*dia-logos*) means journeying consciously, critically, and creatively through the logos—the source, structure, meaning, and dynamics of the active intelligence of our cosmos—together. Transformation is not an experience of dualism but of bi-unity.

Since the drama of transformation is no puppet play, its participants must have the capacity and the freedom to say yes or no to entering each Act or Scene of this drama. And the participants are concretely each of us and also the archetypal force which moves the sacred face of our being within each Act.

When we are anxiously eager to preserve the initial new inspiration of this drama, to make sure that it remains certain in shaping all we do, we turn ourselves—our whole web of life—into an embodiment of this mysteriously overwhelming sacred force. We arrest ourselves in emanation as our way of life and enforce it through our beliefs and through all our networks of relationships.

Or else, inspired anew, we rebel against these fixed limits, but then, instead of exploring the underlying meaning, purpose, and justice of this new sacred inspiration, we feel empowered to polarize with anyone who would limit our ego's new efficacy—and so we arrest ourselves in perennial institutionalized competition. Since the single sacred container that had intertwined all beliefs and conforming actions is now dissolved, but since we also did not complete our journey to discover and explore a new wholeness of being, all that our separated egos can now compete for are fragments of life.

Therefore, as scholars, scientists, socialists, capitalists, as any human being living in the service of fragments as a way of life—that is, incoherence—we cannot know the ultimate meaning, purpose, and justice of life. We cannot hope to find agreement on the substance of these issues because—to speak of two modes of fragmenting our life—subjectively we differ, and objectively we cannot deal with such matters. We also cannot recognize that a sacred force still patterns our life—though no mere rational calculation inspires our drive for power and success, our willingness to blame ourselves for our failure, or our uncritical devotion to this way of life.

The State can help us only to organize (and, at its best, limit the violence of) the competition for (temporary) power and control our fragments of life. Liberal social democracy is by far the best drama (certainly in contrast to authoritarianism) for organizing the insecurity of incoherence as a way of life.

Emanation and incoherence are ways of life that mean to persist in being only partial, that is, incomplete and biased. They are fragments organized for the defense of the sacred force and its concrete manifestations that serve to halt and repress the process of change toward the fundamentally new and better. But in a cosmos of continuous creation, arrest constitutes not only an illusion, not only a repression of transformation, but a growing risk of becoming vulnerable to being sucked into the third way of life, deformation.

The threat of deformation exists from the outset of our stopping ourselves short in the process of transformation. By living within a fragment of this process, and therefore within an intrinsically fragile way of life, we diminish our being. We reduce our capacity and freedom and we cannot help—however powerful we may seem to be—being and becoming more anxious. We are therefore often tempted, especially in relation to the other who lives with us or near us but will not accept our particular enactment of emanation or incoherence, to ally ourselves with the sacred force of deformation to keep the other vulnerable in a less than human status or to push that person on the road to destructive death. We shall analyze this infectious relationship between all three of these ways of life in great detail, for the menace of deformation is growing in our world.

As long as we remain unconscious of them, archetypes have the mysteriously overwhelming possessive power of sacred forces. Since some of the most potent of them keep us biased and incomplete in our lives, and deformation leads us into evil, the fact that they are all sacred is no reason to respond to their inspiration by saying Amen! About a thousand years ago, philosophers of transformation living in Jewish, Christian, and Muslim communities in the Mediterranean amended Socrates to say, "To know yourself is to know your Lord." We can free ourselves to know which sacred forces now mold our lives, and to say no, for I can find within myself the deepest source of being and choose henceforth to participate with that source, and never obey and conform to any Lord.

That knowledge also frees us to understand the radical difference between belief and faith as we make these choices. Belief molds our practice and secures it against any fundamental questioning. Faith, by contrast, means freeing ourselves to risk trust in an experience during which, with care and compassion, we keep testing our hope, and understanding that we can participate in turning it into an experience of transformation. It is not a question of just taking a chance, or of converting and being saved, or of a revolution finally consolidated.

It is not a question of simply discovering our identity. Every drama and every overarching way of life defines our identity and our role differently. We shall explore the experience of every individual not simply as an individual but as a being with four faces. We shall therefore critically inquire whenever any of our faces are being repressed or are not allowed freely to interconnect anew and ask why and what we can do about it. Only transformation can help us find and empower the fullness of our being. Indeed, the most immediate test of the theory of transformation open to us is our own life.

This particular work is only the latest attempt to contribute to a long counter-tradition of theories of transformation. I have learned vital knowledge from Heraclites, Lao-tse, Buddha, Jesus, Alfarabi, Ibn Arabi, Meister Eckhart, and Kabbalists—to mention only a few people long dead. I also *disagree* with aspects of their ideas and with some of their principal interpreters. This counter-tradition has suffered in the East by concentrating (because of political oppression) on the personal and sacred faces of being and repressing the political and historical. It has suffered in the medieval West from being fiercely persecuted, and in the modern secular West especially from a deep reluctance to try to understand the sacred anew, and lately, to create any theory at all that tries to show that there are vital underlying connections between crucial aspects of life.

Because of political persecution, earlier works were often written esoterically (unlike, I dearly hope, this one) that hampers later readings. And while they deal with genuine mystery (and we shall, too), they have misled readers into thinking of them as mystical. People have written about transformation since writing began and practiced it since the beginning of humankind. (If intuition about archetypal patterns could not lead into new choices with respect to practice before we have any theory, we could never develop theory; theory about human choices cannot precede practice.) But now, for the historical reasons I have cited, we begin our present dialogue almost from scratch.

PART ONE

The Heart of the Matter

1

The Archetypal Drama of Transformation

Transformation is a process of participating in creation so that we may give birth to something fundamentally new that is also fundamentally better. However committed we may be to preserving what we have inherited from the past, we live in a cosmos of continuous creation. We can nourish any experience which is already fruitful, loving, and just by asking and learning what is needed for its persistent renewal. But trying to solidify and preserve any particular human situation becomes always an ever more costly fantasy.

If we are yearning instead for change to overcome our present sufferings, most of us now live in a way of life that restricts our vision and our practice to repeating our past troubles in ever new guises and being startled again and again with unexpected changes. At most, we are free to bring about incremental improvements or to change again who bears the costs and who gains the larger fragments of organized incoherence. Or else, in our despair, we fantasize a return to glory at whatever the costs—and the price is always the construction of a road to destructive death. Hope for any fundamental change remains utopian as long as we arrest ourselves in any Act or Scene of the archetypal drama of transformation—the core drama of life. These first two chapters will describe, explain, and evaluate this drama. We shall explore how our conscious, critical, creative participation in each Act and Scene enriches our capacity and freedom. If, however, we convert any Scene of it into a partial way of life, that arrest of our still incomplete experience will limit and lame us—as we shall see. If we exit from this drama, we shall experience deformation.

ACT I SCENE 1: WE ALWAYS BEGIN IN EMANATION

Every experience of our life is a concrete manifestation of living underlying patterning forces—of archetypal dramas. As long as we have not freed ourselves to understand these forces as they flow through us—and through others we encounter—we begin in an emanational relationship to such mysterious, overwhelming sources. We are inspired to be their concrete embodiment with every fiber of our being. The more we succeed, the more we seem to achieve a deep sense of security. We believe we are doing things right, however much others may disagree and struggle against us. We may complain at times about the burden we carry or become anxious about our adequacy in carrying it, but we do not yet know how to detach ourselves from any source of emanation to criticize the source itself—indeed, we cannot imagine criticizing it. We experience its overwhelming power as a given fact of life—in fact, as a blessing.[1]

In the past, we were raised to perform all the stories of our life in the service of emanation as the whole web of life for our entire community. The most embracing story that arose in Act I Scene 1 thus decisively determined all the other underlying stories of our life for all of our life. In our time, many are attached only to fragments of this web or to none of it. But emanation as a way of life is not the only emanational power in human experience. Every living underlying pattern—every archetypal drama—of which we have not yet become conscious continues to possess and command us through an emanational relationship.

In the service of incoherence as the now dominant way of life, we feel inspired to be free to pursue our self-interest as we see it. But what in fact most deeply impels us, what holds this organized insecurity of competition for fragments of life together as a story, is the fact that it constitutes an overarching archetypal drama to which so many of us are emanationally bound. (That fact is to be demonstrated in Chapter 5.) We begin—and remain—in a relationship of emanation as long as any archetypal drama unconsciously shapes our connections to our mother, father, ruler, lover, community, ideas, values, norms, or practices. Mere flesh and blood, mere words, cannot have this compelling power over us unless we experience them as concrete and symbolic manifestations of a deeper force.

We always begin the process of transformation in emanation because we cannot experience any concrete moment of life except as an expression of an archetypal drama in the service of an overarching way of life. That also means that our consciousness always begins as an emanation—a flowing forth from an archetypal source of whose true nature we are initially still unconscious, though we may name its most powerful embodiments *father* or *mother* or *lover* or *fatherland* or *god's*

---

1. Chapters 8–14 will systematically explore archetypal sources as the living patterning forces of our being. Until then, we hope to help the knowledge of archetypes grow in the reader's mind by way of examples of their structure and dynamics.

will. We begin life as the growing embodiment of archetypal sources that shape the containers of our being, conscious only of our need to learn or to develop the concrete manifestations for enacting these stories.

Our father or mother or church may legitimately punish us if we offend their authority or their rules. Our country may ask us to die for it. But we devoutly know and accept (whatever our moments of neglect or sin) that any sacred container must be defended against attacks from within and outside. We know we deserve the punishments it imposes on us; we know we must make the sacrifices it asks of us. We also feel tremendously reassured by how rewardingly our container helps us to store and preserve the past, to cook up a secure present and future, to secure acceptance through our conformity, to receive counsel and consolation, and to share sorrows and joys with people who are like us. How can we be receptive to anything new under these circumstances?

ACT I SCENE 2: CHALLENGED CONSTANTLY BY NEW SOURCES OF EMANATION

Since the core drama of life is constantly being created anew, and since we are open to it by virtue of being human (whether we are aware of that story or not), we constantly hear afresh from the archetypal sources of our being. Even the youngest child, though intensely in the emanational embrace of the first Scene, hears from the depths again and again, causing the child to defy, rebel, experiment, and assert autonomy from the beginning. When these new voices, images, thoughts, or feelings reach us, they compel our attention. We feel deeply stirred, but in the light of our experience in the first Scene, their power and meaning remain mysterious to us. We may be profoundly attracted; we may act them out, but we cannot assimilate these new inspirations into our dominant archetypal story. They confront us as new emanational forces that are trying to pull us into the second Scene of Act I.

What are we hearing? What is its meaning and value? At this point, we cannot know. All we realize now is that, perhaps for the first time, we seem to be at odds with ourselves. A significant part of our life has become problematical. Are we in fact on our way to a fundamentally better experience of life? We cannot know until we have completed our exploration in Act III.

What forces are powerful enough to enter our archetypal container that was molded by a mysteriously overwhelming force? It could only be another archetypal force of still greater emanational power. Who are the candidates? It may be the deepest source of our being, once again opening the drama of transformation. It may be the sources of the other three ways of life—the archetypal forces within the core drama that we can consciously, critically, and creatively enlist in order to move through all three Acts, but which, when we lack the kind of hope, faith, love, and critical consciousness this chapter will soon explore, enlist us instead to stop the process and say no to any movement beyond their own power.

One of these forces may then draw us into a different emanational way of life that promises an even more powerful and secure embrace. Another such force may inspire our rebellion—but nothing more than rebellion—to make us enter and stay in incoherence as a way of life. Or it may be a force of despair dragging us toward destructive death. What usually attracts us initially may be a startling new insight, a particular new person, an urgent impulse, a surprising action, or a powerful drug. But everything concrete represents an aspect of an archetypal drama and no archetypal drama can be enacted except in the service of an overarching way of life.

We are never alone. Each of us has four faces of being—not only our unique personal face, but also our political face, that is, what we can and need to do together; our historical face; and our sacred face, constituted by the living underlying patterning forces of our life. The inspiration of continuous creation that enters us ever anew may be for good or ill. It depends crucially on the quality of our participation—our freeing ourselves from all emanational containers to discover and to understand what hitherto shaped the faces of our being and to choose the fundamentally better.

In view of these facts, our slogan as this drama opens cannot be "Become whatever turns you on." At this point, we are faced by two conflicting mysteries: one emanational force whose power still holds us, though it can no longer prevent us from also feeling drawn by another emanational power that we also cannot yet understand. What can we do? If the emanational force that molded our being in Act I Scene 1 recovers to become once again the stronger one, then we will indeed know what to do. We know that if we continue to break the taboos of that sacred container, we will lose all its previous security and rewards and be severely punished instead. We say, "I cannot do it," and that seems to reassure us because it affirms that, being in the first Scene of Act I, we must not do it, and hence we are indeed rendered unable to move ourselves to do it. Emanation by its very nature contains and embraces us, and tells us how, if we sin against it, we can reenter by way of repentance and doing penance.

This is one of the most compelling and seemingly most stabilizing capacities intrinsic to any emanational story—the power it gives us to contain ourselves. We feel the necessity to render ourselves unconscious of any thought, feeling, image, or action moving through us that is illegitimate in terms of what the mysterious power underlying our story has patterned that story to be.

But if we nonetheless remain vulnerable to hearing or feeling that new emanational force, then we may try to repress it, but repression is costly. Repression can make us unconscious of what we cannot bear, but it cannot make the unbearable go away. We cannot eliminate archetypal forces from our lives through repression, but only through the liberation of advancing through the drama of transformation. Repression (as we shall discuss) is a mode of deformation. Emanation is only a segment of the core drama of life. If its hold becomes uncertain, we may be tempted to protect ourselves through an alliance with a fiercer fragment (indeed, a fragmenting power)—deformation. Still, what we repress keeps us anxious. Out of our shadow, it keeps hitting us and our neighbors destructively from behind and below, and we do not know why. To repress ourselves is to know ourselves even less than before, for "to know yourself is to know your Lord."[2]

When repression no longer works (for reasons we shall soon examine), suppression—the use of naked force—is used to enforce the power of emanation. Suppression is justified by the most powerful people of that story not only because they are in fact threatened by our disobedience. They are also threatened by the same deeper forces that had previously led us into repression. And suppression may work. If it is successful, its success seems to demonstrate above all the overwhelming power of the sources of emanation—even in alliance with the more brutal force of deformation if terror and destructive death are thought to be required. But if suppression fails to restore the supremacy of emanation, it all the more powerfully undermines the deepest justification of the hitherto prevailing story.

But do not emanational containers constitute a mercy of safety when life challenges us beyond our comprehension and our own present capacity to deal with it? Do they not offer ideas, values, and networks of relationships we can truly count on? Indeed, that is why we are so deeply attracted to the container within which we first grew up. And this is why, when its power over us is weakened or our loyalty to it is diminished, we are so tempted to enter the emanational enclosure that converted us in the second Scene of the Act of emanation.

An emanational container is truly an act of mercy when we are still too young or (later) too sick or (at last) too old to know what we need to do, or to do what needs to be done. But that embrace is merciful even under these circumstances only if it arises from the compassionate understanding of people who do not seek to preserve our present limitations, but who help us to become capable and free again as much as possible to continue in our own process of transformation. Whenever the mercy of emanation is not, or is no longer, a manifestation of that process, it becomes intrinsically unreliable, even when we worship its source as a sacred source. All archetypal stories which inspire us to believe and act—or simply take for granted—that they are final and permanent truths lead us to live only a partial truth, that is, an incomplete and biased truth, which is in fact to say, a lie. For none of the sources of such "truths" allow us to reach the deepest source of our

---

2. Alexander Altmann shows us how this idea came to be developed and shared in "The Delphic Maxim in Medieval Islam and Judaism," in Alexander Altmann, *Studies in Religious Philosophy and Mysticism*, 1–40.

being—the source that constantly reopens the opportunity of our participation in continuous creation in order to help bring about the fundamentally better.

To live in any emanational relationship—to a person, idea, or norms; to an archetypal drama; or to an archetypal way of life—is to experience its source as a mysteriously and powerfully overwhelming force. As a result, however passionately, earnestly, and vigorously enlivened and certain it makes us feel, we are never fully ourselves, but at most a half-moon, visible only because we reflect a light. We live in a seemingly enclosed but in fact partial (that is, incomplete and biased) relationship, and therefore we are always vulnerable.

In our time, even the most embracing and professedly the most certain of all such forces—emanation as an entire web of life—has become more fragile than ever. It is always fragile, because it constitutes only a fragment of the core drama of life. Today, emanation as a way of life is not yet dead, but it is dying. Within any concrete manifestation of this overarching drama, we have never been permitted to ask fundamentally new questions or experiment with fundamentally new answers. When established relationships in all realms of life are breaking as rapidly and as pervasively as they are now, neither repression nor suppression can preserve the cohesion of any way of life.

When the new drama to which we are drawn basically contradicts and conflicts with the old drama, when the sacred container around the old story will not permit us simply to add the new story, we would go mad if we tried to hold on to both of them. We cannot merely distance ourselves from an otherwise persisting present or simply turn our back on our past. Unless we separate ourselves from such emanational bonds, they will continue to hold us as living underlying patterning forces we do not yet understand, and that therefore will often leave us depressed at our deprivation and essentially unprotected against being sucked back in.

What moves us to rebel? We come to realize that what had once been so reassuring has now become unbearable, untenable, or at least unfruitful in the light of the far more attractive inspiration we received in Act I Scene 2. These realizations demonstrate that we are hearing a new self speaking from our depths.

But there also remain serious obstacles to our rebellion. We do not yet understand what we are rebelling against. We do not yet grasp why these ideas or values or norms or why this mother or father or ruler (these sets of words, these human beings) had so much power over us. We do not yet appreciate how their authority was in fact infused by deeper sacred sources. Since we are not yet able to understand this deeper power and therefore fully to free ourselves from it, what enables us now to enter into rebellion? We are able to resist and thus depotentiate one powerful embodiment of this archetypal drama only because our feelings and intuition are being animated by a new and more powerful emanational force.

Our new source of emanation leads us to feel that our former bonds have become unbearable. If we stayed there, we would die of it, psychically or physically.

It has become untenable. We cannot live it or support it. It has become unfruitful. At best, we would be stuck where we are, passive, sterile in thought and emotion. But our old emanational source still deeply scares us.

To break with any emanational relationship always leads to a profound feeling of betrayal—or else, suicide. In the first Act of the core drama, we were nothing more than the reflection of a powerful light, never fully ourselves. When we break with that archetypal source or with what we had hitherto experienced as its powerful human embodiment, that human being, in the name of the archetypal source we had shared, feels betrayed—and, therefore, feels justified in killing us. It may actually try to kill us, or else resort to symbolic substitutes that hurt but are not bound to end in our death: to banish, to disown, or to publicly denounce us. And we feel suicidal, for never having been fully present, we have no experience of standing on our own two feet. Suicide may indeed become our impulse, but it, too, has symbolic substitutes—among them, withdrawal into deep apathy, depression, or utter cynicism.

Rebellion in the service of transformation certainly does not require our killing anyone—and no single human being can kill an archetype. (But if enough people reject constituting themselves as its concrete face, it weakens and dies.) Rebellion requires breaking our emanational bonds with an archetypal drama and its concrete manifestations when they have become unbearable. The greater risk of killing ourselves arises when we find ourselves pushed out of Act I Scene 1 against our will, desire, and expectations. For example, the most powerful human embodiment of the source leaves us for reasons of his or her own, or that source no longer has any answer to new problems we face, or the bonds of our community—indeed of our way of life—have been undermined or destroyed. When we therefore feel deeply depressed, we either enter into despair or else grab a fragment of fantasy of glory to come. Both can lead us into deformation. Otherwise, what will normally protect us against suicide at this point is the still mysterious but more powerful new source that encourages us to rebel against our former source—so that we may be free to link with the new source.

That new source, which we initially experience as a source of emanation (it is indeed beyond our power to understand it, even though it deeply inspires us), could also be our first encounter with transformation. We experience it as an emanational relationship because it guides us while, with respect to this experience, we are still a child. It guides us into a process that dissolves emanation—a process that will not keep us overwhelmed, but turns instead into a movement that also, but not only, inspires awe and wonder:

<blockquote>
"To know can only wonder breede
And not to know is wonder's seede."[3]
</blockquote>

---

3. Sidney Godolphin (1610–43), cited by Sir Geoffrey Vickers as a motto for his book, Geoffrey Vickers, *Value Systems and Social Process*.

This emanational beginning of the process of transformation is a gift that guides us to become free and probing, to tune in also to a deeper structure of movement, to intuit and feel it, even before we can find words for it.

With the guidance of theory, or of a person who has previously experienced and become conscious of transformation, we can learn in advance that a menacing anxiety will come upon us as we break with our former emanational source, and then we will not be caught unaware. And as we enter next into Act II (incoherence), in what would otherwise have struck us as constant threats of chaos, we shall be able to recognize a helpful underlying pattern. In this way we shall be enabled and stirred in our process not only by the urgency to break with what has become unbearable, untenable, or unfruitful, but by our hope and desire for the joy of knowing and loving, and of being known and loved. We shall be learning how to *practice* consciously, critically, and creatively—not simply to embody—a way of life that is altogether more understanding, fruitful, compassionate, just, and true—a way that is never to be simply believed, but rather is to be explored and tested.

ACT II SCENE 1: INCOHERENCE; MOVING INTO REBELLION

In a particular instance, we have now broken with a relationship that we had once experienced as naturally, permanently, and most preciously right. And if we are moved by transformation, we shall soon discover that the breaking is far from over. In Act II Scene 1 there is no longer any assured continuity. Changes constantly occur but most of them are unintended and beyond our control. Conflicts arise everywhere around us. Collaboration with others is limited to fragments of life. At best we can agree on procedures between individuals and groups driven by rival inspirations, limiting competition to actions short of killing each other. Our link to what we now appropriately call our "unconscious" (if indeed we consider it appropriate to pay any conscious attention to it) is intended to be a one-way street—we use it to repress much of our being. But in ways we cannot fathom, it nonetheless keeps getting us. This is certainly an as yet incomplete description of incoherence. We shall attend to its deeper roots when we enter and explore ourselves in Act II Scene 2. But already we can see enough reasons for new anxieties.

Since Act II (incoherence) is in fact constituted by a living underlying pattern, we can move through it with growing awareness of this pattern and of what concrete critical and creative participation it requires of us—or we can arrest ourselves within Act II Scene 1 and try (at increasing cost) to *stay* within it, or even to return to Act I. If we want to arrest our progress in Act II Scene 1 (and we have the power to do so), we need to turn incoherence into a whole way of life. Although this first Scene constitutes the enactment of rebellion as an intrinsic part of the core drama of life, in this arresting response we feel incited to institutionalize rebellion—or, to put it more accurately, to turn Act II Scene 1 into an overarching archetypal drama in whose service we join with its source in creating many additional stories of repeated rebellions in its service. (Chapter 5 explores this in detail.) Our reaction in this instance is based on the fact that we have freed ourselves from one previously all-powerful force and were strong enough to escape the risk of death and suicide. Our response is also based on the unexamined fantasy that therefore our power is now our own.

In fact, however, our being is vulnerable in new ways. We have not completed the process of becoming fully and freely ourselves. Instead, *we are possessed* still by the new emanational force which led us into rebellion. We seek the added security of institutionalizing what we now believe to be legitimate forms of rebellion. But we remain unconscious of this still deeper emanational commitment to a whole way of life. Instead, we now believe that we have freed ourselves from all forms of emanation—by whatever words we call that experience if we even recognize such depths—for we believe we cannot know the ultimate meaning and purpose of anything.

We realize that the only thing we share with others now is a *way of life* that allows us to organize and reorganize the insecurity of perennial competition between individuals and groups. We believe that we have nothing we can ultimately count on, only our own immediate power. And therefore we know we have no real foundation on which to trust others or (though we try to repress this thought) even trust ourselves. Not just capitalism and liberal democracy but all modern revolutions have thus cut short our development and growth as human beings. In the case of revolutions, a particular new ideology (the expression of a new emanational voice) inspires rebellion—which is then consolidated by a revolutionary minority and not allowed to change in any fundamental way.

What drives and forms us in the service of incoherence are, in all instances, the unexamined emanational force behind this way of life and the emanational force of each drama in its service. We rebelled against the emanational source that had previously possessed us, but we have not yet detached ourselves or even understood the emanational stories that newly compel us—which inspire our desire to succeed in business or politics, to demonstrate our competence in our profession, to satisfy our self-interest, and to die, if need be, for the sake of our nationalism.

What worries us in our time, however, is that many archetypal stories which move us in the service of incoherence are not shared or respected by others in the same way as all our archetypal stories had been authorized, joined together, and enforced in the service of emanation as a way of life. (Modern authoritarian rulers certainly know that contrast—and fear it in their bones.) In emanation as a way of life, all stories held our devotion as parts of a sacred pantheon ordaining for us a single web of life. Emanation involved a commitment to permanence. Though we still live within each story in the service of incoherence as if it were all that mattered now, we know it is under attack by others who are now free to pursue quite different stories.

We recognize that it is also under attack even by people who are committed to the same story, but who feel free (unhindered by the panoply of mutually stabilizing and reinforcing stories as in the service of emanation—or by its shared sense of shame, sin, and guilt) to attack our very role and presence (and not just our concrete acts) in almost any story (except the few in which a role, but not necessarily its actual player, is legally protected). And our own power to compete (especially now that individual power matters so much more) has been intrinsically weakened by the fact that we are still only a fragment of being (caught in Act II Scene 1 of the core drama) and therefore are not wholly present in our personal, political, historical, and sacred faces to oppose such challenges effectively again and again in our history. Of course, most of our fellow citizens are unfortunately lamed in the same way, but that means that what we can and need to do together is not much more solid. We experience this unending and unresolved struggle within the family, political parties, corporations, and the nation-state.

If we turn Act II Scene 1 into a way of life, changes within it can only take three forms. One is to change the concrete manifestations of existing archetypal stories. We elect a new officeholder; we find a new romantic love; we make incremental changes in the tax structure or in welfare payments; we defeat a particular competitor for a while or once and for all, but never all who challenge us. Another possible alteration within this Scene is to change from one emanational drama to another—as long as the dramas remain in the service of incoherence which deeply shapes their dynamics and limitations. We can shift from democratic liberalism where many are free to compete, albeit with different power, to authoritarian liberalism, where only a small elite is allowed to compete within sharp limits—or vice versa. Our third choice is to engage in *re-formation*—to create new stories in the service of incoherence. Nationalism, for example, did not come into being until the late eighteenth century.

Most of us living an entire way of life within the confines of this scene of the core drama have difficulty realizing that we have three other fundamental choices open to us in life. Repression is a powerful tool of deformation. Considering that we have stopped short in a drama that constitutes the road to the deepest layer of everyone's being, it greatly diminishes us.

Most of us recall emanation not as a web of life but only as a set of institutions, beliefs, and rituals whose dominance or potent alliance with the state Westerners defeated several centuries ago—though others in the world are still struggling with its authority, or at least with powerful fragments of it. We can return to it—so anxiety-ridden by Act II Scene 1 in all its various forms that we are ready to give up our sins, or so frightened that we feel we need shelter again as crippled souls. But when we return to emanation as a way of life in our time—say, as a reborn Christian—we face three problems we cannot solve.

First, even as a way of life, emanation can only serve as a fragment within incoherence, the dominant way of life (unless we isolate ourselves in neighborhoods or countries as if no one else lived there). President Jimmy Carter, though a reborn Christian, spoke of a deep malaise in the United States, but he could not heal it—neither as a reborn Christian, nor as the President (another fragment of power). He has, however, been effective since then in organizing, financing, and training people in a cooperative effort that focuses on a particular task—building housing for tens of thousands of the poor in the United States and abroad through Habitat for Humanity. Second, emanation at any time cannot let us ask fundamentally new questions (it has already answered all questions) in a fundamentally new situation (the sacred source will act as it wills, and, indeed, it has already spoken and acted on all fundamental questions). And third, emanation as a way of life is dying as an archetype in our time.

As we shall explore in detail in Chapter 6, even while we live in the service of incoherence, given its restricted and hence fragile nature, we often ally ourselves with, and therefore accept deformation—within underlying patterns seldom discussed, publicly or privately—as a necessary or inescapable underside of life. It took people many centuries before they abolished slavery, and racism is still alive, as is the treatment of women as inferior to men. For decades, the world's most powerful democracy has engaged in covert actions that succeeded in killing tens of thousands of people all over the world, not to speak of millions killed in internal wars in which we intervened to support one side against another.

It is too easy to offer specific examples. In the service of incoherence, we tend to see each example as a separate case. That all these dramas in fact take us on the road to destructive death is still obscure to us, or is quickly repressed or forgotten. The only point I want to make here is that, because of this largely unexamined alliance between incoherence and deformation as ways of life (fragments of life are always desperately seeking reinforcement), people in the service of incoherence are seldom alert in time to the emergence of the forces of deformation to a full monopoly of terror.

Transformation as a radically different choice would require us to enter into incoherence with incoherence as a way of life—meaning moving this time not only into the first Scene but also into the second Scene of Act II. That would be the least familiar and scariest path—unless we have finally found incoherence as a way of life unbearable, untenable, or unfruitful because it deprives us of full freedom, capacity, understanding, love, and justice.

I have spoken so far of getting lost in the process of transformation by arresting ourselves in Act II Scene 1 of incoherence and consolidating it into a whole way of life. But there is deep anxiety haunting us in the service of incoherence—not only the intrinsic limitations of our being within the confines of this fragment of life, but also the repressed fact that our rebellion is quite incomplete. We broke with something concrete that had possessed great power over us; we also broke away from the underlying force that had once so overwhelmingly empowered that particular manifestation of it. Why do we still feel so apprehensive and unfree? It is as if we had left home, but we still do not understand why.

We have not yet come to understand the archetypal story that had once held us in Act I Scene 1; we have therefore not yet liberated ourselves from it. That great rebellion freed us enough from the old story to be taken over by a newer, stronger, and more attractive archetypal story. But as we incorporate ourselves into the first Scene (only) of Act II, we remain vulnerable to being seduced by new concrete manifestations of the old story, or to being taken over by emanational relationships to other, new archetypal stories—without understanding their nature and implications any better than we did those of the old story. It is a step of great courage to move into Act II: Incoherence. But after we experience the first Scene, we are left with vital questions we cannot yet answer.

There is nothing intrinsically wrong with incoherence, nor with emanation. They are necessary transitions in the process of transformation. It is not incoherence that is the most dangerous part of this drama. Far more dangerous to us are the defense mechanisms that are intended to repress or mask incoherence as coherence by seemingly stabilizing our life by institutionalizing rebellion. We seek to profit from the vanity of flaunting or exploiting our part in these legitimized rebellions by raising victory piles for ourselves by digging holes for others. We build ourselves ever larger (defensive or actively aggressive) fortresses in the desert, but we are unable in fact to grow.

It is not only unnecessary to enter into incoherence as a way of life for the sake of transformation, but it is counterproductive. It creates a great barrier. It cannot and will not lead into transformation through any action intrinsic to its own dynamics. Creating incoherence is a human capacity grounded in the archetypal roots of our nature. We need to rebel against it only when it is an affliction created by others or is enclosed into a way of life by ourselves. Incoherence as a relationship—not as a way of life—can be a mercy: What if every living connection continued and repeated itself in its present form forever?

Our task in Act II is not to persist as a splinter created by others (or by us). It is not to continue to live the problem as it was originally defined by our former source of emanation—or under the still unexamined spell of our new source of emanation. We need consciously and deliberately to enter into incoherence with this first experience of incoherence—to negate this negation. But that does not mean finding merely an opposite position. Transformation is not a linear experience, nor an encounter of binary oppositions. We not only need to reject the original bondage as unbearable, but also to avoid letting ourselves be stranded in the first Scene of Act II. We enter into incoherence anew in order more fully to discover ourselves and the potentials of life.

ACT II SCENE 2: INCOHERENCE; EMPTYING OURSELVES

To liberate the wholeness of our being, we need to uncover, analyze, and empty ourselves of the sacred force that—by way of the powerful particular personal, political, historical, and sacred face of an individual, idea, feeling, value, or practice—colonized us and used us as its setting. We seek to understand for the first time also the new sacred force that reached us in the second Scene of Act I, to see if we need also to empty ourselves of it if it attaches us only to a new and different fragment of life—for, so far, our escape from that earlier powerful concrete manifestation has been a freedom gained at the expense of becoming more powerfully attached to a new emanational force. (To be newly and deeply committed to skepticism, cynicism, or materialism would also be evidence of an emanational relationship to an archetypal drama.)

Emptying ourselves is no small analytical and practical task. Earlier, the particulars that had grabbed us constituted manifestations of larger, deeper forces. Each expressed the structure and dynamics of an archetypal story—a story enacted in the service of an archetypal way of life. If we want to experience what fundamentally better life exists beyond Act II, we need to empty ourselves on three levels of being.

First, we need to empty ourselves of the concrete manifestations of the archetypal story that held us in the first Scene of Act I. (We did that as we entered Act II). We need also to break with the new concrete manifestations we developed or found for the archetypal story that inspired our rebellion. And we need to break with the concrete manifestations of the way of life of incoherence, if that is what had above all kept us within the first Scene of Act II.

Second, we need to discover the actual underlying patterning forces of the drama that held us within the first Scene of Act I and the story that pulled us from Act I into Act II—and we need to empty ourselves of both. Third, we need to come to understand the overarching ways of life which kept us in Act I and retain us in Act II—the ways of life that most deeply shaped these stories—and empty ourselves of them. That is what the process of transformation requires of us. There are no shortcuts.

We all have experience in breaking concrete relationships, though that is not easy precisely because these particular persons, ideas, norms, institutions, and systems of action captivate us by their strong embodiment of emanational sources. In the service of emanation, living underlying patterning forces represent the will of god, to be uncritically obeyed. In the service of incoherence, archetypal forces constitute what we (at most) call our unconscious. As long as we do not free ourselves from these underlying patterning forces, they will readily inspire us with new concrete versions of the same restrictive kind.

But how can we exercise this astonishing human capacity to say no to the sacred—forces that have hitherto commanded us, that we could not command—and empty ourselves of them? We who were prophets once—people compelled by the sacred to speak (and to act it out), but who had not known what we were talking about—need to turn ourselves into philosophers. We need to become philosophers in order to discover the four faces of being of any prophecy and its reality, truth, and purpose, so that we can prepare ourselves to become participants in transformation.[4]

Just as being a prophet in Act I does not require a long beard, flowing robes, or speaking in chapter and verse (nor seeing God face to face or being the first in history ever to say and do what we now hear), so becoming a philosopher in Act II does not require us to qualify as a professor of philosophy, nor simply, as the saying goes, to take life philosophically. The Talmud says a dream uninterpreted is like a letter unanswered. The new inspiration we receive may be for good or ill—we do not yet know. It produces a crisis, and we need to discover how to respond to it.

Our task as philosophers is to inquire into what living underlying patterning forces are shaping the practice of our life and whether it is wise for us to say yes to them. In our time, we still have little experience in probing for archetypal dramas. That is why most of this book seeks to exemplify and explain these underlying patterns. While we will analyze only a handful of quite pervasive archetypal stories, we will in subsequent chapters analyze in detail each of the four overarching ways of life, the most powerful of all archetypal stories at every moment of our life.

Here is a brief sketch of how we might begin any archetypal analysis. We start by telling the story of our own adventures from Act I Scene 1 to Act II Scene 1 as vividly and honestly as we can. We listen for sequences within each Scene that seem to happen again and again. The explicit details differ each time, but certain types of sequences—feelings, conflicts, frustrations, crises, satisfactions—seem to

---

[4]. I have been moved by the work of Alfarabi—a theorist of transformation who was born in 870 and died in Damascus in 950—to speak of Act I of the drama of transformation turning us into prophets, and Act II turning us into philosophers, thus preparing us to become participants in Act III. Alfarabi uses these terms to explain what is required of us to experience the transformation that comes from our connection with the "Active Intellect," meaning (unlike Aristotle's use of this term, *nous poietikon*) the creative face of God. For the third phase, Alfarabi uses the term *Imam*, by which he did not mean the leader of the community in prayer as in Sunni Islam or the leader of the entire community inspired, blessed, and appointed by God, as in Shi'ite Islam, but simply "guide," which is what that word means in Arabic. This process does indeed enable us also to become guides for others, but since Alfarabi's presentation of transformation is only potentially democratic (he addresses his work only to those among an educated minority who are ready), I prefer to emphasize the role of *participant*. For references to the Active Intellect in Alfarabi's work, see especially his "Philosophy of Aristotle," in Farabi and Muhsin Mahdi, *Philosophy of Plato and Aristotle*.

arise again and again. A pattern emerges in our mind. Can we describe it in terms of a structure and dynamics that always mark this story—or else never do? Are we ready to ask, who are all the people, living or dead, whom we have to have on stage with us for this story to recur again and again? Who or what, crucial to this story, is missing now? In answering these questions we shall identify an archetypal story in our life.

Many people in our time will say, "But my life does not hang together." And they are right. That, too, is an archetypal pattern. What we can count on in that case is that whatever story is being enacted, it is certainly in the service of incoherence. It could be any of a large number of such stories—which one it is is still to be identified. Or it could be that the story we first told reflects on unresolved conflict between archetypal dramas in our life—a conflict within ourselves or a conflict with others.

As we begin to see underlying patterns, we search not only to clarify what is happening to us personally. We cannot hope to transform ourselves by ourselves, as if we alone counted in this world. Consider this story: Our mother often beat us and the trauma of it has caused wounds in our being that diminish and hurt us to this day. Why did our mother beat us? Her father often beat her. We cannot stop our inquiry into our story here. No person acts but as an expression of all four faces of being. Why do certain cultures stir parents to beat their children? What historical and political structures and dynamics are at work expressing a sacred force?

Stalin was brutally beaten by his father. Such a fate was not unusual in his culture; he was also beaten as a student at a theological seminary. Given the archetypal dramas his culture legitimized, he had at least three choices. He could yield to this story of beatings in all its adult manifestations as well and submit himself to be a permanent victim in life. Or else, he could decide, as Stalin did, to gain supreme power to make certain that he would never be a victim again, but that he would beat and kill millions—who (so he—correctly or incorrectly—believed) might kill him. Stalin moved beyond the alliance of emanation and deformation as ways of life into the dominance of deformation.

There is a third choice for children who have been beaten—to work to transform the personal, political, historical, and sacred being of themselves and of a society that gave rise to millions of Stalins without whose help Stalin could not have enforced his power. Changes in outward personal behavior alone or in political institutions alone cannot overcome our history or the underlying sacred patterns—whose prophets we are inspired to remain in word and action—until we recognize them and liberate ourselves from them. Our so far only unconsciously inspired opposition to them moves us only into mere variants or opposites of them.

In the service of emanation, we do not need philosophers. We already know what to do; we know that a source (or sources) of unfathomable wisdom—or will—has revealed it all to us. We only require priests, rabbis, or theologians to interpret for us how it applies. In the service of incoherence, many philosophers by the end of the twentieth century have sought to put an end to philosophy except, as Richard Rorty puts it, as "an edifying conversation." They have tried to show that we can say nothing about ontology (the study of being) or epistemology (the study of the grounds on which we base claims to knowledge). We can at most clarify the language (or power games) which organize our thinking—and we can thereby also undo earlier structures of thought. Of course these will remain the limits of all philosophers who arrest themselves in the first Scene of Act II or who enter Act II Scene 2 solely to be inspired anew by the sacred source of incoherence as a way of life. They cannot therefore come to know archetypal forces.

Most individuals work, struggle, and long for concrete rewards. The concrete certainly matters. But most of us in our past and present are unaccustomed to looking for deep forces moving and shaping the entire context of meaning and purpose of each concrete event. Only by inquiring into the underlying archetypal story, however, can we learn whether our rebellion and the particulars to which we are now attached have led us into the service of incoherence, deformation, or transformation. No choice is more crucial in our life.

"To know yourself is to know your Lord." To free ourselves of Lords that possess us in emanational relationships is to free ourselves of all mysteriously overwhelming masters, and instead to participate with the sacred in new creation in a healing life. To practice transformation requires theory—or, until we have gained more systematic understanding, demands a consciousness that is as free, attentive, and probing as possible and that tests its new awareness in the practice of Act III.

The kind of consciousness that guides us toward understanding and emptying ourselves in Act II will seem initially strange to many of us. (So we shall explore it much more extensively in Chapter 10.) Our consciousness, as C.G. Jung has shown us, is constituted not only of thought and sensation (sensation is our capacity to identify and distinguish between concrete items) but also of two other aspects—intuition and feeling—which modern philosophers and scientists ignore, or at least banish into the privacy of the context of discovery, being concerned publicly only with the context of verification.[5] And our consciousness always reflects our unconscious—the archetypal source of the stories we enact but which (except in the drama of transformation which opens us to reject and to renew connections to our unconscious) we do not consciously and critically understand. We repress much of our being and, within such hobbling limits, restrict our creativity solely to expressions appropriate to dramas in the service of overarching fragments of life.

We cannot empty ourselves of something we do not understand. Emptying ourselves in Act II Scene 2 means, first, letting ourselves sense, feel, and intuit in all

---

5. On these four aspects of consciousness, which C. G. Jung calls *functions*, see C. G. Jung, *Psychological Types*.

its depths how unbearable (or untenable or fruitless) this underlying force which has hitherto patterned our life and molded its concreteness has in fact shown itself to be. Emptying ourselves means, second, coming to detach ourselves philosophically from the emanated power of the archetypal force so that we can see and understand it as a patterning drama.

The philosophy of transformation is a form of gnosis—that is, a kind of knowledge that brings about understanding of a process that helps us participate in the creation of the fundamentally new and better. This kind of gnosis involves diagnosis (seeing through surface appearances to the root of the matter), and prognosis (knowing the path of destruction that will grow if the old process continues, and the capacity and freedom that will grow if we persist in our new direction). Emptying ourselves means, third, taking courage from our new critical consciousness—ridding not only our consciousness but what previously seemed to be our unconscious of the domination of the old Lords, thus freeing ourselves to move into Act III to hear anew and to test the new in practice.

It takes courage to learn to unlearn what we had hitherto believed and felt to be of deep value, and that had inspired and molded crucial aspects of our life. It is not easy to say no to a whole way of life that we shared with so many of our neighbors who are still bound by it. It takes courage to learn how to destroy, not the other or ourselves, but instead the once precious concrete and underlying connections—courage to treat the others and ourselves as fully human. What brings this new courage into being? We are experiencing the process of wooing, and being wooed by, the deepest (and yet previously unknown) source of our being into becoming known and connected so that we may participate in creation together. We are freeing ourselves to be inspired with courage and understanding by that source. We have learned to recognize that we had previously clutched only a few fragments of the drama that this source continuously creates anew—and had limited all the stories we enacted by constricting them in the service of the Lords of these fragments.

We need courage to stand on our own feet even though we now stand empty, empty not with respect to everything, but with regard to a vital problem of our life. We desperately need new connections, but we have not yet realized and experienced them. But as we reach the end of Act II, we are not simply empty. At the beginning of this second Scene of Act II, we know that rebellion was necessary but insufficient; it leaves us still possessed.

Possessed by what? All we know is that we do not know. That knowledge turns us into philosophers, trying to gain the kind of theoretical understanding that will lead to new and better practice. By the end of that second Scene, we gain understanding not only of the Lords from which we need to free ourselves but also at least a strong intuition that this drama, even in Act II (incoherence), has a fundamental structure and dynamics.

It arises from the very nature of this archetypal process of transformation—its structure and dynamics—that its forces cannot move without *our* ever more understanding participation. We cannot simply pronounce an established script. If the inspiration that first drew us into this process in Act I Scene 2 was the archetypal force of transformation, it too would have seemed to us to be an emanation. At that point (in the very nature of this process) we could not yet have understood it. However attractive, it was also mysterious to us. It surely sparked our rebellion, but it did not inspire us to turn rebellion into a way of life.

Separating ourselves from this emanational beginning of transformation in Act II Scene 2 does not involve our separating ourselves from the core drama of life. Rather, we separate ourselves from its initial *appearance* of emanation, for no archetypal force in the service of transformation ever truly possesses us. At least intuitively, we recognize from the beginning its desire and need for us truly to come to know its nature so that both we and our source may grow in freedom and capacity for love and justice. Transformation is the only archetypal force that enriches our understanding and clarifies the underlying patterning forces of life so that it enables us to advance into the second Scene of Act II—there to turn us into philosophers who can see beyond the enchantment of emanation. That is no small distinction!

Here is another crucial example of the unique nature of the core drama: We cannot empty ourselves of these previously mysterious and overwhelming archetypes unless at the end of Act II, there also exists an exit for them. We do not have the personal strength to destroy archetypes, but we can free ourselves from them so that they will depart at this exit from the now transforming story of our life. Hence, though we are empty, we are not nothing. Our conscious and conscientious breaking into emptiness—our capacity to say no, to understand why we say no, and to turn our negation into actual practice—possesses an essential form. It exists as the middle passage between two Acts; we have readied ourselves to be filled again. It is amazing how precious a moment this is. Henri Poincaré, the French mathematical theorist, tells us how, again and again, answers to questions in his field came to him after he had worked hard but had given up and had stopped thinking about it. Then while, say, waiting with an empty mind for the bus, the right answer suddenly came to him.[6]

I have had this experience many times. My mind goes blank whenever I wait for the arrival of what moves in its own time beyond my control, for that is, symbolically, what slow elevators, municipal bus lines, and creative new images have in common. What is crucial is our arrival at the point where we know that we do not

---

6. Henri Poincaré, "Science and Method," reprinted in Brewster Ghiselin, *The Creative Process: A Symposium*—a book filled with revealing essays on this subject by creative people in many different fields.

know. What we do not need to empty ourselves of is the loving desire to transform. When Socrates says again and again, "I am ignorant of everything except love," he knows that even at the moment when we and the sacred are silent, our being's essential capacity for transformation remains. The more often we have reached this moment in prior experiences of transformation, the more solid our hope, faith, and love that we shall experience the high value of this moment once more.

Here is a story to illustrate this middle passage:

Once a student came to a Zen Master and said, "I finished all my studies at a monastery some distance away. Then troubles broke out in that region and I fled here. Since I completed all the necessary work, all that is left for me to do is to get a certificate from an established institution. I am ready to be examined and to receive the certificate." "Fine," said the Zen Master, "please go and see what work is needed in the garden." A few weeks passed. The student became impatient. He approached the Zen Master as he was walking in the garden and said: "I believe I was misunderstood. I needed only to be examined and to be certified." "If the garden is not for you," replied the Zen Master, "please work in the kitchen." Only a few days passed this time before the student asked to be allowed to bid farewell to the Zen Master; he felt deeply misunderstood. When he presented himself for the final tea, he watched the Zen Master pour the liquid into his cup. The Master poured and poured and as he kept pouring, the student could no longer contain himself, "Master, Master, how can you keep pouring into a cup that is already filled?" "That is your first lesson," said the Master.[7]

EXIT ACT II: INTO DEFORMATION
OR ON TO TRANSFORMATION

At the end of Act II—and only at this point—there is an exit from the core drama of life. Until then, we can only halt and try to consolidate our place of arrest. Now we may empty ourselves of our unbearable Lord—now that we have come to know that Lord and that Lord's sacred way of life and the story we enacted in its service—so that we may be reborn. We free ourselves of these archetypal forces and let them exit here into the abyss (in German, the *Abgrund*) where their overall strength diminishes even unto death the more they are deprived of their concrete faces. Thus we ready ourselves to conjoin in Act III with the deepest ground of our being (the *Urgrund*). Or else we may ourselves exit in our own concrete being into the abyss of destructive death, still enthralled by an archetypal fragment in the service of deformation.

How can deformation arise in the first two Acts of the drama of transformation? The explanation would be short and simple if it were true that original sin

---

7. Paul Reps, *Zen Flesh, Zen Bones*, 19.

from the day we were born reduces, twists, and damns us into evil again and again, or that evil manifests itself only as a particular thought or action. We would not be able to notice deformation in time if we could see it only as it pushes the last survivors into nothingness. Deformation, like transformation, is a process. It constitutes a road to destructive death. We can therefore discover where and why people are on this path and try to stop and change their course. All of Chapter 6 explores the threats of deformation and how we may analyze it and respond in time. Here, briefly, are examples from that exploration.

If we are gripped by deformation during Acts I and II, our exit is our moment of final destruction. For more and more people in our time, deformation disrupts Act I Scene 1 because it comes all too soon to a traumatic end: The loving, caring emanational security children need when they are young is denied them. Their parents are on killing drugs or they cannot provide enough food or medical care or safe shelter, or they abuse their children with incest or other forms of cruelty. If we do not die of such misery, such trauma—the shock of being denied or torn out of an emanational container while we still need it—may make us feel inadequate, unwanted, and needy for the rest of our life. We may again and again seek new emanational relationships in order to be contained by them and within them because of our grave anxiety about its opposite of being abandoned or even abandoning ourselves. Or else, we may be inspired to revenge ourselves against life—against ourselves or our neighbors or against anyone else.

Alternately, in ever larger numbers, people are finding their life in Act I Scene 1 (often their entire emanational way of life or subsequently their emanational relationship to incoherence as a way of life—because both are intrinsically only fragments) shattered by others whose personal or political power far exceeds their own. As these others destroy the concrete relations on which our security had rested, and as they demonstrate that the emanational sources reflected in these relationships can no longer protect us, we find ourselves, against our will or desire, without help and in despair, in the first Scene of incoherence. And as we cannot bear living a life of competing for fragments, the new and demonic source which infused us along the way in the second Scene of emanation sends us either into deep apathy, cutting us off more and more from ourselves and others, or else renders us totally dependent on someone who believes he alone knows the road to new glory.

As we become enthralled by this great leader and join his movement, we usually fantasize our great new bond to be emanational, because other than incoherence, that is the only kind of relationship we have known and experienced. That is why we trust this new demonstration—or at least new promise—of overwhelming power so deeply. We do not yet understand the deforming nature, though in fact it raises our hope of glory by diminishing our being to one figment of fantasy: Only our race counts; only our nation counts; only our beliefs are true; only I count—or their mere opposite: nothing really counts, not even I.

As we are sucked into Act II Scene 2 by the archetypal force arising from the abyss, the power of our fantasy keeps us from turning into philosophers. Absolute powerlessness—like absolute power—corrupts absolutely. Instead of breaking with this deforming archetypal force which possessed us since Act I Scene 2, we move toward and through the exit in bondage with it, killing ourselves and others.

That is why Act II Scene 2 is so crucial. Unless transformation inspires us in Act I Scene 2, we move into Act II only because a more powerful emanational or pseudo-emanational force takes hold of us. We then repress the emanational force that had formerly possessed us—repress it because we do not yet understand it and thus have not yet learned how to liberate ourselves from it. And if we turn Act II Scene 1 into a way of life in incoherence, we also repress the fact that our deep attachment to it is in fact also an emanational relationship.

Repression is a form of deformation since it controls and diminishes our being. Unless our growing intuition, hurt, and sharpening perception leads us to become critical philosophers in Act II Scene 2 in order to understand what has so far wrenched our being out of its true and full shape, our increasing desire, even desperation, to preserve or magnify our fragment of life (an increasingly costly task) will move us downward on the road to destructive death for ourself and others.

Deformation is the great fall from the core drama of life—the only fall that leads us into damnation. The worst dangers by far lie not on the path of transformation but arise from departing from that path. The coherent structure and dynamics of the drama of transformation are demonstrated by the fruitfulness of its movements, the limitations engendered by its possible arrests, and the radically different uses of its exit. We can move *beyond* the exit to the fundamentally new and better or *through* the exit into the fundamentally new and worse. It is not a drama held together by iron laws of history, by mere probabilities, or by sacred omnipotence. It is an exercise in the freedom of creation in which we may participate according to a known underlying pattern, but never according to any preprogrammed concrete steps or conclusions.

ACT III SCENE 1: CONNECTING ANEW TO THE DEPTHS OF OUR BEING

In Act III Scene 1, we have emptied ourselves three times over—of concrete particulars and relationships, of the underlying archetypal stories they embodied, and of the overarching way of life in whose service they were enacted. Since we have freed all four faces of our being at least with respect to the problem that would not let us stay where we were, we can count on being filled again, filled from our own well.[8] We can count on being filled, for this is a universe of continuous creation in which the core drama of life is being recreated again and again, awaiting our participation. We can count on being filled from our own well—from the deepest source of our being, the source that creates the archetypal drama of transformation, and therefore allows all of us to join in drinking it to vitalize us to become and to be fully human.

If we did not believe in this deepest source of our being, we could not experience transformation. We would be caught in emanation instead. What we experience now is that we hear or see something in relation to our problem at hand that we never knew or understood before. To be transforming for our life, it need not be something nobody ever knew before. What matters is that it is fundamentally new and better for *our* life, and in any case, the concreteness of it is always personally unique. This time, we do not turn into a prophet again. We are not only being inspired from the deepest depths of our being but we also understand what we are being inspired by. We are not only moved by that sacred face of our being, but we understand what kind of participation we are risking our trust in. We will, in the next Scene, turn this personal experience consciously, critically, and creatively into political practice to see if in fact it leads to the fundamentally new and better in our own unique history and the history we share with others.

While we still live in the service of incoherence, we remain deeply skeptical about such a drama. We have no awareness of being anchored in sacred forces. Indeed the underlying forces that compel us inhibit our hearing from our deepest source of being. We may still long for such groundedness, especially in our time when socialism in the East and West has run out of relevant words or action, and when capitalism encourages above all the pursuit of self-interest, however many are thereby rendered insecure or superfluous. But in the service of incoherence, we have no memories of transformation. In the West, we have rarely heard about transformation, and this talk about sacred forces may uncomfortably remind us of religious conformity. In the East, the two dominant movements are to follow the Western model or else to oppose this trend through a fundamentalism that is in fact ignorant of the actual foundations of the past and does not know how to find foundations for continuous renewal in our time (and hence resorts to despotism and terror).

For most people still in the service of emanation, God (or the gods) has already spoken once and for all. But in Act III Scene 1 we approach the deepest source of being in order to ask it again, to hear it again, and to understand it anew—an experience that any believer holds to be beyond our capacity, and to be heretical if we persist in such a claim. Ibn 'Arabi (who died in 1240 in Damascus) said

---

8. A phrase first used by Bernard of Clairvaux and now the title of a book by Gustavo Gutiérrez, *We Drink from Our Own Wells*—a discussion of liberation theology which has inspired a contemporary movement of transformation we shall discuss in Part Two.

that one of the worst mistakes Muslims had made was to create Shariah law—rules based on the revelations of the Koran and on the sayings and actions of the Prophet Muhammad. What was recorded in these original reports was what God or his Prophet did or said that particular morning or that particular afternoon in response to what was being asked or done at that moment. These are precious reports, said Ibn 'Arabi, but if we are to discover whether any particular statement of that time applies now, we need to see if the same archetypal story was being experienced then that we are experiencing now. If not, we need to empty ourselves to reach that deepest of sources again.[9]

What do we hear in Act III Scene 1? We hear a particular statement or see a particular image or feel a particular feeling and we also experience these particulars as concrete aspects of a new archetypal drama and way of life. What we hear is a response to the problem that first moved us into this process, though usually this response also shows us that our original questioning had been shaped by the structure and dynamics of our former story and way of life. We now recognize that that was not really the question (though, fortunately, it first sent us on our way), and we realize as well the value of this new and different response. What we now receive from the depths is not only a new inspiration but a new understanding which, in the next Scene, we will proceed to practice and test with others. Since our relationship to this sacred source of being is the least familiar aspect of our life (though it is the deepest source of our capacity and freedom to understand and act), Chapter 9 will greatly enlarge upon this subject.

ACT III SCENE 2: PRACTICING TRANSFORMATION WITH OUR NEIGHBORS

Insight, even a splendid new vision, is not yet complete liberation. Only people who have freed themselves to find new resources within themselves can begin political movements of transformation. But liberation remains unfinished business until we create new links for all four faces of our being within ourselves and with others. That is why, in the final Scene of transformation, we become a participant with others and a guide who helps them to continue their process.

We do not put ourselves in command of the next step—testing in practice with our neighbors what we learned in Act III Scene 1—for it is humanly impossible to transform others *for them*. We can be guides because we have actually experienced the drama of transformation at least once. But we cannot be more than guides, for

---

9. See James W. Morris, "Ibn 'Arabi's 'Esotericism': The Problem of Spiritual Authority"—though my summary speaks more simply and plainly than Ibn Arabi does—whose approach and substance Morris elucidates with exceptional understanding. For a similar response of earlier transformers to the need to open ourselves to hear again, see Moshe Idel, *Kabbalah: New Perspectives*.

if we now inspire others with our new ideas and new understanding of the process of change—and particularly as a living example of transformation, that inspiration will help them move into Act I Scene 2 of emanation—they are energized by a new spirit, but they do not (and cannot) yet know what it means. We may supply the embryo, but it grows in *their* womb, and as guides—not as hierarchical fathers, not as overprotective mothers, but as midwives and as nonpossessive lovers—we can only (but indeed we can) help to deliver and care for what is being born from within those we inspired in that opening Scene.

At this point, there arises all too often a severely detrimental temptation in the minds of guides of transformation, and also of those who are drawn to them. Both may be seduced by the power of the new experience—one into being the great guru from now on, the others into following the great guru or great teacher or great new charismatic political leader. That great one, experienced henceforth as a mysteriously overwhelming source of "wisdom," may lead us deeper and more intensely into the experience of this new moment. But in that case, transformation is arrested and turned instead into a new emanational way of life of perennial intercourse and perennial (but arrested) pregnancy. "Right opinion," in Plato's sense, may indeed be preferable to wrong opinion or sheer dogma, but opinion generated and enshrined by a source of emanation keeps us from coming to know ourselves—and from giving birth to the deepest ground of being we can share with others.

No immediate political victory is possible for transformers. Having ourselves arrived in the last Scene of this drama, we now have the freedom and capacity, the energy and understanding, not only to heal but to renew the personal, political, historical, and sacred faces of our own being. But we cannot do that without being with our neighbors. As we seek to form a nucleus of transformers (politically and historically we are starting from scratch) so that we may work toward a critical mass (that is, a majority), most others—among those eager to find out more about who we are and what we say and do—begin in Act I Scene 2 of their life.

No grand strategy is relevant now. As we build new political networks, each unique person who hopes to become a full participant in transformation counts, and so do those who are simply baffled. We need to face them as actual, unique persons and to help them see themselves as manifestations of limiting stories which they still uncritically accept and enact. Even as our understanding of the nature and power of the underlying stories that move us grows, we need to respond to all where they are here and now. There is no other place or time to begin.

We need to enter through the door of those who have indeed opened it, but who have not yet experienced the rest of the process—to be with them and help them leave with us through a common door. We must enter through *their* door, for what has become unbearable, untenable, or unfruitful about the experience of the first Scene vitally affects which door the second Scene will inspire them to open. If, in Act I Scene 1, we accept as our fate being treated as lesser—or even invisible—human beings, then the next Scene may well arouse us to fight for our civil rights. We may win, but discover that we have won only a fragment of power in the service of incoherence. Martin Luther King, Jr. recognized this fact, and therefore sought to mobilize the new inspiration and energy for a struggle also against poverty and war. Then he was killed.

Once people recognize that their continued acceptance of their inherited story will not let them be fully human, we can (from the perspective of transformation) help them see that other related stories—and their present way of life—all present obstacles to living a full life with justice and compassion. Entering a radically new Act of the drama of transformation is the heart of the matter.

People, who have enclosed themselves within the present stage of their life, if they listen when they hear about the drama of transformation, will not understand it, or they will see it only as a threat to their way of life. But if they have become anxious about problems which their present story cannot resolve, deteriorating conditions may cause their door to crack, or may lead them to open their door a crack. They may hear questions that open their door entirely to the second Scene of Act I. Incoherence as a way of life requires me to be in charge of my own life, but why is there in fact no one in charge or at most, in charge only over large or small disconnected pieces of life? Why is unemployment so high and so permanent for so many? Why don't we care about (though in fact we fear) the fate of the powerless? (Chapter 5 will raise many more such questions that cannot be resolved through incremental changes.)

Questions that call into doubt the very nature and limits of our present story of life, that cannot be answered within it, but that we recognize need an answer because the lack of working answers lames and even endangers our being—these are the most powerful forces to open us, not only to a new inspiration, but to the entire process of transformation. Such questions are ever more likely and ever more strongly to arise in our time. Repression and suppression are becoming ever more costly, and because they are so costly, they work ever less successfully. Successful achievement of wealth and power and of freer subjectivity leaves us still deeply dissatisfied; we cannot yet truly experience our self or connections to our community. Compassion and justice remain too scarce.[10]

Who is likely to become the nucleus of a transforming society—the initial nucleus of a developing majority? Karl Marx did not know. Marx, who could not tell us why the son of a successful bourgeois lawyer, after gaining his doctorate in philosophy at a first-rate university, became a revolutionary Communist, also could not tell us how workers turn into conscious, critical, creative proletarians. Lenin, unable to find enough proletarians, created a revolutionary elite instead,

---

10. Robert N. Bellah, *Habits of the Heart* offers a most perceptive report on what is lacking and its costs.

only to discover, after a successful revolution, that he did not have enough socialists to help create a socialist society.

Gamal Abdel Nasser, President of Egypt, rediscovered the same lesson. Having announced in 1956 that he would turn Egypt into a socialist society, he was asked in 1962 by a Member of Parliament why there was still so little evidence of socialism in Egypt. Unlike two dozen other authoritarian leaders who had made the same claim in other countries, Nasser acknowledged that he had learned something: "You cannot create socialism without socialists."[11]

Socialists around the world range from deeply concerned humanists, to advocates of the economic and social welfare of the most deprived, to power-hungry centralizers, to people increasingly baffled about what can be done for the general good in our world. All of them enact their quite different repertoires of stories in the service of incoherence. The deepest source of our being remains unknown to them—cannot be known, they say. (They think of the sacred only as based upon traditional beliefs—from which happily they have liberated themselves.) Much of the personal, political, and historical face of our being—interpenetrated by far more aspects of the sacred than was ever authorized by organized religions—remains therefore unrecognized by socialists.

It is also true that we cannot create a transforming society without transformers. That role is even more unfamiliar.

The defeat of tyrants does not in itself begin the process of transformation. It only enlarges our opportunity. As the many changing, conflicting, largely unconnected reforms and their quite unevenly distributed costs in the former USSR, Eastern Europe, and China most recently demonstrate, the drive for personal political and economic power—the desire to gain the benefits of the way of life that now dominates the world—most readily comes to the fore. Even most reformers of the same persuasion still lack new local and countrywide political networks. Reforms so far have above all spread incoherence as a way of life, with growing differences between those trying to organize it as an incremental improvement for the many and the few profiting from it in new power and wealth.[12]

What kind of leaders do we need for a movement of transformation? None. We need *guides* for this process. Genuine guides of transformation always demonstrate their success by putting themselves out of business with regard to the problem at issue. Good parents, teachers, and therapists do so now. Guides are

---

11. But he never found out how to help create socialists. That same year, Anwar Sadat, then Vice-President of Egypt, told me in an interview that after four unsuccessful attempts to create a political party, the government would now organize an Arab Socialist Union on the basis of the files of the national security police—to find informers most in touch with their neighborhoods, and for them to select the most loyal followers.

12. For a most illuminating comparable study of these changes, see Minxin Pei, *From Reform to Revolution*.

therefore always part of a community of mutual guides. We guide people so that, next time (if indeed not already during the present process of transformation) they will know how to guide us (or others) with respect to a problem they have learned to resolve but we (or others) have not yet understood. Guides are people who have come to exemplify and explain what concrete and underlying forces we need to free ourselves from and what opportunities can open up instead.

What kind of followers do we need for a movement of transformation? None. With regard to each problem, we need to discover what kind of network, small or large, we need to build so that all the people who need to be on stage with us for us to be able to enact this new story in the service of transformation are in fact connected anew. It is not a job of *institution building* in the conventional sense of that term. We always begin with new face-to-face relationships, creating political parties, elected assemblies, and task forces upon that face-to-face foundation—not upon the impersonal processing of people according to impersonal rules.

The people most likely to be attracted to new forms of organization are those for whom there is no room or no equality in present networks for what we can and need to do together—people treated as lesser or invisible human beings, and hence exploited, their suffering ignored; people punished or banished if they do not treat themselves as lesser or invisible in the presence of the dominant; people who know they have been deprived of connections to life. Such people are especially likely to rebel against incoherence as a way of life. This most likely constituency may not yet move this way. The majority of them still accept the same archetypal story that drives the dominant: Prepare yourself to gain a place within the established structure. If you find no room or fail in this competition—the governing story says—it is your own fault. You did not try hard enough. Renewed cultural pride (reinvigorated precisely because it is under attack—for it is not part of the dominant culture) may keep us within our inherited emanational containers.

Some of us convert a fragment of capitalism (which is otherwise foreclosed to us) entirely into deformation. To make money quickly, we sell drugs. To rise high quickly, we consume drugs. We create a local "state" that seeks to establish a monopoly on coercion. We may try to conquer or kill off our competition, thus putting them into recession or depression. Consumption of drugs will have the same effect. It may also kill us.

Are the oppressed the only people likely to seek transformation? Buddha was a prince when he began his search. Moses was not a slave, unlike other Jews in Egypt, when he was sparked to lead them into the desert toward a more promising land. Muhammad was a member of the leading family of Mecca, the most important commercial center of the Arabian Peninsula. He was also successful in the caravan trade when he despaired of endless battles between Arab families and tribes and the fruitless inspiration of about three hundred different gods enshrined in different temples in Mecca. He entered a cave for forty days and forty nights and came forth with the idea of a new kind of community based on a new sense of justice uniting "helpers of God."

Even such great people can make mistakes. None of the Jews who traveled for forty years through the desert, not even Moses, could empty themselves enough of old or new stories of emanation or of sheer rebellion. None of them could actually enter into a more promising land to create a transforming community. Muhammad soon accepted the conversion of entire extended families and tribes to augment his power, but in fact these helped to turn the new community of Islam into an overarching emanational container that would more effectively preserve the emanational container of kinship groups.

In our age of specialization reflecting the predominance of organizing and reorganizing fragments of life, even people who have reached Act III with respect to one issue may remain focused solely on that issue and not see and act on its interconnection to other deeply impairing or even destructive dramas in the service of incoherence and even deformation. Only spotted owls, only whales, only peace, only feminism, only the spirit matters.

It is vital for each of us to contribute especially what our talent and need and understanding awaken and energize in us to do. We may well concentrate on creating new photographs or poems that open us to new visions and insights, composing a new liberating musical rhythm, freeing ourselves first of a relationship we discovered had enchained us, tuning in more deeply on the sacred or becoming a political activist on a particular issue. The question is not how big a change, but how fundamental a change. In the service of transformation, however, we will also need to understand and, as far as we have ability and time, to deal with our interconnections (or the still crucially missing gaps) with other stories. Otherwise our own contribution cannot make much of a difference to the quality of our life.

It is indeed essential to begin specifically—but also in depth—where people are now. By the middle of the twentieth century, an ever larger number of poor, illiterate peasants in Latin America experienced growing discontent. Transformation has by now engaged several tens of millions of them, even in the face of despotic regimes. The liberation theology movement begins from the fact that these peasants are Catholic, illiterate, and powerless. They are Catholic: hence the focus on Jesus—but not in order to reinforce belief in him and in the Church's interpretation of his commands, but in order to guide people to risk faith in experiencing *being* Jesus (not to be crucified and resurrected after death, but the ever renewing experience of "dying" in order to be "reborn")—according to the uniqueness of each personal human being, thus becoming empowered also fundamentally to change their historical and political being. People begin (initially with the help of priests or, increasingly, laity) to guide each other to form a new community—*una comunidad eclesial de base*—usually translated as "basic Christian community" but, more faithfully to the actual words and practice, spelled out as "a community assembled upon its foundation." These communities are face-to-face communities of about twelve people each, interconnected with each other through collaboration and by members who join more than one of them, but not impersonal mass movements led by one charismatic chief.

The first shared activity is usually learning to read—to read a book whose vital importance all have heard about but have never been allowed to read on their own in their own language until Vatican II permitted it in 1962. The edition of the New Testament used by these people contains the original text on the top of the page and on the bottom half, questions about its meaning for their daily life here and now. For example, Jesus said: "For I was hungry and you gave me food; I was thirsty and you gave me drink; I was a stranger and you made me welcome; naked and you clothed me, sick and you visited me, in prison and you came to see me.... I tell you solemnly, in so far as you did this to one of the least of these brothers of mine, you did it to me."[13]

As these peasants learn to read and freely to discuss such texts, they realize that Jesus (unlike their rulers, landlords, hierarchic priests, and local police) respects them, cares about them—"not because the poor are good but because God is life and the poor are dying before their time."[14] They now feel empowered to ask: Why am I poor? Why are my children hungry? ("Your body is the temple of the Holy Spirit which is in you."[15]) What can we do about it? Jesus came to form a community, not to save isolated individuals. They study the text as their own story, thus building self-confidence and solidarity. They organize action on specific needs: water, clinics, daycare, cooperative buying and selling. They help each other's families in sickness and also as some of them are tortured and killed by their oppressive regimes.

They constitute still only a small minority. What would it require to succeed? Their task is not to capture the state but to build linked communities that can substitute for the hierarchic, bureaucratic state. That will take time, but surely not as many centuries as it took to develop the nation-state.[16] Affinity groups—each composed of eight to twelve people—constitute the most basic and most pervasive social tissue of a transforming society. People in affinity groups help each other most concretely, face to face, with sympathy and understanding to go through the experience of breaking and recreating to enrich each other's lives. They interconnect with other such groups to constitute the nuclei of what we can and need to do together.

13. Matthew 25:35–40. (All translations from the Bible, unless otherwise noted, are drawn from (1985). *The New Jerusalem Bible*.
14. Gustavo Gutiérrez in a speech given at Maryknoll, NY, December 3, 1984.
15. Corinthians I6:19.
16. John Resenbrink gives us a deeply informed and helpful analysis of the difficulties and opportunities of a newly organized beginning in a "secular" society, the United States, in John Resenbrink, *The Greens and the Politics of Transformation*.

These are the people whom we feel closest to, with whom we live every day, with whom singly or as married couples, we share our lives. We experience affinity in part for reasons we cannot put entirely into words, in part because all of us in this group care deeply about a particular aspect of life—feminism, art, ecology, racism, education, the poor. Many people are likely to belong to two or even three affinity groups because they share more than one such deep concern with others.

Springing from these affinity groups are various larger networks, crucial among them are political parties based on membership dues and not on money from already powerful elites. (When such a rooted party has five million members and dues are two dollars a month, the party collects one hundred twenty million dollars a year, with which it can sponsor many more activities than electoral campaigns.) Political parties that meet to discuss and organize on local, state, and national problems also help to elect members to legislatures at these levels that actually debate issues and then authorize task forces not to issue reports but to actually resolve problems.

These task forces are composed of people who have studied a problem and its interconnection to its larger context, but they also include people whose problem it is. These task forces prove their ability to deal with a problem by putting themselves out of business. That is the proof that they have found a solution which people themselves can practice—if necessary, with funds appropriated by the legislature.

2

Questions about the Drama of Transformation

Transformation is a process of participating in creation so that we may give birth to something fundamentally new that is also fundamentally better. This book is addressed to all, whatever their gender, who hope to plant seeds, become pregnant, and be midwives of transformation in history within themselves and with others.

We need to learn how to free ourselves and to help others to sever unbearable, untenable, and unfruitful relationships—relationships that lack love and justice—so that we may liberate ourselves to be filled anew. We cannot manufacture transformation. We can learn to tune in to this nonlinear process at work as the pregnancy is still developing in the womb and to move caringly in the midst of hope and pain even before there is any practical outcome.

This work is addressed to the pregnant, to those wondering about the risks and joys of pregnancy, and to those in the process of giving birth. Anyone who reserves theory for the ears of impregnators and midwives is not a true guide of transformation, but is striving instead to create a new elite. If we tell people how to collaborate in new ways (or worse, coerce them to) so that they may experience new forms of justice, but don't show them how to achieve consciousness of underlying patterns so that they may find their own link to the deepest source of their being and so become creative themselves, we deny them full participation in a transforming society.

Each person is essential for the politics of transformation, for the personal face of every being is unique and valuable. Only each individual person can free herself or himself to connect to the deepest source of being. We can encourage people to enter this process and help them to find their way. We can be care-fully present to its travail and share in its joys, but only each person can reach his or her deepest depths—becoming conscious of what was previously unconscious about the dramas that had connected all four faces of his or her being, or indeed repressed or distorted some of them. Only a person can be creative and contribute with others to the resolution of shared problems. Only such a conscious, critical, creative person can fully link with others to form a transforming society. Only such a person, linked and moving in these ways, can know whether justice is being experienced in her or his own being and in all that we can and need to do together. No one else can be a substitute on personal, political, historical, or sacred grounds for any face of our being. Any politics that does not make room for this kind of personal participation falsifies our lives—falsifies the very nature and purpose of our being.

As I review the richest and most fruitful archetypal drama—that of transformation—my purpose is not to summarize it for a second time but to try to answer questions that can only be clarified in the light of the entire story.

Nothing being offered here is to be believed even for a minute. Believing in transformation would put us into an emanational container within which we would experience our life sometimes with great (though sometimes with diminished) intensity, but we would never develop into a whole being. It is not belief that is of any help. Instead, it is a question of faith[1]—of risking trust in the practice of transformation as described by a theory which is thus tested again and again by each person and by experiences that are concretely never the same but infinitely varied, yet reflect the same underlying pattern of this drama—or else the pattern of one of its three fragments. If the dynamics of this drama were not aspects of the very structure of human nature (including its depths), inventing a story such as this would not help, for it would remain an illusory artifice.

QUESTIONS ABOUT EMANATION

We always begin this drama of transformation in emanation for reasons stemming from our political, sacred, and personal history. Consider the political. When we are born and for some time after—when so much of the world is still mysterious to us and we have so little power to cope with it—we need someone whose mysterious power we can trust to take care of us. But our parents also share with others of their community (however large or small) an overarching way of life and many archetypal stories in its service. Our parents become for us—and seek to become for us—the immediate embodiments of these underlying forces, thus to inspire us concretely and in our very depths to be like them as much as possible. Most of the

---

1. I owe this radical distinction between belief and faith to Wilfred C. Smith, *Faith and Belief*. Smith does not speak of archetypal dramas, but his comparative study of Christian, Jewish, and Muslim experience profoundly helps to illuminate this contrast.

powerful people, institutions, and media as we grow up will seek to reinforce these emanational attachments. What makes us so deeply vulnerable to their influence?

Consider our sacred history. We have been created in the image of our creator, namely, to be creative. When we reach out to the deepest source of our being, the one that constantly creates anew the drama of transformation, then we are truly free and able to be creative. But the other sacred forces are also transpersonal. They flow through us when we become vulnerable to them out of our personal, political, and historical anxiety as we are stopped, or stop ourselves, in the course of the core drama of life and seek certainty (through unconscious repression and conscious suppression) instead. The archetypal forces of each Act and Scene of this drama have the capacity and freedom to try to consolidate their power and reach out to us, and, if we are vulnerable, to recreate us in their image. That is why problems of stability and change run much deeper than social scientists—working with whatever refined abstraction or precision in the service of incoherence—are able to perceive.

Because human nature has been created as an image of its deepest creator, but also with the freedom and responsibility to say yes or no (and also *maybe*) along the way, it is also in our nature to be vulnerable to the archetypal forces of the other three ways of life and to be recreated by them. But they mold us through emanational relationships, or beyond containment (through a pseudo-emanational beginning) into deforming destruction. They render us creative only within the constrictive terms of their emanational container. Only the creator of the cosmos of continuous creation needs our freedom and capacity to learn how to participate ever more fully with all four faces of our being. Our growing personal relationship in what we can and need to do together with the sacred thus also has a historical face.

Consider our personal history. We always begin any new story in an emanational relationship because the really new (not the incrementally new) is truly unfamiliar and therefore mysterious to us. In Act I Scene 1, we are overawed because we begin as children. But even as we grow up, no established emanational relationship is ever critically analyzed and evaluated by the powers that be, nor by us. (We wouldn't dare.) We remain deeply impressed by the power of the powerful people, norms, values, ideas, and institutions because we experience them not only as mortal creatures or creations but as manifestations of a deeper, mysteriously inspiring reality. That is also why we consider the threat or actual use of naked force against deviants to be entirely legitimate.

In the second Scene of Act I (emanation), we are inspired by what is once again mysterious to us because we cannot understand the new in the light of the established form of emanation. We are baffled this time all the more that there could exist anything so new, so much more wonderful, and also so objectionable to our present stories and way of life—and yet, so powerful. But emanation is always vulnerable because of its intrinsic internal contradictions—it is intensely inspiring but, as a fragment of experience, encloses and thus constricts our life as long as we try to preserve it—and because, contrary to the very belief it always arouses, it is *not* the only way to live. There are competing emanational sources and entirely different ways of life.

All forms of emanation—from stories like romantic love to ways of life like orthodox Judaism, Christianity, and Islam—are also vulnerable to history. This is contrary to the idea that all these forms of emanation inculcate in us—that unless we fail them, they will endure; that they had a beginning long, long ago but they will never change and never end (except perhaps on Judgment Day). Each one of us, by our very nature in this cosmos of continuous creation, also has a historical face of being. All archetypal stories which possess us emanationally face ever new historical challenges for which, within their present underlying pattern, they have no satisfactory answers.

What is most powerfully and pervasively new in history is that emanation as a way of life is dying, both as an archetype and in its concrete manifestations, and hence the overarching reinforcement behind all emanational dramas has fundamentally weakened. And in the service of incoherence, our parents (even if they stay together in marriage) are increasingly less certain what archetypal dramas they want to continue unquestioningly to embody. This is an uncertainty that also faces schools and other institutions and all ideas and norms inherited from earlier centuries or earlier decades. Clutching emanational fragments and turning in their defense to deformation as a way of life (and death) is therefore increasingly becoming the response around the world in order to kill off threats to emanation—threats that can no longer be effectively repressed or suppressed. We shall discuss this historical trend extensively in future chapters.

I have been speaking of our emanational relationship to emanational dramas. That may sound as if that relationship were an additional factor, even an additional story, apart from the emanational story we are enacting. That is not the case. I phrase the matter this way for two reasons. First, I should like thereby to underline our being drawn into this drama, tied to it not only by performing our particular role but also by being unquestioningly enthralled by and living in support of this drama as a whole. And second, I hope thereby also to call attention to a process that allows us to radically change our relationship to this drama.

However deeply we enter into emanation, we still have a unique personal face of being. We have stifled it by our conformity, but however much repressed, it is not dead. A new emanational source can reach us and we can enter into a detached relationship to the old emanational drama. From a relationship that pulled us inside that story, we now are attaining a relationship to it from our own ground in a new story.

Once we live some or much of our life in the service of transformation, we can recognize more quickly how emanation can serve once again to open us to that way of life without retaining us within emanation:

Two Buddhist monks were walking down the wooden sidewalks of a town after a great long rain. The streets were slippery with mud. At the end of the sidewalk, one of the monks noticed a beautiful woman in a festive long dress hesitating, fearful of crossing the street. He picked her up and carried her across the mud. Then he and the other monk walked on. After a silence of half an hour, the other monk could contain himself no longer. "How could you, a monk, dare to pick up a beautiful woman and carry her in your arms for all the world to see?" Replied the first monk: "I put her down half an hour ago, but I see you are still carrying her."[2]

Containers in the service of transformation are not temples within which to hide and from which to ward off what is always to be taboo. In this way of life, we are free to be spontaneously and deeply inspired as new needs arise on each crossing and even in the mud.

In Act I Scene 1, a force we cannot comprehend (symbolized by the squiggle in the diagram) flows into us and animates us, but it prevents us from being whole (hence the symbol of the half moon), for it keeps us in this first step of creation. In the next Scene, a new source of emanation reaches us. There are indeed more sacred forces in the world than we have usually hitherto experienced in our lives or than we now usually call sacred. I have symbolized this new sacred source as a snake, for in the belief of established emanational authorities (and not only of monotheistic religions) a poisonous animal has now infected our body and soul. If this snake comes to possess us, it is indeed poisonous; it may keep us in its spell even more than the previous emanation, and could in fact be a guise for deformation.

Monotheistic emanational authorities, especially Jewish and Christian ones, long ago raised our fears about this snake, since it offered us not only knowledge of the difference between good and evil (knowledge, not commandments) but also invited us to gain knowledge of the tree of life. Before the arrival of these religions, this snake had been a symbol of transformation—carried in the arms of statues of goddesses to signify the kind of wisdom that comes from being able to hide below the ground, move along the ground, and climb above the ground, from shedding one's skin again and again, and from experiencing fertility. Subsequent sacred containers began by arousing our fears especially against this kind of snake—but also against any snake enchanting and enchaining us within its hold.

Rebellion (represented by the snake) against established emanational authorities is the most serious sin they (and, as long as this drama is still alive in us, we) can imagine. But rebellion is not necessarily a radical act—radical meaning coming to grips with the roots of the matter. Initially, no rebellion is possible for us until we are inspired by a deeper emanational source. (This is true even for scientists who are inspired to rebel against the prevailing scientific paradigm by ideas they cannot yet prove. Their final published report will, of course, tell us no word

---

2. Another story from Paul Reps, *Zen Flesh, Zen Bones*, 33–34.

about this context of discovery. We will only be offered verifications.) Rebellion may turn out to be for better or for worse. It may end by subjecting us to a new emanational authority. We cannot discover the root of the matter until we reach Act II Scene 2 in the service of transformation and most of us in our time have never gotten that far.

We have many choices as we reach Act I Scene 2 of the core drama of life. If the story of Act I Scene 1 still enfolds us, we will repress the new inspiration and persist in the life we lead now. If that old story has become problematical for us, but we still cherish aspects of its mysterious power, we may distance (but not yet separate) ourselves from parts of it—or try to reform it. We may attempt to live in both the old and the new story, at the cost of great personal and political conflict which we may also seek to hide, even from ourselves. But to become skeptical, restrained, detached, cautious, ironic, or doubting is already to have entered into Act II. These two Acts can be seemingly reconciled only for the sake of maintaining power, and hence as a commitment to hypocrisy.

If that powerful emanational source of our being weakened or deserted us for reasons we cannot yet comprehend, or we have come to believe that we failed it, we may feel drowned in depression. We may feel suicidal, or we may enter a new way of life that we do not even recognize as suicidal—namely, deformation. Then indeed it becomes much harder for us to be enabled by the waning or breaking of the old emanational force to see or hear something new that is not destructive. Our personal relations to the political and historical faces of our being at every moment also deeply affect our vulnerability to radically different sacred forces. This is a question we shall have to explore in more detail again and again. We may also rebel—indeed, we are inspired to rebel—against life as we lived it in Act I Scene 1. We cannot simply substitute one emanational tie for another; that kind of bond is too strong to be merely interchanged—hence the need for the passion of rebellion. We have choices—made available by the underlying structure and dynamics, meaning, and purpose of the core drama.

These last paragraphs have pointed only to the choices that open up in Act I Scene 2. Further choices will emerge in Act II, thanks to the nature of that Act.

Why would we choose to enter the process of transformation? At this point, we are able to offer only part of the answer: The sacred source of transformation constantly initiates this process anew while all sacred sources of emanation seek to secure permanence in this cosmos of continuous creation. The latter sources energize us to conform. The deepest source of our being inspires us to intuit and to feel (even in Act I Scene 2) that there is a unique person at last emerging—a person who is on the way not toward securing his or her self-interest or already inculcated common goals, but toward making a contribution in the context of all four faces of that person's being. That intuition and feeling is all we know at the outset—before we know how to analyze and evaluate any such evidence. But, unfamiliar as this kind of knowledge is (hardly any teacher in school ever mentions it), it does animate us, not only into rebellion but also beyond it.

QUESTIONS ABOUT BREAKING INTO INCOHERENCE

We rebel. As the image of Act II in the diagram of the drama of transformation seeks to symbolize, the source that had originally dominated us has lost its mysterious power. Its circle has broken, but our new relationship with others is not based on shared values. The people with whom we had previously shared our life had experienced that same emanational relationship. But now incoherence marks most of our relationships.[3] This diagram does not try to symbolize any particular Act or Scene as a way of life, but only as our relationships in the drama of transformation. In this first Scene, we have not yet in fact freed ourselves from that old source or from the new source of emanation—which, in Act I Scene 2, led us into rebellion. We still need to free ourselves from both in the second Scene of this Act and send both archetypal forces into the abyss.

Rebellion can move us in radically different directions. Entering Act II Scene 1 is no guarantee that we are sure to reach the justice and love that will resolve the problem at stake in our life. In our time, rebellion leads most pervasively into consolidating rebellion into a way of life. We tend to think of rebellion as an illegitimate assault on established authority. How then can it be lived as an entire way of life?

Incoherence is an overarching drama that institutionalizes rebellion by patterning in its service many stories of never-ending competition for fragments of life. People deprived of enough fragments and people eager for bigger fragments rebel again and again—to oust or diminish the power of those who control these fragments—in order to get hold of them. For more and more people, there is no longer a web of life that once kept individuals from pursuing solely their own self-interest. Self-interested individuals can at best agree on procedures that limit the violence of this kind of rebellion, but they cannot reach a consensus on the ultimate meaning and purpose of life that would lead them to share the fragments of life equitably or indeed, to agree to overcome incoherence as a way of organizing and reorganizing the insecurity of being, and possessing, only fragments of life.

---

3. I have not spoken on anomie, deviance, or alienation in this account of incoherence. *Anomie* is a term usually used in sociological literature to refer to the loss of values and norms previously enshrined by ways of life in the service of emanation or incoherence. But the term is seldom joined by sociologists to a criticism of this inheritance. *Deviance* is a term used to refer to departure from norms established by these two ways of life, usually without intending to entail any criticism of these ways, but rarely without, in fact, being at least implicitly critical of deviants. *Alienation* is a term normally used only with negative implications, as if there were no conditions in which alienation is a necessary condition for change for the better. Above all, discussions of anomie, deviance, and alienation conventionally pay no attention to organized incoherence as the very core of a way of life.

Today, more and more people live in the service of a way of life in which we cannot know the ultimate meaning and purpose of anything. We therefore perceive incoherence as secular, ever changing, and offering no certainties. But many of us also take it for granted as the only way of life worth living and defending; we live in fact in an emanational relationship to this overarching story. And we therefore cannot understand the basic reason for its limitations and fragility—that it is only an arrested fragment of the core drama of life.

Once incoherence turns into the dominant way of life, it becomes ever more costly and difficult to restrict the contestants of institutionalized rebellion to members of the elite. The spread of information and education, of desire for increased consumption, wealth, and political power, may for a time create only political instability and attempts to restore political oligarchy, but it may also open the door at least to wider competition for fragments through liberal democracy. The most fundamental reason why we are now so deeply engaged in stories of rebellion is that these stories constitute all we are and all we have. We have not yet reached the fullness of being that we can find only through our migration into Act III. Hence the most pervasive tendency of our time is to consolidate this fragile, anxious Scene into an overarching way of life, and within it, to try to reduce the rebellion of others by amassing power, fame, or wealth—or all of them—as evidence not indeed of material success alone (though we tend to think that way) but of our being the ultimate source of emanation. I alone count. I alone am to be taken seriously as the great one in my field of action. (Ego, we now think, is the ultimate sacred source of being.)

Or else, we compete to be some ego's principal assistant. Or else, since we are not among the powerful, we are drawn again and again to different dramas of rebellion. As with the emanation that originally stirred us to rebel, we do not yet understand the underlying pattern, meaning, and purpose of any emanational story, but its mysterious power over us is so attractive—precisely in the face of the inadequacies of our fragments of life, and their frequent crumbling. Incoherence as a way of life is not the kind of overarching container that can more deeply reassure us regarding our emanational attachment to any story in its service. Our emanational relationship to incoherence itself as the overarching way of life at most keeps us from questioning it as readily as we do particular stories in its service, even though it lacks the kind of certainty we had once experienced in emanation as a way of life.

If we live in the face of much greater insecurity (with only fragments of life and with ourselves as only a fragment of being in the service of incoherence), then longing for persons in public and private life who will feel like a mysterious source of strength, safety, and responsibility becomes much more prevalent. Our dominant ideology encourages rational calculations, but we long for new charismatic leaders, for a new romantic love, and also for new kinds of weapons systems that will really help us triumph. We long for relationships that will seem right and empowering beyond question.

Doubts remain—at least in the back of our minds—about these emanational bonds because we know that we cannot in this way of life experience or know ultimate meaning or purpose. We also remember the history of these emanational stories. We know when these stories first appeared in our life. We know that they come and go. We learn that many of them are the product of personal or political covert manipulation. Nonetheless, rational calculation alone cannot help us appreciate the nature of archetypal dramas or our emanational ties to them. We recognize again and again that such ties do not—cannot—last, and that when they last longer, they also become costlier.

Rational calculation alone cannot help us see how entire sets of stories hang together, how they reinforce each other, how they conflict with each other, what their underlying patterning forces are—and on what grounds to choose between them. At most, rational calculation appears to be helpful in deciding whether to support particular persons and particular actions at particular times. It cannot offer adequate criticism of archetypal stories that themselves limit our consciousness to rational calculation. It cannot enlighten us about why we are so deeply moved beyond calculation by certain persons or events. (We are moved because they manifest and symbolize the still powerful and mysterious structure and dynamics of the underlying archetypal story—or else they represent a threat to it.)

We pay a price. Human beings unaware of—or repressing awareness of—the sacred face of their being, not knowing what kind of sacred source they in fact embody, cannot be responsible manifestations of emanation or a link in a chain of emanations for others. Instead, they become merely inflated (and hence even less reliable), thanks to the worshipful love and admiration of others.

In the service of incoherence, we may raise our emanational devotion—to such dramas as stamp collecting, money making, rock climbing, being a wife and mother, or soldiering—into our only or principal story which we cannot imagine calling into question. But even when we ourselves do not yet ask whether this is indeed all or truly what we are, others certainly will feel free to raise it as a crucial or at least a practical issue. More and more often in the service of incoherence, we therefore search again and again for seemingly richer, more intense, and more secure emanational relationships or else we move in anguish into deformation.

Because of our greater availability—or as it strikes more and more people, vulnerability—to unexpected changes in stories in the service of incoherence and even in the overarching drama itself, deformation is becoming ever more attractive as (in its initial understanding) an especially powerful kind of rebellion. Deformation in its many concrete forms arouses us to rise up to defy others beyond (as we fantasize) their right and capacity to change or defeat us—whether we raise ourselves to these heights through drugs, extremist fundamentalism, racism, or aggressive nationalism. That kind of rebellion does not keep us in Act II Scene 1, but leads us first into psychic death and then into physical death—the death of the enemy we must destroy, and our own death.

But if our rebellion takes place in the service of transformation, then what awakens and motivates us is our growing realization of the fact that, at this point, we are still a partial being. Even the most powerful, who have succeeded in consolidating the organization of their power and wealth, are not fully alive even at the heights of their powers, and they often lose their position to other rebels. Even the most energized no longer have any sense of ultimate meaning and purpose to reassure their being and their practice. But if what inspired us in Act I Scene 2 was transformation, and if we broke out of emanation for that reason, we were never caught up in rebellion for the sake of acquiring fragments of life we had not possessed before (or had not been allowed to possess before). We at least intuited that we needed to empty ourselves of what would otherwise hold us up in the middle of the process.

QUESTIONS ABOUT EMPTYING OURSELVES

Why empty ourselves? Our culture never raises this question and therefore offers no answer. On the contrary, incoherence as a way of life is a story that raises hopes of success and makes us believe that if we fail, we must try again, and if we do not try again, then failure is our personal fault due to our own lack of responsible behavior. That is the governing public story; the powerful and the powerless are shaped by the same archetypal story. Any other story is private and merely our subjective opinion. Only power counts; we need to train ourselves to accumulate power. If there is no solid power, there will be no stability, only anarchy. If things get tough in the city, the successful move to the suburbs. Our isolation in these fortresses of separate anxiety may delay our recognition that, however successful, we can never acquire anything in this way but fragments of life. So, why empty ourselves?

In a world of incoherence and growing deformation, there is increasing anxiety about invasions from outside, and ever more danger of internal warfare. Who, in the face of such threats, would dare to empty themselves? Anxiety tempts us to seek the certainty of emanational relationships, or even of deformation, or else greater immediate power in the competition of reorganizing fragments of life. In this political and historical context, we are also led in our personal life to build defense mechanisms to shroud and protect ourselves against dangers we are not able to deal with. Empty ourselves? Human nature is not a barrier to transformation. But when we are captured by such seemingly powerful yet actually fragile and anxiety-provoking stories in the service of fragments of the core drama of life, then we are unable as yet to undertake this process.

Many powerful archetypal sources inspire us to repress or distort or harm one or more faces of our being. Incoherence, for example, leads us to repress our awareness of the deepest source of our being. It limits severely, even in its liberal democratic form, what we can and need to do together in our political life. And it keeps us arrested in repeated rebelliousness or—its mere opposite—a sense of defeatism. Incoherence makes it difficult and painful even to develop our ego, yet this is a task all the more desperately necessary in this way of life. We know there are no longer any permanent containers, and we therefore often substitute our ego as our final source. But since all connections are encounters, and only encounters of a true and genuine other can help to prove the truth and reality of connections, it has become far more difficult to create a reliable history of consciousness for our ego. Our present society can no longer validate our awareness, our choices, or our next step beyond temporary moments of consensus. In the service of incoherence, who knows what it is to be American or Latino or Black or White or a man or a woman—or human?

Nonetheless—but also therefore—when people who live in incoherence are told that the first step out of suffering and anxiety is to break with this way of life and then to empty themselves of this ego, they are aghast. For their experience tells them that this ego is all they have, and that there are no depths to draw upon. When we recognize that our society—given its present way of life—cannot help millions of us make connections to enough food, shelter, education, and work, or help any of us to discover and express our full value as human beings, we begin the most fruitful rebellion: we enter into incoherence with incoherence as an entire way of life.

Our own liberation is likely above all to make us more clearly and more urgently aware of how much work remains to be done, together with others, to put an end to the narrow, distorting, and hence damaging limits of our present way of life. We cannot enter into a fundamentally new and better way of life without our neighbors. This fact now establishes our political agenda.

It is a fantasy to suppose that any body politic will ever die of its own internal contradictions and, upon its death, will inevitably be reincarnated in a transformed state. A body politic in the service of incoherence will deform itself and even destroy itself and others if, for example, it persists in relying upon conquering heroes. But its deepening incoherence cannot and will not of itself lead to transformation. Only individuals, individually and together, can put an end to their participation in such dramas.

Why take risks we cannot now understand to empty ourselves three times over—of the concrete, of the archetypal story, and of the overarching way of life? Why risk being filled anew with understanding, love, and justice with respect to our present problem? Who could take seriously what now seems like sheer idealism? The obstacles and threats we now fear in such a process lie deeper than expressed by this sense of unfamiliarity and skepticism.

Speaking of living underlying patterning forces (archetypal stories) as sacred forces has not been a mere metaphor or a figure of speech in our discussion. As we shall explore much more deeply in Chapter 9, all archetypal forces but one possess mysteriously overwhelming power to shape our lives. But that one exception cannot transform without us, and we cannot transform without it. To empty ourselves of all these other archetypal stories is therefore to empty ourselves of our Lords, and these Lords will struggle to prevent it and to punish us as we struggle to free ourselves.

These Lords who first caught hold of us in Act I Scene 1 may be sources of frozen truths, partial truths, or even deadly lies. (Originally we did not and could not know.) Often we symbolically personify these sacred forces, whether we assume them to reside in heaven or on earth, but their power is expressed above all by their being Lords of a story. To stop believing is therefore not enough. We need to be able to free ourselves not only from their stories but more importantly from them.

Happily, we are not alone in this struggle, for we do not have the power to defeat a sacred source without the help of another sacred source. The deepest source of being is with us from the beginning. The evidence of its being is constituted by the structure, dynamics, and concrete manifestations of the experience I have been describing. This new experience of participation is strange to us at first, though it becomes easier the more often we experience it. We feel strengthened by what we have learned during earlier such experiences, for example that even the Act of incoherence has an underlying pattern—so that, in contrast to so much fruitless destruction in the world, we can count on being filled again. We must not wait to regain our security first, however, before we take courage to empty ourselves. But even as we empty ourselves, we are not alone in the depths of our being.

That is also why, as we empty ourselves, we do not become more vulnerable to archetypal forces in the service of other ways of life. We are not invulnerable to them, but we have already learned so much more and freed ourselves from such great burdens that we know much better than ever before what faces us—ever more so the more often we have directly experienced the drama of transformation.

It is, however, far from helpful—indeed it is misleading—to be told that it is "suffering to the point of despair" which leads to transformation. Such suffering, by itself, is not good for our souls. It can leave us forever anxious, stranded in darkness and numb—even dead. It is true that many people, including myself, are slow learners. We may not ask why we suffer until we are in despair. Despair may help us realize at last that a relationship or a whole way of life has become unbearable and cannot be remedied by any means hitherto known to us. Suffering exposes the fact of our deep pain, but it cannot by itself, help us to find its causes or the way out.

The greatest of all suffering is not any suffering in the service of transformation, but is the suffering that comes from not being engaged in the process of transformation. It is in this sense that I understand the Buddhist conception of suffering—suffering because one is attached to *maya*, to a world of illusion. It is not that caring deeply for these individuals or those mountains or this flower is illusory. It is suffering in this world as if there were only suffering and as if there were only this world in its present appearance—as if there were not the reality of transformation, even for this very world—that is the illusion that recreates suffering. Our deepest need is not to persist in suffering but instead to die, in order to be reborn.

To empty one's self is not to become devoted to renunciation, asceticism, or self-abnegation, or to elitist fantasies that only spiritual understanding matters or that only transcendence counts as the great awakening—that concrete problems, even archetypal forces, do not really matter at all, only the void beyond being and nonbeing. Such archetypal stories, nonetheless, turn Act II Scene 2 into a desert, returning us to emanation as a way of life. In this desert, we are, we say, awakened to practice vacating our personal, political, and historical face of being in order to reach union now, or else after our death, with our transcendent sacred source. But by so doing we have deprived ourselves of our freedom to continue our process of transformation here on earth.

Transformation is not easy. We may stop along the way in uncertainty and doubt. As long as we are pausing—yet still inquiring, still exploring—we have not arrested ourselves. Once we begin this process, our very experience of it also opens and enlarges our capacity for it, since our capacity arises out of our very being. But if we have arrested ourselves anywhere along the way, we shall not proceed until the story—which had embraced us and which we had embraced—becomes for us unbearable, untenable, or at least unfruitful. Hamlet was quite aware that there was something rotten in the state of Denmark: "O cursed spite, that ever I was born to set it right!" He had grave doubts about what he could accomplish within already established ways: "O God! God! How weary, stale, flat and unprofitable seem to me all the uses of this world." But he could not free himself from the force of that archetypal story which his father's ghost had reinforced.

What does it mean to empty one's being? Just as we come to feel bereft of connections that had once reassured us, just as we desperately need new connections but have not yet experienced them, the advice we seem to hear at this point from the people of the counter-tradition of transformation is terrifying: Drop your ego! Annihilate it! If we were to take this advice literally, dire consequences would follow. We would be overwhelmed by the sources and, since the sources can be destructive (as well as constructive), we could become possessed in the worst way. We could become dangerously psychotic or psychically infected by a cult led by a Charles Manson or a Reverend Jim Jones.

There are other misconceptions we might draw from a literal reading of the counter-tradition. We are told, for example, to be like putty in the hands of God or to be like a corpse in the hands of the Sufi master. There are indeed moments in our lives when we must be putty, even dead, in order to be formed again in transformation. But it is of no help to the deepest source of our being or to us to turn these moments into becoming nothing altogether. That source needs our participation in this work. Certain advice can no longer be taken.

Kabbalists for many centuries—and Carl Gustav Jung in our day—advocated that people acquire an ego in the first half of life before they devote themselves to transformation in the second half of life. There are several difficulties with this counsel. It was based on the assumption that one would be devoting the first half of one's life to learning the outward meaning of a tradition and to working and marrying according to its outward rules before coming to understand the inner, that is, the symbolic meaning of that life. Such an education of the ego is scarcely available any longer today. More importantly, we cannot move beyond incoherence by first developing a self-interested ego, shrewd in looking out for his or her material power and advantage. That many of today's young people reject the pressure to develop such an ego and the way of life it represents demonstrates that it is possible (and necessary) to begin much earlier than the cautious once held possible.

We must not annihilate our ego. The Sufi term *fana* (as used, for example, by Jalal ad-Din Rumi, 1207–73) has often been translated as "annihilation." But it is better translated as "emptying."[4] What is our ego and what is the content that we must empty from it so that our being may be filled in the service of transformation?

In the last four paragraphs, I have deliberately used the words *ego* and *being* interchangeably, as is not normally done in modern theories. I mean thereby to say that the ego, if seen solely as the more or less conscious, deliberate, and egotistical "I" is a partial version of being when seen or enacted in the service of incoherence. That ego certainly exists in hundreds of millions of people, but at a high cost to the four faces of being. I used the two terms interchangeably for a brief moment in order to call attention to the need to look at our ego, anyone's ego, through the eyes of being.

Being is the incarnation of the source—of whatever source or of conflicting sources—of the sacred depths of our being. To know ourselves is to know our Lord, and there are many Lords. But the deepest source with whom we can participate to reach wholeness (but never complete perfection) of being is the one source who, happily, is no Lord and cannot command and control us. Our deepest being remains alive in us even though we may have crippled our relationship to it. It regains the chance to become fully alive when we empty ourselves of what has crippled us.

Being does not stand in contrast to becoming, but is constituted by becoming being again and again more deeply and more richly. Being is the depth and concreteness that constitutes our presence—able to create and nourish; to arrest ourselves; to hurt, be hurt, and repress; and to break away and recreate. Only after we empty our being of biased, incomplete, and hence warping Lords can we stop

---

4. Anneliese Schimmel, who has written extensively and illuminatingly on Rumi and on Muslim mysticism, suggested to me in a conversation that *fana* might best be translated by the German word *Entwerdung*, for which there is no single English equivalent but which signifies the reverse of becoming—that is, the antithesis of persisting in solidifying more and more the person one was turning into. I therefore speak of "emptying" one's self.

living someone else's story—someone who most immediately and most powerfully embodied such a transpersonal source for us—and find and experience our own true history and connect freely and creatively in politics with others. Only then will we at last be fully incarnated, able to conceive and become pregnant, able to impregnate and care for others as we care for ourselves. Only then will our own senses become, as William Blake said, "the chief inlets of soul in our time." Only then will the deepest source of our being be able to hear through our ears and see through our eyes in such a way that that source, too, may experience transformation.

In Act II Scene 1, as long as we reject only the concrete manifestations of an earlier archetypal story, we are not free of its underlying patterning power. We may reject our mother and instead, in a new and younger version, marry our mother again, or else her exact opposite. We may fight and sacrifice lives to overthrow an authoritarian regime and then substitute for it an authoritarian regime. If we conquer only the external dragon but do not rid ourselves of our corresponding inner dragon as well as the dragon in the sacred realm that energizes both, the dragon will have been killed only in the realm of appearances. The underlying patterning dragon who had stood at the gate to bar our way to liberation—who thus defined our most crippling problem—will pull us back into the same archetypal relationship, the same story, the same way of life.

To come to understand the sacred forces at work is to be able to redeem our history and end the doom of having to repeat it. Through this kind of exegesis—this return to the original roots and their meaning and purpose—we come to appreciate the true significance of where we had earlier been stranded. No sacred force intervenes in our life solely through this or that event. The unexpected or what strikes us at first as chance is always part of an entire archetypal story. If we try to repress out of fear and anxiety or simply to control that aspect of life, it can come even unconsciously to dominate us or wreak violence on us. But we can also treat it as prophecy—as something powerfully new from which we need to detach ourselves enough to understand its underlying story, and to see whether that story can be lived in the service of transformation, or needs to be struggled against.[5]

What does it mean to empty one's being of sacred stories (*stories*, plural)? Since every archetypal story except transformation intrinsically possesses emanational power over us, it is very difficult to free ourselves from more than one story at a time. In the service of incoherence, we may well be concerned enough, as troubles befall us and we try once again to reorganize our fragmented life, to notice that

---

5. I owe this insight into "events as prophecy" to Alexander Ulanov, in "The Grammar of Creativity," a paper first presented to a regional meeting of the Group for the Study of Transformational Politics at Princeton University, November 7, 1992 and subsequently revised for the annual meeting of the American Political Science Association in September 1993.

more than one problem is threatening us. But as long as we live within that way of life, we are unable to create any but incremental changes—whatever unintended, uncontrolled developments may burst forth—because of the structural limits of our capacity. When we have actually freed ourselves to find a fundamentally more just resolution to one problem, we are quite likely to recognize that the story from which we liberated ourselves had been reinforced by other stories—stories whose power may well have colluded in making it much more difficult and frightening for us to fully free ourselves from the one we had begun to reject. That is why the drama of transformation involves a process we can never complete once and for all.

Emptying ourselves is helped by reasoning, but it is certainly not a case solely of rational decision making. Only that kind of analysis—a word meaning "separating"—works that helps to distinguish and separate us from the archetypal dramas that possess us. Some counter-traditions of transformation focus on disciplined exercises to cut us away from established routines of acting and thinking. The practice of meditation also quiets us so that we can hear anew. We can go that far without words, but I do not think we can go far enough without at least intuitive—if not yet explicit—theoretical understanding of the underlying depths of the practice at stake.

It would be nice and easy if calling people's attention to their concrete errors were enough to make them and the world fundamentally better, or if having a marvelous new experience would always constitute the entrance into a splendidly better story. Such could begin our beginning. But unless we go through the process of transformation, neither outcome will come into being. What keeps us from growing this new fruit is that until we enter Act II Scene 2, we cannot know why the new is better and what held us down within the old. We have not yet become a philosopher.

However deeply and happily we are moved by our new spirit, we can not know whether it was only an intense new fragment of life or indeed likely to fragment our life altogether. The philosopher—who comes into being within us as we free ourselves from the burden of our past, including the limits of philosophy in the service of incoherence—is moved above all by a passion for truth and reality. That passion is kept from exploding into mere opinions, polemics, or dogmas by the underlying archetypal pattern of this drama. And the philosopher's conclusions still remain to be tested in Act III.

THE EXIT FROM ACT II

Shall we or our story disappear through the exit at the end of Act II? On the path of the core drama of life we can seriously damage ourselves only if we arrest ourselves at crucial turning points along the way and thus remain still partial beings, unable to participate in a cosmos of continuous creation. The worst danger by far lies not on this path but in our exiting from it. This peril arises most often when we are torn out of Act I against our will, and when we never come to understand the limitations of the life we lived then or the risks and opportunities that face us. The most powerful source which seemingly most resembles what we lost, that is, emanation (offering us utter certainty instead of growing understanding) is deformation.

We may symbolize the sacred force carving out incoherence as a way of life as the Devil—cutting life into fragments again and again. We may symbolize the sacred force of deformation as Satan, meaning adversary. When, in the service of transformation, we liberate ourselves at this exit from an unbearable or unfruitful archetypal drama, Satan draws the archetype into the abyss. Minus its concrete personal face and its diminished political and historical face, it loses its strength. If enough people reject it, it could die in the abyss. Emanation as a way of life and patriarchy as a story are thus dying.

But if at this point we remain deeply attached to a story in the service of deformation, that fragment of life will now fragment *us* as we enter the abyss with it into destructive death. Our own consciousness is profoundly reduced from the beginning as we are sucked into this path toward the exit. Repression of our personal awareness does not and cannot rid us of the anxieties and desires that lead us to clutch deformation. The cost of personal and political defense mechanisms is exceedingly high: witness defense budgets around the world. In the service of deformation, we either inflict ever greater damage upon ourselves, or we fantasize a single enemy to be the great destructive force in our life whom we need to kill soon—or indeed, we happily martyr ourselves in this political and historical task, for we feel it also to be a sacred task.

The way to destructive death is, in time, harder to leave than the other two fragments of the core drama which we may also constitute as ways of life. But it is a process; we can be helped to turn elsewhere in time. (All of Chapter 6 will be concerned with this.)

In the drama of transformation, no partner—neither we, nor the deepest source of our being, nor our neighbors—can *force* someone to take part. None can be compelled to remain in it, yet nothing fruitful can come of it unless we go through it together. It is not a drama held together by iron laws of history or by sacred omnipotence. It is an exercise in the freedom of creation in which we may participate according to a known underlying pattern, but never according to any preprogrammed concrete steps or conclusions. The outcome depends on the quality of participation of each unique individual.

RE-VISIONING CREATIVITY

Creativity does not begin in Act III, for the entire drama of transformation constitutes our ever more compassionate and insightful participation in continuous creation so that it may turn into the fundamentally better. Our pregnancy begins in the second Scene of Act I, but what we receive then remains incomplete until we have in fact moved through all three Acts. In this story, we need to become virgins again at the end of the second Act, so that, having freed ourselves to interpenetrate with the depths at the opening of Act III, we can now participate in creation with understanding and love.

Even at the outset of this drama, we are not held within a new embrace, but we are inspired and moved to risk a path of hope and faith leading not only to healing a past problem but to the birth of new justice and love. We give birth to new being as we enter, not into union or fusion, but into bi-unity with the deepest source of our being. We shall need this new strength and insight, for as we enter the second Scene of Act III, the landlord of the establishment will tell us that there is no room at the inn.

The politics of transformation—involving our participation with ourselves, our deepest depths, our neighbors, and the concreteness of life—is not a work in which our present lords and masters, elected or unelected, have any experience. It requires a new constituency which will take politics as seriously as the alchemists came to take matter seriously. They sought ways of transforming matter even though the sulfur they used smelled, mercury was hard to contain, the fire was hot and the work was held to be dangerous by the guardians of established matter and by authorized souls.

The alchemists knew what was worth looking for. They did not seek to enter into a process in which they would emerge with greater power and profit. They were not seeking to turn lead into gold for profit—though there were also such pretenders, as there are in every line of work. They worked to understand how the transformation of any matter would help us understand the process of transformation in all the relationships of our being. They recognized that what we can and need to do together is sacred work and part of a single opus.

Our established authorities are above all interested in preserving, enlarging, and enforcing their power at least in whatever area of life they are the authorities. The dominant philosophical distinction (newly created in the seventeenth century but by now taken to be as natural as the air we breathe—if that phrase still works) is between what is objective (which this theory of transformation admittedly is not) and what is merely subjective (as this theory then *must* be, but is not). The established authorities therefore are left without a serious clue as to how we may hear from the depths and test what we hear—and they therefore fear what looks like an unknown, uncontrollable threat against the present order.

Our society knows little about creativity. When we are faced with great problems, we normally resort to substitutes for creativity: disjointed incrementalism, established competence, crisis management, heroism, diversions, and repression, among others. No one, before being admitted to any university, is ever tested for her or his creativity. Nothing like the SAT (the Educational Testing Service's Scholastic Aptitude Test used by most American colleges) exists for testing creativity. But there are sound reasons for not being able to judge creativity in advance or after the fact by asking only the person under inquiry. We are all open to experiencing the drama of transformation even if we have never before experienced it. If we are in the middle of it, we cannot yet know the outcome. Any past outcome has not only a personal face but a political, historical, and sacred face that is also to be tested in actual practice.

"An artist is not a special kind of human being," said Meister Eckhart, "but every human being is a special kind of artist." Nothing I have been saying about creativity is addressed solely to people of genius, if by genius we mean people of exceptional talents. Originally, however, *genius* referred to the spirit within us that gives birth to our true nature.

There is no telling in advance how long it will take us to enact this core drama of life. Sometimes we move slowly through its Acts and Scenes. Sometimes the whole story moves amazingly fast. Sometimes, Act III Scene 1 leaves us speechless for a while. Sometimes it gives us the right words—or else inspires the right action even before we find words for it. Act III need not produce ecstasy or peak experiences. These can arise in the service of any way of life. At any time during this process, we may experience great joy or great trepidation at the first intimation of profound change. Creativity in the service of transformation is not a means, not an end, but the very essence of life.

How much does it matter who created or discovered (meaning "uncovered") or invented (meaning "went into it in order to develop it") something first? Only individuals interested in the invidious use of power or the vainglory of fame care enough to make certain that everyone knows they came to it first. Besides, no ego can create anything by itself alone. What is crucial is that we at last have discovered something of value in our own lives and can now help others to discover it too, even if it has been discovered many times before.

Actually, we all know that this is what really matters. Not one of us has ever said, "I have heard that there are already joyous, creative adults, so I do not need to grow up to be one." Even in order truly to assimilate what someone else has discovered, we need to make it our own by going through the three Acts of the drama of transformation ourselves.[6] Otherwise, other people's theories, art, or experiences of transformation remain only conclusions, finished products, mere information, or discomforting intrusions.

The creation of creativity involves being able to receive and to respond in a spirit contrary to the ideals of competence and successful competition in the

---

6. I read Hegel again and again and each time learn more from him. But I did not really come to understand Hegel until I had done most of my own work. Only then did I see what he was seeing and what vision we share, how we differ, and how he got lost and moved into liberalism instead.

service of incoherence. For example, the best way to get out of Act II may well be to do nothing. Just be. We have learned by now that defense systems cannot overcome incoherence. We no longer need to protect our personal being with the mask of a persona. We have gained the most precious knowledge we need at this moment; we have come really and decisively to know at this point that we do not know.[7]

We start in Act III as a reborn child. Our first attempts to translate our new creation into words or actions may well be childish, given our inexperience, before we become courageous enough to let it become childlike instead. We all need to learn to let this child be born again and again. Often, one of the best ways to begin this turn into Act III is half asleep and half awake or by moving sideways. People often have their best thoughts or images come to them before they are dressed or after they are undressed. But it can, precisely in the same spirit, happen in broad daylight, while waiting for the bus. Or if we listen with a third ear while we hear a lecture or anyone else (even ourselves) talking or while reading a book we are supposed to attend to fully. It pays to have some paper always available or to take notes on two different pads simultaneously. What the third ear hears may be an entirely different theme. It is likely to be at least as important as what the other ears hear.

It also helps, especially when we are stuck and nothing fruitful seems to appear, to move sideways instead of pushing against a wall or a void. Go wholly elsewhere—and, therefore, without the commitment or anxiety that attends our present search. What we are then likely to see or hear or read or do may well be of utmost value. It may simply refresh us when we most need a fresh breath and could not possibly have found it in the place we had stood. Or we may learn something entirely different, which turns out, by sheer synchronicity, to let us leap to an insight. Sideways and elsewhere is sometimes the best way to go, for the sources of transformation do not and cannot work out a preprogrammed concrete design. We need only to be open to recognize a new inspiration or insight wherever it arises.

---

7. It is part of the irony of our time that it is easier for the less powerful to acknowledge that they know that they do not know than it is for the more powerful.

At Princeton University there was a student who received mostly Cs and Ds. He was also captain of his team, and almost every time he led them in a race, they lost. His father had also been a student at Princeton before him; so had his older brother. Both had done well in their studies; both had also led their teams to many victories. He could not understand why he, by contrast, was faring so poorly. Then it dawned on him. He himself had never arrived at Princeton. The person who had come instead was somebody else—an embodiment of his father and of his brother. He could not hope to do well being somebody else. He quit school and spent a year discovering who he was. Among other things, he found he was a painter.

An Office of Intelligence Analysis makes one of its most important contributions to policy making when it reports that we do not know when we do not yet know what is really going on in another country. Most of the time, in my experience, this fact did not deter policy makers from moving aggressively forward. To the powerful in the service of incoherence, almost nothing seems more frightening than admitting ignorance and failing to apply power.

None of this advice must be turned into rules. For example, consider deadlines. At certain moments they concentrate the mind; at other moments, they attack, frighten, and dissolve it. At times we may need to be entirely elsewhere, at times constantly alert to the threat of repressive authority against our becoming fully alive. But even at the end of Act II, we are in far better shape to tune in than we were. The forces that once patterned our life no longer possess us. Once we enter Act III, the deepest source of awareness has opened within us. Now we can be "as wise as a snake (that snake of transformation being now fully present in us and for us) and yet as innocent as a dove" (a dove of peace, since violence can never serve transformation).[8]

The philosopher who emerged in Act II does not disappear in Act III. As a participant—as a philosopher of practice—she or he now actively tests this new understanding by evaluating it in shared practice. Examples of transformation are always concrete, but concrete in a concrete specific personal, political, historical, and sacred context—and not only concrete but also rooted in archetypal depths of which, this time, we are conscious.

What is a concrete face of the sacred? It is exemplified by the actual experience here and now of love and justice in the service of transformation, and hence the truth and reality of life. Without that living experience, we could not be witnesses of this archetypal drama, but as we shall see—especially in our discussion in Chapter 10—love, justice, truth, reality, and the archetype of transformation also refer to a genuine mystery, hence our reference to the sacred.

Testing the reality and truth of new love and justice in any concrete case obviously does not follow well-known standards. We have not been designing, making, and controlling this experiment. We have not exercised solely our will power or our power of rational decision making. Creating is quite different from making. In this last Act, Act III, we are crafting with others concrete expressions of what we have learned. We are creating concrete faces of the images we discovered in the depths and with a strength and skill that draws upon these depths. Of course, we try to develop these new expressions within the resources available to us, but we are not under the illusion that only the concrete actually exists (and therefore that what counts is only the clearly causal—the increase that is also chiefly cost-efficient and profitable as we respond to precisely defined goals).

Can we measure the results and replicate the procedures? If we want to join this kind of work, this kind of craftsmanship, we can replicate the procedures only by our experiencing first the drama of transformation. And the concrete outcome will always be concretely different, though not fundamentally different in kind. Creating and giving shape to a fundamentally better quality of being in all four of its faces cannot be quantified. The criteria of formal, quantitative theory leads us to select

---

8. Matthew 10:16.

only precisely cut fragments and thereby miss the four interpenetrating faces of being, and our greatest needs, and our freedom and capacity to deal with them.

In Act III, democratic political participation is at last being realized in the personal and sacred faces of being. The deepest source of our being is infinite in its potential but it cannot command us. We would not experience the power of constantly renewed inspiration and the reality of an underlying pattern for this process without its help. And it would have no full understanding, no concrete manifestation, and no enactment of this drama without us. Our participation involves a conscious choosing of the best of the underlying stories and a fundamentally better concrete expression of it for this moment. If such a radically democratic participation is not yet available in the political and historical realms, then we know exactly not only what our next task is for completing this transformation, but we have far more solid grounds than before for offering our help.

In the diagram of Act III, we symbolize ourselves as for the first time becoming whole—a circle filled (in so far as we have emptied our being) by the deepest source of our being. In contrast to Act I, two lines connect us to this new source. We hear and we know what we hear and we respond; it hears and knows what it hears and it responds. Together we respond by creating ourselves as a new self and in creating a new idea for action (or already a first action).

Why does that new Act also give rise to a half moon? It is not a new emanation dependent on our will or the will of our source. It is the fruit of the bi-unity of our being. It also has the light of the deepest source. It is an open vessel—open but incomplete because it needs completion by the response of our neighbors if the process of transformation is to grow into a new network of human relations. But what has come forth—our being, understanding, and practice—can engender and nourish a new inspiration and receptivity in others, though they will thereby begin their process, as we always begin, in the second Scene of Act I. Thus, every drama of transformation reaps a harvest that produces new and better seeds. Hence we are not about forming chains of emanation but links of transformation.

We did not necessarily get the best answer. How could we ever prove for all time to come that this moment is the best of all possible moments? If we decide that anything is perfect and therefore try to preserve it forever, it is bound to degenerate—for this is a cosmos of continuous creation. But we can test in practice whether we received a fundamentally better answer than we had before. "The most authentic statements of the Buddha are always prefaced with this phrase: 'So I have heard on one occasion.'"[9]

We did not enter nirvana. Act III will fill us with deep strength and courage, but transforming politics is not likely to be a tranquil activity in our time. Even if we had reached nirvana, then, (as with the Buddha) compassion would demand that

---

9. Guy Richard Welbon, *The Buddhist Nirvana and its Western Interpreters*, 300.

we turn back and help in the great unfinished work on this side. Certainly we shall not ever look for a Messiah to come in order to redeem creation now that we have a sense of how to redeem creation through creating.

What we gain even from one experience of transformation is an irreversible consciousness of what is fundamentally possible in life, thanks to the depth of capacity of human nature and the nature of the cosmos of human relations. And now we can build not only on this kind of consciousness but also on the joy and love and fruitfulness that has been released. The fruit of transformation is not only change but also this kind of nourishment that fires and enlightens us. And to him or her who has, shall be given.

The more we come to know and rejoice in our first experiences of transformation, the more we long for more of them. The more readily we come to empty ourselves again in order to hear, the more often we shall hear. Transformation becomes easier not because the problems still before us become easier but because we enter the process of transformation—even Act II (incoherence)—with ever growing knowledge and confidence. We do not wait to act until things have become unbearable, untenable, or unfruitful. We move because what we face is no longer (or never was) a manifestation of love and justice.

This creation deserves to be celebrated and shared because it has not been a subjective, private experience. Neither has it been only an archetypal experience—exclusively a display of the will of the sacred realm—no mere *a* reiterating *A*, nor merely a pale reflection or inevitable corruption of what are supposedly perfect archetypes. But such a new creation is also not merely a new additional fact. It constitutes a new *Gestalt*—a whole new form, that is, an essential part of a new archetypal story. Every experience of transformation is an individually unique, particular experience that leads to a new way of being. At rare moments, we may even help to bring new archetypal stories into being. (In our time, such new stories of being feminine are coming into being.)

REFORM AND RE-FORMATION

I wish I understood why I once believed and wrote that it is possible to engage in transformation in the service of the other three ways of life.[10] I said plainly then that such "transformation" could not bring about anything that was fundamentally new and better. But why call it transformation then? There have long been available two other concepts: *reform* for significant changes and *re-formation* for great

---

10. Manfred Halpern, "Choosing Between Ways of Life and Death and Between Forms of Democracy: An Archetypal Analysis." Another central aspect of the theory of transformation had not yet dawned on me—that three of the four ways of life were intrinsically shaped and indeed harmed by the fact that they constituted arrested scenes—hence, distorting fragments—of the core drama of life.

changes, but both within the prevailing way of life. There is no clear-cut distinction between these two terms, but there certainly is between both of these and trans-formation. (I spell and pronounce it *re-formation*, lest *reformation* remind readers solely of great changes in particular religions.)

Significant or great changes—but always still partial—can be brought about. We move from childhood to adolescence and from adolescence into adulthood—but we remain in the service of the same way of life. We create computers that can greatly improve our power to gather and organize data to increase our efficiency and our speed of communication—in the service of incoherence. New medicines can cure us—so that we may die of other causes in the insecurity of competing for fragments of life. We can move from one already established story to another within our way of life. We used to act in movies; now we act as the President of the United States. We can revise an existing story; we can amend the Constitution to limit a president's tenure. We can also modify the concrete expressions of any story again and again.

I would especially apply the term *re-formation* to the creation of new dramas—other than transformation—within any way of life. Augustine, appalled that Christians in large numbers were sinning personally and politically even with each other, though Christ had spoken more than three hundred years earlier, was inspired for the first time in the history of Christians to develop the story of original sin: Since Adam and Eve, we are all born with a nature easily tempted to disobey God. Augustine therefore justified the elaboration of an authoritarian Church to control our sinfulness. It was the most enduring, but not the last, re-formation to preserve Christianity as an emanational way of life. Similarly, President Franklin Delano Roosevelt's introduction of the welfare state to save a liberal democratic and capitalist society was meant to increase stability and human survival within incoherence as a way of life.

Our longing for at least re-formation in our life, given what a hard and painful place we live in now, requires the creation of a new archetypal story. Otherwise we cannot really move or if we say no to where we are, we have no new place to live. A drug addict who is sick and tired of the lows that always succeed the highs, of the need to rob to gain enough money to buy drugs, of the constant risk of being jailed, or killed by others, or dying of drug use, may well wish to say no to drugs. But what new story of re-formation can he or she enter? The old stories that were already available have lost all their emanational security, and hence led to the despair that inspired the deforming turn to drugs. Neither the threat of punishment alone nor a resort to therapeutic drugs that render us sober enough to see plainly the horror of our life is enough to reform us. We need therapeutic help to discover within us a capacity and strength to join other already reassuring existing stories if, indeed, there are any openings available. Among such better fragments are support groups whose members know that they can always count on each other's help whenever anyone feels tempted to return again to addiction to drugs or alcohol. But therapy that helps us most helps us to join with others in experiencing transformation.

The trouble with all re-formations in the service of emanation is that they mean to keep us inside the newly altered container. The trouble with all re-formations in the service of incoherence is that, at best, we can only create a better fragment of life. When the archetypal story of the state first appeared some time between 6,000 and 4,000 BC, it was a larger and more powerful weapon than hitherto available (the state always claims to have a legitimate monopoly on coercion) for making larger numbers of people pay and obey even if they are in disagreement on matters of belief or practice. It was—or sought to be—the most potent fragment of society with the power to unify people, who are not in fact unified, for the sake of the state's power.

In the modern age, as incoherence became deeper and more pervasive, a new archetypal story—nationalism—came to be created to reform the growing disunity within societies controlled by one state or to free people who did not want to obey the ruling state. Nations, that is, groups transcending the extended family and the tribe, have had difficulty everywhere in the world coming into unified being. Nationalism did not come into existence until the late eighteenth century as a way of unifying larger fragments against other such fragments—unity at the cost of regional and international incoherence, and often deformation.

Under what circumstances do we open ourselves to the re-formation of a particular archetypal drama or way of life? How do we come to be inspired with a new vision of what to do? When we realize that crucial concrete expressions of this story no longer work for us, we can empty ourselves of those manifestations. But in contrast to the process of transformation, we do not empty ourselves of the underlying archetypal pattern. And therefore we open ourselves to hear again from that same sacred source.

For example, when the military-scientific-industrial complex lost its belief in the power of intercontinental ballistic missiles located in hardened silos (because our enemy knew exactly where to find them and might destroy them before they could be fired), they moved into the first Scene of renewed incoherence. Then they went back to the drawing board—that is, they returned to Act II Scene 2, to the sacred source of the drama of war, and heard, "MX!" And when they lost belief in the mobile missile because they could not find people in the southwestern United States who would let them continuously, day and night, move missiles around their neighborhoods, they returned once more to Act II Scene 2 and they heard, "Star Wars!"

The kindred spirit of these inspirations is not surprising because, had they known their Lord, and had they not depended on the false intelligence that their Lord died about two thousand years ago, they would have recognized that an archetypal source long symbolized as Mars had inspired them each time around. If we do not empty ourselves of the Lord of the archetypal drama of war, or if we do not empty ourselves of the overarching drama of incoherence, we can count on these Lords to fill our empty cup again in their already established spirit of Act II Scene 2.

If we do not empty ourselves of our deep longing for a way of life that seems to give us a deep, intense, ultimately unfathomable but immediately regulated sense of assurance, and if for some important concrete reason we can no longer live in our particular Christian story of emanation as a way of life, we may become a different kind of Christian. If we find the competition of institutionalized rebellion becoming too dangerous to our fragment of power, we may re-form our liberal democracy into an authoritarian drama in order to reinforce our domination of incoherence as a way of life. Re-formation can also take us in the opposite direction.

By *re-formation*, I mean any change, however great, which remains short of transformation because we do not empty ourselves of one of the other ways of life which now dominates us. This vital distinction helps us to see beyond what have become highly ambiguous and confusing terms like *revolution*, *liberation*, and *basic reforms* and to ask, "Is this transformation or a re-formation of incoherence?" And since each of the four ways of life is radically different, I offer no word at all for any change from emanation into incoherence, from either of them into deformation, or from deformation into incoherence. The precise terms just used can do the job; none of them are cases of transformation.

Reform is also possible in the service of transformation; we can modify stories as we learn more. But new stories in the service of transformation come into being only by way of the experience of transformation—a fundamentally better story in the context of a fundamentally better way of life.

What is the difference between the drama of transformation and transformation as a way of life? There is none in kind, only in degree. The other three ways, being fragments of life, establish fixed overarching limits to our experience since they exist in order to embody a particular Scene of the core drama of life. Living in the service of transformation accurately describes us even before we reach Act III if we are proceeding with growing hope, faith, understanding, and love. Transformation as a way of life also describes our situation when we live more and more aspects of our life as fruits as we proceed through the drama of transformation.

TRANSFORMATION

Is transformation actually a different story than the one told here? In telling the story of transformation, we said that the first time we hear from an archetypal source is in Act I Scene 1. That first time, what reaches us is a story that shapes us before we are able to choose any other way of being. What reaches us—for the first time—in Act I Scene 2, is a new inspiration that we have to confront and (in one of several possible ways) deal with. But in fact what we have seen in the telling of this tale is that new inspirations, for better or worse, can arise at any point. The sacred sources can reach us anytime, anywhere, though how well we can hear and respond to them, and where we stop or go also depends on us. But since this is true, does the drama of transformation in fact always begin in Act I Scene 2?

Our answer is yes—but, by now, this answer requires a deeper understanding of the underlying realities of this story. One crucial fact which shapes our reception of any new inspiration is the way of life in which we live. Except for deformation, emanation constitutes the strongest overarching barrier to our listening to and coming to understand anything new we hear. Of the three fragments of the core drama, incoherence is the most vulnerable to new inspirations. It is especially open to new forms of organizing, aggrandizing, and controlling fragments of life. But because incoherence as a way of life is itself archetypal, its emanational bond to us, while that endures, is strong enough to keep us from rebelling against it as an overarching story of institutionalizing rebellion—rebelling against the arrest and consolidation of the very structure and dynamics of Act II Scene 1.

But precisely because each of these three ways constitutes only a fragment of life, we live as fragments simultaneously on two levels of reality. In the service of incoherence, we live in part consciously as self-interested, as rationally calculating, and as passionately demanding as possible. And in part we live unconscious of all sacred forces, including the sacred force that keeps us tied to this way of life. On this second level, we still live Act I Scene 1.

When incoherence as a way of life becomes unbearable or weakens in its power over us and for us, a new inspiration, that is, the second Scene of Act I, will dawn on us, and the part of us we had previously repressed enters afresh into rebellion—into Act II Scene 1. Without that new inspiration and its new passion we would lack the strength to renew our efforts. But, how far we go depends on us; there is no other story of transformation.

Here are two other notes that may help to clarify the nature of transformation. In our discussion of re-formation, we recognized at last that we cannot resort to transformation in the service of the other three ways of life. Within these ways of life, we may at most reject or reform a particular story—going as far as the second scene of Act II only to be re inspired by our old Lords.

Can any one of these three ways be used in the service of any of the other two? No. No way of life can be used in the service of another. But for millennia, the three of them have entered again and again into prolonged alliances with each other. These three are only fragments; the people trying to live within them often become desperate for additional support. In later chapters, we shall examine examples of alliances between the forces of emanation and incoherence, emanation and deformation, and—especially in our time—incoherence and deformation.

Can people live in several ways of life simultaneously? Yes, as long as they live in the service of different overarching dramas with regard to different problems.

We may, for example, find our way into transformation with regard to one story of our life without yet recognizing the high price we are paying for persisting in other inherited stories or yet knowing why they seize us as they do. But once we have discovered how to transform ourselves even with respect to one story, we are likely to become ever more aware of the need—and even become eager—to enter the process again and again.

NOT YET A CONCLUSION

If this process of transformation could not be undertaken, we would have no way to reach the fundamentally better. All solutions would be merely subjectively preferable to someone (but not to another) or merely objectively more efficient and less costly in solving this particular problem (never mind its deeper and larger context or its connection to justice and love). If the capacity and freedom for entering this process were not the richest (but often buried) aspects of our nature as human beings, we would only have given voice to a utopian dream.[11] And if our only other three choices could not have been shown to be only fragments of the core drama of life, thus explaining the intrinsic limits and dynamics of their nature, this theory of transformation would instead have been relying merely on a convenient matrix of four categories, and thus offer no real grounds for critical comparisons.

Because this story is real, the more often we experience turning from prophets into philosophers into participants in the drama of transformation, the more our hope, our faith, the strength of our love, and our understanding of the truth and reality of our life justifiably increase.[12] These are fruits that cannot be produced as if they were goals. They cannot be willed into being. They arise both with, and out of, our participation in the core drama of life.

Though we have in our first experience of transformation resolved only one problem, we possess ineradicable theoretical knowledge about our world because we recognize that no concrete problem is concrete only or exists in isolation. It

---

11. It is typical of utopian novels that they do not tell us how we might get there—except through a most fantastic or accidental journey. Actual utopian communities have normally deliberately cut themselves off and insulated themselves from the rest of society, and attempted to perpetuate themselves as if they could put an end to history. Utopians have therefore remained vulnerable to society's pressures and temptations and, after not too long a time, are overcome by what they had tried to ignore.

12. I have often in this chapter referred to Paul's statement about faith, hope, and love (I Corinthians 13:1–13)—a statement much richer in that text than just these three words. But it is also a statement marred by hope of perfection after we die. Only "then I shall know as fully as I am known." I do not know what we shall see and know then. Transformation deals with our life—and what we can understand and practice—while we are alive.

is always rooted in an archetypal cosmos. No problem can be resolved unless we proceed to confront its roots in that cosmos. Unless we learn how to uproot our connections—even to the most embracing story of which any problem is a part (our present way of life)—we shall not experience transformation.

Every specific experience of transformation releases new energies earlier repressed and nourishes and enhances our capacity and desire to transform again. Every such experience, beginning with the first, enlarges our theoretical understanding of its structure and dynamics and therefore of what we need to do to practice it. To care about concrete problems (even as we come to grasp their underlying structure and context) allows for a much wider participation by more people in fully realizing transformation again and again—much more than some earlier theorists of transformation could envisage when they focused on the requirements of becoming a sage, guardian, or philosopher-king.

To achieve excellence in transformation is to attain wholeness—fundamentally better interconnections between the personal, political, historical, and sacred faces of our being—with respect to one problem or at most, several interrelated problems at a time, never everything at once. But if not at once, we can persist in a process that allows ever more people to discover and practice the wholeness of our personal, political, historical, and sacred being, to pay attention to our health, to work together as human beings and not as the tools of others, and to share all products essential to life. To be perfect (except for a precious moment) is foreclosed to us and also to the deepest source of our being who is also still in the process of becoming.

Transformation is not a one-time experience and then—"Hallelujah, we are saved!" Neither is it a life of perennial change. We begin again only when it becomes necessary or fruitful to do so in order to renew love and justice:

> He who binds to himself a joy
> Doth the winged life destroy;
> But he who kisses the joy as it flies
> Lives in Eternity's sunrise.[13]

What matters, as William Blake tells us, is not our possession and preservation of joy, but our becoming a new gift of life and therefore feeling free and eager to nourish and to share it.

We can nourish any outcome of the drama of transformation by drawing upon our new depths—on the new story that has been born in us—to create new concrete expressions of it again and again. We can compose new songs of that variety,

---

13. William Blake, "Eternity," in William Blake, D. V. Erdman, et al., *The Poetry and Prose of William Blake*, 461.

new ideas of that kind, new ways of reaching out to a community we are getting to know better the more we work together. If we only concretely repeat ourselves, it is a sign that life is departing from this particular way of responding to this situation. It may be that our task has been achieved. Otherwise, we need to look and explore again.

If critics find grounds for revising this theory or indeed in destroying it altogether, we shall all benefit in learning from their work. The most serious danger to the theory and practice of transformation lies in our personal repression and/or our political suppression of it. Those are dangers that we will certainly analyze more thoroughly. The most insidious and subtle threats come from those who turn this theory into a belief or into an ideology or approvingly or disapprovingly into a formula or set of labels of about two dozen categories. I cannot believe that these threats will not arise. I wish I had a recipe for avoiding them, but I do not. They will need to be exposed again and again as humbug.

These first chapters have led us into the heart of the matter of transformation. Now we shall elaborate on the most fundamental choices open to our faces of being—the four radically different ways of life. Then we shall discuss choices within each way of life. We shall describe in some detail several examples of archetypal stories: democracy, capitalism, being competent, and the difference between the drama of romantic love and the drama of transforming love.

We shall also examine nine archetypal relationships—the only ones that allow us in qualitatively different ways to express in any story all five facets of performing in relationships: continuity and change, collaboration and conflict, and the achieving of justice. Each of these nine archetypal relationships is based on a qualitatively different capacity to express those five aspects of performance. That capacity is constituted by the patterning force of our unconscious (or archetypal source of being), our consciousness, our creativity, our capacity to link with others, and our just use of resources.

Then two chapters will deal with the deepest grounds of this theory—the nature of the sacred and of archetypes. We shall also explore how we can justify a theory that, in contrast to any other theory, deals within a single structure with the personal, political, historical, and sacred faces of our being.

Our last chapter will analyze one of the most important practical implications of this theory: justice—as contrasted with biased and incomplete justice, and with evil. In that chapter we shall also explore what kind of injustice, but also what kind of justice, is brought about through the process of transformation.

At this point, the only conclusion we may offer was found at Nag Hammadi in Egypt in 1946. The Gospel of Thomas, not part of the orthodox bible, but dating back to the time of the other four gospels, tells us, "When you will come to know yourselves, then you will become known. . . . But if you will not know yourselves, then you will dwell in poverty and you are poverty. . . . If you bring forth what is within you, what you bring forth will save you. If you do not bring forth what is within you, what you do not bring forth will destroy you."[14]

This threat of destruction is not produced by the process of the core drama of life. Violence cannot bring about the transformation of anyone. This threat arises if we, together with the archetypal forces that also have the power to say no to the continuation of this process, inhibit, repress, and suppress most of the nature of our being. But as each of us liberates ourselves from our partial or destructive life and brings forth what we participated in creating with the deepest depths of our being, we will also no longer seek to seduce or coerce others into living their life within our story, or allow ourselves to be seduced or coerced into living within theirs. We shall instead devote ourselves to creating a new and better story together.[15]

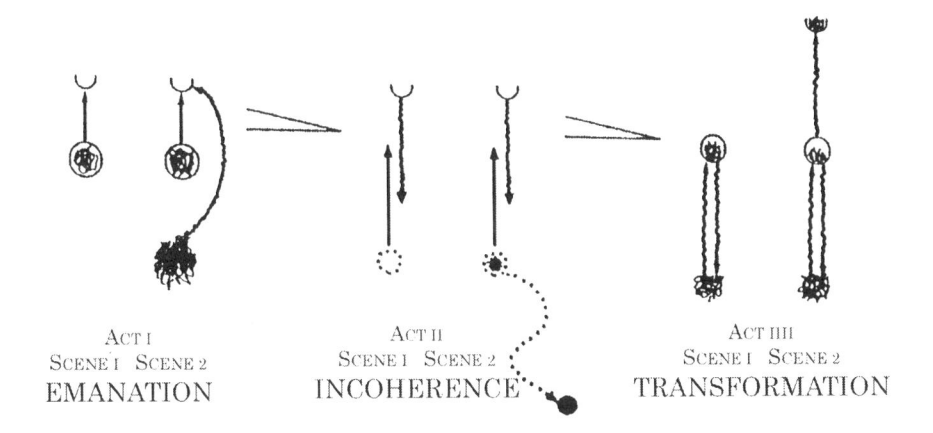

ACT I
SCENE 1 SCENE 2
EMANATION

ACT II
SCENE 1 SCENE 2
INCOHERENCE

ACT IIII
SCENE 1 SCENE 2
TRANSFORMATION

---

14. These two quotations from the Gospel of Thomas, *Logions* 3 and 7, are to be found in Elaine Pagels, "The Orthodox Against the Gnostics" in Peter L. Berger, *The Other Side of God*, 61–73.
15. One of many valuable insights I owe to Dr. Marga Speicher.

3

Who Are We?

Knowing, Interconnecting, And Fulfilling The Four Faces—And Also The Source—Of Our Being

In this work we are trying to discover, explain, and evaluate the most crucial choices of our life and how to free ourselves to make fundamentally better choices. But who are we? Each of us is a being with four interconnected concrete faces of being—a personal face, a political face, a historical face, and a sacred face. And our being is also constituted by an archetypal—or sacred—source that patterns the underlying structure, dynamics, meaning, and values of the dramas (stories) through which we express the faces of our being. *Being* is both a noun and a verb. It describes the form and substance both of our constitution and our practice of life in a cosmos of continuous creation.

Freely and fully to be, we need to liberate ourselves from any sacred source of being which compels us to repress or distort any one of our faces or the links between them. Otherwise, we hurt ourselves and our relations with others. We cannot then truly be ourselves or help others to find their own true being. I shall now describe and analyze the four faces and also the sacred source of our being as we can most fully experience them—and also, by contrast, in some of their limiting and harmful forms.[1]

---

1. I use the word *face* as symbolic of the incarnation of aspects of an archetypal drama that are essential to our being's embodiment and performance of that drama. Our face, among other practical characteristics, expresses and is responsive to seeing and being seen, hearing and being heard. It can express (or seek to hide or put forth a mask regarding) what we are experiencing. It is also an active manifestation of what we are and what we are actualizing. It is therefore also a term that can symbolically refer to the outward embodiment of a deeper reality. The four faces being discussed here express underlying structures and dynamics which this chapter introduces from a new perspective and which this entire book will further explore.

OUR PERSONAL FACE OF BEING

"Know thyself," said Socrates. How few are the people who know themselves, then or now! To begin with, what is our personal face of being? From the perspective of transformation, our personal face is not merely subjective nor solely our own self. It is the face of our being that is responding to the inspiration to free itself to participate creatively with the deepest source of our being and is thus discovering its authentic personal uniqueness in the presence and process of that very connection. Such emerging being needs to augment and fulfill itself by engaging also in creative and just participation—politically and historically.

This is obviously not our conception of our personal face when we conventionally speak of ego, individualism, or subjective preferences. We shall explore this fundamentally richer experience of our personal face, and especially its relationship to the deepest source of our being, before this chapter ends, and we shall return to these unique, creative connections again and again throughout this work. But first, before we look into our other three faces, we shall analyze our personal face when it expresses only our partial being.

In the service of emanation, we seek to be either the most powerful, or else (often as a challenge to the most powerful) the most perfect embodiment of the sacred source who once and for all time established our way of life. Or we aspire to become the most powerful embodiment at least of the sacred container of our family or tribe or community. Or else we try to be the best or at least the most loyal follower; or else, though we try, we secretly have our doubts (or we even sin).

Conformity to the will of the sacred and its embodiments is the dominant order of the day. Hence, emanation as a way of life (and indeed any emanational relationship) diminishes our personal face. We try instead to be the embodiment of the mysteriously powerfully greater other.

But emanation does not lead to uniformity; to similarities, yes—even to points of sameness. But even as we adhere to the same archetypal story, even as emanation inhibits the uniqueness of our creativity, we each conform through our own expression of it. There is no one else like you in the world, not even those with whom you share the same nation, the same religion, the same gender, the same race, the same class, or the same family.

Emanation also may not contain us forever. Not only does its sacred source give rise to varieties of conformity, but our personal face, by its nature, remains capable of hearing from—and of repressing, suppressing, misunderstanding, or saying yes to—one of the sacred sources of the other three fundamental choices of life.

In our time, many are the ways in which we put forth or hide what is never more than a portion of our personal face. We worship our ego—or the property we own—as if it were the deepest source of emanation. We diminish it as merely subjective, but then perhaps imperialize it in the privacy of our own home or of our corporate empire. We mask our personal face by exhibiting it as a persona—for a role that we feel is not us but that we are required to perform in a world of organized insecurity or else, to get us the role we really want. We employ others eight hours a day as mere tools, as extensions of a machine or, as yet, the lack of a machine. All day long, workers rapidly cut chickens into six parts. Their arms often cannot stop moving when they go home. We teach students to learn by rote or, seemingly more sophisticatedly, to prepare themselves above all to do well on standardized tests, so that they may become the effective instruments of others, or rise successfully in already established roles. And if we fail in this way of life which nonetheless possesses us, we feel too unworthy to come forth with a personal face of our own.

The underlying patterning sacred force of incoherence thus diminishes our personal face of being by inspiring us to experience ourselves as merely subjective—or else inflates us, if we gained power in this way of life, to hold only our ego as important. Correspondingly, we experience the ego of powerful others as threatening and the presence of lesser others only (as we publicly explain) objectively: How much do we need them for our purpose, if at all?

By arresting ourselves in Act II Scene 1 of the core drama of life, we can only be partial selves—biased and incomplete and therefore, however powerful, still brittle and anxious. We have not yet discovered the wholeness of our being, not of any of our faces or their deepest source. *Ego*, *self-interest*, *subjective*, and *objective* are our names for fragments of our being.

In the service of deformation, our personal face has shrunk into apathy or despair or else is readying itself to destroy itself and (or) others.

Our personal face is not simply a reflection of what we do alone by ourselves. (Even to be alone, to be left alone, and to be lonely are expressions of our political and historical fate, and of a particular archetypal story.) Our personal face is not and cannot be shaped solely by what we do alone but indeed is created by what we do with ourselves—how we connect (or unconsciously remain connected) to one sacred source instead of another, thus enacting our role in one story rather than another. Unless we consciously, critically, caringly, and creatively engage in this kind of work with ourselves, and then reach out as truly ourselves, the other three faces will dominate our personal face or else we will project our personal fantasies upon the world. Without our personal face, we could not see, hear, feel, understand, or connect to the other three faces of our being or to our sacred source. But unless we thus connect, we cannot fully be ourselves.

OUR POLITICAL FACE OF BEING

From the perspective of transformation, our political face is expressed by what we can and need to do together—together within ourselves (for none of us is only one person living in only one story), together with others, together in history, and together with the sacred. The political therefore does not, as we commonly believe, refer only or above all to competition for public power. It includes loving, playing, creating, learning, teaching, producing, consuming, risking trust in testing new experiences of life, and organizing with others—to give only a few examples. Every relationship, every story in which we participate is political. The theory and practice of transformation gives us grounds for taking the whole human being—and every human being—seriously in politics at all times. Transformation thus puts into question the very roots and branches—and the scarce and diminished fruits and the possessive and exclusionary harvests—of our current public politics.

Consider what we can and need to do together—*can* and *need* are closely linked. We need to free ourselves in order to participate with the deepest source of our being so that we can fully express and interconnect the four faces of our being. Only then can we attain our full capacity to understand our needs and the needs of those who are on stage with us to enact the shared stories of our lives. In the service of emanation, charity for those in need is extended only to those who have accepted our sacred container (or will feel obliged to join it in view of our charity). In the service of incoherence, the needy are also seen as powerless, and hence rendered dependent on what the government and private charity will—or will not—do for them.

In the service of transformation, however, need is seen and experienced as grounded in the very nature of our being. Need is not only particularized or responded to in terms of generalized abstract rights, or ignored because people in need (but still powerless) have not yet achieved legal rights, or met only in uncertain and unreliable moments of compassion. From the perspective of transformation, need is invoked not only by the dire lack or shortage of material necessities like food, shelter, health, and education. We recognize that human needs arise primarily from two sets of roots. One is the deprivation that is rooted in our living stories in the service of partial ways of life. In these stories, much of our being and of our suffering remains unrecognized and indeed repressed. (Even accidents and diseases break out more frequently and are not adequately dealt with.) In these dramas, we cannot achieve more than incremental changes in dealing with these needs. That is why our greatest political need is to say no to these ways of life and organize movements of transformation.

The other roots are needs which, through the experience of transformation, we all come to recognize with deep care. The satisfaction of these needs leads to the full incarnation of our being.[2] I mean the need for understanding our shared life

---

2. Throughout this chapter and throughout this book, whenever I refer to the fullness or wholeness of being, I mean no one who is complete or finally stable and integrated or perfect or who *knows* or *is* everything, but someone who is at this moment and under these circumstances—for as long as they can be creatively nourished—experiencing the richest way of life.

and the need to experience justice, friendship, love, joy, and beauty. Then *can* and *need* are most fully joined in our being.

The question of what we can or cannot do also raises the question of responsibility. When we normally speak of being responsible, we mean being answerable for having done—or having failed to do—what authority has asked of us. In the service of transformation, we cannot partition our life and assume that someone can or must take sole personal responsibility or (but only if duly authorized) public (a limited form of political) responsibility. Instead we ask, "What response-ability do we have now?" Our ability to respond, personally or politically, depends upon all four faces of our being, how well they are interconnected and to which sacred source.

In the service of transformation, we do not simply confine ourselves to responses that conform to already established answers, or else to attempts to modify or undo them. We ask anew what can and needs to be done together. And the answer never exempts our own personal responsibility, but it also necessarily includes all the other faces of our being. If at this point I am powerless to respond, is it solely my fault? Is conceiving, feeding, and raising a child solely my responsibility? Is my child solely mine; is our child solely ours? Is learning, finding a job, being abused, being cured of my illness, living in a slum, or breathing this polluted air solely my responsibility?

In our time, the fragments of society, including our institutions, set ambition against ambition—a story without room for the powerless. In the "free market," corporations find it more profitable to move out of our community, even out of our country, or to substitute automated machines for workers. And we are told by our elites to assume individual responsibility or family responsibility where there are no jobs, no communities, even in our neighborhood. Currently, our political networks are not connected, not made for participation—for part-taking in a network that needs our collaboration.

"Every gun that is made, every warship launched, every rocket fired signifies, in the final sense, a theft from those who hunger and are not fed, those who are cold and are not clothed. This world in arms is not spending money alone. It is spending the sweat of its laborers, the genius of its scientists, the hopes of its children. . . . This is not a way of life at all in any true sense. Under the cloud of war, it is humanity hanging on a cross of iron." That is what President Dwight D. Eisenhower said to the American Society of Newspaper Editors on January 17, 1961.[3]

People's stories—or their disintegrating stories—are more and more entering into other people's stories around the world. We may try to reinforce and even fortify the present boundaries of our political connections, but all of them become less secure. People who needed to be on stage with us in stories we once shared increasingly leave

---

3. *The New York Times*, January 18, 1961.

us. Hence, politics has become more difficult than before. We have not only more but also new political needs and fewer working connections for what we need to do together. We experience discontinuities far more often than continuity. Changes are largely unintended and uncontrolled. Many conflicts proceed without shared rules and too often lead to injustice for all sides involved in it.

When (if) we try to be of help amid this incoherence (and ever more often, this growing deformation), we tend to focus solely on particular causes and particular relationships or on particular effects. We do not question the heart of the matter—the stories which these relationships and causes and effects reflect, or the way of life we continue to serve which keep us all, sufferers and helpers, from being freely and fully present to ourselves and to our world.

When (if we have power enough) we concentrate instead, even in this context, on pursuing our own self-interest, our own success creates enclaves (that is, fragments) of power we mean to protect and enlarge, thus reinforcing our present way of life and its advantages for some and its costs for all.

In the service of incoherence (as in the other two partial ways of life, emanation and deformation), how much we are limited in what we can and need to do together! But how comprehensive is this transforming conception of the political? It includes what we normally separate from the political as constituting instead the economic, social, racial, ethnic, cultural, religious, gender, and family realms of life. From the perspective of transformation, these realms are *not* separate abstractions or fragments, but are different sets of archetypal dramas which emphasize different political issues in our life.[4]

All archetypal stories, by their very nature, have a political face. If we are to live any story, others will need to be on stage with us. Even ascetic monks who live by themselves or in monasteries cannot survive unless nearby farmers and pilgrims supply them with food and clothes. And the story of their insulation gains its meaning in part from its dissent from how others live. No political power is more fragile or more costly than power that connects within the same archetypal drama only a small elite—and denies capacity to the rest of the people.

Does this conception of the political—what we can and need to do together—exclude conflict? No relationship can endure unless it offers us the opportunity for continuity and change, for collaboration and conflict, and for achieving justice.[5] And when it does not, conflict and injustice become dominant, and we need to face this travail and discover what we can do to overcome it. Only to say no, only

---

4. We shall discuss archetypal dramas focused on culture, race, ethnicity, gender, and class in Chapter 11, archetypal dramas focused on religious issues especially in Chapters 6, 7, and 14. Social issues, since *social* has so many different meanings, will be raised in every chapter.

5. We shall enlarge upon and exemplify this point in Chapter 8 when we analyze nine different archetypal relationships, each expressing continuity and change, collaboration and conflict, and achieving justice in qualitatively different modes.

to rebel—to stop our selves in Act II Scene 1—cannot be enough to end such a crisis. Nor can superior power alone resolve the underlying causes of any conflict. The best way is to move through the drama of transformation. As we said in the preceding chapter, that process cannot be accomplished without entering into conscious, critical, creative, yet caring conflict with ourselves and with others with regard to all four of our faces and the present source of our being.

Does this perspective on the political destroy what we now regard as a precious distinction between public and private? How valuable is this distinction in a democratic liberal society? At best, it gives us the right not to speak if we are not ready, if we do not want to incriminate ourselves, if we mean to share our thoughts only in confidence with a few friends. It protects our dwelling, our possessions, and our mail from governmental inspection unless a court has issued a search warrant. The vote we cast in public elections remains a secret. We may organize private schools and colleges. We may own property and also invest it in private enterprise. It is for us alone to decide how to save our soul—or why not to worry about it.

No one actually living in a liberal democratic society will have read this preceding paragraph without rightly having raised qualifications about it. I shall add to them: The preciousness and precariousness of privacy in our time stem from the fact that these enclaves are emanational relationships in the service of incoherence. But their emanational roots (they feel sacred to us) are thought, in this way of life, to have no deeper roots than our subjectivity. Since that self-interested subjectivity is something we believe constitutes the core of our nature, we agree not to invade each other's privacy and in certain respects also to protect privacy's inward and outward expressions and manifestations.

But the very nature of the structure and dynamics of any emanational relationship keeps us from attaining any autonomous knowledge of ourself—even privately. It arouses us to create a chain of emanations by becoming the strongest source of power over others, or obversely, to insulate ourselves as much from others as possible. Emanation also inspires our private ego (or our collective ego, for instance, the nation-state) to define all other people as either insiders or outsiders. We know insiders, however, to be moved above all by their self-interest. The outsiders strike us as not fully human, and therefore to be either impotent or mysteriously threatening.

In such a world, privacy also constitutes a valuable fortress for two quite different purposes. For many, it frees us from a sense of caring responsibility for others and prepares us to be ruthless imperialists over their lives. For some, this fortress of privacy is a blessing, because it allows us to exhibit outward conformity while inside rejecting the limits which the dominant rules of incoherence (or of the remnants of emanation) impose upon the creative uniqueness of our being or upon what we can and need to do together.

But in its conventional form, this emanational experience of privacy moves us to create not our true self, but substitute selves—for example, to enclose ourselves entirely within the embrace of our own property: these are my workers, and I will use them and pay them as I please; this is my land, my forest, my resources, and I will exploit them as I choose; this is my wife and in the privacy of my home, I will use her or beat her as I please. Private property remains the most important enclave of privacy for the powerful. Only in recent decades has the rising power of the previously excluded been able to limit somewhat this kind of "private" power.

Even in liberal democratic societies, the powerful in private life utilize the occupants of public office above all for their "private" purposes, and not for shared public purposes. In this respect, the political becomes the extension of the personal face of the powerful. The "privately" powerful can personally reach the most powerful public officials in order to protect and augment their "private" power.[6] Only the less powerful or the powerless are governed by bureaucracy, which denies their personal face altogether by processing them impersonally according to impersonal rules.

The nation-state, one of the most pervasive archetypal stories in the modern world, diminishes and often even eliminates the distinction between public and private, even in liberal democratic societies. We must be loyal to its cultural values even if we do not belong to its dominant culture. If we are suspected of being disloyal, our privacy will be secretly invaded. If another country (meaning, during the past forty years, not only the USSR but also the United States) does not trust the government or the opposition in our nation-state, it will engage in covert action to bribe, threaten, lie, and kill within our public realm. And all nation-states demand that we give up our lives, if necessary, to protect or advance "our" national interest.[7]

The nation-state, though it constitutes one of the most powerful dramas in the service of incoherence—powerful in the resources it accumulates and consumes and in the emanational devotion it attracts—illustrates, in its costs, its insecurity, and its tendency to invade both the domestic and foreign spheres of private and public affairs, the bias and entanglements of the public and the private. No privacy is possible without public protection of privacy, but the possessors of private power are the principal shapers of how public power is used to protect—or not to protect—privacy. These policies may be used to exploit, hurt, and neglect in "private" life those who lack power in "public" life.

Transformation is not an invitation for the public realm to invade and control the private realm or vice versa. Neither the public nor the private is a face of our being. They are fragments for organizing our insecurity while living in the service of incoherence. That way of life diminishes, when it does not repress and sup-

---

6. For one of the most recent assessments of the power of the "private" in "public" life, see William Greider, *Who Will Tell the People: The Betrayal of American Democracy*. Greider is a former assistant managing editor of *The Washington Post*.

7. See "A Theory for Transforming the Self: Moving Beyond the Nation-State" in Stephen Woolpert et al., eds., *Transformational Politics: Theory, Study, and Practice*, 45–55.

press, a greater treasure—the personal and political faces of our being. Without our political face, we could not connect ourselves to the persons growing or conflicting within ourselves, to others, to the experience of our past, to the process that moves us through the present into the future, and to the sacred. How deeply, broadly, and justly we can make these connections, how well we can understand our shared needs and discover and develop resources for dealing with them, differs in each drama and above all in each way of life.

OUR HISTORICAL FACE OF BEING

Our historical face is constituted by our memories—personal and political, conscious and unconscious, true and false—and by the living inheritance of the archetypal stories and ways of life and their concrete manifestations that arose in the past and that move us through the present into the future. If our past no longer nourishes us and confines our vision and our capacity, we can also create turning points into a different future—historical turning points also in the personal, political, and sacred faces of our being. Our historical face is our experience over time—not only our past, but also our present and future—of being possessed by stories, trying to preserve them whatever the cost, being wounded by them, or else truly nourishing and being nourished by them, and breaking with them to participate in creating new stories.

Our historical face thus is not simply the reflection of a shared or individually developed—or officially developed—narrative. The account of inquiries into the stories of the past, and into the stories that move us through the present into the future, always have three—often three different—archetypal foundations: the archetypal stories and ways of life that still unconsciously shape the outside observer's vision and which they now project upon their narrative, the stories and ways of life that still unconsciously shape the participant's memories and present experiences, and the stories and ways of life we can free ourselves to understand from the perspective of knowing in fact what underlying and fundamental choices we have in life.

Historians in the service of emanation (to speak only of those in the service of its three monotheistic forms) believe that nothing basic ever changes unless we sin or unless God in his unfathomable wisdom intervenes to alter our life or the world. Historians in the service of incoherence recognize that order takes different forms and that change is often the order of the day; they offer different explanations for continuities and discontinuities. But these analysts offer us no adequate explanation for the depth of commitment to emanational relations and ways of life, how and why stories hang together, or the process by which we can free ourselves from them. Historians in the service of deformation envision the past, present, and future as part of an apocalyptic fantasy.

Each of us has a rich historical face. It is constituted not only of our past, whether we are conscious of it or not, but of the present and future we can help to shape. "Indeed, whenever a culture or a community stops taking responsibility for the stories they live, because they unconsciously repeat and enact them, such a society becomes ahistorical."[8] Thus the past and our historical face are not synonymous. Our past is not beyond change. We can liberate ourselves from inherited stories—from their roles, relationships, ideas, and imperatives we had once taken as already settled. We can work to discover and recover a past whose repressions and defense mechanisms we had taken for granted and made into our own. What were the barriers to transformation in our past? The only thing that is humanly impossible is simply to stop and never look back. We need to uncover where we have been and where we are, for each human being and each group can begin its transformation only from the actual turning point of here and now.

We free—or inhibit—our historical face in the context of all four of our faces of being. Our historical face is not merely our public past, present, and future. The history of the capacity of our political face matters. All we can and need to do together—or were or still are not free or able to do—with our family, with the groups to which we belong (or are still not allowed to belong), with our human species, and in relation to other species. The history of our personal face—to speak of only one kind of challenge that arises again and again—is filled with moments of unexpected fortune and misfortune, of accidents and intrusions, of new things happening we cannot understand. The challenge is this: Can we absorb these strange events into archetypal stories that already shape our history, or must we find new ones?

To reinforce the existing archetypal stories of our lives or to search for new ones is to face the sacred aspect of our history. The sacred sources of our being are not exempt from history. They are weakened or strengthened as underlying patterning forces as they enter into conflict with each other in the personal, political, and historical aspects of our being. They are weakened as we say no to them and strengthened as we say yes to them. Indeed, we help them come into being as we fantasize or imagine what stories we need to develop but cannot enact without the power of archetypal sources. Thus we helped bring the archetypal drama of the state into being around 3,000 BC, but not the nation-state until the late eighteenth century.

It is crucial for us to try to understand the interrelationship between the historical and the sacred face of our being so that we may come to understand how to choose the sacred source that, by its very nature, cannot and will not dominate

---

8. David T. Abalos, "The Personal, Political, Historical and Sacred Grounding of Culture: Some Reflections on the Creation of Latino Culture in the United States from the Perspective of a Theory of Transformation," a paper prepared for a National Conference, "Latinos and Religion in the United States," at Princeton University, April 16–19, 1993.

us. For as long as we do not understand the structure and dynamics of the historical process that any archetypal story sets into motion, we will not be able to understand, for example, under what conditions a liberal democracy in the service of incoherence will at last agree to a civil rights law, but then treat its newly recognized fellow citizens merely as new fragments in the ongoing competition. We will also remember only the millions who died in holocausts, but we will still not understand, especially before it is too late, the process that moves people into such deformation.

OUR SACRED FACE OF BEING

We experience and express the sacred face of our being whether we are believers, agnostics, atheists, or transformers—whether we are conscious of it or not. We experience it as the presence of a living underlying patterning force. We experience it most strongly and particularly as the process of creativity, as courage, as deep attraction and caring, as enthusiasm (which means literally, the condition of the god within us), as loyalty or commitment even in the face of threats from others, and as various forms of hate or love—all experiences that cannot be fully put into words. It is the sense of the process of new birth; or of the compelling presence of reaffirmation, reinforcement, or reassurance; or even of being overwhelmingly shaken, possessed, or deeply threatened. It is a presence that arises out of our sacred depths—that could not deeply confirm, move, or alter our being unless it were from such depths.

Since what we hear or see or feel or intuit is always part of an archetypal story (though the story may not yet be clear to us), we need to explore the interconnection of our sacred face to the other three faces of being. Any story which eclipses our personal, political, and historical faces in the name of what is usually termed the spiritual—or any story that eclipses our other faces in the name of political power or in the name of scientific methodologies—squeezes and warps the wholeness of our being however much it may strengthen our power in limited and limiting realms of life. We need to honor our sacred face—not simply to yield to it, but critically and creatively to understand and express (or reject) its archetypal force.

In our time, we have curbed our freedom to choose between different sacred faces of being by believing in only one as defined by a particular organized religion. Or else, we altogether deny the existence of any sacred face because we see ourselves to be secular and scientific. Under these conditions, the archetypal stories that shape the sacred face of our being prevent us from recognizing what living underlying patterning forces shape the data we can recognize and the realities we cannot see.

Since all four faces of our being in their concreteness constitute manifestations of the sacred—that is, of archetypal sources—why do I call only one of these faces sacred? It is to call attention to the fact that sacred sources have the capacity at every moment to emerge and express themselves concretely in our being. Our sacred face actualizes and expresses the rise, reinforcement, or weakening from the depths of each archetypal drama (or aspects of it) that need then to be shaped into concrete manifestations of this story through our other three faces of being.

We can personally, politically, and historically enshrine and idolize prior manifestations and thus, at a cost, protect ourselves from actually listening to what we hear now. But we can succeed in repressing new sacred forces only with the help of an already established sacred force whose emanation is still strong enough to keep us within our present story. Concrete personal, political, and historical obstacles are not enough to hold us where we are. That is why talents previously unknown to us can emerge within us as reflections of sacred archetypal forces stronger than the ones that bind us now.

FROM OUR SACRED FACE TO OUR SACRED SOURCE: A PROSPECTUS

As we seek to understand the connection of our sacred face to our sacred source of being, belief would prejudge and circumscribe our discoveries. The journey of transformation is a way of faith—of risking trust in the experience of moving into the depths of being and testing our understanding of it in shared practice. The crucial questions are these: What sacred source is patterning our life now? Do we need to free ourselves from that source? Can we feel or hear or intuit a face of the sacred that will guide us to the sacred source of transformation so that our personal face is inspired to find and test the personal and political practice that will transform our selves and our history? Our personal face of being must always take the initiative in this. Our political and historical faces possess no consciousness of their own, though their present manifestations of previously accepted archetypal dramas may have weight enough initially within us to block our way.

To understand our sacred face as part of a living underlying patterning story involves an entirely unfamiliar exploration while we live in the service of any of the three fragments of the core drama of life. In one concrete manifestation of the way of emanation, most of us have no sacred face (we are laity) and priests have one, only by virtue of their office—and saints do, by virtue of God's grace. In others, we are subject to the overwhelming power—or at best the unfathomable mercy—of God. (Or only charismatic persons possess the grace of a sacred face. And yet, if we believe and conform, we may yet be saved by that mysteriously overwhelming sacred source.) There are many other emanational varieties, but all keep us from asking fundamentally new questions and seeking fundamentally new answers about the choices open to us about our sacred face and its relationship to different sacred sources.

In the service of incoherence, we have freed ourselves to become more conscious of the concrete, but we are still largely unconscious of what at most we indeed call the unconscious and have repressed therein. We now believe in and enact the powerful fiction that the relationships and stories of our life (except for certain remaining fragments of emanation as a way of life) have no sacred roots. We therefore prevent ourselves from discovering them. At most, we worship certain experiences, but we worship no sacred source (because we have enclosed ourselves to hear no sacred source) beyond our ego, the egos of certain others, and our nation-state.

In the service of deformation, an apocalyptic cause (and its leader and followers) constitute the embodiment of a demonic sacred source.

In the service of transformation we participate in a bi-unity of our being and the deepest depth of our being. Only our participation with the deepest source of our being—a source reachable by all human beings—can help free us from these other incomplete and biased Lords.[9]

OUR BIOLOGICAL FACE OF BEING?

Each of us has a physical face, and a whole body filled with blood, nerves, and genes—with altogether far more interconnected and vital forms of matter than can even be mentioned in one page or explained in one book. We cannot live without a body. Why, then, only four faces of being? Have we no biological face?

I see our body in a different light—as the essential vessel of our four faces of being.[10] But does the term *vessel* not seem to diminish the force of the body? No. The birth or our body gives rise to our being. Death puts an end to it. Illness can weaken or change it. The response of other human beings to our body can exploit it, hurt it, or strengthen its health. Drugs—physical products—can change not only our physiological experience for better or worse, but also our body's relationship to the four faces of our being. Drugs in our body can deepen or lessen our passion, anxiety, depression, clarity and depth of mind; our openness and receptivity to others; our memories and inspirations; our happiness, courage, and caring.[11] The changing structure and dynamics of our body can enhance, warp, or destroy our life—and create new life.

---

9. Our experience of participating in bi-unity is so crucial that any abridged version might well remain unclear or misleading. Chapter 7 will be concerned with this.

10. Dr. Marga Speicher opened this door of inquiry for me.

11. Peter D. Kramer, *Listening to Prozac*. A psychiatric analysis of how antidepressant drugs can change our being has taught me a great deal on this subject, thanks to his detailed case studies and his deeply concerned questioning about the larger implications of chemically producing such changes. Much of my basic understanding of these themes has grown out of many conversations with another psychiatrist, Jeffrey K. Halpern.

Nonetheless, the four faces of our being possess a qualitatively different capacity and freedom than our bodily vessel—a conscious, critical understanding and creativity that allow us, within limits, to alter the conditions of our body in many crucial cases more decisively than the body can alter the four faces of our being.

Even with respect to birth, we can decide to practice celibacy, birth control, or abortion—or to provide good prenatal care.

Even with respect to death, we can consciously, critically, and creatively develop methods for curing diseases in order to prevent death before old age; we can deliberately choose death or inflict it. We can damage the four faces of our being by letting our memory of the dead carry more weight than the needs of the living. We can enrich our lives by recalling the thoughts and deeds of the dead—to build on them or to recognize what can no longer nourish us and to begin anew. Even the birth and death of our physical body is usually less decisive than the quality of our being (performing in its capacity both as a noun and a verb).

Our being can express the greatest freedom and capacity when we act consciously, critically, creatively, and caringly in the service of transformation. Then we are able to reject stories and ways of life that limit and wound us, to create anew and to act caringly with respect to a problem before us—together with all involved in it, because they share the experience of the bodily vessel and the four faces natural to our species.

Certainly this is a perspective radically different from that of much of conventional science. For example, one of the dominant trends in the study of evolutionary biology is to say that what mainly moves human and animal behavior is the desire to have our own genes reproduced—ours instead of theirs. But in fact we do have the biological resources to live hundreds of different stories in the service of four radically different ways of life that differ profoundly in their limits and potentials, and in their experience of understanding, compassion, and justice. Science based on the study of fragments can offer us only limited perspectives.

That kind of science can offer us specific drugs that can affect not only our pains but also our feelings and behaviors. We can thus prevent our body from dominating us. We can also choose other products like tobacco and alcohol by which we will (whatever our conscious intention) slowly destroy our body. If the only way we know at this moment to remedy acute physical or psychological suffering is to use medicine created and investigated by doctors, let us put it to work. But in focusing at such a moment on our body, let us not forget the four faces that we can free to help us overcome our disease and our suffering. Are we taking medicine, or suffering one pain after another, or having parts of our body cut off because the archetypal stories and ways of life in which we live have been deprived of much of our political face? Have we never had access to adequate—or to any—medical care before this emergency hit us? Have we seldom or never had adequate food or shelter? Have we been beaten and abused again and again, but—since politically and historically, such actions have been treated as invisible because they are part of our private life—even our doctor, looking at our wounds, did not ask about or deal with its causes?

In our time, drugs can be prescribed for us that will alleviate our anxiety and depression, indeed, that draw us toward ordinary and even noble human activities—that can, in fact, change not only a symptom but a person. But such drugs accomplish these feats without our discovering what made us feel anxious or low before or why we are now drawn to new activities. Such effective drugs—acting solely within our bodily vessel—may also effectively keep us from discovering the actual personal face of our being, why historically and politically we are still in deep trouble, what sacred sources shape the stories of our life and what deep choices we can in fact free ourselves to make consciously, critically, creatively, and caringly. Instead, such drugs leave us psychologically unconscious (even while they somatically change our psyche) of the psychosomatic illness we had or the psyche we have now—and of the problems of the world in which we live.

The most powerful force shaping our body is constituted by its own archetypal structures that shape its nature and its many parts, and the interconnection of these structures and their dynamics within and beyond this vessel. This is a way of looking at our body (and the bodies of animals and of trees and plants and of such matters as crystals and molecules) that we have not yet attempted. Hence there are a lot of forms, processes, and interactions in these realms of which we remain ignorant.

I am not a believer in any religious dogma. I find it equally impossible to bring myself to believe that human beings and their bodies have come into being as a result of random changes tested solely by the survival of the fittest. Human beings by virtue of their nature have the capacity not only to choose between radically different ways of life, but also to participate in bringing new archetypal stories into being and others to their end—joining with the sacred depths not only in creating and destroying concrete manifestations but also their underlying structure. Bodily vessels, however, can create and destroy only according to already established archetypal structures and dynamics.

Yet there is one major exception to this bodily limitation that occurs again and again throughout history. Whales decided to leave the land and live in the sea. Certain apes, but not others, decided to walk straight on their legs, as part of a new beginning. We currently do not know how to create a new body and its relationship to our four faces of being. It is a genuine mystery to us—but it has been done. How can we—how did we—participate in fundamentally altering the interaction between the four faces of our being and the archetypal structures and dynamics that shape our body?

Because of this unsolved mystery, because our bodily vessel lacks the capacity (except at such rare historical moments) to move through the drama of transformation again and again to create the fundamentally new and better, I have not called our body a face of our being. Our body can reform itself in various modes but, like the butterfly, only according to already established substantive stages. Our being's greatest freedom and capacity stems from its ability to transform. Our body is also a face of the sacred, as is our biosphere—as is everything that exists in the cosmos. The sacred is incomplete without such manifestations. Our body is a necessary and precious vessel for our being, despite its one (but not permanent) limitation.

THE ECOLOGY OF OUR BEING

Our biosphere, reaching from the depths of the earth and oceans to the outer reaches of the atmosphere, is the physical environment and interaction we share with all other living and inert entities on this earth. We can ignore it, or relate to only fragments of it, or try to dominate it. But our very capacity to breathe, to eat, to have room for being—to live—depends more and more upon our recognizing our responsibility as partners within this ecology.

BEING TRULY INTERCONNECTED AND KNOWING AND BEING WHO WE ARE

Nowadays, when we are personally disturbed, most of us remain frustrated and hurt, or we simply blame ourselves, or we try to repress our awareness of such travail. After all, so many of us accept that our principal personal task in life is to succeed by attaining power or competence or at least becoming a marketable commodity. Some of us enter therapy in order to be prescribed a drug or else (or also) to discover the roots of our difficulties in our family history. Our personal history matters, not only when we were young but to this very moment, including the future we are now trying to create. But we also have a larger shared history, and what we can and need to do together, even from the beginning, never involved *only* our family. Focusing at any moment on one particular face of our being can be quite fruitful, but only in the context of the interconnection of our four faces and the sacred source of our being. That context becomes fully known to us only in the service of transformation.

Some of us, in the face of personal, political, and historical pain and sorrow turn for comfort exclusively to the sacred—instead of merely reserving it for pre-scheduled days of the week. Such a belief may strengthen us by concentrating us, but it keeps us from understanding and acting in time upon the dangers and potentials of the political and historical world or from dealing fruitfully with people whose lives reflect different sacred sources. Being concerned only with the spiritual fragments us. Every archetypal story, by its very nature, has four faces and needs a bodily vessel. But there are many sacred sources that compel us to repress or limit one or all of the faces of our being and the connections between them.

For example, in the service of incoherence, our emanational relationship to this way of life keeps us from even knowing grounds for taking the whole human being—the four faces and their source of being—seriously. As long as we can see the political only as a contest (between the self-interested) for power in the public realm, we are unable to recognize that it is our inalienable right to demand that relations—between men and women, parents and children, employers and workers, and the individual and our inner dreams—be recognized as political issues. Now only bits and pieces of us are wanted as competent instruments, loyal citizens, eager consumers, obedient soldiers, regular voters, acquiescent poor—unless, as happens often enough, the powerful consider us to be superfluous. Only when we turn our back on conscious, critical, creative, and caring participation by the whole being of every person does politics become a realm dominated by power and powerlessness, by violence and utopia.

No one face of being can do it all. There has never been a self-made man, or an iron law of history. We have never experienced survival by bringing all four faces of our being and its source under our control. We have no such power. If we were simply the product of nature and nurture, no source or face could rise through us with our participation to free and change us fundamentally. We are not simply fixed entities defined by one of our faces: *man, woman, ruler, ruled, American, Latino, alien,* or *I think, therefore I am.* We are not only individuals; we have four faces and a source of being. No one else can define and shape all four faces of our being unless we are possessed by a sacred source which that person or that group embodies. Only then does our personal face melt into "our" political face, well cemented by the political command of "our" sacred source. What is left of our personal face of being then is a deep fear of dissenting, lest we be treated as an outcast.

Thus there are archetypal stories that can render us apolitical, ahistorical, impersonal, and not concerned with the sacred—also anti-political, anti-historical (just forget history; I hate it; only now counts), anti-personal (conform and shut up) and anti-sacred. It takes a strong sacred force—embodied by persons seeking to control political bonds among others who feel lost and anxious—in order to achieve such repressive interconnections, for none of these four faces can be made to disappear. We pay a dear price for repressing them or repressing their interconnection. We can deeply harm them, but we cannot eliminate them.

There are times when we need to be alone in order to meditate, to get work done, or to relax. But creating such opportunities requires the collaboration of others to agree to our isolation, a historical past and present that does not compel us to keep working or to keep looking for a job that can support us, and the inspiration of the sacred for us to tune in to. Even as we sit alone with an empty mind, or search for explanations, or create a painting we cannot yet fully imagine, we experience a variety of archetypal stories, some being held together or torn apart by our political relations with others, and some being preserved by us at ever increasing cost thanks to our unexamined history. Every moment in our life has four faces and a sacred source.

We cannot ever act as if it were the truth that what we are doing is solely our business. Even if we isolate ourselves to drink or smoke whenever we feel like it, all others we are in fact connected with are emotionally and financially affected by our private acts.

At one crucial moment, it would appear that it requires only two for one to get pregnant, but even this moment which most of us would not want to be public is also not simply private. Do these two actually know each other as persons? What precautions, if any, did they agree upon? What force, if any, was used? Which story of love, if any, was being expressed? What happens if in fact they find that this moment fitted into different stories in each of their lives? How helpful will society be to the new child? Will it become invisible because its mother is on welfare, because the condom broke or abortion is illegal or unaffordable, or the mother has one child too many to be allowed to remain on welfare? But we have trouble talking with each other, and practically and ethically resolving even the most intimate matters because only those fragments of any of our faces are allowed to become apparent—which our archetypal stories and our largest fragment (our way of life) allow us to raise.

In the service of the ways of life that arrest or expel us, our four faces of being are the preordained concrete manifestations of our sacred source of being. In the service of transformation, however, we free ourselves to look anew at our own face, the faces of our neighbors, of our past and present and of our sacred source, and ask whether we can still fruitfully express and share these faces of being. We also join in bringing ourselves into being through a still larger and deeper conscious, critical, creative, and caring participation—namely with the deepest source of our being. This kind of understanding, dialogue, and interaction enlightens, empowers, and shapes the wholeness of our being.

OUR BEING PRACTICING BEING

All descriptions of our experience of being in the service of transformation reflect the reality of bi-unity. What we can be conscious of, what we can manifest and enact through our faces of being, constitutes the being, and the being practiced, of both our concrete self and the deepest source of our being—and the process of participation between our concrete self and our deepest self. The deepest source of our being is not fully, concretely conscious, and cannot fully manifest and enact itself without our concrete faces in being—and in practicing being. Neither can we in our own unique way at every particular moment be our being without also being the source of our being. We, together with our sacred source, constitute a bi-unity of being.

Through the experience of transformation with respect to a particular problem—that is, through the process of participating concretely and intimately with our deepest source—we become an incarnation of that source for as long as we can nourish this emergence of the fundamentally new and better. We cannot ever manifest the deepest source of our being in its entirety. We cannot even manifest ourselves only in our concreteness. The deepest source of our being never exists solely in and for itself. That source needs us too; it is not complete, perfect, or immutable. It, too, is still in the process of transformation. That source is therefore reachable by all human beings *through* the process of transformation.

This description of our experience of being—of who we are and who makes practical choices between four ways of life and the relationships and dramas in their service—is based on the fact that every archetype is a sacred source that manifests itself as well in four concrete faces. Archetypes of the cosmos of human relations also give rise to a being created in the image of its creator, namely a creative being. Archetypes in the service of partial Lords therefore give rise to a different image of their creators—namely, to incomplete and biased roles within such stories. Archetypes are not abstract ideas or forms but structures and dynamics of deep and concrete reality.

This disconcerting, often disturbing, certainly unorthodox description and analysis of being offer nothing supernatural, nothing dualistic contrasting the material and the ideal, nor any simple monism. (Clearly there exists more than one sacred source.) It offers nothing to believe in, nothing to obey or to worship, but instead invites trust in risking the exploration and expression of the actual fullness of our being. But because this image of our nature is initially strange to many readers, we will devote much of Chapter 14 to an amplification of it.

For our being, the greatest practical importance of this structure and dynamics of reality is that only our personal face of being can creatively reach out directly and anew to its sacred source—or to a new one—and participate in creativity. Only our personal face can hear or see or feel or intuit in Act I Scene 2 what new thought or inspiration or feeling the sacred face of our being gives rise to from the depths. Only our personal face can respond next with repression—or rebellion and further exploration. That is the uniqueness of our personal face. The political and historical faces of archetypes—and thus also of our being—cannot take the initiatives our personal face can. But we also cannot fully express our being without reaching out, listening to, respecting, or questioning our present political and historical relationships (and those of others), and discovering in manifestations of their sacred face—and of ours—the source that now endows them (or their institutions or their texts) and us with political and historical power or powerlessness.[12] We need personally to discover where we are, here and now, in our being and the being of our neighbors if we want to bring about change.

In all our discussion, *personally* refers always to our personal face—to only one face of our being, though a face unique in its capacity for conscious, critical, creative, caring participation with all our other faces and our source of being. But this distinction between our personal face and our fullness of being is no small matter. In our time of the "subjective," of the "psychological," of "individualism," of legal rights defining or neglecting what we can and need to be and do (personally, together, or historically), and with the sacred reserved for organized religions, we have segmented, segregated, and repressed aspects of our being.[13]

Most philosophers have stopped thinking about ontology—the study of being. Most scholars are specialists in only one aspect of one of our faces. Most jobs confine us to the efficient, instrumental use of some aspect of our bodily vessel or some facet of our personal—such as the mask underlining or covering some slivers of our being. All archetypal stories except those in the service of transformation assign us to roles—to parts that call forth only a portion of our being and thus crucially diminish us. To accomplish more than others, to star, to gain power and fame, to be the most dutiful servant—these become, unconsciously, compensations that cannot repair our pruned being. No nation-state, no interest group, no scholarly discipline now cares about the full human being.

In the service of incoherence, we cannot tune in on the wholeness of our being or of anyone else's being because we have not yet experienced the whole journey through the core drama of life. We do not yet know what we are missing in our life. We cannot comprehend the depth of suffering—and the repressed and ever more open rage—in us and around us. We all have the capacity to free ourselves to enter this process. But we cannot choose with understanding and courage to cre-

---

12. Contemporary law slivers the political face of our being into hazardous slices. Haitians who suffer economically because their brutal dictatorship rules to make the rich richer, and will imprison and kill people who object to this life, are in their vast majority rejected when they seek asylum in the United States. The U.S. government says they do not qualify as political refugees. They are called economic refugees instead. For the first time in American history, the immigration board granted political refugee status to "an Ecuadorian woman who had suffered ten years of domestic violence, including marital rape. In a decision made public in June, board members declared that the woman would face persecution if she were returned to Ecuador where her husband had threatened to kill her and the police had refused to protect her." *Ms*, vol. 4, no. 2, September/October 1993.

13. I have not referred, as C.G. Jung did, to the *Self*, which emerges through what Jung called the process of individuation. Jung had a deep understanding of the personal and sacred faces of our being, and I have learned most valuable ideas and practices from him. But he had little sense of the political and historical faces of our being, and since all four faces are always interconnected, focusing on the Self in this way creates no small omission.

ate a fundamentally better way of being as long as we do not find it unbearable to remain only partial beings within our present way of life.

Love your neighbor as you love yourself. Why did sages put loving yourself first? Why bother to love your neighbor as yourself? Until we ourselves have experienced the drama of transformation, we cannot know what love is, what understanding ourselves and our neighbor requires, and why we need to—and can—risk trust in ourselves (our deepest source of being) and in our neighbors. Until we have learned to love and trust ourselves, we cannot know what love and trust is or how to love and trust others.

The very task of transformation requires understanding and coming to love and enjoy the fullness of our being—thanks to the connection to our deepest source and the connection between all four faces of our being—in order to risk faith to test the practice of a fundamentally more nourishing form of justice. How can we do that without our neighbors? We need groups—beginning with one of us connecting with another—in order to do what we can and need to do together, but groups need to be composed of actual beings. Institutions cannot truly mask this reality.

"To know yourself is to know your Lord." We are not only the outward faces of the archetype we enact. We are either a partial being constituted as the embodiment of one of the partial Lords, or else we live in a fully unique way in bi-unity with our deepest source of being. The four most fundamental choices open to us for creating the substance of our being—that is what we shall now analyze in the next four chapters.

PART TWO

The Four Ways of Life

4

Enclosing Ourselves in Emanation as a Way Of Life

At every moment of our life we live somewhere in the core drama of life—moving through its three Acts, arresting ourselves in its first or second Act, or exiting from it into destructive death. These four ways constitute the largest contexts of our life, not only in terms of structure and dynamics, but also in terms of providing us with fundamentally different experiences and understandings of the ultimate meaning, values, and purpose of our being and our life.

If *ultimate* here were to mean in the unfathomable long run or on Judgment Day, we would have no way of gaining such understanding. By *ultimate*, I mean the deepest ground we can discover here and now for why we are who we are and why we are doing what we are doing. Three of the four ways of life, because they are fragments of the core drama, can only give us an incomplete and biased understanding of the ultimate ground of our being and our actions. To put it all too briefly, emanation tells us that only the great mysteriously powerful source knows why ultimately we are who we are, why we are doing what we are doing, and why life has the consequences it does. Meanwhile, we must do exactly what we have already been told to do. In the service of incoherence, we may sacrifice our life for the nation-state or let others specialize in ethics while we concentrate on the acquisition of money or power—or we may be deeply attached to other fragments of life. In any event, a life of organizing fragments in the service of a fragment of the core drama keeps us from being able subjectively or objectively to discover the deepest ground of our being. In deformation, only one leader and his movement knows the answers and inflicts them on everyone else.

Through the experience of transformation, however, we attain a fundamentally better understanding of who we are becoming and where we are moving with respect to one particular problem (never of everything at once) in the context of the stories we are enacting in the service of the core drama of life. We understand the ultimate meaning, value, and purpose in this instance because we have reached the deepest source of being we are capable of experiencing. We will always test this understanding with others before we claim to know. The outcome of any particular experience of transformation can be nourished, often for many years, but life will change again because this is a cosmos of continuous creation.

We also have the power to curb our freedom and say no and to arrest or indeed to destroy ourselves. These four ways of life remain our choices at every moment. We cannot experience any concrete moment of life except as an expression of our being enacting an archetypal story in the service of an overarching way of life. This is not only a cosmos of continuous creation, but the basic issue always is whether our participation moves this new moment of reality toward the better or the worse. Only the core drama of life opens the possibility of our taking part not only in the creation of the fundamentally new but also the fundamentally better.

THE RISE OF GREAT PROPHETS

Since the new which presents itself also as the final word is one of the four faces which possesses the archetypal strength to emerge within us again and again, why are people not creating new emanational ways of life again and again and then going no further? Even in the United States in the late twentieth century, there do exist hundreds of new prophets. The founders of the Mormons and of Jehovah's Witnesses in the nineteenth century were not the last ones to come forward.

But there are many strong barriers to the rise of new emanational ways of life. Before the modern age, offering any new and different way of life turned that prophet into a heretic, and normally raised the threat that she or he would be exiled or killed. In our time, we also hear new inspirations, but if we do not understand how they would help us compete in the service of incoherence, we tune out what most of us would now call fantasies or superstitions. Or we turn them into what we call subjective experiences, or reinterpret them in terms of still existing fragments of emanation as a way of life. In the service of deformation, we already know all the answers and would not dare risk raising any different view. In the service of transformation, we do not remain in Act I and we come to recognize that its original emanational quality was never truly emanational, and its overpowering mystery dissipates as we grow to understand the new archetypal drama to which it gives rise.

But since the remnants of at least ten thousand different emanational ways of life still exist today, how can they all be manifestations of arrest in Act I of the core drama of life? This is no small fact we need to face—no small test through which we can examine in practice the reality of the living underlying patterning forces which this theory of transformation addresses. First we shall ask what accounts for the differences between emanational ways of life. Then we shall examine what they have in common in the light of three cases that exemplify both the fundamental sameness and variations within emanation as a way of life.

The differences between the concrete manifestations of emanational ways of life arise again and again from the fact that we all have four faces and also a sacred source of being. No sacred source can speak except through a prophet whose personal face is, of course, unique, who lives at a particular moment in history among people who can (or who are unready or unwilling) to tune in to the same sacred source and to do what they need to do together in a new way. If a prophet remains only a prophet, he (few women indeed have so far been taken seriously as prophets) cannot know what he is talking about. The prophet also needs to turn into a philosopher and into a critical, creative, caring participant so that he may be able to guide others. He needs to participate with other human beings in creating new archetypal stories in the service of this new way of life.

Since each of us has four faces that manifest our present source of being, diversity of response begins during the life of each new prophet. Moses succeeded in leading the Jews out of slavery in Egypt into the desert. He battled against Jews who decided at Sinai to worship a golden calf; he also had other dissenters killed. But none of the people who had spent forty years in the desert of incoherence, not even Moses, made it into the Promised Land.

Christ was crucified in his early thirties. The devastatingly punitive last book of the Christian Bible, called "The Revelation to John," does not sound at all like Christ's Sermon on the Mount.

Muhammad had to flee his hometown of Mecca because he was inspired to found a new community that would transcend loyalty to tribes or the rivalries between them. It was to be composed of "helpers of Allah," guided by a new sense of justice. Since the dominant faction of his own extended family, long the ruling dynasty of Mecca, fought his new movement, Muhammad felt it necessary to accept the conversion of other tribes as tribes (not as new individual helpers). And after his victory, he also accepted the conversion of his family which soon became the ruling dynasty of Islam.

None of these three prophets erected emanation as a way of life. With varying personal understanding of themselves and the other faces and sources of their being, with different political and historical connections (or forms of opposition), they sought to discover the road to transformation. The people who arrest themselves in Act I are devoutly convinced that they have enshrined themselves within the only true version of the original experience. No doubt there were always a few who became thus enthralled during the life of the prophet. But what in pre-modern and modern times both believers and observers regard as the orthodox version was usually not created until decades or even centuries after the prophet's death.

Thus we see again why the manifestations of emanation as a way of life—though they all share the same underlying structure and dynamics—are so diverse, even among those who claim the same prophet as their one and only true origin. Turning that new inspiration into a way of life once and for all is a task that was (subsequently) accomplished not only with a new (not necessarily the original) sacred inspiration, but also at another particular moment in history (not in eternity) by unique persons in the face of political collaboration and opposition within and outside the emerging community. No emanational way of life was ever created *without* us at a moment *beyond* history and politics.

Each emanational way of life, contrary to its own claim, limits our vision and practice with respect to the ultimate meaning, value, and purpose of our life. Ironically, in the face of this fact, each of the more than ten thousand emanational ways of life proclaims that it alone possesses the deepest and best truth. So why do we arrest ourselves in such a way of life?

Max Weber tells us that the only way to keep a new revelation alive is by "routinizing charisma." But turning grace (the meaning of *charisma*) into an institutionalized routine is not only impossible, but Weber's analysis also does not adequately tell us how such a seeming miracle is achieved. We cannot arrest ourselves in Act I of the core drama and consolidate that portion into a way of life without the help of a sacred source that also serves to keep us inspired to stay within this new sacred container. The sacred source that catches and keeps us in emanation as a way of life is not the initially still mysterious but not truly emanational source that turns Act I into the first Act of the entire drama of transformation. Rather, it is a partial sacred Lord who means to arrest us there. Routines alone, except as reminders and reinforcements in the service of this biased and incomplete Lord, could not keep such ways of life potent enough to endow us with a deep sense of absolute righteousness and security—and with a profound fear that if we do wrong, God will punish us and we could be doomed forever.

The truth is that indeed no other Act of the core drama of life can give us this kind of assurance. But since the core drama constitutes an intrinsic capacity of human nature, we are, in the service of emanation, at least unconsciously aware—and certainly the authorities in the established chain of emanation will also have told us, but in their version of the further journey—that rebellion would mean sinful betrayal and would open up a suicidal exit from this only divinely ordained container. Outsiders could then also more easily threaten us with destructive death. If we experienced transformation and gave voice to it, we could bring about fundamental divisions within this already blessed group.

But in this cosmos of continuous creation, the drama of transformation as a fundamentally better journey (or else, another of its fragments) can arise through our being and the being of others again and again. Repeatedly throughout history, emanational ways of life have tried major re-formations or have come to an end because they could not meet these new challenges within the confines of their established web of life. Emanational ways of life usually have a far more conflicted history than their still believing members dare to remember. For no community and for no individual in any period of history can it be taken for granted that all they ever experienced were the already fixed manifestations of emanation. Only by an actual inquiry into their actual experience at a particular place and time can we discover through what dramas, and in which service, particular individuals or particular groups in a community lived their lives. Such care is all the more important since none of the four ways of life are "ideal types"—conceptual constructs intended as heuristic instruments of analysis. Instead, each of these four ways describes a living reality.

That is why we shall now explore the fundamental nature of emanation as a way of life and ask why, despite the seeming certainty and fixity of their moment of origin, they experienced long delays coming into being and why they then endured so long—but neither forever nor without perennial differences and conflicts within and around them. We shall illustrate this analysis with examples from three emanational ways of life, all of which are monotheistic and all of which arose in the Middle East, yet which are different from each other—and also, over time, from themselves.

EMANATION AS A WAY OF LIFE

All the final, eternally valid revelations that are believed to be at the heart of all ways of emanation still alive today began late in human history. The first Act in which peoples arrested themselves was not the first Act of human history. To speak only of the three monotheistic ways (which together still have the largest number of believers in the world), each began at a moment of great conflicts and suffering.

The Jews who had begun in the days of Abraham their migration from what is now Iraq were then slaves in Egypt. A Jew named Jesus lived at a time when his people were deeply divided (in the Promised Land) over whether to struggle against or collaborate with the Roman rulers of Palestine; whether history would end apocalyptically and soon, or would have to be endured; how to interpret emanational beliefs; and whether to persist in the service of the Judaic emanation or turn to Hellenism or to Rome. Jesus offered not a new emanational kind of community to an already chosen people (though some Jews and Romans saw it in that light) but a community of transformation—open to all who are willing to experience again and again dying and being reborn. Muhammad lived in Arabia at a time when hundreds of different gods were being worshipped and persistent bloody conflicts dominated relations between Arab tribes.

No new emanational way of life united many people into a new community as the prophet died. After Joshua had led the second generation of Jews into the

Promised Land (the first generation of the exodus had died in the desert), and after Joshua, too, had been buried, the Jews "then went away, each to his house and each to his town," and they "worshipped Astarte and Ashtaroth and the gods of the nations round them. Hence, the Lord put them into the power of Eglon, king of Moab, who oppressed them for eighteen years."[1]

The Twelve Tribes of Israel continued for a long time to have trouble maintaining a tribal confederation. At times, they fought each other. After several decades, they held general assemblies to deliberate on legislative and military issues. They elected a Judge to resolve disputes and lead their battles. When Gideon, one of the early Judges, had been offered kingship, he said: "I will not rule over you, neither shall my son rule over you. The Lord shall rule over you" (Judges 8:23). Why, in the face of such earlier opposition, and in the face of arguments that have forever rendered the First Book of Samuel divided against itself, did the Jews decide to make Saul their first king? "We want a king, so we in our turn can be like the other nations" (I Samuel 8:19).

Their community was no longer pious or united enough to enforce the law on its own. Saul's predecessor, Samuel, had been an honest Judge, but his sons took bribes. The people did not want them as Samuel's successors. Yet the Jews wanted a king whose son, regardless of his qualities, would normally inherit the throne. And King Saul gave his daughter to David as a wife in the hope that this would make David fight all the more loyally and persistently against the Philistines, and that David would thus at last be killed, since Saul's own attempts to kill David had failed. For the first time in Jewish history, King Saul created a professional army to fight the Philistines and others for most of forty years, but he was defeated by them. He *did* defeat the Amalekites, however. Commanded by God, he killed almost all their men, women, children, and animals, but then decided to save a few for a special sacrifice on the next day. For that disobedience, god rendered Saul mad.

David then became the most cherished king in Jewish history—the first ruler to establish Jerusalem as the capital. But even at its best, this alliance between two fragments of the core drama of life—emanation and incoherence—left life splintered and partisan. David inspired his son Solomon to build the first Temple to centralize the focus of emanation as a way of life. (Solomon married, among many other wives, a daughter of the Pharaoh of Egypt and built the Temple with slave labor—a resort to deformation.) David, whose royal bodyguard was composed not of Jews but of Philistines, was also far shrewder than Saul in making sure that the enemy could kill his chief army commander, a Hittite named Uriah, so that David

---

1. Quoted in the Greek "Septuagint," the earliest translation into Greek of the Hebrew Bible, dating from the last two centuries before Christ; here drawn from footnote j in *The New Jerusalem Bible*, the translation normally used in this book. For further details on the same deep internal divisions, see Judges 1–12.

could marry Uriah's wife, Bathsheba. The rise of David to kingship also led to a civil war between Israel and Judah.

Such wars between Jews recurred, and many of the kings to come were unjust, as the Bible tells us. The bonds between kings, the rich, and the priests of Jerusalem—and also the worship of other gods, especially of goddesses by Jewish women—gave rise to the protests, warnings, and renewed inspirations of prophets whose words constitute no small portion of the Bible. The experience of Jews (and, as we shall see, of Christians and Muslims) with the state—allegedly in the service of emanation, but in fact in the service of incoherence and at times also deformation—was not an experience of the rule of God's justice. Why then did the Jews choose the state?

The governing explanation around the world is that the only way a people can live and enforce their own way of life and defend themselves against their enemies is to create a state of their own. But the Jews of that time were confronted by powerful challenges to the development, protection, and enforcement of a shared emanational way of life. The damage done reflected the particular manifestations of the historical, political, and personal faces of those times. But, at all times, they are archetypal faces of the domestic and external dynamics of the state acting, as always, in the service of incoherence.

Leaving Egypt, the Jews could scarcely have gone to a more exposed position in the Middle East than Palestine. Other people already lived there. For centuries before and after the Jews arrived, every powerful state within a thousand miles of it recognized Palestine as an essential steppingstone for conquering either Mesopotamia or Egypt. Those were the great prizes, because in this region of mountains and deserts, those two had the great rivers and therefore the great continuous harvests—and so at least the economic potential for building great, enduring civilizations. (The Jordan River has about one percent of the water of the Nile.) Therefore, everyone—Hittites, Assyrians, Babylonians, Persians, Egyptians, and the great sea-people known as Philistines—all moved first to conquer Palestine in order to reach the farther, larger, and more enticing target and also to use it as the nexus for international trade routes. As a result, the Jews who had been living within two states, Israel and Judah—for most of the time from the reign of King David (about 1000 BC) to the time of the Babylonian conquest (and exile and destruction of the first Temple) in 586 BC—had experienced many foreign attacks. From the return of many (but certainly not all) Jews from exile in 537 BC, until the Romans destroyed the second Temple in AD 70, Jews in Palestine lived almost always under foreign rule. The Jewish community was divided between collaborators with and opponents of foreign rulers, and they differed about their way of life.

A significant number of Jews never returned from Babylon. They chose to remain in exile for over 2,500 years, staying either in what later became Iraq or migrating as far as Germany and China. They lived under the rule of others. And later, when the Romans exiled all Jews from Palestine, new ways of emanation were consolidated among Jews, especially in terms of "Our Homeland: The Text."[2] Did only the history and politics of the Jews change again and again? Did only Jews pay a high price for the alliance of incoherence and emanation—or later for being without such alliance? We shall now look still more closely into the issues at stake.

All architects of emanation as a way of life responded to the fact that most people in their community after the death of the prophet were still experiencing the power relationships, conflicts, and suffering of earlier days. They were also faced with many people who, however much drawn to the new conclusions, had not known how to empty themselves of their former being while moving through the desert of incoherence. They had not, like Muhammad, meditated for forty days and nights in a cavern to discover why it was not bearable for them to be contained within the underlying patterns of their present lives—in Muhammad's case, to remain a successful caravan merchant within the most powerful family in Mecca. Faced with such people, these architects concentrated on inspiring and organizing a conversion from an old arrest in Act I Scene 1(or in unresolved incoherence) to a new arrest in Act I Scene 2.

The task that drew all such architects was that of establishing a larger political and sacred community (larger than the previously existing dominant units), so that its power and inspiration would tie every individual into a new web of life—a web that would henceforth endure unchanged throughout history (until the final Day of Judgment) because that sacred source of being had ordained its very nature and its many particular rules (though many of these rules are not to be found in the original texts).

Let us look at the first of several inner tensions intrinsic to emanation as a way of life—intrinsic because we are holding on to this fragment of the core drama of life. We are trying authoritatively to consolidate and translate into definitive thought and practice the final revelations of a sacred source whose underlying patterning story now enchants us, and so also prevents us from freeing ourselves with full critical consciousness to understand and evaluate. Emanational ways of life are based politically, historically, and personally on the authority, judgments, and interpretations of individuals who must be able to present themselves as sources of emanation drawing upon a chain of emanational relationships that is ultimately inspired and created by God.

History must now cease to be a vital face of our being. The specifics of life are repeatedly constituted by our obedience and preservation of rules and commands. History, which opened for us through this great revelation, will significantly reopen only once again when God in his mercy reveals himself again on Judgment Day. The political is a face of our being, above all, as it preserves this community of

---

2. The title of a deeply and creatively informed essay by George Steiner in *Salmagundi* 66 (Winter/Spring 1985), 4–25.

believers—or seeks to expand it—in continuous strong solidarity and obedience. Our personal face bows to this political order and to the suspension of history in the name of this most powerful emanational source. We bow, but we cannot fully understand what we are bowing to.

To be an emanation of such a source is to flow forth and radiate as an embodiment of it. That creates another inner tension intrinsic to this way of life. In one respect, emanation attracts us deeply to a mysteriously overwhelming power that has blessed us by being on our side—and not on the side of others. And to please it, we desire as much as we can to be and do what that source wants of us. We are grateful to be the creation and under the protection of the greatest of all powers. In another respect, we must not come to believe that we are ourselves an emanation of this source. For then we—any of us—might believe ourselves empowered to speak in the name of God, and that would undermine the fixed and final word and structure of our present emanational way of life.

That is why Jews in the service of emanation declare that God (who had entered into dialogues with Adam and Eve, Noah, Abraham, and Jacob, to mention only a few) would never again show his face or say something fundamentally new after his appearance at Sinai. The later prophets who heard from God, including his threats of exile from the Promised Land, spoke of the need to return to the original way of life. That is why Muslims in the service of emanation call Muhammad God's final prophet to humankind. That is why the emerging Catholic Church at the Council of Nicea in 325 declared that Christ was indeed an incarnation of God—but that he was God's only begotten son, meaning that no one else must think it possible actually to follow Christ's way and thus enter upon the path of transformation. Belief and conformity were the central requirements. At Nicea, it also became an article of dogma that if you thought that you had heard from God, there were only two possibilities: either what came through you was redundant, because Christ had already said it and the Church Fathers had already understood and rightly interpreted it, or else it came from the devil. So, if we accept this new inspiration, we must be excommunicated or killed.

But this rejection of any direct experience of embodying the source of this way of life—though we are to enact that Lord's way as perfectly as possible—raises a third internal tension. What is to legitimize the rule and interpretation of authorities in this way of life except that they are part of a chain of emanation, thus putting their judgment beyond possible questioning? On what basis can they claim to be empowered by a chain of emanation when they deny it to others in their community? The three monotheistic forms of emanation responded to this problem in different ways; different archetypal stories in the service of the same archetypal way of life inspired their response.

Among Catholic Christians (the largest group of Christians to this day), only one man came (though officially not until Vatican I in 1870) to be infallible in knowing what God wants us to believe and do. From this perspective, the Pope's office is blessed by the Holy Spirit since Christ established this office by appointing Peter as his first Vicar. In turn, all the offices of the Pope's hierarchy, down to the local priest, are also blessed by the Holy Spirit. However human the priest may be, whenever he speaks and acts for his office and under the orders of the hierarchy, he comes forth with the authority of the Holy Spirit. All Christian believers must therefore manifest themselves as emanations of this Church.

This form of Christianity did not begin to take this shape until more than three hundred years after the death of Christ. By that time still, Christians constituted only a minority in the lands of the Mediterranean Sea. They were suffering oppression from pagan rulers and even from fellow Christians. They were deeply divided among themselves as to the very meaning of being Christian. Some of them lived together in communities of transformation. Others did not see Jesus as a living example of the way of transformation but instead, as the Messiah, the savior who had died to redeem their sins (but had left a world still dominated by sinners). There were Christians who rejected the world by becoming ascetics living alone as hermits or in desert and mountain monasteries, rejecting their world and their very bodies as sinful. Others concentrated their worship on the dead—the tombs of martyred saints—so that these saints might intercede for them with God. Several dozen different Christian sects had emerged. Many of these accepted their local bishop as their actual ruler (instead of the official non-Christian one). Conflicts in all realms of life were growing. People longed for the security that only mysteriously overwhelming power seemed to promise. Many, but certainly not all, sought a shepherd who would rule them as a flock of sheep.

At the beginning of the fourth century, the Emperor of the Roman Empire said he had a dream. He saw a cross in the sky—a cross bearing the inscription: "By this sign, conquer." Why did Constantine want to rely on a Christian minority, divided by different ethnic and cultural backgrounds, different client-patron relationships, differing beliefs, differing philosophies? He hoped Christianity, which had grown above all in the cities of the empire, would give his army and his empire a new and fiercer legitimacy and loyalty. It was not easy. At the Council of Nicea in 325, the bishops invited by Constantine debated fiercely, and sometimes kicked each other in the stomach with their boots as they adopted new dogmas. In the days of Augustine, about a century later, the Goths and Visigoths who sacked Rome—the capital of the Christian Emperor—were themselves Christians.

Augustine (354–430) was born about a generation after Christianity had become the official religion of the Roman Empire—an event that had raised great hopes among a number of Christians. But the Christian Emperor was certainly corrupt and oppressive. Many were the Christians who were still sinners or also heretics. The Christians who had sacked Rome were now on their way to conquer Christian North Africa, where Augustine lived. Augustine responded to this deep crisis by re-forming the Christian emanational way of life anew. No one can compare with Augustine's dramatic and pervasive influence on Christian life for centuries to come.

He was inspired to establish above all a new article of belief: We are all fundamentally flawed by original sin.[3] Adam and Eve's sin of disobedience to God arises in all of us again and again by our very nature. Because we are all born as the fruit of lust and because ineradicably we lust also to disobey God's law, we are intrinsically lamed and cannot bring about justice on this earth. Personally, politically, and historically, we can only build a fallen order. God is all good. The City of God is all just. But we reach that city only through our death. As long as a human being is "in this mortal body, he is a pilgrim in a foreign land, away from God."[4] When we die, however, God will elect only a few for eternal life, and in his infinite wisdom, he may even select some who were great sinners. In the meantime, ours is a terrible knowledge and a terrible burden: Human beings alone bring all evil into the world.

Hence we need to be disciplined by both Church and State together, with the State accepting the Church as final authority. And Martin Luther—who, like many Protestant reformers, continued to adhere to Augustine's dogmas—declared, the State is "God's hangman." We have, said Augustine, "no abiding city" on this earth. Here, rulers are often the latest gangs of robbers. But in fact we are all sinners and need to be kept under control. At best, Church and State together might bring about "a persistently precarious convalescence"—provided people with humility acknowledge their basically flawed nature and their dependence on authority.[5]

Augustine seeks to prove that he draws his conception of original sin from the New Testament. He quotes from the Letter of Paul to the Church in Rome: "Well, then, it was through one man that sin came into the world, and through sin, death, and thus death has spread through the human race because everyone has sinned" (5:12). But in his *City of God*, Augustine does not quote *at all* other parts of Paul's letter which put this quotation into a completely different context and give it a radically different meaning. In the very same chapter, just four verses later, Paul adds, "One single offense brought condemnation, but now, after many offenses, have come the free gift and so acquittal" (5:16). Why this good news? "It is God's power for the salvation of everyone who has faith . . . for in it is revealed the saving justice of God" (1:16–17). How does faith save us and bring us justice? We justify our faith

---

3. Augustine and Henry Scowcroft Bettenson, *Concerning the City of God against the Pagans*, especially Book XIII. Peter Robert Lamont Brown, *Augustine of Hippo: A Biography*; Peter Robert Lamont Brown, *The Making of Late Antiquity*, The Carl Newell Jackson Lectures; 1976. Elaine H. Pagels, *Adam, Eve, and the Serpent*. We shall look at that story of Adam and Eve from the perspective of transformation in Chapter 14.
4. Augustine, *The City of God*, Book XIX, Chapter 14.
5. Brown, *Augustine of Hippo: A Biography*, 365.

by re-experiencing the death and rebirth of Christ: "When we were baptized into his death, we were buried with him, so that as Christ was raised from the dead by the Father's glorious power, we too should begin living a new life. . . . Give yourselves to God, as people brought to life from the dead, and give every part of your bodies to be instruments of uprightness, and then sin will no longer have any power over you—you are living not under law, but under grace" (6:4–14). "The law of the Spirit which gives life in Christ Jesus has set you free, free from the law of sin and death" (8:1–2). "All who are guided by the Spirit of God are sons of God (8:14).

This is not the only Paul.[6] But there is no Paul like Augustine's Paul. There is a Paul who spoke of the capacity of all of us for transformation, provided we empty ourselves so that we may be reborn. What Augustine believed he saw and experienced instead were human beings all crippled by original sin—a sin that leads us by our very nature perpetually to break rules, that therefore puts us in dire need of authority powerful enough to limit the outbursts of sin as much as possible.[7] Augustine was inspired to re-form the Christian way of life through a nucleus of emanational power that is not only hierarchic but seemingly impersonal in its utter potency on this earth (with the assistance of the State) over life and death, body and soul. No priests of the Church claim to be a source of emanation but instead, the exclusive spokesmen and managers for the sacred source which blesses, inspires, and empowers their offices and hence their work—the Holy Spirit.

An example of seemingly not being a personal link in a chain of emanation but instead acting officially as manager for the Holy Spirit is Augustine's response to the Donatists. In his own region of North Africa, many Christians were Donatists who would not obey a priest unless he was also a man of morally inspiring character. The office itself was not enough proof of sanctity. They remembered that Christ had said, "You must not allow yourself to be called Rabbi, since you have only one Master, and you are all brothers. You must call no one on earth your father, since you have only one Father, and he is in heaven. Nor must you allow yourselves to be called teachers, for you have only one teacher, the Christ. The greatest among you must be your servant. Anyone who raises himself up will be humbled and anyone

---

6. For an inquiry into the actually and seemingly different manifestations of Paul, see Elaine H. Pagels, *The Gnostic Paul: Gnostic Exegesis of the Pauline Letters*.

7. Augustine himself was a richly complex human being long in deep struggle with himself and the world. Even when, for the first time, he firmly committed himself to Christianity and wrote his *Confessions*, he did not yet sound like a person lamed by original sin, but as someone who had overcome his sins. When he encounters god, he speaks to him: "I have learnt to love you late, Beauty at once so ancient and so new! I have learnt to love you outside myself. I searched for you outside myself and, disfigured as I was, I fell upon the lovely things in your creation. You called me; you cried aloud to me; you broke my barrier of deafness. You shone upon me; your radiance enveloped me; you put my blindness to flight. You shed your fragrance about me; I drew breath and now I gasp for your sweet odor. I tasted you, and now I hunger and thirst for you. You touched me, and I am inflamed with love of your peace." From Augustine and R. S. Pine-Coffin, *Confessions*, L114.

who humbles himself will be raised up" (Matthew 23:8–12). They also recalled that Jesus had said, the Holy Spirit "blows where it pleases" (John 3:8), and that Paul had said, "Do you not realize that your body is the temple of the Holy Spirit, who is in you and whom you received from God?" (I Corinthian 6–19). Therefore for the Church to be in control, it needed to insist that it had harnessed the Holy Spirit.

Augustine sent eighty black stallions from North Africa to Rome in order to gain the Emperor's authorization to burn Donatist Christians at the stake. He burned many of them. To reduce future controversies, the Church soon forbade Christians who were not part of the hierarchy to read the sacred text themselves, and certainly not in their own local language. They declared there was no need for such reading; the Church fathers had already read it and had already established its only authorized interpretation.[8]

Nonetheless, there was nothing inevitable about the triumph of Augustine's dramas of original sin and allied hierarchic authorities for governing this way of life. For centuries after his death, history moved against him. The Roman Empire decayed and fragmented. The predominantly Christian cities lost population, cohesion, prosperity, and influence. In the seventh century, the Muslims conquered most of the lands of the Mediterranean. Many Christians converted to Islam. In 800, the Pope crowned Charlemagne as the Holy Roman Emperor, but after Charlemagne's death, that new Holy Roman Empire crumbled. What were later called "The Dark Ages" began.

But the Church now also sent out missionaries to the tribes of Western Central and Northern Europe. Their warrior leaders found Augustine's vision powerfully convincing. They had read no more of Augustine than the rulers of recent Marxist regimes around the world had read of Marx, but the essential dynamics and values of Augustine's central archetypal story appealed greatly to them.

Their thinking went like this: We are now justified in our authority by the need of all sinners to be kept within bounds. We now exercise power in the name of God, and with the support of the hierarchic Church, and not only on the basis of oaths of personal loyalty or in the name of our noble family and the emanational loyalty of our tribe or of our serfs. Now the question—Are you with us or against us?—is a question sharpened by our obedience to the only true God. "By this sign, conquer." Are the conquered or our own people discontented? That is no excuse for rebellion. Justice cannot be achieved on this earth—only our sanctified law and order.

That kind of law and order, however, points to a fundamental and intrinsic incompleteness in Augustine's re-formation of emanation as a way of life. It cannot succeed in limiting incoherence without an alliance with organized incoherence as

---

8. This edict barring the laity from reading the sacred text was not changed until the Second Vatican Council in 1962.

a way of life. But each state, as the most potent story of that way of life, did not base its power solely on the Church (which both supported and challenged the State by seeking to enlist it in its service). The Church had to contend with rulers who were themselves recognized as sources of emanation—thanks to their heroic deeds, or as heads of their noble families and tribes. Moreover, they possessed the power of naked force, whether they used it on behalf of the Church or of their own interests. They usually knew no limits to power except rival power. But considering that the Church required the State, and considering that the Church's higher ranks were often related by blood to the nobility and often directly served in State offices, the Church was also at times the State's acquiescent ally.

The Church was never strong enough to create a single, unified Christian community. Because each state depended not only on the Church but was also inspired by the emanational bonds that connected its own individual and kinship loyalties, Christian states attacked other Christian states again and again for centuries. The alliance between people living in only fragments of the core drama of life thus led to repeated expressions of great power and devotion and also great insecurity and discontent that produced repeated conflicts. And, as we shall see in the next chapter, after a deeper split arose among Christians with the rise of Protestantism, the State triumphed over all churches—but, once again, in alliance with a new emanational story, this time a drama in the service of incoherence, namely *nationalism*.

Alliance with the State is not the only way to try to deal with the internal tensions—by now we see that they are indeed inner contradictions intrinsic to a partial life—within emanation as a way of life. Let us now look at two different archetypal forms of maintaining consensus in the service of emanation—as practiced by Jews and Muslims—in order to discover their benefits, constraints, and tensions. In contrast to the dominant drama of Catholic Christianity that we have been analyzing, Jews and Muslims in the service of emanation have never ceased to discuss the meaning and practical implications of the sacred text and its earliest commentaries and also its later commentaries upon the earlier commentaries. No living authority or interpreter claims to possess any direct or hierarchic link to God.

It is the text of the Hebrew bible or of the Koran that constitutes the central symbol of God's presence—the word incarnate. That belief generates a deeply binding focus for all discussions. It also generates an inescapable need for discussion; the meaning of God's original word is not exhausted by its concreteness. It touches all aspects of life without exception, and hence the discussion cannot end—both in order to honor and appreciate what has hitherto been said and done, and to discover how further to apply these texts and interpretations in the present.

This dialogue embraces not only rabbis (and among Muslims, ulema) who have been studying the original text, the commentaries, and the rules that have been established. Among Jews, it also involves all men—but no women, for all men have studied the sacred text and its major commentaries at least until the age of thirteen even if they devote themselves thereafter to other occupations. Among Muslims, literacy has not been as widespread, but the community draws upon its ulema also to settle social and legal conflicts and thus tests the value of their judgment. And at every moment and in all aspects of life, men, women, and children experience and evaluate themselves and their neighbors as embodiments of these interpretations of their sacred way of life—sacred not as distinguished from being secular, but because of what these textual interpretations ask of us in every aspect of our being.

These interpretations are not all of one school of thought, neither among Jews nor among Muslims. Focusing now on the Jewish experience, we shall examine first elements of variety, then of unity. We are speaking of a bible that was written by several different authors and editors, and many chapters of it millennia or at least centuries after the events recorded therein, with several of the crucial stories, including the beginning of the world, reported in different versions. It is a book that vividly tells both of divine actions and of human actions as being performed not solely in the service of emanation, but indeed again and again in all four ways of life. Not surprisingly then, even the first basic interpretation of the Bible, called the Talmud, exists in two different versions, one written over many years in Babylonian exile, one written over many years in Jerusalem—and also an oral tradition, based on two different versions, one by the school of Shammai, the other by the school of Hillel. Then, in the second and third centuries after Christ, there also emerged the Mishna, a commentary on all the preceding texts. Henceforth were produced commentaries upon commentaries by rabbis living in different communities of Europe and Asia—and later, America.

How much did these commentators differ? The Talmud tells this story about Rabbi Akiba, one of its principal authors: When Moses climbed up Mount Sinai for the second time to receive tablets, he asked God whether their fate would be any better than that of the first tablets which Moses had smashed in anger as he saw the Jews worshipping the golden calf while they had grown impatient waiting for his return. God gave Moses a vision. He saw Rabbi Akiba lecturing to his students, but Moses could not understand anything Akiba was teaching. "Is this what will happen?" Moses asked God. But God let the vision continue: A student asked Akiba how he knows what he knows and Akiba replied, "I have it by a tradition from Moses at Sinai"—and then Moses understood.

No rabbi ever became the sole authorized interpreter or final authority, even within a single locality. Instead, this continuous discussion both perpetuates and, within fundamental limits, changes interpretations of the text. The written commentaries do not veil differences of views. Indeed, they carefully report them, but they veil changes, once they have been accepted, by presenting them as deeper and better understandings of the original.

There existed differences among Jews in the service of emanation. For example, Jews in parts of the Islamic world were permitted to marry two wives. But what united all Jews, living in communities stretching over thousands of miles in all directions is that at the center of study and interpretation for all Jews in emanation rested the Torah—the five books of Moses, and the same early commentaries. They also read the other four-fifths of the Bible, but they concentrated upon the story before the Jews entered the Promised Land, before they created an alliance with the State in the service of incoherence, and entered into battles with each other and were conquered by others. For all, the emphasis fell on conforming to 613 central rules of life. What happened in history since the second exile was assimilated into a liturgy, into rituals and holy days of grieving, atonement, celebration, and affirmation.[9] Since everywhere Jews constituted only a small minority, they also needed internal cohesion because of frequent persecutions and renewed exile from countries in the Christian world—and because of living under constraints, but rarely persecutions, in the Muslim world.

Consider the deep limitations within which arrest in emanation, even in this version of it, fixates our life. We can develop or experience no fundamental change in history until the Messiah comes. In the meantime, we assimilate all new suffering into our already established liturgy. We do not know how to analyze or understand history anew. Politically, we can only act to preserve and protect, if possible. We must not ask fundamentally new questions about our one and only sacred source. Within these bounds, we can personally enter into endless discussions and even re-formations amid deep commitments.[10]

Did all Jews remain within this sacred container until the modern age? For several centuries, a majority of them moved into the path of transformation instead. We shall discuss the kabbalists before this chapter ends, but now, we consider one other set of archetypal dramas for organizing life in the service of emanation—namely, Islam.

Why did Islam arise as a new emanational way of life about two thousands years after Moses and six hundred years after Christ? Not ignorance; both Moses and Christ are quoted extensively in the Koran, which was given to Muhammad by God through the voice of the Archangel Gabriel, as the perfect and final version of the same revelation received earlier by Moses and Christ. But the Jews who were then living in Mecca and Medina were living in exile. The most powerful Christian sect in the Middle East in the early seventh century was that of the Byzantines who almost fused Church and State in their way of life. Dozens of other Christian communities were in conflict with them. And the tribes of the Arabian Peninsula were fiercely at war with each other.

---

9. See Yosef Hayim Yerushalmi, *Zakhor, Jewish History and Jewish Memory, The Samuel and Althea Stroum Lectures in Jewish Studies*.

10. For an insightful and deeply sensitive discussion of such re-formations, see Edward Feld, *The Spirit of Renewal: Crisis and Response in Jewish Life*.

At the heart of Muhammad's message are two concepts. The first is this: "*La ilaha illa'llah*" there is no god but God—no prophet, no ruler, no dogmatic opinion is god, only God is God. The second is this: There is a new *umma* (a community in Muhammad's original version) composed of companions, helpers, and friends of God—a community not of kinship but of shared faith. The Muslim calendar begins in AD 622, the year of founding this community of the faithful. A Muslim is a person who surrenders, not to Islam—Islam is the act of surrender—but to God, generating the fruit which Muslims wish for each other as they greet each other: *Salam aleikum*, peace be with you, the peace that comes from surrender to that god. (All three words—*Muslim, Islam,* and *Salam*—are rooted in the same three consonants: *SLM.*)

Within a hundred years after Muhammad's death, Muslims ruled an area from Arabia to Spain—an area soon expanding to twice the size of the Roman Empire. Islam was the overarching emanational umbrella, but existing kinship groups based on extended family, clan, tribe, and ethnic solidarity now felt endowed by the overarching umbrella as the blessed local emanational umbrellas of the Muslim community. This system of umbrellas—of the sources and reach of archetypal stories and of the overarching way of life—created permanent tensions between patterns of conflict and collaboration, difference and conformity within the community of Islam which we shall soon examine—when we shall find still more sources of local power.

During the first two centuries after Muhammad, the *ulema* (the scholars who study the legal meaning of the Koran, and also of the sayings of Muhammad and his companions) began to develop Shariah law—a law kindred to the Jews' *halakha*. Almost from the beginning, four somewhat different schools of jurisprudence developed. Shariah law explicitly defines behavior for all aspects of life under five categories: obligatory, recommended, neutral,[11] recommended against, and forbidden. But just as among the Jews, the discussion of application to specific cases continues.[12]

Rulers never insisted on enforcing all of Shariah law. They usually developed laws of their own, copying, revising, or differing from Shariah law. Their judges, *kadis*, were appointed to make binding judgments, but putting them into effect depended on the ruler's willingness and ability to carry them out, and the individual's or the community's readiness to accept it without resorting to personal influence, bribery, or rebellion. Muftis were appointed by Sultans to give advisory

---

11. When the radio was first introduced in Saudi Arabia, the question was this: Which of the five categories applies to its use? The ulema read the Koran over the radio and found that it could be heard clearly and without alterations on the loudspeakers. Not a demonic device to be forbidden, it was declared to be neutral.

12. The veiling of women is not mentioned in the Koran. That rule was not introduced into Muslim society until about two centuries after the death of Muhammad.

judgments, which influenced people according to the character of the person issuing it, the wisdom or prudence of his views, and the agreement of other Muslims. Most Muslims in conflict were likely to resort to negotiations or submit the dispute to a mediator equidistant from both parties.[13]

There was no center for the entire Muslim community. Islam never deified its prophet, and never developed a Church or priesthood or an absolute king ruling by divine right. One to two percent of all Muslims made a pilgrimage to Mecca once in their life. Of the first four caliphs of the new Muslim empire, the only ones in Muslim history ever called "pious" (*caliph* means "successor" to Muhammad, not as a prophet or lawgiver but as head and command-in-chief of the community), three were assassinated. In one of its longest lasting and largest states, the Ottoman Empire, sometimes the Sultan's writ was not effective in his own palace, sometimes it reached from Istanbul to Aleppo—but more rarely, to Cairo. *Sultan* means "man of power." Before and beyond the Ottoman Empire, Sultans who rose to power at the top of the page of *The History of the Islamic Peoples* seldom lasted to the bottom of the page.[14] The Arabic word for "dynasty" comes from a root meaning "taking a turn."

How did Sultans come into power and why did they so often lose their turn again? In the case of the original Muslim empire and later the Ottoman Empire, the answer is persistently more far-reaching conquest from a single center of power, but then increasingly less reliable ability to exercise full power all the way from that center. For most other cases, Ibn Khaldun—who died 63 years before Machiavelli was born—with great insight developed a theory from the experience of more than 750 years of the Muslim community.[15]

The cycle that Ibn Khaldun describes and analyzes moves through four phases:

1. A tribe—that is, a large kinship group—sees an opportunity to gain power by capturing a center containing far more resources and prestige than they possess, a city in their region where the ruler's power is weakening. (Why is that ruler's power weakening? We will find out at Point 3, when this cycle turns downward, and at Point 4, when this cycle begins again.) This tribe wins

---

13. Lawrence Rosen, *Bargaining for Reality: The Construction of Social Relations in a Muslim Community*; and Lawrence Rosen, *The Anthropology of Justice: Law as Culture in Islamic Society*, Lewis Henry Morgan Lecture Series.

14. Carl Brockelmann, Moshe Perlmann, and Joel Carmichael, *History of the Islamic Peoples*. Almost any page will tell this tale.

15. Khaldun Ibn, Franz Rosenthal, and N. J. Dawood, *The Muqaddimah: An Introduction to History*. Khaldun served four Sultans in North Africa as vizir before he was 24 years old. The fourth Sultan jailed him in the desert of Algeria, where he wrote these three volumes of theory. Later he became Chief Justice of Egypt. For an especially helpful interpretation of Ibn Khaldun's philosophical, historical, and sociological work, see Muhsin Mahdi, *Ibn Khaldun's Philosophy of History: A Study in the Philosophic Foundation of the Science of Culture*.

power because (provided that) it is far more inspired by *asabiyah*—intense solidarity and courage—than any other group in this region. From our perspective, but not alien to Ibn Khaldun's, the tribe's *asabiyah* expresses the strongest link of Islamic emanational umbrellas—the tribal chief, as the most powerful individual source, drawing on tribal solidarity as a political source, drawing on God's will as a sacred source to legitimize its rule over others in the larger Muslim community.
2. The tribal sheikh rules as Sultan from the city as far as power can extend.
3. The heir of the Sultan begins to fear being ousted from power by rivals within his tribe. The son (or grandson) cannot claim credit for the great initial victory. At that time and still in our present age, there is a saying (at least among the Arabs) describing a pervasive practice: "I against my brother; my brother and I against our cousin; our cousin and I against the family; the family and I against the clan; the clan and I against the tribe; the tribe and I against the world." The Sultan therefore no longer relies upon his tribe, but creates an army of slaves or mercenaries.[16] He also tries to create support by paying off his closest followers within his own and other tribes through expensive construction and luxurious consumption. Waste and rivalries grow.
4. As *asibiyah* within his own tribe decays, the rule of this Sultan—within three or a dozen generations—is overthrown by another tribe which conquers the capital and that region, thanks to its stronger *asabiyah*.

To explain these underlying dynamics reiterated in many parts of Muslim society, I will rely upon forms of archetypal relationships.[17] Islam (a word meaning "surrender") is no simple, single type of relationship among Muslims. Whether the demand for surrender is to the will of father, ruler, or God, each Muslim had at least four choices. He could entirely yield himself up—to the best of his power for yielding—to becoming an emanation of the mysterious and overwhelming power

---

16. From the ninth to the nineteenth century, most of these slaves had been kidnapped or bought as children, especially from among Balkan Christians, Circassian Christians living north of the Caucasus Mountains, and from non-Muslim Turkish tribes of Central Asia. They were educated as Muslims in special palace schools, and then placed according to their talents into posts ranging from palace officials to the military. These slaves were not permitted to pass on their offices to their children. They had no local ties, no local loyalties. But they had the largest practical power to coerce—and the result was that this slave military often turned the Sultan into their tool.

17. I first analyzed Muslim society in terms of these archetypal relationships (and in greater detail than in the present chapter) in "Four Contrasting Repertories of Human Relations in Islam: Two Pre-Modern and Two Modern Ways of Dealing with Continuity and Change, Collaboration and Conflict, and the Achieving of Justice," in L. Carl Brown and Norman Itzkowitz, *Psychological Dimensions of Near Eastern Studies, Princeton Studies on theNear East*. Eight of the nine relationships available to all of us had become clear to me by then, but not yet as archetypes. And knowledge of the four ways of life and the process of transformation was just beginning to dawn on me. In Chapter 8, we shall explore all nine archetypal relationships.

of father, ruler, or God. (We now speak of emanation as a relationship, not as an entire web of life.) Or, he could subject himself in deliberate response measured to the displayed power of the other. Or, he could bargain directly with God no less than ruler or father, saying in each case: In return for my submission, I anticipate rewards. Or, if he possessed neither the power to bargain nor the will to bow with the wind or wholly to yield, he could resort to buffering—that is, he could ask an uncle to mediate with his father or a local saint to intercede with God, or use an amulet to filter out the evil eye, or seek or offer an ambiguous bureaucratic response to cushion and soften the decree of the ruler.

In relation to others, most Muslims sought, if possible, to represent himself or herself as a source of emanation. In addition, every male Muslim who could not present himself to outsiders as the source of emanation for his family, tribe, or faction sought at least to present himself as their outward emanation. Thus, most Muslims were forever entering into rivalries with each other under the banner of the most overwhelming power available. Each struggled with the other to guard or radiate the magnetism of himself, or of the vessels of kinship, or of the other hallowed poles of the Community of Believers. This kind of battle kept Islamic society from being static. Emanation draws upon a most powerful energy for struggle—but the kind of energy whose nature, while we are possessed by it, we cannot truly understand. Emanation also draws upon the least reliable energy— for it is not ours to command—yet the most overwhelming, and therefore also the most inspiring and the most tiring. Its tolls constantly create opportunities for newcomers. Also, since no source of emanation can ever hope to establish a fixed boundary—except when it is reified, that is, turned into a thing which is to serve as fetish—but only a horizon which waxes or wanes from moment to moment, the battle cannot end.

Among the most powerful, no less than among the less or least powerful, the relationship of emanation (based on a mysteriously powerful source) could also turn into a manifestation of covert manipulation, trickery, fawning, or ingratiation to achieve one's aim. Such actions do not necessarily indicate disrespect for the divine origin of the chain of emanation but, rather, fundamental doubt that the other truly represents it.

This constant competition, fed and altered by constantly shifting alliances, renders the execution of justice arbitrary and uncertain. Indeed, it creates a strong bias toward injustice motivated by considerations of power. But there are some important and fundamental limits to tyrannical power. One of the greatest sins every Muslim recognizes is the sin of putting anything or anyone equal to God. Only a handful of rulers over many centuries forgot this injunction with respect to themselves, but their people always remembered. Moreover, the alliance between the people of emanation and the people of incoherence in Islam is never an alliance between two hierarchies, but only between individuals.

In addition, the limits upon tyranny derive from the fact that each family and tribe is united by its own emanational bonds and seeks, as far as possible, to resolve disputes within its own confines—or with other such units—or with rulers, through mediators. Muslims in the service of emanation know no autonomous institutions, no autonomous principles autonomously enforced. But in contrast to the feudal societies and later royal dynasties of Europe, the desire to be a personal source of emanation—since all Muslims are equal in the eyes of God—is widely present and sought throughout Muslim society. For the same ultimate reason, the right to engage in direct bargaining or to seek mediators in all areas of life is also recognized as a legitimate right of all Muslims, regardless of status.

Muslims in emanation see no possibility of agreeing that we will abstain from actively collaborating or conflicting with each other or from trying to change each other. Everyone is expected and expects to be counted on. Seeming fatalism is the result of fully accepting being an emanation. Enforced passivity is the result of subjection which cannot be escaped. Such periods also existed in history, but so did frequent rebellions and also migrations away from tyrannical or exploitive rulers.

One of the types of archetypal relationships which endured through most of Muslim history was direct bargaining in the form of antagonistic collaboration between the Sultans and certain influential *ulema*—between the most powerful in the service of incoherence and the most influential in the service of emanation.[18] The men of power needed legitimacy through the support of those who had studied and interpreted sacred law. The *ulema* needed rulers who would enforce, or at least endorse, Shariah law. As in all archetypal relationships of direct bargaining, intrinsic to its bargaining is also the threat of (to give a modern example) going on strike or resorting to lock-outs if an agreement cannot be reached. The *ulema* could always try to curb a movement toward tyranny by threatening to withdraw their support and encourage rebellion instead.[19]

The *ulema* came from all social classes, and they worked not only in such antagonistic collaboration—or direct bargaining—with the Sultan. Many of them also engaged in the archetypal relationship of buffering, acting as political brokers or mediators between groups and individuals from the top to the bottom of society.[20]

---

18. I first learned the concept of "antagonistic collaboration" from Joseph R. Levenson, *Confucian China and Its Modern Fate*. Levenson used it to describe and analyze the relationship between the Chinese Emperor and the Mandarin bureaucrats.

19. One of the *ulema*, Ibn Tamiya, declared in the thirteenth century that "sixty years of tyranny is better than one hour of anarchy," but that position was rare among *ulema* of the pre-modern age. Indeed, no small number of *ulema* refused, at peril of beatings and imprisonment, to accept the Sultan's appointment as judges. They often did become the Sultan's bureaucrats because that empowered them to engage subtly and even covertly in direct bargaining and buffering—though the Sultan's intention was that they be embodiments of him as the emanational source of their power.

20. Ira M. Lapidus, *Muslim Cities in the Later Middle Ages*.

The pursuit of justice thus remained always uncertain and the outcome remained open to challenge. But all archetypal dramas and archetypal relationships (direct bargaining, buffering, subjection, and emanation) were lived in the service of emanation. "There would seem to be no word in Arabic or indeed in any Islamic language meaning 'orthodox.' The word usually translated as 'orthodox,' *sunni*, actually means rather 'orthoprax,' if we may use the term. A good Muslim is not one whose belief conforms to a given pattern, whose commitment may be expressed in intellectual terms that are congruent with an accepted statement, but one whose commitment may be expressed in practical terms that conform to an accepted code."[21] I now add that by *orthopraxis* I mean the actual Muslim practice of emanation as a way of life that I have been describing here. It is a community which, as Muhammad had already said, believed that it would always hold to seventy-two different opinions but would never all agree on error. And whatever happens, the Koran says, God is "compassionate and merciful"; God "knows best."

Nothing in the Muslims' past resembles the fantasy of contemporary fundamentalists who declare that they seek to restore the past by once again having the ruler, in close alliance with the *ulema*, enforce Shariah law in all of life according to their only true standard. But as we have seen, with all the mobility of its individual and collective parts, this way of life *was* static as a whole. The sacred container it provided for ultimate values, meaning, and purpose left no opening, rendered no help for reaching anew the deepest source of our being to discover the fundamentally better. It perpetuated strong obstacles against organizing relationships based on brotherhood (not to speak of sisterhood) beyond kinship ties.

From the beginning of Islam, there were nonetheless also Muslims who organized to explore together the journey of transformation. By the twelfth century, they were in the majority.[22] We shall explore their alternative ways before this chapter ends.

EMANATIONAL WAYS OF LIFE ENDURE

How and why did emanational ways of life endure for so long? From their beginnings to this day, there has never been a single kind of Jew, Christian, or Muslim. At times, members of a particular emanational way of life constituted the majority among people who shared the same collective name—but only at times. Why, in

---

21. Wilfred Cantwell Smith, *Islam in Modern History*, 20.

22. Most Orientalists had told us a different story, focusing their studies on Sultans and *ulema*. H.A.R. Gibb, Director of Oriental Studies first at Oxford and later at Harvard, entirely changed his mind as he retired. His new sense of Islam is reflected in his Preface to Seyyed Hossein Nasr. *An Introduction to Islamic Cosmological Doctrines: Conceptions of Nature and Methods Used for Its Study by the Ikhwan Al-Safa, Al-Biruni, and Ibn Si*, A Revised edition. This Preface was unfortunately only a condensed version of a much longer, but still unpublished talk Gibb had given at Princeton University.

the face of perennial inner differences and conflicts, did emanational ways of life endure for centuries, even millennia?

Such sacred containers all offer a tremendous sense of community, a community that shares the only fixed and final truth about life, a truth that the only God (or gods) ordained for us—the people who believe in acting in the only right way within our web of life. What protective shelter could offer more security and righteousness of being? The very experience of belief and acting upon that belief together with others connects us to an awe-inspiring depth. Since that depth is so mysteriously powerful that, whatever it has already revealed, it nonetheless remains beyond our comprehension, emanation as a way of life helps us to bear suffering no less than joy. We trust God's judgment even if we cannot understand its mysterious wisdom. How far most of us are in our time from living in such a community!

This awesome magnetism is a significant part of the story of endurance—but not all of it. The endurance of emanation as a way of life requires not only deep attraction but also enforcement, for we are being held by and holding on to a fragment of the core drama in a cosmos of perpetual creation. Hence, contrary to its most profound intention, this way of life cannot hope to remain fixed. People remain at least unconsciously aware of other fundamental choices and feel troubled being confined, anxious in the face of inadequate answers and of changes that cannot be explained. Each person also has a unique personal face, so responses vary, often a great deal. And if people act in a mode that does not conform to God's explicit judgment, or if injustice can be remedied by human hands, will the powerful help us to mend things or must we generate conflict with established authority?

What limits conflict even before authorities intervene? Emanation as a way of life has legitimized which stories and archetypal relationships may be used for conflict and for regaining consensus. It has also established firm limits to conflict. We have heard from God—therefore we know none of us *is* God, however much endowed by our place in the chain of emanation. Even in the most extreme version, where we are all seen as crippled by original sin, we must not say, "Ha! I am doomed; anyway I'll do what I please!" If human beings fail to catch you, God certainly will.

Most of our daily life in the service of emanation requires no centralized authority in order to ensure our devout observance of it. Our own belief moves us to proper action. This way of life has permanently codified all four faces of our being. We are not free in any aspect of our being to act except within the authorized stories in its service. Therefore we observe absolute distinctions between what we can do and must not do, between men and women, between us and those who do not belong to our way, between what we can criticize and must not imagine criticizing. If our sense of obedience weakens, our foreboding of sin and shame rises. If we do transgress, fortunately there exist also ways of returning to salvation through humiliation, penance, and penalties. It is not easy to be hesitant or evasive; an emanational community governs itself continuously through that nucleus of political relationships that are based on face-to-face communication. Such relationships render solidarity immediate and vivid—the expression of a shared communal enterprise always touching people in their daily lives.

As long as emanation is practiced in this spirit, as a way of life which inspires and enforces relationships to mysteriously powerful human beings, texts, and gods, the question of conflict may not even arise. The very nature of emanation, while we are possessed by it, prevents us from feeling that we are being dominated. We feel ourselves instead to be a personal actualization of what these mysteriously powerful sources want of us. And these sources—and their earthly representatives—expect far more than obedience. They feel entitled to unquestioned reverence and honor.

Such a way of life therefore makes it profoundly easy for the powerful to feel legitimated and blessed in their control over others, and in their material and spiritual rewards, and in doing what is needed to secure and enlarge their power. Correspondingly, emanation deeply justifies and puts beyond question the necessary submission by the dominated—its lower ranks, the exploited, women, and slaves—who in fact constitute its majority. This great and pervasive tension between suffering and believing suffering to be the justified or unfathomable will of God is another travail intrinsic to living in the service of emanation.

Why do conflicts nonetheless arise within this way of life? The power of emanation is never permanent, not even the emanational power of any sacred Lord. Although all sources of emanation claim that power shall endure forever and that pronouncements are final, life changes always and offers no final answers. That is an intrinsic and inescapable challenge to emanation. However powerful the source, it needs embodiments for it to be fully alive. But in our constantly changing world, new sources of emanation constantly arise to challenge the existing one—from the realm of sacred sources and also from human beings who claim to be much truer or more powerful embodiments of the prevalent sacred source in behalf of our family, tribe, faction, or community, or who present variant versions of our source or offer interpretations of its will, or who even offer a different sacred source. Every flow of emanation creates not only a definitive set of facts but also an aura, a horizon that is impressive but also obscure—and therefore vulnerable to ambiguities, to shrinking, and to incursions.

These intrinsic aspects of emanation, contrary to its seemingly infinite power, render it problematical, not yet to speak of challenges from relationships and stories outside of emanation as a way of life.

How can emanation as a way of life be preserved? None who consolidated Act I into a way of life were simply overwhelmed by the sheer inspiration of emanation. From the beginning, they clearly feared the recurrent danger of the rise of new forms of emanation, of incoherence, deformation, or transformation. Indeed, all founding fathers lived in such threatening times. However much their prophet had spoken of God as compassionate and merciful and of the crucial importance of loving our neighbor as ourselves, those were reflections of the journey of transformation. Emanation values caring for our fellow believers, but it cannot be consolidated above all through compassionate kindness. The very fact that the consolidators sought to establish what must and what must not be done—and how to enforce this new order—shows that they and their successors in fact recognized the threat though not its true cause. The threat is intrinsic to closing ourselves off within a fragment of the core drama of life.

Under the most favorable circumstances, emanation as a way of life offers an intense attraction. We alone are the great insiders; we alone have been given God's only true revelation. Now at last we have the best of causes for inspiring courage and solidarity and for defending ourselves against all others around us. And one of the strongest reasons for our sinners to repent is that otherwise they, too, will be treated as an outsider. But because no single manifestation of emanation has converted the entire world, outsiders almost always worry us, even in times of peace. Just beyond our horizon live people who have consolidated a different vision of the sacred into a way of life. Since we heard the right voice, their voice must be fundamentally mistaken, yet they prosper and are also powerful. By their very existence, they challenge our very way of life. Or, they are hearing a new prophecy and they are moving into the path of transformation. Will they thus undermine the very structure of our existence?

Such grave fears often turn into fiercely destructive arrogance—into deformation. Jews heard their God order them to commit holocausts—the killing of all men, women, and children of the Midianites and the Amalekites.[23] But they also heard and experienced God punishing Jews most severely with destruction, death, and exile.

Catholic Christians during the Crusades killed Jews and Byzantine Christians—heretic Christians—on the route to the Holy Land where they killed Muslims. From the early days of Western imperialism to the late nineteenth century, mass killings of inhabitants of the Americas, Asia, and Africa were often justified on the grounds that not being Christians they were without rights and doomed to go to hell anyway. By contrast, Muslims fought no Holy Wars after the ninth century and whether in Holy or other wars, seldom killed people except during actual combat.

We have so far observed how the anxiety raised by living locked within Act I leads into an alliance with deformation with respect to outsiders. But suffering the torture of hell now or after we die is a threat often voiced by the Lord of emanation—thus intimately allied with the Lord of deformation. Few texts of sadism

---

23. Exodus 17; Numbers 31; I Samuel 15.

can compare in their joyful hate with that which God speaks through the prophet Ezekiel to tell the Jews what they will experience as God destroys Jerusalem and as they barely endure exile.[24]

In a further discussion of how the preservation of emanation can lead to an alliance of emanation with deformation as a way of life—to a holy hell on earth, a hell which can at least be demonstrated—I will focus on Catholic Christian experience. As we have seen, at the heart of the Jewish experience is not a State's or Church's enforcement of authority and dogma but, as reflected in their Bible, many centuries of struggles and discussions to develop a shared understanding and practice of emanation—and also departures from such consensus. They often had no state under their own control even while living in Palestine. After their Second Exile, they had no state at all, but relied on their communities to develop and enact emanation as a way of life. Among Christians, though not among Muslims, Jews often experienced severe persecution.[25] Muslims also did not build any hierarchic structures to enforce Islam but relied above all upon community consensus. They accepted Jews and Christians as inferior—but not alien—People of the Book (earlier written versions of the word of God).

Why, by contrast, did the people of power among Catholic Christians resort so often to an alliance with deformation for more than a thousand years, not continuously, but too often from the fourth to the seventeenth century? In this case, its leading figures were inspired to create a set of dramas reflecting one of the most elevating, yet also most laming tensions of any emanational way of life: We are the only people—indeed the only kind of Christians—who will be saved, yet we are all crippled by original sin. Those who know how we may be saved—or at least how the temptations of original sin can be frustrated—need supreme power. But how can even the best or the most powerful of Christians be trusted, given the universality of original sin? Power becomes the central theme of their stories—justified by the need for salvation; this is an intrinsic strain.

The Church began by making lifetime appointments within an emanational hierarchy empowered to carry out the work of the captured and institutionalized Holy Spirit. This was not enough power. From it's beginning, the Church also allied itself with the most powerful instrument of naked force in the service of incoherence, the State. Let us look at the tension between sin and salvation and power within and between Church and State. Naked power by itself cannot even hope to preserve its own rule. Since nothing but raw power can sustain it, its lead-

---

24. See especially Ezekiel 5–12, 21–22, and 33. God's reasons for bestowing death, destruction, suffering, and exile upon the Jews—and for offering hope for the future—is to be found in other chapters of Ezekiel.

25. For a thoroughly scholarly comparison, see Mark R. Cohen, *Under Crescent and Cross: The Jews in the Middle Ages*.

ers can never sleep—night or day—lest they be taken by surprise and defeated. Raw power needs emanational (or deformational) grounds on which it can rely. But when emanational powers believe they cannot fully rely on the many personal and communal forms of attraction and enforcement to sustain their way of life, they will employ naked force and use it not only against crimes but also against impiousness. This naked force is legitimate, of course, because it is wielded in the service of emanation.

But this alliance involves resorting to the enactment of archetypal stories that, however much advertised as being in the service of emanation, are in fact in the service of incoherence—and often deformation—on the part of both Church and State. Machiavelli spoke plainly of what is required: The State must ensure that religion is "well used" to "inspire virtue and terror."[26]

In the service of incoherence, the archetypal story that inspires and structures the exercise of hierarchic power—in this instance in both Church and State—has costly dynamics of its own. It demands not only that we constantly struggle to keep people outside the hierarchy obedient, but there also arises a constant need to keep the members of the hierarchies obedient. Power is therefore asserted not only to dominate, but also to demonstrate that the powerful are truly powerful. Such demonstrations often expose instead the vulnerability, corruption, and viciousness of the powerful and thus, the actual values and dynamics of this story of competitive power. This revelation damages the image of their overpowering mystery allegedly derived from being in the service of emanation—tempting people to challenge their very legitimacy and not only their particular acts.

In this historical instance, however, threats to the legitimacy of their power were experienced by the powerful as unpardonable and often led to reactions of deformation. This form of emanation is organized as an absolute authority enforcing absolute truth—a deep irony, since absolute truth (though I personally know of none) is presumably absolutely convincing even without official enforcement and would not be damaged by lack of enforcement (but absolute authority can thus be damaged). Absolute authority, however, is also dogmatically said to be required to keep sin from prevailing since all of us are rendered unwholesome and damnable because of our original sin (but so also are the men of absolute authority who are seldom good examples of virtue). In the very nature of this case, the men of absolute authority are fearfully not truly absolute but feel themselves required to act so in the name of a truth they consolidated in seemingly absolute form.

In the face of such a vulnerability, anyone within the community who could no longer feel possessed and commanded by such a sacred container became a threat

---

26. Niccolò Machiavelli and Leslie Joseph Walker, *The Discourses of Niccolò Machiavelli, Rare Masterpieces of Philosophy and Science*, Chapter 15.

to authority and had to be destroyed—often to be burned, even before he or she would also be burned in hell.[27] To find such people even before they could harm established authority, the systematic torture of the Inquisition was justified. Especially from the fifteenth century to the seventeenth century, millions of women were burned in Western Europe, accused of conspiring with other sacred forces (in this monotheistic universe), thus threatening the established way of life. In the seventeenth century, Protestants and Catholics killed each other for thirty years in the center of Western Europe because each considered the other the wrong kind of Christian. No single paragraph such as this can adequately express the grievous costs of this alliance—between emanation and deformation as ways of life—to preserve the most powerful certainties of a way of life.[28]

We shall have more to say about emanation as a way of life when we compare it with the other three ways in Chapter 7, when we explore the sacred sources of our being in Chapter 14 (for emanation has no monopoly on the sacred), and when we analyze justice in all four ways of life in Chapter 16. But we cannot end this chapter until we have overcome a possible illusion that could arise from the conventional conception that, before the modern age, all societies were "traditional" and that *tradition* must therefore be a synonym for *emanation*.

EMANATION—NOT OUR ONLY PAST

I have offered only three particular and unique examples of emanation as a way of life. Even so, none of these cases describe all Jews, Christians, or Muslims. They describe members of these communities only if and as they are contained within these particular examples of emanation. Emanation is not a synonym for a singular orthodoxy. The actual beliefs and practices of people we call, or who call themselves, *orthodox* within the same community often differ from each other. In today's Jerusalem, some orthodox Jews walk around in long black coats and hats that they believe to replicate Jewish models before exile from Palestine, but which no Jew wore before the seventeenth century development of a certain form of orthodoxy in Poland. In the Israeli Parliament, six different orthodox parties contend with each other—only six because other orthodox parties did not succeed in gaining seats.

Also, what I have presented here is not an image of Christianity, not even an image of Catholic Christians, but of those particular Christians who believed in particular

---

27. For exactly these reasons, the Grand Inquisitor in Fyodor Dostoyevsky, Charles B. Guignon, and Constance Black Garnett, *The Grand Inquisitor: With Related Chapters from the Brothers Karamazov* tells the returning Christ he must be crucified again.

28. Elaine H. Pagels, *The Origin of Satan*. This work analyzes why Satan played such a powerful role in the later development of Christianity.

manifestations of emanation.[29] Since this theory of transformation is applicable only if we analyze concrete moments of being as well as their living underlying patterning force, it cannot give rise to stereotypic or abstract designations. If conformity to the dominant form of Catholic Christianity had simply constituted the order of the day, suppression—even to the point of terror and death—would not have been as prevalent. No small number of Christians devoted their lives above all to providing compassionate help to their neighbors. Guilds rose to achieve political, economic, and moral autonomy. Peasants more than once rebelled for justice. And just as the Church from time to time became more rigorous and then more tolerant, so the Church also did not always succeed in immediately curbing—or in modifying in order to assimilate—the impact of such courageous, original thinkers as Francis of Assisi, Ignatius Loyola, Nicolo Machiavelli, or Thomas Aquinas. Aquinas often differed with Augustine, drew importantly upon Muslim philosophers of transformation, and several months before his death, rejected his own work as "straw" (to offer a polite translation), spending his time instead reading especially the Song of Songs.

Christians from the beginning to the present have lived their faith in a great variety of different manifestations, often so deeply at odds with each other that they would, even into our time, often fight rather than talk with each other. Contemporary Catholics conform less and less to the dramas we have described, and it is doubtful that the majority of those who ever considered themselves good Catholics were fully committed to all those dimensions and dynamics of the drama of emanation which so deeply moved its leading hierarchy.[30] This majority was and is grateful that this drama also preserves the reassurance and solidarity of participating in sacred links to God, especially at the most crucial turning points, but also at frequently recurring moments of life.

I focused on the hierarchic, repressive, and suppressive aspects of this particular case so that I could compare it with two different (but also monotheistic) cases of emanation as a way of life. Every one of the more than ten thousand instances of emanation is shaped by the archetypal dramas in its service, and by different unique persons and political and historical events expressing these dramas or finding themselves in conflict with competing dramas within themselves or with others. Demonstrating the similarities and differences among archetypal patterns opens the door to systematic comparative analysis.

---

29. Pope John Paul II, in a letter on the third millennium of Christianity, spoke of the Church's obligation to express profound regret for the "acquiescence given, especially in certain centuries, to intolerance or even the use of violence in the service of truth." But the Pope blamed not the Church but "the weakness of so many of her sons and daughters who sullied [the Church's] face." (*The New York Times*, November 15, 1994.)

30. In May 1988, Seton Hall University, New Jersey's largest Catholic University, awarded the author of these pages an honorary Doctorate in Humane Letters for the "theory of transformation with which he has inspired—and help[ed] us to shape a new vision of education."

Given the limits and strains intrinsic to emanation as a fragment of life, it is impossible to think of "pre-modern" societies as static, or as people simply possessed by a "participation mystique."[31] But as long as a particular manifestation of emanation endured as a way of life, all changes—including re-formations—took place within its container, though some "Reformations" put an end to it.

The question is not whether we honor our past or the past of others, but this: Which way (or indeed, *ways*) of life constituted our past? And from the very beginning of humankind, all four choices have formed our lives in fundamentally different ways. We have already looked at major instances of alliance between emanation and incoherence—and emanation and deformation—as ways of life. Certainly there were also times when deformation triumphed over the life of people in slavery, persecution, and brutal wars, and when incoherence, for example, after the decline of the Roman Empire, was the dominant order of the day.

We also experienced transformation in our past. Beyond the Western world, we practiced it, for example, in forms inspired by Buddha, Lao-tse, and Zoroaster (though not in all the forms bearing their names). In the Middle East, all three prophets entered into the experience of transformation, but as we saw, so did *none* of the consolidators of the original transformation experience.

Transformation was the way of life even among large numbers of Jews and Muslims but, because of intense persecutions, among a much smaller number of Christians. The kabbalists among the Jews did not limit their understanding and experience to the received text and the interpretations and rules of that text. They sought to participate with the deepest source of our being, which they called *ein-sof*, the endless one, in this world of continuous creation, not a world completed in six days. They considered the unwritten Torah (in part passed on orally to those ready to hear, in part not yet heard by anyone) to be even more important than the written Torah. They saw our task as helping *ein-sof* to overcome the sickness, fragmentation, and evil of the world by helping ourselves, our family, our neighbors, and the animals, plants, and stones in the field to discover the sacred spark of *ein-sof* within them so that they could join us on this journey.[32]

From the twelfth to the seventeenth century, kabbalists constituted the majority of Jews. The kabbalists' reopening of our relationship to the sacred led a number of them to experience and to teach and write on how we can reach the deepest

---

31. Lucien Lévy-Bruhl, in *The "Soul" of the Primitive*, used this term to speak of "primitive peoples." Anyone anywhere may be vulnerable to being totally seized by an emanational experience of "participation mystique," but the evidence quite clearly makes it a mistake to suppose that all or even most people once called primitive are in fact primitive in this way. And as we have seen, people in the service of emanation cannot avoid also experiencing its intrinsic tensions.

32. See the pioneering works of Gershom Gerhard Scholem, *Major Trends in Jewish Mysticism*; and *On the Kabbalah and Its Symbolism*.

source of our being again and again.[33] Others ritualized the process of meditation, and became disciples of a particular teacher, turning kabbalah into a new emanational container. Still many others among the kabbalists were so deeply moved by the experience and possibility of great change—and the need for great change, but change beyond their present capacity—that instead of persisting themselves in the process of transformation, they longed for and expected the Messiah to come to transform the world for us.

The Messiah, Sabbatai Sevi, announced his arrival in 1665. Hundreds of thousands of Jews from the Mediterranean to Central to Eastern Europe became his followers. In 1666, the Sultan of the Ottoman Empire, fearful of a Jewish revolt, threatened Sabbatai Sevi with death unless he converted to Islam. He converted; so did tens of thousands of Jews, believing they had to follow his road.[34] Only if we ourselves consciously, critically, creatively, and caringly experience the drama of transformation will we also come to recognize that no one else, not even the Messiah, can do it for us and that there is no sudden, final salvation.

Among Muslims, especially after the twelfth century, Sufis came to constitute a majority until the modern age. Though they seldom became rulers, they sometimes influenced, subverted, or rebelled against them. Politically, they offered an alternative society to the Islam of Sultans, local kinship bonds, and Shariah law—namely, brotherhoods of transforming experience and mutual help. Like the kabbalists with respect to *halakha*, the majority of Sufis observed most of the rules of the Shariah, but as a symbolic reflection of a deeper reality they sought to understand. They saw themselves as "friends of God" and believed that God needed and desired their participation in creating the fundamentally new and better.

But as among kabbalists, not all who called themselves Sufis were practicing transformation. Guides of transformation after their death were often turned into saints to be worshipped as intermediaries to God. Some guides while still alive were tempted to turn themselves from teachers and exemplars into idols to be venerated. Some of them announced themselves to be messiahs. But many Muslims over the centuries—many of the leading philosophers, poets, writers of stories, and artists—devoted themselves to the exploration of the experience of transformation.[35]

Christian communities of transformation existed for several centuries after Christ.[36] They were persecuted and destroyed by the emerging alliance of Church

---

33. On this aspect of the kabbalist experience, see especially Moshe Idel, *Kabbalah: New Perspectives*.

34. Gershom Gerhard Scholem, *Sabbatai Sevi: The Mystical Messiah, 1626–1676*.

35. Essays and books by James Winston Morris offer truly original and profound insights on this theme. Also most helpful are the works of Henry Corbin, William Chittick, Seyyed Hossein Nasr, Tushihiko Izutsu, and Annemarie Schimmel.

36. These communities and their experience of transformation are analyzed in Elaine H. Pagels, *The Gnostic Gospels*.

and State. Those who spoke up in later years were normally either excommunicated or burned at the stake. People of transformation came forward (or went into exile or hiding) again and again. Transformation as an experience is intrinsically open to us by virtue of our nature. But in the Western past, in contrast to the past of the other two monotheistic ways of life (and in contrast to many other communities dominated by ways of emanation), transforming communities were not free to build their own widespread movements. Hence, in the West, our contemporary knowledge of transformation is slim and has little memory to build on.

Dissent from the dominant emanational way of life in the past was not limited to transformers. Many local communities and individuals beyond the effective control of established authority held to their own inherited or revisionist ways with respect to beliefs, rituals, and values. Incoherence as a way of life, and in some regions of the West, Protestantism as a fragment in the service of incoherence, became the most decisive challenge to emanation as a way of life, as we shall see in the next chapter.

The purpose of this component of our discussion has been to enlarge our view of the past. We have always had four radically different choices—emanation, incoherence, deformation, and transformation—about how to organize all the stories of our life with respect to their underlying meaning, purpose, and values. Our focus in this chapter has been to clarify above all one of these four choices—the first arrest upon which we can be tempted to fixate in the core drama of life—that is, emanation.

Pre-modern experiences of incoherence often did not turn into a way of life but remained a tangle of incoherent relationships. People could not escape being in the same place and time with each other but they could no longer agree on shared modes of collaboration and conflict for seeking continuity, avoiding changes (most of which proceeded beyond intention or control), and achieving a shared conception of justice.[37] Incoherence as a way of life contributes to, and cannot easily avoid, such frequent breaking of relationships. But its overarching drama constitutes a way of organizing (and reorganizing) insecurity through archetypal dramas that inspire, structure, and justify competition and its limits and consequences for losers no less than for winners. In pre-modern times, adherents to this way of life and its dramas lacked the power and rewards created in our age to prolong their domination and to inspire others in large enough numbers to be drawn into its dynamics and values. That is why even the State, the most powerful fragment of life in the service of incoherence, needed its alliance with the forces of emanation.

Deformation arose again and again in pre-modern times, but primarily in alliance with emanation and incoherence. The anxiously powerful know that both of

---

37. Incoherence as a way of life is analyzed in the next chapter, but incoherence as an archetypal relationship is analyzed in Chapter 8.

these ways of life are by their very nature and at all times incomplete and hence vulnerable.

In the next chapter, we shall explore why emanation as a web of life is dying in the modern age and why incoherence became dominant everywhere in the world. But even though emanation did not constitute our only past, why did it endure for so long, despite all its limitations and intrinsic tensions?

Once the opportunity arises, through being born into it or finding a new consolidation of *the* certainty, *the* answers, *the* solutions of Act I Scene 1, we want to stay within it. Given the constant rise of new unexpected and even threatening moments of life, we remain eager (because we also remain anxious) to conform to a mysterious, powerfully overwhelming source that not only provides certainty, but also justifies human enforcement of this certainty—or else necessarily justifies uncertainty, only because we do not have the source's infinite wisdom. Such certainty molds the meaning, purpose, values, and ways of living for every story of our life from its beginning to its end.

Being confined to a sacred container is conducive to a deep intensity of experiencing piety, serenity, and commitment, and of kinship with one's fellow believers past, present, and future. The daily enactment of particular obligations and prohibitions expresses loyalty and gratitude for the blessing of security among insiders—and against outsiders. The most intense or ambitious adherents experience even greater rewards by dominating established personal, political, historical, and sacred relationships not through power alone but within a chain of emanation. They take the lead in enforcing, restoring, mediating, healing, elaborating, benefiting from, and refining life ordained in this way.

The Lord of emanation seeks to compensate us for our partial being (for we have not completed our journey of transformation) by asking us to believe in him who is eternal, all-knowing, and all-powerful—though all such Lords are in fact sources of a fragment of life and hence themselves inadequate and impermanent.

Our arrest within this sacred container entwines our life with many deep tensions intrinsic to this way of life. No person is as infinitely powerful as this Lord; we are only finite. We therefore need the overpowering sense of security this way of life offers. Yet we cannot feel secure; we must try as perfectly as possible to embody God's revelation and rules in our life, yet we are imperfect. We often desperately need God's protection, but nothing ends our suffering. Martin Buber acknowledges "the risk of having to despair of God in view of the actualities of history and life." Buber's answer is this: "Only through the fear of God does man enter so deeply into the love of God that he cannot be cast out of it."[38] We cannot

---

38. That statement, which Buber never applied to any relationship involving "I and Thou" comes from "The Two Foci of the Jewish Soul," in Martin Buber and Will Herberg, *The Writings of Martin Buber*, 269.

resolve the many tensions intrinsic to any arrest in the core drama of life. We can only suppress and repress our selves and others in order to achieve seeming certainty and security.

Emanation also turns most fellow human beings of our earth into outsiders and, depending upon the particular manifestation of this way of life, ignores the other as invisible, whatever their pain and suffering; or treats the others as a lesser human being, whatever the cost of treating them that way; or seeks to convert the other, or else deems them not worthy of conversion; or, if they do not convert, treats them as truly inferior; or else looks upon them as people to be exiled from the areas we dominate—or to be exterminated. Emanation is thus a way of life that diminishes the being of both the more powerful and the less powerful within their sacred container and puts all outsiders on stations on the road to destructive death. Most concrete manifestations of emanation, at least during the past several millennia, have also reduced half of their own people—women—to a lesser station in life.

This chapter has sought to demonstrate the reality of sacred Lords of emanation by describing and analyzing the living underlying patterns—our three examples—that inspire and shape human beings and their practice. In most conventional analyses, a review of such Lords would have been seen as rendering unnecessary any further our discussion of the sacred. But this chapter has spoken only of a limited and incomplete sacred source of our being. The most crucial impairment intrinsic to all manifestations of emanation as a way of life is that such beliefs deny us the freedom and capacity to risk faith in participating in continuously creating the fundamentally new and better. It denies us the experience of the deepest sacred source of our being—the one that does not seek to control us—but participates in our movement toward wholeness again and again.

Our four faces and their interconnection come into both their particular and their ultimate being through their link with a sacred source. We need to free ourselves to understand our fundamental alternatives and to choose—lest we be commanded and possessed. After considering one more arrestingly partial sacred source and its way of life (incoherence), and also one fragmenting sacred source and its road to destructive death (deformation), we shall explore transformation as a sacred way of life in contrast to these others.

5

In the Service of Incoherence

For the first time in human history, we are bringing about the demise of emanation as a way of life—not only more and more in its inherited concrete manifestations but also as an underlying sacred force. And we are giving rise to incoherence as the dominant way of life everywhere in the world. Deformation is the main competitor with incoherence, when it is not already its ally. What is coming apart in our time is the connection between Church and State or what we now call the sacred and the secular. Established relationships are dissolving again and again because an entire web of life is irrevocably dying (though it is not yet dead), and its now dominant successors are intrinsically unstable and destabilizing.

In this chapter, we shall seek to understand why emanation is finally breaking and how incoherence—persistent rebellion in organizing and competing for fragments of life—nonetheless reflects its own underlying sacred order. Our explanation will be based on the structure and dynamics of the core drama of life. Emanation is dissolving as a web of life because never before in history have so many individuals risen in rebellion against all ties that keep them from securing the freedom and power to attain whatever interest leads to still greater power and payoffs for themselves. Never before have individuals linked so many magnifying aspects of knowledge, dominance, production, and consumption into new and large competing networks of power and profit.

What produced this shattering and this great opening? Such shatterings are not new. Emanational ways of life have dissolved again and again in the face of successful conquests by neighbors who did not share that same version of emanation or by the rise of new forms of emanation within the community, especially in response to fundamentally new problems which the inherited sacred container could not absorb within its established bounds. Prolonged periods of incoherence therefore also broke out in the past. But why, in contrast to experiences in the past, did incoherence as a way of life triumph this time and fatally cripple emanation?

Our analysis must initially focus primarily on Western Europe, because the changes that took place there were subsequently imposed by imperialist conquest upon the rest of the world. Through summary statements and examples, the next few paragraphs will only point to these changes. The Catholic Church as the most powerful network of the largest emanational form of Christianity had weakened itself by what it believed to be a necessary augmentation of power (over human beings impassioned by original sin)—its alliance with the State.

As kings—thanks to their own increasing power to amass arms, taxes, and organizations—triumphed over those unable to rise beyond being feudal lords, the State became far more powerful than the Church. In the sixteenth century, King Henry VIII of England could break with the papacy and establish his own Church. In the seventeenth century, the Thirty Year War in North Central Europe was a battle over which form of Christianity was right—Catholicism or Protestantism. It left one-third of the people of that large region dead and another third maimed. The winner was the State. The Treaty of Westphalia in 1648 gave each monarchy the right to decide what religion its people would be free (or required) to practice.

The rise of Protestantism as a re-formation of Christian emanation moved people into various directions—into new and separate sacred containers of conformity believing, once again, that the State was needed to curb and punish the eruptions of our original sin. But other forms of Protestantism (for example, the Quakers) moved people to form communities expressing their own newfound inner light and consciences reopened by autonomous understandings of the personal, political, historical, and sacred meaning of Christ.

Martin Luther illustrates this divergence of Protestant views in his own person. First he translated the Christian Bible from Latin into a German that made a major contribution for centuries to the creation of a language connecting people above all the many different German dialects. When peasants—having read or heard that Christ cared deeply for the poor and did not offer legitimacy to the rich and powerful—joined each other in rebellion, Luther (like Calvin and certain other Protestant reformers still attached to Augustine) supported the State in its bloody suppression. The invention in the same sixteenth century of movable-type printing—also in peoples' own languages—opened the door to the circulation of religious, scientific, and philosophical ideas on a much wider scale, so that the issues we are discussing touched far more people than ever before.

Another crucial distinction arose among Protestants (and later also among Jews and Catholics) as their new freedom of personal interpretation turned them into at least two different roads beyond the reach of organized religion. One direction, as in the case of the English Levelers and later of democratic socialists, led from new individual consciousness, criticism, and caring to a concern for freedom, equality, and justice in the community. The other became the direction for many of the newly dominant. The personal for them became the legally private, and the private realm included not only subjective thoughts and feelings but the right to acquire and control property—and also to control the workers and the wages and working conditions of men, women, and children employed by them. Through their private and public influence upon the State, they also succeeded in curbing, in most countries through most of the modern age, the power of the poor.

The property of women upon marriage until the nineteenth century became the private property of men, and so—for most practical purposes—did women. With the breaking of emanation as a way of life, there also arose for the first time in Western history "organized religions." The term *religion* had never been used in this sense of being a distinct organization until the seventeenth century.[1] From then on, believers had indeed to organize the fragment of emanation that remained or that had been re-formed of the original web of life—that is all the "religion" that could now be organized. Until this point in the book, we have not been discussing religion in this modern sense.

That newly organized distinction, and increasingly the separation of such religion from the public political structures of the newly dominant way of life, is what most of us now remember and understand only within the limited vision of the separation of Church and State—of the private and the public, the subjective and the objective. But in fact, our current experience—and usage of the term *religion*—shows that we lost a whole web in which an only incomplete and biased sacred source shaped every aspect of our being by interpenetrating with all the faces of our being. We are therefore also mostly unaware, despite our official, scholarly, and private separation of the sacred and the secular, that a new incomplete and biased sacred source now shapes the overarching drama of our search and competition for the largest possible fragments of life. Even conservatives know only how to speak of the loss of crucial pieces of life—patriarchal, constrictive family and community values, absolute moral values and forms of discipline, and belief in a particular god.

The loss of that web of life has deeper roots and consequences than even many conservatives can recognize. For most who now call themselves conservatives are also heirs of the rebellion against that emanational web. They also seek to magnify and protect whatever they in their own self-interest desire. For anyone who has moved in rebellion from Act I to the first Scene of Act II of the core drama of life,

---

1. Wilfred C. Smith, *The Meaning and End of Religion: A New Approach to the Religious Traditions of Mankind.*

but then seeks to consolidate and preserve this Scene, cannot yet understand the underlying patterning forces involved in the past or in the present. That understanding cannot be reached until we take courage to discover, in Act II Scene 2 of incoherence, the roots of our being that in fact we have not yet reached and that therefore cannot yet nourish us.

Conservatives are seldom guardians of the actual past but partisans of particular fragments of the past and present. Many people in the service of incoherence (not only conservatives) and many people in the United States (and not simply in developing countries), are still devoutly attached to—or searching for—various sacred sources. But their concern, now that religions have been organized, is for an additional archetypal drama or relationship that can give them far more security, meaning, and connection—with a deeper level of life and with a community—than do the other dramas of their life while incoherence remains the overarching reality. Or else, they seek authoritative inspiration and approval for the career or for the immediate desire or long-term hope they are pursuing or the easing of the grief they are suffering.[2]

We have not examined all of the major challenges that confront people in the service of emanation, but we have seen enough to illustrate the heart of the matter. Any emanational way of life breaks when its very nature can no longer deal as a single web with fundamentally new crises and opportunities. At issue are not only particular fissures, but a chain of emanations no longer able to hold life within a single sacred container.

Emanation began to unravel in most of the rest of the world when the West conquered it, because most people failed to preserve their web against this imposition of foreign-controlled regimes that organized incoherence instead.[3] For more and more of the native elites, emanation remained alive only in major fragments (such as the caste system) reflecting still unchallenged political power or powerlessness. The West's success in imposing and profiting from incoherence as a way of life in the rest of the world also inspired a growing number of people everywhere, with whatever new power they could muster, to follow on their own the path of incoherence.

THE LIVING UNDERLYING PATTERNING FORCE FOR
ORGANIZING INCOHERENCE AS A WAY OF LIFE

In ever larger numbers around the world, people rebel against inherited emanational relationships and ways of life, but then arrest themselves—or accept the pre-

---

2. Robert Wuthnow, *God and Mammon in America*.
3. Especially for Spanish and Portuguese colonies, imperialism in the service of incoherence was also in alliance with the drama of Christianity.

vailing arrest—in Act II Scene 1 in the service of incoherence. To cite a relatively early report on this arrest by the poet John Donne in 1611:

> An Anatomy of the World
>
> ... And new philosophy calls all in doubt
> ... 'Tis all in pieces, all coherence gone;
> All just supply, and all relation:
> Prince, subject, father, son, are things forgot,
> For every man alone thinks he hath got
> To be a phoenix, and that there can be
> None of that kind, of which he is, but he.
> This is the world's condition now. ...
> Reward and punishment are bent awry
> ... proportion is dead,
> Since even grief itself, which now alone
> Is left us, is without proportion. ...
> And false conceptions fill the general wombs.[4]

Thomas Hobbes, writing *Leviathan* forty years later, said that what above all moved all men was self-interest. But now that they had become "masterless men," their life would become "solitary, poor, nasty, brutish and short" unless an authoritarian ruler enforced rules governing competition. A generation later, John Locke proposed democratically liberal ways for agreeing on procedures that would keep free competitors from killing each other. (Throughout this work, by *liberal* I mean solely what it meant at its beginning and in most countries today—free to pursue one's self-interest.)

But why is the pursuit of self-interest now the most pervasive order of the day? Why are both authoritarian and democratic liberalism consonant with the pursuit of self-interest? What holds this way of life together in the face of its very rivalries? Hobbes and Locke and most of their successors were worried on this last score, but offered no answer on what underlying patterns could keep this show on the road.

Hobbes thought self-interest to have always been the dominant force that sets individuals into motion, however much it had been repressed or suppressed in the past. It is true that from the beginning of human history, we have been moved again and again to liberate ourselves from past emanational constraints and to rebel in behalf of whatever now inspires our own spirit, including our self-interest. But never before in history have so many freed themselves from emanation as a way of life and from inherited emanational relationships in so many areas of life.

---

4. John Donne, "The First Anniversarie," published in 1611, not as the first anniversary of incoherence but of his friend's daughter's funeral. John Donne and (ed.) J. T. Shawcross, *The Complete Poetry of John Donne*, 270–86.

But what neither Hobbes nor any liberal thinker since has appreciated are the fundamental choices in fact open to a fully free self.

As we explored in the first chapter, whatever inspires our spirit to rebel, and thus to enter Act II (incoherence), cannot become known to us until we free ourselves to move into the second Scene of that Act. Not until then can we understand the living underlying patterning force that thus inspired us. But as liberals, we do not yet recognize the most fundamental choice open to us as rebels—to enter the process of transformation to discover and put into practice the fullness of all four faces of our being and of its deepest source, or to arrest ourselves in rebellion, or to move toward destructive death. At no time before in human history have so many human beings halted their emergence in Act II Scene 1 of the core drama of life, thus living under the illusion that they already know their self and their interest.

All arrested ways of life also terminate all the dramas in their service—at the same point at which that way has been halted within the core drama of life. In the service of incoherence, all archetypal dramas inspire our ego to defend the fragments of life we possess now, but if possible, to enlarge such fragments or invent new ones. But since even success leaves us only a fragment of being with enhanced power over fragments of life, we are driven to renew our competitive rebellion again and again.

If we mean to perpetuate life in the first Scene of Act II (incoherence), continuous rebellion becomes a necessity. Those who lack the power to rebel within this Scene indeed do worse and worse in life. To remain only a partial being living this time not within a mysteriously powerful sacred container but only among fragments of life is to be left always dissatisfied.

Even the greatest power, wealth, or fame we attain has no ultimate security—or meaning and purpose—that we can discover from within this overarching fragment of the core drama of life. All success and all power are now temporary. No problem and no conflict that arise within this way of life can be fundamentally resolved; caught where we are, we cannot know how to transform anything. Since all power and all victories are therefore temporary, competition for power and success constantly reopens. This kind of political competition always limits the realm of what we can and need to do together regarding issues of power and the advantages gained from the use of power.

In this way of life, most people, certainly most political leaders and political scientists, can no longer imagine what else politics could be about. But given the very nature of this competition, there is no one else but ourselves and our power we can really count on. So we seem to have only our own ego, but it too is frail and anxious since it is not consciously, creatively, and critically connected to the deepest source of our being. And we experience a great and perennial scarcity of anything but transient connections to others who have some useful share at present in our interests. More power than we possess now seems ever more vital and somewhat more reassuring while we can hold on to it. But power can be attained only—as in every rebellion—by ousting or at least reducing the position of one now more powerful, or developing new means of power. And since rebellions in this way of life persist, we can count on others—sooner or later—to try to oust us from our position of power.

As Lee Iacocca, the former Chairman of the Chrysler Motor Company put it, "Lead or follow—or else get out of the way." Does this kind of competition between rebels encourage people to reach their highest potential—to sell more soft drinks than anyone else, to be the quarterback of the football team that wins the Super Bowl, to be the most competent lawyer in town? Yes, but only within the constraints of being molded by this way of life. Let us therefore now look at the underlying patterning force that shapes all dramas of rebellion and that actuates our initiatives—and if we stay in it, also actuates the intrinsic limitations upon our potential, even at its most powerful.

We can, at any age, enter an archetypal drama of rebellion—for example in the form of adolescence. This surge of youth "is a time of enthusiasm, idealism, and commitment. It is a time of courage and open-heartedness, of genuine warmth, kindness, love, creativity and a love of life . . . of opening to a new world, and loving the world one opens to."[5] But this is what we experience only when, regardless of age, we leave the security, domination, and dependence of emanation to open ourselves to the journey of transformation.

Historically, it became much easier to rebel as the millennia-old force of patriarchy, backed by the force of emanation as a way of life, was losing its power so that "masterless men" could spring forward. Less and less does any mysteriously overwhelming sacred source still inspire and justify people keeping themselves in their place. No longer must sons wait until their patriarch dies before they can rise to the top and succeed. No relationships remain stable for long. All the dominant dramas in the service of incoherence—including liberalism and capitalism—exemplify the persistence throughout our life of the archetypal drama of adolescence.

That is not what we have conventionally been taught in the West. We have been told that the great rebellions between the seventeenth and nineteenth centuries (and now also beyond the West) have increasingly brought democratic liberal societies into being. Rebellions now would therefore seem to undermine these great achievements. Conventional history refers to rebellions as movements against emanation as a way of life and more recently against regimes of authoritarian liberalism or deformation. What persistent rebellions are taking place now?

---

5. The first analysis of the archetypal drama of adolescent rebellion originated with Cynthia Leslie Perwin who wrote about it almost two decades before I came to see this drama in the light of the core drama of life. See Cynthia L. Perwin, *The Ego, the Self, and the Structure of Political Authority*, doctoral dissertation, Department of Politics, Princeton University, 1973 (p. 645).

Now, within the family, adolescents rebel against the dominance of more powerful egos. That manifestation of the archetypal drama is a rite of passage—but it has also become a passage into participation in incoherence as a way of life where we rebel (if we can) against more powerful egos again and again not only so that we may be free but also so that we may gain more power and its rewards.

But incoherence as a way of life in the modern age was also shaped from its beginning and until recent times by two fragments of emanation as a way of life. Only men had the right and the power to persist in rebellion, and only men of one particular group—this time meaning white men not only in the West but throughout the world while it endured under Western rule. Incoherence and almost all the dramas in its service therefore emphasize masculine values—power, domination, control, and competition to achieve such gains. For those who do not or must not make it to the top, the corresponding roles demand loyal service, or acceptance of becoming lesser or invisible beings—stations on the road to deformation (which we shall explore).

Until quite recently (and too often even in the present), men have remained the patriarchs for most women, and white men the masters of men and women of other ethnic and racial groups. The first few openings for women and for people of other ethnic and racial groups living within the same nation-state have been limited primarily to those who are willing to assimilate themselves into this drama of masculine adolescence and its kindred archetypal dramas.

What are the constraints intrinsic to persisting in stories that begin and end in Act II Scene 1? We shall now examine more closely their interconnected dynamics. We focus our life upon our self and its interests but we cannot really know our being and our needs. We live a life in which we constantly compete with others and hence remain deeply disconnected from them—and from ourselves. And these limitations and their accompanying anxieties all the more rouse our desire for more power to acquire what can only be more fragments of life. We see no alternative to being powerfully self-centered and self-interested—an effort caught in profound irony since we cannot at this point constitute more than a partial self and cannot yet know our full depth of being.

But the fact is, arresting our selves in any Act or Scene of the core drama (of participation in continuous creation of the fundamentally better) demands *power*—in order to consolidate life in that fragment. And in the service of incoherence—since there no longer exists any belief in an ultimate power and its eternal rules—all dramas for gaining power are also dramas of rebellion against the present holder of power to acquire whatever fragments of life these others already possess or would inhibit us from possessing. No mere agreement on procedures, no social contract, no particular and always changing outcomes could hold together dramas or a way of life for organizing and reorganizing insecure power and its rewards and losses.

What institutionalizes rebellion in all these dramas are not simply the currently prevailing constitutions, laws, institutions, or our latest pragmatic arrangements.

They, too, are concrete manifestations of the living underlying patterning forces that give structure to our arrest and inspire and shape our rebellious movement within this reiterating Scene. To keep rebelling to secure our own self-interest, to seek more and more power over who gets what, when, where, and how is to conform to that kind of archetypal drama. That kind of underlying source of being animates rebellion in order for us to be seen as at least powerful enough to be accepted as a useful ally by the more powerful, and also inspires conformity to the most powerful by those who cannot gain the top, and acquiescence by the defeated who therefore come to believe that losing was solely their personal responsibility.

Only archetypal dramas that we unconsciously share with others could integrate into enactable stories so many deep intrinsic tensions. This ego has freed itself to be, above all, bent on gaining whatever it feels to be in its private, subjective interest, but it also needs to use its power effectively in the public realm to protect and enlarge its ownership and control over its private property. This ego seeks public freedom to rebel and take the place of present occupants of superior power—but also seeks to secure and enlarge its own new power as long as possible. Even the greatest power can provide this kind of ego only with larger fragments of life—fragments not part of any web, not secure in any sacred container. And being focused upon fragments gives us both more control over a particular aspect of life—and also less control, for no such fragment (a particular office, product, skill, area of expertise) is exempt from being challenged by renewed rebellion and competition. None connect us to any fundamental meaning and purpose. It is a power, however great, that separates us not only from the wholeness of others but from the wholeness of ourselves.

Hence, all these dramas work only because they organize both our seeming power and our insecurity. The overarching power of our present way of life is reflected by the fact that in all these dramas, having halted ourselves in the process of transformation and confined ourselves to rebellion, our own ego is not (contrary to our dominant view) acting as a mechanism in a mechanistic universe. Instead, we in fact see and enact ourselves as if our ego was our ultimate source of being and we are its embodiment. Speaking in public of course from an objective, mechanistic perspective, that is not how we would or could describe ourselves. But our ego feels such great power because the archetypal force of the overarching drama has taken possession of our unconscious. We connect to incoherence as a way of life in fact as a source of emanation. That is the mysteriously overpowering source of our ego, but we do not know our Lord.[6]

The Devil is the sacred source of incoherence as a way of life. (I do not believe in a Devil stalking or flying about this earth; I ask no one to hold such a belief.) I use

---

6. For a different but importantly helpful analysis, see Albert O. Hirschman, *The Passions and the Interests: Political Arguments for Capitalism before Its Triumph*.

the word *Devil* to symbolize the living underlying patterning force at the turning point and into the experience of rebellion in the core drama of life. (We experience a sacred face of being and its sacred source at every moment of our life.) If we do not understand the sacred source that moves us now (and therefore are not able freely to say *yes* or *no* to it), it comes to possess and command us as our Lord. The Devil—as the meaning of his very name implies—always inspires us to cut and separate what held together before.

This is a necessary part of the process of transformation as we move into and through Act II Scene 1, and also when separating ourselves from Scene 1 in order to move into Scene 2—there to separate ourselves even more deeply from Lords we recognize as unbearable. In the service of emanation, we are denounced for letting the Devil separate us from the revealed container and into the sin of any movement beyond it. In the service of incoherence, we remain with the Devil and perpetuate rebellion again and again, but only within the same Scene.

Our point therefore is not simply to denounce the Devil, but to ask, as we would as concerns any sacred source, "In the service of which way of life is this source moving with us and through what archetypal structures and dynamics?" The devil is "he who throws across"—and thus throws open, throws out, throws over, throws together, throws up, throws away, overthrows, throws through. We cannot tell in advance what throwing across will produce next (initially, it may simply confuse us), but its value, meaning, and purpose will depend on the way of life in which we experience it. For example, analyzing—separating a previous unit into parts and examining them—can lead to our being rejected and condemned for throwing away our conformity. It can lead to our coming to recognize and cure a specific disease, but without being moved—if we act only as a specialist disconnected from other aspects of life—to ask what personal and political problems help to cause this illness. Analysis can reveal the vulnerability of an opposition group that the authoritarian ruler seeks to throw into destructive death. Analysis can also help us understand and overthrow sacred sources that had possessed us.

But the Devil is not only a sacred force who can incite separation. He is also a Lord with the power to incite us to remain within this kind of motion. He can tempt or throw us into seeking power over fragments that will be destructured again—the only kind of structuring we can engage in under such conditions. That is how the Devil can keep us in his own story of a deep, ever renewed, and ever unhealed incoherence. While still immersed in the service of incoherence, we cannot understand these living underlying patterning forces.

Most academics now define politics as the extraction and allocation of resources, including human resources. Rational calculations and experiments—concerning the present balance of power and its likely trends, efficient cause, the logic of games, and the tendencies of passions—sharpen our understanding, but within all too limited a framework. The sacred Lord of incoherence as a way of life even cuts us off from being conscious of its being (and its coming through us) as a living underlying patterning force. And that turns us into a cutoff fragment in relation also to our deepest sacred source of being. We cannot therefore know the ultimate meaning, purpose, and value of who we are and what we do. Yet ironically, living in the service of a sacred Lord—all the more powerful for being unrecognized by us (it is much harder to rebel against a covert Lord)—and conforming to that Lord's command to rebel (for larger fragments of our self and of our interests) currently constitute the "ultimate" nature of our self, our interests and our life.[7]

THE ARCHETYPAL DRAMA OF DEMOCRATIC LIBERALISM

We shall now explore one of the most unchaining and empowering archetypal dramas in the service of incoherence, namely democratic liberalism. *Democracy* is a word that, consonant with its very practice, does not conclusively and finally define a fixed state. *Democracy* does not mean rule of the people. It means power of the people. It refers to a persistent dramatic problem—the continual reopening of the process of participation by the people as they discover new grounds and new capacity to reshape their life together and as they join in nourishing what they hold to be good.

The suffix *-archy*, as in *monarchy* or *oligarchy*, is not to be found in *democracy*. That suffix, *-archy*, means "rule" only derivatively. It means ultimate or original root and therefore the principle and action consonant with that original root—hence also the word *archetype*. That does not mean that democracy is not an archetypal drama. *Kratia* ("power") would be an empty word if it did not signify an archetypal force. Whenever democracy arises after people have lost power or have never yet gained power, it is to be expected that democracy is seen by the established elite as lacking any legitimacy, and is seen by both elite and the people as the power to put established roots and principles into question. But all power deserves to be regarded with a wary eye, even the power of the people, and certainly the tyranny of the majority.

We must always ask these questions: What are the sources of power? What are its meaning and purpose? The sources, meaning, and purpose of "power" and of "people" change fundamentally within each overarching way of life. In speaking at this point of democratic liberalism, its dominant structure and dynamics—thanks to incoherence as a way of life—are shaped by our enlarged freedom to pursue our self-interest. Hence we shall also soon be discussing authoritarian liberalism within the archetypal drama of capitalism, even in alliance with democratic liberalism. Only in the service of transformation can democracy empower each of us

---

7. In the following chapter on deformation, we shall speak of Satan as the symbol of the Lord who molds the archetypal way of life that leads us to destructive death.

each day anew to use our capacity to discover the riches of the cosmos of human relationships and to participate in sharing them.

Democratic liberalism offers us great freedom and opportunities in contrast to the fixity and enforcement of emanation as a way of life, in contrast also to modern authoritarian liberalism and the deforming power of totalitarianism. We can gain freedom of speech, press, and assembly; religious tolerance; protection of property; the right to elect our governmental representatives, to establish and limit governmental jurisdiction, and to seek agreement on legal and political rights and procedures, and on taxes and budget allocations. Democratic liberalism opens a road to liberty.

Thus, in the United States, white men without property were at last allowed to vote a hundred years after the founding of this republic; all women achieved the right to vote in 1920; all African-Americans gained the right to vote after 1963. And a minimum welfare safety net for those who had fallen to, or could not rise from, the bottom in the competition of self-interested individuals came to be established in the nineteen-thirties, though conservative liberals and left-of-center liberals continue to differ and to fight over which human beings are entitled to such help, what kind of help, and how much help, if any. These gains make a democratic liberal society the best of available choices while we remain also within that drama of incoherence as a way of life.

But is democratic liberalism a government of the people, by the people, and for the people? Democratic liberalism is most crucially an archetypal drama for organizing competition and its rewards for those with power seeking more power, not for collaborating to help create a fullness of being for each and all. This institutionalized form of rebellion of democratic liberalism makes the already powerful deeply reluctant to open democracy also to be of, by, and for all the people. Why let more competitors enter what is now our arena? New competitors may take our place, or seek quite a different distribution of resources—or indeed, a transforming democracy. That is why it has taken such a long time even in the liberal democracies to let everyone participate in voting, and why the struggle to enable everyone to receive a good education and to compete for any economic or political position is still only in its beginning.[8]

The more powerful in a liberal democracy not only limit the majority in its access to higher positions where we can compete with them for power and resources, we all handicap ourselves even in the best of cases: "Congress shall make no law respecting an establishment of religion, or prohibiting the free exercise thereof; or abridging the freedom of speech, or of the press; or the right of

---

8. See, for example, *The New York Times*, March 17, 1995: "White Males and the Manager Class; Report Finds Prejudices Block Progress of Women and Minorities." We shall discuss this issue further in Chapter 12.

the people peaceably to assemble, and to petition the government for a redress of grievances." This first Amendment to the U.S. Constitution magnificently enlarges our public rights. But the dominant philosophical interpretation reflecting incoherence as a way of life greatly diminishes this Amendment's significance. It frees us to offer both our subjective and objective opinions in the marketplace of ideas. But subjective opinion does not and cannot tell us anything objectively true, while objective opinion is true in part because its findings are testable and because it will not let itself be influenced by subjective opinions. But this philosophical stand (in contrast to the kind of understanding, capacity, and needs we shall explore in the last four chapters of this work) holds that with respect to justice, love, compassion, beauty, and the ultimate meaning and purpose of anything we become or do, we can only offer subjective opinions. We have been freed, but the significance of what we express subjectively on such vital issues has been devalued—unless we are powerful.

At stake in a democratic liberal society is what power we can accumulate to pursue our subjective interest (even our subjective interest in gaining objective knowledge) and with which interest groups we can ally ourselves. For most candidates for public office, there is no chance of running unless they can collect hundreds of thousands or indeed millions of dollars. Therefore, lobbyists working for clients seeking favorable treatment from legislatures and governmental executives contribute large sums of money to candidates and office holders.

Precisely because people in need lack such resources, little or nothing is supplied for such people. According to the U.S. Bureau of the Census, among 11.9 million designated as poor in 1987, 7.6 million received no cash stipends from welfare or Social Security. And 4.6 million received neither cash nor non-cash benefits.[9] In 1995, the number of the poor permitted to receive grants was cut further, and also cut was the amount of aid. The archetypal drama of democratic liberalism alone does not organize all of society. Its structure, dynamics, and values are affected by its interaction with other archetypal dramas also in the service of the overarching way of incoherence—witness the contrasts between the United States, Sweden, Italy, and Japan. What the drama of democratic liberalism has in common in all its manifestations is that it inspires and organizes the enactment of political competition of all who can compete (but certainly not all and not all with equal power), striving to satisfy their subjective or intersubjective desire for particular gains (but certainly not the wholeness of personal and shared being).

Intrinsic to all the dramas of rebellion in the service of incoherence is a constant tension between the power to enlarge one's liberty and the power to attain authoritarian control—for freedom to compete for the dominant heights one has not yet reached but also to dominate these heights for as long as possible. There is

9. William Greider, *Who Will Tell the People: The Betrayal of American* Democracy, 429, n. 14.

intrinsically little room at the top. Otherwise, there would be no top. The institutionalized rebellion of masterless men thus also produces a new kind of master.

In regimes of authoritarian liberalism, freedom to compete is restricted entirely to a small elite, which seeks to perpetuate its mastery by organizing (and oppressing, providing minimum welfare for, or neglecting) all others for the sake of those now in power. Such regimes have been losing ground to more democratic liberal regimes in the past two decades in many parts of the world. Yet the drama of authoritarian liberalism is the dominant order for most people most every day even where democratic liberalism shapes the political system.

We impose authoritarian liberalism upon ourselves. We have submitted ourselves to arrest in the midst of a quintessential process and at our strongest, at this point, mold ourselves through what we term self-mastery, self-control, and self-direction when, in the nature of our case, we have not yet developed the wholeness of our self. We may then, in our self-interest, impose our mastery, control, and direction on others—for competition with others does not disappear simply because we have already sharpened ourselves. Many are the bureaucratic hierarchies, based on democratically voted laws and legally appointed or elected officials, in which authoritarian liberalism is the actual practice. Even in democratic liberal societies, the most powerful experience of authoritarian liberalism that dominates the economic aspects of what we can and need to do together is the archetypal drama of capitalism. Through this drama, a few people decisively control not only the working conditions but also the living conditions—indeed the conditions of life—of the many.

THE ARCHETYPAL DRAMA OF CAPITALISM

What about capitalism as a living underlying patterning force? Capitalists appear to be concerned solely to calculate concretely (and to some scientific extent, abstractly) about ever-increasing material advantages for themselves in producing, possessing, controlling, buying, and selling products and services—and therefore also in using their power to rule people who work for them and to prevail among those who compete with them or who can affect the terms of competition. Increased power over relationships and over matter to increase profits has generated more products and services than ever before in human history. Capitalism has also turned more human beings than ever before into mere tools that have not yet been replaced by mechanical tools, and into people with dire needs that are ignored because meeting those needs is not profitable—or would reduce profits, by way of taxes, if they were met.

What inspires so intense a personal drive and such worldwide acceptance of capitalism? We have already explored the basic form of the underlying patterning force that also inspires the life of capitalists:[10] the drama of persistent rebellion. All dramas in the service of incoherence reflect this same character of rebellion because of our arrest in Act II Scene 1—except for those dramas that are intended to compensate for this organized security by providing us still with the seeming security of emanation.

The difference between each drama of rebellion is its goal—and hence its modifications in its structure and dynamics. Capitalism is the most materially gainful of all dramas in the service of incoherence for those who move toward the top. Such power and profit is the heart of the matter. What one produces or serves matters in terms of selling, but what it is does not matter. The people at the top of the ladder are concerned to place efficient, inventive, disciplined managers and workers below them. But for the controlling owners or managers at the top, the skill required is above all the use of power and knowledge to reap more power and profits in the face of the competition of others moving toward the same goals. This is true even in those rare cases when the corporate executive is the inventor and designer of production. And the devotion to profits may often involve polluting the environment, endangering the health of workers and consumers, building weapons also likely to destroy civilians, and (as we shall soon examine in greater detail) exploiting workers. But all capitalists lead lives which, however much wealth they have achieved, leave them little time to enjoy their wealth. Their days are filled with long hours of work; their social life is intended principally to improve business relationships.

And no single capitalist can control other recurrent aspects of this story—new, competing, and more profitable inventions; the value of currencies, stocks, and bonds; and depression or rising prosperity that may improve this capitalist's lot or the lot of some competitor instead. A capitalist needs to be ready to endure losses, and not only to be propelled by profits. However successful, capitalists remain insecure. Which competitor will challenge them next? Even more significantly, no capitalist, however powerful over others in his corporation, in the market, and in the community, can overcome remaining a biased and incomplete human being—the deepest cause of the capitalist's insecurity.

Is capitalism a story that moves us because of our desire for particular large gains or a series of such gains? If we are successful, these are our concrete payoffs. But such concrete results cannot alone explain the dynamism and the manifold content of this story. The underlying patterning forces of capitalism are not solely economic. What inspires and shapes such a life is an archetypal drama that

---

10. By *capitalist* I mean individuals who own or, as managers, control enough capital to take a leading role in their enactment of the archetypal drama of capitalism. We shall soon be discussing the role of other participants in this drama.

constitutes the most empowering—and disempowering—rebelling in the service of incoherence. It would not be necessary to seek living underlying forces that pattern a drama of capitalism, if products, profits, and organizing power were all straightforward, rational entities or processes.

The fact that this drama is enacted in the service of incoherence means that every aspect of it fragments life and itself constitutes only a fragment in conflict with other fragments with deeper implications than its own incomplete and biased story is able to tell us.

For example, does the quality and safety of a product matter to a capitalist? Only if profits are affected by such problems or the State is prepared to enforce rules. How often do dangerous pesticides infuse foods? Are cars constructed with unsafe features? Does lead in paint, water pipes, and car exhausts—and hence into human tissue—continue to move children to increased aggressiveness and delinquency, and lower intelligence?[11] How often do medicines carry dangerous side effects? Are stocks and bonds sold with less than full and honest information? Are cigarettes or firearms sold that are bound to endanger our health? These are only a few examples.

Is anything as important to a capitalist as are profits? Steel mills have been closed without warning, leaving an entire community without its dominant, indeed often sole, industrial employment. Skilled and hardworking employees may be fired by the thousands to raise profits for their company. Capitalism is not a drama limited in its business to increasing production and profits from material goods and services, or buying or selling corporations or stocks. Quite undemocratically, even within democratic liberal societies, it creates deep inequalities not only in the distribution of profits but in the quality of our lives.

The economic is an expression of all four faces of our being, but especially of the political—of what we can and need to do together, or of what frustrates us in that work. As we showed earlier, all archetypal dramas of rebellion in the service of incoherence move us to enact two dominant desires and always they produce the same type of outcome. All three of these dynamics are in such deep tension with each other that rebellion is thereby also perennially renewed and also inhibited. One dominant desire is to be free to rebel within a drama that also allows others to rebel. Another desire is to be free to be powerful enough to stay at the top. But any top, by definition, has room only for one or a few—raising the temptation of alliance with the dynamics of the drama of authoritarian liberalism.

The natural outcome of this kind of rebellion is always inequality, even within democratic liberal societies—an outcome that both renews the desire for rebellion and, for many, discourages or represses it. Capitalism is a drama especially potent in producing these three manifestations and the strain between them. Rational

---

11. *The New York Times*, February 7, 1996.

calculation—of such keen and often exclusive concern to corporate managers, academic economists, and many political analysts—is only one limited outward manifestation of this archetypal drama. "Self-reliance" exaggerates the reliability even of the self in this drama, which focuses us on our (still limited) conception of self-interest—a self-interest we cannot pursue without relying upon a shared archetypal drama whose structure and dynamics rational calculation cannot truly fathom.

From the perspective of capitalism, the attraction of democratic liberalism lies solely in its present comparative advantage, not in any intrinsic or sustaining advantage. Against the power of absolute kings, feudal lords, or warlords with no sympathy for capitalism, democratic liberalism was clearly a better course for capitalists to join in rebellion. Against a modern state that predominantly owns and controls property and all political institutions, aspiring capitalists are also eager to join the same cause of rebellion.

But what kind of democratic liberalism are capitalists likely to favor? Historically, we know that capitalists have not been eager to open the doors of democracy to people not already among the competitors to whom one is compelled to pay attention. Until the late nineteenth century, only men of property could vote. Until the early twentieth century, half the population—women—could not vote in such democratic societies. And there certainly exists an institutionalized distance between the voter's right to choose between candidates and actually to influence (as do lobbyists and powerful individual leaders) what laws will be enacted.

And if the now dominant capitalists attained their present power in alliance with an authoritarian liberal group, and this alliance assures them of property rights and contract enforcement (and of ways of diminishing new competition at home and from abroad and of curbing political opposition to capitalism), these capitalists are *unlikely* to work toward democratic liberalism. Freedom (for capitalists) to rebel is then limited to competition for power within corporations, between corporations, and for new capitalists able in their rebellion to find allies within this system.

Even democratic liberalism, like all dramas in the service of incoherence, is capable only of fashioning incremental changes. Such a democracy would have to be undone before changes for the fundamentally worse or fundamentally better can take place. No democratic liberal society can therefore be expected to put an end to capitalism. Given the power of capitalism in such democratic societies, the powerful receive more from the government than the powerless. What *does* worry capitalists in democratic liberal states is that the powerless are, in the very nature of the case, far more numerous than the powerful. However, as we shall see, the inequality intrinsic to the drama of capitalism deeply depotentiates the less powerful, and the drama itself legitimizes their defeat.

Inequality in liberal society is a consequence not only of capitalism but also of its form of democracy. That democracy has at last come to offer equal rights to all citizens to speak freely, to vote, and to seek office. But these constitute opportunities to enter a competition for power within a deeply fragmented society. To speak is not yet the power actually to be heard; nor does free speech lead to sensitivity—born of being in open, searching, and caring dialogue with others. To seek office is not yet the power to be selected as a candidate or to gain the money to run.[12] To vote is not yet the power to be consulted between elections on the laws and executive decisions to be made. A liberal democracy is not a community of human beings freeing themselves fully to express and interconnect the four faces of their being by participating in creating fundamentally new and better lives for each unique person and all neighbors.

The most powerful authoritarian constraint in a democratic liberal society—upon most men and women, and in most of the world, even children—is the drama of capitalism. For most people, it determines who works, who is not hired and who is fired. It sets the working conditions, however harsh or intense, without flexibility or adequate time for employees to participate in other dramas, including family life and community life. It pays most workers as little as possible—unless unions or the state set higher standards. Capitalism decisively shapes the conditions and quality of most lives. Within each corporation, one boss makes all the crucial decisions—on hiring and firing (on grounds of power and profit, not only with respect for the quality, and certainly not the needs of each worker); on what to produce and how to produce it (once again on grounds of power and profit, not only the quality of the product and certainly not on whether all people who need it can afford it).

Boards of Directors and stockholders are the only people who can vote in corporations. Stockholders are often left uninformed by the boss on crucial issues—on the company's pollution, risks of health damage to workers, gifts to politicians, or the quality of goods. Members of Boards of Directors, on the other hand, are either so closely connected to the top executives or they are themselves, as officers, so involved in their own corporation's daily machinations to avoid regulations that they have become increasingly unwilling to become involved in the daily activities of the corporation for which they serve as a board member. Dissent within corporations is very dangerous unless the dissenter is powerful enough to have a good chance to win. Whistleblowers—who reveal defects of products, health risks to workers, or pollution—are normally fired. Every boss knows that he is working even within his own corporation in the company of critics and competitors.

To speak of capitalist bosses is like speaking of despots who, as Alexis de Tocqueville said, "themselves do not deny the excellence of freedom, but they wish

---

12. Senator Phil Gramm, announcing himself as a candidate for the American Presidency, said, "I have the most reliable friend that you can have in American politics, and that is ready money." *The New York Times*, April 23, 1995. It turned out during the primary elections that others had even larger reliable friends of this kind. And, of course, rebellion in the service of incoherence is always uncertain in its outcome.

to keep it all to themselves." But in the case of capitalism, should we not be focusing on the market instead? Many are the elements of the market that no single boss can control, though the more powerful he is the more he can influence it. Witness the military-industrial complex, tax laws, government subsidies, and tariffs. The market is one of the shared stages of this drama—but not for the vast number of people who do not have the money to buy or resources or products to sell.

But since bosses are the principal actors in this drama, they recognize that since they are not fully in control of market forces and are faced by rivals, each tries to be as fully in control as possible. There would be no need for authoritarianism if authority were in fact not at risk of being challenged. The capitalist market constitutes part of the drama that depersonalizes—reduces the being of—the less powerful even more than it does of the powerful. Competitors, investors, customers, and workers are seen on this stage only as threats to the power and profit of successful rebels—or as supports for power and profit, as purchasers of commodities, as hired tools—not as fellow human beings. No single boss alone has shaped the conditions and qualities of life we have been describing. But this biased and incomplete life replicates itself for all its actors because even the most powerful among them are shaped by a shared drama.

Let us look more closely at the painful costs of inequality created by the authoritarian enactment of the drama of capitalism. I will focus this discussion on the United States not simply because I know it best but because it is one of the most advanced cases of capitalism and takes place in a democratic liberal society. In the United States, as in Western Europe, capitalism began before the pursuit of self-interest needed also to pay serious attention to the demands of the drama of democratic liberalism. The great majority—that is, people without property, women, and slaves—could not vote.

In many mills and factories of the northern United States until the early twentieth century, more than half the workers were children, some younger than eleven years old. Child labor was not outlawed until 1937. Most workers (until the early 1920s) were compelled to work twelve hours a day, with only every other Sunday off. (Especially among steel workers and miners, this burden created a high accident rate.) Strikes by labor unions were not legal until 1937. (Until then, powerful capitalists were often able to call upon the National Guard to kill strikers.) Some years after the Great Depression of 1929, which for a time weakened the power of capitalists and created deep suffering and discontent on a greater scale than before, a number of Democratic Party presidents led toward legislation providing social security retirement and also Medicare payments for the elderly, welfare payments and Medicaid for the poor, and a minimum-wage standard—in the mid-sixties at 25 cents per hour, and by the early nineties at $4.25 per hour, leaving most of such employees below the poverty line.

Maintaining or raising profits counts far more than anything else as the material demonstration of power in capitalism. When capitalism is the most pervasive way of earning any income, and therefore the jobs and livelihood of most people is dependent on it, capitalists do not ask, "At whose expense are we making profit? What contribution do we need to make to the livelihood of people we have fired for the sake of our profit?" Does capitalism indeed simply reflect the workings of an "impersonal market?" To Westerners, economics in Soviet-dominated Eastern Europe were once known as "command economies." Indeed a single center sought to dominate all forms of economic enterprise. But obviously it too faced resistance—or else its exceedingly tough enforcement would not have been necessary.

Capitalism, even when not oligarchic or monopolistic, is also based on power over people. The boss insists on conformity, on hard work according to his rules to prove conformity, and at best, on shrewd suggestions that will increase his power. This demand for loyalty is a one-way street. Even high-ranking managers (never mind workers) are treated by their superiors as possessing no other stories of life that matter and no ultimate human value.

Sometimes individuals who are truly conformist are appointed as the successor at the top—and then soon demonstrate their lack of imagination, initiative, and courage. How could authoritarian bosses emerge if they had in truth been conformist beings? Beneath the required surface of conformity of the ambitious— deeply moved by capitalism as a drama and by incoherence as a way of life—lives rebellion. It is not an easy contradiction to live. In the course of a forty-year corporate career, three-quarters of the people in management careers had at least one boss they found unbearable. On the average, they changed jobs every three to seven years. For those seeking to be on the fast track, the job-hopping rate is closer to once every two years.[13]

That is why I speak of rebellion as the most basic force in all dramas in the service of incoherence, including capitalism. Even for analyzing capitalists, the conventional term "competition" is inadequate. It is not only striving in the face of rivalry that is at stake. The way to the top requires at least covertly resisting the controlling power, seeking to oust those who are now in power so that we can take their place. At the top, it may often lead to rebellion against our fellow workers (fire them!) against our community (close the single, large industrial plant—our company's—that now above all sustains the people of this town!), against our own company (sell it so that the proceeds may be used to buy another company to enlarge our conglomerate while the new owner sharply diminishes the old work force!), and against our own country (take our manufacturing jobs and the finan-

---

13. From a study by Michael Lombardo, a research psychologist at the Center for Creative Leadership in Greensboro, NC, quoted in *The New York Times*, December 28, 1986.

cial assets we earned here—but not our workers—and move them abroad). And then be sure to anticipate, if I can, the rebellions of others who seek my power.

Who are the most powerful participants in a democratic liberal society when it comes to gaining, protecting, or increasing material resources? Those who are the major source of financing and therefore vitally influencing the election of officials, who abundantly finance and control lobbyists, who control most public media, and in these ways shape laws and regulations and their actual enforcement—namely, the leading capitalists.[14] How well are the majority of voters informed and organized to counter this small minority?[15]

Capitalists are freer now to exploit governments and peoples also because no democratic or even authoritarian liberal state can effectively alter the actions of corporations that are multinational. They cannot be kept from moving their manufacturing abroad and, there, more easily exploiting cheap labor and polluting the environment. As early as 1982, one-quarter of American-owned manufacturing had already been moved abroad.[16] The United Nations estimates that the total annual sales of the 350 biggest multinational companies are equal to one-third of the combined gross national product of the industrial world and exceed by several hundred billions of dollars that of the developing world.[17]

At the same time, many are the workers who are required to work twelve hours a day, six days a week so that the corporation need not hire additional workers and thus pay additional job benefits. Many also are the workers who have been displaced altogether by high-tech automation—or else have been put on revolving twenty-four-hour schedules to service machines that run all the time. In the last decade, many American corporations have embraced a view of capitalism that put workers last, cutting costs, laying off workers and pressing those who remain to labor harder, longer, and more efficiently. These kinds of working conditions do great damage to family and community life and thus also to workers' political participation.

---

14. For a deeply informed and vividly detailed description and analysis of this situation in Washington, D.C., see William Greider, *Who Will Tell the People: The Betrayal of American Democracy*. More recently, the excellent but disturbing work by Kevin Phillips, *Wealth and Democracy*, traces the strategies of the rich to stay in power since the beginning of the Republic.

15. In this analysis I have concentrated on this minority of the most powerful of capitalists and about whose behavior we know relatively more. In the United States there are also 14 million businesses with fewer than 500 employees, constituting 97 percent of all American companies. They employ nearly half of the nation's non-farm workers and create about 40 percent of its gross national product. Leonard Silk, *The New York Times*, April 9, 1986. All of these capitalists are moved by the same drama, with all the personal uniqueness that a partial self is capable of.

16. James Hines and Glenn Hubbard, "Coming Home to America: Dividend Repatriation by U.S. Multinationals," National Bureau of Economics Research Working Paper 2931.

17. Robert Heilbroner in a review of Paul M. Kennedy, *Preparing for the Twenty-First Century*. *The New York Times*, February 14, 1993.

Slavery has been abolished, but suffering—indeed violence done to body and spirit—has not come to an end under capitalism today, for the employed no less than the unemployed. Caring about human beings is intrinsically not a concern of capitalists—for reasons we shall examine in the concluding part of this section.

In the United States, 14,500 people are killed each year on the job. These figures, for 1969, compare with 9,414 Americans killed in Vietnam that year and 14,950 murders in the nation. Another 2.5 million experienced disabling injuries on the job.[18] A hundred thousand more die each year from occupation-related diseases.[19]

If the government of a liberal democracy refuses to help, and the less powerful cannot fundamentally change this system (for reasons we will examine toward the end of this chapter), will the more powerful capitalists ever act differently? The chief executive of the International Business Machines Corporation—then the world's largest computer company—was asked whether his corporation should withdraw from South Africa in protest against that government's brutal racism. He replied, "If we elect to leave it, it will be a business decision. What other kind of decision would it be? We are not in business to conduct moral activity; we are not in business to conduct socially responsible action. We are in business to conduct business."[20] (The powerfully rich do engage in charity. People with income-producing assets of more than $1.3 million a year on the average give away half of 1 percent of that wealth annually.)[21]

Have I been presenting a one-sided picture of capitalism? In actual historical experience, capitalism has been by far the most productive of all dramas through which we have organized and delivered the largest quantity and variety of often innovative and efficient goods and services. More people than ever before have thus succeeded in greatly increasing their income—from salaries, stock ownership, and sales—as compared to the days before capitalism or to the earlier days of capitalism.

I chose the United States as our principal example because it is, in spite of the current problems of the economy, one of the most successful stories of capitalism at this time. In 1995, American industrial production was 40 percent higher than in 1980, 350 percent higher than in 1950.[22] Stocks during the last decade rose by more than 2,000 points. The growth rate, inflation rate, and unemployment rate are performing more favorably than those in most of the industrial world.

---

18. Report of the U.S. Department of Labor, cited in *The New York Times*, September 21, 1970.
19. Senator Edward M. Kennedy, quoted in *The New York Times*, May 7, 1992.
20. *The New York Times*, April 23, 1986. The context of these remarks was South Africa, but its application was clearly much broader.
21. *The New York Times*, April 30, 1995, quoting from C. N. Rosenberg, *Wealthy and Wise: How You and America Can Get the Most out of Your Giving*.
22. George F. Will, *The Trenton Times*, January 18, 1995.

Capitalists will, of course, agree that particular corporations or the entire economy can go up or down. In 1951, the United Kingdom industrially produced more than Germany and France combined. By 1985, French industrial production was twice that of the UK, and Germany's had increased to three times that of the UK. But we have deliberately been discussing one of the most prolonged successful cases precisely because what is at stake is not solely the material payoff, even for those who receive some part of it. Even in the best of cases, this drama does not—indeed cannot, thanks to its very nature—put an end to the authoritarian domination, exploitation, inequality, and poverty of the great majority of people.

Even in democratic liberal societies, no workplace is democratic. The State is welcomed to protect private property, to maintain order, to support the monetary system, to invest in education that will help create a useful workforce. But a minority of powerful capitalists as we have seen is often strong enough in such a democracy to limit the State's power to clean the air we breathe, to curb the dangers to our health (and even to our lives) that we face at work, or to help the poor. As for customers in this type of market system, human need does not count, not even demand for supplies, only "effective demand"—meaning, demand supported by enough money. The price we pay for capitalism is not only in money gained, lost, or denied but also in the very nature, value, meaning, and purpose of our lives. As we have seen, this drama too often leads us into the road to destructive death—a deformation we shall discuss in the next chapter.

Karl Marx saw with powerful sensitivity and insight that capitalism estranges and even cuts us off from our "species being." It mutilates us into "a fragment of a man." But he based his criticism of capitalism above all on "production relations"—and no other underlying structure and dynamics. He did not recognize that there is an overarching way of life from which we also need to free ourselves if we are to liberate ourselves from capitalism as a drama. Thus, even democratic socialists remain in the service of incoherence. Communists resorted to aspects of authoritarian liberalism (with actual or subversive rebellion confined to the elite) and also joined this drama in the service of incoherence with many dramas in the service of deformation.

Marx did not know the process of transformation that could in fact lead workers to turn into proletarians who rejected capitalism. He spoke of workers who failed to make the journey as possessing "false consciousness," but he did not recognize what underlying forces thus held them enchained.[23] He believed that capitalist productivity was a necessary prelude to socialism. He wrote little on the personal and political process that would lead from socialism to communism and

---

23. Toward the end of this chapter, we shall discuss why people wounded or defeated within the drama of capitalism nonetheless continue to adhere to it.

he wrote only about a dozen pages on the experience of communism.[24] He offered no analysis of "species being." In fact, he could not because he had ignored the deepest sacred source of our being as if it were a synonym for organized religion.

EMANATIONAL TIES IN THE SERVICE OF INCOHERENCE

In the face of remaining only partial beings, whether we are successful in gaining large fragments of life or possess only an insufficient fragment of life, we all seek more security here and now. The fragments of emanation as a way of life no longer possess the power for us they once had. They are no longer part of a whole web of life. Today, in the service of incoherence, they have become the shared subjectivity of some (though not of others) in our society, molding our perspectives in some stories of our life but not in other stories.

When in the past, as we saw in the preceding chapter, the leaders of emanation as a way of life felt inadequate to enforce their monotheistic way as they had arrested and consolidated it, they sought the State (though in fact always in the service of incoherence) as an ally. In the modern age, the leaders of capitalism, especially in twentieth-century Germany and Japan, formed an alliance with selected aspects of emanation. In corporations, what came to count was the mysterious absolute power of the top leader, loyalty, discipline, and (nonetheless—or, indeed, naturally under these conditions) rivalry between various in-group alliances. Corporations then conducted their daily work as if they possessed managers and workers body and soul, and—although (godlike) they can exile them—they meanwhile offer security in return for total commitment to disciplined hard work. In such cases, the state is also a partner in the alliance between these two ways of life. Success is the blessing that reinforces this alliance of incoherence and emanation. How long will people be willing to bear such costs?

In these same countries, but also in many other societies, fragments of emanation as a way of life have survived as a double-edged but rusting sword. One side of it still makes us obey and yield uncritically to our leaders—to calls to war, calls to unity—because we are still moved by the powerful mysteries of office, hierarchy, and group consensus. This side of the old sword also inhibits democracy through its repressive morality, its justification of heroic aggressiveness in behalf of individual self-interest or the national interest, its distrust of the feminine, and its rejection of any person or group who does not share our emanational container.

The other side of this inherited sword still provides emanational values that living with incoherence can never provide on its own as an archetypal way of life:

---

24. Shlomo Avineri, *The Social and Political Thought of Karl Marx*, 220–39, and "Marx's Vision of Future Society," *Dissent*, Summer 1973, 323–31.

compassion, trust, and the commitment to take an oath seriously when—judging on the basis of self-interested, rational calculation—it appears highly probable that we could get away with lying. It is the survival of these latter fragments from the way of emanation that makes life bearable in the service of incoherence. It follows that as the two-sided sword from the past continues to rust and therefore also fragments further, thus freeing us from earlier constraints, its protective edge will also cease to be of help. Consequently, our lives, dominated by incoherence, will get worse.

Others, who are already deprived of the once seemingly complete and final truth and security of emanation (as the only prevailing or at least the dominant way of life in this seemingly secular society), look above all for renewed security through emanational relationships. What are these overwhelmingly powerful forces, whose nature remains mysterious to us even as they come to possess and command us? All of them are archetypal dramas.

While we remain arrested in the service of incoherence, we remain unconscious of the fact that we adhere to this allegedly secure way of life through an emanational relationship that commits us to its sacred source. Of course, the Lord of incoherence speaks in a different vein than the Lord of emanation. The Devil says be sure to commit yourself, as I inspire you again and again, to the structure, dynamics, and purpose of stories of change in my service.

Compensating yourself for the intrinsic insecurity and incompleteness of this way of life or asserting yourself are the two main themes of the archetypal stories in its service. Often, both themes are present. In nationalism, we respond to the fact that we have no deep human bonds with each other in the society of perennial rivalry and rebellion, so let us be united as a nation-state and at least against rival nation-states.[25] Through the drama of the conquering hero we seek to assert new and decisive potency in the face of grave danger or else, far-reaching ambition. In the drama of romantic love, we seek passionate compensation for feeling so alone. Being competent is a drama in which, when we enact it in the service of incoherence, we focus solely on developing a special skill and compensate for our lack of human wholeness by dedicating our talent to contributing to the power of others to assert themselves. We shall devote chapters to each of these dramas later in this work.

These dramas—and a few others we shall now mention briefly—sometimes augment each other but basically raise rival attractions in our lives and compete with each other, for they reflect the Devil's inspiration and work. When the Devil is in control—instead of being a force that helps us break to make a new move

---

25. Both nationalism and the nation-state are always in the service of incoherence and are obstacles to practicing transformation.

into a Scene of the drama of transformation—he arrests us in a life of separating. Meanwhile, for the sake of survival or greater power, we seek fragments that will also separate us from ourselves and others and that will also come apart again. The Devil, through his persistent acts of separating, prevents us from understanding the fundamental grounds of our being—and even from knowing the Devil. And therefore we look at archetypal dramas—all of which connect the four faces of our being to a sacred source—at best as a poetic manner of speaking about connecting things, but not as analyzable within our present perspective.

The most important figure on stage in every drama in the service of incoherence—as we see it—is our ego, even when we desperately seek to compensate for our incompleteness by becoming even more romantic or more nationalistic. Because we do not understand the living underlying patterning source of passion that inspires us, we experience ourselves within the archetypal story, to which we have an emanational relationship, above all as the embodiment of our ego—as if our ego were the deepest source of our being. And our ego then turns this drama into the only fragment of life that really counts, or else, in intense competition with other dramas in our lives—as capitalist and romantic lover, as worker and mother. Dramas in the service of incoherence—either within their own dynamics or in relations with each other—bring no wholeness, love, or justice into our lives.

As a matter of mysteriously potent empowerment, we seek an emanational source that enables us to declare, "I am the embodiment of Chrysler Motor Company." "I am the embodiment of the best American (or Russian or Japanese) values." "I am the embodiment of the Teamsters Union." The underlying source inflates some part of our being at the expense of our selves and of others. But we do not understand at all the underlying archetypal drama; we do not understand very much its concrete manifestation in this instance. Any emanational tie keeps us from such understanding. And therefore, however hard-nosed we become in our judgment, however much we attain in fame and in material gains, we are caught in deep uncertainty and anxiety. For with our enlarged and driven ego, we continue to live in a world of colliding egos, competing about who is to be the ego embodiment who can become the source to inspire or control others: Enter into my chain of emanation, so that I may be obeyed and propitiated no matter how seemingly unreasonable my demand.

If the rebellion of our ego has not raised us toward the top, we may clutch links to charismatic figures or movements that seem to offer the solidarity and certainty of emanational relationships. But within the overarching drama of incoherence, we cannot know on what grounds ultimately to trust that person, for our historical memory is largely anecdotal—fragmentary and short. Or we find an ideology that galvanizes and convinces us that it is the only set of convictions that will lead us to success. Or we become deeply devoted to a team competing with other teams—

the scholars who specialize in sharing our paradigm for systematizing political analysis through rational quantitative calculation; the Pentagon officers (who only wrote analyses of Soviet capabilities but never of Soviet intentions, who dogmatically interpreted capabilities to mean intentions) committed to fighting the Cold War; the followers of the Dallas Cowboys football team, who cannot imagine anyone favoring another team. Or we try gambling, to find out if there is a mysterious source of good fortune with us.

If others do not respect our emanational aura, try covert manipulation, as if indeed a mysterious power were with us. This is turning into an ever more prevalent form of activity in creating images and manipulating strategies in many areas of our life. Or we try being protean—to change our emanational embodiment in the service of incoherence again and again.[26] This kind of shifting has become more and more common as incoherence as a way of life dissolves more and more the inherited fragments of emanation whose original status we could not have questioned without filling us with a sense of guilt and shame—and they could have enforced their sanctions if we had violated established codes. Today, not only parents but presidents and royal families are no longer treated with deference or even respect. We know that even the most authoritarian or authoritative individuals are not likely to endure in their positions as long as once they did. We therefore feel much freer to rebel against prevailing emanational relationships by re-forming or creating new archetypal dramas in the service of incoherence—to remain attached to them only for a spell, until we rebel again.

In this way of life, we have no capacity for ultimate judgments about the meaning, values, and purpose of life. Since we cannot, in the very nature of this situation, find any emanational source that can "save" us or give us a security backed by a community-wide consensus, the Devil remains free to throw open, throw out, throw together, overthrow—or, in more conventional language—possess, desert, trick, and trip us. Any separation in any emanational relationship is experienced as either betraying or having been betrayed, demanding either murder or suicide or their psychological equivalents. If we soon discover a new emanational bond or have become more accustomed to such changes, we may survive. But killings and suicides for these reasons are also increasing.

---

26. The Greeks saw Proteus as a sea-God who assumed many different shapes again and again. Robert J. Lifton, *The Protean Self: Human Resilience in an Age of Fragmentation* presents vivid examples of such people living—from our perspective—in any of the four ways of life, but he does not make any such systematic theoretical distinctions. And when he speaks with great sympathy of "proteanism on behalf of species consciousness," he does not tell us by what underlying process we can move in that direction. I speak of protean changes taking place solely in the service of incoherence, since a return to emanation as a way of life renders any further changes sinful, a movement toward deformation ends in our death sooner rather than later, and the journey into transformation cannot be achieved in this fashion.

Happily, there also exist people who are deeply committed to caring for other people, helping them with food for the day, working politically to improve the lives of the poor and the disabled and the people against whom society still discriminates. Such compassion may have its roots in emanation as a way of life, but now re-formed to apply charity not only to one's inherited group but also to anyone in need. Or else such a sense of responsibility springs forth from seeds of transformation, but as yet without a theoretical and practical appreciation of the actual process of transformation. The great majority of such people in our time confine themselves to trying to accomplish what is incrementally possible within the present way of life. To do as much as we can here and now is indeed necessary. But we shall explore the fundamental limits of incremental change in the next section.

What we have tried to show in this section is that the hoped-for reward of rebellion in the service of incoherence is not simply naked power over matter and people but also emanational empowerment. But in contrast to the earlier web of life, these emanational bonds are only vertical individual relationships. They can connect us to others only if they are inter-subjective—that is, if others share this same bond. We can work together, govern together, only if we share the same way of life and also the same archetypal dramas. But since all the archetypes focus on the me-now, in contrast to you (and who are you moving to be?), all the stories leave us insecure even when we share them. Each of us in emanation is apprehensive because we are only a half-moon in reflecting the outflow of our source—or even a full moon, hiding or unaware of our dark side.

CAUGHT IN DISJOINTED INCREMENTALISM

Many are the damages we suffer in ourselves and in our community for having terminated the journey through the core drama of life already in Act II Scene 1. And as long as we remain arrested within it, we do not—cannot—even have the mind and heart to be fully present to our suffering and take action to overcome it. That arrest persists until something happens within us or to us that cannot be contained or borne within this way of life. But as long as we do not rebel against incoherence as a way of life, all that is possible within its service is incremental change. We can struggle to make it (or us) bigger or smaller; we can make it (or us) rather better or rather worse—but not fundamentally better. We can create what is new—concretely, or by changing our life from one drama to another, or by re-forming existing dramas or generating new dramas—as long as whatever we do remains in the service of incoherence. We are also free to oppose any such changes, though that is not easy in a life of rebellious competition for fragments—a life of constant change.[27]

---

27. We shall discuss this point more fully in Chapter 16.

No fundamental choices are open to us in the service of incoherence. As long as we live with this way of life, we cannot really know what such choices are. And even incremental changes are limited—if any of them threaten the power and the rewards of the currently powerful. And the theoretical thoughts available to us in the service of incoherence limit our vision. To be effective specialists, we divide our study of life into separate disciplines. Which academic discipline now explores the interconnections of the personal, political, historical, and sacred faces of our being and our choices between sacred sources?

To be as accurate and efficient as we can be in our exploration and use of cause and effect, we analyze primarily efficient causes: What specific actions are required to get this machine moving? What human genes probably cause a certain illness? However powerful these findings, all that we learn is that A leads to B. What then happens to C, or D, or even K—or to anything beyond the already established alphabet—we do not yet know and may not even care to find out. We resort to pesticides as soon as we have ascertained that they kill pests, without asking what other animals, farm workers, and consumers they may also injure or kill. After all, I only discovered this pesticide; I don't sell it. After all, I only sell this pesticide; I didn't make it.

The more powerful normally define our thoughts and actions about any fragment and its place and value. The work of women is normally paid less than the equivalent work of men. The domestic labor and child rearing by wives or single mothers does not count as work. In most countries, prostitution is a crime charged only against women—as if no male clients had ever been present. A mistress is no prostitute, however much a married man rewards her. Married women must never have lovers. Could we possibly permit women to marry women or men to marry men?

Systemic problems cannot be resolved by making particular incremental changes. Certainly it is possible to make changes for the worse. (Move the homeless out of our sight!) It is also possible to make changes for the better. (Provide them with shelter and food!) But we are inhibited within this way of life from asking each homeless person why he or she or their child is homeless (since no single concrete cause is at work) and asking why there are so many of them (there are certain archetypal dramas in the service of incoherence here at work)—and therefore to ask what needs to be done to put an end to homelessness.

We may at last pass laws to put an end to centuries of legally established racial discrimination, but we do not, as a body politic, seek to discover what we can and need to do together to overcome racial, ethnic, and gender discrimination—and our indifference to the poor—in all the other realms of our daily life. And in the service of incoherence, we normally do not act on such issues until we see the actual flames of destruction. And even then our first impulse is usually to restore law and order, not to work toward a community based on a shared sense of justice. Even the rebellions (not the ones led by Martin Luther King, Jr. or César Chávez) are usually based on a fragmentary surge of incoherence (or deformation)—flames and other forms of violence! Then what do the rebels plan to do?

It is essential that we struggle for incremental improvements today if that is the most we can do today. But even today we need also to work toward transformation even if all we can accomplish politically is to expose the limits of incoherence as a way of life.[28] Nothing we can achieve will ever be perfect. Even in the service of transformation, we can only attain a fundamentally new and better concrete resolution. But we can also attain the understanding of and capacity for a radically different way of life in which to renew such transformation again and again.

THE DEFEATED ACCEPT INCOHERENCE

Why do the defeated accept incoherence as a way of life? Why is there no rebellion against this way of life by the exploited, the deprived, the diminished, the excluded, the abused? The issues at stake are not small or the burden of a few. Even in many jobs, we face risk of hurt or even death, and our pay may not be sufficient to raise us beyond poverty. Even with jobs, we may not be able to afford doctors or medicines or have access to a good education or breathe clean air or drink clean water. Without jobs we will not have enough food and may have no safe place or any place to live. We may well die long before a life without such risks and pains would have come to an end. Those above us rebel again and again—but only within this way of life. What prevents rebellion *against* this way?

The barriers are great. The liberal State was established (among other vital reasons) to prevent the most ardent pursuers of their self-interest from killing each other—and to prevent those alienated by this way of life from putting an end to it. Bloody outbursts by the discontented have occurred everywhere from time to time, and democratic liberal states have given way to authoritarian liberal states and vice versa. But nowhere in modern time has incoherence as a way of life been brought to an end except by forces of deformation. The most successful rebels within incoherence as a way of life also achieve the power to make sure, for the sake of their self-interest, to limit any political help that would increase the number of competitors. And for the powerful, those who do not have the money to make an "effective" demand for supplies do not count. And the workers they no longer need no longer count for them as human beings that they can and need to care about. Private property is protected by the public realm. Suffering by contrast

---

28. "Public policy problems are too complex to be well understood, too complex to be mastered. One develops a strategy to cope with problems, not to solve them." Decision-making therefore becomes and needs to be "disjointed incrementalism." Professor of Economics and Political Science at Yale University, Charles E. Lindblom, *The Intelligence of Democracy: Decision Making Through Mutual Adjustment*. The title for this subsection comes from page 148 of his book.

is seen as a private matter without public obligations. The powerful are no small obstacle to change on this score.

Is not the welfare state an important limit which a democratic liberal state can add to its agenda to inhibit the damages of capitalism and more generally of incoherence as a way of life? Such a limit has been advocated at least since Thomas Hobbes in the seventeenth century wrote in *Leviathan*. He wrote that since this system has been created to keep people pursuing their self-interest from putting each other to death, those in danger of dying from hunger because of their lack of success have the right to rebel against it. This kind of reasoning has given rise to one quite limited form of the welfare state. Measures are taken to keep the poor from rebelling—measures of control as well as aid—not on grounds of justice and compassion but out of self-interest on the part of the powerful. The so-called safety net for the poor in fact reflects a calculation of what minimum action will constitute a safety net for the people at the top and in the middle against rebellion from below.

The other form of the welfare state arises when the unemployed, and union-organized workers, and even parts of the middle class form nationwide organizations—as social democrats, Christian democrats, and (as a competitive threat also to the left) even Communists—strong enough to be taken seriously, separately or together, as a possible or frequent majority within a democratic liberal state. (These groups never gained this kind of strength in the United States where workers usually get fired if they go on strike.) In this kind of welfare state, people can count on healthcare and housing, regardless of their wages or employment, and can receive sufficient help to survive if unemployed.

Certainly it is better to live in the latter welfare state, but even there, everyone continues to pay the fundamental and serious human costs of living in the service of incoherence and its dominant dramas. The problems that put people on welfare and face them in that life cannot be solved within this way of life. The democratic liberal left has found no way of overcoming incoherence. Its supporters, even the poor, the sick, and discriminated against, are seen only—and many act only—as one special interest competing against others. Some of its party and trade union leaders replicate this way of life in their own kind of leadership and in colluding with leaders of more conservative parties. And as long as there is a safety net that insures survival, why rebel against this way of life?

The answer to that question—and to why any of these barriers to rebellion against incoherence as a way of life possesses a power to which we yield—is that we still remain enchanted and enchained by a living underlying patterning force. All these barriers are concrete manifestations of this still overarching drama.

As long as the defeated and not only the winners are still possessed by this archetypal story, all will persist in casting their lives in accordance with it. Its concrete examples matter—no archetype can exist without them. But it is the empowerment of the concrete through their sacred force by which we are defeated. That is why we accept its established authorities (even if not its particular representative) and its established modes and uses of power (even if not that person or his or her particular action). Indeed we fail to see its underlying patterning force because that very force focuses our attention on incremental concrete changes and short-term consequences and leaves us baffled by movements toward personal and political disasters.

What choices do the defeated have within this way of life—or beyond it? They must return to "industriousness, sobriety, thrift, self-discipline, deferment of gratification." This is the declared ideology at the top (never mind their actual behavior or the actual dynamics of this drama), and since the top is in fact at the top, many are the people at the bottom (given the authority of this view) who accept it. I blame myself for my defeat; I failed in my responsibility; I was not good enough; I can—I will—try again; meanwhile, I will try to survive as best as I can, though it is very hard. Some give up. I have no chance; they say they do not need me. Others accept that defeat by yielding to apathy—into passivity in the shadow of this stage.

Partial beings can, at most, take only partial actions, and when the less successful are condemned—not only by the dominant but also by the very spirit of this drama—as less worthy, their part diminishes even further. Not only have they lost the chance to be successful rebels; they are in fact no longer needed as a marketable commodity. They now belong to the underclass—powerless.[29] Unwanted even as a fragment within this way of life, their rebellion now, left unaware of the potentials of transformation, is more likely to lead into crime and drugs—into deformation.

In the daily travails in the service of incoherence, the central issues are limited to struggles over who can capture, enlarge, or build a new fortress, who is needed to supply the fortress while it lasts, and who is to live in the desert. Its living underlying patterning force enshrines and legitimizes not only its victories but also its defeats. This sacred force inflicts not only suppression of rebellion against this drama but also repression—rendering ourselves unconscious of who we can fully be as human beings, and of what now warps all four faces of our being and their interconnections.

The lives of the successful are materially more rewarding and physically safer, but even they are turned against themselves—against the wholeness of their being by all the dramas of incoherence. Even they are—at least unconsciously—starved.

---

29. At times, there are moments of recognition that incoherence as a way of life therefore becomes more and more costly even as it persists in one of the most prosperous and democratic societies. "Consider a different part of the reality of America today: a violent, drug-ridden, drug-infested reality; a reality in which the institutions of civilized social life have broken down; of disintegrated families, boarded up storefronts, schools that have become armed camps, and crack houses replacing community centers as the focus of neighborhood life." These are the words of Senator John Kerry of Massachusetts, speaking at Yale University, quoted by David Broder, *The Trenton Times*, April 2, 1992.

Conservatism—that is, policies trying to preserve what already exists, or once existed—therefore lacks solid foundations for enduring. The dissolution of emanation as a way of life has put in doubt all forms of legitimacy, a justification rooted more deeply than in the concrete text of particular laws—a legitimacy justifying the State, all duly passed laws, and community and family values. As we saw, there exists therefore all the more of a hankering for emanational relationships, but those also remain unstable. What has remained in place so far has been our emanational connection to the overarching drama of incoherence and to the archetypal stories in its service. But within that way of life, we have no awareness, no understanding, no acknowledged feeling of anything anchored in the depths—of nothing in which we can truly risk trust. That incapacity intrinsic to this way of life also makes it easier and more necessary for us to mask the human costs of incoherence.[30]

We are told again and again in this way of life to take personal responsibility. Yet our ability to respond (the content of the very word *responsibility*) is severely handicapped by the fact that our autonomy—*auto* meaning "self," *nomos* meaning "underlying order"—is constricted. And the very price of freedom is constituted not simply by our working within particular established procedures and with particular established authorities, but above all by our conformity to incoherence as the overarching drama as well as to the dramas in its service. That kind of freedom inhibits our caring and capacity for creativity, empathetic neighborliness, understanding, love, and justice.

Happily, while rebelling to enter Act II Scene 1 of the core drama of life is an essential step on the journey of transformation, consolidating incoherence as a way of life is not a requisite stage of human history. But since most of the world has already entered into this overarching drama, liberation will remain fundamentally incomplete if we now free ourselves only from particular dramas. To put an end to the basic limitations we have been discussing, we need to free ourselves from the way of life that gives birth to these foreshortened dramas. If there were no such living underlying patterning force, we would not know in our present being how to keep incoherence going by organizing it.

Just as emanation is not a synonym for all ways of life that were pre-modern, so incoherence is not a synonym for being modern. We have ample cause to reenter Act II and this time to go on to discover the underlying structure and dynamics of

---

30. Before I had come to be able to say what I am writing now, an undergraduate student of mine had written this in a class essay: "The Hobbesian man is a man in flight, always from himself. This is the true fear of the self. The fear that self-confrontation may expose him to experience which he would not be able to repress. This flight into objectivity, then, is a refuge from himself. This false rationality not only provides a shelter from himself, but also gives that flight a stamp of legitimacy. He is thus freed from any moral obligation, any links with . . . love and justice. The external world . . . becomes a place of desperate escape, a place where he can try and repress the fear of the self by gaining control over others." Praveen Kumar, May 13, 1977.

incoherence as a way of life. Thus we gain the insight and courage to empty ourselves of it and to be inspired in a fundamentally new way by our whole self and its interests and a life we can and need to share.*

One of the discussions we often had about the theory is its capacity to point out what is taking place on the level of the concrete as well as on the deeper level of our lives. We spoke often about the way of life of incoherence that arrested our lives as partial selves who were not fully present and therefore not able to respond to new kinds of problems. And because this way of life creates anxiety and urges us to be in a state of constant rebellion against those who would threaten our power, stories in its service such as capitalism, can turn violent.

Millions of Americans lost their life savings as a result of the accounting practices that inflated the earnings of corporations and thus drove up the value of stocks based on dishonest practices. The story of capitalism, as we have seen, in order to enhance power, again and again turned the workers in American corporations into commodities. This is evident from a comment by Robert S. Rester, a former plant manager who was with the McWane Corporation—one of the world's largest producers of cast-iron pipe—for twenty-four years: "The people, they are nothing. . . . They're just numbers. You move them in and out. I mean, if they don't do the job, you fire them. If they get hurt, complain about safety, you put a bull's-eye on them."[31]

At this point, capitalism as a drama is no longer enacted in the service of incoherence but enters a violence that profoundly wounds the four faces of our being. Our personal face is erased because we are treated as "nothing"; our political face is the recipient of a politics of anger, revenge, and exclusion, caught in a freefalling spiral of despair; our historical face cannot create new and better stories; and our sacred face is possessed by the Lord of deformation. Capitalism, at its worst, turns people into faceless consumers and workers who are considered as the acceptable casualties of the market. This expels the perpetrators *and* the victims from the core drama of life into the abyss of deformation.

---

* Manfred Halpern died before the tragedy of September 11, 2001 and the events following that have so challenged us as a people. So much of what he wrote about in this chapter regarding the power of the drama of capitalism to continue to possess us has, unfortunately, been confirmed even in the midst of the war on terrorism.

31. As quoted in *The New York Times*, in an article by David Barstow and Lowell Bergman, January 9, 2003, A1, A20.

6

Deformation

A Way of Life Moving Us toward Destructive Death

Deformation is an overarching drama that from the very beginning takes us beyond partial justice—justice that is biased and incomplete, and is therefore, in fact, often injustice—into evil. Like all archetypal dramas, deformation is not only shaped by its ending—an imposed premature death. It is also a process of inflicting or being afflicted by deeper and deeper evil. Its living underlying pattern can be recognized, halted, and overcome before it destroys us. To help us achieve such insight, so that we may intervene in time and counter with a healing response, is the main purpose of this chapter.

All of us are capable of entering into deformation—creating in our lives and those affected by it a fundamentally new and also fundamentally worse ordeal, just as we are all able to experience the other three ways of life. None is inescapable. Fascism is not a peculiarly German disease. Fundamentalism is not a strange Muslim aberration. We shall discuss these two particular cases of deformation, but nearly everywhere, today, dramas in increasing numbers are being enacted in the service of deformation.

We shall examine deformation as an underlying patterning process and not, as is usually done, by analogy to past historical events or by abstracting particular examples of it. That kind of analysis is often misleading. Hitler did not resemble any previous German ruler; many, therefore, could not recognize his nature in time. Mussolini was not an exact replica of Hitler; nonetheless he lived in the service of deformation.[1]

---

1. Robert Laurenty is currently at work on a book analyzing Italian fascism in the light of the theory of transformation. Eric King is writing a book on experiences of deformation in the Wynnefield section of Philadelphia from the same theoretical perspective.

The United States supported Saddam Hussein with weapons and money before his invasion of Kuwait. Did this invasion of Kuwait turn him into a Hitler, as President Bush put it, or did his prolonged warfare against Iraqi Shiites, Kurds, political opponents, and Iran have no aspects of deformation? Did our bombing of many tens of thousands of Iraqis during our attacks have no deforming face? The American Constitution outlaws punishment that is "cruel and unusual," but in war we still take much cruelty for granted because it is not unusual. Deformation is not a single concrete entity or an abstracting label, but a way of life which as a process can come to destroy us.

What renders us vulnerable to deformation? All of us, as we have seen, begin all the stories of our life in the first Scene of Act I of the core drama of life—at a point where, thanks to our birth into this story or our becoming enchanted with it, we feel as certain and secure as possible about where we are, thanks to the emanational power of the source of our story. In the service of emanation, we halt ourselves within the confines of this overarching way and the stories in its service. But how can we still be in Act I Scene 1 if incoherence as a way of life has arrested us in the first Scene of Act II?

To arrest ourselves in the core drama of life requires our submission to the emanational power of a living underlying patterning force. In the service of emanation, we cannot believe that this sacred source would desert us, though it is dying all over the world. In the service of incoherence, we remain unconscious of our sacred source even though its force holds us in adherence. Consciously, we devote our life to organizing rebellions, but unconsciously we are being held in a new emanational embrace, a new form of Act I Scene 1. When, in the service of incoherence, such unconscious emanational relationships break, we become vulnerable to deformation—vulnerable, though not inevitably caught.

Whenever that kind of emanational power is breaking or else is being threatened beyond its own present strength, and re-formation in the service of emanation or incoherence has come to be beyond anyone's power (or can no longer constitute an adequate response), we have only two choices left—transformation or deformation.[2] Transformation never keeps us within an emanational relationship but even from its inspirational beginning gives us a conscious, critical, creative, and caring capacity we can grow and test again and again through the core drama of life.

Deformation, as we shall see, attracts us through its powerful fantasies of pseudo-emanation. What deformation seems to offer us in such crises of power is not simply more power, but absolute power. That is its greatest attraction—and

---

2. Re-formation in the service of emanation or incoherence may bring about a major incremental change, but arrests, even new arrests, continue to render us vulnerable, by their very nature, to new crises we cannot effectively deal with within the prevailing overarching drama.

its seemingly most familiar aspect, for we think we already know what power is about—power rising within ourselves, over ourselves, and over others. And now that we are at serious risk of losing or have already lost our present form of power, here is a way of life that seems to promise total power. In fact, in every instance, deformation offers us not even an arrest within the core drama of life, but only a fragmenting fragment of life whose sacred source inspires us to move ourselves, and all those over whom we have total power, through the only exit of this core drama—into the abyss.

This road always begins in Act I Scene 1 when—despite its seemingly extraordinary security, and despite the power of our emanational way of life, or of our emanational relationship to incoherence, or of a drama in its service crucial to us—our present life is being destroyed. Destroyed not because of a new inspiration that attracts us and leads us into rebellion on behalf of a new form of emanation, incoherence, or transformation—but destroyed by the overpowering actions of others.

This is no small fact. We do not initiate deformation as long as our present relationship to ourselves and to others in the dramas of our life is bearable, tenable, or fruitful. When we initiate our desertion of our present emanational source, our rebellion always leads us into ways other than deformation. We yield to the attraction of a more potent pseudo-emanation only if our present emanational source has weakened beyond our needs, and does not or cannot tune in to our needs. The archetypal source of deformation can reach us so that we burst out in anger and say to the other (or say it only within ourselves), "I could kill you!" But we do not kill because sources of emanation (if not yet of transformation) still hold us back. But we cannot prevent the risks of deformation because sources of emanation—as long as they possess us and they remain mysteriously powerful even to themselves—are beyond our and their own timely understanding of what they (and we) are still doing.

Always, when any emanational relationship dies because of what the other does, we experience a deep sense of betrayal. How could such a powerful, mysterious source of great security—or its concrete embodiment—have deserted us? How could anyone have dared to desert such a source of emanation or its concrete embodiment? Without such a bond, we feel we cannot bear this loss or survive such a crisis. Such a betrayal leads us to what we feel is a deeply justified right to murder, or if by now we lack even that much power, to suicide—or to resort to their moral and symbolic equivalents.

Having been contained within an emanational relationship, we cannot yet truly know who we are or how to stand on our own feet. Our move into rebellion in the first Scene of Act II is therefore a brutally harmful step. And our past trauma and our compensating fantasy of the new kind of power we require is so overwhelming that in the second Scene of Act II, we can gain no new understanding; we cannot free ourselves of anything that now possesses us. Instead, in that Scene, we attach ourselves more fervently than ever to our new fantasy of power and exit into destructive death. As we shall see, all the many different dramas in the service of deformation take this same path.

Deformation is a fall from the core drama of life—the only great fall that leads into more and more evil. Powerlessness, like power, corrupts. But absolute powerlessness, like absolute power, corrupts absolutely. This kind of response to the loss of power brings leaders and led together for the absolute fall into evil.

Deformation is not simply a road to death, and is certainly not the only road to death. There is no deformation in dying peacefully of old age, or in dying in the cause of defending the good, the helpless, or oneself against tyrants, or in dying wisely—seeing life as Socrates did, as a ripening for a continuing (if different) and even more fruitful journey. That kind of death is not an arrest, but a change in landscape.

Deformation is not merely a way of death, but one of degeneration, destruction, and dissolution in the service of evil leading toward destructive death. People around the world have long recognized that death of the body is not the only thing that counts. For all people in the service of emanation and incoherence, as we have seen, vital aspects of being are repressed, and hence not allowed a natural or fruitfully creative life. In transformation, we die—but not in body—in order to be reborn. In deformation, the dying begins with treating someone else—but also our self—as less than human or as not visible as a human being, and rolls downward toward extermination.

We will not notice deformation in time if we see it only as it pushes the last survivors into nothingness. Deformation is not only Hitler presiding over the Holocaust. And holocausts are not the only examples of deformation. We have trouble keeping our eyes and ears—and our hearts—open to cases of deformation on our side. Great Britain and France, after winning the war against fascism and broadening democracy at home, tried brutally to prolong their domination over peoples for whom Western imperialism and colonization had involved many decades and sometimes centuries of institutionalized deformation. Directly and through surrogates, the United States organized and funded the killing of hundreds of thousands, the largest number of them civilians, in Southeast Asia, Africa, Central America, and elsewhere—all in the name of preventing the spread of Soviet deformation.[3]

Unhappily, the seeming security of Act I Scene 1 of the core drama of life can be gravely damaged when we cannot yet be ready to leave it. We may be abandoned even while we are still children and cannot know how to take care of ourselves. Or we may, even as children, be beaten or abused—which can lead to feeling stranded, intimidated, and always at risk. No recognition is given to who we actually are.

---

3. "It became necessary to destroy the town to save it," declared a Major of the U.S. Army, Ben Tre, in Vietnam in 1968 as quoted in Don Oberdorfer, *Tet!* 184.

Many are the societies that legally allow children to be beaten by their parents and teachers, and few indeed are the societies that are prepared to intervene and protect. Such a child may grow up fantasizing about becoming free at last to find someone to cling to who actually wants to enlist our rigorous obedience to a cause of seeming glory—or indeed to become at last a truly dominating person, or to rebel at any time and occasion it pleases us.[4] It is indeed difficult but not impossible for such a child to imagine or to respond to a fourth alternative—to rebel against all these archetypal variants and to work to transform the society that gives rise to them so that no child will be beaten again.

Deformation begins with the first blow with which a parent strikes a child in order to turn him into an obedient puppet. It begins at the moment a young girl is made to understand that men are always superior in their very nature. However seemingly small the beginning, it is life-threatening. There is in this movement into the abyss no natural stopping place. When one's status as a lesser human being has been ritualized (as in the case of castes or women) in the service of emanation, or routinized (as in the case of races, workers, or women) in the service of incoherence, is that deformation? Yes. Deformation can become custom or routine.

When evil is integrated in these ways it becomes almost invisible to the dominant—and to the dominated who have assimilated the same archetypal drama into their being. At least until the 1980s, battered women in the United States gained no protection—no action at all—even if they did call the police. There were few, if any, shelters for battered women. There is no natural halt to the process of being battered. For a long time, doctors took the diseases of women less seriously in their research and treatments than the diseases of men. They used the white, male body as their template for research—thus excluding men of color and all women and children from their field of vision.

Cases of deformation differ in intensity and scope. But from its first moment, deformation constitutes a force moving us out of the core drama of life—an increasing distancing from the opportunity to become a whole human being. No countervailing power then inhibits the dominant if the oppressed still arouse the oppressors' wrath. Nothing awakens their compassion, since indifference to the suffering of the lesser is consonant with the internal dynamics of the drama of

---

4. Alice Miller, *For Your Own Good: Hidden Cruelty in Child-Rearing and the Roots of Violence*. Miller tells us that "among all the leading figures of the Third Reich, I have not been able to find a single one who did not have a strict and rigid upbringing" (p. 62). "The men and women who carried out 'the Final Solution' did not let their feelings stand in their way for the simple reason that they had been raised from infancy not to have any feelings of their own but to experience their parents' wishes as their own." Though I have since read Miller's book, her deeply revealing work was first brought to my attention by Find Findsen who drew on her insights in his splendid analysis, "The Road to Evil in the Holocaust: How Ordinary People Were Enlisted in the Service of Deformation," Junior Paper, Princeton University, 1993.

deformation. If the lesser protest, they must next at least be rendered invisible. This is the moving reality—as we shall explore in later chapters—of institutionalized racism or sexism as forms of deformation.

That there is so much deformation in the world—that hundreds of millions of lives this day are being pushed or pulled into the abyss—does not lessen the significance of the evil of one holocaust, or of one child being battered. Everyone is unique and a face of the sacred; everyone is a potential participant in the transformation of the cosmos of human relations.

Considering that deformation is a process that ends in the evil of destructive death, why call the battering of women, men, and children evil? Why call segregation or pollution evil? While we are talking, most of the people suffering at this moment in these ways are still alive. If a woman dies because she is too poor to pay for medical care, nobody in particular killed this person. That this kind of death is a routine fact of life that does not merit our attention demonstrates how evil becomes institutionalized in an environment in which some people are considered lesser human beings.

In the service of a way of life of organizing and reorganizing fragments, there is indeed no way of talking objectively about evil until we have conclusive evidence of death and its causes, that is, after it is too late. Meanwhile, in that vein, we can at most speak only about probabilities. As for evil, in our seemingly secular society, we shrink away from the use of this term in everyday or scholarly discourse—except for subjective or religious outcries.[5]

We lack a process-oriented language able to give full voice to the process-oriented theory of transformation. Every archetypal drama, including even the ways of life that arrest us, patterns a process that from beginning to end shapes the structure, dynamics, values, and purposes of our enactments. In the drama of transformation, we live from Act I Scene 2 in the process of creating the fundamentally better even though it does not fully emerge until the second Scene of Act III. So also the creation of the fundamentally new which is fundamentally worse is not evil solely as a final judgment. Deformation becomes completely evil at its ending in the abyss, but it is also evil to push or to be pushed into this path to destruction. Its ending is not inescapable, but it will end in calamity if we stay on that path. While we stay on it, it becomes more and more evil as it hurts, damages, diminishes, and cripples us psychologically and physically. Evil is the experience of this process.

If we say that deformation leads us into more and more evil, are we relativizing our evaluation? No. We are not saying, "Oh, you are merely an exploited worker

---

5. In the United States in the late '90s, "good" has also practically disappeared from our language. If we say "that's good," we usually mean that at most, it is acceptable. If it were really good, we would call it at least "cool" or "fantastic" or "terrific."

employed in an unsafe factory; at least you are getting paid. At least you are still alive, though your arm still hurts from last year's injury. At least you are no longer a slave." Deformation is not a path to evil but a process of evil from its beginning—which also too often ends in destructive death. This view of the reality of evil deeply and greatly enlarges our realization of how widespread and frequent evil is in human lives.

But we are not crippled from the beginning of our exile from paradise to overcome evil because Eve and Adam sought to eat the fruit of the tree of the knowledge of good and evil. We are not each one of us crippled again by that original sin from the day of our birth, as Augustine proposed. We can enact fundamentally better alternatives to the injustice of partial justice. We can even enact fundamentally better alternatives to evil.[6]

Everyone at every moment constitutes the four faces of the sacred. We are threatened with losing the protection of and confidence in any present sacred source of our being whenever any drama or the way of our life fails to help us deal with the problems we confront. That does not immediately mean that we give up on the Lord who inspired us to enact these living underlying patterns. We can instead see ourselves as an individual who failed because we are a sinner or because we made inadequate efforts or errors in the pursuit of power. We try again. We re-form our participation or the drama at stake. Or we accept our failure or even our punishment as justified by the very values of the drama we enacted. But if we are still powerful in the existing drama or way of life, but cannot hope to maintain our power in the face of threatening or actual failure, we may be tempted to resort to deformation or at least ally ourselves with it.

We may, as did the Pope, resort to brutal inquisitions, or we may, as a feudal lord, go to war against all those who oppose our becoming absolute monarch of the state. If we become truly powerless within the existing drama or way of life, we may be tempted to assert or deny ourselves even if our response leads to destructive death. We may be tempted, but deformation is not inescapable.

There is no escape from sacred sources. Even when our god is dying or has left us bereft in this particular crucial instance, the realm of the sacred has not come to an end. Instead of searching to understand why it has become necessary and helpful to empty ourselves of our old Lord and that Lord's patterning forces, we can be drawn above all toward clutching what seems like a new and more powerful emanational source. Deformation initially strikes most of us in this fashion because emanation is a familiar experience to us. But deformation is always a case of pseudo-emanation. It does not serve to arrest us but sends us upon an apocalyptic way of destroying and being destroyed. Its often exceedingly rigid order or sudden, seemingly

---

6. We shall augment this discussion of evil in the chapters dealing with justice and with our connection to the sacred.

spontaneous bursts of compulsiveness exist solely for that purpose—enforced through the obverse threat: "Oh, I know I'll die if I don't do that."

What sacred force inspires us not to ask why we feel rage, terror, and panic but to make ourselves the agent of terror or to succumb to such a deep sense of disillusionment that we sink apathetically out of despair into the same exit? That force is symbolized by Satan—the adversary of life. As we shrink, he inspires us to turn life into a fantasy: This leader or this dogma or this drug will increase our power to satanic proportions—final and unquestionable power, with anything justified in its name! No fragment could keep us devouring and being devoured in this great fall unless there were an archetypal power behind it. That mere figment of reality which inflates us—or adversely deflates us into nothingness—acts as a prison that allows the darkness of Satan's abyss to focus onto us and to become our source of destruction. Our new seeming omnipotence therefore renders us—and others—more vulnerable than ever before. If we join with Satan, we are deformed until we are formless.

From the perspective of the core drama of life, evil is an ever more wounding process as the drama of deformation moves on toward destruction. We do not reserve the term evil only for its ending. We experience evil from its beginning. I want to underline this point again because of the reality and truth of such evil from our perspective. The perspective of the drama of transformation makes us aware of the power of evil in all its phases and enhances our sense of need and our capacity to act to prevent, to stop, and to heal deformation.

From the standpoint of Augustine, we are prone to do evil thanks to our very nature and we therefore also lack the capacity to overcome evil. Reinhold Niebuhr writes, "The Tragedy of human history consists precisely in the fact that human life cannot be creative without being destructive, that biological urges are enhanced and sublimated by demonic spirit and this spirit cannot express itself without committing the sin of pride."[7] Niebuhr's viewpoint was not fatalistic but was intended to encourage American leftist liberals to take stronger measures against communism and domestic poverty. But later (and without his knowledge), it encouraged the CIA to justify its covert violence against possible Soviet influence all over the world.[8]

Carl Gustav Jung, despite his deep concern for transforming people's lives, was bound by a vision of a fundamental limit to change: "It turns out that all archetypes spontaneously develop favorable and unfavorable, light and dark, good and bad effects. In the end, we have to acknowledge that the self is a *complexion oppositorum*, precisely because there can be no reality without polarity."[9] Jung taught us

---

7. Reinhold Niebuhr, *The Nature and Destiny of Man: A Christian Interpretation*, 10–11.

8. In the late 1940s, I served for two years with Reinhold Niebuhr on the Executive Committee of the leftist liberal Americans for Democratic Action and later heard about his influence directly from members of the Central Intelligence Agency as I worked as an intelligence analyst in the Department of State.

9. Carl G. Jung, *Aion: Researches into the Phenomenology of the Self*, 267.

how to recognize its manifestations. But he did not recognize how the darkness of archetypes was strengthened in two ways of life, turned into deadly evil in a third way, and how darkness and evil can be understood and overcome in a fourth way. Evil is no mere opposite of good—no mere absence of good. To break with evil relationships is creative without entering into destructive deformation. If we do not know how to stop it and also overcome it, evil harms us to the point of early and unnecessary death.

Satan is not an inescapable source of evil. I use the familiar name of Satan in an unfamiliar way to symbolize the sacred force of a way of life arising from the exit from the core drama of life—a force to which we can enable ourselves to say no by emptying ourselves of and sending into the abyss the sacred force we have come to understand as unbearable. Satan is not an external cause of evil and certainly not an abstraction. Satan can arise within our being, for we cannot be a being without also a sacred source. We can come to know our source, however, and say yes or no through our very being.

DEFORMATION BEGINS IN FANTASY

The different kinds of movement into deformation are shaped by the archetypal dramas in its service. All of them begin in fantasy and animate us toward destructive death thanks to the very nature of fantasy.

To clarify this matter, we need to rediscover the distinction between imagination and fantasy—two concepts that we have tended in recent times to use as if they were synonyms. Imagination is our intuitive capacity to appreciate the image of something we had not previously realized in our thought or practice. The empirical test of imagination is that this image, once put into practice, allows us to make ever more fruitful connections with ourselves and with others, and to resolve the actual problem we face. By contract, fantasy is our intuitive power to become so fascinated—so possessed—by one small part of reality that we are bound to distort the nature of this fragment, just as it is bound to distort much of the rest of our vision and action.

The empirical evidence that we are involved with fantasy rather than imagination is that, as we try to realize our fragment in practice, it cuts us off more and more from ourselves, from others, and from the problems that confront us. Fantasy, too, draws upon and creates reality—lies also constitute a reality—but this is a distorted and distorting kind of reality.[10] Fantasy can keep us at a loss, disconnected, while otherwise we still remain in the service of emanation or incoherence. But fantasy by its very nature can attach us so intensely to a fragment that

---

10. We shall explore the distinction between true and false realities and between the four aspects of consciousness—thought, sensation, intuition, and feeling—in greater detail in Chapter 15.

it distorts and breaks our being even while it totally seizes our sense of being and our sense of our world. Fantasy, by disconnecting us from the rest of reality and certainly from truth, always frightens us—and compensates us for our anxiety by binding us (within ourselves and with other followers) to such a fragment against all the rest of the world.

On a large billboard (a sign that went up all over Germany), which I could see right across from our apartment in my hometown once the Nazis came to power, I saw this: "You are nothing. Your folk is everything." The Nazis had taken a real part of our life (blood) and turned it into a fantasy ("pure blood")—and this "pure blood" into the mysterious and overwhelming source of life (in fact, of death) of the master race and all it touched. To bond the folk—the followers of this fantasy—against the rest of the world, against the rest of reality, another slogan, on thousands of billboards, said this: *Ein Volk, ein Reich, ein Führer*—"One people, one empire, one leader." The first message says you are not merely a partial being, but nothing. Yet at the same time you are also all you can be, because you now embody the only source that counts. Deformation acknowledges that you have been abandoned and offers the opposite of abandonment—total possession.

The fantasies of deformation warp our past, present, and future. We are the only ones who count and who know what to do—only our gang, only our religious group, only our political movement, only our nation counts.

Our past? Khomeini declared that Muslims must restore a society in which the ruler strictly enforces all the sacred laws of Islam. But no such ruler ever existed. Our present? The point is not to solve the problems of the present; they only spell out doom. Our task is to put an end to the present. Our future? It is apocalyptic redemption—to achieve "ultimate freedom, ultimate happiness, and ultimate joy."[11]

People in some dramas in the service of deformation may also resort to scientific research, technical and bureaucratic efficiency, and hard work, but all of it is warped by its overarching values and purpose. In many of these dramas, people also experience a solidarity of community with their fellow followers far more intense than—or indeed in sharp contrast to—the life they had hitherto experienced in incoherence. But then our community is constituted only of us or of potential converts—but not of any other human beings. Resorts to modern means of power and to an intensely united community may well attract followers who do not yet recognize that these are means toward a death-dealing half-life.

We shall soon discuss a number of different dramas in the service of deformation. But there is also, both in our past and in our present, another frequent path of

---

11. The words in court of Shoko Asahara, the leader of the Aum Shinrikyo movement that organized a nerve-gas attack on the Tokyo subway system. *The New York Times*, April 25, 1996.

deformation onto which we push and station other people while we remain otherwise within our prevailing way of life. Both emanation and incoherence as ways of life can arrest us from further destruction, but arrest requires power to defend the established stability and its limits. Since arrests in the core drama of life render our existence more fragile in our incompleteness, especially those more powerful—in order to sharply, widely and persistently limit threats to their power—have compelled others to live in stations on the path of deformation.

INCOHERENCE IN ALLIANCE WITH DEFORMATION

The three stations of seeming arrest in the service of the still dominant way of life are in fact, as we shall see, stations on the road to destructive death. At first glance, the first two of the three stations we are about to analyze seem simply designed to keep "them" in "their" place. But as we shall see, this alliance of what are conventionally called respectable people with deformation deeply harms "them." These stations seriously diminish the four faces of our being and hence our capacity to take ourselves seriously or to be taken seriously.

The first stage on this path is to be treated as a lesser human being. But if anyone is not needed by the dominant even as a lesser one, he or she is compelled to enter the stage of the invisible. The third and last stage is in fact a time to die—the end of this path. It is not an inevitable ending, but all too often, the ending for the lesser and the invisible who suffer an early death because we have neglected and rejected them as human beings. We shall now explore this crowded path.

"They"—the lesser human beings—constitute the majority of human beings in most societies. "They" are, for example, the weaker sex—weaker, since only "we" know what constitutes a real human being able to occupy any position of power, including any position that requires hard-nosed decision-making, beginning with being head of the family. "They" are, for example, members of a different race or—in the United States at least until the 1940s—"they" are members of a religion different from ours. When injustice is done to them, it does not matter as much. We recall being told why slaves had to be beaten so hard: "they" felt it less; or why "they," the Vietnamese, kept fighting so hard from 1942 to 1973: Asians value life less.

Certainly, if a woman is not related to us (or of our social class, as class is defined by men like ourselves), we can treat her without respect. Unless we need her to serve us in other roles as a lesser being, we shall indeed treat her as invisible. If a woman from the middle or higher classes is raped, she had better become invisible—or else destroy herself, at least psychologically. But if she is from the lower classes, why not have her assimilate this experience and become a lesser being, that is, a prostitute? The abuse of women became a political issue only quite recently when "they"—women in our country—dared to turn this matter, which men had rendered private and hence invisible, into a political issue.

But if compelling still larger numbers of lesser men and women to come under our control will bring us more power and profit, then let us be imperialists and colonialists—until the 1960s on a vast scale. We knew from the beginning that they were lesser human beings. In the days of emanation, we realized that they lived outside the only sacred container—ours. In the modern age, we saw that on their own most of them did not know how to modernize, that is, how to westernize—as if the West had solved the basic problems of the modern age.

Human beings in the service of incoherence are still only partial beings, but they are free and able to compete for power. Lesser human beings are not permitted to do so, but their reduced position has also tamed them in their self-confidence and purposeful self-discipline.

We cannot trust any of the lesser to support our power. Why? To translate covert or overt assertions of bias into the terms of transformational theory (but still to express their prejudiced nature), we say this: We regard all others who do not obey and conform to our source of emanation (the archetypal drama of incoherence)—or by their very nature seem unable or unwilling to do so—as deep threats to our very existence. In the service of emanation, most of the powerful and their followers felt the same way about these alien others.

"They" are invisible. We do not want to see "them." We certainly do not need them. They are not permitted to be visible. James Baldwin, in *The Fire Next Time*, wrote of growing up in Harlem and never being allowed as a teenager in the 1930s to go south of 110th Street, even to the main building of the public library at 42nd Street. I can vouch for it. I lived on West 83rd and went to school on 89th Street. No Black teenager was ever visible there. As President Reagan said during his campaign in 1980, in his youth we had no race problem in the United States. Now segregation has come to an end, but the unassimilated have no choice but to remain in ghettos—invisible in exile.

We remove beggars and the homeless not from suffering in our society but from our neighborhood. Many people on welfare in the United States will be made invisible if they cannot find a job within two years. Why keep the "structurally unemployed" in our mind—or in our heart? No one among the lesser and the invisible is ever understood or treated as an individual, but only as a stock character in this drama. But I, by contrast, have an ego!

In the Muslim world, until recently (and in some countries even now), half the population were rendered invisible as soon as they reached puberty—except for their eyes under the veil—lest they risk the honor of men. Until the other day—and all too often still today, even in the West—we could not imagine seeing a woman at work in any significant political, economic, or academic position nor, in the West, anyone not white.

Being rendered lesser or invisible is often to be left to die before our time. Even at the end of the twentieth century, about 40,000,000 Americans never get to see a doctor in their entire life. Indifference can kill, too often while the invisible are still young.

The road from lesser to invisible is very slippery, at home or among the people abroad who are foreign to us. During the nineteenth century and the first half of the twentieth century, the British viewed the Near East (that is, nearer to Europe than the Far East) as involving above all the security of "the road to India." The British and French were forced, by growing nationalist movements among the over one hundred million people who actually live there, to surrender their domination of this region. But as its oil became a major resource for the West, President Eisenhower became worried. He called the Near East "a vacuum."

In fact, the West played a major role in shattering emanation as the dominant Middle Eastern way of life, but no Western government has deemed it necessary to understand and deal helpfully with the fundamental human problems that have arisen all over that region. The exploitation, poverty, and suffering of the majority of people around the world remain invisible to most of us most of the time. But within our anxious unconscious, the invisible remain "hypervisible."[12] Even when those in danger of extermination render themselves invisible at home by surging into exile abroad, many of us still find it hard to treat them as human beings in desperate need of our help.

Extermination: When we are entirely enlisted in the service of deformation, we must not trust those who are or seem to be invisible. We will kill—if they rebel, or might rebel—all who cannot or will not assimilate our beliefs. Stalin killed millions of peasants unwilling or unable to accept the collectivization of farms. He killed millions of Communists who did not share his own fantasy of Communism. But even in the service of incoherence, we often ally ourselves with deformation to conquer others in order to enhance our power and profits. During what officially we called the Cold War, we exterminated (and subsidized others to exterminate) many hundreds of thousands of human beings lest, as we fantasized, the Soviet Union use them to conquer us. Authoritarian liberal regimes in the service of incoherence will often torture and kill dissidents.

But most of the premature dying of the lesser and the invisible is brought about by the inflicted withering of the faces of being and of the bodily vessel. These stages diminish our capacity to take ourselves seriously. They diminish our chance to be helped by others while we are compelled to live there. We are denied adequate food, education, healthcare, or housing. We receive less protection or no protection

---

12. I borrow this term from Katharine L. Balfour and Princeton University Dept. of Politics, "The Evidence of Things Not Said: Race Consciousness and Political Theory," a doctoral dissertation which contains revealing analysis of race and politics (vii, 228).

from the law; indeed, we are likely to suffer from the way its enforcers treat us in court and in prison. We make a living in jobs that can poison or mortally wound us as we work.[13]

Since the governing drama imposed upon us does not treat us as fully human, and since we are told and shown that there is little or no room for us in society, one possibility still open to us is to depress ourselves into apathy or despair. What emanational source could now possibly inspire discipline in us or help us gain self-confidence or give us a sense of response-ability? Our psyche is dying, because what is the point of facing the fact that we are suffering, that we are nobody? We withdraw, even from our self, because there is nothing we can do about it anyway.[14]

Or else we assert ourselves underground and try to gain the power and profits of crime. If poverty alone were the cause of crime, crime would be higher in poorer than in richer countries. That is not the case. To be inspired by one of the archetypes of crime (there is no single such archetype), when we live a poor life in a country that is not poor requires essentially also to have been rendered a lesser or invisible being—and hence to feel threatened by still worse risks than crime.[15] Crime, depending upon the drama enacted, throws the victim upon the station of being lesser or even of being exterminated while criminals themselves intend to remain invisible—on their own terms, in order to avoid exile in prison.

THE POWERFUL INTERNALIZE THE THREE STAGES ON THE PATH TO DEFORMATION

While we arrest the major dramas of our life in the service of incoherence, we cannot diminish the life of others even beyond our own biased and incomplete nature except by also rendering ourselves lesser or invisible and threatening our very own existence—at least with respect to our actions toward people we have thus stationed. In outward appearance and in its effect upon those thrust upon the stations of the path of deformation, the behavior of the powerful afraid for their power looks like the obverse of these three stations: I treat them that way because

---

13. From a different theoretical perspective but a similar ethical perspective, Iris Marion Young has written a vivid, carefully documented scholarly book on "five fundamental and grave categories of oppression" in the United States: "exploitation, marginalization, powerlessness, cultural imperialism, and violence." Iris M. Young, *Justice and the Politics of Difference*, 40.

14. American Indians in 1988 committed suicide at ten times the rate of White Americans.

15. Richer people who still more rapaciously resort to crimes of theft or disobedience of laws on worker or consumer safety may also have fantasies (or indeed may be right) about their power to (politically) avoid prosecution or successfully bribe possible prosecutors. Have such people ever been treated as lesser at home—as unloved unless totally successful in their rebellion to achieve great power and profit? Certainly rich criminals are able to steal far larger amounts than poor criminals. But they seldom receive as much time in prison as poorer robbers who seize far less money.

only I count. I am bigger than anyone. I am the only one really visible. They cannot, must not reach me. If I let them, they might destroy me.[16]

But when we dehumanize others, we also dehumanize ourselves, even if we do it under the illusion of grandeur. As long as a man does not treat a woman equally as a human being, he also denies himself the free and full experience of the archetypal feminine (which concretely will emerge differently in a man) through his own being as well as in and with a woman. He will know and experience even the archetypal masculine only within this lesser and, in part, invisible framework.

How many children, even of the powerful, are raised in alliance with deformation? Yes, we want you above all to learn to be competent in our dominant way of life, but now you are still a mere child, to be seen but not heard. But now stay with your caretaker, or go upstairs or go away to a boarding school. I cannot afford to be home with you; business calls me. You do not matter—just as I do not matter—unless we devote all seemingly awake hours of every day to becoming instrumentally competent or powerful. "What shades we are, what shadows we pursue."[17]

CAPITALISM IN ALLIANCE WITH DEFORMATION

Capitalism (and all forms of authoritarian liberalism) makes a major contribution toward the alliance between incoherence and deformation. Capitalism provided one of the major inspirations for colonialism and imperialism. But this sense of authoritarian capitalism remains alive both at home and abroad. Workers, in most countries, must not assert themselves. They are only doing what machines cannot yet do. Workers are often injured by the work they do. The adequacy of their income, their ability (given their work schedule) to participate in family and community life does not matter to us. As human beings, they do not matter as much as profits do, as we capitalists do.

Capitalists are not in favor of increasing competition: "Why should we let vast new numbers of others join the competition for the heights of power within our institutionalized rebellion? We are the only ones who matter, and we still have the power to enforce our domination." This governing view is often shared by the middle and lower classes—a position within capitalism even more fragile to hold on to.

Capitalism often reduces the partial beings within its ranks to lesser human beings. Workers are treated solely as a commodity harnessed to perform preprogrammed routines. Even the trained and educated may be treated only as a more

---

16. "Many people believe that in order to raise themselves, they must put others down. I realized a long time ago that by putting others down, you are effectively putting yourself down, because it is a naked display of your own inadequacies and insecurities." Kebba Jobarteh, in an essay for my class on Personal and Political Transformation at Princeton University, 1994.

17. This is a statement made on his deathbed, in the early nineteenth century, by British Prime Minister William Pitt.

useful commodity, never to be consulted beyond their specialty on the value and purpose of service or products. And the authoritarian way in which many bosses treat their employees also dehumanizes them. There is a thin line between being partial and being treated as a lesser human being, but one condition is still fundamentally worse than the other is.

The invisible? The invisible are not even part of the market, for they cannot demand supplies. *Demand* means "effective demand" and they do not have the money. We pollute the air, the water, the earth—but we do not live here; we live *there*. Indifference and inaction by the powerful, which hopelessly cuts off the powerless from the present and the future, can kill. For example, in "advancing" agricultural societies, more and more millions of human beings have had their land taken away (having worked their land for centuries without a written title) by government-supported landlords who primarily use machines to grow and harvest crops for export. Except in the less than two dozen capitalist countries that offer adequate state-supported welfare, the lesser and the invisible die much sooner than others living within capitalist countries, regardless of growth in gross national product.

Can we escape the three stages on the path of deformation through assimilation? Is not our assimilation into the dominant culture and of the most promising dramas in its service the proper path to success? Most societies around the world in the service of emanation refused to assimilate even neighboring outsiders. That sense of sacred insulation is still very much alive today. That sense of containment has remained a source of cohesion or has taken a new shape through the nation-state.

In the past, Christians far more than other emanational adherents worked and prayed to convert nonmembers—and often even forced them to convert—lest they go to hell when they die.[18] And since those who remained non-Christians were destined to go to hell, it was also morally right to kill them without regret. In the modern West, these dynamics of *convert or die* are not dead. The sacred source of incoherence, even though we do not call it God, is nonetheless our only true Lord. And sacred also are the archetypal fragments of the ethnic, racial, and cultural past which still inspire the powerful. *Assimilate or be rejected*.

But such a form of assimilation—if you mean to rise upward in the service of incoherence—always demands uncritical acceptance of the canon of the dominant way of life. You, who had been one of "them," must now turn yourself entirely into the only triumphantly right way of being human, or else you will never be trusted. You must give up your critical consciousness, even more so than the

---

18. The Southern Baptist Church in 1993, taking the population of each county in Alabama and subtracting the number of those who belonged to churches that do not closely match the beliefs of the Southern Baptists, concluded that 46.1% of that state's population are at risk of going to hell when they die. (*Trenton Times*, September 18, 1993.)

main shapers of the society into which you have been incorporated, for you must *not* now speak—within the business or executive governmental organization in which you work—of what you once knew most immediately: the suppressed and repressed needs and suffering of your own former group. Once you have been incorporated—that is, taken over—you must abandon them and join the powerful in treating the unassimilated as lesser or invisible. In French colonies, such native collaborators were called *les evolués*—"the evolved ones."[19] But they were on "perennial probation,"[20] for their skin, their names, and their accents didn't match those of the white ruling elite.

The growth of democratic liberalism and the demand for loyalty to the nation-state created opportunities for assimilation of men (not yet women) in Western Europe earlier than in the United States. In these democratic countries of Europe, labor and socialists were able to organize more effectively than in the United States—in part because the emanationally inspired boundaries between different ethnic groups were (in contrast to today's Europe) not as high as they have been in the United States. But since this kind of assimilation opens the door only to a new arrest—to becoming a partial being instead of remaining lesser or invisible—all the changes have been incremental in terms of welfare for the poor and with respect to legal (but not yet fully human) rights for the less powerful or the powerless.[21] But even the highly competent—as we shall see in a later chapter—are valued solely for their competence and not fully as human beings.

Now that assimilation is growing, so also is a counter-movement—a national response in a way of life based on freedom (though greater for the powerful) to pursue our self-interest. Why should the currently powerful enlarge so greatly the opportunities for competitive rebellion and thus threaten their own position?

---

19. In the early 1950s, American academic scholarship joined this trend. In 1952, the Social Science Research Council issued its first report to encourage the comparative study of "non-Western" societies—a phrasing that accurately reflected their former invisibility: the study of non-A, as compared to A. Though an important minority of scholars came to explore the actual nature and dynamics of people previously largely neglected by Western academia, the majority of Western theorists concerned with "modernization" initially were quite explicit in saying "modernization" in fact could only mean "westernization." Subsequent scholarly literature has for the most part rested on abstracted conceptions of political and economic development in which the identity of modernization as westernization has remained uncritically implicit. This trend has been encouraged, of course, by the assimilation of many of these conceptions into the actual practices of many nations in the Third World. These nations recognized the successfully dominant in the world—the "First World"—and assimilated their underlying pattern.

20. An evaluative description by Lois Benjamin, *The Black Elite: Facing the Color Line in the Twilight of the Twentieth Century*.

21. To be a human being does not yet count. In the United States, only in the late 1980s was a federal law passed requiring all agricultural field workers (most of them migrant workers) to be supplied with water and toilets while they worked for twelve to fourteen hours a day on the land. Dangerous pesticides are still often being sprayed while they work.

Obviously, I have not been using *assimilation* as a term for freely discovering, choosing, and coming to understand and integrate previously unfamiliar ideas, values, and feelings into one's own unique being. Such people may act as both insiders (they have come to understand the structure and dynamics of incoherence as a way of life) and also as outsiders. In the service of transformation, they try within the present system to stop or change as many costly or evil steps as possible.[22] That is different from at least a critical acceptance of the dominant way of life, seeking to speak for the continuing suffering of your group, but thus being seen within this system as solely pleading for a special interest group, and not for people seeking to be fully human. I have been using *assimilation* as a synonym for conversion into a particular set of dramas in the service of incoherence as established by a dominant elite. From our perspective, each individual can only be judged by what that individual is in fact doing. Assimilation is not a single box. I have been focusing on its narrowed but most pervasive type for turning people at last into partial beings who thereby join from a relatively more powerful position in the alliance between incoherence and deformation.

WHY IS DEFORMATION INCREASING THROUGHOUT THE WORLD?

Never before in history everywhere at the same time have so many underlying forms and concrete manifestations of relationships been breaking at the same time. Coming apart are our relationships to established ideas, values, groups, and people with whom we had been connected. The most powerful cause of this growing alienation and division is the dying of emanation as a web of life, the vulnerability and cost of incoherence, and the alliance of incoherence with deformation.

We cannot enact archetypal dramas or relationships except in the service of a way of life. Incoherence is not yet dying as an overarching archetypal patterning force, but the only solution it can offer for its travails is incremental change. If the re-formations of incoherence cannot overcome the fundamental reasons for our discontents with a biased and incomplete life, we have only two alternatives left—deformation or transformation. The great majority of people have never faced this pervasive and fundamental a challenge before.

To live in any emanational relationship to a way of life which we uncritically accept puts us into exile from the source of our being that is fundamentally deeper, richer, and more creative than any of the sacred Lords. Hence we are rendered

---

22. This is a strategy of subversion, turning around from below, practiced by an insider/outsider who creates strategies for practicing transformation within a context of both obstacles and opportunities.

more vulnerable to deformation—especially in a cosmos of continuous creation whose current dimensions of change are beyond our capacity to understand and recreate for the better.

Emanation is meant to give us tremendous security despite the fragility of life. To preserve our security, we sought the help of many sacred sources, a pantheon of them. When it is a pantheon, we know they represent all kinds of different forces— some quite destructive, which we cannot overcome except with the help of another Lord of the same pantheon. When we believe in monotheism, we also recognize that our sacred container is not always safe. Jesus on the cross, cried out in a loud voice, "My God, My God, why have you deserted me?"—a plea already voiced centuries earlier in Psalm 22.[23] The Lord of emanation may test our righteousness even to the point of collaborating with Satan to impose deformation upon us—as in the vicious treatment promised to the Jews in exile (in Ezekiel) or imposed upon Job to test the firmness of his belief.

We nonetheless remained in the service of emanation because we believed that a mysteriously most powerful source had offered us (indeed imposed upon us) the best and right web of life for connecting our community through what we did and held dear in its light at every moment. We recognized that we were prone to sin, but sins would be rightly punished by God and by our community—and that there were also ways of redeeming us from sin. But we knew that leaving this sacred container is the deepest of sins, punishable by death and by experiencing hell—on earth, or after our life here comes to an end.

But what if our emanational way of life can in fact no longer help us deal with the problems we face and cannot avoid facing? What if our resort to naked force in its behalf no longer has the support of all who once shared our emanational bonds, because they have lost confidence and trust in the adequacy of our web and in the ultimate power behind it all?

For those who are appalled by the kind of superior human power which incoherence has given us and its uses in contrast to emanation—and who reject the heresies of transformation—deformation remains the only other choice as emanation dissolves as a web and only leaves us with fragments or fantasies of our past. Deformation under these circumstances becomes all the more inspiring because of the very dynamics of emanation. As we have already discussed, the very nature of emanation inspires suicide or murder when it breaks. That impetus is all the more profound when so many emanational links to dramas and relationships in the service of a sacred source are breaking. The Lord of emanation always justified a resort to deformation against those who deserted or threatened to break our

---

23. Jesus's last words cited in Matthew 27:47; also in Mark 15:34. See also Psalm 89: 46–51 for a similar plaint.

bonds. But when the Lord of deformation becomes the dominating Lord, promising us in the present crisis far more security and certainty than even emanation, it is a final answer to be enacted here and now.

Incoherence, like emanation, is a fragment of the core drama of life. In contrast to emanation, it frees us to keep rebelling, but being an arrested fragment, it is also vulnerable to decay and dissolution. There are aspects of incoherence that open it to the peril of deformation. The rebellion for power and the subjection of the powerless has already led to a widespread alliance with deformation. Our sense of remaining only partial beings, even when we gain still more possession of seemingly the most solid substance of life, namely property, fills us with a longing that this way of life in no way can satisfy. When we are not powerful, when the few emanational relationships that gave us a sense of belonging and security disintegrate, when the job provider we thought we could rely on—especially when our whole life had been that of a workaholic or else could not be sustained without such a job—finds us "redundant," we may have no other adequate fragment of life left.

Organizing and reorganizing incoherence also often leads to mere incoherence—a coming apart of connections. Scarcity in many realms of life is the governing reality of incoherence. Yet incoherence cannot compensate for our losses by offering us any experience or understanding of the meaning, value, purpose, and potentials of life beyond its outward manifestations. The core of our being and our continuing journey of fruitful renewal has been repressed, yet we—and even most of our scholars—cannot understand the underlying dynamics and intrinsic limits of incoherence.

In the service of incoherence, we are always deeply alone, in contrast to emanation as a way of life. If, left to ourselves, we reach a point at the bottom where we have lost any power for successful rebellion within incoherence, or we reach a point at the top, but the present institutions of incoherence do not appear to be adequate to ward off a threat to our very chance to remain powerful, deformation may capture us. Almost every country in the world now has movements of deformation—and they are not only composed of groups proclaiming the fantasy of restoring emanation through deformation. They also offer other vehicles of destruction—moved, as we shall see, especially by their hostility to what incoherence did to their lives.

WHAT DO DRAMAS IN THE SERVICE OF DEFORMATION HAVE IN COMMON?

Deformation may arise out of a particular problem while initially we still remain in the service of emanation or incoherence in other stories of our life. But any drama of deformation has the potential power to take over all of our life—and to kill us.

All dramas in the service of deformation, as we have already discussed, begin with the destruction of the seeming security of life in the first Scene of the first Act of the core drama of life and our attachment instead in the second Scene to a fantasy that compels us to rebel and also to cling to the powerful seduction of an embodiment of the source of darkness that can take us into the abyss. That source always offers us something fundamentally new (new at least for us) that is in fact also fundamentally worse—a total connection to what has become for us the only thing that counts but that is in fact a fragmenting fragment.

Rarely do dramas in the service of deformation arise entirely at our own personal initiative. The destruction of our existing emanational bond may begin even before we leave the womb. Drug use by our mother or inadequate nutrition because of poverty may harm our being before our birth. We may be severely beaten, abused, or abandoned even before we become adults. Our sense therefore of powerlessness, anxiety, or rage—in the absence of any help (and how little help is being offered within incoherence as a way of life!) can turn us toward deformation. When an essential story of our life is harmed or destroyed, when a whole way of life dissolves, what can save us except a resort to far greater power and, at the same time its obverse, an intensely passive self-denial? Who knows of transformation?

One difference between dramas in the service of deformation is whether seemingly only one person enters on stage (in some forms of crime), only a small group (in gangs), or as large a group as possible.[24] Another difference is whether its participants are made more aware of the likelihood of dying or only of illusions of glory. The most crucial similarity of all these dramas is that the commitment to deformation by anyone also inflicts deformation upon others.

We shall now examine some dramas in the service of deformation in more detail, but unhappily there is not space enough in one chapter to examine all of them or even most major historical cases of the infliction of deep suffering.[25]

FUNDAMENTALISM

One of the most pervasive movements of deformation in the world is often called *fundamentalism*, although in no instance does such a movement accurately remember the past or offer new foundations of wholeness for our time. Fundamentalists

---

24. Seemingly only one person; others were on stage with that person beforehand and loom behind the scenes even now, politically and historically.

25. Since my immediate family is composed, among others, also of one psychiatrist and two psychologists, and also of three psychiatrists, two psychologists and one social worker as relatives-in-law, I recognize that I do not know enough to analyze different types of neuroses and psychoses as dramas in all four faces—personal, political, historical, and sacred. I also do not know how to discuss deformation arising in the world because of diseases that can kill us because we do not yet know how to cure them, the very existence of murderous viruses, or the meaning of natural disasters.

select fragments of the past now fantasized out of context and turn them into indisputable, immutable, and transcendent foundations to be imposed by force upon those who cannot devoutly believe in them. This road of deformation has been opened and empowered by a deep, double sense of loss—not only the dissolution of emanation as a way of life, but also the failure of the nation-state, of capitalism, and of modern thought in the service of incoherence to create a real new community of true meaning and social justice. Most of these movements of deformation turn to charismatic leaders who will lead them to the restoration of glory through vengeful terror.

Under fundamentalism, the group that has perhaps paid the greatest price—as the traditional way of life of emanation decays—is women. All over the world, as change becomes more accelerated, women are not allowed to adapt their lives, but are told to be the guardians of the traditional way of life and the conduits for nurturing and socializing the next generation.

Fundamentalism caused a backlash in moderate Muslim societies when women made progress. Men caught in the throes of the death of emanation as a way of life sought to return women to normal, that is, back to the patriarchal world of unquestioning obedience as the will of God. If women resisted they were often subjected to violence. Angry young men who have not been able to make it in the emerging economies from Algeria to South Asia turn to hatred, intolerance, and the abuse of women. Lower-middle-class men are especially vulnerable to these feelings of rage and the call of leaders to follow them into the breach against the West. But even some women are in favor of the extremism because they are afraid of the changes that would cause them anxiety outside of their traditional roles. The issue of gender is crucial to progress and modernity.

Because most of us now live in the service of incoherence, it is difficult for us to appreciate and understand that what most deeply moves the so-called fundamentalists is the loss of belief in a mysteriously powerful sacred source. Many of us no longer share this sense of loss of the sacred. At most we try to preserve fragments of the sacred in our private lives. We do not recognize that our way of life is being organized and reorganized in our arrest under the Devil, a symbol, pointing us to the underlying way of life that drives us to participate in the competition for fragments of power. What we hold to be our own power—organizing, increasing, and defending it—is now our central concern.

I would like to illustrate this dominant response in the service of incoherence by way of a brief tale of my own experience in trying to bring the danger of what I then called "neo-Islamic totalitarianism" to the attention of the American government. In 1951, working in the Office of Intelligence Research of the Department of State in Washington, I wrote an analysis (given the focus of those times) on "Islam as a Barrier to Communism." I showed that, contrary to our own official view, Islam was not a strong barrier to Communism, for its traditional form (what I now call its emanational form) was deteriorating. But a new response to this crisis, namely neo-Islamic totalitarianism, now referred to as fundamentalism, was becoming a far greater menace to other Muslims and to the West than Communism in that area. (In 1952, I received the Meritorious Service Award from the Department of State, the first time such an award had ever been awarded for research analysis.[26] This work never had any impact on American policy.)

In 1953, when in the light of this same perspective, I wrote an analysis that began, "For at least the next decade, Communism in the Middle East is likely to remain *impotent*," the secretary typing it could not believe it. She typed the last word as "*important*," but I corrected it in time. When this analysis reached Kermit Roosevelt, the head of the CIA's covert action division on the Middle East, he asked me to come to his office and requested that I withdraw this analysis. I did not. For Kermit Roosevelt, who organized the overthrow of Iranian Prime Minister Mossadeq (because he had undermined the power of the Shah, our barrier to Communism) and who stoutly convinced the CIA and other U.S. government agencies to support the Shah after his restoration (unaware of how the policies of that alliance would strengthen the forces supporting Khomeini), only the menace of Communism mattered to American power.[27]

Nowhere in the world does fundamentalism constitute a return to emanation as a way of life. Nowhere does it mean to be merely a new form of "organized religion." Fundamentalism is a case of pseudo-emanation. People in the service of incoherence cannot recognize the Devil as a symbol of a sacred source, the underlying way of life of incoherence that organizes the whole of life into a world of competing fragments. People in the service of deformation cannot recognize Satan, the Lord of Nothing—except in their fantasy of projecting satanic images upon their opponents. Neither can they recognize or understand the deepest sacred source of our being and thus participate in bringing forth truly critical and creative responses to our contemporary problems.

---

26. What I wrote in "Islam as a Barrier to Communism," and what I learned on that subject thereafter is reflected in a number of chapters, including the chapter on neo-Islamic totalitarianism in my work, Manfred Halpern, *The Politics of Social Change in the Middle East and North Africa*. By that time I had also learned a lot from the then still unpublished manuscript of Richard P. Mitchell, *The Society of the Muslim Brothers*. Most recently, my understanding has been greatly enlarged by Roxanne Leslie Euben, *Islamic Fundamentalism and the Limits of Modern Rationalism*, accepted as a doctoral dissertation at Princeton University, June 1995. Euben offers a greatly revealing analysis of Islamic fundamentalism, not only from the viewpoint of comparative politics, but also in the light of comparisons and contrasts with Western political theory. The dissertation was published in 1999: Roxanne Leslie Euben, *Enemy in the Mirror: Islamic Fundamentalism and the Limits of Modern Rationalism: A Work of Comparative Political Theory*.

27. For a first-rate analysis of this period of Iranian history, see James A. Bill, *The Eagle and the Lion: The Tragedy of American-Iranian Relations*.

Even as we stay with Muslim fundamentalism, as our principal case of what is in fact a worldwide movement, most of its particulars exemplify the general case. As in every instance of emanation, Muslims in its service believed they had been given god's final revelation to humankind. Yet Muslims everywhere in the modern age were defeated by more powerful foreign secular forces. So say all fundamentalists: We also failed ourselves; we had come to misunderstand our past. I, your new leader, truly understand the past. Example: Khomeini declared (correctly) that the Koran requires the appointment of trustees to take care of widows and orphans. Khomeini added that all Iranians are now widows and orphans and he is now their trustee—the vice regent of the jurist of god. Never before had any Muslim claimed to be the only one entitled to interpret the sacred laws of Islam.

Fundamentalism can be found in any religious garb that gives rise to forms of pseudo-emanation leading to deformation when a society based on emanation is crumbling for its adherents. In Israel, locked in a struggle with the Palestinians, Israeli religious political parties are literally fighting to breathe their religious spirit into the government. Which sacred source becomes dominant in Israel will determine if there is hope for peace.

It is not only the failure of emanation that raises support for fundamentalism. It is also the failures of incoherence to provide opportunities for jobs and status, or indeed opportunities that could restore any deep sense of community and a devotion to shared values. Also, other manifestations of deformation are already damaging the community. Predominant among followers of the Muslim fundamentalists in Egypt and among the group that exploded poison gas in the Tokyo subway were educated people trained in the sciences but unemployed, and disenchanted with the role of science and scientists in the service of incoherence. Now they experience a new sense of purpose.[28]

And these fundamentalists demonstrate that they do care for those in distress. Sayyid Qutb, the leader of the Egyptian fundamentalists said, "The entire community is obligated to be the caretaker of each individual in need."[29] At the time of the earthquake in Cairo in 1991, the government did not show up for several days to help restore injured people and their environment. The fundamentalists showed up immediately. Their local leaders and followers reside in the same neighborhood. They build many new mosques. They pay if necessary for doctors, teachers, housing, healthcare, after-school programs, kindergartens, and lending libraries.[30] Such actions are means to an extremely different end: to cement a community—but only our community—that will triumph by whatever force is required not only at home but also in the world.

28. For the evidence on Egypt, see Roxanne L. Euben, *Enemy in the Mirror*, 159.
29. Ibid., 177.
30. From a lecture by Eva Bellin at Princeton University in 1992.

TOTALITARIANISM

Totalitarianism is a seemingly secular movement for establishing true glory for the first time in history. To be totally dominant over all aspects of life is its ambition. A single leader is always the controlling source, whether in Stalin's USSR, Hitler's Germany, Mussolini's Italy, or Mao's China.

But in fact in every case so far, totalitarianism was imposed—by what was at the outset a minority—upon a different-minded majority. None ever fully succeeded in being in total control of everyone's four faces of being. No small number of people continued to live in archetypal dramas in the service of incoherence or even emanation which weakened or corrupted or modified the dominant way of life. Hitler in distrust even killed thousands of Nazi Storm Troopers. Later he organized a new secret police, the *Sicherheitsdienst*, to spy on his already existing secret police, the Gestapo. Stalin killed millions of Communist officials and party members. At one time, he said, "I trust no one, not even myself."[31] To live in the service of a fragmenting way of life that is based upon a fantasy of wholeness cannot even in its supreme leader overcome a deep and justified anxiety. Instead, deformation leads them to blame such deep threats not only on actual opponents but to project this menace upon people who by their very existence are fantasized to threaten their cause—which is also their being.

Why do totalitarian movements succeed? To cite one example, why did Hitler and the Nazis win power over Germany in 1933? On November 8, 1923, a few months before I was born in Germany, Hitler tried in Munich to stage a Putsch. His coup failed. By that time Germany, against all its aggressive expectations as the most successful industrial country in Europe, had lost the First World War, and the German Emperor had been forced to abdicate and to leave Germany. The payment of enormous reparations inflicted upon Germany by the peace treaty of Versailles had caused an inflation in which a loaf of bread that had once cost one Mark now cost about one billion Marks. My father had therefore lost his hat-making factory and ownership of the local theater. I was born on the kitchen table of a small apartment we had to share with another family.

In a society kindred in some ways to the Japanese, namely based on an alliance of emanational values of hierarchic discipline and loyalty with such values of incoherence as nationalism and capitalism, both the aristocracy and a significant portion of the middle class felt deeply shattered: What is the use of strict obedience and discipline when, under these past regimes, you can nonetheless be defeated? What is the use of hard work and savings when under past and present regimes, you can nonetheless lose it all and thus also lose your social status and security?

---

31. Stalin's remark is quoted in Nikita S. Khrushchev, *Khrushchev Remembers*. It is cited in Robert C. Tucker, *The Soviet Political Mind: Stalinism and Post-Stalin Change*, 117.

In Germany, under the democratic Weimar Republic, a new freedom and creativity was emerging in politics, philosophy, art, values, and morality that was also undermining established values. Hence, members of the traumatized upper and middle classes also feared for their children. And in 1929, an economic depression hit Germany before it had much recovered from these earlier blows, and great unemployment ensued. A way of life was being undermined against the majority's hopes, expectations, and intentions.

My mother and father began again from scratch after the inflation ended, designing, making and selling hats in their small stores. My mother tried hard—very hard—to train me to conform once again to bourgeois values of disciplined competence and hard work. My father became very active in the Social Democratic Party, discontented with its depotentiating belief that capitalism will inevitably and necessarily come to an end, and hence unwilling, despite its large electoral support, to initiate policies to deal with real political and economic problems now.[32] He helped to organize a number of community actions in our town of Mittweida: cooperative gardens, an adult school, actual help for people in need.

In the last free election before President Hindenburg appointed Hitler to be Chancellor—but in fact dictator—of Germany, the Nazi Party received only 33 percent of the popular vote. Neither Hitler's victory—nor that of Stalin, Mussolini, or Mao—was inevitable. What makes such a victory possible is the destruction, for many, of the emanational relationships to a way of life and to crucial dramas in its service for those who had been the powerful concrete embodiments in these archetypal stories—and for those once dependent on these relationships for the very spirit and material rewards of their life. Nonetheless, totalitarians gain power and their opposition cannot stop the still powerful but anxious members of the threatened elite from appointing totalitarians to top power positions because that elite is under the illusion of thus restoring its position (in the case of Hitler and Mussolini)—or they are not powerful enough to stop the totalitarian resort to force (in the Communist instances).

The best way to prevent totalitarianism, as we shall discuss at the end of this chapter and in the following chapter on transformation, is to deal with the underlying issues created by the decay of now existing ways of life.

HOLOCAUST

Holocausts are not dramas enacted solely in one final Scene. Much of our incomprehension of the horror of the satanic endings, and our failure to prevent the

---

32. An excellent analysis of the contrast between the politics of the Swedish and the German Social Democratic Parties is to be found in Sheri Berman, *The Social Democratic Moment: Ideas and Politics in the Making of Interwar Europe*.

extermination of millions of human beings again and again even in the modern age, is the result of our being spellbound solely by the massacres. We remember and lament only the ending. Holocausts also begin in the second Scene of the first Act of the core drama of life. There will be more holocausts among various peoples unless we learn to recognize this road to destructive death so that we may stop it before its end.

My mother held that Hitler was a demagogue. You do not have to believe what demagogues say, and they do not last long. My father was an atheist and had raised me as an atheist. He recognized from the beginning that that fact would not keep Hitler from putting us to death as Jews. He therefore also cared about the fate of the Jewish community. I only knew a few of the Jews of the five Jewish families in our town of 18,000 people. But from the age of ten to thirteen, I was the only Jew in town who kids my age could, and often did, beat up. Hitler declared that Jews needed to be eliminated lest they continue to control and racially poison Germany. At that time Jews constituted one-half of one percent of the German population.

We escaped from Germany a year and a half before we would have been eradicated. Most of my aunts, uncles, and cousins suffered death. At least a third of German Jews did not leave in time or entered other parts of Europe only as visitors, to be killed after Hitler's conquests. Why? Many indeed were refused permanent visas (by countries in Europe and beyond Europe). Most countries wanted no immigrants, especially not Jews. Many German Jews also had assimilated into being Germans, and while they and the majority of Germans, until Hitler was appointed dictator, felt themselves threatened by the deepening of incoherence, they had not yet taken the growing danger of deformation seriously. As many restrictions were put upon their lives by decree, many Jews still said to themselves: "It has happened before, but we have survived anti-Semitism before. Despite past programs and exiles, we still exist."

Anti-Semitism has led to outbursts of killings before. Historically it manifests a station on the road to deformation—expressing the ruling culture's alliance of emanation or incoherence with deformation. In emanational Christianity, Jews were deeply distrusted and feared because they had rejected the greatest Jew, Jesus Christ, as their savior. They were members of a community that lived across all borders, while Christians often fought each other. Jews were sometimes used by rulers to finance loans, in part because they had such connections, in part because they could be ousted if the loans could not be repaid. Later, they were seen as dangerous initiators of incoherence as Jews became prominent among those who philosophically and politically questioned established beliefs and institutions—and subsequently as dangerous critics of incoherence as a way of life. It was therefore deemed vital by many—certainly not by all—to treat Jews as lesser human beings or as people to be rendered invisible, that is, to be exiled. When Jews failed or became suspected of failing to adhere to these stations, they were perceived as deserving death instead.

Hitler's regime began by treating Jews as lesser or as people to be exiled. But when deformation becomes dominant as a way of life, it does not limit itself to the archetypal drama of tenuous stations. By its very nature it opens the door to destructive death of all the "wholly others." Exile into concentration camps or gulags often ends in torturous death. Totalitarianism as a drama is committed to the extermination of all those who will not or cannot be totally loyal to its only true top source.

It was not inescapable for any totalitarian to pick Jews as that kind of enemy. The history of anti-Semitism as a path of stations helped to inspire Hitler, and so did his new fantasy of Germans as the master race and hence the need for those of pure blood to recover and purify all German soil, including that now occupied by other "inferior" races East and West. But if not race or class as the enemy, nonetheless any and every kind of opposition must be totally eliminated, if necessary or possible by civil war, aggressive war abroad, or through Holocaust—no stations short of extermination. Their very existence violates the deepest nature of our being; their very existence puts us at risk of dying. We cannot risk any compromise. We kill Jews regardless of their political or religious or nonreligious views, whether they are assimilated or not.

We kill anyone, even a professed Communist, who does not agree—or only seems to agree—with particular policies of Stalin. Stalin killed 20 million people. Anyone not like us is wholly other and therefore a menace to us as long as he or she is alive.[33] That is a common element in all manifestations of totalitarianism. Extermination of others proves that we are the only ones with power, including the power to revenge ourselves—at last. It proves that we alone have the only true cause.

What could have been done in time to prevent the Nazi-organized Holocaust? Certainly German Jews could not have done it by themselves. Also, German Jews were as divided as other Germans on political grounds, on religious, agnostic, and atheist grounds, in cultural divisions between German-born and Eastern European Jews, and on assimilationist and nonassimilationist grounds. There were Social Democrats, Communists, and Catholic Center Party members who favored a united front between these parties who together would have constituted a parliamentary majority which could have prevented the President—despite his proclamation of emergency power under Article 48 of the Constitution—from appointing Hitler as Chancellor. The great majority in each party opposed such a coalition because of deep ideological divisions between the parties.

Besides, why worry about the Nazis? In 1928, the Nazis still had only three percent of the popular vote. In July of 1932—three years after the depression began in

---

33. Similarly, as Yugoslavia crumbled, the horror of "ethnic cleansing" reflected not simply the renewal of past hatreds and discriminations, but the rise of movements of deformation.

1929—support had risen dramatically to 37 percent, but by November of that year, but two months before taking power, it had fallen to 33 percent. Why worry?

As we showed in the preceding section on totalitarianism, a deep crisis had begun much earlier in Germany, with the defeat in World War I—a crisis that in its underlying causes was not being faced or resolved, whatever particular changes for the better sometimes took place for a time. Deformation in the hands of Nazis was not only a threat against the Jews but against all people in opposition. It threatened a new war that would eventually cost altogether 55 million lives. Anyone who read Hitler's *Mein Kampf*, which was published in 1925, listened to his speeches, or experienced (as I did as a child) brown-uniformed and black-uniformed Nazis, even before they took power, marching through towns and shooting at counter-demonstrators, could have been on alert to all these dangers. To prevent victories of deformation means above all tuning in to the existing causes of deformation and dealing with them—as we try to show in the last section of this chapter. It is far too dangerous to wait until political movements and other expressions of deformation gain more than one-third of popular support.

I have in this section spoken of the Nazi-produced holocaust in totally inadequate detail. Millions of unique men, women, and children were brutally killed through a highly organized mass production of death. Each holocaust is unique in its concrete manifestation—slaughtering particular human beings in a particular political enactment of a particular historical sequence in the name of a particular sacred inspiration. Even so, the analysis of this particular example of the archetypal drama of holocausts in the service of deformation is meant to show that all exterminations of real or fantasized opposition in the service of a deforming fantasy constitute holocausts. Even when done by Jews: "Samuel said to Saul: 'I am the man who Yahweh sent to anoint you king over his people, over Israel, so now listen to the words of Yahweh. Thus speaks Yahweh Sabaoth, "I will repay what Amalek did to Israel when they opposed them on the road by which they came up out of Egypt. Now go and strike down Amalek; put him under the ban with all that he possesses. Do not spare him, but kill man and woman, babe and suckling, ox and sheep, camel and donkey."'"[34]

Even when done by Americans—to cite only one case: On March 10, 1945, we firebombed Tokyo. The United States Strategic Bombing Survey estimated that "probably more persons lost their lives by fire in Tokyo in a six-hour period than at any time in the history of man." At least 100,000 persons died and hundreds of thousands were injured.[35] It would be miserably easy to add to this list from all over the world, even if we limited our vision to the twentieth century.

---

34. I Samuel 15:1–3.
35. Richard Rhodes, "The General [Curtis LeMay] and World War III," *The New Yorker*, June 19, 1995, 47.

Holocausts arise not only in association with dramas of totalitarianism, but can arise in connection with any form of deformation which controls one aspect of our life even while in other aspects we remain in the service of emanation or incoherence. Holocausts are not joined with every drama of deformation, but forms of destructive death arise in every one. The issue therefore is not only to prevent holocausts—kill them all or kill as many of them as we can kill now—but to prevent any destructive death.

TERRORISM

To clarify terrorism as a drama in the service of deformation is difficult for reasons kindred to the common view of the holocaust. We tend to attend only to the final explosion. Most terrorists live in isolation from the rest of their own community and from the rest of the world, though sometimes with links to regimes that feel a similar isolation, fear, and rage. What is true both of underground terrorists can also be the case with officially armed forces. The latter may fire on crowds or bomb civilians. Both mean to intimidate and if possible also to stop the others from continuing on their path—but neither know of any effective ways of actually doing so.

For example, in 1985 Abu Nidal, a Palestinian terrorist group, bombed airline offices in Rome and Vienna; hijacked an Egyptian airplane which cost 59 lives; bombed a British Airways office in Rome, and threw grenades at a Roman café, in both instances injuring tourists from all over the world; bombed two hotels in Athens; attacked a British Airways office in Spain; bombed two restaurants in Kuwait; tried to down a Jordanian airliner; assassinated a Palestinian in Amman; and murdered a Jordanian publisher in Athens.[36] I stop even before the list of attacks for 1985 ends. Abu Nidal's terrorist acts were intended to contribute to an all-embracing Arab revolution and the liberation of all of Palestine. They accomplished no such goals.

In the 1940s, Yitzhak Shamir was a commander of the Stern Gang which, in what was then still British-ruled Palestine, among other terrorist acts, assassinated Lord Moyne, the British minister-resident in Cairo, and Count Folke Bernadotte, the UN mediator at work in Palestine. In a 1991 interview on the Israeli army radio, Shamir who was by that time Prime Minister of Israel, defended the Stern Gang's actions: "There was justification and usefulness in using this extreme method." By contrast, the Palestinians were "fighting for land that is not theirs."[37] The Stern Gang's terrorism did not play a significant role in the creation or international recognition of the State of Israel, nor even in the rise of Shamir to become Prime Minister.

---

36. *The New York Times*, January 1, 1986.
37. Karin Laub, Associated Press, *The Washington Times*, September 5, 1991.

Let us take an example of seeming success in terrorism: In 1954, the U.S. Central Intelligence Agency violently intervened in Guatemala and overthrew the democratically elected government of Jacob Arbenz on the grounds that otherwise, Communists would take over. It called people Communists who were eager to overcome virtual slave labor on the plantations owned by United Fruit, persistent malnutrition, and anti-Indian racism. The CIA not only organized a dissident Guatemalan army group and supplied them with weapons, but handed the new regime an initial list of more than a thousand names of people to be killed by newly organized death squads.[38] The new regime drove impoverished peasants and Mayan Indians from the lands restored to them under earlier land reform programs. In 1961, peasants, Indians, and others opposed to the new military dictatorship began to rebel. Thereafter, in thirty-five years of army combat with these guerillas, more than 100,000 people were killed, above all by the army—the longest and deadliest of Central America's civil wars.[39]

Terrorists gain such successes only when they are intimately connected to local or outside forces powerful enough to have a chance to gain control of the national governmental apparatus—and then they inflict their augmented power with great cruelty. Most terrorist groups or individuals do not possess such connections and they fail. Even the Khmer Rouge, led by Pol Pot—who killed more than a million human beings in Cambodia—failed. Even the United States failed, though our forces killed altogether about 3,000,000 Vietnamese, most of them civilians; our forces, in particular in Operation Phoenix, killed 23,000 Vietnamese (smaller numbers do not matter; each one is a human being) and tortured many more to find people suspected of cooperating with the Viet Cong—in a war we lost, despite connections to some powerful Vietnamese groups.

Terrorists who express the power of the very powerful no less than of the still powerless feel free to inflict destructive death. Both feel compelled to demonstrate such naked power: the other is not a human being. What matters is not who dies but the terrified response of the still living—as if terror could lead to deeper understanding of the problems of life. Demonstrating my power—our power—of destruction, that is the heart of deformation. Even if we have no further ideological explanation: whoever exploded a bomb at the Atlanta Olympics in 1996 nevertheless spoke up for a fantasy to provide a particular aura for the core cause of terrorism. Only we count, but you do not yet listen to us. Hence we need to impress the still established that they are quite vulnerable—really vulnerable, by depressing them to the point of death and destruction. To stop terrorism through

---

38. I was told about this fact by a colleague in the Office of Intelligence Research of the Department of State who was shown this list by the CIA agent while they were both flying on an airplane to Guatemala after the coup.

39. *The New York Times*, September 20, 1996.

intelligence operations before or after a killing may help in specific instances, but it doe not—cannot—lead to eliminating this road to destructive death.

WAR

War—except for one different archetypal form of it, as we shall see—is one of the most repeated, pervasive, and costly dramas in the service of deformation. It would be exceedingly long to list all the wars we know about. To speak only of wars within Europe between the Thirty Years War (1618–1648) and before the beginning of the second World War in 1939—in the part of the world that prides itself on being the most civilized—over seventeen million soldiers died in battle, not counting the large civilian casualties[40] and also not counting the many casualties of European imperialist conquests.

What are the costs of war? Here are a few specific examples: Napoleon left for Russia in 1812 with 422,000 men. Only about 10,000 remained alive to return to France. In just one day on the Somme River on July 1, 1916, the British suffered 21,000 killed, most of them by German machine guns.[41] For eleven months at Verdun in 1916, the Germans and the French persisted in battling each other. German casualties: 434,000; French casualties: 542,000. The First World War, then in its second year, continued for two more years. Successful conquests end in prolonged domination over others—or else in revenge. Despite the great human cost of World War I, Hitler started World War II just twenty-one years later—at a far higher price.

Not only soldiers die in large numbers in war. Civilians die in bombings because they live near weapons factories or airports or in towns into which armies retreat or advance.[42] But the saturation bombings of many German and at least 63 Japanese cities, and the "free-fire zones" in Vietnam, exterminated mostly civilians, millions of them.[43] Intended to destroy the morale of the enemy people so that they would seek surrender, that kind of bombing, even of Hiroshima and Nagasaki, was nowhere decisive in achieving that purpose. But increasingly in war, even democracies have moved from killing the armed forces of the other to destroying their civilian populations.

War is almost always a deforming drama supported by many in the name of our cause and shaped above all by one Commander in Chief. One Commander

---

40. Charles Tilly, *Coercion, Capital, and European States, AD 990–1990*.
41. "100 Years of Maxim's Killing Machine," *The New York Times*, November 26, 1985.
42. In the U.S. war against Iraq in 1990, the U.S. government referred to civilian casualties as "collateral damage." A Harvard University study estimated that more than 170,000 Iraqi children would die from malnutrition and infection by waterborne diseases in the year after the war. (*The Trenton Times*, May 22, 1991.)
43. In Vietnam, nineteen million gallons of Agent Orange, a toxic herbicide dropped by U.S. bombers, destroyed not only crops and forests but caused many cancers.

in Chief, Dwight Eisenhower, recognized even its larger deforming dimensions: "Every gun that is made, every warship launched, every rocket fired signifies, in the final sense, a theft from those who hunger and are not fed, those who are cold and not clothed. This world in arms is not spending money alone. It is spending the sweat of its laborers, the genius of its scientists, the hopes of its children.... This is not a way of life at all in any true sense. Under the cloud of war, it is humanity hanging on a cross of iron."

Eisenhower was speaking in the eighth year of the Cold War—with thirty-six years more to go. Despite these insightful words, he and his successors did not recognize the fantasy behind the Cold War. Throughout the Cold War, no agency within the U.S. intelligence community was allowed to write analyses of Soviet intentions, but solely of Soviet capabilities. Capabilities were judged to be the equivalent of intentions. Yet if the Soviet Union had intended to capture the only valuable treasure—the industries and highly skilled workers of Central and Western Europe—it could have succeeded only if it used troops without weapons heavy enough to damage its intended human and industrial gains. That was certainly unworkable. In the highly unlikely case of a successful Soviet advance, the USSR knew it would be faced with the infliction by the West of short-range nuclear weapons on East Germany and Eastern Europe and of long-range nuclear weapons and bombs on the USSR.

The only new invasion beyond its own already existing satellites (invaded during the war against Germany) and initiated by the Soviet Union after World War II was the invasion of Afghanistan—a landlocked country without important resources, no capacity to counterattack the USSR, deeply split among tribes and political factions—a lost cause even if we had not intervened by supporting fundamentalists. How enormously heavy in human and economic cost was the fantasy of the Cold War! The decision to use nuclear bombs upon Hiroshima and Nagasaki was centrally connected to President Truman's intention to intimidate the Soviet Union, the only other major power—but in fact a country largely destroyed by the time World War II ended.[44]

Are there no just wars? I fought as a battalion scout in the 28th Infantry Division against the Nazis and, when the fighting ended, was transferred to Counterintelligence in order to find, arrest, and interrogate important Nazis. It was a just war against an evil force. If we had not—even belatedly—stopped Nazism, Hitler would have killed many more civilians, meaning men, women, and children, especially in the East but also in the West and North of Europe and would have tried to conquer still more countries. We allied ourselves with the deformational regime of Stalin and with Western European colonialist powers who had used deforming

---

44. Gar Alperovitz, *Atomic Diplomacy: Hiroshima and Potsdam: The Use of the Atomic Bomb and the American Confrontation with Soviet Power.*

violence before World War II—and for years afterwards—to retain their colonies. By the time we entered this war, we could have defeated Hitler no other way.

Was there ever any alternative to our joining even this war? Once again, as in the case of any road of deformation, we could have acted earlier; we needed to have acted earlier. But that requires recognizing the menace of evil before it ends in destructive death. In the early thirties, the left and the center failed to ally in order to stop Hitler within Germany. When Hitler broke the Treaty of Versailles in 1935 and sent German troops to occupy the German Rhineland—which had previously been occupied by French and Belgian troops but now had, by agreement, become demilitarized—the Western Allies did nothing. Had they intervened, Hitler would at that time (two years after becoming dictator) still have lacked the power to resist effectively, and his failure to do so could well have ended his rule. But living in the service of incoherence—a way of life based upon competitive rebellion and partial justice, which is often injustice—it is very difficult to recognize evil or agree that it is evil. The West exaggerated the Soviet menace to the world of capitalism/competition, and for a time even saw Hitler as a possible ally against that menace.

Is war always in the service of deformation? No. There is a different archetypal drama—a war of self-defense—in which we do not initiate a road of evil toward destructive death, but in which we engage in inflicting destructive death in as limited a form as possible solely in order to compel people in the service of deformation to get off that road.[45] Violence in any drama in the service of emanation, incoherence, or transformation can be justified only in self-defense against violent aggression if other measures for stopping such aggression have failed. We need then in self-defense to target solely the aggressor, seek his capture if possible, his death only if unavoidable in order to preserve our life and the lives of others. In the service of emanation (we alone are the right people of right belief) or in the service of incoherence (our power is at stake), it is not easy to be persuaded that self-defense does not justify every form of counter-violence.

This is not an easy path. In self-defense, we attack not only the aggressor's adherents but also those he has conscripted into his armed forces and to work in his military supply factories. If they desert and refuse to cooperate, the aggressor is likely to kill them, but if they remain with him, they will be killing others in an evil cause—a terrifying but real choice. In my battalion, the majority of my comrades did not know why they were risking their lives against Nazis. They, too, were conscripts, told they must fight for the country against "the enemy"; most of the enemy's army was also conscripts. This was a deep moral failure of education on our part. To come to understand the deeper meaning of this struggle is to experience personal and political transformation.

---

45. David Abalos helped me greatly to clarify this exploration of self-defense.

It is not inevitably the case that our side is the good guys and the other side is the bad guys. It always depends on what each of us does in what type of war. As weapons on all levels become more cleverly and more powerfully destructive, as deformation moves more and more into our world, as all can fall in a nuclear war, acting to heal and overcome deformation—before war becomes the only choice, even for self-defense—is more essential than ever.[46]

GANGS

We do not need the power of the state or of a political movement to organize deformation. Since we all possess a capacity for deformation, all that is needed to incite us is an environment in which emanation and incoherence are decaying and at most, stifling and oppressive, and transformation, which requires our conscious, critical, creative, and caring participation, offers no living examples. We shall now look briefly at a number of additional dramas in the service of deformation—first, gangs.

Most gangs engage in warfare for territory, economic domination (usually in drug traffic) and unifying pride. They lack the legal right of sovereignty of the nation-state, but they enact the same archetypal drama of war. If there were no gangs in the menacing world in which they live, what else could they belong to? How else would they have status? How else would they be safe? "Everyone has got a gun, so I got to have one."[47] And they are tough: "Happily, you can die only once."[48]

Coming from below, their assertion of power is only the obverse—and hence the perverse expression—of powerlessness. The often abused turn themselves into abusers of the enemy or of vulnerable outsiders. This kind of adolescent rebellion, in contrast to incoherence as a way of life, has no father—no authority position—one can rebel against in order to attain power now and to preserve it for any truly encouraging length of time.[49] To put an end to gangs requires us to help in building new caring and fruitful communities.

---

46. Are we entitled to intervene in other nation-states in order to help put an end to the road of evil within their society? I tried to deal with this question in "'The Morality and Politics of Intervention'"—an essay first published in a pamphlet by the Council on Religion and International Affairs in New York in 1963 (and then reprinted in somewhat revised form). See also James N. Rosenau and Woodrow Wilson School of Public and International Affairs Center of International Studies, *International Aspects of Civil Strife*, 249–88; Richard A. Falk and American Society of International Law, *The Vietnam War and International Law*, 39–78; and Kenneth W. Thompson, *Moral Dimensions of American Foreign Policy*, 75–104.

47. *The New York Times*, November 5, 1990.

48. Gertrude Samuels, "Why 'The Assassins' Can't Be 'Punks,'" *The New York Times Magazine*, August 16, 1959.

49. An adult gang like the Mafia for that purpose requires the attainment of powerful political and economic corporate connections.

DRUGS

Let us ask not only why people consume illegal drugs but also legal drugs and drinks that are known to produce premature and destructive death. Cigarette smoking kills three million people worldwide every year, or one person every ten seconds, and these numbers will continue to mount. If current trends continue, these deaths will reach ten million a year, about half of them in peoples' middle age, losing twenty to twenty-five years of their life expectancy. Smoking cigarettes is killing more people in Western countries than all the other causes of death put together, including illegal drugs, car accidents, fires, AIDS and homicides.[50] In the United States, according to the Surgeon General's office, in 1989 fewer than 9,000 lives were lost due to hard drugs, but 390,000 were lost due to cigarettes, 100,000 due to alcohol.[51] In 1993, at least $20 billion (out of a total of $87 billion spent by Medicare on inpatient hospital care that year) was due to excessive drinking, illicit drug use, and smoking—about $16 billion of it for conditions attributable to smoking.[52] Americans spend about $26 billion a year on cigarettes.[53]

Smoking does not generate the personal criminal acts that often stem from alcohol abuse, nor the robberies and killings that are stimulated by the use of illicit drugs. Smoking cigarettes and drinking large quantities of alcohol are intended as compensations for the merely partial reality of incoherence as a way of life, but they can turn us into lesser and lesser beings until our early death. Though the consumption of illicit drugs does not kill as many, its sale and use places many millions on the road to destructive death.

Underground capitalism in the production and sale of illegal drugs manifests many of the most deforming aspects of that archetype. The crack business for most of its workers is "a modern, brutalized version of a nineteenth-century sweatshop." People making crack work twelve hours a day, six to seven days a week, earning about two hundred ten dollars a week. Those who steal any amount of crack are severely beaten or shot; those who become their own best customers never make any money. Hustlers, who can make up to $500 a day, distribute the drug to runners who do the actual selling and who can make $500 a week.[54] The jobs of

---

50. From a report prepared by scientists and epidemiologists from the Imperial Cancer Research Fund in Oxford, the World Health Organization in Geneva, and the American Cancer Study in Atlanta, Richard Peto, Imperial Cancer Research Fund (Great Britain), et al., *Mortality from Smoking in Developed Countries, 1950–2000: Indirect Estimates from National Vital Statistics*. (*The New York Times*, September 21, 1994.)

51. Harry Sayen, *The Trenton Times*, July 1, 1990.

52. Report by Joseph A. Califano, Jr., head of the Center on Addiction and Substance Abuse at Columbia University, *The New York Times*, May 17, 1994.

53. George Will, *Trenton Times*, December 28, 1992.

54. Gina Kolata, *The New York Times*, November 26, 1989.

runners do not last long. They are the most likely to be arrested and imprisoned—by 1996 in the United States, in excess of one million people a year.[55] Both runners and hustlers are also most directly involved in and vulnerable to the violence of turf battles. The local and international wholesale dealers—the capitalists in charge—make enormous sums of money. Worldwide revenues are estimated to exceed the Gross National Product of three-quarters of the world's 207 economies, or $180 billion to $300 billion annually.[56]

People working for these underground capitalists see no legitimate opportunities for themselves. Hence they risk their lives in search of power, respect, prestige, and wealth—for proof that they can succeed. But in this instance, capitalism is a drama being enacted entirely in the service of deformation. It is a life that serves to empower them until they are overpowered by it, also empowering and, toward the end, overpowering others along the way. For the lesser and the invisible of our society, the "high" provided by such drugs—which lifts us incomparably higher than our daily life—soon drops us to an even deeper low, and to a more desperate shortage or lack of money to buy a new dose.

What alternative do we have then to working for the drug dealer or to robbery, whatever the cost? People surrounded by so many dramas of deformation in their lives know nothing more powerful or glorious than a drug. Others around us either treat us as nothing, offer us nothing, or else they are our enemy. Drugs and excessive alcohol—and seemingly more gently, cigarettes—for people of any social class, constitute a form of consumption that is meant to uplift us because otherwise we would feel at least vacant or down and abandoned. But in fact it consumes us. This is a fantasy real enough to be inhaled, injected, or swallowed, and for our body to come to demand as a requirement for life. But its pseudo-emanational effects can destroy the very container as well as the faces of our being.

Legalizing cocaine and heroin consumption would empower some of the most vicious among capitalists to enlarge their political and medical impact at least to the present effects of cigarette consumption in all levels of society. While legalization would leave present local gangs unneeded for drug distribution, it would greatly enlarge the opportunities and the violent quest of addicts to acquire drugs.[57]

55. *The Trenton Times*, September 22, 1996.
56. Paul B. Starres, *Global Habit: The Drug Problem in a Borderless World*, cited in a review by Christopher S. Wren, *The New York Times Sunday Book Review*, August 18, 1996.
57. The psychedelic drugs which are consumed primarily in the middle and upper class seldom produce violence against one's self or others (except at times from LSD and physiological damage from other drugs). They may produce for us an extraordinarily wonderful fantasy or vision or feeling of empowerment about this moment. But they cut us off from any understanding of the underlying personal, political, historical, and sacred issues that in fact confront us. They create an illusion of our being fully present that cannot, when they wear off, be sustained in critical consciousness. Marijuana is a milder version of such psychedelic drugs.

Under present conditions, where are the resources now within us or in the society around us that would enable us to take the advice: "Just Don't Do It"? In the United States, most of the war against drugs focuses on curbing foreign suppliers and arresting and imprisoning drug law violators at home. In 1994, almost 30 percent of all inmates in federal and state prisons, and certainly two-thirds of all inmates in federal prisons, serve time for drug sale or drug use. This war has made little difference. Only a small fraction of the money spent in most nations in the war against drugs is used to prevent or treat substance abuse. Increasingly we teach about the risks of illegal drugs, but how great do these risks sound when we experience so many other grave risks all around us. We hardly open any doors for participating in more fruitful archetypal dramas in the worst of neighborhoods—or any place else. We do not actually sit down with people afflicted by drugs to discover not only what their personal problems are but also the political, historical, and sacred forces which moved them into deformation, and to help them overcome and heal these problems. Personal drug therapy is often successful in returning people from deformation to incoherence as a way of life—no small accomplishment, but therefore also into all the travails again of that partial service.[58]

VIOLENCE

Violence involves a range of actions—or inactions—far larger than the infliction of illegal physical damage upon others or ourselves. Violence constitutes not only a specific concrete act but is also the manifestation of underlying patterning forces without which violence would lack meaning, context, and deeper motivation. From the perspective of transformation, violence is any use of power that damages human wholeness physically or psychically by compelling people to act against their present understanding and readiness, or which denies them the opportunity and diminishes their capacity to attain wholeness. Violence can be justified only in self-defense, and only if we also attend caringly to why this danger arose and how to remedy it—not simply self-defense as an act of suppression. This conception of violence does not yet cover the subject.

What if we are not already whole, and are therefore living in the service of emanation or incoherence, still doing violence by hurting or denying ourselves and others? In so far as we commit violence to the wholeness of our being, are we therefore also engaged in deformation? When we arrest ourselves in a fragment

---

58. For a thorough analysis of what methadone and therapy can achieve and how it can best achieve it, see Mark W. Parrino and (U.S.) Center for Substance Abuse Treatment, *State Methadone Treatment Guidelines*.

of the core drama of life, we need to suppress those who fail to uphold our beliefs and thus also fail to repress themselves and hence become sinful or shameless instead—or else suppress those who break the laws and rules governing the dramas of rebellion.

The infliction of punishment, even of death, is not called violence by any such governing order. Violence is a term only used for physical violations of the established order. This incomplete and biased view of violence remains uncritically accepted by the participants in these partial ways of life because they recognize, correctly, that no way of life can be sustained by coercion alone. Their ways require acceptance, obedience, and cooperation with the powers that be. We therefore accept the legitimacy—a justification open at most to particular criticism in particular cases—of violence that diminishes the being of offenders against the established order.

Are such punishments for violating the law not justifiable—punishments which we in these ways of life do not call violent because law and order define and judge what must be done? Within the service of partial ways of life, there is no escape from the need to employ power to repress and suppress. From the perspective of transformation, we can plainly see emanation and incoherence thus in alliance with deformation. But deformation as a way of life, unlike these two, knows no limits to violence.

I have in these preceding paragraphs focused primarily on the requirements of law and order in the service of emanation and incoherence. But it is vital to recall the violence also done in these ways of life to people treated as lesser and invisible and crippled by life on the stations—among other blows, denied the opportunity to make a decent living—ending up in early and destructive death.

The deep frustration and rage that arises from the repression and subjection characteristic of a partial way of life—experienced but not understood—gives rise to violence especially within homes where that apparatus of the State is not present. In the United States, whose history has greatly inhibited gun control, about 40 percent of all homicides are committed within the family. Banning all guns would lessen such deaths, but not physical and sexual abuse within the home. Angry men in authority at home but unsure of being entirely obeyed or respected (in compensation for how they are treated beyond their door) will be enraged enough to manifest their power.

Violence is the breaking or damaging or diminishing and thus the deforming of any face of our being through powerful suppression or self-repression, or through deception, manipulation, or insult—each expressing the infliction of an archetypal drama upon us or our yielding to it. There is no shortage of violence in our world, not only as we commit ourselves to fragmenting fantasies but also because of the costs of power in arresting our lives.

OBSTACLES TO LEAVING THE ROAD
TO DESTRUCTIVE DEATH

Many are the dramas we have not discussed that can also move us into deformation. The point of this chapter is to offer only enough examples to help us understand the structure and dynamics on this road so that we may come to recognize them, even in dramas we have not examined here, and to intervene in time.[59]

As we have seen, it is so easy for us not to become aware and to acknowledge that we and others are moving into deformation. These obstacles are rooted in our depths. They stem from our attachment to our present way of life. In the service of incoherence (as we shall discuss in the chapter on justice), we know of no objective criteria for evil, only, at best, inter-subjective ones—if our self-interest, and perhaps also a fragment of emanation we still share, turn a number of us in the same direction.

Was slavery evil? How long it took us and how bitter the battle to put an end to it! Is racism or sexism evil? That struggle is still underway. Was Hitler evil? First let us try to appease him at Munich. Now that he has taken over Austria, let us also give him at least part of Czechoslovakia to keep him content. With respect to all these questions, I have spoken of the response to evil of democratic liberal societies—the second best of all our political alternatives.

In addition, in both emanation and incoherence, we remain often uncritical of evil when people in authority (not only within the state but within any drama in these ways of life) do what they declare must be done in order to preserve our way of life or the enactment of any drama in its service. In these fragments of the core drama, our political face is not sufficiently awake to what we can and need to do together but primarily to what the more powerful embodiments of established archetypal forces seek to achieve.

Our historical face of being sustains what may be evil actions by acknowledging that indeed we have had to do such things before or else, by contrast, we need to do them now because we face a crisis. Hence our sacred face accepts these evil acts as absolutely necessary or as emanationally justified by our bond to our way of life when in fact such explanations constitute pseudo-emanational cover stories for evil. We may be able to recognize evil only when it arises from outside our way of life, but given the frequency and pervasiveness of alliances with deformation within our own way of life, even that realization does not come easily.

Our personal face of being in emanation and incoherence often also serves to blind us to evil. Except in the experience of transformation, we hold on to the power to repress what we saw and heard and felt when it is too powerful for us to respond within our own present power and too awful to remember. But repression does not empty us of any such experience. Instead, it moves that encounter into the shadow

---

59. We shall be discussing racism, sexism, and culture in chapters 11 and 12.

of our being and erupts again and again from behind our back, especially through projecting its darkly negative image upon others and seeking to scapegoat them in the hope that therefore we shall be saved.[60] We thus become the carriers of deformation. And if we are still more powerful during a crisis than the people we identify as our necessary scapegoats, they may become psychically infected and accept the identity we have projected upon them: Yes, we are members of an inferior race; yes, god did declare that we deserve to be persecuted and to suffer.

Are there any barriers to evil? None that we cannot in three of the four ways of life be moved to break. Are there any obstacles—even if not barriers—to evil? I know of only two: We can arrest ourselves in Act I or Act II of the core drama of life. Such overarching arrests inhibit evil as long as they remain powerful and stable, and can still be counted on to punish those who—however deforming our punishment—commit such evil as these ways allow us to recognize. But to arrest ourselves in a constantly changing world, especially in our time, is to be tempted, as we saw, to move increasingly into alliance with deformation. That alliance increases the power of the powerful but diminishes and warps the capacity and performance of all of us. And when vital connections within the dominant way of life break, the experience of that alliance leads the powerful to reinforce the seemingly still greater and more impressive power of deformation—and more of the devastated and enraged powerless to strive for it too. When society's arrests in revealed or procedural law and order begin to dissolve, deformation can have devastating effects even without being executed by the State. Cut off from our former emanational roots, isolated and damaged in what we can and need to do together, harmed by our history, we move toward destroying ourselves or our family and former friends.

But there is an alternative to evil stronger than any inhibiting obstacle. We can free ourselves to tune in to the breaking as it takes place and to help the people who are being moved by a sense of betrayal or suicide to enter with new hope, faith, love, and understanding into the drama of transformation before deformation gains in power. The last section of this chapter will begin to elaborate on this alternative. Even now, we need to acknowledge that our power to blind ourselves to such an alternative or to reject it is not small.

Here are still more—but not all—of the obstacles to leaving the road to destructive death: I am regarded as useless, unwanted, inferior, and unworthy. I have nothing. I can find no opportunities for a fruitful new start. Why should I—how could I—live up to their standards? Why then would I not resort to the satisfaction of drugs or robbery? It gets me something now. I killed the man I robbed. Hell, I do not expect to live very long either. You are talking about the need for a world in

---

60. For a sagacious and most helpfully revealing analysis, see Sylvia B. Perera, *The Scapegoat Complex: Toward a Mythology of Shadow and Guilt*.

which men and women practice critical consciousness, compassion, and creative action. I've never met anybody like that. Where are they?

That increasingly disconnected person counters times of despair with momentary highs of power. Why not move into a (merely) opposite direction—rage? Rage, unlike anger, explodes beyond any limits. The other is turned into a dreaded thing, not entitled to any human respect and understanding. Rage, like rage repressed, produces a seeming void—not the emptying needed for transformation.

Both despair and rage in the face of betrayal lead to victimizing either ourselves or others. These are both powerful fantasies of destruction. Would transformation give us even more power? No. It would give us the capacity for a journey that these people never heard of and cannot now imagine.

Whenever I became afraid that I was about to be completely rejected and abandoned by the powerful person at home because I had not yielded to that person and conformed to that person's demands, I would seek to avoid that person's revenging final blow by making myself emotionally invisible to that great power and to myself. I wanted to survive upon a station short of destructive death. I turned myself even as a child but also as an adult into the Old Man of the North—an archetypal drama in which I appeared as frozen stiff, seemingly already dead (not really dead but also not really alive)—disabled from actually dealing with the problem at hand and not worth bothering with any longer.

It is also possible to focus with great skill, energy, and devotion upon one fragment of the process of fragmenting and claim that I am not killing any Jew: I am a bureaucrat making sure that the trains are filled and run on schedule to the death camps. I do not deliberately kill Jews; I am a doctor experimenting with their living bodies for the sake of new scientific findings. I do not use poison gas; I am a scientist testing it, or I am a worker working hard to package it. These claims may have been excuses after defeat, when in fact they were originally deep commitments to the fragment I could best augment in the cause of total power. Or they may indeed have been blinding commitments to details turning us with rigid insensitivity from a person into a *persona*—our personal face into a mask that also defined us for ourselves.

Add together all the indices of what American scholars used to call "modernization"—not only high per-capita income and a high growth rate but also high literacy, high media consumption, highly developed transportation and communication networks, high use of nonhuman energy harnessed to technology, a high degree of national consensus, highly effective execution of law and order, a highly efficient bureaucracy, at least one political party connecting ruler and ruled in common public purpose—and no country in Western Europe in the late nineteen-thirties would have ranked higher than Nazi Germany.[61]

---

61. Manfred Halpern, "A Redefinition of the Revolutionary Situation," *The Journal of International Affairs* 23:1 (1969), 56.

Focusing only on one fragment or analyzing only variables—being clinically or professionally detached without any critical consciousness of the underlying forces at work and their moral impact on human lives—is how we learn to behave in the service of incoherence. Emanation as a web of life is no longer with us in most of the world, and transformation is least familiar to us in our time. I suspect that when President (and former General in World War I) Hindenburg appointed Hitler to be Chancellor, the powerful strengthening of order and stability (and perhaps revenge for the German defeat in the First World War) was uppermost in that President's mind—not any commitment to totalitarianism. Like Hitler's German high capitalist allies, Hindenburg may have minimized Hitler's totalitarianism as demagoguery used to gain power but not actually to be practical.

The path of deformation has no inescapable beginning or ending. Its forces can come into power at the top of the state without first gaining a majority. Elites in the service of incoherence often deliver the final blow.[62] Even movements of transformation can be turned into targets of deformation. Jesus was crucified. In our time, many thousands in the liberation theology movement have been killed. Movements of transformation can even be perverted by their enemies into movements of deformation: witness the projection of being satanic upon those who did not follow what came to be established as orthodox Christianity.[63] Witness the actions of the Catholic Church we already discussed in Chapter 4.

To be alert to the very beginnings and early growth of movements of deformation and to organize effective ways of healing human lives are therefore essential.

WHAT INHIBITS RESISTANCE TO DEFORMATION?

What depotentiates our ability to resist deformation are the suicidal alternatives to varieties of murder when an emanational way of life or a once deeply possessive emanational bond to incoherence as a way of life, or to any dramas in its service, breaks and hence also breaks us. This is the underlying, archetypal explosion that patterns our responses. We have, against all expectations, ceased to be the embodiment of a deeply and powerfully protective source. Now we do not know who we are. The mysterious and mystifying quality of emanation kept us from knowing who we really were. Now we have nothing, none of the energy and sense of direction that source once gave us. All we have now is great pain.

In most of the preceding sections, we have focused on the satanic alternatives to murder. Now we focus on the suicidal varieties of responses by which Satan

---

62. See Nancy G. Bermeo and P. G. Nord, *Civil Society before Democracy: Lessons from Nineteenth-Century Europe*. This shows that none of the thirteen European countries that turned into dictatorships or totalitarian regimes did so by majority vote. Elites delivered the final blow in every case.

63. For a superb analysis of this rise of Satan, see Elaine H. Pagels, *The Origin of Satan*.

leads us (and therefore also others whom we thereby neglect or injure) toward destructive death. Evil takes place not only when others initiate it, but also when we do nothing. I will cite many conventional ways of speaking about this response in order to reveal the actual underlying pattern of emanational dissolution so that we can come to know from what deeper forces—and not only from which concrete obstacles—we need to free ourselves.

When the shock of losing crucial emanational ties leaves us lonely, loveless, feeling meaningless, and powerless so that we no longer know of any alternative to freezing ourselves into apathy, we may not even feel capable of understanding or responding to the slogan "You are nothing; your folk is everything." But neither will we be emboldened to resist such a movement of deformation. Our depression exiles us into what we hope is safe invisibility.

One obverse of apathy, if we still have the strength of some other emanational bonds in our life, is to remove ourselves from the memory of our crisis. I am too scared to find out what is disturbing me so much; it might destroy even what I am still hanging on to. Such an act of repression leads us to being indifferent to our own pain and that of others: I am too busy (now all the more so); I am too tired to figure things out. Or in another obverse of apathy, we become nihilists. We clutch the satanic inspiration that nothing matters.

Why can we linger in such a state? We live in incoherence in a world often reduced to atomistic individualism, in a world also in which by now too often we can say this: My mother also did not care, nor did my father. We are thus only conforming to what there is—or is not there any more.

Once forces of deformation gain power, we may in our present state of deprivation feel all the more afraid of resisting. Now either we are dominant and can terrifyingly prove it, or else we are scared. What else is there? Covertly manipulating such forces is possible only for high-ranking insiders. If we do not share their dogma, only a highly prudent yet deeply ambitious devotion to careerism could save and even promote us. Yet appeasing such an arbitrary ruler (or parent) is a task we need to have the presence to attend to every moment. And how often we fail!

It is all too easy for those without the mysterious power of emanational support and its seemingly protective confines to be pessimistic—now any situation seems beyond our justified right to change. According to a Gestapo-organized public opinion poll (surely valid, in the light of results not hoped for by the secret police) 90 percent of the German people opposed the Nazi violence against Jews on Kristallnacht, but these Germans did nothing. Indeed, if we are to survive at all, we must not try to change anything; just try to survive.

These defense mechanisms demonstrate that the road of deformation already seriously afflicts our lives—that oppression already dominates us. The repression necessary for all of them deeply damages our insights and our feelings and our capacity to help ourselves and our neighbors. Repression conceals, disguises, distorts reality.

Within such warped containers, we cannot recognize or understand the underlying forces that have now enchained us. A laming anxiety hits us from the shadows of our being again and again and drains our energy. Depression (in contrast to conscious sadness) cripples our capacity to understand and to act. If we possibly can, we focus what energy is left on repressing our anxiety. We don't want actually to face the fact that our life and the lives of others are becoming unbearable.

MUST WE SUFFER?

Can suffering lead to transformation? In the service of emanation—at least within its three monotheistic forms—what is required is not only our righteousness but also the grace of god and his mercy. For we suffer because god is punishing us for our sins or is testing our righteous obedience. Or, even if we are obedient, our suffering may be a mysterious expression of the will of god. Or, in some forms of emanation, god will finally send us a Redeemer. To accept suffering on these grounds gives us seemingly deep security, at the cost of seeking no fundamental solutions except, at best, a compassionate attentiveness to suffering human beings who do not persist in sin and who do not live beyond our sacred container.

In the service of incoherence, suffering for long was treated as a private issue—as a matter solely of personal responsibility—until the rise of the welfare state in some societies began to attend to some problems of economic survival. The rise of scientific freedom, which also accompanied the dying emanation, led to the discovery of drugs and surgical operations that can cure personal physical pain. But most people living in societies in the service of incoherence around the world still remain deprived even of these economic and physical alleviations of suffering. All still experience the personal, political, historical, and sacred suffering of arrest in a partial way of life. Arrest in emanation or incoherence is a substitute for really facing the task of overcoming suffering even short of deformation or as the result of alliances with deformation. (We examined in earlier sections the grave toll of the fragmenting impact of deformation upon its suffering victims and also upon its seemingly triumphant leaders and followers.)

Is suffering required in order to enable ourselves to recognize what has gone wrong and to give rise to our responsibility to empty ourselves of it in order to empower ourselves with new understanding and courage and to help create a life of love and justice? The only helpful aspect of suffering may be that it could help us reach a point where we cannot avoid facing it. Suffering until we find it unbearable is a possible road to transformation, but deformation, as we have seen, can also (even if not inescapably) keep us overwhelmed too long, even at the cost of our life. Suffering can, at its very outset, lead us to move toward transformation much sooner if we therefore discern our situation or that of others to be already unfruitful and likely to become untenable and unbearable.

Suffering is intrinsic to human life. We cannot prevent all suffering. Human beings will never be in full control of life; happily, this is not a cosmos that is or can be automated along predetermined lines. To alleviate suffering as soon as possible—that is our task.

What is crucial for transformation is not suffering. Suffering, as we see every day, can be seemingly justified, and also imposed and accepted, without leading to transformation. We can also rebel against suffering, as the Jews rebelled against slavery in Egypt, migrated through the desert of incoherence for forty years, and received a new inspiration. But that generation of Jews had not sufficiently emptied itself, said god, to be allowed to enter the more promising land.

Christ, the emanational Christians tell us, died for our sins. But Christ did not seek or tell us to seek crucifixion. He said: Die again and again to be reborn again and again. We do not need to wait to suffer. We can free our capacity to empty ourselves now of ways of life and dramas vulnerable to or already in alliance with deformation because we can come to understand the great cost of the underlying dramas now at work. Then we shall have the strength, insight, and compassion to help ourselves and others to leave this dreadful road.[64]

HELPING OURSELVES AND OTHERS TO TURN AWAY FROM THE ROAD TO DESTRUCTIVE DEATH

People are open to transformation only when they find their present way of living unbearable, untenable, or unfruitful. Must we wait then till they find deformation unbearable—a moment all too close to destructive death? No! As we have seen, people enter this road to destructive death because they find already unbearable the breaking of emanation as a way of life, or the breaking of their emanatinal bond to incoherence and to crucial dramas in its service. Our most fruitful response is not trying to restore their past connection to a once mysteriously powerful source but to help them understand what happened, or is now happening, and to turn them from deep resentment, or crippling passivity, or passion for revenge, and guide them toward a fundamentally new and better connection to themselves and to others. That kind of help and guidance is at the heart of this last section and also of the next chapter on transformation as a way of life.[65]

People possessed by deformation will not find it easy to hear this. Their being is currently severely damaged and diminished. They do not understand—not even their leaders do—the underlying dynamics of their movement toward destructive

---

64. In Paul Edwards, *The Encyclopedia of Philosophy*. There is no entry on the subject of suffering. For an analysis of suffering rooted in a deeply informing and critical analysis of the causes of past philosophical neglect of this issue and its present conceptions in modern and postmodern theory, see Cynthia Halpern, *Suffering, Politics, Power: A Genealogy in Modern Political Theory*.

65. We shall explore this great and unfamiliar task in greater depth in Chapters 8–14.

death. In their trauma, anxiety, and despair—or its obverse, their commitment to a fantasy of glory—they cannot muster the strength and detachment for critical evaluation. Above all, they want to drown their sense of loss by raising themselves high through their attachment to the one absolute fragment of life that still draws them. Why trust anyone who disagrees? These others must be our enemies. And if people on this road were now to desert their new mission, they fear that their leader, their gang, or the absence of drugs will kill them. Or, in the darkness of what they already suffer, they are afraid to explore where they are now. They are afraid we will subvert their defense mechanisms.

These are no small barricades against transformation. Can we help them now to restore the emanational relationships that have been broken against their will? For reasons we explored earlier, emanation as a permanently anchored way of life can no longer securely preserve us at a time when we face fundamentally new questions. Emanational relationships to people and stories in the service of incoherence are intrinsically vulnerable. The devil is the dominant sacred source, and loyalty, love, power, desire, intellectual conviction, and property possessed in that service are at risk again and again. To face deformation as soon as it breaks out, or threatens to break out, while most of us still live in the service of incoherence, is a challenge to which we need to attend also with the partial resources of incoherence.

We can even now struggle to persuade our society to provide care for deserted and abused children, adequate health and welfare for all, methadone drugs plus therapy for cocaine addicts, and an end to threats to our environment—many such specific programs. But the heart of the matter is freeing people from the tolls exacted by the breaking of past emanational bonds to existing relationships and ways of life—and from the toll of incoherence's alliance with deformation. We can help them to gain a new capacity to understand and to enter the new opportunities of transforming stories. Incremental change and incoherence as a way of life cannot be relied upon to prevent or overcome the underlying forces leading to deformation.

As long as we live in incoherence as a way of life, having rendered ourselves biased and incomplete—even those of us who feel free to speak, to seek power and profit—even reformers cannot yet understand why the modern age, thanks to the dying of emanation and the limits of incoherence as a way of life with its frequent breaking of established relationships, has rendered all of us more vulnerable to deformation. We do not know how to evaluate the ultimate meaning, value, and purpose of anything, and hence have great difficulties tuning in to the underlying patterning forces and dynamics of the fundamentally worse or that move us to seek the fundamentally better. We may come to agree on issues of law and order. But we remain much more divided, indeed lamed, by existing power structures and scarcity of empathy and understanding regarding how to heal connections that are breaking—or that lesser or invisible human beings are not allowed to make and are thus creating problems of law and order (and much deeper problems).

Germany, Italy, Russia, and China have turned away from deformation into incoherence. People—with some exceptions in the latter two countries—are no longer being destroyed. That is a great gain indeed. But as we have seen in the preceding chapter, even in one of the best of cases of serving incoherence—in the United States—there persist major alliances with deformation. And all the cases of deformation we have examined in this chapter arose initially out of the vulnerability of incoherence to incoherence—to the breaking of relationships that we lack the power to reorganize. Incoherence as a way of life cannot offer us nourishing foundations for preventing deformation or solidly moving us beyond any such outbreaks. It can only motivate us to act out of a partially developed yet deeply moving self-interest.

As long as we remain only partial beings, we normally fail to be alert in time to the emanational dissolutions that lead to deformation. We are only prepared to meet with counter-force rebels who do not act according to agreed upon procedures. We arrest and imprison them—but we do not attend to them as human beings before their arrest or even after we have them under our physical control.

We have in this century discovered one other alternative: individual therapy. Therapy can indeed be of great help in moving people out of preponderantly personal manifestations of deformation. But therapy is not available to most people in dire trouble. There are far too few psychologists, psychiatrists, and social workers. Their fees are unaffordable to most people in trouble. The government spends very little money indeed to help people who need such care. Few therapists go out into neighborhoods to help those in need to discover this path to healing.

And at present, almost all therapists focus entirely on the personal face of our travail—on neuroses or psychoses, or the experience of inadequate, inhibiting, painful, or breaking relationships, ignoring the damage to our political, historical, and sacred faces that also lead us into deformation. Social workers may also try to help us with particular problems of legally or currently politically defined cases of injustice—if it is indeed within their power to do so.

The great majority of therapists take it for granted that, while they can help us resolve the personal problems in a particular drama of our life, we need to learn to adjust to the dominant way of life. That is a public affair. They may at best help us find and enact a different drama already available in the service of incoherence. Hence we may find a new security blanket, rendering us biased enough to feel less incomplete in our renewed arrest in the core drama of life. But we have not yet found our way to our true and deepest self, or toward helping to build a new kind of community. A very good therapist *can indeed* help us to find and open the door toward that transforming experience.

In analyzing various dramas in the service of deformation, I have emphasized understanding how we move onto that path. The earlier in time we act on that understanding, the more readily the people on that path can still hear us and change—when what we have hitherto experienced as the most mysteriously powerful relationships of our life are about to break or have just broken. They can hear us because their old defense mechanisms no longer work. Hence they are more vulnerable also to new insights before deformation takes over. If we cannot understand how and why we are moving into deformation, it is extremely difficult to move out of deformation. We certainly must not wait until deformation is about to control our government. That may well happen before such a movement gains a majority. Then it may become too difficult or too dangerous for us even to mobilize a self-defensive counter-force. We need to act together with our neighbors as a counter community as our society begins to be undone by deformation.

We cannot transform anyone else by putting ourselves in charge of their life. We certainly can never coerce anyone into transformation. Once they recognize us as compassionately and insightfully understanding, they will feel free to express their rage and resentment at what happened to them. Obviously, we shall not reject them as irrational or depraved or (to use a scientifically detached term) nonconformist. We realize (and so will they) why we empathize with their feelings. Through our compassion and understanding we are helping them to become strong enough to freely open and to empty themselves. We cannot transform what is in fact evil, but we can free ourselves from its power. "Perhaps everything terrifying is in its deepest cause helpless, wanting help from us."[66] Even within emanation, incoherence, and deformation, we still keep hearing from the deepest source of our being—it is a very part of our nature—but we cannot comprehend it. But when we are being helped to see truly why we have reached a crisis—a separation that does not allow us to turn back—we may well begin to understand and to bring forth what is most enriching within us.

Our task is to engage ourselves in face-to-face encounters to explain the experience of the drama of transformation so that people can recognize and practice it—knowing how to help them along this way because we have gained insight and courage as living examples of it. And our task is also to organize politically with them and with others so that together we can create a new community that finances such guidance on a full-time basis and that connects us with people and resources to overcome the underlying causes of deformation.

Are we ready for such a task now? Now is certainly already the time to begin. But we are starting from scratch. The sad fact is *not* that there is nothing we can really do to stop deformation, but that there are not yet enough people with the understanding and experience needed to do it. All forms of deformation are self-destructive, but at the cost of great suffering while it endures. And we have reached

---

66. Rainer Maria Rilke and F. X. Kappus, *Briefe an einen jungen dichter*, 48. This does not mean that Rilke or I believe in enantiodromia, a supposed psychological law that when one position is carried to its utmost extreme, it is transformed into its opposite. Nothing so automatic.

a time when even a few thousand nuclear warheads can destroy most of the world.[67] Even a small elite can ally itself with a force of deformation to inflict "order" upon the majority of people. Small numbers of transforming people cannot yet prevent or overcome the horrors of deformation.

We live in very dangerous times in our country. In the name of "God" many want to cleanse the world of evil at any cost. We are daily faced with the fear of terrorism and thus many are willing to give up constitutional rights for security. The military budget continues to grow while programs for the elderly and children are being cut because of a weak economy and tax cuts that will largely benefit the wealthy.

It is therefore all the more vital that we begin now to organize movements of transformation within ourselves and with others. That journey leads us not only toward the fundamentally better but helps us to overcome a life that is fundamentally worse—and also to move beyond ways of life that render us vulnerable to deformation or seduce or force us into alliance with it.

Deformation always offers a "final" solution. Transformation never does. It helps us create a community in which people are free and capable of fully expressing and connecting all four faces and the deepest source of our being. And that enables people to go through the drama of transformation again and again as new questions and problems arise—as they always will—in order newly to nourish what we are where we are, and to find new answers. We shall now discuss transformation as a way of life, contrasting it with our other three choices.

---

67. In 1961, Daniel Ellsberg at the White House was shown a top-secret document estimating how many people would die in a full-scale nuclear war between the United States and the Soviet Union. The number was 350 million dead in the USSR and China, 100 million in Eastern Europe, 100 million in Western Europe, and 100 million more in Finland, Afghanistan, and Japan as the radioactive fallout spread around the world. (No figures on American deaths were included.) However, by 1996, the power of nuclear weapons had greatly increased. The atom bomb dropped on Hiroshima was equivalent to 15,000 tons of TNT. Today, when the nuclear weapons stockpile has by international agreement been reduced from 18,000 to 8,000 megatons, U.S. bombers alone can carry 8 million tons of nuclear TNT. Sea-launched cruise missiles can hit a target 1,500 miles away and ballistic nuclear missiles are now accurate to within four hundred feet. (On Ellsberg's speech at Princeton University, see *The Trenton Times*, November 4, 1996. On current U.S. nuclear power, see *World Military and Social Expenditures*, published by World Priorities, a Washington Research Organization, cited by Jane Ciabattari, *Parade*, October 27, 1996.)

7

Transformation as a Way of Life

The search for a life based upon fundamentally better understanding, love, and justice began at least millennia ago. What is novel about it in our time is that for the first time in human history, the archetypal force of one of the four ways of life open to us is dying. The way of life that has become dominant around the world fashions us only into partial beings competing solely for larger fragments of life, and deformation is becoming a growing threat. Transformation is now the least known and the least experienced way.

Transformation is not an ideal—something visionary but actually impractical. It is not utopian. The journey of transformation does not begin in a boat that gets lost in a storm and suddenly comes upon an island where a wondrous society blooms. In this chapter we shall first discuss the most fundamental obstacle now in our path— the way of life that now dominates us. Then we shall explore moving toward the actual practice of transformation open to us as a fundamentally better way of life.

I never knew that transformation was an alternative until I had written a book in 1963 that for the first time compared the problems of modernization for the countries from Morocco to Pakistan. For almost all policy makers and academics of that time (beginning in the 1950s and at least until the end of this past century), modernization meant westernization, even as the next term used was seemingly less culture-bound—namely, *political and economic development*. But the essential meaning of *development* consisted of Western concepts of stability of political order, efficiency, and increased production.[1] If it became feasible under existing

---

1. See, for example, Harry Eckstein, "The Idea of Political Development: From Dignity to Efficiency," *World Politics* 34:4 (July 1982): "In developmental theory, one wants, ideally, to identify a general motive force that operates throughout developmental time (akin to physical inertia) and also

conditions, increased political participation was also explored as an issue—but all these were issues solely of new power.[2]

OPENING DOORS TO TRANSFORMATION

Writing that book, *The Politics of Social Change in the Middle East and North Africa*[3] had begun to alert me to two vital facts. First, this part of the world faced many issues beyond increased order, efficiency, production, and power. It could not overcome its new, deep, and ever-recurrent crises unless it also freed and helped human beings to discover the basic causes of their modern problems and how to resolve them. How can we change the present connections—indeed the growing lack of connections—between human beings and the growing absence of community? How can we put an end to the new and increasing causes and burdens of political, economic, and military exploitation by the newly powerful? How can we find new grounds of being and justice as our fixed inherited concepts and rules of the sacred as well as our experience of modernization limit our own deeper vision? The second vital fact is that no part of the world can grapple with the basic new problems of the modern age without facing these same questions.

I therefore decided to write a book that would deal in a systematic comparative way with modernization as a worldwide problem. First I called it *Violence and the Dialectics of Modernization*. I wrote all the chapters—except the last one—of what I had re-titled *Dialectics of Transformation in Politics, Personality, and History*. I only knew the title for the last chapter: "Where Does the Fundamentally New and Better Come From?" I did not want to write a book that was only critical of where we all currently existed. I wanted to be able to show that there was a much better road to a far more fruitful and richer life. The Princeton University Press, unusual in the face of an unfinished manuscript, signed a contract in 1968 accepting this book. It turned out that I did not have a glimmer of an answer to that question at the top of the final chapter: Where does the fundamentally new and better come from?

That threw me into a deep depression that affected all aspects of my life, for I recognized that I myself was caught in a way of life that, even for its successful

---

special forces, generated in each earlier stage, which similarly lead to each later stage. The general motive force at work in the sequence of stages I have described is surely the drive for the direct and indirect benefits of efficient primacy in and over society—the direct benefit of social elevation and indirect perquisites, such as material goods. . . . The long trajectory from social polity to [modern] political society can also be considered a modulation from 'dignity' to 'efficiency' (the most fundamental quantitative social change conceivable)" (pp. 484, 486).

2. Lucian W. Pye, "The Concept of Political Development," *The Annals of the American Academy of Social and Political Science*, March 1965: "[Participation] may be either democratic or a form of totalitarian mobilization, but the key consideration is that subjects should become active citizens and at least the pretenses of popular rule are necessary" (pp. 11–12).

3. Manfred Halpern, *The Politics of Social Change in the Middle East and North Africa*.

relationships, exacted a high cost. Hence its human connections were often inadequate or dissolving. I felt that we all needed transformation, but I did not know what it meant. I could think about it only in terms of concepts supplied by our present way of life. For example, I wrote, "Transformation, at any time in history, may be defined as that kind of alteration of a system which results in the exclusion of some existing elements and linkages and the entrance of some new elements and linkages sufficient to be recognized, at a given level of abstraction, as a new system. (By *system* I mean simply a patterned interaction of elements.)"[4] What I had written did not enlighten me about the process of transformation.

What helped me to discover a fundamentally new and better answer? I needed to discover the archetypal dramas that had held me enchanted and enchained and that had kept my feelings of discontent still much repressed—archetypal dramas that had kept me from freeing myself to hear and understand anew.[5] I needed to become emotionally and not simply intellectually free to experience and to say, "I now really know that I do not know." Modifications and augmentations of my existing vision did not—and could not—help. I did not know what caused these pervasive human problems that afflict so many millions of us, including me—wars, exploitation, poverty, racism, tyranny.

Until we have succeeded in emptying ourselves of the living underlying patterning forces that insulate us, we cannot hear and also understand anew. We—and not only I—we, any of us, can discover and experience the fundamentally new and better, for the capacity to experience the core drama of life is intrinsic to human nature.

But it is not easy. Emanation as a way of life in most of the world no longer has the power to bar us from asking fundamentally new questions or to punish us for that sin if we do ask. But incoherence *does* stand in our way. We cannot, while we remain arrested within incoherence, imagine that we can find out the ultimate reality, meaning, value, or purpose of anything. On what grounds therefore can we possibly raise any fundamental criticism of what is taking place or justify any radically different response?

Certainly the powerful see no reason to ask or encourage any questions except about what is likely to lead to their next success or could threaten their present power. Even thinkers in the natural and social sciences who challenge existing

---

4. Manfred Halpern, "The Revolution of Modernization," in Roy C. Macridis and Bernard Edward Brown, *Comparative Politics: Notes and Readings*, third ed., *The Dorsey Series in Political Science*, 513, 514; published earlier as "The Revolution of Modernization in National and International Society" in *American Society for Political and Legal Philosophy*. See also Carl J. Friedrich, *Revolution: Yearbook*, 8.

5. What also helped me was finding a guide for this road. In 1971, I entered Jungian therapy with Dr. Edward Christopher Whitmont. He greatly deepened my understanding of archetypal forces shaping my life, and helped free me enough so that subsequently, I came to recognize archetypal dramas—not only archetypal forces, of which Carl Gustav Jung and his students spoke.

paradigms are usually deeply opposed by their colleagues unless their ideas aid the already powerful.[6] Thinkers in the service of incoherence are specialists; they focus their work solely on a fragment (or at most, several fragments) of life.

The less successful see no way of moving upward except by trying again to work within this *system*. I emphasize that it *is* a system because we actually face at this moment in history all the concrete persons, ideas, values, institutions, and patterns of interaction that prevail, but all of these manifest above all—even within ourselves— the overarching archetypal force that empowers but in fact also diminishes us.

Incoherence as a way of life seems to be a success in a growing number of countries—especially in terms of the three most dominant archetypal dramas in its service—liberal democracy, capitalism, and the nation-state.[7] Why should any of us be critical of this way of life, except about particular insufficiencies or errors? Liberal democracy has given us more freedom than we had before. Capitalism has given us more wealth, more goods and services, more jobs than we had before. But as we have discussed in the last two chapters, however great a success we experience in these two archetypal dramas, since we arrested ourselves in Act II Scene 1 of the core drama of life, we can only get hold of fragments of life and of our own being and the being of others. Whatever our power, we experience a poverty of human relationships. We are not yet fully participating authors of our own being. We are at war with our selves and others on many fronts. We feel a sense of claustrophobia within the boundaries of our self.[8]

We pay a high price for our freedom and power to preserve or augment our arrest. But from within incoherence as a way of life, only incremental changes are possible, thus keeping our real, underlying problems disguised. Why then do most of us now still adhere to this way of life? Incoherence as an archetypal way of life also supplies us with defense mechanisms aggressively to justify or defensively to hide its costs to us and to others. To those of us who now get its payoff, that is justification enough for our life. Transformation is unnecessary; we are already the most successful in power and productivity. For those of us still seeking to rise, we know we always have to pay a price for anything. I cannot afford to risk my job by raising questions. You say that only fragments of life are all I can get now? Why would you have me risk not getting the most I can now get under these circumstances? There is now no other game. If I lose out, it will by my fault.

But being caught within such defense mechanisms is a symptom of a far deeper and greater enchainment. As long as we are possessed by this archetypal bond, we

---

6. Thomas S. Kuhn, *The Structure of Scientific Revolutions*. We shall further examine how theories are shaped by being in the service of incoherence when we take up such matters in the chapter on theory.

7. See the archetypal drama of capitalism as discussed in Chapter 5.

8. The last three sentences are drawn from a lecture by Jeremy Goldman at Princeton University in 1995.

would feel completely vulnerable or deeply enraged if we dropped these defenses and betrayed our emanational commitment to our present way of life. We do not know how to deal with such a challenge in any other way as long as we do not know and cannot even imagine any alternative—but only the fantasy of totally re-empowering ourselves through deformation.

And why, in the face of challenges to incoherence as a way of life would the powerful not want to defend their power in even greater alliances with deformation than they already do now? Arresting ourselves within the core drama of life requires us to repress ourselves or else be suppressed by the powerful. When these defense mechanisms disintegrate because of a challenge, we do not know how to deal with them because repression (or suppression) has succeeded in diminishing our being and the being of others. The insight and courage required for moving toward the understanding, love, and justice of transformation is hard to discover. We still lack the full freedom, capacity, and understanding we can discover only as we consummate our journey through the core drama of life.

Why, then, is there any hope for transformation? The answer is this: Not all people in our time are still possessed by incoherence as a way of life nor are they being drawn into deformation.

UNDERLYING FORCES SHAPING THE FUNDAMENTAL DIFFERENCE BETWEEN INCREMENTAL AND TRANSFORMING CHANGE

Many of us desire to change and improve our lives and the lives of others, but until we free ourselves from its living underlying patterning force, we are being limited in all our actions to incremental changes by the very structure and dynamics of our present way of life. It is only possible for us to try for more or else for less—or at most for re-formation, that is, for a new and different archetypal drama that nonetheless fits within the basic limits of our present way of life. All arrested ways of life terminate all the dramas we enact in their service at the same point at which that overarching way has been halted within the core drama of life. This is the basic cause of our being confined solely to incremental changes within such ways of life. In the service of incoherence, no drama takes us (or *can* take us) beyond Act II Scene 1—institutionalized forms of rebellion to possess or enlarge or change or create new fragments of life.

At most, within these limits, we may criticize burdens or discriminations or failures from within incoherence as a way of life. We may ask, "What does their particular action do to our particular interest?" Or we may struggle—especially as women, members of ethnic minorities, and the poor often do—to enter the capitalist and democratic archetypal dramas of competitive self-interest and group-interest in order to become insiders at last within incoherence as a way of life. Or, if we fail, we may still accept these dominant dramas and blame ourselves for not having taken enough responsibility to gain power for our success. Or we join such forms of underground capitalism as the drug trade, or such underground forms of democracy as doing whatever we individually or as a small group can get away with.

The largest kind of change that may sometimes be achieved within incoherence as a way of life is re-formation—by that I mean something more specific than reform or a religious reformation. I mean the dissolution of an existing archetypal drama or the creation of a new archetypal drama—but only in order to re-form incoherence as a way of life. Examples are the abolition of slavery, the rise of the nation-state, the welfare state, and the ending of colonial rule.[9]

I have not spoken of revolutions since I know of no revolution in the modern age that began or persisted as a process of transformation. Revolutions have changed elites, the ownership of production, and, unless they also moved into deformation, they have redistributed the costs and benefits of incoherence.

Yes, all particular problems matter. Let us do whatever is possible today to help us to reduce people's pain or to improve their lives. But what is not possible through any kind of incremental change is overcoming the intrinsically partial nature of our solution and the still partial nature and experience of our being and of all our relationships—partial, biased by our arrest, and hence incomplete. No incremental changes in human life can ever become transforming. With respect to any particular problem, the heart of the question is this: What will it take to overcome this archetypal drama and incoherence as a way of life that give rise to this kind of problem?

PRACTICING TRANSFORMATION AS A WAY OF LIFE

Even in incoherence and not only in emanation as ways of life, thanks to the power of our emanational relationship to archetypal forces and their concrete exemplars, our hearts and minds are closed to the humanity of the Outsider, and also the lesser and invisible within our society. Our understanding and empathy is diminishing even for all partial others within our society—including ourselves. Our concern, if any, is primarily about possible threats to our power. These threats may come from the deprived *other* and sometimes from the compassion still alive within us as fragments inherited from emanation as a way of life.

Transformation can only begin within a person, but it always produces new insight, courage, and capacity not only to bring fully alive the personal face of our

---

9. As I stated in Chapter 1, I deliberately offer no term for movement from one way of life to another, for example, from deformation under Hitler to incoherence since his defeat. I prefer that kind of precise reference to any general term. *Transformation* is a word I reserve for moving into transformation as a way of life.

being but also our political, historical, and sacred face—and to help others to enter and experience this way of life with us. This book therefore began with a chapter that concentrated on the personal experience of the core drama of life. Now we shall focus above all on our political and historical experience in turning transformation into a way of life. Chapter 14 will explore our manifesting the bi-unity of our connection (in transformation) to the deepest sacred source of our being.

This present chapter is shockingly short in a book dedicated to transformation—shorter than the chapters on the other three ways of life. We have as yet so little practical experience of it.

Who shall lead us into transformation? No one. We are looking neither for leaders nor for followers. We need guides—people who, thanks to their own experience of transformation with respect to at least one kind of problem, can offer themselves to others as living examples of transformation, and hence are free, capable, and deeply caring enough to help others experience this most fruitful of all archetypal dramas.

Guides never present themselves as gurus. They may at first, thanks to their enabling wisdom and empathy, seem to be a source of emanational inspiration. But guides of transformation never seek to arrest people in any emanational bond. Belief in transformation is of no help whatsoever. What matters is faith—meaning risking trust and testing the actual experience of transformation. For true guides of transformation are always not only in the process of helping but also of making themselves unnecessary as a guide with respect to that particular kind of problem.

When the guided ones reach Act III, each will have experienced the underlying structure and dynamics of transformation—and will have experienced the message from a prophet (initially the guide may be heard only as a prophet), but then that message is also experienced within. Hence the guided one begins to hear the guide's new kinds of questions and joins with the guide in gaining new understanding of the underlying patterning forces that were so costly in shaping this problem. Now the guided ones become ready on their own to reject these forces and to turn into participants in testing out with others their fundamentally new and better inspiration. That experience also enables them to become their own guides and the guides of others.

Hence there is no hierarchy of guides and the guided. Sometimes you will be able to guide me and sometimes I will be able to guide you—always a temporary, moveable, response-able (that sense of *responsible*) interaction. There is no possibility of a universal guide who understands all problems. Guides, on the basis of their own practical and theoretically informed experience, begin by helping people who feel betrayed by the breaking of their emanational relationship to an archetypal drama they had counted upon to secure and shape their lives—and others who are deeply dissatisfied but do not yet realize why in terms of the living underlying patterning forces now ruling their lives. Guides help them to discover what process of liberation of all four faces of our being is truly needed, and to remain compassionately in close presence with them while they need guides. This is the first vital political step toward transformation—toward what we can and need to do together in a fundamentally better way.

As soon as there are people who have begun to experience transformation in their own lives and hence have freed themselves fully to explore and connect all four faces of their being, the next step is affinity groups. Affinity groups are composed of people who feel a deep empathy with each other and who mean to share insights, feelings, and actions in a concern they share especially with regard to two or three problems of transformation. Affinity groups constitute the core of a community of transformation, for such a community is based upon face-to-face relationships—people who can learn from each other on a daily basis, nourish each other and act together also beyond their particular group of eight to twelve people. If there are more than about a dozen people within one affinity group, face-to-face links become impractical, though it is also possible for most of our group members to join at least one more such group concerned with similar or related problems and thus help to interconnect and shape our larger transforming community. Issues literally come to life as we learn how to communicate with each other about what we can and need to do to practice love and justice together. Such a network of affinity groups can move us toward fruitfully supplanting, not overthrowing, the existing power structure through a radically democratic form of politics.

We can also enlarge our political network through a political party that, in a democratic liberal society, can move us from interconnected nuclei to becoming a critical mass, that is, a majority. But this party is not above all a mechanism to attract campaign money and voters every two, four, or six years for what in our time are ambitiously competing individuals and factions. Transformational politics is not focused upon capturing power within existing structures. Yes, we need to win a majority in order to be legally enabled to transform society. Yes, in the meantime, we also act simultaneously as insiders and outsiders, accomplishing as much incremental change as is currently possible in order to help people who need—if they are to survive—to gain a larger fragment of life. A political party cannot ignore the present and be oriented solely toward the future.

The heart of what a political party of transformation works for is our initiating and persisting in changing living underlying patterning forces and their concrete manifestations—so that the causes of poverty, exploitation, violence, bias, and scarcity of community can truly be overcome. It can do so because it is a party of people with experience in transformation, working together to gain insights for entering and accomplishing more and more vital changes for the fundamentally better.

The candidates for office of a party of transformation emerge not from hierarchic control groups usually also composed, as in our time, of eight to twelve people, but from face-to-face affinity groups. Parties of transformation are present not only at election time or in legislative bodies. For example, they collect monthly dues from their members not by mail but through a person living in the same neighborhood knocking at their door. But money is not the main purpose of knocking. Your fellow member will ask you about whether you need any kind of help and what you think needs to be done politically, locally, and within the larger society and pass on such information in relevant ways. If a political party of transformation agrees on dues of five dollars a month, and after a while gains five million members (still, only a beginning), it will collect $300 million per year—no small amount of resources for action, and not only for electoral campaigns, especially once we have transformed the financing of campaign funding. That's a lot of money collected without any dependence upon the rich and powerful.

One of the transforming moves for local, state, and federal legislatures would be to create task forces to discover and initiate action on major problems. Task forces will ask, "Why is this a problem? What archetypal dramas now still hold us enchanted and enchained—or bereft as they are dissolving—and prevent us from dealing with this problem? Thanks to our own experience with the drama of transformation, of what do we need to free ourselves in this case in order to see and understand afresh? What needs to be done anew? Who can we find to help us with this new work?" The authorization to act and to use money comes from the legislators. The actual work is done by the guides of the task force and their transforming helpers—and, as soon as possible, through the very lives of the people of society.

CAPACITY IN CONTRAST TO POWER

The majority of our contemporaries focus their lives on power; so therefore also do political scientists. *Transformation* is currently a term used simply for any big change. But power cannot bring about or nourish transformation. Arresting ourselves within fragments of the core drama of life does indeed require power—the power of the archetypal force that inspires and molds our partial lives and holds us back from continuing our journey, and that also shapes and legitimizes our concrete power structure and its enforcement, its gains, and its costs in repression and suppression of ourselves and others. We need power because we lack the capacity that comes from our having become fully connected to all four faces and the deepest source of our being.

Power hides the absence of true capacity, veiled by our ability instead to concentrate our energies, resources, and attention on exploiting and diminishing others—and accumulating, protecting, and enforcing our power. For others thus to be rendered less powerful, or even powerless, is one of the costs we pay, but even the most powerful cannot use their power to become more than partial human beings. The most important reasons why the forces of organized incoherence are more powerful now than ever before is that we have achieved more freedom to create new fragments of scientific knowledge and skills, especially of power over nature, matter, and people, and more control over larger organizational (but still fragmented) economic and political nets—more effective products all, in the first place, for the sake of power and profits. But the personal, political, historical, and sacred incompleteness and vulnerability—even of the powerful—remains the governing fact, and both their power and their incapacity prevent the emergence of a true community of people.

What is capacity, in contrast to power? Capacity is our human (and sacred) endowment that enables us with freedom, courage, compassionate caring, and critical and creative insight to move through the entire core drama of life again and again and also with others—to thus create a fundamentally better life. Do we always find answers as soon as we need them? No, but exploring our capacity with this new freedom, depth of being, and understanding of underlying patterning forces and of our basic choices, and with many more people asking and moving in this way, we will be able to find more fundamentally better answers much sooner.

For the sake of power, we need other people to be our allies, or else to be defeated or (if possible) ignored. For the sake of capacity, we need others to open up their capacity to help us find, test, and experience new transforming inspirations. The political face of our being is what we can and need to do together. In the service of transformation, we realize that we share the need to experience understanding, love, and justice. And each one can now contribute according to the capacity of her or his being.

Power does not work unless those who succeed—as well as those who fail—in the dramas of power continue to be possessed and commanded by the same living underlying patterning force. As more and more dramas in the service of incoherence—for example, those of the family and of communities and their once established bonds and values—lose their commanding archetypal power, the attraction of total power rises and leads into movements of deformation, that is, toward destructive death. We need to develop our capacity to help people leave that path in time, and move toward transformation instead. Power alone—manifested through incremental changes or official acts of deformation to suppress deformation—cannot put an end to the causes of deformation. The meek cannot inherit the earth this way. Being meek is merely an opposite of being powerful. Only people with capacity can truly nourish the world.

CONCLUSION

Transformation as a way of life is not *overarching*—a term for possessive and commanding shaping I have used to describe the other three ways of life—nor do we live "in its service." Transformation enhances our capacity for participating in all aspects of our being—and with our fellow human beings. The process of transformation and its results are intrinsically democratic. The living underlying patterning force is always the same, but our personal experience of it and its outcome is always unique in its concreteness. Its concrete outcome can never be preprogrammed. But when we share this way of life, the uniqueness of each person is deeply appreciated and constitutes no barrier to participating with each other in a variety of relationships and dramas. Such unique contributions can enrich us.

Great damage arises out of the core drama of life if we arrest ourselves during the process. The worst danger arises from exiting from it into the abyss. But persisting again and again through the entire core drama of life as an experience of transformation is impossible unless we open ourselves to be truly caring and concerned about the basic and pervasive suffering of our time. We have turned ourselves into only partial human beings, and indeed we treat many others, and at times even ourselves, as lesser or invisible. Facing this deeply limiting reality as unbearable, untenable and, however profitable for some, certainly at least unfruitful to our being, means seeking to understand through a new, testable theoretical vision why we are where we are and how we can indeed discover and experience a fundamentally better way of life.

Transformation will advance us toward ending ignorance and bigotry, eliminating poverty and oppression, nourishing peace and beauty, and also both nourishing and being nourished by nature. And thus also the core of our being is moved toward being understanding, loving, just, and joyful with ourselves and with each other—hence, toward our becoming fully present and complete beings.

This chapter is only a beginning of our discussion of the politics of a transforming society. In each of the next nine chapters, we will explore how radically our actual enactment of an archetypal relationship and of an archetypal drama changes in the service of each of the four ways of life. Then we shall offer three chapters to deepen our understanding of the meaning of transformation. And we shall end by contrasting justice in each way of life.

PART THREE

Choices within Each Way of Life: Introducing Archetypal Relationships and Stories

8

Nine Archetypal Relationships

We have emphasized all along that, in order to create transformation, we need to break not only with the concrete manifestations of relationships, dramas, and ways of life, but indeed also with their underlying patterning forces. Hence we need to learn more about this unfamiliar deeper ground in order to be able to free ourselves to live a fundamentally better life. We have so far explored the most potent of these archetypal forces: the four ways of life. Now we shall analyze archetypal relationships and, thereafter, a number of major archetypal dramas, and then look more closely into the very nature of archetypes.

There exist only nine archetypal relationships shaping our capacity (or power) and our performance with any others we encounter in our life—*any* others, not only other human beings. When I mean to include all others to whom we relate, I shall call them *poles*, because I know of no other term that covers so large a constituency and because *pole* means "turning axis" in a flowing field of connections. I speak of poles because hardly any concrete human being is shaped by only one single kind of relationship, and because *the other* may or may not be human.

Here is only a small list of poles: We have relationships to this nation, that corporation, this idea, that value, some event, a moment in time, an object, an archetypal drama, a particular way of life. Our exploration of the enactment of nine archetypal relationships allows us to analyze any concrete moment and any change experienced by an actual concrete person—in relationship to whomever and whatever. Any human relationship may take only one or several of these nine forms but *only* in these nine forms—a hypothesis easily testable. If we were all capable of enacting a repertory of *ninety* such archetypal relationships instead of just nine, the human species would have far worse trouble understanding each other than we have now.

Our analysis of the potentials and limits of each archetypal relationship can explain a lot about life, but no such relationship can be experienced except within archetypal stories and, most decisively, within ways of life. We shall analyze these relationships by way of examples also within this larger context, to show how our being, and our being with others, hangs together or fails to hang together and why.

Writing a theory of transformation is itself an experience of transformation. I returned to the Middle East and North Africa after the publication of my first book to discover which inherited relationships were breaking down in the modern age—and why. I had learned from a splendid book about pre-modern China that the Mongol Emperor of China and the Chinese Mandarin bureaucrats were engaged in "antagonistic collaboration."[1] The Emperor could not retain the legitimacy of his rule unless the Mandarins verified that at least at crucial moments he remained within the confines of Confucian rules. The Mandarins could not have their rules enforced unless the Emperor authorized them to do so. This was a perennial tug between two sources of power who also needed each other.

I saw such a relationship in many areas of life from Morocco to Pakistan, but becoming less reliable and often breaking in our time for its would-be participants. After fifteen months in this region, however, I came back in 1966 having discovered five different relationships at work. After two years of testing them out with my students, I had found there were eight.[2]

I published them as "A Redefinition of the Revolutionary Situation." These eight types of relationships (which I then called *polarities*) allowed us to deal in qualitatively different ways with our performance—not only with continuity but also with change, not only with collaboration but also with conflict and the achieving of different kinds of justice. I showed that six of these types of relationships were breaking again and again in our time, landing us in the seventh (incoherence) but not yet in the eighth (transformation). But I called these eight polarities "socially accepted abstractions." How could every one of these relationships have spread throughout the world if they were simply abstractions? I knew nothing as yet about archetypes or about the four faces of our being and our deepest source—and so nothing about how to bring about transformation.[3]

---

1. Joseph R. Levenson, *Confucian China and Its Modern Fate*, vol. 2, pp. 25–31, 35.

2. I also benefited greatly from discussions organized by William R. Polk through the Adlai Stevenson Institute of International Affairs at the University of Chicago.

3. Nonetheless, the focus of "A Redefinition of the Revolutionary Situation" upon types of necessary relationships and why they were in their concrete manifestations breaking more and more in our time within and among individuals, groups, ideas, and values attracted much attention. First published in *The Journal of International Affairs*, vol. 23, no. 1, 1969 (the revision of a paper originally presented to a National Conference on "'The United States in a Revolutionary World," sponsored by the Woodrow Wilson School of Public and International Affairs, Princeton University and the American Friends Service Committee in April 1968), it was republished repeatedly in somewhat revised form or in new contexts in Norman Miller and Roderick Aya, *National Liberation: Revolution in the Third World* ;

Now I turn to a discussion of the nine archetypal relationships in this new light as aspects of the basic underlying structures and dynamics of all archetypal dramas.

PERFORMANCE AND CAPACITY—OR POWER

I shall speak of nine forms of relationship that allow us, each in its distinct way, to deal with five crucial issues that are problematical in every human relationship— with our self and with others. We need to assure continuity of the relationship yet also allow (or else try to avoid or prevent) change. In order to achieve continuity and to deal with change, we need to connect with each other in collaboration, yet also be able to deal with the possibility of conflict with the other pole. Continuity and change, collaboration and conflict—in order to attain the shared goals or justice possible within that particular type of relationship. No heuristic matrix is being offered here, but facts of life. We shall soon examine the qualitative differences of performance in each of the nine forms.

What kind of capacity is required to engage in this kind of performance? As we shall see, in the service of ways of life other than transformation, we can

---

in Jules Hymen Masserman and John J. Schwab, *Man for Humanity: On Concordance Vs. Discord in Human Behavior*; in L. Carl Brown and Norman Itzkowitz, *Psychological Dimensions of Near Eastern Studies*, Princeton Studies on the Near East; and most recently in Alexander J. Groth, *Revolution and Political Change*, International Library of Politics and Comparative Government.

The following doctoral dissertations utilized these relationships to shed new light on major issues: James A. Bill, on relations between groups and classes in Safavid and modern Iran (1968); Faruk Logoglu, on Ismet Inonu as an innovator in Turkey, 1945-65, (1970); Kay Doherty Boals on modernization and Egyptian Intervention in Yemen (1970); David Abalos, on the changing authority structure in the Catholic Church (1971); Gabriel Ben-Dor, on the impact on the Druze community of innovation and national integration in Israel (1972); Aggrey Brown, on the relationship between race and class in Jamaica (1973); Badi Foster, on the political consciousness and political participation of a family living in a bidonville in Casablanca (1974); and John H. Lorentz, on modernization in nineteenth-century Iran: the role of Amir Kabir (1975).

Three Masters theses at the University of Texas in Austin also utilized unpublished materials of this theory under the guidance of Professor James A. Bill: Kathrine Hubbs Gundersen, on changing rural relations in Iran (1968); Edna Louise Koenig, on nation-building in Tanzania (1970); and Sharon Lee Wiggins on teaching children (1971).

At Princeton, several dozen Senior and Junior theses have applied and tested this early beginning of the theory of transformation. These valuable contributions both enlarged my understanding and led me to ask new questions I could not yet answer. But it is still an incomplete beginning and a highly unfamiliar perspective that has led scholars to try to assimilate this new theory into their already established perspective. For example, Ira Katzelson, looking at this first essay on the theory of transformation, decided that incoherence and transformation "need not detain us here," and treated the other six as if they were Weberian "ideal-types." Then he classified these "according to their relative distribution of power," namely as "uni-directional," "bi-directional," and "non-directional." As a result, he missed the radical implications even then of the theory of transformation for his own radical analysis in *Black Men, Cities, Race, Politics, and Migration in the United States, 1900-1930 and Britain, 1948-1968*, 25-28.

possess only various kinds of power (instead of capacity), or else we are rendered almost powerless. We shall examine power or capacity in detail in each archetypal relationship. The question is this: In each relationship, how can we express—or not fully express—the five aspects of our capacity for enacting all five aspects of performance? 1) Our unconscious: What living underlying patterning force has hold of us or participates with us? What aspects of our unconscious do we have to repress—given our present archetypal commitments? How much of our unconscious—of the depth of our being—is presently beyond our understanding? 2) Our consciousness: Our consciousness is also shaped by our archetypal connections—and by four of its aspects: sensation, feeling, intuition, and thought.[4] 3) Our creativity: How free are we in this relationship to be creative? To what kind of incremental changes does this relationship limit us—or does it enable us to act with fundamentally more freedom? 4) Linking with others: How freely and broadly does this relationship allow us to interact with the other pole? Does this relationship as such limit the relationships we can have with others? Or does it simply intend to include more, but within this same type of relationship? 5) The just use of human and physical resources.[5]

In each of the nine archetypal relationships, the ten aspects of performance and capacity are interconnected and expressed in qualitatively different ways. This analysis will help us ask a critical and creative question: How are we really interconnected with our self and with each other?

THE ARCHETYPAL RELATIONSHIP OF EMANATION

Emanation is a relationship in which the self lives to the maximum extent possible as an extension of, or at least in unquestioning conformity with, the other. The self accepts the denial of freedom for exploring and expressing her or his own capacity in order fully to experience and accept the mysterious and overwhelming power of the source of emanation—a yielding which is rewarded with a sense of seemingly total security, or at least of a fundamentally right commitment and a sense of power flowing through us from that source.

Most of us began our life in this relationship. We were children and therefore without capacity adequate to deal with all the poles of life we encountered. From the beginning, we also rebelled against the mysterious and overwhelming power of our mother and father, but if we had not also experienced the seemingly total security of that expression of emanation, we could have died or remained filled with anxiety.

---

4. We shall discuss our unconscious, consciousness, and creativity in far more detail in Chapters 13 and 14.

5. We shall, of course, discuss injustice, evil, and justice in detail in Chapter 16 of this book.

I used the term *seemingly* when I spoke of total security. No archetypal relationship—no archetypal drama or way of life—can in fact offer us total security, though emanation and deformation can seize our unconscious and our consciousness with this deep impression. Even parents who raise children as participants in transformation will be unable to avoid their understanding, loving, and just guidance initially being experienced by their child in an emanational spirit. But such parents will increasingly be able to help their child move toward experiencing transformation herself or himself. Most other parents in our time will find their child becoming an adolescent rebel (again and again, however much older) in the service of incoherence. Those who mean to preserve "traditional family values"—seeking to retain their children throughout life as emanations of themselves—are becoming less and less successful because emanation as an entire way of life is dying.

The dying of that way of life does not put an end to all emanational relationships. That way of life, as we shall see again, also legitimated certain other archetypal relationships in its service—but never all nine of them or every possible concrete manifestation even of the legitimized ones.[6] Many such inherited emanational relationships are indeed weakening or dying in our time—established offices of authority, standards and ranks of honor and social class, rules of morality, and ties of community (no small list).

Until we transform ourselves, however, our connections to incoherence as a way of life, and to any dramas in its service, constitute our present emanational bonds.[7] Incoherence could not hold us as a way of life if it were solely based on rational calculation or if it were in fact based on a comparison with transformation. And we compensate for the fact that incoherence as a way of life by its very nature cannot give us the seemingly total security of emanation as a way of life by seeking new emanational relationships. We may be devoted to our property as if it were a source of emanation or as if we alone were its unassailable source of creation. We may require our employees to treat us with unquestioning loyalty as the dominant source of emanation. Or we may look for a romantic relationship in which we treat our lover as a source of emanation, or else as the emanational embodiment of ourselves. We may be captivated by moods or popular fashions. We may also search in crises for charismatic leaders and movements. Or we may seek to attain the pretense of emanational power and self-satisfaction through covert manipulation or seduction—or by seeking good luck through gambling.

6. In Chapter 4 on different manifestations of emanation as a way of life, we showed that the relationship of emanation can also be utilized in quite different forms, for example, in enforced hierarchical chains of emanation or as sources of competition for renewed tribal solidarity.

7. Emanation as an archetypal relationship can connect us to archetypal dramas and even to emanation and incoherence as ways of life. The archetypal relationship of deformation and transformation connect us to dramas and ways of life of their kind. The other six archetypal relationships cannot do so. They gain their power or capacity from the drama and way of life of which they are an intrinsic part.

In the service of incoherence, emanational relationships are more vulnerable than in the service of emanation. In the latter case, they may become vulnerable as particular manifestations, but not as the kind of relationship that must be practiced in that drama. In incoherence, the mysterious power of any source of emanation becomes testable and hence vulnerable through new experience and analysis, or simply because we feel free now to rebel, or because it becomes impossible for any emanational source (within its inflexible embrace) to deal with continuous change.

The archetypal relationship of emanation also becomes more tenuous in the service of incoherence because covert manipulation too often becomes a deliberate substitute for what still seems to be genuinely mysterious power. Thus, when news first appeared regarding the Iran-Contra affair (the U.S. government's covert illegal sale of weapons to Iran in order covertly and illegally to supply funds to anti-government guerillas in Nicaragua), "'The fundamental question is that some means has to be found to give appearances of controlling the situation,' said one Senior White House official who did not want to be identified."[8]

Or individually we may try to create ourselves not as the person we are but as a persona that will, although spurious, captivate others. Or we may find ourselves dependent upon someone whom we know we have to treat as that person desires to be treated—that is, worshipped—but we do it solely because we cannot afford to conflict with that person. All people in emanational relationships perceive the one outside that relationship as lesser or invisible. Or they see the one outside as dangerous and to be eliminated, if possible—and in this way for example, thanks to their unquestioning and exclusive devotion to their ethnic group or nation-state, they may thus ally themselves with deformation. Civil rights legislation compels us at minimum to treat the person who was once seen as that outsider as someone whom we need now to tolerate, even if we do not yet value her or him as a human being.

There are no emanational relationships in the service of deformation. There are pseudo-emanational sources and links—the dose of crack which initially seems to give us only a high; the policeman who tortures because of his seemingly overwhelming, and mysteriously powerful authority; the confidence man who succeeds in having us give him our money. All these may at first be experienced as emanational. But they are instances of the archetypal relationship of deformation.

All persisting emanational relationships—whether in the service of emanation or incoherence—do great damage to our capacity and performance. We repress any sense of conflict with that mysteriously powerful source in our unconscious.

---

8. *The New York Times*, November 30, 1986. The seeming appearance of emanational power and trust may also be found outside the government. One of my students wrote, "Most of the respect I showed my elders was not earned . . . but a costume I assumed on my parents' command. . . . I was like a window which my parents' friends and elders could look through and see the respect of my parents."

We are conscious only of what that source requires, or forbids, or allows us to see or experience, but we do not and cannot within its confines understand its real nature—or that of others. We must not be creative, except to find ways to be more intensely devoted with awe—or at least with uncritical trust and respect. We must not link as deeply with anyone else, and we must reject all those who are not entitled to enter into relationships with our source. When we have loyally served our source of emanation, that source justly gives us all the security and rewards within its power—and within the particular archetypal drama and way of life.[9]

Hence, continuity and not change is our shared purpose of performance—unless the source compels us to change ourselves or to change others. We exercise only collaboration, never conflict with the source, but certainly conflict with those our source opposes. Any means our source holds to be just are therefore just—unless our larger drama and way of life say no.

Thus, even the source of emanation has no capacity, but instead has total power within this relationship while the embodiment of the source gains whatever empowerment—or deep yielding—this source engenders within its confines. Emanation produces an intense, highly focused performance of great power—but at great cost to our being freely and fully present with all four faces of our being.

THE ARCHETYPAL RELATIONSHIP OF SUBJECTION

Power, which in emanation is experienced as overwhelming and mysterious, becomes in subjection demonstrably strong and naked—naked in its source and imposition, and specific in all its requirements. With emanation now weakening, subjection is the next most potent relationship for providing unequal control.

Subjection has been used in the service of emanation in order to punish sinners—or against competitors when its authority is challenged. It may be used by an individual who is being defied as a source of emanation, because even such poles often lack the power they claim to possess. But if even subjection fails in its enforcement, that source's emanational power is thereby also severely damaged or even destroyed.

Here are some examples of the archetypal relationship of subjection in the service of incoherence: the empire founded upon conquest; the parent focusing on disciplining the child so that it will always obey and copy the parent's model until the child has internalized subjection in the form of self-control; the employer treating his employees as if they were machines (and they yield because they need the job

---

9. We shall discuss in detail in the final chapter how ways of life produce partial justice that is often injustice, or else produce evil, or else the good. Though we will speak here of the just use of resources and of justice with regard to each archetypal relationship, their content is most decisively shaped by their way of life.

and lack other resources); the government enforcing civil rights legislation, since otherwise the naked power of citizens inspired by deformation might triumph.

Subjection is also exemplified in archetypal dramas of science by the naked power of deductive logic and instrumental rationality, and by the sequence of efficient causes by which we can make a machine work. Subjection is a more efficient relationship than emanation or any of the other seven we will explore. When instrumental rationality, efficiency, and discipline as means to the ends of the powerful become dominant in our life, such subjection will compel us to neglect or ignore other aspects of our being.

Subjection encourages the dominant to enhance and secure their single-minded power and control by turning it into a monopoly, for when subjection is no longer in the service of emanation or no longer at least legitimized and thus enforced by an emanational relationship, it becomes less likely to succeed or to endure. Enforcing subjection through violence, within the family or in gang warfare or international wars leads into deformation. Indeed, the physical and psychological control intrinsic in this archetypal relationship often entails its alliance with deformation—or its turning into the archetypal relationship of deformation.

In the archetypal relationship of subjection, conflict is not primarily repressed, as in emanation, but suppressed. But if the pressures and limitations imposed upon us through subjection become too painful, we may also repress them from our consciousness. People being subjected, however, must remain conscious of what specifically they fear and therefore specifically what to do and what they must not do. Within subjection, one yields to necessity, but only as long as one calculates it *is* necessary. Certainly, people in subjection are conscious of their loss of power—the loss of their right to create changes, except perhaps subversively.

In subjection, collaboration is based on explicit rules defined solely by the dominant pole and is most likely to exclude permission to collaborate freely with others similarly subjected. The one in power seeks to assure continuity and change solely in order to serve his or her power and its rewards. Any means legitimized by the drama and way of life at stake that perpetuate the power of the dominant pole and the survival of the subjected—as long as the subjected is still needed—is seen as just by those in control. Survival is the form of justice for the subjected. Mere survival, even when it is harsh in its conditions, is hard to achieve in most of the world. More power for the powerful and its rewards is their form of justice. Power is a necessity if we arrest ourselves in the core drama of life to seek the partial fruits of emanation or incoherence.

ISOLATION AS AN ARCHETYPAL RELATIONSHIP

In this form of relationship, the poles involved agree to collaborate—but solely in avoiding all conflict intended to lead to any change in the relationship between the self and the other. Since the energies of life remain in motion, self and other must in this case use their energy to repress, suppress, or deflect their energy lest it reach the other. No human beings can ever completely insulate themselves through their own inaction, or solely through their own action—except thereby to enter the archetypal relationships of incoherence or deformation. It is a mere fantasy for a person to call himself "a self-made man."

A person who wishes to be alone to relax or to meditate needs this kind of collaboration from society. To isolate women after puberty from all men except men within the family could not work in Muslim society in the service of emanation unless the whole society collaborated in enacting and enforcing such isolation.

In democratic liberal societies in the service of incoherence, the initial and still widespread agreement to keep two fragments of life—the public and the private—isolated from each other creates areas of freedom, especially for the powerful, but also of unattended suffering by workers, women, children, the poor, and the sick. In its most useful form, umpires separate the personal feelings from their impersonal decisions, but bureaucrats, in separating the personal and the impersonal, will often ignore the real and entire problem at stake. Virginity is protected by isolation as an archetypal relationship, but like a truce, may yield to different types of relationships.

A policy of isolation by a nation in international politics—sometimes also called neutrality—is an entirely one-sided assertion, and in fact depends decisively on the will of the more powerful and aggressive nations. Secession by dissidents is likely to lead to conflict.

Both solitary withdrawal and uncaring response to suffering lead into incoherence, not isolation. Telling a child only to be seen but not to be heard is a one-sided imposition of seeming isolation that is in fact at least subjection. Isolating people of a different religion, ethnicity, or race in ghettos constitutes a unilateral imposition allegedly of the archetypal relationship of isolation but is, in fact, a station on the road to deformation. For many who live in suburbs in order to isolate themselves physically and psychologically and who pay no taxes for the city in which they actually work—their "ghetto" constitutes self-centered incoherence and not a relationship of isolation.

Narcissism may look like isolation, or may be an aspiration to become a source of emanation, but is likely in fact to be an archetypal relationship of incoherence. For scientists to "isolate" variables hardly ever has the explicit agreement of human beings being examined, and cannot have the explicit agreement of fragments of matter. (This is no small matter of fact and value.) The prevailing distinction between subjective and objective ideas creates at best a deep relationship of isolation—but often indeed of incoherence—within our lives.

Continuity if possible, but no change, no conflict—that is the purpose of collaboration in the archetypal relationship of isolation and, as far as possible, of the just use of resources between self and other. Justice means self-determination, but where our unconscious may be, what isolation does to our thought, sensation, feeling, and intuition, and to our creativity depends very much on the drama and the way of life within which we practice this archetypal relationship

BUFFERING AS AN ARCHETYPAL RELATIONSHIP

Buffering is managed most crucially by intermediaries. Such a position may be occupied by a mediator, arbitrator, or political or economic power broker; or by a concept, theory, or standardized procedure; or by habits, conventions, routines, or rituals. Money often serves as a buffer through which we see, evaluate, and deal with the other. So do social and official roles. So do the media, which inform us and interpret life for us.

Who or what is our buffer depends on the archetypal drama we are enacting. Each drama makes us see data in a different light. As with all other archetypal relationships, buffering is most deeply molded by ways of life. Two medieval knights, who have agreed to fight each other even unto death, are guided by buffering (among other archetypal relationships). They do not start until the trumpet sounds. Unless one is gravely injured or dies, they do not stop until the trumpet sounds again. They agree not to reach out at each other through illegitimate moves or weapons. Competitive games in our time and their adherence to rules and the loyalty of their followers are in some crucial aspects—but with greater freedom for members of different social classes to enter into such competitions—a survival of this emanational inheritance. The buffer sought in various aspects of life may also still be a source of emanation, for example, a saint or a prayer or a ritual to intercede for us.

In the service of incoherence, the powerful feel much freer than in the service of emanation to shape and manipulate buffers. Among the buffers available to them are political campaign contributions, control of the media, and advertising. Concepts about aspects of life—its expectations, needs, and requirements—are buffers that in our time change frequently. We know we cannot fully rely upon them; we say there is always a gap between the ideal and the real—between words and actions. Established language is one of the prime filters of our experience, but increasingly we are aware that it can mislead us. Instrumental needs change; fashions change; values change. Some buffers are masks intended to fool us—to offer gestures, external appearance—while the problem remains unsolved. The less powerful may be quite dependent on buffers—if they can find them—to reach and persuade the more powerful.

Scientists produce new concepts and even new theoretical paradigms again and again through which to explore and explain some fragments of life. To stereotype other human beings, to be prejudiced against them, to see the other solely as a sex object, to treat others solely as tools, is to move buffering into the service of deformation.

By *buffering* I do not mean one-sidedly raising barriers to a relationship. That, as we shall see, is an example of the archetypal relationship of incoherence—or even of deformation. In the case of the Berlin Wall, the assault on peoples' lives who tried to cross it was, of course, a case of deformation. But as long as both sides agree to a barrier also open to traffic under negotiated rules (for example, to a border between two countries), that is a case of buffering. One other case that might conventionally be called buffering—an overprotective mother holding her child always in her embrace—constitutes, in fact an emanational relationship.

Buffering limits our consciousness to what we can see, experience, and express through its filter. It can help us to avoid (or at least establish rules for) conflict—but only in the service of emanation and incoherence, at the cost of indirect and limited exchanges. Bureaucrats treat the less powerful impersonally according to the rubric under which their problem is ruled to fit—or not even fit at all under any present rubric. Abstractions usually distance and even distort our vision of the pole to which we relate. Change through such collaboration with others is thus still inhibited. And, within established relationships of buffering, creativity is also inhibited. We shut off from our experience what is not already clear through such lenses. We cannot thus see or experience the depth of ourselves or of the other. Unless our unconscious rebels on its own, our knowledge of it remains dim. The just use of resources is set by the buffer we agree upon. Justice in buffering is the attainment of ends circumscribed or enhanced by such particularly focused encounters. Not enough of the self or the other can emerge through this relationship, however, to bring about the kind of understanding and compassion, or justice, of which we are otherwise capable.

DIRECT EXCHANGE AS AN ARCHETYPAL RELATIONSHIP

So far in our list of archetypal relationships, direct exchange is the first archetypal relationship in which individuals, groups, and other poles collaborate and conflict with each other directly and on the same terms of encounter—though in the past, and in our present, seldom as equals. Its justice in the service of emanation and incoherence is temporary. It is the bargain we can achieve now, but its use of just means is constituted by the reciprocal capacity to seek a different bargain as the balance of power changes. The particular advantage that may accrue to one side or the other at any moment serves primarily to fuel or diminish new energy into this form of encounter. Any attempt to take all, or to preserve any particular outcome against unfavorable change, puts an end to open and free direct exchange between its present participants.[10]

Direct exchange in the service of incoherence is, of course, reflected in the most common way in which businesspeople agree on a deal—via direct exchange. In the West, in contrast to the Middle East,[11] consumers are usually not in a position to bargain with retailers—except on some single big item, such as a car, or by buying a rival product instead, thus communicating via a buffer. Workers in most countries have also been denied power to bargain collectively over wages; certainly their human capacity is not enhanced by this situation. Buying, however, is not a case of direct exchange but of buffering (via money)—unless it is an example of bartering.

Direct exchange is augmented for the self who is more powerful, even in liberal democracies. The more powerful can usually enlarge their power in direct exchange through an additional repertory of relationships that also gives them unquestionable or naked control through emanation and subjection and through buffers more under their influence to reshape our vision of the issue at stake in the direct exchange.

Voting in public elections or in legislative assemblies reflects direct exchange. What can I count upon for you to do for me? What financial or public support can I bring to bear now to have you vote my way? How far off is the next public election? These concerns are among the manifestations of direct exchange as bargaining is renewed again and again within or from outside of legislatures.

Doing favors in the service of incoherence both in private and public life are often not expressions of generosity or caring but a mode of creating or maintaining a sense of indebtedness between self and other. Favors in this way of life are seldom extended without a price, but as an unwritten contract that sets the ground for further direct exchange: You are now in debt to me. What have you done for me lately? In the worst of cases we must turn ourselves into a commodity which

---

10. This fear of speaking out reaches into the highest places. In 1975, Vice President Nelson Rockefeller was asked why, as governor of New York, he had never spoken out against the spending of $140 billion and the loss of 50,000 American lives on the war in Vietnam. "I see that you never ran for political office, young man," the Vice President said. "I was elected Governor of New York, and my responsibility was to the people of New York. You don't kick people in Washington in the shins if you expect them to do something for you" (*The New York Times*, May 7, 1975).

11. In the Middle East and North Africa, emanation as a way of life is still alive enough to connect the archetypal relationship of emanation to any direct exchange involving bargaining. I was present in a rug store in Tunis when a tourist entered and said, "I want to buy this rug and I know your custom but I have to hurry to catch a plane. So when I ask how much is this rug? You say the equivalent of 100. Then I say I offer 45. Then you'll say 80. And I'll say 55, and you'll say 75. And after some more discussion along these lines, you'll come down to 70 and I'll go up to 60. I'll agree to 68 now, so please sell me the rug." The owner responded, "I am not a mechanical doll. I won't sell you a rug." The more powerfully effective you demonstrate you are in direct exchange, the more your reputation as a source of emanation rises—probably also in other regions of the world.

we trade for a job—or indeed we are told the powerful have no need for us. That moves us closer to the way of deformation.

In international relations, direct exchange is one of the most necessary relationships for the sake of peace and collaboration. Yet direct exchange is often deeply inhibited by the predominance of the other archetypal relationships. In the worst of cases, the powerful seek to intimidate instead, or they agree to a bargain only because conquest is not yet feasible. Even within democratic liberal governments, "confidentiality" severely limits the number of participants who have full access to the facts in any free discussion of foreign policy. Diplomacy is too often performed as an art of manipulation for which the term *direct exchange* would be misleading. That relationship is often desperately needed, but direct exchange requires at least shared norms. To be told by your parent, "Only if you finish your work on time can you go out today to enjoy yourself," expresses not only direct exchange but also subjection.

Scientific experiments are an example of direct exchange—though, as we have seen, other archetypal relationships are also involved, for example subjection, which sets limits to the changes that are possible or that are to be examined. Here the relationship constitutes a test of whether that pole responds as we hypothesize it will as we interact with it, and as it interacts with other poles.

Within this relationship, change can never be avoided. But continuity and change persist within a pattern of conflict and collaboration that is accessible to both poles. Our consciousness, even our unconscious, needs to be alert to change.

But our creativity remains limited in incoherence as a way of life to what we can do about becoming more powerfully effective, and what direct linkages with others can help our power and the results it can produce.[12]

AUTONOMY AS AN ARCHETYPAL RELATIONSHIP

In the archetypal relationship of autonomy, both poles are entitled to claim an autonomous zone for our unconscious, consciousness, creativity, continuity, and change for gaining justice—a claim based upon an explicit principle agreed upon

---

12. When a sense of this relationship first dawned on me (while reading Levenson's work on Confucian China), I used his term—*antagonistic collaboration*. See Joseph Richmond Levenson, *Confucian China and Its Modern Fate: A Trilogy*, first combined edition. Certainly it also marked the relationship between rulers and *ulemas*, and also between others in the emanational days of Islam, as we saw in Chapter 4. But it has never been the only form that direct exchange has taken even in the Middle East. Then I published essays calling it "direct bargaining," being unconsciously influenced by the dominance of incoherence. But as we shall see when we explore this archetypal relationship in the service of transformation, "direct exchange" describes it much better—the first of the relationships we have so far discussed that allows that kind of exchange, even within the limits of its power-ridden usages in the other three ways of life. (In deformation, this relationship is used only while power cannot yet be totally applied to the poles of that form of encounter.) I did not call buffering "indirect exchange," because we also need to focus our analysis on the buffer involved.

by both. The basis of this principle may be custom, reason, law, status, ethics, revelation, utility, value, or competence. What matters is that a principle has been made explicit so that each participant in this relationship can enact it autonomously—for example as a fellow citizen—but in this form, can also collaborate to maintain and expand a common ground.

In the United States, the archetypal relationship of autonomy allows us to link through both collaboration and conflict the three branches of the federal government. It also serves to organize, coordinate, and define the tasks and relations within and between bureaucracies—though lower bureaucrats may be limited to being buffers or enforcers of subjection in their relationships. This relationship serves to protect and enhance the autonomous jurisdiction of private corporations—for the most powerful, even on a global scale. It also creates and shapes autonomy for professions and scholarly disciplines and through the award of tenure for professors. It is currently the officially championed relationship governing international relations, though of course powerful nations have often reduced the autonomy of the weak to merely outward form.

Our autonomy—the making of law (*nomos*) by and for ourselves—is based upon a relationship which, through shared principles and not solely through particular laws, defines and helps to enforce the autonomy we have agreed is available to all participating in this particular manifestation of it. We usually define this autonomy in terms of procedures—freedom and its limits, not its substance. Congress can legislate, but not execute laws. Yet nothing in this relationship defines the contents of the laws it can make, but only their topics, dimensions, and limits. For example, the first Amendment to the U.S. Constitution states "Congress shall make no law respecting an establishment of religion, or prohibiting the free exercise thereof, or abridging the freedom of speech, or of the press; or the right of the people peaceably to assemble, and to petition the government for a redress of grievances."[13]

Autonomy as an archetypal relationship arose late in human history and hence was still rare in the service of emanation.[14] Among Jews, the covenant with God also granted permission to study and interpret what God intended us to believe and to enact. If we do right, God will reward us; if we do wrong, God will punish us. The emanational relationship with God remains decisive. Autonomy is limited

---

13. Already by the late eighteenth century, when the first ten Amendments to the U.S. Constitution were ratified, autonomy had already spread among the powerful. The ninth amendment says this: "The enumeration in the Constitution of certain rights shall not be construed to deny or disparage others retained by people." Among the autonomous property rights of those days was also the right of Whites to own Black slaves.

14. One of my students, James A. Beha, showed in his essay in 1970 that this archetypal relationship arose rather late in human history—not, for example in Greece until the fifth century BC ("Gods of the Younger Generation: A Study of the Transforming Agent in Aeschylus' *The Eumenides*").

to exploring—and differing over—means of being rightly connected in emanation. The *ulema*—the scholars of sacred law in Islam—took a similar position. Even so limited a sense of autonomy allowed the rise from within of a sense of "I feel guilt in having failed to understand and to do the right thing"—and not simply, as in the hierarchic interpretation and enforcement of the emanational code by the Catholic Church, a sense of sin because I disobeyed.

In the alliance between the Catholic Church and the states of Europe, between emanation and incoherence as ways of life, both sought autonomy for themselves, and not only a form of "antagonistic collaboration." But this Church also saw the State as its instrument for enforcing above all its law—a conflict that ended with the supremacy of the State, but also an autonomous Church, in the seventeenth century. What persisted in the Church was its tradition that the Holy Spirit sanctified the power of office regardless of the personal qualities of its occupant. Strangely, a similar notion of the emanational quality of each otherwise autonomous office (regardless of the person elected or appointed) has persisted in the secular state. (In the Byzantine Christian Empire, the Emperor also headed the Church—no autonomy.) With the coming of the Protestant Reformation, both private and public forms of autonomy grew among members of some of the new sects—a movement that grew even more with the spread of secularization.

In the service of incoherence, autonomous boundaries grew because this archetypal relationship constitutes the most secure way of organizing fragments for collaboration and conflict, for continuity and change, and for gaining justice for the autonomous. Now we know what boundaries (under the law or new custom) we share, we are entitled to defend, or (under agreed-upon rules) what areas we can try to enlarge or diminish. This archetypal relationship also allows large numbers of individuals and groups to collaborate on a sustained basis in explicitly connected roles. But it also permits individuals to sustain and defend their own distinct mode for expressing the autonomy of being a citizen. The archetypal relationship of autonomy created one of the most solid grounds—even amid incoherence as a way of life—for the rise of the modern age. Autonomy enhances our power for sustained action even while setting agreed-upon limits to power. It makes large-scale organization more feasible while also enabling the expression of individual rights, and opens autonomous claims to principled—and not only particularistic—debate.

The principles underlying autonomy in the service of incoherence involve not only one *auto*—one self—but an agreement between selves that creates or preserves impersonal rules and procedures to construct a type of public space for protecting the public opportunities and limits of defined polar occupants. That is the kind of freedom the archetypal relationship of autonomy creates in that way of life—not independence or self-sufficiency nor any principle that connects each person to the deepest self and thus to each other.

Principle was originally a term expressing the deepest origin and foundation of an idea. In the service of incoherence, even in democratic liberal societies, we cannot know or agree upon any ultimate ground for any principle. We can at best only come to agree that our self-interest demands new space—or the protection or enlargement of established autonomous spaces—that provide us with access to power, and the freedom to employ that power. Hence, this kind of relationship not only joins but also separates. It limits autonomy to the already powerful.

Even American democracy for many decades excluded the property less, women, and nonwhite citizens from voting. The powerful did not have to worry about what could happen to them in the next election, except that a different faction of the already powerful might win. Even today, the already powerful win more often, thanks to their legislative lobbies and their ability to hire more expensive lawyers and lobbyists. Even today, millions of the poor and the sick lack enough legislative influence to be cared for as human beings.

Autonomy in the service of incoherence suffers from additional serious handicaps intrinsic to this way of life. Its participants, as we explored in Chapter 5, are only partial beings. This fact not only limits the freedom and capacity of the explorations, discoveries, experiences, and interactions of such autonomous people, but it creates frequent conflicts and inequalities of power. Within autonomous domains, hierarchy based on emanation and subjection may run the show, justifying discretion in informing or not informing others, and demanding devotion, dedication, and trust—thus in fact undermining the autonomy of others by acting as a sovereign. Sovereign states have long had this same tendency in their relation to other states. Coordination (or competition) between hierarchies of autonomous jurisdiction may also inflict costs. In New York City, it takes seventy-one steps through ten different agencies for the city to buy equipment, such as a desk or a sanitation truck.[15] Sovereign states moving beyond autonomy inflict exceedingly high costs.

But any challenge to the already autonomous lacks legitimacy if it comes from those not yet autonomous and hence not part of the existing collaborative link. Thus the autonomy of the private realm established and executed solely by men for a long time (and even now) deeply limited the freedom and capacity of women and of the employees working in a private company. Partial beings are naturally eager for more autonomous power, and fearful of less, given their intrinsic incompleteness. The archetypal relationship of autonomy is thus the most authoritatively

---

15. Or at least it did so in 1971. (*The New York Times*, January 11, 1971.)

In earlier publications, I called the archetypal relationship of autonomy "boundary-management"—a crucial aspect of it in the service of incoherence. But that term missed pointing to the heart of this matter, which is autonomy. Boundaries can be established through other archetypal relationships. And "management" restricts our vision of what this relationship requires of us, especially, as we shall see, as we participate in transformation.

sustained form of self-interest—even in the drama of democratic liberalism—in the service of incoherence.

Autonomous relationships can also depersonalize us in the service of incoherence. Instead of emerging more freely and more fully as our self—or as a group collaborating as such selves—we present our self as a "bureaucratic officer," a "mayor," an "owner of this property," an "executive of General Motors," a "specialist," or a "citizen." Autonomy defines above all the nature, extent, and limits of our authority and hence of our persona as coordinated role-players within an established zone of autonomy. In this way of life, not only do the lesser and the invisible lack autonomy, but autonomy also shrinks in the time and space left to the deeper self of the powerful. Hence, direct contact between fully present human beings does not take place within this archetypal relationship of autonomy when it is practiced in the service of incoherence.

But even within this way of life, autonomy constitutes a major gain in freedom of inquiry and practice, especially for scientists and their various disciplines. However, because of the defense of established paradigms of science, interdisciplinary inquiries are still rare. Actually related aspects of life are therefore often neglected, and radically new ways of thinking that challenge the existing ground and boundaries of inquiry are usually, to put it gently, not encouraged.

Can we ever proclaim autonomy by ourselves? Proclaim and assert, yes—in art, science, philosophy, and in our personal and political lives. But our claim to autonomy will turn into an accepted relationship at this point in history only if our claim is accepted in the service of incoherence by enough democratic others so that we can defeat the opponents of our attempt to gain autonomy.

In the service of deformation, bureaucracies may be able to maintain their autonomy in relation to each other but certainly not in relation to the political leadership and its apparatus or in connection with the tasks of deformation.

Archetypal relationships of autonomy limit most conflicts to attempts to change within the principles agreed upon and the boundary of jurisdiction between self and other. Indeed, no participant is allowed to change another's behavior directly. Instead, the one whose zone has been effectively reduced may as a consequence have to consider a change of behavior—but does it autonomously. However, no one is likely in the service of incoherence to maintain the boundary of our autonomous claim for us—no one, except us. If Congress lets the President take almost sole control of foreign policy, if corporations are allowed to pollute air, water, soil, and (by extension) people, we yield our right of autonomy. But why can any democratic government—a government that possesses autonomous power thanks to the autonomous consent of citizens—tell its citizens that gays may not legitimately marry or that the poor are not entitled to the welfare they need? In the service of incoherence, it is the power of those who already possess autonomy that defines and protects the principles and exercise of anyone's autonomy.

INCOHERENCE AS AN ARCHETYPAL RELATIONSHIP

The archetypal relationship of incoherence comes into being whenever one pole within a currently practiced archetypal relationship will not or cannot enact even a single aspect of its type of capacity or performance. My unconscious—the living underlying patterning sources which now inspire me (even if I do not yet understand them) will no longer allow me to join with you. My consciousness no longer understands or else no longer agrees with what you or this relationship requires of me. I cannot any longer express or keep my creativity within these limits. I need to link with others in a different type of relationship than this relationship (or you, the other pole of this relationship) allows. I lack the means to persist in this relationship, or I no longer consider the means to be just. I cannot or do not want to continue to experience this relationship. I must not be limited to the changes—or I can no longer stand the changes—intrinsic to this relationship. You in fact no longer collaborate with me or I will not collaborate with you on these terms. I conflict with you beyond the limits within which I am bound within this relationship. I no longer share with you the same sense of justice.

These grave changes exemplify what it means for a relationship to have become unbearable, untenable, or at least unfruitful. The breaking of one of these ten aspects of any relationship is sufficient to create incoherence, but any one such break is usually only the first of more separations to follow. For one pole then to try to purchase continuity at the cost of change, or to repress our consciousness of this break through false consciousness, is likely only to create further incoherence.

Incoherence is a relationship, not the absence of a relationship, as long as the interaction between the two poles persists but on terms involving all five aspects of capacity and all five aspects of performance—but now on basically different terms that are shaped by the negation of the particular preceding archetypal relationship and by the new relationship and way of life one of us seeks to enter instead. *Crisis*—a word that means "separation"—describes this kind of break.

If the break is only about a particular concrete manifestation of an existing archetypal relationship—as we shall also discuss—such a rebellion could be repaired through still prevailing types of relationship in the larger repertory between these two poles. If aspects of our capacity and performance are diminished—that is, they are biased and incomplete but not altogether lacking—incoherence is prevailing as a way of life, but not yet in a particular instance such as the archetypal relationship.

As we said in the chapter on incoherence as an entire way of life, it could not possibly hold together if it were based solely on incoherent relationships. That way of life is rooted through an emanational connection to its archetypal fragment of the core drama of life. This arrest allows us to create and enact archetypal dramas within which we can repeatedly engage in rebellions against particular possessors of power and their particular uses of power and its results—not necessarily to put an end to established archetypal relationships or dramas, but at most to re-form them or create new ones in the service of incoherence.

So why are archetypal relationships in the service of incoherence in fact turning more and more often and pervasively into relationships of incoherence—into the experience of discontinuities rather than continuity; of change, yes, but uncontrolled change, and of conflict without shared rules, thus leading to injustice for both self and other? Why is such breaking of coherence taking place even in societies that offer more jobs, more pay (thanks especially to greater capitalist power), and more freedom and pleasure? Let us ask why the archetypal relationships we have discussed so far are breaking more and more often.

The dying of emanation as a way of life does not put an end to all relationships of emanation, but it separates not only that relationship but all others in its service from what had once been a securely sacred and unquestionable web of life. Today, in the service of incoherence, we feel more free to question any emanational relationship—or any other type—in order to deal with new problems which cannot be dealt with through established answers, even if they are still being pronounced by such once secure emanational sources as the Pope, the President, our parents, or our spouse.

New qualities and quantities of change now enter our daily lives. To remain more intensely bound to established emanational answers—even answers that arose within incoherence as a way of life—disconnects us all the more from others who do not or cannot share our persisting connection. Thus, greater success cuts off most capitalists all the more from the poor who are not needed by their network of relationships—even if both were once connected within the same community.

Resort to naked power in the form of subjection cannot reconnect ideas, individuals, and groups that have already broken apart. When subjection does temporarily work, as in authoritarian liberalism, the cost is high in pain and frustration, and in our inability to deal with unintended changes which, in incoherence as a way of life, do not cease. Means of naked power have indeed been greatly magnified in this way of life to the point of alliance with deformation, but its effects on the currently subjected are also undermined through new forms of education and communication with respect to new ideas, methods, and values—but also through new weapons available to terrorists.

People who had once agreed or yielded to isolation are being swamped by the better or worse results of change and are no longer willing to deny themselves new opportunities. To insulate ourselves by remaining strictly orthodox or by becoming solely spiritual—and hence not to care about others or their growing problems—is in fact to live in incoherence with most of the world. Indeed, parochial self-interest today imperils the ability of the human species to cope with those problems that only the species as a whole can hope to solve.

In relationships of buffering, using shared concepts or finding a mediator works only as long as people continue to share the same perspective or the same range of convertible values. But increasingly people are saying, "I can no longer see clearly, or explain things this way, or share these values."

Depending on the archetypal drama within which it is enacted, a relationship of direct exchange may—as we shall shortly discuss—legitimize a form of rebellion that, in fact, constitutes another mode of bargaining. One is entitled to remain angrily or reservedly present while refusing as yet to bargain in order to improve one's bargaining position. But increasingly, in the service of incoherence, the powerful attain power for more unequal bargains, resulting each time in quite unequal payoffs rather than direct exchanges leading to sustained investments in shared political fruits. For example, when national economies are severely damaged, national and international aid by the World Bank and the International Monetary Fund is given primarily to the still powerful, and new opportunities arise primarily for global corporations and their investments.

Autonomous boundaries are being challenged because political, economic, environmental, and intellectual problems often can no longer be dealt with within already established jurisdictions. Or, in the case of the growing autonomous power of global corporations in a global economy, the citizenship of many is being further delimited in its political and economic rights and opportunities.

The costs of the relationship of incoherence are not small. As we have shown in the chapter on deformation, breaking a relationship of emanation is not only a break between specific participants but also with a mysteriously powerful source that possesses and commands our unconscious and all other aspects of our capacity and performance. That break therefore creates a deep sense of betrayal leading its former participants to murder or suicide—or to symbolic equivalents such as exclusion from any human relationship under the control of the other or to laming apathy or cynicism. The end of subjection may lead to its opposite, a total lack of discipline. Or it could lead to our seeking to become master now, since in that relationship we gained no knowledge other than how to be master or servant. Our former master will not care at all about our survival. What happens after isolation is demolished depends upon what moves the poles once they are separated and what opportunities each means to grasp.

The dissolution of buffering compels its participants to manage tensions and conflicts through an archetypal relationship of direct exchange instead. If they cannot do so, conflicts can become quite destructive. When direct exchange also breaks down, we can lose all we once bargained for, and we are tempted and freed to try to get hold of what we need or want unilaterally.

The absence of a relationship of autonomy appears to justify utilizing our freedom and power to exploit those without it—to use child labor or to colonize those whose autonomy as a people we do not recognize. Within nation-states, people of different cultures than the officially established one are often deprived of autonomy to explore and experience their culture, and hence are treated as lesser or invisible in many crucial aspects of life—as we shall explore in Chapter 11.

In the service of emanation, any breaking with any sacredly endowed relationship is a sin, and hence subject to punishment by human beings and by this Lord. Within organized rebellion as a way of life, at least six modes of resorting to incoherence as a relationship are frequent and seen as legitimate, and hence are less costly than the breakings we have just discussed. One is resorting to incoherence as a bargaining device, for example, by going on strike. In most cases, the disagreement is over concrete manifestations of the previously existing relationship. The strikers remain angrily present while striving for a new and better concrete response. Business people often act in the same manner when bargaining with each other.

A second mode is breaking with the present concrete manifestation of an established archetypal relationship in order to substitute a better manifestation of it with another person, group, or pole. We change our job or our investment. But if we break our present marriage in order to marry a new spouse, divorce can throw our former partner into incoherence, especially if that person cannot find a new mate or even adequate financial support, and especially if the children's emotions are neglected or ignored.

A third mode is an often tenuous and temporary agreement not to talk about a problem lest we are confronted by the fact of incoherence between us. A kindred fourth mode is hypocrisy: Affirming agreement while acting otherwise—as long as we can get away with it.[16]

A fifth mode becoming ever more popular is to resort to incoherence not only within previously major relationships but also within established archetypal dramas. Princess Diana, for example, divorced the Prince of Wales because he did not really love her and, in fact, betrayed her. But divorcing is not a customary way of treating a future king. Indeed, she rejected the required but inhibiting archetypal response of being royal. She openly and boldly immersed herself in archetypal dramas of pleasure and of caring for those in need, while also still trying to discover and define herself. But these also were already existing dramas in the service of incoherence.

A sixth mode of rebellion, legitimate in democratic liberal societies, is to refuse to persist in an established archetypal relationship in order to achieve a reformation within incoherence as a way of life. For example, the prolonged courageous demonstrations, in the face of government-directed police brutality, at last achieved only civil rights legislation—but not a new sense of community—in the United States in the 1960s.

---

16. Hypocrisy may last longer as a deliberate cover for incoherence if it is mutual: "Pretend, pretend that you are just and true and I shall make myself believe in you." Molière, *The Misanthrope*.

We are happy with our freedom deliberately to initiate these forms of incoherence, especially when they render us more successful in becoming more visible and more powerful as a result of the ensuing change. But I have focused this chapter on far more pervasive and deeply damaging kinds of incoherence to which we tend to pay far less attention. In spite of the impressive growth of production and sales and the stability and spread of democratic liberalism during the past fifty years, the very nature of our arrest in the core drama of life tends to blind us and render us insensitive to the widespread experience of incoherent relationships caused by this arrest.

Many are the ruptures that the powerful can initiate. "You are fired!" "But what if I now cannot feed my family and I lose my home?" "What you do now is not my business!" This last statement is not only literally but also symbolically true—in terms of the heart and mind of the powerful but care-less.

Hundreds of millions around the world are sick and could be cured but they receive no help. Half of all the people around the world have not enough to eat and could be fed, but they receive no help.[17] Hundreds of millions around the world receive no adequate education or no education at all. All these people are thus cut off from vital aspects of themselves and others—and hence experience deformation. In the service of incoherence as a way of life, we sever ourselves from taking such responsibilities. At most we may help some particular people, but we do not deal with the basic problems at stake. We cannot. As we saw in the preceding chapter, people in that way of life cannot move beyond particular incremental changes, even when the breaking of relationships increases.

There are two major reasons why so many relationships are breaking in our time. One is that the decay of emanation as a way of life is destroying what we once believed to be the unquestionable view of who we are, the meaning and purpose of life and the legitimacy of family, community, and other authorities. The other reason is that as long as they are constantly employed in the service of incoherence in the face of new questions and problems, all the archetypal forms of relationships we have so far discussed share one crippling characteristic—each permits only modifying changes.

To cite a few examples, in emanation, self and other can modify the intensity of the experience; in subjection, the pain, the rewards, or the precision of control; and in isolation, the degree of social distance. In buffering, we may be able to modify the tolerance, distortion, or degree of resolution offered by our intermediary; in direct exchange, the relative gains and losses achieved; and in autonomy, the aids or obstacles in readjusting boundaries. Yet in the service of incoherence, we no longer possess the power to repress or repair the break into incoherence by treating

17. Gerald V. Poje, director of international programs at the National Institute of Environmental Health Science, quoted in *The Johns Hopkins Magazine*, February 1998, 46.

it as a sin. And in the face of so many unintended and uncontrolled changes, our deliberate intention to preserve a relationship in its present concrete manifestations may even help to break it asunder—to break with others or within ourselves: I will continue to do my best to preserve our political machine as the governing force in this city; I will continue to do my best to remain, above all, a workaholic.

In the service of incoherence, there is also a great temptation to ignore or even dismiss the experience of incoherence as an archetypal relationship: They need help? Never mind them; I don't even need them. Let them learn to accept and live with suffering. They got themselves into it; it's their problem, not mine. I must not disobey or even protest, or I will lose my relationship to my parent or to my spouse. (Though in fact I do not yet realize it, I have thus lost a crucial relationship to myself).

In the service of incoherence, there is also a great temptation to try to live with it without seeking to remedy it: I lost only a fragment of life, but hell, I still have the power and shrewdness to conflict through my rebellion; that's what counts, even though I have not won yet. You have doubts? You are skeptical? Those, too, are expressions of incoherence. Living with incoherence? That's also life in our way of life. We're doing the best we can. Let's have another drink!

In a world focused on competition for particular fragments, it seems justifiable, as long as incoherence does not yet appear to threaten us, to change the subject or, with a sense of ideological justification, to declare the opposing stand of the other as irrelevant, though it is currently "being exploited by a vocal minority of agitators." How can I remedy incoherence within this way of life? I make a living by working eight hours a day as the manual extension of a machine, disconnected from the rest of my being. I do not even get paid enough to connect to an adequate or interesting life. But how else can I make a living?

All archetypal relationships we enact in the service of incoherence or emanation diminish both our capacity and performance even before they dissolve into the archetypal relationship of incoherence. That can take place whenever just one aspect of capacity or performance breaks within or through the reaction of just one of the participating poles, or through the inability of just one of them to deal with a shared problem. The recognition of these facts and of the persistent breaking and increasing scarcity of relationships in the modern age led me to take the first steps of exploration of this theory of transformation. For when I discovered that there were only nine (though at first I saw only eight) forms of relationship giving us such capacity for such performance, I recognized that our age was not merely an age of strain or tension.

Incoherence as a way of life is not intrinsically doomed to destroy itself, but the very structure and dynamics shaping this kind of life prevent us from understanding and overcoming the fundamental causes of incoherence. At best, we understand and resort to the forces that still lead to power and success within any fragment of life. But indeed too often, precisely the increase of power and success by some leaves more people bereft of connections. We, however, tend still to see failure as solely our individual fault or the fault of particular others.

Given the intrinsic limits of incoherence as a relationship and as a way of life, we have—in the face of the growing frequency of breaking archetypal relationships—really only two alternatives that are fundamental and not merely incremental: deformation or transformation. Both allow us to create new repertories of archetypal relationships.

DEFORMATION AS AN ARCHETYPAL RELATIONSHIP

We can experience deformation as an archetypal relationship, as we do transformation as an archetypal relationship, beginning as a new inspiration in Act I Scene 2 of the core drama of life. While transformation, because we cannot yet fathom its meaning, may seem to us at first to be an emanational relationship, it cannot and will not retain that appearance as it moves us through the core drama. Deformation at its start may also strike us as emanational because we are more familiar with that kind of relationship, and it may retain its pseudo-emanational power over us much longer as we seek to repress our growing awareness of how it warps us and how it threatens us with quite a different ending than emanation. The relationship of deformation disconnects us from our self and from most others and their real problems and instead glues us to a person, idea, or substance that seems to magnify us (or negate us) as it pushes us toward doing evil to ourselves and others and toward premature death.

The archetypal drama of deformation deeply harms our capacity because our unconscious is possessed by a satanic force. Our own consciousness consequently fantasizes the world and ourselves in the reflection of that darkness. Our creativity seeks to give expression to that fantasy not only through compulsive forms of construction but also, and especially, through compulsive forms of destruction. We link only with others like ourselves. Deformation gives us no capacity but instead inflames our power for evil.

We seek to secure performance through absolute control of all five of its aspects. Yet our intense commitment to the continuity of our performance cannot prevent our movement toward destructive death. Change—above all to increase our power, yet deformation by its very nature imperils the power of its participants. Collaboration takes place—but only with people like us, who accept the same source of deformation. Conflict is the result—with all who are different from us, hence with others vast in number. Justice becomes not merely injustice, but evil.

There are so many kinds of manifestations of the satanic force that can draw us into a particular relationship of deformation and pull us into a drama in the service of deformation. I feel like a no body, but this drug or this political movement makes me feel really great. Or we may not be attracted to but rather overwhelmed by deformation: I am being beaten again and again in this relationship but I don't want to end up dead, so I see no evil, hear no evil, and speak about no evil. Or we may have been incapacitated to resist a deformational force that is organized to exterminate us.

The archetypal relationship of deformation shapes the concreteness of many relationships in dramas in the service of deformation, though as we have seen in our earlier discussion of such dramas, "fundamentalists" may help the needy in direct exchange, but only if it is direct exchange for their commitment or likely commitment to this movement. Hitler, for example, needed bureaucrats with enough autonomous power to administer his state.

People for whom incoherence is the dominant way of life may, in order to preserve their present form of power, resort to the threat or the actuality of a deformational relationship to force people who entered into incoherence with them back into a relationship of emanation or subjection. Or the powerful, in the service of incoherence, may be compelled by threats of forcing a deformational relationship with the Mafia to persist in paying them off. Or they may institutionalize a deforming relationship to many others by treating them as lesser or invisible. Consider—in the light of our earlier discussion of the four faces of our being, and now of each of the five aspects of capacity and the five aspects of performance—how much we lose by being rendered lesser or invisible!

The archetypal relationship of deformation, with its unsolved anxiety and overpowering fantasy, sucks us from its beginning to move toward the abyss at the end of Act II. The archetypal relationship of transformation inspires us from its beginning to move through the entire core drama of life into Act III.[18]

TRANSFORMATION AS AN ARCHETYPAL RELATIONSHIP

The archetypal relationship of transformation connects us to the deepest source of our being and thus enables us to participate in bringing the fundamentally new and better into being. In earlier publications, before I had come to understand the archetypal drama of transformation, I wrote that the relationship of transformation constitutes a reversal of the flow in the relationship of emanation, producing emergence rather than submergence of our own inner and transpersonal self. But I did not know how, nor did I understand that this experience is in fact not emanational.

In light of what we have learned, what are the differences but also the connections between the archetypal relationship of transformation, the drama of

---

18. I first published an essay on the eight archetypal relationships in 1968 in "A Redefinition of the Revolutionary Situation," cited above. I did not experience the transforming capacity to recognize deformation as an archetypal relationship until 1993.

transformation, and transformation as a way of life? Transformation as an archetypal relationship in the first place constitutes our connection to the sacred source of the archetypal drama of transformation—a connection that inspires us and moves our courage and insight to grow and to enter even into the relationship of incoherence with those archetypal dramas and their concrete manifestations that had previously possessed and commanded us, and then to practice different and fundamentally better relationships with ourselves and others. The archetypal drama of transformation helps us to enter into and enact a variety of archetypal relationships and not only that of transformation—a variety we shall shortly explore. And when we participate in transformation as a way of life, we enact the drama of transformation again and again in order to become free and capable of creating a variety of new dramas or basic changes in the quality of present dramas to augment this fundamentally better way of life—as we shall explore in the chapters to come. And in each such drama, with all its various relationships, we always include the archetypal relationship of transformation in our repertory connecting us to all the concrete poles. We help to bring into being and to nourish each concrete manifestation as an expression of the deepest sacred source of being, thanks to our own connection with that source.

Since we discussed the drama of transformation in the first chapter before we could clarify archetypal relationships, readers will see the structure and dynamics of that drama even more clearly in the light of this brief exposition of how the relationship of transformation connects us to our deepest ground—in contrast to being embedded in emanation. Chapter 14 (about the sacred) will tell us still more about the deepest source of our being as we participate in bi-unity with it, and hence also achieve the capacity to participate in the relationship of transformation with others.

When we are moved by a new inspiration in Act I Scene 2 of the core drama of life, we are drawn by what seems to be the archetypal relationship of emanation into the drama of transformation. But that mysterious source turns out in fact to connect us to the archetypal relationship of transformation. Guides of transformation may also as persons or in terms of their ideas inspire this same seemingly emanational beginning for others. A human being in need of reassurance may well initially experience our embrace as emanational. Only when we temporarily resort to emanation to take care of children, or of adults in difficulties who do not yet know how to take care of themselves, can emanation be temporarily justified from the perspective of transformation.

When we enter the first Scene of Act II, we rebel—but we do not arrest ourselves in a way of life that institutionalizes rebellion within prevailing archetypal dramas in its service. We move on into the second Scene of Act II where we enter into the archetypal relationship of incoherence three times over—with the archetypal drama, with the way of life that had possessed us, and with their concrete manifestations in this instance. In order to experience transformation, we never destroy another person but only break with the relationship, drama, and way of life we shared. This is no small matter, however, especially in our days of so much breaking within incoherence as a way of life. Hence we shall examine—in the chapter on justice—the injustice that transformation can initially inflict on those with whom we break.

Can we use the archetypal relationship of subjection while transforming? In deep contrast to all revolutionary ideologies, the answer is no—with one exception. We can use subjection only temporarily, and not in order to enhance our power, but simply to restrain the enraged until we can further show our capacity to help the other overcome such rage. We use subjection only as long as necessary to prevent an attack and to prevent self-destruction—only until we can help to open the other to a different response, thanks to the other's own capacity.

Because we remained in the service of incoherence, we engaged only an important fragment of that kind of response when the United States in 1963 passed a civil rights law. We enforced the new regulations by lawful subjection, if necessary, but we did nothing to nourish a new individual and community capacity for treating people not of our race as fellow human beings. Thus it was only a re-formation.

There may be times when—for a time—we need to discipline ourselves in order to concentrate on a particular moment of transformation. But focusing especially on scheduling and meeting deadlines is to be out of tune with the dynamics, rhythm, insight, and caring that help us to realize in practice the drama of transformation.

Certainly we cannot stay within isolation as an archetypal relationship and connect to all others collaborating with us in transforming a situation. But to agree that for a time you or I or we need to focus on meditation in order to recover our capacity or more fully understand who we are and also what is at stake in this transformation can be quite fruitful. We may need to organize and nourish a Women's Center or a center for a particular racial or ethnic group or culture or religion, not in order to insulate ourselves from others in our society but in order freely and honestly to discover together with people like us where in fact we have come from historically, where in fact we are now, and what we need to do to transform ourselves. All of us also need time off to enjoy ourselves concretely and to connect to the very depths of our being.

While transforming, we can resort to buffering, for example by way of a mediator empowered not by being a clever, shrewd, and pragmatic person—but one who is fully human and can help solve problems by interpreting human beings to each other and helping them test out the next fruitful steps. We can develop and utilize concepts that help us see and understand the value of human beings and of human work rather than concentrating on issues of profit and power. When we trade in old lenses for new lenses, we now also know that we are still using lenses. We know what they exclude and are free to capacitate ourselves to test them out again and again, so that we change them as soon as their limits render them unfruitful, and not only after our suffering from distortions and blindness has rendered our life unbearable or untenable.

New lenses arising from the experience of transformation can give us new theoretical knowledge—for example, of different archetypes. But fully to understand such a ground of being is different from knowing about it. Such understanding needs our own experience of transformation—a difference between knowledge and understanding, indeed between knowledge and compassionate wisdom, that we shall further explore in the chapter on theory.

The archetypal relationship of direct exchange is crucial to the drama of transformation. What we have learned and been energized to do from the depths of our being, thanks to our connection through the relationship of transformation, we translate into practice most often through manifestations of direct exchange—certainly not through naked power. And in contrast to incoherence as a way of life, the point of direct exchange is rarely a bargain, except in the case of political coalition. We resort to direct exchange to discover who the other actually is now, with what understanding and what capacity and what needs—and how we therefore can best be of help to each other. We exclude no one from this kind of relationship—not even ourselves, as we connect and reconnect to our own being. Direct exchange is intended in this way of life to lead not to a new balance of power but to a new empathy, reciprocal understanding, and collaboration. Our direct exchange involves all four faces of our being and of our fellow beings and the deepest source of our being that we share.[19]

In the service of incoherence, we are authorized to withdraw behind and defend present autonomous jurisdictions or seek to enlarge them. When we participate in transformation as a way of life, the autonomous self arises, thanks to its connection to the deepest source of life—thus discovering who each uniquely and truly is, and recognizing and respecting that potential, even if not yet its actuality, in all others. It is this potential freedom and capacity (in all five of its aspects) within all human beings that allow us to achieve this kind of autonomy. Because that is the sharable ground and origin of autonomy, we in this way of life deeply respect this relationship and all its participants. This is certainly one of the relationships that link affinity groups. In transformation, the principle underlying the relationship of autonomy is thus indeed recognized as an expression of the deepest archetypal force.

Autonomously participating in transformation does not cut us off from the wholeness of life because our concentration is not on the defense of our present

---

19. In Chapter 10, we shall discuss transforming love as an archetypal drama especially also expressing such direct exchange. Then we shall see why "love" is not a single archetypal relationship, but requires a whole archetypal drama; indeed, it can be expressed in qualitatively different ways through different archetypal ways of life.

jurisdiction. On the contrary, we remain eager especially because of the strength of our autonomy to enter also into direct exchange—for example in affinity groups—in order to learn what boundaries are worth crossing or changing or ending in order to learn how to collaborate more fruitfully, and to innovate afresh.

Can we use the archetypal relationship of deformation in the service of transformation? Never. The only case of destructive death—killing in self-defense when there is no other way left of defending our life—is not a case of deformation—as I discussed in Chapter 6.

Except for encouraging only temporary resorts to emanation and subjection (and thanks to excluding deformation entirely), transformation as a way of life frees everyone to utilize our capacity—and not our power—to enact more archetypal relationships with more varied concrete manifestations than the other ways of life allow.[20]

IN OUR DOMINANT WAY OF LIFE, ARCHETYPAL RELATIONSHIPS INCREASE OR DECREASE OUR POWER OR RENDER US POWERLESS, BUT THEY GIVE US NO SHARED CAPACITY

What we have further uncovered in our preceding analysis is the crucial contrast between power and capacity. In the light of how all archetypal relationships deny us capacity when we enact them in the service of emanation and incoherence, but at most give us only—or not even—power, we can now enlarge our understanding of this vital difference. Even in the face of the greatly increasing spread of incoherent relationships, all archetypal relationships in the service of our now dominant way of life leave us at most only with the power of incremental change within our unconscious, our consciousness and creativity, and our ability to link with others and to resort to just means. This is the power—but not the full capacity—we can use to deal with ourselves and others and the problems we face as continuity and change, collaboration and conflict, and the achieving of justice are increasingly in trouble. And when the coherence of such relationships can no longer be maintained, unilateral power or powerlessness becomes more precarious and more fearful, yet even unilateral power also becomes more precious to the previously connected powerful. Power is intended to dominate and control, but power also creates new incoherence again and again and often leaves us stranded.

Only capacity can overcome such incoherence—and also take the place of the power of still persisting archetypal relationships that have left us therefore (and

---

20. In earlier publications on these archetypal relationships, I presented a diagram of only eight and mistakenly connected the different sacred sources of emanation, incoherence, deformation, and transformation to a single center circle.

nonetheless) diminished as human beings. We cannot change our performance so that it brings about fundamental changes for the better in all ten aspects of any relationship unless we have first freed our capacity for transformation. Capacity, unlike power, arises from our renewed connection to the deepest sacred source of our being, and hence is also intrinsically connected to our new critical and caring response—ability to link our new freedom and understanding and acts of justice with those of others.

The archetypal relationship of transformation can arise only in the service of transformation. Its first emergence in Act I Scene 2 and our rebellion against our earlier confining containment, as well as our conscious rejection of these bonds in Act II Scene 2 are not reactions based on our power but on our deeper and greater capacity. To be *in authority* is to have power to command obedience. To be *an author* is to be someone who helps to originate, to grow. We shall discuss this deep contrast between power and capacity again and again in the coming chapters.

REPERTORIES AND NETWORKS OF ARCHETYPAL RELATIONSHIPS

So far, we have explored what all the different expressions within any archetypal relationship hold in common. We shall now clarify four important practical aspects of relationships that our conventional use of language tends to hide. When, for example, we say "I am his father," we have phrased our connection in a way that can be expressed in nine different kinds of relationships, and certainly will most often be expressed in more than one of them. We shall next examine in a number of examples how archetypal analysis can open up our insights and our capacity by overcoming such ambiguities.

Secondly, we also often use the phrase "our relationship," when in fact not only a single but a plurality of archetypal relationships connect us to the other pole. That kind of analysis helps us clarify what repertory of archetypal relationships is open to us—and which ones would give us greater capacity but we are not permitted to use, or now deny our capacity but we are not permitted to reject (no small blows to our capacity).

Thirdly, we shall ask which archetypal relationship is dominant in this repertory. For example, within that autonomous corporation or government office, are emanation and subjection the dominant relationships? And fourthly, we shall by way of examples also explore networks of archetypal relationships, to discover what capacity is—or is not—ours to connect (with respect to a particular problem) to more than one pole involved in it. What networks, for example, now give us capacity to help the oppressed or to eliminate pollution?

We shall now raise questions and re-envision examples of relationships in this light. By limiting repertories and networks, societies perpetuate the unequal distribution of the costs and benefits of dealing with continuity, change, collaboration, conflict, and justice, and thus also mask and repress our awareness of incoherence. Thus, most campaigns against prostitution only move against the women, as if no men were involved. How often do we resort to pesticides as soon as we have ascertained that they kill pests, without asking what else they will affect? We call ourselves a "nation" as if we were indivisibly united, but what repertories and networks of relationships in fact hold us together which also give us the capacity to create a community, or which in fact divide us? The lack of relationships that could enhance our capacity to deal with the problems of our community is everywhere one of the greatest deprivations of our time. To create new strong communities is especially important in our time since no single individual has the capacity (not even the power) to deal with the new global economic corporations—or with most other new problems.

Repertories and networks are indeed literally vital for each individual. Even when we seem to be alone in the archetypal relationships of isolation or incoherence, both are in fact relationships. But in both we cannot survive for long except in a larger repertory at least within ourselves and a network with others. We did not originate ourselves; we cannot exist solely by ourselves. The theoretical perspective of transformation allows us to ask what forms of archetypal relationships exist in this repertory and network but also to evaluate what capacity therefore exists or is missing for us and the people with whom we now connect. In this respect, too, our theory does not present us with an abstract matrix for this crucial test, but our evaluations are based on the fact that our very nature allows us to express any of these nine relationships.

Only by way of analyzing repertories and networks, and which of the nine relationships are missing and why, can we discover the full capacity—or else the power or lack of power—we are experiencing even before we deepen and expand that kind of analysis by inquiring into the archetypal dramas and ways of life being enacted.

Let us look at repertories and networks that can be enacted (or, significantly, not enacted) by many high school teachers in democratic liberal societies—in the best of all societies in the service of incoherence. Emanation—I know lots of things you don't know, which you can't even yet understand when I tell you. But just listen to me and believe me. Subjection—I will strictly enforce these rules. (I am sorry that I am no longer allowed when students disobey me to punish them physically in or after class.) Or, I am committed to teaching you self-discipline. Combining emanation and subjection—I inculcate, above all, rote learning.

Isolation—I will never tell you my personal views on any subject. Do not tell me yours. Do not use the personal pronoun "I" in any of your essays. Always in class be impersonally objective. Buffering—These concepts constitute the right view of the subject at hand. Or, now let us autonomously and also by way of direct exchange test these concepts. Direct exchange—Only if I have a question for you or you for me. Any other direct exchange? Only outside the classroom, or let us also learn from each other and why we agree or disagree. Autonomy—For both teachers and students? Incoherence—As open disagreement or as rejection by the teacher or truancy by the student?

Deformation—Do the courses taught—or not even taught—lessen or render invisible those people and their problems who are not successfully assimilated to the dominant culture? Transformation—We have been discussing a repertory in the service of incoherence where teachers do not act as guides through the process of transformation.[21]

I focused primarily on only one pole in this repertory, teachers, and asked implicitly which archetypal relationship dominates their teaching, and therefore which relationships can (or cannot) be enacted in the same repertory—and in what manifestations. I have not yet inquired into the network that is also at stake. What, for example, are the archetypal relationships between students? Who decides how much money to spend on education, or on repairing school buildings in bad condition? Who decides which textbooks to use? How do teachers and parents relate to each other? Do schools remain open "after school" for adult education, for community meetings, for shared student activities? Why do these links differ so much from neighborhood to neighborhood?

Our theoretical perspective always takes us to the roots of life. Having discovered the wholeness of reality open to us, it informs us and frees us to ask not only about what we are experiencing and in what underlying forms, but also to understand what we are looking for and on what fundamental ground we can find it. What are we missing in our life now?

Thus we can discover, even before we look at archetypal stories and ways of life, how limited the repertories and networks of the poor and powerless are, and therefore why, under these circumstances, they cannot solve their basic problems. Scientists, as we have also seen, have one of the richest repertories, but their network often does not relate their specialty to other problems of life, and may even deny them the power or capacity to do so. Who shall now in fact be able to receive this new medicine? Who shall prevent nuclear war, now that we have invented its weapons?

CONCLUSION

Archetypal relationships acquire their substantive content, context, underlying motivations, values, and purpose through their enactment in archetypal stories and their service in one of the four different ways of life. This fact does not change

---

21. See David Abalos's book, *Strategies of Transformation toward a Multicultural Society* that deals with education as teaching and learning and how to transform all four faces of our being at all stages of our lives.

the underlying structure of any archetypal relationship, but it shapes their actual expression, and also what kind of relationship, repertory, and network might be, must be, or must not be expressed. It is through the perspective of archetypal dramas that we discover who needs to be on stage with us and in what kind of archetypal relationships.

Who is on stage with us? Am I (are we) only a pole—a unit solely in a particular relationship—or are we beings? Are we only role-playing or are we beings seeking wholly to enact in our dramas our four faces—for being is also a verb—and to help others to do so too? Are crucial poles in our relationships occupied by people we have reified—that is, turned into things? Are there poles occupied by ideas we have vivified—that is endowed with a life of their own? Are we alive to these vital questions in every relationship in stories we enact? Only when we participate in transformation as a way of life are we that fully present and critically, creatively, and caringly alive.

Is the group to which we belong in the drama we enact in fact based on an open repertory and network of relationships, or is it in fact a drama of the nation-state or of capitalism controlled by an elite? What problems does our repertory and network leave us unable to deal with? Have these dramas and our way of life—thanks to their effective socialization—led us to internalize our roles and their requirements? Is that all the being we are?

No society, as yet, encourages the discovery and expression of our full human capacity.

9

The Archetypal Drama of Being Competent

My search for a theory of transformation began because I saw established relationships breaking all over the world, but then I recognized the problem we shared was much greater. Many stories of our lives, indeed entire ways of life, were also becoming unendurable or coming apart. What were the living underlying patterns that had held such relationships and dramas together? How could we free ourselves from them before they exact much higher human costs? And how could we discover how to enact much better dramas?

Most of us have trouble telling our stories. We know only how to tell anecdotes or at most, narratives—one thing happening after another—when, in fact, different dramas interact in our lives. Not only concrete events but also deeper underlying forces shape all four faces of our being. Yet, unless we understand archetypal dramas, we cannot get out of them. If they break, they leave us stranded. We need to gain insight into the stories we enact—stories that inform us and that we incarnate. It is not enough simply to recognize their particular advantages or penalties.

Now I shall offer an introduction to archetypal dramas as we begin to discuss a particular series of them. I postponed a detailed exploration of the nature of archetypes till now because, had I presented them first, given our present state of knowledge and scholarship, archetypes would have seemed unreal, mystical, or abstract. It is always more fruitful to have understanding grow in us as we examine particular cases in a new light.

One of the most potent empirical tests of any description of any archetypal drama is that any of our descriptions of its underlying structure and dynamics and of its purpose and meaning *always* hold true, or else that certain actions can *never* take place within the drama—as long as it is enacted within that particular way of life. A single test case to the contrary will either call for a revision of our description, or it can undo what we have said about that archetypal drama or that way of life. We cannot predict whether any particular concrete manifestation will arise at any particular moment, but we are speaking of what interconnected underlying patterns will or cannot arise to shape such concrete manifestations.

Our exploration of the archetypal stories in this chapter and the chapters that follow (and those we have already explored—for example, the archetypal drama of capitalism) test these propositions. These chapters will also demonstrate that each of the four ways of life remold the substance, meaning, values and purpose—and the forms of conflict and collaboration—of each drama in vitally different ways, so much so that giving a drama once again the same name can become problematical as we change our way of life. I do not know how many archetypal dramas exist altogether. Certainly there is not only one drama within which we can enact being a father, or only one for enacting being a lover or a mother. I suspect that there exist several hundred archetypal dramas. If there were many more of them, human beings would have even more difficulties understanding each other than we already do. There is clearly much more pioneering exploration of archetypal dramas to be accomplished—pioneering that, unlike the analyses of Plato or Jung, explore all four faces of our being as manifested in any particular drama and its way of life.

We now begin with an archetypal drama that a large number of our readers will already have experienced, especially as enacted in the service of incoherence: being competent.

BEING COMPETENT IN THE SERVICE OF INCOHERENCE

First our parents, then our teachers, and soon our own ambitions—and then also our bosses and our own sense of what really matters—have concretely inspired us to be competent from early morning till late at night. If any of these superiors threaten to punish us if we are not doing our best to be competent, we certainly believe their threat or their actual punishment to be legitimate. We have grown up in the conviction that we wanted to get educated above all in order to join—and to rise to the top—in this drama.

Is not the drama of being competent a story of becoming especially skilled, expert, practical, objective, and proficient? Why am I about to suggest that it also has a sacred face—expressed by our enactment of its archetypal drama? But where else could its deeply inspiring strength come from? What else could hold it together as the same entire underlying story, especially however different its concrete manifestations from moment to moment?

The word *competent* is a first cousin of the word *compete*—and that is indeed the immediate family of behaviors when we enact this drama in the service of incoherence. The infinitive of the Latin root in both words—*petere*—means to fall upon, to assail, to strive after. And in the modern age of incoherence, the people in this drama strive to become especially skilled to enhance their own competitive power and the power of those whose interests they serve.

How do we achieve this kind of competence? We are required to turn ourselves into a fragment in order to focus solely those specialized skills that allow us to gain knowledge to control solely those efficient and effective causes that lead to immediate or at least early payoffs solely within those fragments of life that are regarded as important by those most powerful over fragments within this drama or in other dramas (also in the service of incoherence). If we are inspired (certainly not from within this drama or its present way of life) to ask what, ultimately, is the meaning and purpose of what we are so competently doing, the answer is this: We can never know.

Enacting this drama in this way of life creates another incoherence. However competent we are, however much appreciated by others for being so competent, there is absolutely no connection between being competent and being valued by you or by others as a human being. There is no convertible currency here. All the specialized competence in the world will not and cannot, enrich our value—or even our sense of what it would mean to be valued—as a human being. We are left at most to feel pride in our achievements thanks to our competence, and pride in the power such competence may give us, to rise still higher in this competition. This is all about power, not capacity.

What about human capacity? That is seen in this drama (when in the service of incoherence) as a purely subjective notion, in contrast to objective analyses of competence and of the power competence allows us to achieve. This split between the subjective and the objective exposes another intrinsic limitation of this archetypal drama within this way of life. Within this type of competence, we pay no attention to deeper underlying forces unless they are of a kind that can be abstracted and quantified. Hence, we cannot imagine exploring the archetypal realities and choices of our being.

But that is also one major reason why this kind of competence often also leads to failure and defeat. This competence includes no concern with the larger and deeper context, with our fundamental choices of purpose and values that cannot be understood and do not even concern us as we focus on highly specialized knowledge, rational calculations, efficiency, and power. Yet these deeper forces—including those breaking relationships, stories, and ways of life in our time—are basic and real, challenging more and more often our power to organize and reorganize fragments of life, as well as challenging our capacity to fulfill our being.

We, the competent, are also lamed by the fact that, thanks to our concentration on what we call the objective, we do not much tune in to or understand what we curb in its full reality by thinking of it as merely subjective. We do not, for example, recognize how much being we had to repress when our parents' love for us was always conditional on our increasing our competence. Are we now laming our children in the same way? By thus being stifled in aspects of our own being in what we call the "private" realm, we in fact also dry up our capacity to care for other human beings in what we call the "public" realm.

Being competent becomes the most important aspect of our political face of being. But what we can and need to do together in our life focuses almost entirely on collaborating and especially competing with those who have the same type of competence, and becoming the most useful instrumental self for those powerful enough to hire us so that we can expertly develop the goods and services others can afford to purchase. The last sentence also describes all those who need to be on stage with us in this drama when it is enacted in the service of incoherence. To disagree with the powerful of this drama—however competent or incompetent they may be—can get us thrown off the stage.[1] What is left then? Who can we be? What can we do?

There are competent people who are moved by a sense of responsibility not only to a particular kind of task or to pleasing a particular boss in order also to gain their own success. They may also be moved by a sense of responsibility to the standards of their profession—for example, in medicine, psychology, and science. They may discover and develop a new fragment in their field. Does this new knowledge challenge the existing power structure of this drama or augment it? Does a deeper sense of morality remaining from an emanational inheritance or arising from emerging transformation put into question what is now established as competence? These are possible movements into an archetypal relationship of incoherence with the existing drama of competence. But the less we value our being, the less likely it is that we are going to speak up and dissent.

Within this drama in the service of incoherence, the archetypal relationship of autonomy predominates in the repertory of the competent, but its boundaries within this drama are limited. Limited, too, is the network of relationships, especially to people not onstage with us within our own concrete manifestation of this drama. Our autonomy within this drama is above all defined by our particular competence and its particular quality, not by being human. We may, of course, live our life in more than one drama, but being competent for far more people than ever before has become the most powerful drama in our life in the service of incoherence. It gives us also a sense of control missing from so much of the rest of our life in the service of incoherence.

---

1. For a vivid, deeply informed analysis of what "prudence or indeed phronesis" (that is, great practical understanding) it requires to struggle successfully (but also unsuccessfully) for new or opposite policies with the most powerful, see James A. Bill, *George Ball: Behind the Scenes in U.S. Foreign Policy*.

But would we not rather be treated by a competent surgeon than an incompetent one? But if we had only these two choices, we would obviously agree unanimously on the answer. But we have four fundamentally different choices, and we shall discuss all of them.

BEING COMPETENT IN THE SERVICE OF TRANSFORMATION

I shall now focus on people who are especially competent in understanding and practicing at least one aspect (one or perhaps two or three aspects, but none of us will ever understand everything) of our being—as a noun and as a verb. People competent, for example, in understanding and dealing with a particular political problem in the service of transformation will also know at minimum how to learn, if not by themselves then with the help of others, how this problem of what we can and need to do together connects (or why it currently fails to connect) to the personal, historical, and sacred faces of our being and (or not yet) to our deepest source.

A surgeon in the service of transformation, in addition to operating on us to overcome our pain, will also ask and seek help to answer these questions: Why did this pain arise? Did someone beat you or infect you? What can we do to prevent that from happening again? Will you neglect your own care (or be neglected by others) when you get home again? What can we do about that with you and with others competent in their specialties (but also in collaborating to deal with the whole problem) in order to restore wholeness of being? This sense of purpose is certainly also a good cause for creating employment for many more people than we seek now.

In the service of emanation, we try to heal in the name of God or Science. In the service of incoherence, we try to heal by restoring this fragment of life—by trying to overcome a particular relationship of incoherence or deformation. To be competent in the service of transformation, however, we try to learn again and again how to be fully present with respect to a concrete problem—to be fully present one's self and with others who can help us to overcome all the forms of incoherence or partial existence—or the deformation—that constitute the problem.

To be competent in the service of transformation is to learn above all how to gain insight, courage, and capacity, to move critically and creatively with others through the core drama of life in order to overcome the particular kind of problems on which we have so far come to focus our competence. This is not competence for the sake of power or in the service of the powerful, but competence that expresses our capacity. And this capacity is at one and the same time singular and plural. At its best, the drama of competence in the service of transformation fills the stage with all who are needed and willing to cross existing boundaries, as necessary, in order to learn how to help.

COMPETENCE IN THE SERVICE OF DEFORMATION

When the fantasy that leads to deformation is our way of life, competence has no place except as it increases or expresses the power of our leader and our possessive dogma. The surgeons at Auschwitz used sadistic methods for their racist medical experiments. Eichmann made sure that the trains to the death camps were running on time. Goebbels, the Minister of Propaganda, became an expert in lying.

What remains all too pervasive, even when people live predominantly in the service of incoherence, is that part of their competence turns into professional deformation. They see and treat themselves and others solely as commodities or sources of profit; solely in logical or quantitative terms or else as invisible; solely in terms consonant with their specialty, or else not at all—certainly not as human beings. When Bob Lund, an engineer at Morton Thiokol at the Cape Canaveral Launching Center expressed to NASA his technical doubts about the safety of launching in cold weather, his boss said to him, "It's time to take off your engineer's cap and put on your manager's cap." As a manager, concerned with future business with NASA and Congressional appropriations cuts if NASA were to cancel the flight, Lund said yes. The rocket carrying the Challenger space shuttle exploded and killed all seven astronauts in the crew.[2]

People whose competence turns toward professional deformation tend to offer purely technical explanations in response to human suffering. The Nixon Administration, in 1973, having already officially declared it wanted to end the war in Vietnam, was nonetheless still bombing Cambodia. Colonel David H. E. Opfer, the U.S. air attaché in Cambodia told the press, "You always write it's bombing, bombing, bombing. It's not bombing. It's air support."[3] And when Secretary of Defense Robert McNamara resigned in 1968 because of our persistence in the Vietnam War, he spoke of what persuaded him solely in terms of cost-benefit analysis.[4]

COMPETENCE IN THE SERVICE OF EMANATION

Competence in the service of emanation is demonstrated by refined and thorough craftsmanship within established lines of work. But are rabbis or *ulema* or peasants solely competent as we understand and practice that term in our time? No, nothing is impersonal—disconnecting their work from other aspects of their personal, political, historical, and sacred being. They are certainly hoping that their compe-

---

2. Amy Gutmann and Dennis F. Thompson, *Ethics and Politics: Cases and Comments*, second ed., The Nelson-Hall Series in Political Science, 117–28.

3. *The New York Times*, August 12, 1973. (Ironically, the Colonel's name, Opfer, is a word which in German means "sacrifice.")

4. This fact was first brought to my attention by Lawrie Balfour in a Senior Thesis she wrote on justice and the Vietnam War—before Robert S. McNamara changed his perspective and, in a new light, wrote Robert S. McNamara and Brian VanDeMark, *In Retrospect: The Tragedy and Lessons of Vietnam*, first ed.

tence would also enhance their emanational relationship to the sacred source of their being and also with their neighbors.

That emphasis on the archetypal relationship of emanation, also in this drama in the service of emanation as a way of life, did limit originality and inventiveness, and set limits on the forms of competence women were expected and allowed to express. But emanation as a way of life and the pre-modern past are not synonymous. All four ways of life have been present at least from the beginning of humanity. How else could that past have given rise to agriculture, alphabets, arts, mathematics, medicines, gunpowder, philosophy, and so much more that is yet to be created?

CONCLUSION

I have not spoken of artists, composers, writers, or scholars enacting the drama of competence. No doubt they also need to be able to perform in that mode, but stories and ways of life that inspire and lead to the enactment of critical understanding and creativity are essential for the core of their experience. I have also not examined competent soldiers and skilled workers because their role is so constricted by the commands of others. Some people differentiate between *competence* and *excellence*. I have not done so, because in the drama of competence, even if someone's performance deserves a C-minus at this moment, the archetypal drive intrinsic to this story in the service of incoherence is to strive for ever more skill within our specialty, and for power and rewards.

Now there are more such people of that kind than ever before and they have in great measure raised the quantity, quality, variety, inventiveness, and efficiency of production and services—but, as we have been discussing, at dramatic cost to our being wholly human with ourselves and with our neighbors. Even when we are highly competent but in the service of incoherence, then, just like even when we are rich and powerful in this way of life, we remain only partial human beings.

("Why are you raising this point again? Don't you know how busy I am already? I need to concentrate on my particular task! Why would I have to be present as a whole human being to make a case for my client in a court of justice?")

By contrast, the core criterion of our theory and practice of transformation in enacting any archetypal drama is this: Are we now moving toward helping to connect with understanding, love, and justice the four faces and the deepest source of our being and of the beings present in this drama with us?

In some archetypal dramas, as we have seen, we cannot fulfill this criterion. We can only enter the path of transformation by entirely freeing ourselves from such dramas. In the case of competence or democracy, we need to free ourselves from the severe limitations and distortions of the structure, dynamics, values, and purpose of such dramas in the service of arresting ways of life. But then we can enrich lives anew by enacting them as a participation in transformation.

10

Transforming Love, Romantic Love, and Other Forms

Contrasting Archetypal Dramas

What is the point of understanding if it does not also help us to move toward greater love and justice? Why devote ourselves to love if it does not also lead to greater understanding and justice? How can we attain and enact fundamentally better justice without understanding and love?

Deep and essential is the connection of love with our most valuable, creative, and caring capacity to contribute to what we can and need justly to do together. Yet the richest form of love—transforming love—is the least familiar to us. Romantic love is the most popular instead.

Love is not simply an emotion; it reflects different archetypal dramas. We shall concentrate on contrasting the stories of romantic love and transforming love—but also mention a few more.

THE ARCHETYPAL DRAMA OF TRANSFORMING LOVE

In transforming love, I am deeply attracted by something fundamentally new and better existing or still growing in the other. I try to grow that same seed within myself where it can develop in its own unique way (no imitation)—and the other person lovingly helps me grow that seed within me. Similarly, the other discovers something fundamentally new and better existing or coming to life within me which the other has not yet experienced, and I help lovingly to grow that seed in the other person. We love each other as beings who are sharing an ever renewed discovery and understanding for bringing forth and enjoying together once hidden treasures in each other—and in our world. We share not particular fragments but concrete manifestations of wholeness of being. We come not only to know each other intellectually and (as the Bible often uses the term *knowing*) sexually, but with understanding and love that helps us to a fundamentally better justice—within ourselves, between us, and in our relations with others.

This experience of the deepest intimacy, joy, and sharing is not possible until at least one of us has already experienced the drama of transformation and hence can express a love that will awaken in others the desire and courage to find and nourish this kind of love. Certainly this is not a selfless or one-sided love. Instead, both become more and more aware that they have something of value to share. Hence both have cause more and more to love their own worth and the worth of each other as they participate in helping to create each other anew to be more truly and wholly their own unique self and also their political selves in what they can and need to do together. This is not simply a passionate eagerness to please the other, as in romantic love.

Transforming love is based on faith—not on belief, as in romantic love. Transforming love involves risking trust in the fruitfulness—in the love, understanding, and justice—that arises as we share our experience and capacity. Transforming love also involves risking trust in the sacred source of our being. Like all transformations of our life, the capacity and experience of this kind of love originates from the deepest sacred source of our being. Love is never ours to command, and transforming love, in contrast to other forms of love, does not overwhelm us. Transforming love comes into being as a new story of our life as we move through the drama of transformation.

Such love is never perfect. Not even the deepest sacred source is perfect (as we shall discuss in Chapter 14). But in transforming love, both of us draw upon the experience of that sacred source in each other—an experience neither of union with that source nor with each other, but of bi-unity with that source and between us. We are thus connected but we also remain unique, indeed become capable more and more—thanks to these connections—individually and together to enrich ourselves and our relationships.

SIX EXAMPLES OF EXPERIENCING THE DRAMA OF TRANSFORMING LOVE

We do not "have sex" or "make love," but instead of such moments of possession or production, we connect our bodies and souls freely in joyous, playful, and passionate intimacy and love. And we thus communicate not only *during* this physical experience of bi-unity, but we also communicate *about* it before and afterwards so that we may become ever more present and real to each other, and experience more intimacy—even within our own being. Expressing such love does not expend it but makes it grow.

We tune in to each other's creative work (which may be expressed through similar or different subjects and forms), deeply caring about what emerges from each of us and how we can help each other both critically and constructively, and keen to discover how we can—each in our unique way—continue to do such work. In the drama of transforming love, we can discover the constraints of our present culture (or within each of the different cultures in which each of us grew up) and explore together, and with others, how we can transform—and thus free and enrich—especially also the historical and political faces of our being. We help each other discover and freely, creatively practice both the masculine and the feminine in archetypal dramas which our current culture—under masculine domination—has shaped one-sidedly as above all masculine in structure, dynamics, and values. Our bodily containers and our personal uniqueness will continue to make a difference in our performance, but in transforming love, we do not accept barriers to experience imposed by others or our own past.

A transforming lover is also a fellow human being we can count on to be with us as in this cosmos of continuous creation we go through Act II (incoherence) again and again. Even in the midst of that experience, the transforming lover nourishes us with love and understanding. Then we begin the test of the fundamentally better with our lover. We begin that test by sharing a new inspiration in practice, and creating a new story together. In this way, we love each other *during* our process of transformation, not only for its fully ripened fruit.

The repertory of archetypal relationships enacted in this drama of love in the service of transformation is far richer in forms and substance than in any dramas in the service of emanation or incoherence. And (as we shall see again and again later in this chapter and in others to come) its networks and hence the experience of its substance intertwines with other dramas in the service of transformation. The repertory does not include emanation, of course, except in moments when we need care beyond our present capacity to cope with a particular problem. (We are not seeking to become embodiments of each other.) Except for those moments we discussed in Chapter 8, there is no subjection—and certainly no deformation. What about isolation? Yes. Not only for times of personal or shared meditation, but to arrange time out from our usual responsibilities—but not from transformation as a way of life—to focus separately or together on enjoying ourselves and the fun and beauty of life. And the repertory includes buffering—as we come forth again and again with an open and curious heart and mind to see and experience our relationship through new images and symbols.

Direct exchange is one of the most enriching of all archetypal relationships in this drama of transforming love. We do not employ it to increase our payoffs in power and profit. We enact it in order to tune in to each other to discover, explain, ask for, offer, receive, and deliver fruits of each other's growing capacity—capacity arising out of each other's opening unconscious, consciousness, creativity, and linking with others—and also our resort to just resources.

Our autonomy arises in this drama from our both being connected to the deepest source of our being—and thanks also to our connection to the archetypal relationship of transformation. Our respect for each other's autonomy—and for each other's uniqueness—arises from this same root. But our persisting experience of transformation also inspires us to ask again and again which existing boundaries are worth crossing, changing, or ending, and which are worth nourishing together.

What about the archetypal relationship of incoherence? We may experience moments of incomprehension or of disagreement and certainly, again and again, the incoherence intrinsic to moving through Act II of the drama of transformation. But we stay connected despite such specific breaks because of our love and the richness in understanding and justice of our existing repertory that helps us to renew relationships.

Can transforming love come to an end? Certainly it can if we try to enshrine it, or if only one of us consistently seeks to lead the way. It can also be at risk if a deep and exciting inspiration comes which our partner refuses to explore even as it is being expressed within us. Transforming love holds no fixed beliefs but again and again risks trusting in being fully present in this process of participation. We do not try to preserve or conserve transforming love, but persistently to nourish it from the growing roots and fruits of our experience of the archetypal relationship of transformation.

Is there room for more than two (and our children) in transforming love? Especially when we participate in transformation, we are conscious of the fact that we have four faces of being and our deepest source which we can share—we are, indeed, being deeply moved to share—with others. Love cannot be solely personal and private. Hence there are additional dramas of transformation that require more people to be on stage with us—for example, affinity groups, task forces, cooperative enterprises, school classes at all age levels, and communities at all levels. What all such groups share is that some of its members have already experienced the drama of transformation at least once and others are seeking to do so in order to experience wholeness based on understanding, love, and justice.

In transformation, we are not being moved to be selfless, in mere contrast to our being selfish. We now are deeply inspired to love our neighbor as we love ourselves because we now have found and have come to understand how and why we love ourselves. We do not love only neighbors who are like ourselves because they live with us in the same emanational container, or neighbors who are like ourselves because they are partisans in the pursuit of a self-interest we share. Unless we intimately understand and practice transforming love with ourselves, we do not have the resources for loving others.

The intrinsic connection between transforming understanding, love, and justice also leads us beyond affinity groups into yet another drama of love which initially begins with compassion. Not compassion, as so often exemplified in our time, as our donating specific things or services needed by others. Of course, such immediate steps are necessary, but I mean compassion in a context of discovering, together with the deprived and endangered, what fundamental changes we need and can together bring about. We seek to connect, even with the powerless or deforming, to bring about a community in which we can help such neighbors to love their neighbors as they discover how to love themselves. We are in dire need of many, many such new neighborhoods everywhere in this world. The more we become filled with love, the more sensitive we also become to the personal, political, historical, and sacred deprivations of others. And thus we reach out to as many actual fellow human beings—not to "the masses," not to "humanity" (abstractions that disconnect us from others)—as we, in particular, have the capacity to do.

The kind of love we have been describing, joined also with understanding and justice, constitutes an intrinsic aspect of all dramas as we participate in transformation as a way of life—even as the particular drama might primarily involve issues of ecology or fundamentally altering economic relationships for the better.

Some years ago, a student of mine decided to write her senior thesis on some aspects of love and politics. She went to the Departmental Representative for Senior Theses, who said, "I can't imagine how love and politics go together." And she responded, "If I said that I wanted to work on hate and politics, you'd recognize immediately how they go together." He agreed and approved the topic.[1]

Some people may say, "But how can we find time to experience transforming love—even with our spouses, much less with our community? Fortunately, my wife and I have focused and crystallized our personalities, our views, and our skills; we both have good jobs. If indeed we are lucky and get home by 7:00 PM, we need to make dinner, to play with our children, and to relax. So where is the time or room for transformation?" Others say, "Look how other people have been treating me at home and at work (when I had work). Love? What's love? I've never experienced it."

We are not likely to move toward transforming love until we find our own life and that of our neighbors unbearable, untenable, and unfruitful for any such understanding, justice, and love—for any wholeness of being. But how can any one or even two deeply connected human beings make so much of a difference, considering that most people are now in arrest, even at best, in only partial and fragmented lives?

We can begin historically, politically, and personally only where we are now. But we can begin to build a new community based on our experience of transforming

---

1. Aline T. Geronimus wrote her Senior Thesis, *Love and Politics: A Penetrating Glimpse into the Obvious*, December 31, 1977.

love that helps us to discover our vocation—what our being now calls upon us with ever greater intensity and understanding to do with ourselves and with others. A transforming community does not demand equally close, equally intense relations with everyone, but it asks us to give what our unique talent can contribute to the lives of specific others and to the resolution of crucial problems we share.

What are our alternatives? Chief among them in our time is—rather than liberating ourselves for capacitating love—to resort to power. In the service of incoherence, we also practice a number of partial and incomplete forms of love—some of which we shall soon discuss. But first, let's look at one of them that attracts us most in our time—romantic love.

AN ARCHETYPAL DRAMA OF ROMANTIC LOVE

There exist different stories of love we usually call "romantic." I will speak here only of the one that is most widespread, at least in our overwhelming desire for it, if not in actual practice. In this archetypal drama, we are enthralled, enchanted, beguiled, and captivated by each other. We want to cherish or even possess each other. At its most intense, we may wish to fuse. Franz Kafka wrote to his beloved: "I wish you didn't exist in this world, but existed wholly in me; or even better, that I didn't exist in this world, but wholly in you; one of us is too many here."[2]

Why am I about to unveil this kind of romantic love so critically? Not because I am moved by sexual Puritanism, instrumental rationality, or cynicism, but because its living underlying patterning forces always give rise to a fantasy that ends in the destruction of every concrete manifestation of this drama—sometimes even of ourselves.

Romantic love within this archetypal way of life always begins as a fragment of fantasy—as the seeming opposite of the merely conditional love we received in our childhood and adulthood and in contrast to our tough competition in the world of power and profits that offers no love whatsoever. We project upon the other our fantasy of who she (or he) is, and if we are "lucky," the other does the same—when in truth we know so little about each other's being. Then we try our best to please the other by living up to embodying that great fantasy. The deepest source of our being did not create us—each of us—as a unique being so that we would lose ourselves again, not even within that source, and certainly not as a lover within our beloved.

We do not together find more and more of our being, as in transforming love, but we both lose ourselves. "I am completely taken by her and she is by me." Yet we believe that this fact at last gives us full value. We believe that this kind of love will compensate us for our wounded self and overcome our incompleteness. Yet this

---

2. Franz Kafka et al., *Letters to Felice*.

kind of love, that even at its best is only another fragment in the service of incoherence, in fact keeps us biased and incomplete in all the stories of our life. It seems to increase our power to experience the rewards of love. But it does not—nor does it do anything to increase our shared capacity of being.

Yielding to romantic love remains shaped by the issue of power. It seems to enlarge our power, or compensate us for our shortage of power, or justify our yielding to power. At most, our shared self-interest counts: Look, we agree on who gets what, when, where, and how! And we give each other so much of what each and both of us want that neither one of us could ever break away! But the "only you and me" is also a reflection of incoherence as a way of life—of the self-interest of only partial beings. We have invested everything in the incompleteness of each other's being. Hence, even romantic love does not keep us from experiencing anxiety over the fact—ripe with the potential for conflict—that the other, despite our deep desire, is not our self, and certainly is not yet a whole being. We fear rebellion of the other and competition from others. Therefore we seek the power to become as possessive as possible, and as indispensable as possible.

What are the deeper risks of such monopolization? When we give our entire life to the will, desire, needs, and power of another, we enter the road of deformation in a seemingly wonderful cause: "All or nothing at all; half a love isn't enough for me." Romantic love can lead us to totalize a fragment of love. We are overwhelmed by the other. Without this lover I would be nothing. Hence I will do anything my lover wants me to do, for if my lover stops loving me, I will die.

We may literally die when this drama thus enters into the service of deformation. This drama always begins as each fantasizes an image of the other. At first, each tries to live up to that image but then, inescapably, one discovers that the other is not really like that, or one or the other can no longer bear to live up to being that fantasy. Thereupon we feel like actually—or at least in terms of symbolic equivalents—killing the one who betrayed our fantasy, or committing suicide in the face of such torment. This drama was the only story of our life that really mattered to us. We therefore end in premature and destructive death, or at least in deep self-wounding apathy, anger, or despair.

Or we can live out this drama in the service of incoherence. For in this drama one of us will always discover that the other is not really like our fantasy. This fact of pseudo-emanation that seizes us as an overwhelming reassurance in the midst of incoherence puts us always at risk of deformation. But the end need not inescapably manifest itself in destructive death if, while retaining expressions of deformation, we still also remain deeply allied with, indeed dominated by, incoherence as a way of life. At least for one of us in that case, love is not fully unconditional. Hence we can see more clearly what is or is not going on, and calculate risks and profits. Romantic love remains a vital and major fragment of our life, but not the only fragment. It becomes only (though certainly not merely) our principal private enterprise.

Under these conditions, romantic love still feels inspiring, uplifting, exciting, and reassuring most of the time. We feel so wonderful that we might even assert that it is "transforming" us. True, we may never have experienced this kind of love before, but given our arrest in incoherence, our knowledge of who and where we are is still only partial. Our unconscious has captured our consciousness. Our creativity focuses above all on this relationship and may well be shaped, even harnessed by what the other expects of us.

What about linking with others? How could either one of us also be interested in others? What of just means? Whatever reinforces our love, even if it is covert manipulation, is justified. What about continuity? Yes, please, please! Change? Never! Collaboration? Yes, please, please! Conflict? Never! Justice? What else exists for us except shared goals?

Are we conscious of how these constrictions limit our relationship, and how they show what we cannot face?

Our networks connecting us to others are obviously deeply inhibited under these circumstances. We are being depoliticized—in contrast to our experience within transforming love. Our repertoire of archetypal relationships is also narrowed: Emanation, yes, if it also exists instead of, or in addition to, pseudo-emanation—that is, deformation. Subjection? If our beloved (if he is the male one) seeks to express his naked power, would we (if we are the female one) not let him? Isolation? We cannot imagine it. Buffering? We do try to seduce each other and to share images and rituals of love. Direct exchange? To please each other, yes. Can we engage in honest conversations and explorations? That is very risky, most likely too risky. Autonomy? We have both yielded it. Transformation? We are certainly not who we once were, but we certainly do not understand who we are now and where we need to go from this re-formation.

Women risk far more than men in this drama of romantic love. For most women, still today, the question "How could I survive without him?" is not only an emotional question but also an economic one. Women may not have jobs or jobs that pay adequate wages. Not by nature, but by necessity, women may therefore respond dependently and submissively or else subversively and all the more seductively. What alternative dramas could I enter? I therefore try to repress my inner torment or I blame myself even if he keeps battering me or if this drama is beginning to dissolve. Unless indeed I can no longer avoid rebelling against being suffocated or swallowed up by an image of me or of him that I no longer see as real.

Most men, by contrast, are now more free to join other dramas—dramas that offer power, profit, and prestige. In the service of incoherence, men can more easily rebel against growing powerlessness in this particular manifestation of the drama of romantic love. But as long as we do not yet understand its living underlying patterning forces, we can just fall for it again, with a different concrete manifestation of our fantasy.[3]

We have been analyzing an archetypal drama of love that pulls our energies and thoughts away from caring for other people. In the drama of romantic love, we are so busy instead in our private, subjective world where, however, neither we nor our lover truly understands or expresses the wholeness of our being. The older we get, the more disenchanted we are likely to have become about romantic love.

Transforming love, on the other hand, can persist throughout our life. And even if we lose the other in such a drama of love, we still have our self. Even if romantic love does not end in destructive death or its symbolic equivalents, even if we enact its deforming expressions instead in alliances dominated by our service of incoherence, look how much we lose (even in terms of love) while we persist in that way of life.

The next section seeks to introduce certain other kinds of love (or its exile) but does not yet have room to discuss them as archetypal dramas. Transforming love and romantic love are not our only choices.

SOME OTHER FORMS AND DISPLACEMENTS OF LOVE

Enriching love—better and longer-lasting than romantic love, but not yet transforming—is a love of caring, warm intimacy. We tune in to each other's need in the face of what we recognize as our partial nature, and know that we can rely on each other to provide attention, stability, and the nourishment of loving friendship. We do not know how to overcome our incompleteness, but happily, as best we can, we give and receive from each other the most caring connection we can imagine and practice in a world of fragments.

In our second example, our analysis begins to move further and further away from love. Love turns, before matters get worse, into ritual and habit—into loyalty, duty, and commitment, or into a mutually acceptable arrangement and routine. We both adhere to a masculine vision of an attractive domestic environment—or the best a woman can yet hope for: In exchange for my sex, my cooking, housekeeping, and taking care of our children (we do have children!), he finances it all. It is the best we can hope for, and I am grateful it still continues. Or, it is the best game we can try to play. People under these conditions often experience friendship, if they have such friends, as much richer and rewarding than love.

Such a marriage can reflect the dominant form of a culture. In Japan, the strength of the Japanese family consists of three ingredients "low expectations, patience, and shame." Low expectations become the "built-in shock absorbers." We

---

3. In the service of emanation as a way of life, romantic love for women usually remained an unfulfilled fantasy—to be rescued by a lover from a family-chosen spouse or to be delivered into a far more glorious emanational container. But men saw themselves mostly as performing patriarchal roles.

have nothing in common? That's par for the course. Patience means "toughing it out, enduring hardship." Husbands are above all devoted to many hours of work—and then relaxing away from home. Hence few husbands and wives talk much with each other, or fathers with their children. Shame? Women cannot afford financially to live without husbands and divorced husbands lose social prestige.[4]

In societies of more competitive domestic capitalism, a woman may be inspired to dress up her persona no less than her body in order to be bought, hopefully for keeps, by the richest (and hopefully the nicest) buyer. But such men (at this point in history much more than women) may diversify their investments in such commodities. Direct exchange as an archetypal relationship is then based above all on the constantly challenged and challenging contractual agreement: I will now do something that will please you; now please me. Love thus also becomes conditional on the market and has to be earned anew each day. (Stimulus/response, nothing deeper.) If my power is far greater than yours, then I shall above all enjoy experiencing my complete mastery over you, and I expect you to want to be mastered—and thus to feel completely cherished.

In this drama, both husband and wife become emotionally empty but see no alternative (as yet) to changing their current investment. Desire (at least on the part of one, but felt only below the waist) becomes the substitute for shared love between two beings. "Ready or not, here I come!" Afterwards? "I now have other things to do. I do not want to be weighed down by someone who wants to be coddled."

If that fragment becomes so inadequate, why not have sex with another fragment, too? We become "tourists in the world of gratification armed with temporary visas."[5] We may have affairs to compensate for our frustration, loneliness, and emotional isolation—our incoherence. Our wife may not be able to find an alternative to passivity. We may resort to promiscuity with prostitutes who link us to nothing in life except moments of passion, though the price may turn out to be far more than money.

For the great majority of women in the world, life (*love* is not even a relevant word) is far worse than we have so far described. There can be sexual mutilation before marriage, the marriage partner selected by her family, the bride required to bring a dowry, and ritualized rape as the first act of marriage. In child marriages, a girl as young as six or seven works for her new family as an unpaid servant even before sexual intercourse begins.[6] A wife can be physically abused by her husband.

---

4. Nicholas D. Kristof, "For Better or for Worse; Who Needs Love! In Japan, Many Couples Don't," *The New York Times*, February 11, 1996. But things are beginning to change, and the divorce rate is rising.

5. *Harper's*, April 1998, 25.

6. This is prevalent on a large scale in Northern India, resulting also in "soaring birth rates, grinding poverty and malnutrition, high illiteracy, and low life expectancy." John F. Burns, *The New York Times*, May 11, 1998.

We are not speaking here of special cases, but of many, many millions. We shall look more deeply into these deformational archetypal forces in the chapter on gender.

EVALUATING LOVE

Love is not simply one particular archetypal relationship or only a single archetypal drama. It is not only a private matter; it deeply affects the world around us. Love is one of the most important manifestations of what we can and need to do together—or cannot yet or can no longer do together—with all four faces of our being and the deepest sacred source we also need to share.

As we have seen, many are the current underlying archetypal obstacles to sharing deep, creative, enduring love. Instead we often, all too often, experience love without understanding and justice. Shall we conclude that "that's what life is like"? No, these obstacles and seductions arise out of incoherence (or emanation, and even deformation) as ways of life. Does the culture of incoherence teach us as a child, as an adolescent, as a competent adult to search for and become ourselves a human being? It does not. Hence we feel so incomplete that we try to compensate for that vital deprivation by falling in love.

We act as if we can care for another more than we care for ourselves. We surrender to love; we submit to the love of the only other person who seems to be able to supply it. Or else, we try to own and control the other. Or we drive for even more power over others as a substitute for the love we cannot attain. Transforming love does not own or control or submit. It constitutes a just sharing of love and understanding of being.

Sexuality arises out of our being—not only out of our body. When our being is diminished by our way of life and sexuality becomes our prime expression of love, all other people are then excluded from our love. But we declare having sex is fun—the fun of seduction, a big power trip, even spontaneity—and there is no fun, no joy in the rest of our life. Hence it is so usefully enjoyable even if these dramas come and go and too often end too soon. But in such service, we do not understand the extent of the deprivations these dramas and our way of life cause.

In the service of incoherence, most of us have learned how to rebel in established ways against present power-holders (especially our parents), or how meanwhile to serve the powerful in order for us to rise in power. So also, when we search for lovers, we look primarily for opposites of our father or mother or current lover—opposites found through our rebellion within incoherence as a way of life. And when dramas of romantic or even lesser love, thanks to their own dynamics, move us into the breaking of relationships, we still tend to remain deeply attracted to them as dramas that already recognize and welcome more of our power or else compensate us so excitingly for yielding to power in these dramas.[7] We may come to find our present participation unbearable, untenable, or unfruitful, but our dominant way of life—as long as we have not freed ourselves from it—can easily seduce us to try a new concrete manifestation of the drama (when we have not died in it). But we are not fully alive to be fully present, especially to love, understanding, and justice.

Love, understanding, and justice are intimately connected. In all four ways of life, they arise from the sacred depth, but only in transforming love do all three come from our deepest sacred depth and need our full participation. In transforming love, we love our selves and our beloved as incarnations of that creator of fundamentally new and better archetypal dramas. Only in transforming love does that love and understanding of the concrete as reflections of living underlying patterning forces and our response-ability for justice shape the entire journey of our life. We do not try to please or to bestow but to value each other as we tune in to each other and help each other grow in love, understanding, and justice.

And it is not just the two of us. Love your neighbor as yourself? In three ways of life, your self is still limited. How much are you truly able under these conditions to love others? Love gains its full capacity by inspiring all four of our faces and interconnecting them, and helping our body, too, to strengthen and express our being. There is no substitute for such love and for a community based on such love.[8]

---

7. Consider Laura Esquivel, *Like Water for Chocolate*. This book was subsequently also turned into a movie. In the story, Tita frees herself from her mother's domination. Her mother had told her never to get married but only and always to take care of her mother. But Tita married her romantic lover, who died of a heart attack in the midst of making love. Tita believed that she would never experience such love again and set herself afire so that, after her death, she could meet her lover again. For a splendid analysis that gives us, from the perspective of transformation, far more understanding of this story than even its author did, see Chapter 3 in David T. Abalos, *La Comunidad Latina in the United States* .

8. Every variety of love (or its displacement) we have discussed in this chapter also applies to gays and lesbians, unless it is shaped solely by the treatment of women as inferiors. Missing from this chapter—which, like the book, is only opening a new kind of exploration—are still other forms of love: our love of our parents, of our brothers and sisters and of our children, of nature, and of animals, especially this one sitting right here, our golden retriever, rightly named Rumi, after the poet and philosopher of love.

11

What Archetypes Shape Culture— and Race and Ethnicity?

In order to find our way to a theoretical and practical understanding of culture and of our choices in this vital realm, let us begin with the confusing, class-structured, and power-structured old and new views of culture that confront us now.

For centuries, the term, *culture*, was defined by the elite and referred almost entirely to established forms of art, music, literature, and highly proper behavior and rituals. The culture of the rest of the community was held to be "common," with the double meaning of commonplace or low, that is, not really cultured. In our time, the word *culture* still often has that inherited meaning or else refers to forms of entertainment.

In recent social science, *culture* has remained a concept in controversy or still obscure. Most anthropologists give us very vividly concrete pictures and particular conceptualized comparisons (for example, types of kinship) of many different cultures, but are hesitant to evaluate them.[1] In political science, the focus now is on a persisting debate over "political culture." But to speak only of political culture is to neglect or ignore the three other faces of our being and to focus instead above all on kinds of stories preoccupied with issues of power—though in fact without analyzing them as archetypal dramas.[2] Hence the

---

1. Robert Klitgaard, "Taking Culture into Account: From 'Let's' to 'How,'" International Conference on Culture and Development in Africa, *The World Bank*, Washington, D.C., April 2 and 3, 1992.

2. For example, Harry Eckstein, "A Cultural Theory of Social Change," *American Political Science Review* vol. 82, September 1988, 789–804.

critical, creative application of the concept of culture to practical problems has remained very difficult.[3]

What constitutes a culture? Each one of the four ways of life and the archetypal dramas we enact in its service provide the structure, dynamics, meaning, values, and purpose of our culture. Are there only four different cultures? No. As we already saw in Chapter 4, even in the constricting way of life of emanation the archetypal dramas and their concrete expressions differ also within different manifestations of such a way of life. But the fundamental structure and dynamics of a way of life shape or re-form all its dramas from the same point of arrest in the core drama, unless the culture expresses the process of deformation—or else of transformation.

Our deep attachment and devotion to the culture we still share with others is based on the fact that every culture is sacred, that is, it is shaped by archetypal forces. Culture is not only a religious, social, historical, artistic, or political fact. Culture's sacred underlying patterning forces shape not only our bond to cultures born in emanation as a way of life, but indeed to cultures in the service of the other three ways, as we shall soon see. This sacred fact also shapes our commitment to differences of class and gender, as we shall see in subsequent chapters. And since our bond to the sacred can change, so can our culture.

But who in fact shares the same culture with us has become ever more a controversial question, with answers all too often warped both from within and from outside, especially when the issues are said to be race, ethnicity, gender, and religion. Those terms are meant to imply "that is how *they* are"—always. Stereotypes shaped by our blind or defensive commitment to archetypes in trouble are being substituted for an open-minded exploration of actual archetypes. As members of the human race, we are able to experience any way of life and any archetypal drama. No particular so-called race has ever permanently shaped or held us within a single culture. Neither has ethnicity—a seemingly polite term for speaking of "those people" but hardly ever about ourselves. Religion does not shape an entire culture. *Religion* is a term, as we explained earlier, that did not come into use until the seventeenth century when emanational webs of life yielded to incoherence or deformation and only fragments of emanation were turned into organized religions.

All Jews, all Christians, all Muslims, all White Americans, all Latinos, all African-Americans—none of them belong to just a single culture of their own. All of them now (and also in earlier history) are divided by four ways of life and by many different dramas in the service of these ways of life. "Our" culture (whoever

3. The Social Science Research Council Committee on Culture, Health and Human Development seeks to "strengthen theoretical foundations by bringing to bear a deep and detailed conception of culture that can be explicitly integrated with existing biosocial points of view." Their summary report in *Items* of the *Social Science Research Council* vol. 49, no. 1, March 1995, pp. 1–22 left me with details and abstractions, but no strengthened foundations.

we are) is far more varied than many of our own groups (and certainly than most outsiders) now tell us. To call ourselves or the "other" by a single name cannot yet tell us if we are speaking of one particular culture. We need to ask what ways of life and what dramas are in fact being shared. Not to ask is likely to encourage racism, ethnocentrism, and other forms of bias and oppression.

Let us look more closely at two examples of people, each with a single label attached from within and by outsiders, in order instead to explore their actual differences in culture. In no case do we have space to tell all of such people's cultural varieties, but enough to show that any single label misrepresents them, and that their cultures (plural in each case) can only be understood if we look at least at the evidence provided here for different dramas and ways of life being practiced. In fact, *multicultural* is a term we need also to apply to every culture to which most of us still normally apply a single label.

JEWISH CULTURES

We begin with a people who have never been large in number. Have the Jews constituted a single culture for over three thousand years? The Hebrew Bible tells us that in the middle of the thirteenth century before Christ (a Jew)—about six hundred years after Abraham—god asked Moses at the burning bush in the Sinai Desert to return to the Jews of Egypt in order to lead their Exodus from slavery to the Promised Land. While Moses was crossing the desert on his way to Egypt, god (without explanation) tried to kill him. But Moses was saved by his wife, Zipporah (not Jewish), by circumcising Moses' son and touching Moses' legs with his son's bloody foreskin.[4]

After forty years of Exodus through the Sinai Desert, god did not allow Moses to enter the Promised Land. That was because, as the Jews once again ran out of water, Moses thought that it would be the blow of his stick upon a rock (god had instructed him to strike that rock) instead of god's will that would produce water.[5] In fact, no Jews who had heard or been told of god's revelation on Mt. Sinai and who had also spent forty years migrating through the desert was allowed to enter the Promised Land: "You are not ready for it," said god, "only the next generation."[6] Not ready, to put it in the words of our theory, for a culture based on a singular emanational way of life.

But that next generation of the twelve tribes, and several generations to follow, could only agree upon a judge to adjudicate their problems and a culture of sharing that single archetypal drama—but within ways of life at odds with each other.

---

4. Exodus 4:24–26.
5. Numbers 20:1–13; Deuteronomy 32:51–52.
6. Numbers 14:20–38.

Eventually, Judge Samuel agreed with some of his people (and with god)—as these judges (even his own sons) became corrupt and the Jews began to worship other gods—that they needed a king to rule over them, "so we can be like other nations."[7] Saul was chosen to be king. But when god asked Saul to go to war against the Amelikites (who had attacked the Jews on their way to the Promised Land) and to kill them all—"man and woman, babe and suckling, ox and sheep, camel and donkey"— Saul did not kill all of them "and God regretted having made Saul king of Israel."[8]

We already described in Chapter 4 this alliance of kingship and priests—that is, between emanation and incoherence as ways of life and its effects on the kingship even of David (who followed Saul) and of his son Solomon. Jews of the Promised Land further split themselves by civil wars between Israel and Judah that followed their reigns. In this early period also, ten of the twelve tribes became lost forever. No one knows where they went. As the Prophets tell us, kings and many of the people again and again worshipped other gods and the rich exploited the poor. Neighboring empires again and again conquered the Jews of the Promised Land and Jews lived under foreign rule. Twice the temple was destroyed and Jews were exiled as a punishment for not obeying god's laws, as the Bible tells us. Many Jews never returned to the Promised Land from Babylon even when they were allowed to after the first destruction of the Temple. They migrated to many other parts of the world instead.

Some Jews collaborated with their foreign rulers; others sought to preserve their inheritance in various ways; still others sought new paths. One Jew, under Roman rule, created a new conception of the sacred and of the commentary, though Jesus in his sermons also used many texts from the Hebrew Bible. For example, Jesus states that one of the two most important laws of god is this: "Love your neighbor as yourself."

Some Jewish priests persuaded the Romans to kill Jesus, since he did not obey the authority of the priests nor of the Romans. Jesus was arrested on the night that he and his disciples had celebrated the Exodus from Egypt during their Passover meal. Initially, most of his converts before and for a time after his death were Jews.

After Jewish rebellions against Roman persecutions led to the destruction of the second Temple and the exile of all Jews from the Promised Land, Jews could not govern themselves again until 1948. From that time to now, for the first time in Jewish history, Israel has represented a *new* archetypal drama—a nation-state.

Many different Jewish cultures emerged all over the world during this exile. Sacred law, Halakha, covering all aspects of life, continued to inspire the vision, rules, and rituals of most Jews for most of the centuries to come, but interpretations of that law differed sharply on vital issues. For example, the kabbalists did

---

7. Samuel 8:6–22.
8. Samuel 15:1–35.

not believe that god created the world in six days but that god needs our persisting participation in continuing creation in order to create a fundamentally better world. They and the early Chasidim were therefore also concerned with seeking renewed direct contact with god. (In the eighteenth century, rabbinic leaders forbade their followers to marry Chasidic Jews.) Other kabbalists—hundreds of thousands of them—accepted Sabbatai Sevi as the Messiah in the middle of the seventeenth century. And when the Sultan of the Ottoman Empire threatened to kill the Messiah unless he converted to Islam, tens of thousands of Jews joined in his conversion in order to stay on his road—which remained in fact closed.[9] Opening yet another (not the only other) door, one Chasidic rabbi declared that all that god had pronounced on Mount Sinai was the letter aleph—the first letter of the alphabet. All the rest is interpretation.[10]

From the beginning, even before the first exile, there were Jews who assimilated to the dominant culture. Or at least they economically, financially, and politically collaborated with it, since there was little or no possibility of survival in total insulation. Moreover, since Jews constituted the only community spread over so much of at least Europe and the Middle East, engaging in international trade and finance was one of their major opportunities. Hence, also, Jews remained open to the ideas of other cultures. Thus, after writing a new commentary on the Mishnah—a further interpretation of the interpretations of Jewish sacred law—in the late twelfth century, Moses Maimonides nonetheless felt it necessary next to write *The Guide of the Perplexed*, drawing deeply upon the transforming ideas of the Muslim philosopher Alfarabi of the tenth century.[11] In the modern age, Jews have been among the pioneers in questioning the established cultural containers in many fields of life.

After you have traveled through the nation-state of Israel in our time—a place the size of New Jersey—never again will you be able to say to someone: "Oh yes, you look Jewish." Jews in Israel are black, brown, or white. People all of "one blood"? They look, dress, act, and think in many different ways. The majority of Israeli Jews try to substitute the nation-state—with its many intrinsic obstacles that we shall examine in Chapter 14—for the absence of a shared community and culture.

Zionism—a nationalist (and originally also primarily a secular, socialist) ideology—did not come into existence until the nineteenth century, and at that time (and even now) only among a minority of Jews. Israel's founding fathers did not seek to restore the Jewish past of the Promised Land—to achieve at last what god had ordered Jews to be and to do. Given the realities of that Biblical past, given the divisions old and new that have remained, that is not the hope or intention of most Israeli Jews.

---

9. Gershom Gerhard Scholem, *Sabbatai Sevi: The Mystical Messiah, 1626–1676*.
10. Gershom Gerhard Scholem, *On the Kabbalah and Its Symbolism*, 31.
11. Moses Maimonides, S. Pines, et al., *The Guide of the Perplexed*.

For the first time in nearly two thousand years, Jews who moved or fled to Israel once again share a common language, but deep are the cultural divisions within this nation-state. Orthodox Jews—about one-quarter of the Jewish population[12]— receive government subsidies so that they can work only part-time and focus most of their life on studying religious law and observing its requirements and rituals. They are not required to serve in the armed forces. But orthodox Jews are also politically strong enough within the archetypal drama of democratic liberalism to be decisive in establishing certain legal rights—for example, who is a Jew and what Jewish marriages are legal.[13]

There are also Orthodox groups who have attacked non-Orthodox Jewish women for daring on the Sabbath to worship at the Western Temple Wall. They accept no equality for women in sacred rituals or public life. They do not allow Orthodox women to study the Bible or to bear witness in court. Some Orthodox Jews hold the state of Israel to be illegitimate, since the Messiah has not yet come and only the Messiah can restore it.[14]

The Israeli economy also divides Jewish cultural life. Originally, the kibbutz—a democratic, communist agricultural community—was one of Zionism's pioneering enterprises. Now only a few are still active in this vein. In 1998, the fiftieth year of Israel's new existence, about 200,000 Israelis were unemployed (about fifteen percent of the population thus live under the poverty-line) yet also 300,000 foreign workers had been imported. And one of the most powerful segments, powerful enough to shape the actual lives of the majority, are capitalists producing especially high technology for a world market and also for a consumer culture—for what many of them now call "a normal life," that is, the archetypal drama of capitalism, the satisfaction of consumption. Several hundred thousand Israeli citizens also live abroad.

Differences in origin and cultural traditions have divided especially Ashkenazi Jews (Jews from Western, Central, and Eastern Europe, hence themselves not all of one shared culture because of various archetypal dramas, many of them assimilated from their differing European experiences) and Sephardic Jews. Most of the latter, Jews from North Africa and the Middle East, arrived after the establishment of Israel. Only then (in contrast to Christian and post-Christian countries of Europe) did hostility against the Jews emerge strongly in Muslim countries. Especially in the nineties, Jews also arrived from Ethiopia. Now Sephardic Jews constitute about 40 percent of Israel's population. Yet Ashkenazi Jews have discriminated a great

---

12. Fully 20 percent in Fosoil call themselves religiously non-observant, only 14 percent call themselves strictly observant. *The New York Times* July 21, 1998, based on a survey by Tel Aviv University.

13. A Jewish movement in Israel called Gush Emonim is one such orthodox group.

14. The followers of Gush Emonim believe that they have the duty to destroy all Christian churches and Muslim mosques on Temple grounds in order (after what it admits will be apocalyptic responses) to build the Third Temple.

deal by denying equal opportunities, economically and educationally, to people of these other Jewish cultures.[15]

One million Israeli citizens are Arabs of various religions and certainly of various cultures who have lived in Palestine more than one thousand years. They are cut off because of their cultures from the very nature of a solely Jewish nation-state and are not entitled fully to all legal rights.[16] About 750,000 Palestinian Arabs fled Israel and became refugees during the 1948 war, and have not been allowed to return. Over a million Palestinian Arabs live on the still largely Israeli-ruled West Bank, next door. Could Israel also annex these Arabs and remain a Jewish nation-state? Israeli citizens—Jews and Arabs—in the fiftieth year of this nation-state of many cultures together number 5.9 million. Israel, which has fought three more wars with Arab states since 1948, clearly is not yet a safe haven.[17] Its capital, Jerusalem, is a Holy City for Jews, Christians, and Muslims.

Among the Jews of Israel, four different ways of life and many quite different archetypal dramas—hence many different cultures—are in deep conflict with each other. One major faction says, "Follow God's law or else God will punish you with a third exodus." The other major faction responds, "If we end democracy, Jews will decide to leave Israel." Eighty percent of Israel expects outbreaks of violence between them.[18] Individuals seeking to develop the understanding, love, and freedom that liberate us and give us the capacity to create new Jewish cultures that are also response-able to deal justly with Arabs as fellow human beings—yes, there are a few thousand such people in Israel, Jewish and Arab.

The majority of Jews have remained in diaspora, but more Jews are assimilating into the dominant cultures, especially in the United States. Here, being Jewish for the majority is becoming at most a culture shaped by a re-formed fragment of emanation as a way of life but now in the service of incoherence. The Holocaust is remembered. Israel is—ever more critically—supported. Half of American Jews are marrying spouses of other religions (or of no religion) and hence of other cultures.

I see four main reasons why Jewish cultures have survived for three thousand years. One is that Jews were the first in history to give rise to a monotheistic way of life of emanation. Everything in life was shown by revelation and interpretation to be the will (or of our failure to obey the will) of a single sacred source of our being. A second and related reason is that after the often more corrupt and risky period of statehood, kings, and priests, Jews came to anchor its emanational culture upon

---

15. Raphael Cohen-Almagor, "Cultural Pluralism and the Israeli Nation-Building Ideology," *International Journal of Middle Eastern Studies* 27 (1995), 461–84.

16. "There shall be one law for you, whether stranger or citizen of the country" (Numbers 9:15, 15:15). Israel has also acknowledged the torture of many jailed Arabs.

17. More than 20,000 Israelis have so far been killed in wars and hostile attacks.

18. Serge Schmemanh, "In Israel's Bitter Culture War, Civility is a Casualty," *The New York Times*, July 21, 1998.

each patriarchal family, community, and the study of its tradition and rituals by all Jewish males. A third reason is that, despite the power of the first two emanational causes, Jews again and again created movements of transformation (for example, the Kabbalists and the early Chasidim) who also kept many of the rituals of emanational Judaism, but from a new perspective. The fourth main reason was the creation by Christians of a costly enclosure for Jews. Among Christians, again and again, Jews were defined and treated with a painful bias, and often exiled, beaten, or killed.[19] To be a Jew was to be treated as a dangerous "other"—even when Christians temporarily allowed that "other" to be of service to them. In the past, assimilation or conversion was the only possible exit beyond persecution.[20]

For Hitler, even assimilation could not keep Jews from being sent into the Holocaust. Another strong but not violent version of this fourth reason is this: As long as emanation as a way of life remained the dominant way for most people around the world, every people in the service of their concrete version of emanation saw all outsiders as "others." The "other" was therefore powerfully defined by that experience. With the rise of incoherence as a way of life, nationalism also took a similar toll. This fourth cause also reinforced the emanational cohesion of many Jews and later also led to their nationalistic Zionism.

But the worldwide growth of incoherence as a way of life diminished and further divided inherited Jewish cultures—as it did the cultures of all other people. Individuals now increasingly make their own choices to express their own new freedom and also for the sake of various forms of new power in this world. To describe the actual past and presently emerging cultures among even one people would take at least one entire book.

ARAB CULTURES

We now explore the cultures of Arabs—a people whose cultures also first arose in the Middle East and a people who also speak Semitic languages. But kindred to what we call Romance languages in Europe, its various linguistic forms are not always understandable to Arabs from different countries. Its equivalent of classic Latin is the Arabic of the Koran. Arabs now inhabit an area larger than the United States. When you travel through the Arab world from Morocco to the Arabian Peninsula and from Egypt to Iraq, Arabs also look remarkably different from each other, both individually and as groups.

---

19. To mention only one case, hundreds of thousands of Jews were massacred in Poland in 1648, many of them exiles from Germany in the fifteenth century—exiles when their lives had been threatened because they had then been accused of causing the Black Plague.

20. Or else, Jews pretended to have become converted, especially in Spain. (For a heritage of such secrecy, even in the state of New Mexico, see *The New York Times*, November 11, 1990.)

There are now over a hundred million Arabs. Arabs brought Islam into being. There are now over a billion Muslims—most of them living east of Karachi. The largest number live in Indonesia, the second largest number in India (even though Pakistan seceded from India in order to create its own Muslim state).[21] Also, as many Muslims now live in sub-Saharan Africa as there are Muslim Arabs in the Middle East.

We begin our story of Arab cultures at a vital turning point in their history when Muhammad, in AD 622, founded a Muslim community in Medina in the Arabian peninsula where most Arabs then lived. Muhammad had been born in Mecca, a major international trade center (also inhabited by Jews and Christians) and filled with sacred shrines for several hundred different gods. But this region was also at that time deeply troubled by many wars of rivalry and revenge between Arab tribes. Muhammad and his first followers were persecuted in Mecca for trying to establish a new community transcending tribes and offering a new form of justice based on a new and final revelation from the one and only god—Allah. But Muhammad was persecuted even by his own politically powerful family. So he fled to Medina.

Setting forth from Medina, the newly converted Arabs within the next hundred years conquered an empire of many different cultures from India to Spain. Arabs also moved to reside in and initially also to rule over all of these areas, supported also by many new converts who, in the early centuries, did not, however, yet constitute a majority.[22]

Did Arabs ever establish a single culture that can unmistakably be called *Muslim*? As we already discussed in Chapter 4, there has never been only a single concrete manifestation—or even a single living, underlying patterning way of emanation—of Islam. (Also, Sufi Muslims tried again and again to bring a transforming community into being.) Did Arabs—as we shall now discuss, ever succeed in establishing a single culture that can unmistakably be labeled *Arab*? In solely a singular way, no; in a plurality of ways, yes. But as we shall see, several of these archetypal dramas were (and still are) patterns that again and again renewed conflicts between Arabs—patterns of disunity within unity.

For despite the rise of and maintenance (till modern times) of various forms of Islam among most Arabs, the archetypal force of the more ancient dramas of the family and the tribe also endured. Every Muslim state (many of them even still in modern times) constituted an empire ruled—after a successful conquest—by one family or tribe over other families and tribes. And, as we saw in Chapter 4,

---

21. Pakistan since its secession has also experienced the secession of Muslims who formed the state of Bangladesh.

22. Christians and Jews—as people of earlier versions of The Book, were not killed or compelled to convert, only to pay higher taxes than Muslims.

archetypal patterns involving structures and dynamics of both conflict and collaboration also existed (and still exist) within each family—including Muhammad's own descendents—despite the persistent struggle to maintain the drama of patriarchal dominance as well.

Did the new Muslim community—*umma*—that Muhammad had sought to create actually come into being? In beliefs, rituals, customs, and rules of justice, yes—for many but certainly not all Muslims. But culture, as we explore its reality, is not only composed of outward manifestations but of underlying dramas that shape the meaning, values, and purposes of all manifestations of our life. Arab Muslims, as we explored in Chapter 4 (and will again in Chapter 14 on the sacred) did not all share the same sense of the meaning, values, and purposes even of the sacred.

And the Arabs' sense of community was split not only by the rivalry of family and tribes but by deep differences in archetypal dramas practiced by nomads, peasants, and urban people. And for Arabs, that sense of *umma* was further undermined when, beginning in the thirteenth century, most Arabs were conquered by Muslim Ottoman Turks and ruled from Istanbul by Ottoman slave armies for centuries (though the dramas of internal conflict and collaboration also persisted) until, beginning in the nineteenth century, they were conquered by European powers and ruled by them until the middle of the twentieth century.

Under the circumstances, Arabs all greeted each other every day and everywhere by saying *Salam aleikum*, meaning "peace be with you." Salam has the same roots (the same three consonants) as Islam and Muslim. A Muslim finds peace by his or her yielding to god. But there is no uniform belief in what god stands for now. For some Muslims, *Salam aleikum* may at this moment be a ritualistic reiteration or acceptance or even affirmation of the prevailing consensus. It could indicate a peaceful acceptance of what we cannot yet resist within the balance of tensions within prevailing archetypal dramas, or an affirmation, or an opening of alliance, or a longing cry of hope. In all these stories, god is still seen as the all-powerful one. But for Sufis, especially those influenced by Ibn Arabi, saying *Salam aleikum* involves no surrender to god, but a compassionate affirmation of the deep peace we can draw upon if we become a friend and lover of god. And Arabs also produced major philosophers, mathematicians, and scientists in several fields including medicine. Only in the worst of days did fatalism sometimes become an expression of *Salam*. Consequently, this common greeting has not a common meaning.

What cultures do Arabs share in the modern age—the culture of the nation-state? In 1963, I wrote, "The persistence of colonial rule in most countries of the Middle East until the end of World War II delayed the resolution of the imbalance between aspiration and resources, education and jobs, population growth and opportunities, revolution and consensus that make present problems so total in scope."[23] Nationalism came to the fore to free Arabs from Western and Ottoman Turkish rule. Religious and tribal organizations were not strong enough to accomplish that. But more than three decades later, no resolution of these problems has taken place.

It is very difficult indeed anywhere to create a cooperating nation-state when its populations to this date have remained so diverse. Here are a few examples:

> *Iraq:* The majority of Arabs are Muslim Shiites—the same form of Islam that is shared by the majority of Iranians. Sunni Muslims constitute a majority only if we count Arabs and Kurds together—but Kurds have been struggling for independence for quite some time.
>
> *Lebanon:* This nation-state is divided by eighteen different religions that have at least twice engaged in prolonged civil wars.
>
> *Syria:* Only about 60 percent are Sunni Arabs. Kurds, Olawis, Druzes, Greek Orthodox, and Armenians each have more than 100,000 inhabitants.
>
> *Sudan:* In this nation-state the size of all European NATO nations combined, people speak more than a hundred different languages and adhere to different religions, especially in the south, where Arabs constitute a minority.

But these diversities do not yet speak of the growing difference between the rich and the poor and people still adhering to emanation, which cannot be revitalized except for certain fragments now in the service of incoherence, newly adhering to the destructiveness of deformation or incoherence as ways of life.[24]

The nation-state in most of the Arab world is constituted primarily by a leader, his bureaucracy and army, his political party, and government-capitalist collaboration (if not collusion). Now that all Arabs live in one or another nation-state, does that experience serve to unite them as Arabs? In 1958 Egypt—by far the most populous of all Arab nation-states—and Syria agreed to form a United Arab Republic. When I spoke with members of the Syrian cabinet in Damascus in 1961, they all said, "Egyptians do not understand us or our problems. They only want to rule us." Later in 1961, the United Arab Republic came to an end. Saddam Hussein of Iraq is still eager to dominate other Arab nation-states. But mobilizing a nation and producing unity among Arabs has come about only in wars against Israel, and after several defeats by Israel, it is at this point no longer a practically inspiring cause.

The coming into being of Arab nation-states produced a victory against Western imperialism. But no Arab nation-state has yet become a creatively cooperative

---

23. Manfred Halpern, *The Politics of Social Change in the Middle East and North Africa.*
24. See for example, Hisham Sharabi, *Neopatriarchy: A Theory of Distorted Change in Arab Society.*

community.[25] Each is deeply divided by radically different ways of life, and also by the fragmentation of incoherence as the dominant way. That deep division is all they share, however much Western forms of industrialization, militarization, and consumption have grown for some. Half of the population in each Arab nation-state—the women—is still far from having achieved equality. Fouad Ajami calls it "a new world of cruelty, waste, and confusion."[26] No archetypal drama—no way of life now being served by the great majority of Arabs—gives them, in the face of such dire needs, the capacity to transform their lives.

ISSUES AND INSIGHTS ARISING FROM OUR TRANSFORMING VIEW OF CULTURE

We have been discussing, albeit with exceeding brevity, "Jews" and "Arabs" who have often seen themselves and each other—and have also been seen by most others—each as a single culture. But even in so brief an overview, we have perceived in each case never only one single culture, not over time, and not even at any one moment. Throughout their histories, all four ways of life have come into being—and different dramas in their service, including dramas which institutionalized conflicts, rivalries, and different schools of thought and values about the meaning and purpose of seemingly similar acts. We have also tried to show (and we will still do more of it) how and why it is fruitful to gain a new understanding of culture by examining it as a synonym for a way of life (and the dramas in its service) by particular people—including their concrete manifestations at and over a particular time.

That is not what our cultural custom is now. Most of us call ourselves and others each by a single common name, as if each such group in fact was bound by a common culture. The individual disappears: "They are all Mexicans!" "They are all Russians!" "We are all Americans!" And we do not pause to discover and analyze the real cultural differences among us and among them. Above all, still, most of us mean to devote ourselves to protect "our" culture against "their" culture, hence also our power against theirs. We do not consciously, critically, creatively, and caringly ask these questions, for example: Is power in most of our cultures primarily the fruit of the power of the archetypal drama of capitalism in our way of life of incoherence? Do Latinos ask this: Is power in our cultures primarily the fruit of macho (male) dominance? And is our powerlessness the result of the bias of people of the dominant cultures against our joining them as capitalists?

25. For a vivid, empathic and insightful analysis of actual fragments of community networks, see Diane Singerman, *Avenues of Participation: Family, Politics, and Networks in Urban Quarters of Cairo*.

26. *The New Republic*, July 15, 1996, p. 30. See also a deeply moving, critical understanding of the lives and works and historical context of modern Arab writers in Fouad Ajami, *The Dream Palace of the Arabs: A Generation's Odyssey*.

As we shall examine next in more detail, all cultures in the service of emanation or incoherence keep us partial beings who therefore cannot discover who we really are or who anyone else really is—and of what wholeness of being we and they are deprived. At best, democratic liberalism allows us procedurally to connect with regard to certain legally recognized issues, but the power of each cultural group to resolve issues is based on its relative power as an interest group.

Our inquiry is intended to penetrate these partisan mysteries of culture. We need always to gain insight not only into dominant or competing or conflicting cultures that in fact now shape the four faces and the sacred source of our being and the being of our group—but also into those cultures that in fact shape our neighbors. We must not simply generalize our answers, however. We must also discover what way of life and which dramas in fact shape each unique human being. We may soundly generalize, but we must not stereotype. Through this kind of inquiry, we may come to understand how emanation or incoherence as ways of life—and how particular dramas in their service—still arrest any particular individual or group, and how we can begin caringly to help each other transform our lives.

EMANATION AS A WAY OF LIFE WAS THE DEEPEST ROOT OF OUR CULTURE, BUT NOW IT REMAINS ALIVE ONLY AS A FRAGMENT OF INCOHERENCE AS A WAY OF LIFE

When emanation was the dominant way of life, all archetypal dramas were enacted in its service—not only what we now call religion. But as we have seen, its believers differed in their interpretations of this way and in the dramas to which they in fact adhered. None even of the monotheistic ways of life of emanation in fact succeeded in creating and preserving a single enclosure of culture. Indeed, among Christians, even before the Thirty Years War between Protestants and Catholics in the seventeenth century, conflicts over the control and meaning of their way of life were often very bloody. For example, in 1204, Crusaders of Catholic Christianity on their way to Muslim Jerusalem massacred many thousands of Byzantine Christians in Constantinople.

Tradition is a misleading term if applied solely to emanation as a way of life. In many past cultures, emanation often could not prevent the rise of incoherence and also of transformation as ways of life. Adherents of emanation also allied themselves at times with forces of incoherence and deformation. Secondly, the compelling power of tradition depends not primarily on the long weight of its past but (at any time) upon its archetypal force in molding individuals and in cementing communities through the inspiration and enactment of dramas which form the web of life of our established culture.

That web has come apart, but not all of its dramas, especially what is now a fragment we call religion, and patriarchy, and what we still feel is the justified exclusion of outsiders. Why are such dramas still alive? They provide deep archetypal certainty to the still powerful or to those fearful of losing their once established power. Every archetypal drama constitutes a sacred force, but when it is no longer in the service of emanation as a web of life—but in the service of incoherence—it connects us to a more fragile way of life. And as we thus miss our earlier sense of certainty, we may be tempted all the more to seek to preserve our power or even to ally ourselves with forces of deformation. We tend not to analyze or come to understand either the limitations upon our humanity imposed by emanation or (through a later arrest) by incoherence as ways of life.

In the service of incoherence, we may still call others by a single label to designate their culture while we are increasingly confronted by the diversity of our own cultures. Nonetheless, for the sake of our power or our conviction, we may choose just one type of culture and call only that archetypal experience—one drama or a few more—"culture." "What you guys call 'pop culture'—no! That 'culture' isn't even the same as it was last year!" Or, "Obey your family's standards!" "But I have only one parent who keeps trying to enforce his own patriarchal rules. Why should I follow such old-fashioned values?"

The culture we share most widely is a consumer culture—not to speak of the deprivation and desperation below, which is a part of this story. The most potent of cultures, affecting also many other cultures in the service of incoherence, is the archetypal drama of capitalism—a drama inspired, like all the others in this way of life, by a particular form of self-interest justified by the sacred force of this way of life. Capitalism is not the only culture to have become global. But the culture of democratic liberalism in most of the world is still a greatly limited drama, restricted largely to voting for those who shall have power. It is a drama of very limited participation in what we really can and need to do together, and indeed has room only for partial selves. This same statement applies to the drama of being competent in the service of incoherence. The nation-state—a highly problematical archetypal drama in the service of incoherence (as we shall discuss in Chapter 14)—constitutes one of the major attempts around the world to encourage, coordinate, and cement cultures that might help to unify that nation-state.

The dramas cited in the last paragraph are the dominant cultures of our time. There is also a growing variety of cultures. However, all these varieties, including the majority of those cultural dramas emphasizing rebellion, are shaped by incoherence as a way of life—a way that constantly organizes, changes, and then tries to reorganize our living with fragments of being. That is the overarching cultural experience of the modern age. We will now discuss how much freedom, how much contrast, how much conflict, how much tolerance, and how much understanding this variety involves.

FROM CULTURAL DIVERSITY TO A MULTICULTURAL CONSCIOUSNESS

A number of democratic liberal societies—not even all of them as yet—are beginning to say, "Let us respect cultural diversity within our society. Let us therefore accept multiculturalism." To speak of the United States, let us have a Latino Month, an African-American Month, a Women's Month—or even allow a self-proclaimed Gay and Lesbian Month. Let us, for example, celebrate Latino Month in town this Sunday with a parade and a fiesta. (Then the vast majority of Latinos can go back to manual labor—with very few of them working for bosses who are also Latino.)

To limit respect for others primarily to ceremonials is not yet to understand them or to share life with them. Such recognition of diversity in fact reinforces our single labeling of "others." We called the original population of the United States "Indians" (because Columbus thought that is where he had arrived) and now we call them "Native Americans." But there are still 554 different Native American tribes in the United States, each with its own cultures. Latinos in the United States come from many different cultures, even when they come from a single Central or Latin American country. "Asian-American" is a label lately invented in the United States. It's amazing how many different peoples we put into one basket. Culture shapes the structure, dynamics, values, meaning, and purpose through our dramas and ways of life, not only through special events and rituals. It is deeply shocking how little we understand others (or ourselves) so that we can share a creative and just life with those who are now "them."

Some societies have come to "accept" diversity, but the domination of the dominant culture is not to be challenged, and assimilation, especially of capitalist values, is still the most decisive order of the day. At best, the people of a different culture are counted in so far as they have become an interest group that must be taken into account. Otherwise, they may still be treated as the lesser or the invisible.

But diversity can also become a mere cover story in another respect. Any group may now feel all the more justified in taking (indeed in demanding of its members) uncritical pride in its emanational heritage—in dramas that diminish or even deprive members even of their own group of their full human rights. A car window sign declares: "I am 100 percent Irish." It is not the only culture that has such signs—but has no one else on earth anything valuable to offer to you? What identity other than partial—biased and incomplete—can any of us attain in the service of emanation or incoherence?

Freedom to express our cultural diversity can become a fruitful beginning only as each of us becomes free at last to learn how our past and present sacred, historical, and political face has come into our personal being. With that understanding of who we really are, and aided by a similar understanding of other cultures—as others also learn to become free consciously, critically, and creatively to understand their archetypal dramas and ways of life—we can for the first time really live together to create a new culture of compassion and justice.

But where are we now? One major example of incremental improvements in the United States is evidenced by these statistics: African-Americans were three times more likely in 1998 to graduate from high school than in 1960; they were five times more likely to attend a four-year college. An improved environment helps us to discover and improve our intelligence. A third of African-Americans now consider themselves members of the middle class. (Where are the other two-thirds of them? Are there now more political divisions of class among them?)

By the middle of the twenty-first century, the majority of people living in the United States may no longer be white. (Given present birthrates, Italy's Italian population could shrink by 85 percent in three generations. Other European countries are now also moving in that direction.) By 2005, according to the Census Bureau, the largest American community of color will no longer be African-American but Latino. In many cities (but significantly, as a matter of class difference, not in suburbs) nonwhites are becoming the majority. For example, Minneapolis, the largest city in the state of Minnesota, was 93 percent White as recently as 1970. By 1997, public school enrollment was 68 percent nonwhite.[27] (Do the current leaders deal with this future that is on its way?)

Our conventional (largely white-generated) labeling does not help us really to understand and collaborate with members of cultures different from us. We have labels of color, geography, and race. Consider color: red, brown, black, yellow, and white—strange, since the actual variations of color within each such alleged group are quite wide.[28] Consider geography: Asian-American (intended to include Vietnamese, Cambodians, Chinese, Koreans, Japanese, and people from Pacific islands and India as well as Pakistan); or Latinos (never mind from which country or whether they are all or partly Spanish or African or American Indian or Catholic or Muslim or Pentecostal or Jewish or many other emanational or religious variants—or secular). Consider race: for example, the black race—though people in Africa speak nearly two thousand different languages, and (like whites) have often been at war with each other. Many American "blacks" have "white" blood in them—among them, Booker T. Washington, Jesse Owens, Martin Luther King,

---

27. *The New York Times*, October 18, 1997.

28. Actually, there are no whites who are white. (*White* was probably intended as a term symbolizing sacred purity.) Certainly whites, like people of other races, are of various shades. In his novel, , E. M. Forster, *A Passage to* India, the author speaks more accurately of some whites when he calls all of them "pinko-grey."

Jr., W.E.B. DuBois, and Malcolm X.[29] And never mind a race's differences of social class; never mind how women are molded by our present culture to differ from men; never mind who he or she actually is. Never mind that we are all members of the human race, in contrast and comparison with other animals.

Yes, color, geography, and race are part of our historical face of being, proclaimed by us or imposed upon us—hence part of our emanational inheritance and of the current challenge to our self-interest and in a different vein, to our true being.[30] "If I spill soup in a restaurant, they tend to see hundreds of me; if I have a baby, ['we'] tend to have a population explosion; if I move into a neighborhood, I come as the forward phalanx of an invading army; if I have an opinion, it is attributed to 'you people.'"[31] Prejudice, as I said in the chapter on deformation, is not merely a mind-set. It has deep archetypal roots.

And these roots are deformational—whether we are so proud of our color, our country, or our race that we seek to exclude or at least dominate others, or we *suffer* this hatred. When I was a soldier living for five days on a troopship from New York to Southampton, Great Britain, in order to join the fight against fascism in Europe, I was deeply shocked and offended when we landed. I saw African-American soldiers marching out of our boat. I had not seen one black soldier on our boat for five days. I was told that they had not even been allowed to come on deck from the lowest storage areas of the boat because they were not white, like us. Not until 1948—three years after that war—did President Truman end segregation in the American armed forces. Why have such changes occurred only so recently? Why have so many changes—concerned with still prevailing prejudice—not yet taken place? Why in some areas in the world—for example in the former Yugoslavia and parts of Africa—have cultural forces of deformation grown worse?

We are living in a historical period of deep anxiety. The cultural dramas of emanation as a way of life are threatened by dissolution. The cultural dramas of incoherence are only fragments that also dissolve from time to time. People increasingly refuse to remain lesser or invisible—stations on the road to deformation. Hence those meaning to retain their power are greatly tempted to resort to outright deformation—to renew the trauma so long imposed upon "their" historical face, to deny

---

29. Cited by George Will, *The Trenton Times*, October 6, 1998. Will also states that the NAACP estimates that 70 percent of those who identify themselves as African-Americans are of mixed racial heritage. He adds that American law once regarded the Irish "race" as non-white.

But in fact in the United States, more than half of all states barred interracial marriages—laws not struck down by the Supreme Court until 1968.

30. Central to any discussion of the issues we are raising is the work of Cornel West, especially his two volumes, *Beyond Eurocentrism and Multiculturalism* and *Race Matters*.

31. Patricia J. Williams, "A Rare Case of Muleheadedness and Men," in Toni Morrison, *Race-ing Justice, En-Gendering Power: Essays on Anita Hill, Clarence Thomas, and the Construction of Social Reality*, 167, quoted in Katharine Lawrence Balfour, *Evidence of Things Not Said: Race Consciousness and Political Theory*, a dissertation, Department of Politics, June 1996, p. 111.

equal rights to "their" political face, to believe "their" sacred face to be menacing to our power, and to deny "them" altogether any personal face of being.

Shall we live and work above all to preserve our culture? In grade school and high school in New York City and in college in Los Angeles, I never had a course that taught me that less than eighty years earlier, twenty percent of the people of the United States had been slaves, with New York City second to Charleston, North Carolina in the number of slaves. (I only learned that we had abolished slavery.) I never had a course that taught me that less than a hundred years earlier, we had conquered half of Mexico, including California. Or that prior to 1940, only one percent of Mexican children—of the population we had conquered in the Southwest—were in school. They were wanted for part-time but heavy manual labor.[32] If I had been African-American or Mejicano, I could not have had the freedom or opportunity to discover my culture. History as told by the dominant culture ignored or misled me, but that culture called itself a "civilization." "We" therefore are the ones who really count!

Many are the cultures in the service of emanation or incoherence that tried or succeeded in being imperialist. And even now the power of the powerful at home is based on a deep sacred archetypal distinction between insiders and outsiders—an archetypal drama. How rich a being can the insider become in the service of incoherence? I do not have to reveal my private identity publicly. (And thus my private life remains only a fragment of my being.) My public individual, political, historical, and sacred identity is shaped by my interest in seeking to become an embodiment of "conventional" patterns of rules through which I can fit with others and thus also find accepted ways toward recognized status and achievement—not to be identical with others but to possess an acceptable identity. This is the cultural environment I need to protect, against others who might undermine it or—by way of assimilation—increase the number of competitors challenging my status within it. That is the reason why I must remain alert to what I define as "their" identity—a parochial identity from the perspective of "our" civilization.

To be free at last, thanks to official tolerance and new academic courses of multiculturalism, to discover our own culture and its true past—is this meant solely to make us proud of our culture? If you discover at last what it is to be Chinese or Latino, will you—your actual being—feel obliged to disappear again except as a symbolic enactment of your culture? If you now also learn self-esteem and self-control, who is that self? Are you now merely a reflection of paternalistic authority? What dramas of our culture are worth not obediently preserving but actually nourishing anew because they will nourish all four faces of our being?

---

32. Alan Pifer, *Bilingual Education and the Hispanic Challenge*, Annual Report of the Carnegie Foundation of New York, 1979, p. 16, cited in David T. Abalos, *La Comunidad Latina in the United States: Personal and Political Strategies for Transforming Culture*, 75.

Conservatives of any culture are now, above all, partisans of fragments of the past that can still secure their power. "If we are to confront radically new issues, we cannot use the tradition as a bulwark to protect us because people do not simply inherit a cultural past but actually make history. Indeed, whenever a culture or a community stops taking responsibility for the stories they live because they unconsciously [and uncritically] repeat and reenact them, such a society becomes ahistorical. We need to be participants in the uprooting, creation, and nurturance of our cultural stories in order to earn our historical calling."[33]

We cannot free ourselves until we come to understand what archetypal dramas have so far molded our culture and thus our being. That demands an understanding beyond what our present dominant culture at its best offers as multiculturalism. We can no longer preserve any culture—even the still dominant one—because emanation as a way of life can no longer help us to confront the problems of this age, and incoherence as a way of life arrests us as only partial human beings. Yet we need now to deal constantly with new challenges.

Yes, the dominated cultures have been maltreated and, until quite recently (and on some vital issues—like poverty, health, housing, and education—even now), have been rendered politically impotent. That is a crucial cause for political and historical solidarity, but not for uncritically preserving a cultural past, a stance that will also serve to divide us even within the same label we still bear.

We need actually to understand our historical past, and hence what we also need to overcome. We cannot build upon what we are ignorant of. We also need truly to come to understand our neighbors—both of us in terms of the living underlying patterning forces that now shape us so that we understand not only who and what we are but why we are where we are in the core drama of life. Otherwise, the type of our concrete experience will repeat itself even if we reject it concretely. Only thus can we move beyond power or powerlessness to true and full human capacity—and also toward our own personal uniqueness, for the transformation of our cultures can only be created person by person.

"Success, recognition and conformity are the bywords of the modern world where everyone seems to crave the anesthetizing security of being identified with the majority."[34] We seek to become emanations of incoherence as a way of life, especially of its most potent dramas—capitalism, and its freest drama, democratic liberalism. Or else, we try to remain emanations of our inherited culture. We are proud of it. But we do not understand the fundamental limits of these ways of life. Such forms of emanation by now repress our anxiety of being abandoned. (Where

---

33. David T. Abalos, "The Personal, Political, Historical and Sacred Grounding of Culture: Some Reflections on the Creation of Latino Culture in the United States from the Perspective of a Theory of Transformation," in a volume edited by A. M. Stevens Arroyo and G. Cadena, *Old Masks, New Faces: Religion and Latino Identities*, 144.

34. Martin Luther King, Jr. in a speech in Memphis, TN, April 3, 1968.

are there real communities?) But we do not recognize how through these bonds we have already diminished our true being.

This is where we are now. That is why we need guides of transformation to reach out to actual persons—not already labeled groups—to help them understand by what dramas they are possessed now. The same basic issues of culture we have been discussing affect us all, but differently within different cultures, and differently within individuals. New cultures, as we shall discuss in the next chapter, are also emerging, for example, of feminists, gays, and lesbians, but most of them remain still in the service of incoherence.

GROWTH AND FRUITS OF CULTURE: CULTIVATING FUNDAMENTALLY NEW AND BETTER ROOTS

Guides of transformation who understand culture as ways of life and archetypal dramas in their service can truly help us to understand and compare cultures and to make new choices among the living underlying patterning forces that are to design the structure, dynamics, meaning, values, and purpose of our lives. The new cultures underlying and manifested by transforming communities are not based on kinship, inherited customs, and already established structures and dynamics of power. Nor are they open only to us. Such new human communities are created democratically through shared understanding, compassionate love, and justice. At last we are practicing "love your neighbor as yourself."

The equality we now need is the freedom to enter, or to be guided to enter, any drama of participation in transformation.[35] After all, any human being, whatever his or her present culture, can learn to practice any drama through his or her unique concrete experience. There are no barriers of culture, race, or gender except as we adhere to them now.

This is no small task. At a time when there exist fewer communities even in neighborhoods than before, we need to find new ways to seek the transformation of cultures even far beyond our neighborhood. "We should regard all human beings as our fellow citizens and neighbors."[36] We come to understand ourselves better when we also come to understand others.

---

35. A transforming perspective on this issue is offered by Michael Lerner and Cornel West, *Jews and Blacks: A Dialogue on Race, Religion, and Culture in America*.

Also two quite helpful analyses are by Marla Brettschneider, *Cornerstones of Peace: Jewish Identity Politics and Democratic Theory*; and edited by the same author with an introduction by Cornel West, *The Narrow Bridge: Jewish Views on Multiculturalism*.

36. Thus wrote Plutarch already two thousands years ago in his book, *The Fortune of Alexander*, cited in Martha C. Nussbaum, "Patriotism and Cosmopolitanism," in Martha C. Nussbaum and Joshua Cohen, *For Love of Country: Debating the Limits of Patriotism*.

We need to overcome past ways of life and dramas in their service—that is, our past culture. There is no way of combining the best of incoherence as a way of life with living in transforming cultures. To transform means giving up our present cultural identity. That is scary. "Think what it will do to my present relations with others!" But we cannot reach out from our true uniqueness to realize and express our full humanity by re-forming, reestablishing, or reclaiming, or by reaffirming the present stories of our society or blindly asserting our cultural past.[37]

We are not creating a new uniform culture of transformation that gives us a universal identity. Each person makes unique creative contributions learned by participation with our deepest being—contributions to our newly shared cultural consciousness, collaboration, change, and justice—and remains free to conflict with present or new solutions that no longer nourish us. By participating in the transformation of cultures, we no longer confine our regard to already cultivated people, we no longer preserve cults of existing power, but we seek the capacity to be and to be together and work together to cultivate new roots and growths and harvests in the soil of our lives.[38]

Consider what a distance we are now from that road! Let us, therefore, begin.

---

37. David T. Abalos, *Strategies of Transformation toward a Multicultural Society: Fulfilling the Story of Democracy*, xvi.

38. One such pioneer—both in scholarship and in community education and organizing—is David T. Abalos. I have learned so much from him! To cite only his extraordinarily insightful and deeply and critically creative books—all based on the theory of transformation, all dealing with Latino culture but as examples of basic issues in all of our lives: *Latinos in the United States: The Sacred and the Political*; *Latino Family and the Politics of Transformation*; *Strategies of transformation toward a Multicultural Society: Fulfilling the Story of Democracy*; *La Comunidad Latina in the United States: Personal and Political Strategies for Transforming Culture*; and *The Latino Male: A Radical Redefinition*.

12

Archetypal Dramas of Being Masculine and Feminine

We all live in the core drama of life in which we need not arrest ourselves to be the kind of man—or else the kind of woman—our current way of life impels us now to be. Instead, we can free ourselves to continue our journey in order to participate in creating new dramas in a fundamentally better way of life—a way that gives both men and women the capacity to experience, each in our own unique way, both masculine and feminine archetypal forces. Our core task is not above all to be a man or a woman but, whatever our biological container, to be truly a human being free and capable to enact any truly fruitful archetypal drama.

Throughout this analysis, I use the words *feminine* and *masculine* to refer solely to archetypal forces that shape the underlying patterns of our lives. By contrast, I use the words *female* and *male*—or *women* and *men*—to refer solely to biologically shaped forms. The concrete expression of every archetypal force differs in each biological form and certainly in each unique person, but being a woman or a man does not prevent us from expressing both masculine and feminine archetypal forces.

Until Act III, we are molded by the partial—that is, biased and incomplete—ways of life of emanation and incoherence, and often, as we shall see, through their alliance with deformation. That is why we shall now explore why we need to empty ourselves of past and present archetypal dramas that inspire and shape our being male and female and create a future in which we are wholly human.

THE ROOTS AND FORMS OF THE MASCULINE AND FEMININE IN EMANATION AS A WAY OF LIFE

We come from a past—and we still strikingly persist within the heritage of that past—in which almost all archetypal dramas allow only men to seek domination through monopolizing the archetypal relationships of emanation and subjection and hence also to gain much greater power in relationships of direct exchange and in establishing their positions of autonomy. Men have also until recently monopolized the shaping of theology, philosophy, and science as buffers that decisively mold our understanding and our linkages from a masculine perspective.

No woman could, until quite recently, openly compete with men. Besides, men believe that women are unable to compete in war or peace;[1] they either are or ought to be pregnant and need to attend to our children. Patriarchy is required to protect women and children against other men who—if their aggression is not intercepted—may seek to rape them. Thus the political face of all beings becomes biased and incomplete. We are not free equally to express the uniqueness of our being in what we actually can and need to do together. Throughout such a history, the four faces of being of both men and women are warped by constrictions.

The emanational source of the sacred—in all of its three monotheistic forms—is masculine. Only men spoke as its prophets. Only men interpreted and enforced its laws. Only the dominant thus legitimized are truly connected to the ultimate Lord—as heretical men and sometimes women (especially "witches") must also be made to understand.

In Catholic Christianity, the Church sought to be in sole control of the feminine. It changed the Holy Spirit—the Spirit of Wisdom which was feminine in Hebrew and Greek—to being masculine. And it dogmatically endowed all offices occupied by celibate priests with the Holy Spirit in order to legitimate their office regardless of their personal being.[2] It called itself the Mother Church. (Only our Father and his only Son and now our masculine Holy Spirit are in Heaven). It became the guardian of the Virgin Mary, of virgin nuns and of married mothers. It recognized no other kinds of women. Its dominant dogma about women is this: "Let a woman learn in silence with all submissiveness."[3]

---

1. Most men cannot remember Joan of Arc or the women participating in resistance movements against fascism and colonialism. Recently, about 20,000 women, some of then commanding entire battalions, fought in the Eritrean army against Ethiopian rule. Now they have been pushed back into their traditional inferiority. (*The New York Times*, May 4, 1996.)

2. This was proclaimed in contrast to Christ who said the Holy Spirit "blows where it pleases" (John 3:8), and St. Paul who had proclaimed, "Do you not realize that your body is the temple of the Holy Spirit, who is in you and whom you received from God?" (I Corinthians 6:19).

3. I Timothy 2:11.

By contrast, Jesus taught women also. Only women (and possibly one of his male disciples) were with him during the crucifixion and initially after his resurrection.

Among Jews in the service of emanation, the domination of men was sacredly enshrined by forbidding women to study the Holy Scriptures or their interpretations. The presence of women at synagogue prayers did not count in establishing the minimum requirement, a quorum, (the *minyon*) of ten human beings present. No woman could be a witness at court. No woman could have a divorce without the husband's permission, but the husband did not need his wife's permission.

Among Muslims, men are allowed to have four wives provided, says the Koran, the husband treats them equally (but as he would treat women, not as if they were his equals as men). The husband is also permitted to have concubines. Genital mutilation of the clitoris among many Muslims (an act not ordained in the Koran) powerfully suggests that there is a great fear of women's own freedom of desire. Are the severe restrictions upon women we have cited in all three monotheistic ways of emanation evidence of a deep fear by men that their domination might be challenged by the other half of the population? That fear is obvious in the deforming response to women by men. These things are done in order to diminish the being of women.

Why is it that, in the past, when feminine archetypal forces were recognized (Sophia, the Greek feminine conception of wisdom, or Shekhina, the feminist aspects of God discovered by kabbalist Jews in the twelfth and thirteenth centuries), such inspiration was supposedly intended solely for men? These forms of monotheistic emanation thus created a huge domain of exclusive male domination, even when feminine forces arose from the depths.

Given the great political distance and inequality between men and women in all realms of life, is their marital relationship—the closest encounter between men and women—any different? In most societies, even today, women have no choice of their own about whom to marry. In many areas of contemporary Pakistan, women are often killed when they marry against the wishes of their parents.[4] Once married, most men "enjoy sexual pleasure from women, not with women."[5] A woman is meant to yield not only to naked power, but willingly to submit to her duty, or at least acknowledge her dependence. And a man must demonstrate at home that he is strong and powerful. Certainly he is entitled to beat his wife to show that he is not a weakling—thus deforming her being.

Men want to enlarge their power also by enlarging their family with children. But do mothers of many children remain sexually active or desirable in such a

---

4. *The New York Times*, February 19, 1999.
5. David T. Abalos, "'The Latino Male and the Politics of Transformation," a paper prepared for the Annual Convention of the American Political Science Association, September 4, 1998.

culture? Men therefore also use various ways of connecting to other women sexually. They are free to do so in many cultures in the service of emanation. Women certainly are not.

The central competition in the three monotheistic ways of emanation we have been discussing is the quest for male domination, thanks to being recognized and accepted as the principal embodiment of the masculine values, ideas, and purposes. There is no room for women in this competition. Throughout most of our past, only a minority of men have been literate, but they have normally left women entirely illiterate. Thus, men have rigged the rules of life to prove that they are morally, intellectually, and physically superior to "the weaker sex."

There have been women in the past who chose the path of transformation in order to gain an understanding and compassionate life. But more frequently, in the face of the male monopoly of power, some women have resorted to seduction, covert manipulation, subversion, and deception—a risky course and a corruption, because men's absolute power corrupts all but is difficult to overthrow.

INCOHERENCE AS A WAY OF LIFE HAS PRODUCED WHAT CHANGES IN THE MASCULINE AND FEMININE?

How much have masculine and feminine archetypal forces—and the relationship between men and women—changed since most of the world entered incoherence as a way of life?

Incoherence is the fruit of men's rebellion against the limitations of emanation—against the limitations imposed by an ultimate power so that instead, the self-interested power of men can triumph as they devote themselves to organizing fragments of life as aggressively as possible (under procedures agreed upon by men) and as defensively as necessary. Here are some of those fragments: men with power and rights distinct from those of women, the personal segregated from the political, sex often separated from love, law detached from justice, our male-dominated culture at odds with other male-dominated cultures, and the material ruptured from the sacred.

Men are moved by and still seek control over women as well, through the male-empowering archetypal dramas which dominate both men and women. Mothers and fathers are moved to love their sons only conditionally—if they are becoming more competent and (within established procedures) more aggressive. A man ran past me while I was on a walk one morning. He was wearing a T-shirt that said, "Your parents will love you more if you win."

Women, until quite recently, were rendered invisible in scholarship and public discourse. We spoke only of *man*kind to cover all of humankind or only of "workmanship" or "craftsmanship". Even when we referred to solidarity, we spoke solely of *brother*hood. To thus render women invisible as human beings is crucially to deform them.

Women are beginning to enter and to rise in this way of life of organized insecurity. But there is still much male resistance to women assimilating into this way of life. Why allow competitive rivals to double in number?

In the United States in 1935, only 5 percent of the women worked outside the home. In 1998, 60 percent received wages—but the average woman earns only 74 percent of a male wage. Only 30 percent are in jobs with pensions, and certainly women remain a minority in the higher ranks of political power, including the institutionalized economic and intellectual fields.[6] But domesticated women who take care of husband, home, and children are called "unemployed."

The emergence of successful women conformists to established masculine archetypes can also delay further liberation. And, of course, even this kind of assimilation has been delayed. In France, women were not allowed to vote until 1945, in Switzerland, not until 1971. In France also, women could open no bank account of their own until 1965. They could buy no contraceptives without their husband's permission until 1968. A woman is still sixteen times more likely to die in childbirth in Thailand than in the United States—and thirty times as likely in Indonesia or Myanmar (Burma).[7]

In the United States, many Latina women who work must hand over all their earnings to the husband. In all societies until recently, all property belonged solely to males. Part of the new competitive arts of women may now also be about developing power to woo and win a successful man. "After all, I do not know who I really am but I know what I want and how to acquire it. After all, I cannot really hope to be successful on my own." Women are still seen as the weaker sex. Many women therefore still believe that they can best be protected by the status of the husband: I am truly happy to be known now as "Mrs. John Smith," and thus to know my place.

Especially on the road to marriage, within marriage, and in motherhood—the greater part of most women's lives—most of her performance and that of her husband is still shaped by the masculine archetypal forces inherited from emanation as a way of life. It is a largely one-sided life of inequality: at her ordained best, to inspire, obey, service, and support her husband; to be always available for sex; to keep the home running well and looking good; and to take care of the children. While occupied by these dramas, to emerge as an autonomous individual—even as autonomy is defined in the service of incoherence—is very difficult indeed.

Worse, as we already saw in Chapter 8, is that the archetypal relationship of incoherence arises more and more often even as fragments of emanation—and indeed of other dramas and relationships—break in the service of incoherence. In

---

6. In 1999, three decades after Princeton University first began to admit women students, only 27 percent of its faculty is composed of women, only 15 percent of its tenured faculty so far are women.
7. Nicholas F. Kristof, *The New York Times*, June 11, 1998.

the United States, for example, four out of ten women and nearly a third of men suffer from disinterest, stress, or other difficulties in sexual intercourse.[8] One-half of all marriages in the United States end in divorce.

Women are now being allowed by men to become—and are perceived by men as being—more instrumentally rational, more impersonally competent, and more competitively free. But can men and women in the service of incoherence become free to be fully human within themselves and in their relationships with others? If not, then can they actually trust each other?

DEFORMATION THROUGH THE DOMINANCE OF MEN OVER WOMEN

As we have already seen, in contrast to the transforming love that connects men and women to the deepest source of their being and frees them to understand and to be just, the power required in emanation and incoherence as ways of life too often leads men to ally themselves with archetypal forces of deformation. Diminishing the being of women to the status of the lesser or invisible leads women—still billions of women—into deformation. There are two widespread examples of deformation: rape and prostitution. Rape of women takes place not only in wars, not only by intruding strangers, not only on dates between men and women when women do not consent to intercourse, but also within marriages when women reject intercourse. Few cases of rape are punished. In Italy, rape was not a crime until 1996.

In most countries and in most American states, women prostitutes are often arrested—but not the men who used them. Child prostitution has become a multi-billion dollar industry. Especially in Asia and Latin America, hundreds of thousands of children are sold by fathers to men who confine them and exploit them as prostitutes.

When manifestations of deformation arise in women, they are hardly ever manifestations of total power, but of total powerlessness instead—and often lead to desperation expressed in forms of self-wounding.

PRESENT BARRIERS FOR BOTH MEN AND WOMEN TO BECOMING FULLY HUMAN

Why does our exploration not accept that "boys must grow up to be men," and that "a man is a man," different from the "weaker sex"? Why not focus simply on helping both men and women to improve their own lives and also their relationships

---

8. This is from a study published in the *Journal of the American Medical Association* and reported in *The Washington Post*, February 10, 1999.

to each other? Yes, once again, I affirm that I am as much in favor of incremental improvements as are now possible. But the question upon which our analysis concentrates is this: How can we now gain the freedom and capacity to create a fundamentally better life for both women and men?

First we need to understand still better the barriers to such a transformation—the conventional assumptions and standards that get in our way. We cannot arrest and hence limit the other without arresting and limiting ourselves, even while our remaining devoted to incoherence as a way of life increases our power—though certainly never our capacity. We will now explore how emanation and incoherence as ways of life keep us, as men and women, partial beings who cannot yet discover who we really are or who anyone else really is—and of what wholeness of being we and they are deprived. And then we shall show that as long as a man does not treat a woman fully as a human being, he will also deny himself the free and full experience of the feminine through his own being and with others. The same is true for women with respect to masculine archetypal forces.

For millennia, men have decided what archetypal dramas we are to enact and what roles men and women are to enact within them. Men have exercised a sacred power to select and enforce living underlying patterning forces. This male monopoly over who may enact masculine archetypal forces and their values and purpose, and how feminine archetypal forces are to be enacted solely by women, has rendered men and women different in their past and present form. In 1869, John Stuart Mill wrote with great insight, even if with no understanding of archetypes, "But was there ever any domination which did not appear natural to those who possessed it? . . . What is now called the nature of women is an eminently artificial thing . . . [put] in practice to enslave their minds."[9]

Most men in our time also still seek to exclude from existing rights and opportunities men and women—gays, lesbians, bisexuals, and transsexuals—who in part reject these dominant archetypal forces. This stereotypical defense of inherited and ruling forms of archetypal domination blinds heterosexuals to the varieties of archetypal dramas in which these others in fact live. A gay man or a lesbian woman may be solely masculine or solely feminine in response to his or her lover. Gays and lesbians may be monogamous, polygamous, sexually promiscuous, sadomasochistic, or in transforming love. Gays may or may not be anti-female. Lesbians may or may not be anti-male. Their sexual orientation may or may not be their dominant archetypal drama. Do they want to become only another socially and legally recognized interest group within incoherence as a way of life—a good incremental change—or do they also mean to free themselves to become and to be

---

9. John Stuart Mill, "The Subjection of Women," in Alice S. Rossi, ed., *John Stuart Mill and Harriet Hardy Taylor Mill: Essays on Sex Equality*.

fully recognized as human beings? The paths of these men and women challenge the present structure and dynamics of male domination of our culture—and the dominant culture's form of devotion to the archetypal masculine. Males may still respond with deforming violence especially against gays.

How do we now conventionally—but in fact archetypally—enact and enforce the masculine and the feminine? We say that women are by nature more emotional and less rational than men. But in the United States, men are four times more likely than women to die from suicide. Homicide by people under the age of thirty is eight times more likely to be committed by men than by women. Men are eight times more likely to end up in prison.[10]

Men, we say, are physically stronger than women. Yet the *British Journal of Sports Medicine* reports that "women cannot close the strength gap entirely, but they can get within five percent of an equivalent body-weight male."[11] Women also live longer than men do.

The distortions in vision, understanding, and practice created by our currently dominant way of life have produced almost no fruitful relationships between men and women in many realms of life. And they have also produced conflicts which are beginning to rise to the surface among women, especially against the shortage of human sensitivity, the reification and abstraction of issues, the emphasis on technique, competitiveness, the bottom line, and the continuing political dominance of men.

MASCULINE AND FEMININE ARCHETYPAL FORCES THAT ARISE WHEN WE PARTICIPATE IN TRANSFORMATION

What masculine and feminine archetypal forces arise when we participate in transformation? We shall only know the answer once we have truly freed ourselves to discover and understand both kinds of archetypal forces. But let us begin our inquiry.

There are major changes under way within incoherence as a way of life. In the United States, for example, women increasingly outnumber men at colleges and universities. By the year 2007, the U.S. Department of Education expects women students to number 9.2 million—men, 6.9 million.[12] Women are more strongly on their way to equal rights and equal pay, but do universities teach their students wisdom or only knowledge—how to become fully human, or only how to become successful?

---

10. Natalie Angier, *The New York Times*, February 17, 1999.
11. Dr. Ellis Cashmore in the *British Journal of Sports Medicine*, reported in *The New York Times*, April 27, 1999.
12. *The New York Times*, December 6, 1998.

Can we, within incoherence as a way of life, discover feminine archetypal forces? "No matter what else they're doing, women are also always nurturing."[13] Women are essentially more nurturing, loving, cooperative, and socially connected than men. Separation and polarization alarm women and they respond through connectedness, intimacy, and interdependence.[14] "In order to nourish herself, a woman must connect with others."[15]

Women are able to respond in these ways, but is it a response also shaped by men's dominance in shaping the role of women? Women can also rebel against such roles. Women can become dominating mothers. How effectively have women so far linked themselves politically with other women against male domination? "Women may manipulate others or even inspire or be inspired by destruction."[16] Or women may feel compelled to limit themselves to being "nice" rather than compassionate and loving; emotional, but not passionate and symbolically expressive; passive, rather than creatively receptive; sociable and dependent, rather than open to profound union with others and capable of creating cooperative supportive groups; benign and motherly, rather than having a capacity for healing and nurture.[17]

What we are searching for is a transforming way of overcoming established archetypal forces. For example, is being aggressive intrinsic only to men? Being aggressive literally means "stepping forward urgently." Why cannot both women and men act with vigor, daring, and courage—with imagination and steadfast and well-honed clarity and skill to help the weak overcome weakness, to struggle against injustice, to rescue and heal people in danger, to fight against war, and to woo whomever we love?

If being aggressive in this sense is a masculine archetypal force, then to be aggressively transforming does not mean for men or women to seek domination. If being loving and caring is a feminine archetypal force, then being feminine does not mean being effeminate. Solely to dominate (or solely to protect) prevents the full human actualization of the ruler and the ruled. Every archetypal force that expresses any part of being human is available to us because we are human, though its archetypal expression differs in different ways of life and concrete expression differs in each biological vessel and certainly in each person.[18]

---

13. Cokie Roberts, Congressional correspondent for ABC news, quoted in the *AARP Bulletin*, January 1999.

14. The last two sentences are drawn from Carol Gilligan, *In a Different Voice: Psychological Theory and Women's Development*.

15. Kathy Kovner, a Princeton University student in her senior thesis, *Medusa*, May 1977.

16. Ibid.

17. Drawn from a paper at Princeton University by Betsy Wright, Spring 1977.

18. There is no biological difference that prevents women or men from learning and doing well all the tasks and possibilities and pleasures of human life. When there are such differences—such as the biological differences that further human reproduction—let us also learn truly to collaborate.

TRANSFORMING MOTHERHOOD, FATHERHOOD, AND MARRIAGE

Does motherhood and fatherhood doom us to persist in already established archetypal dramas? Is our most enticing diminution of the bonds of marriage—unfaithfulness to our partner—another traditional path? Does not motherhood, above all, shape a woman? No man can become pregnant, give birth, breast-feed or, given our present male-dominated dramas, devote most of his life to raising children. Fatherhood takes far less time for men, and requires far fewer risks, such as dying in pregnancy or childbirth.

Certainly it is possible for communities to exercise real care for pregnant mothers and their children and to dramatically reduce injury and death. But is it only a mother who can devote herself to being always with her child? One deep attraction for a woman of being always present is to be her children's source of emanation. In turn, children give her the only love, meaning, and purpose in life that she can count on. Or motherhood, like fatherhood, can be expressed in a possessive archetypal drama—the child to be the only sure possession she can count on.

But now, more than half of all women in the United States are fully employed at jobs. Soon, most will be—even as most men are—fully employed. Both men and women work at least eight hours a day—and more and more often, even longer. It may additionally take as much as two hours a day to commute to and from the job. A child asks, "Who is going to be with me?" And when half of American marriages end in divorce,[19] the child asks again, "Who is going to be with me?"

In the United States (in contrast to a small number of capitalist societies which are also serious welfare states), there exist only a very small number of daycare centers. At the best of these, children are taught how to do things, how to have fun, and how to be disciplined. But do they also receive love? Or do you have a childless woman come to your house? Or a woman who must therefore leave her children at home? Can you pay someone to love your children? Or shall the mother seek only a part-time job? Under competitive capitalism, the answer at higher job levels is likely to be this: Then you are not here when we need you! And the mother asks, "Why did I get a full-time education to get only a part-time job for the first eighteen years of my child's life?"

We cannot move beyond present archetypal dramas of motherhood, fatherhood, and marriage unless we also say no to other related dramas of our life—indeed, until we say no to our present way of life.

We need a life of transformation that inspires us to create loving and just relationships of collaboration in all our dramas of life. Men and women will be free

---

19. But only about one-third of all mothers who have court orders requiring fathers to make child support payments actually receive the money in most of the United States. *The New York Times*, April 25, 1999.

and enabled to have no children or only a small number. New life then comes into being as a true choice. Men and women both share or arrange daily turns in raising and in every sense nourishing their children. That requires working in an economic drama whose participants care deeply not only about production and consumption but the creation and quality of whole human beings. Much shorter workweeks are essential. It requires collaboration between part-time workers also as human beings, so that they can in fact achieve their tasks together. And both mother and father recognize and connect with the political face of children—long before children become old enough to vote. Yes, actually listen to each other in order to come to understand and to collaborate with each other. Disciplining children effectively is not our dominant political task.

Affinity groups can also organize raising their children together. Daycare then remains a matter of personal and loving contact within a small group of people.

Why should we persist in the backwardness of a way of life in which fathers are enchained by the living underlying patterning forces to be seldom as immediately concerned about children as mothers are? Why are fathers still entitled to keep the problems of mothers and children primarily a private concern?

BECOMING AND BEING NOT ONLY A MAN OR A WOMAN, BUT A WHOLE HUMAN BEING

Both men and women need to discover not only the particular burdens they now bear but the nature of the dramas and ways of life that render both men and women biased and incomplete. Only this kind of penetration by both men and women will allow both to open themselves to becoming pregnant with the fundamentally new and better. Thus, both will also discover that such creation comes into being through the intimate collaboration between the masculine and the feminine in our deepest depths and within our concrete relationships. We need such loving intimacy with ourselves and with others—with whole and hence real human beings. We need greater capacity, not more power to overcome lesser power or powerlessness. To love our selves in this way is also to learn and deeply to desire to love our neighbors as we love ourselves.

Once both men and women experience and express the masculine and the feminine, will they still be attracted to each other? Yes, human beings will be attracted to each other and come to love each other sexually—in various forms—and also and above all as human beings.

Both men and women need to become prophets, philosophers, and guides of participation, for our task is to create fundamentally new and better archetypal dramas so that we may discover and enact fundamentally new and better understanding, love, and justice for both women and men. What will these dramas concretely be like? Only through our experience of the drama of transformation can we find all the varieties of the fully and truly feminine and masculine. To change a whole way of life is for each of us a personal movement through the core drama of life. There is no vast architectural design or edifice. Can women, the more oppressed half of humanity, become our pioneer guides on this journey? Yes, but only if oppression has not led them instead to seek the mere opposite, or merely a place of power in our present way of life. Men will not be pioneer guides unless they recognize the partial nature of their power—in contrast to their potential human capacity.

In transforming ourselves, we do not move from one-sided dependency to mutual dependence. Men and women both give birth to new forms of being fathers and mothers to themselves. We learn how and why to authorize ourselves to become uniquely who we are; we learn what we can and need to do with others. We also learn how to nourish ourselves and others. We are lovingly close to ourselves and hence also understand how to be close to others—but not as a substitute for being close to ourselves.

We no longer feel compelled to say, "I need you, therefore I love you." Instead, when we have freed ourselves to understand the being of others, our depths call upon us to declare, "I love you, therefore I need you. I need you so that we can both help each other continue to transform our lives and the lives of our neighbors."[20]

---

20. I have here augmented a statement from Erich Fromm, *The Art of Loving*, thanks to a very fruitful discussion on this issue with David Abalos.

PART FOUR

The Theory and Practice of Transformation

13

The Nature of Archetypal Dramas

Now that we have offered empirical evidence for the archetypal core drama of life and its four radically different archetypal choices, and empirical evidence for nine archetypal relationships and more than two dozen different archetypal dramas/stories in the service of these basic four archetypal choices, we can more deeply explore the nature of these living underlying patterning forces.

Nothing concrete takes form in our life except as the manifestation of archetypal dramas. They shape the structure, dynamics, values, meaning, and purpose of all our stories. Each archetypal drama—and most of all the way of life in which we enact it—shapes the nature of our being, including our deprivations or wholeness of being. But as we have explored, we are able not only to enact ourselves and to interact with others within such dramas, but also to re-form them or to create new dramas of deformation or transformation.

What is the empirical evidence for the existence and nature of any particular archetypal story? We can always see and experience its enactment through the four concrete faces of our being—personal, political, historical, and sacred. And the description and analysis we have offered of the living underlying patterning forces of any archetypal relationship, archetypal drama, and the four ways of life always hold true and are never otherwise, and it can be demonstrated that certain experiences can never take place within it. Such archetypal structures and dynamics, though only as long as they historically endure, remain the same even though their particular manifestations differ from moment to moment. A single case to the contrary of these theoretical and practical criteria calls any hypothesis regarding any particular archetype into doubt. Anyone using this theory of transformation necessarily accepts these same criteria of proof.

As our case studies have exemplified, I use the word *drama* not as a metaphor but as a description of how these forces are actually structured and actually work. We may be initially attracted to an archetypal drama by the immediate textures, colors, rhythms, sounds, and feelings it generates—or by its arguments, calculations, and rewards. We may be prevented by our current way of life from understanding its underlying structure and dynamics. Nonetheless, archetypal ways of life and dramas inspire and shape the very nature and character of our participation.[1] Archetypal analysis allows us to see beyond concrete personal, political, historical, and sacred manifestations and also to understand why life is as it is and what basic choices are in fact open to us as human beings.

The greatest power of the powerful is the ability to limit our capacity (and, in fact, their own as well) by culturally inflicting upon our lives the archetypal dramas that above all empower them. Archetypes are the deepest existing grounds of what we call *legitimacy*, even when we speak primarily of "rational-legal" justification. Any power, any force, even any legitimate monopoly of coercion is fragile unless it manifests a significantly shared archetypal drama. Our full human capacity, on the other hand, can only be understood and expressed when we participate in transformation.

Is all the world a stage and all its people players? No, our concrete words and actions are not already scripted nor are any of the concrete outcomes. We are not mere players in a design beyond our capacity to change. Yet, at every moment of our lives, we enact aspects of an entire drama in the service of an entire way of life. What many of us neglect is to ask what human beings are in fact on stage with us in this drama; we render invisible the wounded and losers. We tend not to ask how this drama limits our repertory of archetypal relationships and the faces of our being and of the being of others. We pay no further attention to human beings who are not allowed to enter our drama on our stage.

Our analysis of archetypal dramas always illuminates our thoughts and actions from the perspective of our capacity to move through the entire core drama of life—a core that helps us to discover and enact a fundamentally deeper and better understanding, love, and justice. No one before this present work has ever presented such an understanding of the archetypal grounds of our being and the choices open to us.

---

1. Genes also matter in our biological vessel. We all have about 140,000 genes within every cell of our body. For example, we need a father and a mother in order to be born and to be raised. Genes affect our ability to join in the process. But what kind of mother and father we have and our response to them is shaped by ways of life and their archetypal dramas. Also, however strong the personality of our mother or father, they could not deeply move us unless they represented the living underlying patterning forces of a way of life and of an archetypal drama. We also find theater plays, films, and novels compelling as they express archetypal patterns with particular and sensuous actuality. Music can affect us similarly.

Why do most of us today not even know about archetypes? In the past, emanation as a way of life stood in opposition to our asking fundamentally new and better questions about the living underlying patterning forces of our life. What we had come to believe to be the best and also the only right answers had already been revealed to us. Only heretics dared to ask questions in this vein, often at the risk of their lives.

As we explained in Chapter 5, incoherence as a way of life became dominant as stronger forms of physical, political, economic, religious, and intellectual power came into being which could not and would not be contained within the limits of the emanational web of life. But these new forms of power created a life of fragments.

In the realm of philosophy, especially since the seventeenth century, empiricism looks only for the concrete and if possible, quantifies it. At the beginning of Thomas Hobbes' *Leviathan* (his book on how we can organize a society based on self-interest), he said, "There is nothing in the world universal but names; for the things named are every one of them individual and singular."[2] There are things we can and need to do together—if we can share self-interested goals and agree not to kill each other when we still disagree. In the eighteenth century, John Locke specifically wrote that we cannot know archetypes. They are the work of god and we cannot know the sacred, only what *we* make. And we start as a *tabula rasa*—an empty canvas on which others—or else, much better, we ourselves—inscribe a picture of our self.[3]

For centuries now we have more and more examined independent or dependent variables—types of particulars—through different procedures, and separated fact from value. We have calculated market forces at work. We have in scholarship and also in daily bureaucratic actions tried hard to be impersonal—as if neither we nor others had actually four faces of being. Rational, logical calculation—so that we can know and shape our efficient, empirical practice—is the primary tool at the heart of our present task to shape what we regard as socially formed reality.

We see no archetypal dramas or ways of life. At most we see narrative stories, simple anecdotes, or maybe analogies. We did not want our attack on Iraq in 1990 or on Yugoslavia in 1999 to become an analogue of our war in Vietnam. Or indeed we may say, "In my life, nothing hangs together as a story"—but we do not know why. We certainly recognize no underlying patterns, not even those causing incoherence. Instead, we try pragmatically to organize and reorganize fragments and hope to find a more powerful path to success.

Most political party platforms in our societies certainly constitute only collections of fragments. We see ourselves and others play particular roles. We do not really see whole human beings. Narratives are told, written, and analyzed above all by the powerful or by specialists. Understanding, love, and justice—we ask, "How

---

2. Thomas Hobbes, *Leviathan*.
3. John Locke, *An Essay Concerning Human Understanding*.

could those be objective criteria? Can understanding, love, and justice be real and true?" We know no way of establishing such criteria.

WHAT ARCHETYPAL DRAMAS ARE NOT

In contrast to Plato's philosophy—which opened me to crucial questions and possibly fruitful answers—none of the archetypal ways of life and dramas we have been discussing are ideal or perfect. Some are evil. They are not eternal entities; they are dramas that can die or be re-formed or renewed or newly created. Plato at one point even speaks of a type of democracy in which people pay no attention to archetypes.[4]

Carl Gustav Jung, who has otherwise taught me much about the process of transformation, actually offers less than one paragraph on archetypes of transformation.[5] He also speaks only of our personal face and, more ambiguously, of our sacred face, but hardly at all of our political face and historical face. His synonym for archetypes—our *collective unconscious*—renders archetypal dramas ancient, but in fact ahistorical. He does not speak of archetypes as dramas or ways of life and hence has no basic underlying grounds for moral judgment.[6]

In the next section of this chapter, we shall try to understand, as best we can, the nature of these living underlying patterning forces. But first, I want to put aside notions that may in our time stand in our way and prevent us from coming to hear what archetypes really are.

Archetypal ways of life and archetypal dramas/stories, as we have already demonstrated by our examples, are not metaphors or models or ideal types or prototypes or conceptual abstractions. They are, rather, descriptions and analyses of actual living experiences and their actual underlying structure and dynamics, as well as their meaning, values, and purpose. Archetypes in our theory do not refer to stereotypic or very typical behavior—but to all forms of being human. If an archetypal drama were only a social construct, the fruit of cultural socialization, it would be so much easier to transform our selves, our stories, and our way of life.

COMING TO UNDERSTAND ARCHETYPAL DRAMAS

Our understanding of archetypal dramas is based upon the testable discovery that we all live at every moment in the archetypal core drama of life, that this archetypal

---

4. Plato, *The Republic of Plato*, Translated with Introduction and Notes by Francis Macdonald Cornford.
5. Carl G. Jung, *The Archetypes and the Collective Unconscious*.
6. For an excellent summary of Jung's ideas about archetypes, see William A. Shelburne. *Mythos and Logos in the Thought of Carl Jung*. Shelburne concludes his book with a chapter examining archetypes as hypothetical constructs.

core drama offers us four radically different choices regarding our way of life, and that all other archetypal dramas are lived in the service of one of these ways of life. And while any archetypal story persists in such service, we offer testable descriptions that its underlying structure, dynamics, meaning, values, and purpose always demonstrate this patterning form—and never any other.

We show how living underlying patterning forces hang together—and also how they can be reiterated, re-formed, deformed, and transformed. This is a theory about a practice that in any of its varieties is open to all human beings through the personal, political, historical, and sacred faces of our being. Understanding such living underlying patterning forces matters because we need to discover whether our present arrest in the core drama of life diminishes our humanity by rendering us biased and incomplete in our living, loving, learning, and working being—or whether our inflicted or chosen path can lead us into the core drama's only exit, into premature, destructive death. Moving consciously, critically, and creatively through the core drama guides us toward a fundamentally new and better life.

Relationships, work, self-interest, and institutions—through thoughts, desires, fears, hopes, means, and ends—move us so deeply (or no longer move us) because of the archetypal drama they manifest. And a single active expression—"be aggressive"—is manifested quite differently in different archetypal dramas for example, organizing and acting in fundamentally new and better ways to help the oppressed instead of being a conquering hero. Nothing can happen outside of archetypal dramas. Our discovery that we have four fundamentally different choices demonstrates a real order in the cosmos of human relations.

Rewards and punishments, calculations, and arguments may reinforce our already existing commitment to an archetypal drama. But to inflict and enforce our archetypal drama and way of life through subjection masks the four real faces of being. Indeed, the power alone of any person or institution cannot survive without shared archetypal support. Submission or consensus will only be temporary at most without such deeper support. The caste of untouchables, for example, accepts its fate as a manifestation of emanation as a way of life. The exploited and the unemployed may accept their fate as long as they, too, are possessed by the archetypal drama of capitalism. Nothing concrete exists except as the manifestation of an archetypal drama. To be connected through an archetypal relationship of emanation to a person or belief is also to be thus connected to an archetypal drama. To enter into an archetypal relationship of incoherence is also to endanger the archetypal drama of which that once coherent relationship was a part. Within any archetypal relationship, story and way of life, we are bound to express in basically predictable ways its underlying structure, dynamics, meaning, values, and purpose, however free we are to shape its outward particulars.

WHO NEEDS TO BE ON STAGE WITH US? WHO IN FACT IS ON STAGE WITH US?

We need to know who needs to be on stage with us if we are to exercise our power or else our capacity to enact any archetypal drama. Even a religious hermit needs to have others on stage with him—to provide him with food and protection and at least at first, with lessons.

Do the people living in poor neighborhoods have adequate transportation to get to jobs? Tools and explanations are also often needed to allow dramas to work—and they work differently in different ways of life. Do we repair schools that are in bad shape? Do we in fact educate students to understand the archetypal dramas in which they are likely to live?

Who is in fact on stage with us? "The tobacco industry reports that it provides jobs for 2.3 million Americans—and this does not include physicians, X-ray technicians, nurses, hospital employees, firefighters, dry cleaners, respiratory specialists, pharmacists, morticians and grave diggers."[7] Nature is also always on stage with us. Are we decimating flora and fauna while poisoning the environment? The people who have been rendered lesser or even invisible human beings by capitalists who have no need for them are still on stage with us even if they do not yet understand how to respond to their neglect or denial and hence may sink into deformation.

Dramas in the service of incoherence render even its active participants biased and incomplete, and all the more unlikely to tune in to human beings in dramas not relevant to—or at least not in conflict with—their own dramas. Even dramas of family kinship have weakened since the decline of emanation as a way of life. Events are shaped by who is in fact on stage with us, even when they enact life in different dramas and ways of life—and hence with differing power and capacity.[8]

WHAT PERSONAL UNIQUENESS CAN WE EXPERIENCE IN ARCHETYPAL DRAMAS?

We are not puppets in enacting archetypal stories. Our concrete expression of them differs at every moment according to the understanding, talent, feeling, experience, and other aspects of our personal being—and also of our political, historical, and sacred faces, which we shall discuss in later sections. Hence, we must never substitute our analysis of a person's archetypal involvement for discovering—as we always need to do as well—the actual, concrete manifestation of the being of that person.

---

7. Ann Landers, quoted in *The Reader's Digest*, March 1994, 150.
8. Events are also shaped by aspects of nonhuman nature whose archetypal character we do not yet understand.

Some people are possessed and enthralled by an archetypal drama and cannot—and do not want to—enact this drama in any other fashion than through their own utter conformity to its structure, dynamics, values, meaning, and purpose. But even in the service of emanation, such people do not always constitute a majority. We can act *response-ably*. We can decide, among other things, to which of the archetypal dramas current in our life to give priority now, or how, personally and politically, to conduct our conflict with other people who emphasize other dramas within the same way of life. Few of us express our being only through a single story. Gorbachev and Yeltsin dealt differently with the same challenges in what had been the U.S.S.R. and had become Russia. Thanks to the fact that we are human beings, we can take the initiative to re-form our present dramas or to transform our way of life. No concrete deeds, no remedies or fundamental changes are possible without our concrete personal face.

It is no small fact that in emanation as a way of life, the entire web allows us to be only a partial being. In the service of incoherence, not only our way of life, but each drama further renders us to be a particular fragment of being. For example, being a capitalist may lead us to corrupt or even reject democratic liberalism. These are among the principal powerful causes that within emanation and incoherence, however able and shrewd we are, we can only bring about incremental changes. There is no archetypal drama of freedom. Our freedom as an archetypal force differs profoundly as an aspect of each archetypal way of life and drama. Our personal roles in three of the ways of life diminish our personal uniqueness. Only when we participate in transformation can our personal face express and interconnect us with others through understanding, love, and justice.

HOW CAN WE COME TO UNDERSTAND THE ARCHETYPAL DRAMA THAT WE ENACT?

No action, no problem is only concrete or is only personal in its nature, its cause, or its effects, however much the personal face of our being may indeed matter at this moment. Public opinion polls cannot really discover anything fundamental by asking for our opinion on specific issues. The same "facts" have radically different meanings in different ways of life and in their dramas.

How can we reach understanding of an archetypal drama, including its characteristic values and risks? Most of us do not yet understand archetypal stories. In the service of emanation, we believe in rules that tell us what to do or not to do. In the service of incoherence, we try to learn as much as possible about our role and the roles of significant others and about specific matters of competence—fragments about a drama that organizes power to accomplish certain aims of power. In the service of incoherence, the more we learn about how the structure, dynamics, meaning, values, and purpose of a drama hang together, the more powerful we can be within it. Few, nonetheless, are the participants or the scholars who understand that much. Many are the people who divorce their spouse and then enter archetypally into the same drama again and are not happier. Only the experience of transformation allows us to understand where and who we now are in the core drama of life and the true meaning and value for the four faces of our being in the archetypal dramas that we now enact. For example, as we saw in Chapter 10, there is not only a single drama of love. The differences are crucial to our life.

EVEN WITH INADEQUATE KNOWLEDGE WHAT CAN WE DO WITHIN ARCHETYPAL DRAMAS?

Even when it is only inadequate, we can use what knowledge we have to employ such archetypal legitimized power as we have to increase our own power and limit or punish others. Thus, we stereotype others—"Get your act together or you'll be in trouble!"—by using our power to fit them into the confines of our archetypal way of life and dramas. We also strengthen our superego—to use Freud's term—to master ourselves in the service of incoherence. The greatest power of the powerful is their ability to inflict their archetypal dramas upon us. But since they do not truly understand the biased and incomplete nature of their way of life or their dramas, the power of their authority and stability is again and again in danger. They do not understand at all the deep and also the concrete cost of archetypes that require the use of power because they arrest us in being partial.

What do we mean by "being partial"? People still fully committed to incoherence as a way of life cannot understand the living underlying patterning forces that give rise to so much poverty in our time. They cannot tune in to the four faces of being of the poor (nor of their own). They cannot see how much and why the unique personal face of the poor has been lessened or rendered invisible, why the poor's own acceptance of the vision and values of the governing drama—it is our fault that we failed—demoralizes and even deforms too many. Hence, they cannot perceive what they can and need to do together. The successful, still committed to incoherence, do not care about the past, present, or future history of the poor. What about the sacred face of the poor? We are glad that there are churches to provide the poor with food. Which sacred source of being moves the poor? That's not our problem. We will, if we do care about their poverty, deal (incrementally) with some of their concrete problems. What archetypal stories and ways of life produce these problems? Who has heard of them? We don't know what you are talking about.

But in so far as we have come to know our main roles in our daily life, and their values and purpose, we may also "role-play" in what we see as our main "games." We may want more power than we are entitled to, or others may want more power than they are entitled to, and so we accept corruption. Our way of life justifies such self-interest, though we may thus secretly enter even a drama of crime. Or we may repress our real being because our governing drama cannot let us express it, and we feel driven by a compelling need to earn a living, or *this kind* of living. Or we may become cagey and dissimulate our role-playing in our present drama until we can enter a different one within our present way of life. Or we may manipulate the truth about what really happened for the sake of our own power or the power of our chief performer. Or we may manipulate others so that what happens is what we want to make happen. In terms of self-interest, only I really count in this drama—or only he, thanks to me. All dramas in the service of incoherence can seduce us into expressing this kind of self-interest.

Can we live outside of archetypal dramas? An-arch-ism cannot work. To live what feels like a life of rootlessness and formlessness is to live with many archetypal relationships of incoherence. We cannot stay there without severely risking losing our very being. Just having sex, we remain unconnected to ourselves and the other. We, still within incoherence as a way of life, need to ask why such breaks of archetypal relationships took place, why they are unresolved—and what archetypal dramas still move us. To be fired and hence not to be able to make a living is still to be powerfully affected by the archetypal story of capitalism. Shall we seek alternatives to capitalism, or accept our failure as our fault, or move into deformation?

A person might say, "But I don't really know what I want to do next. I feel lost. I don't really want to accept the patterns of life most people follow." The proficient guide will ask, "But have you reached Act II Scene 2 of the core drama of life? If you don't understand that move, what dramas still preoccupy you?"

ARCHETYPAL WAYS OF LIFE AND STORIES ARE VULNERABLE TO CHANGE

Archetypal dramas constitute no universal truths, no immutable laws. The core drama of life—but not its arrested or destructive ways of life—may persist forever, but not its concrete manifestation. Archetypal dramas can be expressed in old or new concrete manifestations or be re-formed, abandoned, or transformed. But any such vital change also constitutes an archetypal process within the core drama of life, as we shall soon discuss. To analyze archetypal dramas and processes is a vital expression of critical theory with respect to our being and our choices at every moment—a theory based on our understanding of the core drama of life and its living underlying patterning forces at work in a cosmos of continuous creation.

I have in previous statements about archetypal dramas said that an essential part of our empirical proof of their existence is that they always or else never move us to enact that specified structure, dynamics, meaning, values, and purpose. But always and never is never a final statement. As we have also discussed, our particular personal (and political, historical, and sacred) response can produce—as long as we remain in the service of emanation or incoherence—incremental changes. But these changes can only take place within the living underlying patterning forces always prevailing in that drama. To re-form or to reject an existing drama is always in response to its always-or-never pattern.

There is also nothing preordained about the specific ending, this time around, of any archetypal drama. Even on the road of deformation, you are not inevitably destined to die—though the danger intrinsically is quite high. Within the archetypal drama of being competent in the service of incoherence, you can count on not being valued (or valuing others) as a human being, but you are not predestined to gain the intended fruit of your competence or to rise in your career.

Archetypal dramas and ways of life are vulnerable to change—because of our discontent and our opening ourselves to new inspiration or because of the incoherence brought about by others first. Archetypes indeed do not and cannot exist without also the historical face of our being. Archetypal dramas become vulnerable in our experience of them, when even one of the ten aspects of any archetypal relationship within it is threatened with incoherence—that is, when continuity or change, modes of collaboration and conflict, and means of justice are not working, or when whatever unconscious conformity, or the expression of consciousness, creativity, linking with others, or the achieving of justice we need in any relationship are no longer within our power (not yet to speak of our capacity). Emanation and incoherence as ways of life, which render us only partial beings dealing with a biased and incomplete life, leave us and our life fragile and vulnerable to change—especially into deformation if we do not yet understand transformation.

What holds us back from breaking with the dramas of emanation and incoherence and still renders us closed to the opportunity of transforming ourselves? We are afraid of moving into incoherence, as required by the second Act of the core drama of life—frightened by the unfamiliar, afraid of offending our present co-participants in the prevailing drama, scared of giving up all of the remaining seeming security and rewards of our present drama. Fearful of this grave disappointment, this defeat, we remain attracted, even if no longer to this drama, still to our present way of life. After all, the powerful still practice this drama. We may understand our problem concretely, but not yet the living underlying patterning forces at stake.

TRANSFORMING THE DRAMAS OF LIFE

If we reject a particular drama but still remain caught in emanation or incoherence as a way of life, then our power—and not yet our capacity—still remains at issue. Then we may be inspired by the sacred sources of those ways of life to re-form a drama or create a new one but still in the service of their living underlying patterning force. In Act II Scene 2, we have emptied ourselves of the drama, but not of its governing way of life. We may even ally ourselves with archetypal forces of deformation to reinforce our power.

But when in fact we also begin to realize that not only this drama but this way of life is unbearable, untenable, or unfruitful, and also that they leave crucial aspects of our being (and that of others) unilluminated, unexplored, and unexpressed, our transformation can begin. How does it begin and move? In the light especially of Chapters 3 and 7, we can answer the question very quickly now. Because we are in serious doubt about our life in what we once unconsciously experienced emanationally (that is, in Act I Scene 1), we have opened ourselves to a new inspiration from Act I Scene 2. That inspiration, if it is transforming, will move to guide us in our journey through the entire core drama of life, but we will need to test it out also with our neighbors in Act III.

The core drama—which is also the archetypal drama of transformation—will help us to understand and to overcome the concrete manifestations and the archetypal force of the drama and the way of life at issue. To speak of this process solely in terms of the archetypal relationship of transformation as it first emerges in Act I Scene 2, our unconscious is now inspired by and connected to new sacred roots. Our consciousness becomes more and more aware of the structure and dynamics of the living underlying forces that have hitherto patterned us, and of the meaning, value, and purpose of its concrete manifestations. We creatively seek new links with the four faces of our being and with those of others, and we search for and test fundamentally better means to achieve fundamentally better justice. These changes in the continuity of our previous relationships, these new forms of conflict and collaboration—thanks to the greater wholeness of our being—lead to improvements in our understanding, our love, and our capacity to help create a just life

That we can free ourselves of archetypal dramas and ways of life and participate in creating fundamentally new and better ones is one of the most crucial facts of our life. We alone of all animals are capable of persistent transformation. Only by way of transformation do we as real people have the capacity to connect ourselves to problems as they really are.[9]

9. This volume has presented an analysis of the core drama of life, the radically different choices it offers us, and several archetypal dramas of major significance in their service. But there exist many more archetypal dramas. I suspect that there may be around a hundred such dramas. If there were thousands, human beings would have even far more difficulties communicating with each other. Even now, we enact many of the same archetypal dramas within different cultures.

David T. Abalos, in his most recent work, *The Latino Male: A Radical Redefinition*, not only presents deeply revealing analyses of archetypal dramas currently being practiced by Latino males but also creatively describes changes of our personal, political, historical, and sacred face that give us the capacity to participate in transformation.

THE FOUR SACRED SOURCES OF ARCHETYPAL DRAMAS

The living underlying patterning forces that inspire and move us arise from four radically different sacred sources—as manifested by the creative force of the entire core drama of life and by the existence of powerful arrests in two of its Acts and the path of destructive death through its exit. The nature of these four sacred sources and of our connection with (or disconnection from) them is the subject of our next chapter.

14

Choosing from Among Four Sacred Sources

Exploring the four fundamentally different sacred sources of our being from the perspective of transformation, we ask no one to believe anything we say. We shall offer nothing that is merely subjective or merely objective. We shall instead ask people to risk faith in what we say—meaning, freeing ourselves to risk trust to discover through our own experience whether these differences between sacred sources are real and true.

People who insist instead on remaining committed—we are believers and we already know that we are right and we do not dare to doubt, or we are agnostics and we know that we cannot know, or we are atheists and we already know that we cannot believe in any religion—will keep themselves from understanding what we are saying here. Secularists reject religion, but that modern term is not what we mean by the sacred. As we shall see, the sacred exists in our lives at every moment, shaping the personal, political, historical, and sacred faces of our being and of our archetypal depths—but in four radically different ways.

THE SACRED DESIGN OF THE CORE DRAMA OF LIFE

I discovered the core drama of life—as all of us can—by asking these questions: What are our fundamental alternatives in life? And, considering the pain and limitations of how most of us live, with so many deadly pulls around us, where does the fundamentally better come from—and how? I discovered, as all of us can, that there exist only four fundamentally different choices for us. No small fact.

When we explore our experience of the structure, dynamics, meaning, values, and purpose of the core drama of life—and we live somewhere in it at every moment—we discover also its sacred design. Here is that fundamental truth: The deepest sacred source of our being created this core drama as a process of transformation leading to our experience of the fundamentally new and better. When we listen and are inspired anew by the deepest sacred source of our being in Act I Scene 2, we rebel in Act II against what had previously enchanted and enchained us in the first Scene of Act I. But we rebel not only thanks to our newly inspired courage to say no, but also with new understanding of our former sacred source, now derived also from our participation with our deepest source. Then, in Act III, we fully open ourselves to our newly inspired understanding and test it in practice to see if in fact our capacity leads to fundamentally new and better understanding, love, and justice.

But there also exist three other sacred sources who have the power to inspire us instead to arrest ourselves within a fragment of the core drama of life (nowhere else)—or to fragment ourselves altogether into death (through its exit). Certainly such arrests or such destruction are not needed at all by us for our journey through the core drama of life. Why then did the deepest sacred source of our being also create these other three sacred sources? I don't know.

I can only speculate that our deepest sacred source—who is not perfect, not all-knowing, and not all-powerful—could not initially create human beings who would be able always to discover and express their whole capacity, and hence always engage in transformation. Considering human history, considering the situation in which even most of us were born and raised, power is still what most clearly, most potently either strikes us down or else attracts us—power to hold on to the security of a web of life, or power to change this or that fragment, or power to destroy so that we alone can dominate. It would be impossible to be inspired, energized, and committed to do these things if there were no sacred sources to create these ways of life and stories by which to structure and move our lives. As long as we are fully possessed by them for the sake of their kind of power—and hence seek at most only to fight one form of power with another form of power—we are unable to understand transformation and the capacity it gives us instead.

Once we find our experience of the way of life inspired by the other three sacred sources unbearable, untenable, or unfruitful, we become more capable of moving into the process of transformation. Since about the sixth century BC—though it probably also happened earlier—we have written evidence of people freeing themselves from the other three alternatives within the core drama of life and moving toward transformation. In not too distant a future, we may increasingly reenter the journey of transformation not only to free ourselves from the ways of life and dramas in the service of the other three sacred sources but also because—in this cosmos of continuous creation—earlier experiences of transformation turn out to be no longer as fruitful as they once were.

The core drama of life structures our fundamental choices in life. But unless we come to better understand this core drama, we will not recognize the fact that something *sacred* is not necessarily something *good* or *eternal*. We can free ourselves to say no to any sacred source, but only with the help of another sacred source. Hence, contrary to the opinion of poststructuralists, my finding is that we—all of us—can find and make choices in the meaning and purpose of our life thanks to the reality of the very structure and process of the core drama of life. For these are not four entirely separate sacred sources. On the contrary, the core drama of life gives us interconnected choices of structuring, or deconstructing, or restructuring, or unstructuring, or transforming stories that contain contrasting values and purposes.

FROM THE SACRED SOURCES THROUGH ARCHETYPAL DRAMAS TO OUR BEING

The sacred sources are incomplete without the concrete. Only through concrete differentiation can a sacred source fully realize itself. Hence, sacred sources manifest themselves through archetypal ways of life and the stories in their service—and through our concrete enactment of them in the personal, political, historical, and sacred faces of our being. Thus, we all participate at all times—in four radically different ways—with the sacred, and this actualizes the sacred sources in our lives.

We would not be inspired and moved by our living underlying patterning forces unless sacred sources empowered—or else capacitated—them and therefore us. No "secular" monopoly of power can do that for an entire way of life or for all aspects of any archetypal story. Any concrete person, idea, feeling, image, or event can move us so deeply only because they symbolize such living underlying patterning forces that express a sacred source.

But in the service of a life of fragments, for example, are we not inspired and driven by our desire for power over money and over others? Indeed, what useful alternative is there within this way of life for any of us except to seek to enlarge or at least hold on to the fragments of our life? Is that not a sufficient explanation of the structure, dynamics, meaning, values, and purpose of our lives, even of most of the exploited and unsuccessful among us? No. It is the archetypal pattern created by a sacred source that has inspired our arrest in the core drama of life—an arrest that shapes our life as a devotion to fragments, and that blinds us also to the fact that we, however successful otherwise, are also still only a fragment of being, biased and incomplete. Our self-interest molded by archetypal forces prevents us from seeing ourselves as only partial, and induces us to treat most others as lesser or invisible beings.

We do not have the power or the capacity to destroy sacred sources or their archetypal forces, but indeed we can free ourselves from them—as long as we connect anew to another sacred source and that source's archetypal dramas. We can collaborate with a sacred source to reform or add new archetypal stories within the limits of that source and our present way of life, or we can achieve freedom to transform our way. We can preserve or nourish or change the concrete only within an archetypal drama, that is, within our connection to the sacred. Those who live in a world they have split between the secular and the religious have no understanding of how our life is rooted and moves or how it can be nourished or transformed. If the deepest source of our being were undifferentiated—that is, formless or wholly other—we could offer no fundamental explanations about our choices in life nor discover which is the fundamentally better. If that deepest source were absolute, it would already be perfect and unlimited in its power. Then why has it put us or left us in the shape we are in? If no sacred sources exist outside the deepest source except as faces of that very source (as I thought until 1990, because I had not yet recognized the structure and dynamics of the core drama of life), then the meaning of justice remains ambiguous.

We can come to believe we know the one and only sacred source. Or we can come to believe that we can ignore that one and any other sacred source. Or we can come to surrender and be totally possessed by one of them. Let us discuss how we come to enact any of these options—or how we come to understand the four sacred sources and then choose our deepest sacred source.

BELIEVING IN THE SACRED SOURCE OF EMANATION AND ITS WAY OF LIFE

We shall focus our concrete discussion only on three forms of monotheism, but most of our generalizations apply to all forms of emanation as a way of life. Hundreds of millions of people still seem to be caught in its service, but for more and more—probably already the majority—what has survived of this way is becoming instead a fragment within incoherence as a way of life.

In the service of emanation, we believe that its sacred source exists infinite in its power, all-knowing, perfect, and finally beyond our understanding. This source, whatever its will, must be worshipped and obeyed in all aspects of our lives according to the rules already revealed and codified for us. Otherwise, great punishment in this life and in eternity is in store for us. Except for its beginning and its expected extraordinary ending, this way of life is ahistorical. Personally, politically, historically, and sacredly we must not change anything—including the status and roles of women—and *certainly* must not free ourselves from these sacred forces.

Though there are ways of emanation which put greater emphasis on god's rewards for the right responsiveness of human beings to each other and to god, many also agree in their own way with Martin Luther's declaration: "For as long as a man is convinced that he can do something for his own salvation, he retains his self-confidence and does not completely despair. For this reason he does not humble himself before God, but asserts himself, or at least hopes and wishes for opportunity, time, and work in order finally to attain his salvation. But he who never doubts that all depends on the will of God, despairs completely of helping himself . . . but awaits an act of God, he is nearest to grace and salvation."[1]

The sacred source of this arrested and hence only partial fragment of the core drama of life must above all seek power to possess, command, and judge us. Any such fragment is in fact fragile. Believers in a different manifestation of emanation as a way of life, for example, may feel proudly inspired to destroy ours—or vice versa. Let us witness, for example, the Thirty Years War between Protestants and Catholics. The sacred sources of the other three ways of life also may succeed in inspiring us instead. These pose additional threats to the power of emanation.

The number of sinners and dissenters was never small. People in the service of emanation as a way of life therefore also tried to enforce god's power and to help create archetypal barriers to threats to that power by extending hierarchic emanational relations throughout society—beginning with kings and popes to priests and family patriarchs—emanational power one cannot or must not dare to imagine questioning.[2] Jews, Christians, and Muslims also tried to reinforce this kind of emanational yielding through an alliance with the more powerful groups within the State.

The State—however much its head is experienced as a prime figure in a chain of emanations—is itself most deeply in the service of incoherence, but therefore can more easily use subjection and not rely solely upon emanation. For Jews after the destruction of the Second Temple, that kind of alliance was no longer possible—though the words of the prophets in the Bible tell us that this alliance had seldom worked well earlier when an elite hereditary line of priests often allied itself with powerful Jews, or even with foreign rulers who had conquered the land. Muslims, as we saw in Chapter 4, were also moved again and again by rival family and tribal loyalties—archetypal stories of emanation not intended by the Prophet Muhammad to be constituent parts of the new Community of Believers.

However powerful any sacred container is meant by its source to be, its partial character, thanks to its arrest in the core drama of life, renders it in fact vulnerable. To preserve and indeed reinforce its power, it frequently also allies itself with the sacred source of deformation. Consequently, none of the three monotheisms speak or act only through one voice within one way of life.

It would take many, many pages to cite from the Jewish and Christian Bibles all the examples of deformation enacted or commanded by the monotheistic sacred source. In the Christian Bible, see especially the apocalyptic end of all sinners

---

1. Martin Luther, "On the Enslaved Will," cited in Ernst Cassirer, *The Philosophy of the Enlightenment*, 140. In June, 1998, the Catholic Church agreed with the Lutheran Church that salvation comes only through our belief in god's grace and not from our good work. (*The New York Times*, June 26, 1998).

2. Pope Gregory XVI, in his encyclical *Mirari Vos* (1832), still strongly condemned republicanism and democracy. Even the writers of the Jewish and Christian Bibles were deeply influenced by the already prevailing chains of emanation, and often referred to god as Lord and King of the universe.

in the Book of Revelation.[3] In the Jewish Bible, in the days of Noah, god killed through a flood all people except Noah's family and all animals except two of each kind who joined Noah on his ark. Why? Because "the sons of God had married as many daughters of men as they chose . . . and had children by them." And God also "regretted having made man on the earth" because they were wicked.[4] In the book of Job, Satan enters into the presence of god and receives his permission to punish a righteous man, Job, in order to test his loyalty to god.[5]

This sort of treatment at god's pleasure is not just in the Book of Job: "Because of you, we were done to death all day long and we are treated as sheep for slaughter. Bestir yourself, Lord: Why do you sleep?"[6] "I am Yahweh, and there is no other; I form the light and I create the darkness; I make well-being, and I create disaster; I, Yahweh do all these things."[7] "I wound and I heal; there is no rescue from my grasp."[8] The mystification that is intended to prevent our questioning any actions of that God says, "The sacred source of emanation works in mysterious ways." Unlike us, that source is all-powerful and all-knowing, hence we must accept what that source wants of us as a single web of life, for "you shall love the Lord, your God, with all your heart, and with all your soul, and with all your strength."[9]

All three monotheistic manifestations of emanation—and not they alone—also taught compassionate love. It existed within such communities, but was seldom the most influential theme of life. But any story of emanation diminishes our being. Neither the source of emanation nor its embodiment can truly come to know itself; we are no longer open to the full realities of life or able truly to understand them. Emanation thus always diminishes both the sacred source and human beings even when it empowers both in certain ways.

How can we explain the fact that a sacred source which seeks its way of life to be preserved forever has inspired so many different manifestations of emanation as a way of life and also inspired a new one while the old one still exists? For example, among Jews, the sacred source of emanation inspired Christianity and then among Catholic Christians inspired Protestantism—while also persisting in inspiring adherence to the old way. In fact, the sacred source of emanation also dwells in a cosmos of continuous creation. To cite only a few successive parts of one sacred

---

3. On Satan in early Christian times, see the splendidly revealing book: Elaine H. Pagels, *The Origin of Satan*.

4. Genesis 6:1–7.

5. Job came to know that "God has put me in the wrong." But when he also said, "I know that my redeemer lives" (Job 19: 16, 25), no transformation took place. God instead restored to Job several times more in number family members and property which Satan had destroyed.

6. Psalm 44: 22–23.

7. Isaiah 45: 6–7.

8. Deuteronomy 32:39. The Koran states that god will punish sinners severely, but does not speak of other threats.

9. Deuteronomy 6:5.

text, in the Hebrew Bible, that source tells quite different things to Adam and Eve, Abraham, Jacob, Moses, and Isaiah.

Why different ways of emanation? Because individuals in different cultures are ready to hear only what they are prepared to hear. Why a new way while the old way still persists? Because all emanational ways are fragile and can begin to die, and as long as people in changing times still seek certainty of belief, they will listen anew to this source offering such certainty.

We also need to explain why no monotheistic way of life began, or else had great trouble beginning, as an emanational way of life. Moses received not only the Ten Commandments but also many rules by which Jews were to live their lives. In the name of this new way and to enforce it, Moses had three thousand Jews killed because they had made and worshipped a golden calf while he was on Mount Sinai.[10] And later, god killed 250 Jews who rebelled against Moses' leadership.[11] Yet god found neither Moses nor any of the Jews who had spent forty years in the desert obedient enough—hence they were unworthy of entering the Promised Land. And after their descendants entered it, few obeyed the law; ten of the twelve tribes departed from the land, and soon Jews of Israel and Judea went to war with each other again and again. The Torah as the authoritative version of the Bible, and the even more detailed rules of the Talmud and Midrash drawn from it or added to it, emerged only about a thousand years after the Jews entered the Promised Land.

At least until the Catholic Church gained in power through the support of the Roman Emperor beginning in the fourth century, Christ's message had been interpreted in many different ways, including a transforming one. Muslims developed no sacred law until two centuries after Muhammad's death, and then in four different schools of interpretation, not to speak of Shiite heretics or of Sufis—the latter, Muslims concerned with transformation, who formed the majority for many centuries.

What is the difference between an emanational inspiration and its further development in various ways, including as an emanational way of life? Since this is a cosmos of continuous creation at all levels of being, we constantly hear, through Act I Scene 2 of emanation (regardless of where we are also located in the core drama of life), new inspirations from four different sacred sources. But since it first reaches us in the form of emanation—or seemingly as an emanation—we cannot yet really understand what this inspiration means. Even if it is in fact an inspiration of transformation, we cannot come fully to understand until we have freed ourselves of present dramas and ways of life that limit us and until we have tried it out in practice with our neighbors.

If it is indeed an inspiration from the sacred source of emanation, we are not being asked truly to understand, but to believe it forever. But any one person may

10. Exodus 32.
11. Numbers 16.

not hear enough inspirations to organize a whole way of life in which all dramas and hence all actions are in its service. It required much collaboration between believers—in the face also of much conflict—to organize the three monotheisms, each as an emanational way of life. Believers may also be inspired anew to re-form and reinforce their emanational way of life, as St. Augustine did. Without such a way of life, believers may turn their inspiration into an attractive fragment in the service of a life of fragments, or let go of it entirely.

Emanation as a way of life has existed all over the world for thousands of years, so there is much evidence for our analysis of it. Today, that way of life is not yet dead, but it is dying everywhere. Why? Because it does not truly permit believers to deal with fundamentally new questions or experiment with fundamentally new answers—the basic challenge especially of our time. It also cannot compete with the great gains of power for the more powerful in the service of the life of fragments. Aspects of emanation are therefore at most becoming insulating or additional fragments in the service of the life of fragments. No new manifestations of emanation as a way of life can deal with this crisis, but movements of deformation pretend increasingly to be able to empower believers to restore their past—however historically inaccurate that "past" might be. However, the dying of emanation as a way of life does not also put an end to all emanational relationships to archetypal dramas, persons, and ideas, though it increasingly calls them into question.

JOINING WITH THE SACRED SOURCE THAT INSPIRES FRAGMENTS WHILE BELIEVING THAT THERE IS NO SUCH SOURCE

Most of the world has now entered into a life of fragments without knowing of any sacred source that inspires its underlying structures, dynamics, meaning, values, and purposes. Indeed, within this way of life, we cannot know the ultimate meaning and purpose of anything. If we think of the sacred at all, we see it at most as another fragment. As the Dean of the Woodrow Wilson School of Public and International Affairs of Princeton University said in the 1980s when asked by protesting students why the School taught nothing about ethics, "You can find out about ethics by going to Sunday School."[12] Incoherence is a more and more frequent experience that fewer and fewer people, in contrast to the past, hope to overcome through repentance and purification.

But there is a sacred source that inspires—through our archetypal relationship of emanation with it—our submission (for a time) to the powerful whom it is promising or already profitable to follow, or else our rebellion against them. This

---

12. Since then, the Woodrow Wilson School has been offering a course, "Ethics and Public Policy," to discuss different points of views on different issues.

is a sacred source that also inspires us to create new fragments that enlarge our knowledge and our control—a sacred source that also inspires us to idolize some of these fragments or its personifications. Who is this sacred source? The Devil—but not the Devil as defined in the service of emanation.[13] Nor is this the Devil of popular lore who runs around in red tights with a pitchfork. No, this is a sacred source who possesses us and inspires us to gather more fragments of power in our haste to acquire security in an increasingly insecure world.

We end up not only with "the ephemeral, the fugitive, the contingent,"[14] but in our focus on gaining power and its rewards, we are inspired to believe in and enact what are currently among the most powerful archetypal dramas of this Devil—being a capitalist and being a competent specialist in the service of a life of fragments. And as we already said in Chapter 5, many of the powerless share the same sacred belief: There is no way of escaping our present fate unless we become powerful. To prevent that additional competition, the powerful often resort to a form of deformation, treating the less powerful and powerless as lesser or invisible human beings. Individual freedom remains unevenly distributed, even in democratic liberal states. But life remains anxious even for the most successful. This Devil will inspire new rebels again and again and even the greatest success gives us nothing more than a fragment.

The State helps to maintain some order lest the self-interested compete for power as if they were all gods—as if it were a case of polytheism on earth. (But some global corporations manage to overcome many State restrictions.) The nation-state also serves to protect us—but often also to separate us—from our neighbors beyond our borders, but nowhere has the nation-state served to create a genuine community.[15]

When we therefore, in moments of freedom and happiness, say to ourselves, "I want to be myself! I am happy to be myself!" we still have not overcome the partial nature of our being or our solitude in this way of life of fragments that offers no grounds for understanding, compassionate love, and justice.

In one of the most successful societies in the service of this Devil, according to a Gallup poll, one in five teenagers said he or she seriously considered suicide; half of the teens believe they will be mugged at some point in their lives; and one-third of them believe they will be shot or stabbed. More than half of the teens said they knew of violent gangs in school who would go after minorities, gays, and lesbians, while 23 percent of the teens admitted they admired Adolf Hitler and the Nazi party. George Gallup Jr. said, "Young people live in a world of fear

---

13. We already described this Devil in Chapter 5.
14. This is Baudelaire's description of modernity.
15. See my chapter, "A Theory for Transforming the Self: Moving Beyond the Nation-State," in Stephen Brim Woolpert, Christa Daryl Slaton, and Edward W. Schwerin, *Transformational Politics: Theory, Study, and Practice*.

and uncertainty."[16] No mere calculation of power or reason holds this way of life together. We are also joined to that Devil.

THE SACRED SOURCE OF DEFORMATION

Just as we described a Devil who is not of the biblical variety, so we now present Satan also in a different vein, and even much more briefly, since we already dealt with this sacred source at length in Chapter 6. Whenever we feel vulnerable and therefore search for greater power when our present power is threatened, this Satan can inspire us to diminish the humanity of others and ourselves even to the point of death.[17]

BEING IN TRANSFORMATION—PARTICIPATING WITH OUR DEEPEST SACRED SOURCE

We now face a sacred source who has never inspired us to pray, "Thy will be done on Earth as it is in Heaven"—a sacred source who has no need of servants and disciples, but of friends and lovers. When we are in need and also realize that it is our present way of life that deprives us in our current situation, we will hear from the deepest sacred source of our being. We will hear also from the more anxious other three sacred sources (because they are narcissistic and partial) who will try to re-inspire us to believe in them and in their ways. But the deepest sacred source asks us to risk trust in participating with it creatively, critically, and caringly in a journey through the core drama of life.

Any human being can gain the capacity to free herself or himself to go on this journey. Our new inspiration leads us next into incoherence—but not into a way of life of fragments in which more and more people are experiencing archetypal relationships of incoherence without yet knowing why or blaming themselves or particular others. We do not now in incoherence enter into the hands of the Devil but are moving with the deepest source of our being who is journeying with us through all Acts and Scenes of the core drama.

That source not only inspired us and gave us new capacity and courage to enter into incoherence in a fundamentally different way, as a rebellion against our earlier position for the sake of something new and better. That source also inspired us to recognize the archetypal drama and way of life of which we were a part in our actual relationships, and to empty ourselves of all three bonds—to reach the deepest incoherence, in order to move on. We sacrifice our previous partial self

---

16. *The Trenton Times,* November 10, 1999.

17. Am I saying that there is a Satan or a Devil? No, I use these terms once again to symbolize the sacred force of each of these ways of life.

in this way, but we do not reach chaos. Instead we reach an essential, emancipating moment in the core drama of life. While we thus break with previous parts of our self, we do not surrender or annihilate all of our self. By thus emptying our self, we are free to reach the deepest depth of our being and to tune in, with our newly emerging ego, to what in the next Act arises from that depth. Despite all the incoherence we experienced in Act II, we were not alone, but even then were participating in the realization of a living and just truth.

All politics—including our political relationship with the sacred—is not only about what we need. Politics is about what we can and need to do *together*. We would be of no help to the deepest source of our being or to our self if our arrival in Act III were based on no new understanding and experience. If either we or our deepest source knew the outcome in advance, it would be calculated manipulation. We both participate in transforming both of us. We are not only materially concrete; we can test the significance and value of the concrete by discovering the sacred source which the concrete is manifesting.

The deepest sacred source is not what Aristotle called it, an "unmoved mover." It does not participate with us as a "Father" or as "King of the Universe" or as a maker or enforcer of specific fixed laws. Our deepest source is not entirely mysterious and unfathomable, nor is it perfect. It is not an undifferentiated source. The deepest sacred source needs all four faces of our being to discover and test in concrete practice what is indeed fundamentally better than what exists now.

There is no fusion between our self and our deepest sacred source, nor do we become its emanational incarnation. We do not become a god. But bi-unity comes fully into being as we enter into Act III. Now we can fully hear and understand and enact all four faces and the deepest source of our being in a particular drama of transformation—not in everything. But we are much more likely, now that we are stronger, freer, and more insightful, to proceed through the core drama of life again and again.

Act III does not constitute salvation, but the fruition of theory and practice—of understanding, love, and justice—with respect not only to an actual problem but also to an entire archetypal story and way of life. We have been strengthened by learning how to respond to a beginning we had not anticipated, a middle that emptied us, and an ending that surprised us, enlightened us, and nourished us. We have come to recognize that we were moving in understanding, loving, and just bi-unity with the deepest source of our being—each growing within the other. Through such an experience of bi-unity, truth makes us free. In the stories in which we participate in transformation, we thus become whole beings in our personal, political, historical, and sacred faces and in our depth—a wholeness which we seek to help our neighbors realize and experience through their being, in theory and practice. Thus we are able to love our neighbors as ourselves.

Wholeness is not perfection. It is a fundamentally better capacity for participating in a drama of transformation. *Capacity* as a word is derived from *capex*, meaning vessel. But we are not an empty vessel at this point. We are a vessel filled with our whole being, concretely and in depth—both interconnected. Wholeness is not power, domination, or control by us or by our sacred source. The deepest sacred source does not want—cannot use—servants. That source needs, as Ibn Arabi told us, friends and lovers—free to criticize and create anew as participants in transformation.[18]

We have been discussing a sacred source not invented by us but experienced and reported on before, though never as the deepest source of the core drama of life and its four fundamentally different choices. We shall now cite only a few of the scarce reflections of the deepest sacred source in the Jewish and Christian Bibles. The other three sources are reported much more frequently in these certified texts (in contrast to the Gospels found at Nag Hammadi)[19] because their editors intended to create a community in the service of emanation.

The following citations open the door to transformation but they do not fully tell how, or else they seem to simplify the way. For example, to free our selves to come to love our own true being and hence to love our neighbors as ourselves, helping them to free themselves to love and be loved is crucial in our experience of transformation. Love is thus emphasized in both the Jewish and Christian Bibles, but without adequate explanation of the necessary process of reaching such love. "You must love your neighbor as yourself," we read in the Jewish Bible, followed just a few verses later by the statement: "If a stranger lives with you in your land, do not molest him. You must count him as one of your own countrymen and love him as yourself—for you were once strangers yourselves in Egypt."[20]

One Jew put the question to Jesus: "Master, which is the greatest commandment of the Law?" Jesus said, "You must love the Lord your God with all your heart, with all your soul, and with all your mind. This is the greatest and the first commandment. The second resembles it: You must love your neighbor as yourself. On these commands hang the whole Law and the Prophets also!"[21] Love of God, ourselves, and our neighbors are what is needed—not obedience.

---

18. I have learned a great deal about transformation from Ibn Arabi, especially through the works of Henry Corbin and James Morris. I am deeply grateful to all three of them who teach me ever anew whenever I read again what I thought I had understood before. See especially Henry Corbin, *Creative Imagination in the Sufism of Ibn Arabi*.

19. See especially, James McConkey Robinson, Marvin W. Meyer, and Institute for Antiquity and Christianity Coptic Gnostic Library, *The Nag Hammadi Library in English*; and Elaine H. Pagels, *The Gnostic Gospels*.

20. Leviticus 19:18; and 19: 33–34.

21. Matthew 22: 35–40.

Paul offers a beautiful long passage that begins, "If I have all the eloquence of men or of angels, but speak without love, I am simply a gong booming or a cymbal clashing.... Love ... delights in the truth.... In short, there are three things that last: faith, hope and love; and the greatest of these is love."[22]

These are not the only passages on love in these two Bibles, but never are we told of the actual process of transformation by which we reach such love.[23]

There are references in the Christian Bible to the need for us to be born anew—not to be crucified but to empty ourselves of our present spirit so that the Holy Spirit may enter us—but here, too, the process is still left unclear. We are not told how we can also come to understand anew and what living underlying patterning forces we need to understand. To acknowledge our "sins" is not yet to understand the great burden of such shaping patterns when they are only partial—but also possessive and warping—in nature. Jesus said, "I am the way." But he did not mean we all need to be crucified and resurrected—or to believe in him—to be saved. To die again and again to be reborn again and again—that way is not explained in the Christian Bible (or in the Jewish Bible concerning the significance of leaving slavery and emptying yourself while journeying through the desert) as much as we need to understand it for the sake of love and justice.[24]

That scarcity in the texts allowed people of power to emerge who authorized and enforced interpretations that were intended to keep people within an emanational container. They say, "We are in charge of baptism. We will clean you just once so that you will receive grace, and we will punish you if you sin against the sacred law as we have defined it."

TO UNDERSTAND YOUR SACRED SOURCE IS FUNDAMENTALLY TO UNDERSTAND YOURSELF

About a thousand years ago, theorists and practitioners of transformation expanded the advice of Socrates, "Know yourself," to say, "To know yourself is to know your Lord."[25] I have in this work reopened this inquiry to learn how each of us can come

---

22. I Corinthians 13: 1–13.

23. Many are the references to wisdom in both Bibles (see especially Proverb 8), but gaining wisdom is never really explained and often is reduced to obedience.

24. In our time, drawing upon this theory of transformation, Pastor Oscar S. Suarez of the Cosmopolitan Protestant Church of Manila, Philippines, offers a deeply insightful analysis of *Protestantism and Authoritarian Politics: The Politics of Repression and the Future of Ecumenical Witness in the Philippines*. It not only helps us profoundly to understand where Christianity stands now but also how we can transform being Christian.

25. Alexander Altmann, *Studies in Religious Philosophy and Mysticism*, 1–40 ("The Delphic Maxim in Medieval Islam and Judaism").

not only to know but to understand which of the four sacred sources now joins our unique personal being in forming our way of life and the stories in its service. I would now say that to understand that sacred source and its role in forming us is fundamentally to understand ourselves.

But the deepest source of our being is no Lord. I use the word Lord with a capital *L* because these are sacred sources who wish literally to lord it over us and to possess us. We have no capacity on our own to resist them. I use the word god with a lowercase *g* when speaking of the deepest sacred source of transformation because this source is not all powerful and all knowing as the Lords of the other three ways of life claim to be. This is a god who needs us and invites us to participate with the personal, political, historical, and sacred faces of our being in the task of finishing creation in love and justice.

In Act III of the core drama of life, our new concreteness comes also to be newly connected—in bi-unity—with our deepest sacred depths. This is our most important choice in life. Where we have three different Lords inspiring us to remain within a fragment of the core drama of life, and commanding us to be a partial self, the deepest source of our being guides us through the core drama of life so that in fact we come to understand and love ourselves and to be with and love our neighbors as our selves. The deepest sacred source of our being, is not, as some Buddhists believe, beyond form or forming.[26]

In the cosmos of continuous creation, we can and will hear, especially in any crisis, from four different sacred sources. They are free– but only within their nature—to try to reach and move us. We are free—but only within the present limits of our way of life, unless we free ourselves also of these limits—to respond and act. No sacred source has the power or capacity to alter human lives without our participation as shaped by our present way of life—unless we are ready no longer to adhere to it. No sacred source can stop any holocaust as long as we remain enclosed within our partial way of life and cannot therefore care about or tune in to the dangers for the potential victims—or even they cannot therefore envision the danger to come from the followers of deformation.

We create in the image of our present creator who created or recreated us in that image. But we also, in each way of life, participate in any creation with the uniqueness of our personal face and our other three shared faces. In the service of three of the sacred sources, creation is above all devoted to the rise of new power or the reinforcement of established power, not of capacity. Hence our participation with these three sources involves no bi-unity.

---

26. *Nirvana*, the term for the highest state a Buddhist can reach, means "beyond forms." Beyond which forms? All forms—including archetypal dramas that can help us bring the fundamentally new and better into being?

Most of us in our time live in exile, even if we have not been forced to flee our native land—even when we now live in our Holy Land. Most of us have not freed ourselves to become truly ourselves and be completely with our neighbors in understanding, love, and justice. Three sacred Lords keep us away from this sacred reality, this sacred truth. Instead we have arrested ourselves—exiled ourselves—into their ways of life, thus diminishing the four faces of our being. We keep ourselves separated—partial. And when our fragment is threatened, as is so likely under these conditions, we ally ourselves with deformation to repress ourselves and to diminish or put an end to others. Exile is the principal source of scarcity in human life—whatever our present power—because it keeps us from participating in the journey through the core drama of life, and thus we also remain crippled in our capacity to put an end to oppression. To empty ourselves (in Act II Scene2 of the drama of transformation) is not to move into exile but to allow us to complete our exodus into a fundamentally more promising land.

We may accept our present life as fate. The contrast between fate and destiny is similar to the contrast between belief and faith. Let us have faith in risking trust in journeying toward a fundamentally new and better destiny.

Our theory of transformation allows us to analyze, to understand, and to connect with the deepest sacred source of our being, and to analyze and understand what it means to connect with the alternative three Lords who command us to be partial or destructive instead. I do not know more about sacred sources than what is revealed to us by the existence and our experience of the core drama of life. Is there a source beyond what I have called the deepest sacred source of our being? I do not see how any of us could know. If it were absolute—meaning already complete, detached, disengaged, absolved—why would it have left us in our present condition? If the deepest sacred source we can experience were already perfect, why would it bother with us? As Einstein said, "The eternal mystery of the universe is its comprehensibility."

But there are vital things we do not yet understand. The four sacred sources participate, each in their own way, not only with human beings but with all of creation. Our universe has already existed for thirteen and a half billion years, and our own solar system for four and a half billion years—but human beings like us only for about fifty thousand years. For every human being, there also exist two hundred million insects. What kind of participation could the four sacred sources experience before we arrived? Why are there black holes, earthquakes, floods, volcanoes, hurricanes, and viruses—to mention only a few deeply troubling facts?

But we can say in the light of our rather recent creation as human beings that it is not surprising that transformation as a way of life has been sought less often still than the seemingly total security of emanation. The recent pervasiveness of incoherence may well scare more people into deformation—or raise our awareness of what now renders us biased and incomplete and what we need to search for anew. Transformation is not dying in the abyss since the few who have so far tried it did not reject it and send it into the abyss.

Could human beings all over the world, without any opportunity of initially discussing it with each other, have come to agree millennia ago to enact the same core drama of life and its four fundamentally different choices? That is why we have been discussing our relationship with four fundamentally different sacred sources and how and why only one of them participates in our journey toward the fundamentally new and better. The fact of this relationship is the basis for the theory of transformation that we will explore further in the next chapter.

15

What Kind of a Theory Is This?

As we have seen and as we can all experience, this theory is based upon the discovery that there is a core drama within which we live at every moment of our life, and through which we can also participate in reaching the fundamentally new and better. To free ourselves to understand this core drama also enables us to become truly and wholly a human being and to help our neighbors to move through that process as well.

Understanding this theory of transformation is also based on the discovery of living underlying patterning forces that shape the structure and dynamics as well as the meaning, values, and purposes of the stories and relationships of our life. That we can choose between only four fundamentally different ways of life within the core drama is an empirical statement; the existence of a fifth way could undo the entire theory. Thanks to this theory, we can come to connect ourselves wholly to ourselves and with others through understanding, love, and justice—instead of relating to ourselves and others through various forms of power, thus turning ourselves and our neighbors into fragments instead.

At this point, no other theory allows us within a single overarching view to understand and evaluate so many different aspects, interconnections, and disconnections of our life and hence to make our life choices much more consciously—both individually and together. This theory analyzes our ways of connecting or disconnecting the personal, political, historical, and sacred faces of our being—within and between archetypal stories and ways of life—with radically different sacred sources of our being.

This theory is always connected to, and tested by, practice. It is about true realization—through understanding and practice. But as we have seen, we cannot basically solve any problem in a fundamentally better way unless we also free ourselves to understand and choose not only new concrete manifestations but also their new living underlying patterning forces. There is nothing abstract in this theory of transformation. It clarifies our alternatives concretely and to our depths, and hence is a critical, creative theory of participation. It is a vital, workable alternative to our being possessed by any combination of the three other ways of life which we can also truly analyze only from the perspective of transformation.

Only this theory can explain what and why we miss aspects of our being and what richness we can experience instead. This theory is radical in the sense that it deals with the roots of our being and frees us to transform them and their concrete manifestations.

This chapter was originally intended to deal with the ontology and epistemology at the base of this theory. But as more and more philosophers became adherents of poststructuralism, we further lost any shared sense of being and we said that our prevailing language is corrupt. I agree with poststructuralists who have demonstrated that past and present theories constitute defenses of existing power structures or seek to create new power structures. But this theory of transformation rejects all forms of power and shows us instead how to free and experience our capacity for understanding, love, and justice based on fundamentally better grounds of being. We need not only to empty ourselves of the dramas and ways of life that have possessed us (as we do in Act II Scene 2 of the drama of transformation). We need also to be inspired anew—critically, creatively, and ethically—with respect to our foundations and our concrete actions.[1]

I am not emotionally detached in the presentation of this theory. This theory is neither subjective nor objective. It is true about real life, including the living underlying patterning forces and the sacred sources of our being. Because the theory covers more aspects of life, interconnects more aspects of life, and clarifies our ultimate choices, it opens more tests for the truth of this theory. Our lives test this theory. This is not *transformationalism*, and in this cosmos of continuous creation, there is no *final* theory of transformation.

We shall now explore how other modern theories intrinsically reflect the limitations of the life of fragments. Thereafter, we shall further examine the core of the theory of transformation.

---

1. I am deeply grateful for the enlightening discussions with Aryeh Botwinick who gave me a greater insight into the underpinnings of poststructuralism and postmodernism. See Aryeh Botwinick, *Postmodernism and Democratic Theory*; and *Skepticism, Belief, and the Modern: Maimonides to Nietzsche*, *Contestations*.

THE INTRINSIC LIMITS OF ALL THEORIES ARISING WITHIN A LIFE OF FRAGMENTS

I will not debate with any past or present theorist. I take this approach because of two obstacles: I would have to insert at least—*at least*—three volumes of discussion; and there are inherent difficulties in any communication between fundamentally different ways of life—a problem certainly also for many readers. The advantage is that we can focus on real, fundamental obstacles and cite a few examples.

No theory originating within a life of fragments can offer us the ultimate truth, meaning, value, and purpose of anything. We cannot come to know such matters within this way of life. Hence we are not supposed to challenge its theories upon such grounds, but only upon its errors or its inadequacies of efficiency, data, or rational calculation. Most of us are not qualified to challenge theories in this life of fragments for we are not specialists within that particular fragment. (We also cannot yet understand what is missing in ourselves and in our life of fragments—if indeed we understand even those fragments.)

But the present possessors of currently powerful fragments are inspired by this way of life above all to defend and enlarge their power. This is true in the field of the sciences as well as economics and politics.[2] They may desire more knowledge but not more understanding. They may try rational calculation especially through cost-benefit and immediate use-effect analyses—but not seek the truth about fundamental problems and realities. The greater freedom of inquiry and analysis within the life of fragments—in contrast to emanation as a way of life—is thus limited by the people of power and also by its underlying limitations.

To illustrate a few of these generalizations, I shall now cite just two examples of how theories in the service of a life of fragments intrinsically limit our capacity to analyze fundamental changes—but I know of no exceptions. Harvard University Professor Talcott Parson told us that there is no use trying to explain the transformation of a system. He wrote, "A general theory of the processes of change of social systems is not possible in the present state of knowledge. The reason is very simply that such a theory would imply complete knowledge of the laws of process of the system and this knowledge we do not possess. The theory of change in the structure of the social system must, therefore, be a theory of particular sub-processes of change *within* such systems, not of the overall processes of change *of* the systems as systems."[3] Some pages later, Parsons adds, "When such a theory [concerning the change of systems] is available, the millennium for the social sciences will have

---

2. In regard to the sciences and resistance to transformation, see Thomas S. Kuhn, *The Structure of Scientific Revolutions*.

3. Talcott Parsons, *The Social System*, 486.

arrived. This will not come in our time, and probably never."[4] By contrast, we have not offered structural-functional systems, but ways of life that are aspects of the core drama of life and the archetypal dramas in their service.

Theories arising from fragments of life acknowledge that there is also a context of discovery, but it is left unexplored. The focus of theories is on the context of verification. Hence the three Acts of the journey of transformation toward the fundamentally new and better are not analyzed or understood. For example, William James writes, "If the grace of God miraculously operates, it probably operates through the subliminal door, then. But just how anything operates in this region is still unexplained, and we shall do well now to say good-bye to the process of transformation altogether—leaving it, if you like, a good deal of a psychological or theological mystery."[5]

This life of fragments has produced also many divisions within academic disciplines that make it professionally impossible to explore, as we have, the interconnections between the personal, political, historical, and sacred faces of our being within four radically different ways of life. The point instead is to be a competent specialist in, say, political science—meaning at least in politics, though not also history or sociology or economics or anthropology or psychology? The point is to be a competent specialist in certain aspects (not all aspects) of normative political theory or formal political theory or comparative politics or international politics or presidential politics or constitutional law or public administration or voting behavior in American politics or feminist politics or Latino politics or African-American politics or urban politics or state politics or something else. Yes, we need competent specialists in every discipline, but as we discussed in the chapter on the archetype of being competent, we who are competent need to understand also to connect our transforming work with the transforming work of others to achieve both concrete and underlying understanding of our life so that we may live in communities with compassionate love and justice.

As we further illustrate the fragments that underlie and are intended to refine theories arising within a life of fragments, we shall recognize how such theories select fragments that help us sharpen our knowledge—but also help us to ignore vital aspects of life, including its fundamental problems and their solutions. We seek to get control of the most efficient causes and effects of action. Instrumental rationality, yes; empathy, no! Efficient assembly lines, yes; the human beings who work there, no—unless they have become a powerful-enough interest group.

Gross national product is seen as an objective fact; evaluations of the justice of its distribution are thought to be merely subjective. The powerful in each

---

4. Ibid., 534. According to Prof. Victor Lidz, however, Parsons's views on social change as reflected in his book, *Societies: Evolutionary and Comparative Perspectives,* dramatically changed.

5. William James, *The Varieties of Religious Experience: A Study in Human Nature*, 270.

field focus on the objective; the subjective is only a private matter—a realm to be reached through manipulation or propaganda or advertising, but only for the sake of increasing the controlling efficiency of the wielders of power. *Subjective* thus becomes a deeply distorting and minimizing synonym for the unique personal face of our being and its sacred source. Democratic liberalism seems to enhance our freedom by declaring that all are entitled to their subjectivity—however unobjective, or even irrational, or merely emotional. All are thus also entitled to their privacy until they challenge our self-interest or that of the objective order.

That objective order of the powerful uses public and private corporate bureaucracy to eliminate the subjective as it deals—not with human beings, but—impersonally with objective categories, such as welfare recipients, customers, safety supervision, etc. Bureaucrats must not ask in whose self-interest their rules function or whether the needs of that human being have been met. Bureaucrats respond solely from within the rules and boundaries of their official positions.

When theorists in the service of fragments as a way of life do decide to examine the subjective, they try to do it objectively—that is, in an intrinsically alien way. We thus cannot discover who the other human beings (or we ourselves) truly are.

Many more fragments of knowledge have been organized by theorists in our currently dominant way of life. What all of them share in common is that the *other* in each case remains cut off from any analysis within the governing theory, and hence is put in a relationship of incoherence with—of cleavage from—the only subject now present. Consider facts, but not values; consider the secular, but not the sacred; consider the rational, but never mind what is not rational. Consider the problems of *our* nation, of *our* culture, of *our* gender, but never mind others unless they threaten *our* power.

Pragmatic, analytical, and postmodern philosophers, each for reasons of their own, tell us that we can only look at particular cases. We can only offer generalizations as to why we cannot generalize. Many more are the people who, in the present way of life, are simply reluctant—or do not know how—to generalize, for they see everything as contingent, transient, or providential.

Nonetheless, it is no small fact that at its best, our way of life of fragments has greatly increased our freedom and our knowledge, our power to do harm and to do good, and our prosperity, though not our power to overcome the poverty of the great majority.

It is also no small fact that, within this way of life, we all live incomplete and biased lives, unable, while we are entwined with it, to recognize and overcome our deep limits in all realms of life, including our thinking about any subject. For we are connected emotionally to a way of life—not a link therefore that we feel free to examine. Nothing in this way of life—not any thought or action—can therefore be conclusively rational or value neutral. However much power we have attained, we have arrested ourselves within Act II Scene 1 of the core drama of life. Hence any expression of it intrinsically and necessarily keeps us from understanding or expressing the true reality of our being, or of any other form of being, or of our four fundamentally different choices in the structure, dynamics, meaning, values, and purposes of our life.

All new discoveries—theoretical, scientific, or empirical—are limited in this way of life. Yes, we empty ourselves of concrete relationships and of a former archetypal drama in Act II Scene 2, but then we return to express and test our discovery in Act II Scene 1—not in Act III of transformation. We re-form by discovering or importantly changing a fragment of life.

Our critical analysis of the limitations of theories in the service of the currently dominant way of life is not simply based on the perspective of a different kind of theory, but on the discovery of the reality of the core drama of life from which such a fundamental difference in understanding and practice is based. This also means that we cannot fully understand the underlying grounds and consequences of our present archetypal limitations until we become more conscious of their burden and constraints and therefore free ourselves from them.

This theory of transformation is different from all theories arising out of the other three ways of life because it is based upon the discovery of the core drama of life which we experience at every moment. Hence it offers not merely another objective or subjective opinion but the truth about reality—as much as we have yet thus learned about both. It is not a theory that is culture-bound, that seeks to preserve or build a new power structure or that treats the concrete as merely contingent—or that offers knowledge of the concrete solely as the product of efficient causes. It does not replace old model boxes with new model boxes, but reveals the grounds upon which we can make four radically different choices in every aspect—personal, political, historical, and sacred—of our life. In every choice, not just relationships and dramas but an entire way of life is at stake. This is a theory about how understanding, love, and justice can—or cannot—arise from our practice.

This theory of transformation also offers more understanding of more underlying patterning connections and disconnections in the cosmos or human relations than any other theory—and thus of the context and choices of our life and our actions. Only this theory allows us fully to understand all four ways of life and hence our most fundamental choices, not as an issue of preference—but of testable reality, truth, and justice.

16

On Justice

How can we know when the fundamentally new, or else what we have long been nourishing, is also fundamentally better at this moment? What is justice? The cosmos of human relations is renewed and nourished—and exists most justly—by virtue of the process of transformation. This cosmos would not exist long without it. Any act—by us or by the sacred—is unjust whenever it prevents us from entering this process, or holds us under arrest in the course of it, or ejects us from it.

We build our discussion of justice upon the foundations we have been exploring in the preceding chapters. We now ask this: What basic ethical choices do the underlying realities of the cosmos of human relations offer us? Why choose transformative justice? What keeps us from choosing transformation and leads us instead to pursue or accept partial justice, injustice, or even evil, that is to say, destructive death? What leads us to be blind to injustice—or to inflict it, and even evil, upon others or ourselves?

Transformation is the core drama of the cosmos of human relations. The other three ways of life, as we have seen, are mere fragments of this drama. Deformation is the most dangerous of these fragments; deformation—psychic and physical violence leading us toward death—is the exit from the core drama, an exiting turned into a whole way of death.

Why is there evil and only partial justice in the world? The enactment of transformation requires a process of journeying through these three Acts. (It is no sudden miracle.) Our participation in transformation requires capacity and freedom; the freedom and capacity to understand the concrete and the underlying depths and how to break and to reconnect. If we are to have the freedom and capacity to join and break, then so must the archetypal forces that constitute this drama.

This is no puppet play. That is why there are four ultimate choices, each grounded in a radically different sacred source (as we saw in Chapters 4 and 14). This is a cosmos of continuous creation—whether for good or ill depends significantly on the nature of our participation. All four ways of life are formed entirely by our response to this central fact.

We can enact three of these ways of life—emanation, incoherence, and deformation—that are fragments of the core drama with only partial consciousness, the consciousness needed for living solely within that fragment. We can enact transformation only if we participate with growing consciousness and love together with the deepest source of our being. Transformation liberates our greatest capacity for just participation. The others limit, repress, and even destroy the capacity and freedom to move creation toward justice.

THE ARCHETYPE OF JUSTICE IN THE SERVICE OF FOUR WAYS OF LIFE

The archetypes and archetypal stories discussed in Chapters 6–13 all derive their deeper meaning, value, and structure from the underlying way of life in which they are enacted. This also holds true for justice. Justice is not an abstraction or a code of conduct or a feeling to do the right thing. Justice needs to be discovered daily in our lives as we confront the problems of people in this concrete place at this time. We need to be fully present as a whole person to be able to respond to injustice. Only in the service of transformation are we fully present and prepared to respond with the four faces of our being to intervene together with our neighbors when we face injustice.

JUSTICE IN THE SERVICE OF EMANATION

If we remain arrested in the first Act of the core drama of life we are partial selves who are capable only of practicing a partial and therefore flawed justice. What is justice in the service of emanation? Justice is whatever the ultimate source or Lord of emanation does or commands we do in this world. Justice means conforming ourselves to that sacred source's code of righteousness, usually referred to as god's will. Human beings are not entitled to decide whether what god wills is just. To be sure, people in the service of emanation are often taught that god is just, arguing the case by way of selective examples, but above all by asking us to bow to his unfathomable wisdom. We are told that it helps to please and plead with god, but god's judgment is decisive, not ours. Only the Lord of emanation as a transcendent ruler, his creation now fundamentally complete, is our true, immediate, and ultimate ruler and judge. (Or else, in the case of polytheism, that one god is Lord who has triumphed over the other gods.)

The value of practicing such justice as has been revealed to us seems clear and potent enough: obedience to sacred rules and customs and rituals and beliefs preserves the solidarity and justice of the community. The belief that final punishment and final salvation is not now to be found on this earth can serve to create some tolerance for disobedience and corruption since such people are sure to be punished in the end. But two kinds of injustice can be counted upon to be taken with utmost seriousness—the betrayal of an emanational relationship or any personal or political act that challenges the very ground of existence of our way of life.

Being confined to a sacred container is conducive to a great and deep intensity of experience of piety and serenity, and of kinship with one's fellow believers past, present, and future. Suffering and turmoil become more bearable under these conditions. The daily enactment of particular obligations and avoidance of prohibitions is, for most, not so much a compulsive adherence to particulars of behavior but expressions of loyalty and gratitude for the blessing of security against threats from outsiders and insiders, from above and below. The most able or courageous or intense adherents experience even greater rewards by dominating established personal, political, and sacred relationships not through power alone, but within a chain of emanations. They take the lead in enforcing, restoring, mediating, healing, elaborating, and refining life ordained in this way.

But the price of the injustice of emanation is too high. Emanation necessarily involves denying one's own and others' participation in continuous creation and hence in the wholeness of life. There is another high cost: the community of believers is endowed with sacred value—but this great blessing is confined exclusively to our *own* community. The outsider is at best a lesser human being; how much worse they are treated—in terms of deformation—differs among communities of believers. The injustice of emanation profoundly injures the four faces of our being. Our personal face is repressed as we ignore, often unconsciously, any doubts or questions that may arise. With our political face, we enact a politics of uncritical loyalty to all those in the golden chain of emanation. Our historical face lives the stories and traditions of the past as if there was nothing new under the sun. And our sacred face is possessed by the Lord of emanation who prevents us from reaching the deepest sacred source of our being.

All communities in the service of emanation have deeply committed views on what is good and what is evil. They are ready to punish the evildoer, but since believers possess no critical understanding of the nature of the road to destructive death, they do not know how to diminish evil, except by repressing and suppressing themselves within the limits of their beliefs—and suppressing and redeeming the sinner.

The limits are clear: Do not move beyond the established limits of our consolidation of Act I. The power of repression that constitutes an intrinsic aspect of emanation is not small. People who persist in asking why this must ultimately be our way of life, or in acting outside of its limits—and who do not stop when warned of their impiety—are rejected as a threat to the being of the entire community. Rejecting a particular outward emanation—for example, the practice of a rule or a custom, or the order of an authority figure—may in less serious instances bring only shame, but not yet sin. But rejecting the ultimate source—the Lord of emanation and its way of life—constitutes betrayal, legitimizing one's death at the hands of the source, or of those who speak in its name.

Changes in conceptions of justice do not come to an end once there has been the kind of consolidation that makes us believe that our past and present has always taken place within the same kind of sacred container. Even within emanation, life bursts forth within the not-always-predictable limits of repression and suppression in the service of the Lord of emanation—who seeks to hold us in the first Act of the core drama with the assistance of revealed texts and the solidarity and justice of the community. Despite all attempts to live within these confines, people cannot avoid the fact that the deepest source remains the source of constant creation—the source also of the interplay in which the sacred source and guardian of Act I is only one of the Lords of the ultimate stories of our lives (the source also of all those faces of the sacred we call archetypal dramas). The fact is that people continue to hear the deepest source of transformation. Guides like Moses, Jesus, and Muhammad were not the only ones to hear the source.

From the perspective of transformation, we are not fully alive until we enter into bi-unity with the deepest source. For anyone who cares about the ultimate foundations of both truth and justice, this question may be phrased this way: How can I know what the sacred source of my being asks of me when justice is at stake? This question does not ask for already established answers nor for the judgment of authorities in established codes. When I ask that question, I seek instead to discover the creative and critical double-link of reality that can come to exist between the deepest sacred source and me with respect to this problem here and now. This reality is not fully validated by the emergence of an inner linkage between the personal and the sacred but needs to be tested as well by the political and historical faces of our being and of the deepest source. It is a question that needs to be asked ever anew. No human being, however revered, is automatically or permanently attuned to the deepest source.

By contrast, we cannot hope to know and embody the source of sources directly while we remain in the service of emanation. We cannot therefore hope to know the deepest and best justice—the justice of transformation. But in the service of emanation, we cannot even hope to know the Lord of emanation directly. We have to believe that the words he has revealed (emanated) have been correctly received, correctly reported, correctly interpreted, and correctly executed here and now to produce justice. In rare instances, the power to know and embody this all-powerful Lord is reserved solely and permanently for the ruler, such as the Pharaoh, who is then regarded as superhuman. But the power of the intermediaries between the Lord of emanation and ourselves is at once ambiguous and decisive.

It is decisive. How else could we discover justice except through legitimate rulers, priests, texts, and interpreters? But their power is also ambiguous. Both of us are human; both of us bear responsibility. The authorities present themselves as links in a chain of emanations. The people may accept them as such; they may also see them as outward embodiments and wonder if they are truly the right emanations of the divine source. Contrary to the very meaning and purpose of emanation as a way of life, this vulnerability and anxiety about being, truth, and justice cannot be overcome within this way of life. This anxiety reinforces the need for certainty, and this kind of certainty reinforces anxiety. It is not possible to remain enshrined within Act I of the core drama of life without paying a price.

All emanational ways of life rest their political strength upon the fact that their single web of life is constituted as a community. How far we are in our time from immediately grasping what such a community may be—a time when the state has become the chief substitute for community, when we do not know most of the people who live with us in our apartment building, yet we speak longingly of "a community of nations."

What is an emanational community? Why do some (including some social scientists) look back nostalgically to *Gemeinschaft*—to the organic solidarity of people? Why do others (including other social scientists) look with gladness at the liberation they have experienced from such a confinement? There existed an irreconcilable tension also between these two responses from the beginning within emanational communities—another cost of living within a fragment of life.

What distinguishes communities in the service of emanation from any other networks in any other way of life is that all political and historical relationships serve to reaffirm and reinforce the already established interconnections between the four faces of our being. Consensus and solidarity arising out of established forms of collaboration and conflict, guided by and renewing a shared sense of justice: this is the heart and substance—the sacred blessing—of emanational experience. Authority figures are required primarily to serve as models, teachers, counselors, mediators, arbitrators, judges, and chief organizers for gathering and supplying resources for shared needs, and beyond the community, as leading negotiators and combatants. In many crucial ways, an emanational community governs itself through personal relationships—rather than centralized enforcers—which render solidarity immediate and vivid and construct the road to justice, even if sometimes long and controversial, into a shared enterprise always implicating more people than the accuser and the accused.

And yet emanation as a way of life, contrary to its dearest intentions, cannot offer any final consolidation of belief, solidarity, and justice. There are three fundamental issues affecting emanational justice: Who is to interpret god's will and the sacred text—and on what grounds? Who is to organize the community—and on what grounds? And how shall we respond to people within our own community who live in the other three ways of life? These are the very questions that prevent a final consolidation of any emanational way of life, and our responses to them shape the struggles over justice and its costs and consequences.

From the perspective of transformation, no idea or image about relationships inspired in us by the source of sources is the final word. Certainly, how it is to be concretely expressed and understood tomorrow can only be discovered tomorrow. But if we are inspired and thereafter possessed by other Lords, our relationships, as best as we are able, become repetitive. The task of the consolidators on this earth of living in an emanational fragment of life is to translate into authoritatively definitive thought and practice the revelations of a transcendent sacred source on whom no human being can be a final authority. How can this be done?

ORGANIZING THE JUSTICE OF EMANATION IN CATHOLIC CHRISTIANITY

In Catholic Christianity, Augustine, unlike any Jew or Christian before him, interpreted the story of Adam and Eve in Genesis to mean that their disobedience has forever infected and lamed all of their descendants. This original sin will always prevent us from creating a just society on this earth.[1] Augustine thus justified the need for an alliance between a hierarchic Church appointed by god for a fallen human race and a hierarchic State in need of guidance and legitimacy—powerful enough to help keep sinners within bounds, since clearly neither emanation nor incoherence alone could hope to do so.

Though the Roman Empire soon decayed, Augustine's new emanational mode of alliance with organized insecurity came centuries later to have a powerful attraction to the pagan warrior tribes of Western and Northern Europe. The pledge of loyalty to the warrior lord became more than a personal oath; it became a pledge to god. Moreover, it became obligatory for all sinners, at home or abroad, to learn obedience—at home through authoritarian rule, abroad through conquest. And if the human lord proved to be sinful, that was to be expected; it could not be an excuse for rebellion. It is necessary for duly sanctified authority to maintain strict control over all other sinners.

Since the Church did not in fact succeed in creating a single universal triumphant emanational way of life, the emanational force of local communities and of rulers remained sufficient again and again to set Christian communities at war

---

1. Augustine and Marcus Dods, *The City of God*, especially Book thirteen; and Elaine H. Pagels, *Adam, Eve, and the Serpent*. Peter Robert Lamont Brown, *Augustine of Hippo: A Biography*.

with each other. The Church, however, granted no individual or group autonomy. It was compelled to grant autonomy to states only after the Treaty of Westphalia, which ended the Thirty-Year War in 1648. It never accepted the autonomy—of personhood, body and soul, or of corporate groups—that Protestantism, in part beyond its intentions, brought into Christianity.

As early as the Council of Nicea in 325, the Church declared Christ the only begotten Son of God. Hence it became unimaginable and certainly heretical to consider that any one of us may prepare herself or himself to walk, like Christ, in the way of transformation. No other way of emanation was as determined, as ruthless, or as successful in exterminating anyone who lived in the service of transformation. None has killed so many dissenters within its own community as this form of Christianity. It claimed that it practiced the evil of deformation for the sake of emanation but in fact it was because emanation failed again and again as a container.

Until the 1960s, when Vatican II officially acknowledged openings which Catholics themselves had been creating for some decades and ever more so now, the Church had persisted in a constant struggle to preserve its version of emanation. There is no escape from persistent battle when a way of life is based primarily on established dogmatic belief, repression, and suppression. The Church's struggle continues, but the underlying archetypal force is now dying, and its people are ever more eager to explore life and to be creative.[2] Witness the practice of liberation theology by millions of Catholics since the 1950s and the recent rebellion of many Catholics in response to the arrogance of the hierarchy as they shielded priests guilty of child abuse.

What I have condensed here is not an image of Christianity, not even an image of Catholic Christians, but of those particular Christians who believe in this particular emanational manifestation. One advantage of the theory of transformation, faithful in its respect for each concrete moment of being as well as for its underlying patterning forces, is that it cannot give rise to stereotypic or abstract designations.

Christians, from the beginning to the present, have lived their faith in a great variety of different manifestations, often so deeply at odds with each other that they would, until recently, often do battle rather than talk with each other. Contemporary Catholics conform less and less to the emanational drama we have described, and it is doubtful that the majority of those who ever considered themselves good

---

2. Here is one small indication of this new spirit: in May 1988, Seton Hall University, New Jersey's largest Catholic university, awarded the author of these pages an honorary Doctorate in Humane Letters for "the theory of transformation with which he has inspired . . . and helped us to shape a new vision of education."

Catholics were fully committed to all those dimensions and dynamics of the drama of emanation which so deeply moved its leading hierarchy. This majority was and is grateful that this drama also preserves the reassurance and solidarity of participating in links to the sacred, especially at the most crucial turning points—but also at frequently recurring moments—of life. I focused on the hierarchic, repressive, and suppressive aspects of this Catholic drama not only because it was potent, but because I wanted to begin showing in a systematic comparative way how similarly and how differently justice may be dealt with in the service of emanation—so that its dynamics may indeed be seen archetypically and not stereotypically.

Sacred texts were written over time. Even the Koran, which was received by Muhammad within half of his lifetime, reports on an experience long enough to require some later verses to abrogate earlier verses. All three texts of Jews, Christians, and Muslims, cover a history longer by far than one person's life. By far the longest and most detailed history—even though it ends centuries before Christ—is to be found in the Hebrew Bible. It is filled with stories and not just rules. It is the story of humankind, and then of a particular community—coming into being, finding and losing itself, in combat with itself and others, told by god to kill strangers, and told by god not to oppress strangers. It included stories of prophets warning the community against persisting in oppression and evil, and stories of god being absent when needed and, alternately, standing by to protect people in the face of almost impossible odds. All four ultimate faces of god appear in the text (and in the other two texts). The task facing such a community is not only understanding rules but also understanding history in the light of the past, present, and future.

People in the service of emanation insist in every generation on remaining in touch with what they believe to be the first and final emanation of the ultimate source—namely, the text. This may curb people asking questions, but they cannot in fact eliminate the freedom of others to hear more or even otherwise. The text is like a musical score. One cannot play it without understanding it, without appreciating its deeper spirit, its contexts, the instruments called upon to translate it into practice, and the audience now attending to it. One cannot play a score of music staying within Act I of the drama of transformation.

Jews in the service of emanation, by making it obligatory to join an ongoing discussion that necessarily included the great (but not final) authorities of the past, are able to enshrine this conversation within a conservative cast. However, since the score itself needs always to be available, the people within the emanational dialogue have no means except dialogue to keep others from trying to hear sounds, rhythms, and meanings beyond the current interpretation of the score. The people of emanation have no argument and no power to deny the fact that the god of transformation, the deepest sacred source, is infinitely richer than the incarnated word, and that it may therefore well be possible to hear and learn more than is contained in the already structured melodies now surrounding these words.

ORGANIZING THE JUSTICE OF EMANATION IN JUDAISM

In the Jewish experience, some Jews held firm to the new emanational consolidation that emerged in the centuries after Sinai. Some Jews saw its hold loosen and, beginning with King Saul, sought to make the forces of emanation more secure by allying them with incoherence through the drama of the State. Such a state was intended to be a new power in the service of emanation, but its rulers, however devoted to god and community, always acted above all for the sake of strengthening their own power. This was even true of David (whose body guard was composed of Philistines) and Solomon. Some Jews therefore were inspired again and again by prophets, who first returned to the desert—remembering the great journey of transformation which had first produced this community—to seek re-formation in the service of emanation or, indeed, transformation itself. Some Jews voluntarily exiled themselves; others never returned from the first great involuntary exile to Babylon and dispersed—usually as communities—from Western Europe to China. Some Jews consolidated emanation anew after the return from Babylonian exile in the sixth century BC.

The concern of the kabbalists was to discover and experience the living light that is god in all of us, indeed in all living things, to help this light lead us into transformation. They interpreted god's word accordingly. They rewrote the story of Genesis into a story of continuous creation. They sought to live their lives as participants in the creativity of the deepest sacred source, for they saw an essential part of god—namely the feminine aspect of god—in exile with us. Neither group of Jews turned exile into incoherence as a way of life. But one experienced exile as a long arrest in Act II longing to return to a secure web of life in the service of emanation; the other saw exile as tremendously unfinished work in Act II already in the service of transformation.

The latter held the unwritten Torah (in part passed on orally to those who are ready to hear, in part not yet heard by anyone) to be even more important than the written Torah. They considered the white space around the letters of the Torah—that is, the words yet to be found, albeit within that space—and interpretations yet to be developed even more important than the letters themselves. One of them said that at Sinai, god pronounced only the first letter of the alphabet—the aleph, which sounds like the clearing of one's throat—all the rest is interpretation.[3]

3. Gershom Gerhard Scholem, *On the Kabbalah and Its Symbolism*, 30.

The kabbalists heard more, and more deeply, from the deepest source of being they could reach. What they heard differed profoundly from the sacred, historical, political, and personal basis of the Jewish community grounded only in emanation. But the kabbalists did not struggle politically for new foundations for that community. They concentrated on the personal and sacred face of those open to the journey of transformation. Outwardly, they lived according to the same rules as their fellow Jews, but with a different appreciation of the underlying meaning and reality of our taking part in continuous creation.

Did the people of emanation ever try to suppress the people of transformation as a danger to their own community? When the Jews had their own state's institutionalized force available for fighting against those who disagreed with them, wars between Jews broke out intermittently in Biblical times. But the Bible itself, written and edited during those centuries, is filled with stories and statements reflecting all four ways of life. When Jews lived repeatedly in Palestine under foreign rule—or after AD 70, in prolonged exile—it was dangerous indeed to speak and act for transformation in terms of what we can and need to do together.[4] But the emanational Jewish community as a whole never tried to kill transformers as heretics. The killing of Christ is the most glaring exception. After we have looked at Muslims in the same light, we will try to examine why Catholic Christianity differed from both in its persecution of transformers.

One seeming exception to the political self-restraint of transformers among Jews was the rise of Sabbatai Zevi as Messiah in 1665—whose appeal was powerful and spread quickly and widely from Palestine throughout the Mediterranean and Western and Eastern Europe.[5] However much his pronouncements reflected the views of the kabbalists, he differed from them in one crucial respect: Sabbatai Zevi announced himself as the final savior. Transformers know that no one, not even the deepest sacred, can solve our problems by a sudden grand move. Only our persistent participation with all four faces of our being can move us toward the fundamentally new and better in more and more areas of life. (When we have completed our journey, the Messiah may come, but solely to ratify our work by saying Amen.)

---

4. Even while most Jews still lived in Palestine, they often did not govern themselves. Christ appeared at a time when the Jewish community had been divided by at least two centuries of especially deep conflicts. The Jews also split on Christ. Some Jews joined him; indeed Jews were initially his only followers. Others opposed him because he challenged the law that the community had discussed and followed for over a millennium, and because he meant to create a new community founded by individuals who had experienced death and rebirth as the word turned anew into flesh, and because he thereby challenged the politically most powerful—the Jewish collaborators with Roman rule.

5. Gershom Gerhard Scholem, *Sabbatai Sevi: The Mystical Messiah, 1626–1676*. See also Zevi Josef Kastein and Huntley Paterson, *The Messiah of Ismir: Sabbatai Zevi*.

PRACTICING JUSTICE IN ISLAM

By simply absorbing existing custom, one is not alive to one's self or one's neighbor or one's past or to the sacred now. Emanation as a way of life has a powerful tendency toward soon freezing what is expected, practiced, and approved and not remembering accurately or at all when it was otherwise.

The pursuit of justice thus remained always uncertain and the outcome often remained open to challenge. Procedures and results were always shaped by the actual presence, ethics, and power of individuals and groups as they interpreted the law in the here and now. In addition to Shariah law, the rulers also developed codes of their own, their impact differing with the stability of rule, the loyalty of bureaucrats, and the distance from the capital. Many Muslim communities also inherited and developed customary law. The geography of this region—from Morocco to China, from Central Asia to Africa south of the Sahara—made centralized rule exceedingly difficult in pre-modern times, however much modern mapmakers color large parts of this world, for example the Ottoman Empire which lasted six hundred years, all in one color. Sometimes the writ of the Sultan was not effective in his own palace; sometimes it reached from Istanbul to Aleppo or (more rarely) Cairo.

Justice in any overarching way of life is also shaped by a repertory of relationships and, especially among Muslims, by two different sources of emanation. One source of emanation is Islam; the other is a particular individual—acting not as an individualist, but as the heroic embodiment of his family, his tribe, his clan, his faction. In each extended family, that individual is the patriarch. But two questions are always ready for reopening: Which family is to be dominant in the village or tribe? Which son is to be dominant in the family—now in the name of the patriarch, and in the future?

In the service of emanation, the repertory of archetypal relationships of Muslim men excludes isolation. Muslim men in emanation see no possibility of agreeing that they will abstain from actively collaborating or conflicting with each other or from trying to change each other. Everyone is expected and expects to be counted on. Seeming fatalism is the result of fully accepting being an emanation of another. Enforced passivity is the result of subjection, which cannot be escaped. The force of emanation—in the form of Islam and in the form of individuals—creates this community's networks of ideas, norms, values, and practices, augmented by direct exchange and buffering (as expressed by mediators, concepts, and rituals).[6] I, as

---

6. For a more detailed discussion of archetypal relationships in Islam, though written when my understanding of archetypal ways of life was more rudimentary, see Manfred Halpern, "Four Contrasting Repertories of Human Relations in Islam: Two Pre-Modern and Two Modern Ways of Dealing with Continuity and Change, Collaboration and Conflict, and the Achieving of Justice," in L. Carl Brown and Norman Itzkowitz, *Psychological Dimensions of Near Eastern Studies*, Princeton Studies on the Near East, 60–102.

the emanation of Islam, of my larger community, of my immediate community, of me—the order of this chain of emanations differs from person to person, from place to place, from time to time. But no individual can hope to act as if this chain does not exist as a very lifeline in Islam. When Muslims fight wars with each other over how this chain is to be organized, they battle with each other as rivals, much less often as outsiders who could therefore be treated in the spirit of deformation.

As against this practice of perennial conflict within the confines of emanation, Sufis, especially after the twelfth century, came often to constitute a majority among Muslims until the modern age. They seldom became rulers, though they sometimes influenced them as persons or by virtue of their political strength. Above all, they offered an alternative society to the Islam of emanation—a society beyond local kinship or political boundaries, a society concerned with the experience of transformation including brotherhood and mutual help. Craftsmen guilds were deeply influenced by Sufis. Like the kabbalists, and Catholic Christian practitioners of liberation theology, the Sufis used the inherited, revealed texts of their community, but offered radically different interpretations of them. Like the kabbalists with respect to *halakha*, the majority of Sufis observed many of the rules of the Shariah but as a symbolic reflection of a deeper reality they sought to understand ever anew. They recognized themselves—and were accepted by all their neighbors—as Muslims, but they saw themselves as "friends of God," a god who needed their participation. (Similarly, some Catholics who identified themselves and considered themselves Catholics were a different kind of Catholic who identified themselves with the poor.)

In Islam, for centuries, many of the leading philosophers—and no small number of poets, writers of stories, and artists—devoted themselves to the exploration of transformation.[7] It was an extraordinary flourishing of ideas and experience.

---

7. The scholar who discovered in his own inquiries that the philosophers of transformation in Islam—among them Alfarabi (died 950), Avicenna (died 1037), Ibn Arabi (died 1240), and Mulla Sadra (died 1641)—are concerned with the interpenetration of all four faces of being and their transformation is James Winston Morris. (Earlier Western writings, when they paid attention to these theorists at all, saw them primarily and variously as philosophers who misunderstood Aristotle, as logicians, metaphysicians, reconcilers of religion and philosophy, or advocates of an inner mystical life.) Among Morris's splendidly clarifying works are James Winston Morris and Mu hammad ibn Ibrahim Sadr Al-Din Shirazi, *The Wisdom of the Throne: An Introduction to the Philosophy of Mulla Sadra*, Princeton Library of Asian Translations.; "Ibn Arabi's Esotericism: The Problem of Spiritual Authority," *Studia Islamica* 67 (Spring 1988); "Ibn Arabi and His Interpreters," *Journal of the American Oriental Society* 106 (1986), 539–51 and 733–56; and 107 (1987), 101–19; "The Spiritual Ascension: Ibn Arabi and the Mi'raj," *Journal of the American Oriental Society* 107 (1987), 629–52; and 108 (1988), 63–77. Also very helpful in understanding Muslim philosophers of transformation are the works of Henry Corbin, William Chittick, Toshihiko Izutsu, Parviz Morewedge, and Annemarie Schimmel. On the history of Muslims of various ways of life, the best overview is provided by Marshall G. S. Hodgson, *The Venture of Islam: Conscience and History in a World Civilization*.

But after the age of incoherence triumphed, this experience of transformation was until recently almost as forgotten among Muslims and ignored in the modern West as kabbala was among Jews.[8] The contemporary memory of most Muslims tells them that, from the seventh century until Western imperialism and westernizing modernity tried to take them over, the great majority of Muslims were Muslims by virtue of adhering to Sharia law. The quite different image of Muslim history I have presented here has largely been suppressed and repressed in the Muslim world, as is evident from the triumph of madrassas—schools where the young are taught an intolerant interpretation of Islam based on Wahabism.

I now add a problem not peculiar to Muslims, but a matter of grave significance for movements of transformation everywhere. Not all people who call themselves Sufis (in the past or today) are committed to transformation. Guides of transformation were often turned after their deaths into saints to be worshipped. Some guides while still alive were tempted by themselves and their followers to turn themselves from teachers and exemplars into idols to be venerated. Both cases move from transformation into emanation. (Certain later Hasidic masters suffered or encouraged a similar fate.) But the movements of transformation were also renewed again and again in Islam—until Muslim rulers under attack from the West saw them as the principal domestic force of subversion and suppressed them, and a new Muslim intelligentsia, looking for defense against Western imperialism, turned to Western nationalism instead.

THE COST OF PARTIAL JUSTICE

This brief comparative overview of justice in the service of emanation practiced within three world religions shows us that emanation is truly an archetypal drama, and not a single stereotype. The underlying dynamics intrinsic to this overarching drama are the same wherever it is practiced, but the archetypal dramas and relationships we add in its service create quite different performances even within the same emanational community and over time. And despite the illusion carefully fostered by the overarching drama that its concrete expressions and underlying forces have remained the same from its origins, reinterpretations and even reformations in the service of emanation are possible.

---

8. For a truly courageous transformation of the views of a scholar who had devoted his life to the study of Islam in the service of emanation as the core of Islam—reduced, as he saw it, by folk Islam and deeply corrupted and mired for centuries by sufism, see H. A. R. Gibb's preface to Seyyed Hossein Nasr, *An Introduction to Islamic Cosmological Doctrines: Conceptions of Nature and Methods Used for Its Study by the* Ikhwan Al-Safa, Al-Biruni and Ibn Si, a revised ed. Nasr was of major importance in helping to change Gibb's view. Here, in an essay shorter than an as yet unpublished stenciled paper, Gibb rejects his earlier focus on the Islam of the orthodox *ulema* and recognizes sufism as the most pervasive and significant experience of Muslims.

From the perspective of transformation, the need for interpreting any manifestation of the sacred is truly inescapable. All sacred texts are initially communicated to particular persons of a particular community (always a community in crisis) at a particular critical moment. These texts—and the experience and understanding they reflect—have since then been understood and enacted by particular people under changing circumstances. What god was understood to have said, god said that afternoon. What Christ said, Christ said that afternoon. These statements may well contain truths of enormous value even now. But such truths need to be discovered anew, both in the light and against the darkness of earlier interpretations, and above all in the light of what we can hear now from the deepest depths of our being—and can test now. They cannot be understood if we examine them, however objectively, as if they had a historical face but no archetypal meaning to be uncovered from its present emanational form and to be revealed anew in its transformational significance. They cannot be understood if we hold objectively that they have no personal and political face to be re-experienced in our life now, because we consider the personal to be merely subjective and the political to be merely partisan.

I have said little about the particulars of justice in this discussion, for the heart of the matter in emanation is not any particular rule or outcome, however important, but that our thoughts and actions serve this one Lord in this way of life. My concluding criticism therefore focuses on this very point—that is, on the limits to justice in emanation.

The people in all three of our examples take seriously the story of Adam and Eve eating the apple of the tree of good and evil and, for their disobedience, being ousted from paradise. However they may differ in further interpretations of this tale, all three communities, in so far as they are committed to emanation, agree that human disobedience to god constituted their most profound sin. From our perspective, Adam and Eve—and that god—stopped too soon. We share the view of the kabbalists. If we separate the knowledge of good and evil from the knowledge of life—if we do not actually eat the fruit of both trees—then we are in dire trouble. Then we cannot experience and know the whole truth and love of life.[9] When we know only what god has already said, we concentrate on god's power and judgment. But this is a lesser and partial Lord who seeks to prevent us from completing the journey of transformation by arresting us in a fragment of the core drama. Our greatest need is to discover and hear the deepest sacred source of being again and again, so that we may participate with the deepest sacred source through our being and thus transform this cosmos through each concrete action.

---

9. Gershom Gerhard Scholem, "Sitra achra; Gut und Bose in der Kabbala," esp. 58–62, in Gershom Gerhard Scholem, *Von Der Mystischen Gestalt Der Gottheit: Studien Zu Grundbegriffen Der Kabbala*.

In any service of emanation, we may recognize that our sense of certainty of what is just and unjust may nonetheless not be satisfied on this earth, but rather in god's own time. We may realize that the security of solidarity within our own community may be threatened by sinners, people without shame, and rival communities. In these respects, we recognize that life is not perfect, even in emanation, but we cannot imagine a better way of life for body and soul, for anyone and everyone, now and in eternity. We certainly know who we are, whom we belong with, what we believe, what we need to do and must not do, and who has commanded us to be thus.

What we cannot appreciate, within any service of emanation, is the perennial wounding and suffering that comes from being cut off from our capacity and freedom to complete ourselves lovingly and justly with others and with the source of all sacred sources. The repression intrinsic to forgetting that we are living in a fragment of life raises our anxiety and strengthens our desire for the absolute of emanation. It prevents us from gaining the autonomy needed to critically and creatively respond to a constantly changing world. We are prevented from connecting as fellow human beings with that great majority of the world whom we now cannot truly see because they are outsiders—to be ignored, to be looked down upon, to be converted to be like us, to be feared, or to be destroyed.

The cost of any justice in the service of emanation thus is too high. Its justice even at its best can only be partial justice—partial in the sense of being incomplete and biased; partial in the sense that a partial truth may hint at the truth but above all distorts it.

LIVING IN THE PARTIAL JUSTICE OF EMANATION: HOW IT LIMITS AND DISTORTS OUR BEING AND OUR EXPERIENCE OF JUSTICE AND THUS OPENS US TO DEFORMATION

Why does deformation arise while people still live in the service of the partial way of life of emanation—the seemingly most secure, most stable of all ways of life? Within a life of emanation we devote ourselves to ritualizing, refining, elaborating, protecting, reinforcing, containing, yet we also remain perennially anxious. Why? Our anxiety is shaped in part by the other two Acts of the drama we have repressed, and by its worst possible exit. We are deeply worried about entering into the rebellion of incoherence that, from our limited perspective, we can only see as sin. Our system of security is powerful and structured enough to make it possible for sinners to repent—or else we turn them into outsiders. We are constantly anxious about the potentials of transformation—a new insight into reality, a new creativity coming into being, a breaking of our present sacred container.

Our anxiety is shaped in large part by outsiders, for all emanational containers are built without doors that may be freely opened for the sake of actual exploration. Just beyond our horizon live people who seem by their very existence to raise the specter of splitting open the worst possible exit from our container by threatening us with deformation—that is, with an opening into incoherence from which we do not know how to return short of the abyss. If—the Lord help us—they have frozen a different vision of the sacred into a way of life, how can that be? Since we heard the right voice and have all the truth, their voice must be fundamentally mistaken, and yet they live and prosper. Is it we instead who are lost? Or—the Lord help us—those people live in the sin of incoherence, and yet they are rich and powerful. Or they are hearing a new prophecy. They, however, are enacting it as the first Act of transformation. They are threatening the very structure of our existence. The outsider therefore appears as a danger in time of peace no less than in times of actual warfare—thus justifying resort to deformation toward outsiders at any time.

But our anxiety in the service of emanation is kindled in largest part by the intrinsic nature of this way of life, because it is only a fragment of the core drama. Its people cannot in fact be what they devoutly believe themselves to be (to speak of our three examples)—the only people truly chosen by the only god, the only people whose beliefs will save at least some of them, the only people to have received god's final revelation to humankind. To live in emanation, as I suggested in Chapter 4, is to live in exile from the source of all sacred sources, and to deny one's self and one's neighbors the capacity to participate in continuous creation. To suggest, as Max Weber does, that charisma needs to be routinized and institutionalized in order to be preserved is to miss not only the fact that to routinize grace is to turn a living experience into an elite-controlled pretence, but is also to miss the tragedy of institutionalizing the loss of our individual and democratically shared participation in the deepest and widest sense and experience of our being.

The built-in limits, fragility, and anxiety of emanation readily move us to resort to deformation and, because we cannot question our own position, blind us to the evils of that road. Evil is defined as breaking out of—or not belonging inside—our sacred container. Or if evil is inflicted upon us by forces our container does not help us to analyze or understand, we ascribe it to god's mysterious will, for we can never blame the source of emanation. Within emanation, this limited but therefore all the more anxious vision of the threat of evil normally leads to four further moves in increasing the bias of an already partial justice.

One bias stems from the terrifying threats of punishment by a Lord for those who break the rules—often threats of destructive death. That Lord, who has barred access for himself and for us to the source of all sacred sources, means to enforce fixed rules forever, for he must ward off renewed journeys of transformation in the face of new problems. But that threat of punishment—however scary to many, for it is voiced by a seemingly absolute power and absolute power knows no limits short of deathly destruction—is by itself not effective in curbing everyone.

To arrest any Act of a drama of ever renewed journeys requires institutions to enforce and reinforce that arrest. In large societies, the more powerful institutions have usually been those of the State. However much priests may organize their own power, the State is normally more powerful. It is armed; it can tax, police, and punish. For the powerful men of religion to collaborate with the men of the State in order to shape the views of the ruler is therefore in most instances an illusory hope. The State is ultimately in the service of incoherence, however much it pretends that it uses its power in the service of emanation. The ruler depends on the organized institutions of emanation, on organized beliefs and obedience—hence on calculations of power, not on god. The established authorities of emanation and incoherence normally forget that there is no god but god. Under the State, incoherence comes to dominate as a way of life. Look at the kings of Israel and Judah especially after Solomon. Look at Christian kings after the conversion of Emperor Constantine. Look at the caliphs—after the fourth caliph (or "successor") of the Prophet Muhammad—who, as the enforcers of the sacred law, came increasingly to be called Sultans ("men of power").

The State in the service of incoherence, in alliance with the dominant groups in the service of emanation, also move together to enforce and perpetuate those archetypal stories in the service of emanation which compel us to accept and perpetuate oppression, exploitation, and inequality, especially of class and gender—and in the past, of slavery as well in all three of the cases we have been focusing on. These dramas demonstrate that when emanation—as a way of life in collusion with incoherence—is deeply threatened, god is used by the powerful to justify a turn toward the abyss in the form of violence against enemies of the community. These dramas are in fact all stations on the road to destructive death—as we shall try to demonstrate later in this chapter.

And the fourth move is to ally the fragments of emanation and incoherence with the fragmenting way of deformation—in the past, when emanation was losing its power in its particular exemplification, and especially now, as emanation as a way of life is dying as an archetypal force.

When this chapter comes to focus on the evil of deformation (after we have also discussed the partial justice of incoherence), we shall analyze five stations on the road to destructive death. But a quick summary of these five ways of relating to outsiders will allow us now to organize systematic comparisons between three examples of emanation.

Anyone living within any fragment of the core drama of life cannot see or experience the wholeness of their own humanity, much less that of someone other than themselves. The other is therefore often turned into a fragment less than human, or else into someone altogether invisible. A third station on the road of deformation offers conversion. Obviously, the other is not human until the other conforms entirely to our sacred standards. Otherwise, the other is doomed to death or to hell—or at least to permanent inferiority. In times of crises, people already living with the anxiety of a fragment of life are likely to impose exile—to incarcerating or ejecting the disobedient and the dissenting. Or, they will try desperately to regain their sense of certainty by resorting to the extermination of the other both at home and abroad.

All people who are enclosed within an emanational relationship—not only in service to emanation as a way of life, but in any archetypal drama which they enact unquestioningly as given—see all outsiders at least as lesser (less significant as human beings, lesser human beings, inferior). When I refer to the reassurance of the experience of being chosen that arises out of the associated experience of outsiders as lesser people, I speak of Jews contained in the emanational relationships of a particular historical period, not of Jews generally (just as throughout this section we have not been speaking of Christians or Muslims but of those people contained in their emanational relationships of a particular historical period). And elites of the rulers, the wealthy, and the high priests tend to see themselves as superior emanations of god. Hence there arise among Jews again and again prophets who speak up for justice for the poor and the oppressed among their own people.

Exile from the Promised Land—to Babylonia in (and to many lands after) the second destruction of the temple by the Romans—and repeated forced exile from many European countries has profoundly reformed the emanational experience of the Jews. "Our homeland: the text" became the heart of Jewish life for many dispersed Jewish communities—arrested in Act II of the drama of transformation, but interpreting this arrest as living with others in the service of organized insecurity (especially in the Christian world often under the threat of deformation), while living with each other in Act I in the service of emanation still. Within this vision, only the Messiah could bring about transformation.

But this interpretation does not cover all of the Jewish past. The majority of Jews (as we discussed earlier) for many centuries turned to the transformation of their personal and sacred (but not their political and historical) faces of being with the guidance of kabbalistic teachings—that the feminine aspect of god is also in exile, and that god needs our active participation to overcome the exile in which all of us still live on this continuing journey.

There also remain major unexplored aspects of the experience of exile among Jews. Many Jews never returned from Babylonia to Palestine when they were free to return. Instead, they remained in what is now Iraq or else migrated as far as Western Europe, India, and China. Why did so may choose exile? In *Ezekiel*, god speaks against the Jews with an extraordinarily sadistic voice before he punishes them by sending them into exile.[10] Why so vicious a scapegoating? Why so prolonged an acceptance by Jews of being scapegoats to be exiled or even killed by god or their neighbors?

God, from time to time, ordered the Jews to commit holocausts—to kill every man, woman, and child of a particular people.[11] The road toward the destructive death of the other has been taken by almost all people in the service of emanation—reducing their humanity so that it leads more readily to early and unjust death. Destructive death through extermination has also been inflicted by many people in the service of emanation—or in the grasp of an emanational relationship (though we often cover this fact under the seemingly more acceptable terms of war, or punishment for past or anticipated betrayals).

Muslims have long been stereotyped by the West as above all champions of holy wars—convert to Islam or die. That is a grave distortion. Of course, Muslims in the service of emanation treat others as lesser folk, but Muslims initially conquered primarily "People of the Book"—people to whom the same one and only god had revealed an earlier, less perfect, and by now corrupt text of the one and only Book of which the Koran is the best and final version. Muslim tolerance for the religious and cultural autonomy especially of Christians and Jews dramatically contrasts with the intolerance of Christians for Jews and Muslims in their midst.

Christianity began as an experience of individuals experiencing, as Jesus did, the way of dying and being born again and again, and forming a new community together. After moving in this and other directions, it came to be dominated after Augustine in the fourth century by a reformed emanational way of life bent above all on repressing all transformation and curbing the sins of incoherence. To these

---

10. To cite a few passages of deformation pronounced by god, as Ezekiel reports them: "Those of you who are parents will eat their children, and children will eat their parents.... For as I live—declares Lord Yahweh—as sure as you have defiled my sanctuary with all your horrors and all your loathsome practices, so I too shall reject you without a glance of pity.... A third of your citizens will die of plague or starve to death...; a third will fall by the sword round you; and a third I shall scatter to the winds.... I shall sate my anger and bring my fury to rest on them until I am avenged. As the butchered fall about you, you will know that I am Yahweh.... When the populous cities have been destroyed and the country has been reduced to desert, then you will know that I am Yahweh" (Ezekiel, 5:10–14, 6:7, 12:20). God also announces in this text that he will inflict deformation on a number of neighboring states at the same time. For a text from the Christian Bible about god speaking and acting in the same spirit, see The Revelation to John, especially Chapters 8–13, 16–20.

11. Genesis 6. There is no shortage of such examples in the Old Testament, and not only of holocausts ordered by Yahweh against his enemies, but also of the near murder of his favorites. In *Exodus* 4:3, he nearly succeeds in his intention of killing Moses, who is on his way back to Egypt in order to lead the Jews out of slavery. And "An evil spirit from Yahweh came over King Saul" so that he hurled a javelin to kill David, the greatest king-to-be in Israel (1 Samuel 19:9–10). Christians who remember only a loving god have to think of god's scapegoating crucifixion of Christ solely as an act of redemption, and may not have read the god who reveals himself in the Gospel of St. John of Revelations, or have looked at the history of Christianity, even in the treatment of fellow Christians.

ends, this form of Christianity resorted to deformation far more than either Jews or Muslims.

Augustine rendered god all-good, all-powerful in his ability in mysterious ways to reach us, but entirely invisible to us and unreachable by us. By denying us any direct access to the deepest ground of our being, Christianity in this way succeeded in deeply crippling us. We are by nature incapable of transforming ourselves and with our neighbors, incapable of bringing justice into the world. On the contrary, human beings alone (not the sacred) are responsible for bringing evil into the world. We are crippled even now by Eve's and then Adam's original sin of disobeying god. That indeed renders the most crucial aspect of each of us—our capacity and freedom to experience transformation through our participation in god's journey—invisible. This is no small deformation.

From time to time, the Church sought to make sure through inquisitions (interrogations marked by torture) that no soul had connected in unauthorized ways to the Holy Spirit—which stood solely behind the office and authority of the Church. Short of extermination by burning at the stake and other violent forms of execution, the Church also resorted to exile—that is, excommunication—of the more prominent dissenters. Dissenters had no place at all in the community. The lesser—especially Jews—were often sent into exile, or else given the choice to convert or die.

Christianity was able for a long time to employ deformation effectively because it could rely on an alliance between a usually strong hierarchic Church and a usually strong hierarchic State. But that is also to say that inflicting such archetypal stories in the service of a chain of emanation whose deepest level is not the god of continuous creation, but the Lord who inspires the enforcement of established sacred doctrines, makes a resort to deformation more likely. People under these circumstances wonder more often in their hearts whether the powerful in fact live up to the standards of emanation and thus deserve to be obeyed. The sanctified glory of power also tempts others to seek power by sinning, if necessary, as much as the already powerful. The powerful of Church and State mean above all to preserve power even if it requires taking the road to destructive death. Both they and those who challenge their power for the sake of power forget that there is no god but God, that all other gods are partial gods.

This alliance between a war-prone political hierarchy in the service of incoherence and a dogmatic religious hierarchy in the service of emanation was at times uneasy, even conflict-ridden, but it justified for both the use of deformation (if the appeal of emanation proved inadequate) to impose their order at home and their conquest of outsiders.

All three of our examples of partial justice were originally produced entirely by men. Men alone shaped the sacred containers in terms of their partial gods—the archetypal sources of being by which the entire community of men and women was to be inspired and constrained. Men alone also molded its concrete manifestations, including those to be put into practice by women. Half the population in each community was thus deformed as human beings by this sacred container—treated as inferior human beings, to be kept invisible in the public political realm. Their three principal roles—virgin, mother, and wife—were by public law and custom solely domestic functions. In all three of our examples of emanation, their fathers and husbands could beat and punish them if in their judgment women did not conform to these limitations upon their humanity. In the Christian realm of Catholicism and early Protestantism, the doctrine—convert (assimilate and conform to these patriarchal dictates) or die—was also applied to women. About one million women were burned as witches.

For the first time in history, an archetypal way of life is dying. Emanation as an overarching emanational container is dissolving as an archetypal force. Humankind has experienced the dying of specific instances of emanation as a way of life again and again for millennia. But now the underlying patterning force of all such experiences of life as a single and unchanging web is dying. That is no small movement into death.

This time, all four faces of this archetypal drama are breaking and dissolving. Never before in history has there been such an explosion of personal assertion by so many—whether freeing themselves to ask new questions, to discover new depths and new opportunities, or to seek new forms of domination and profit. Never before have the political bonds of all communities around the world irrevocably come apart—bonds which had previously been held together by codes and authorities based on fixed sacred revelations. Neither the new questions nor the new answers can any longer be absorbed and assimilated by personal beliefs and customs or by the political structure or culture of these emanational containers. A cosmos of continuous creation was bound to undermine emanation as a way of life as the millennia passed, especially when people no longer live in as much isolation from each other as they did before the modern age.

To cite only one example of growing incapacity to deal effectively with new questions, the infallible Popes have been unable to prevent the rise of Protestantism, secularism, science, the dominance of the modern State, capitalism, and (more recently) liberation theology, or the increasing freedom of women to deal with their own bodies and souls—all of which the Church has denounced and struggled against.

When we break with any form of emanation, we create a vital beginning on the road to transformation. But if we do not open ourselves to the faith, hope, and love of this journey, this breaking can move us into deformation instead. This is becoming an increasing threat in our time. The great sundering of emanation, especially since the seventeenth century, is dissolving not only emanation as a way of life, but also, interrelated with this great illness unto death, a dying of many concrete emanational relationships and also a dying of many of our connections to established archetypal dramas once in the service of that way of life. (As long as we remain unconscious of our connection to any archetypal drama, our bond to it is emanational). Altogether this constitutes an enormous movement toward an underlying and concrete dissolution of relationships and stories in which we hitherto lived our lives. Why does this movement also increase the threat of deformation? Why does it so often draw us beyond incoherence into the abyss?

Challenged by new problems that cannot be understood or healed from within the established sacred container, its defenders further diminish their human freedom and capacity under the fantasy that this consolidation will strengthen their power. Interpretations become more dogmatic; the enforcement of rules hardens; violence against outsiders or internal factions (which also tend now to increase) is more easily justified than ever before; the only hope is moving toward the apocalypse, which surely is closer now.

The ending of the road to deformation in destructive death becomes more and more inviting. The breaking of emanation releases on the part of any source of emanation a desire archetypally rooted in this drama to kill its previous embodiment for having betrayed its loyalty. When we are still in the service of that source, we experience its killing power through its capacity to make us desperately ill while we remain in sin. When we deliberately break away once and for all, the established hierarchy or its self-appointed representative—or the person by whom we were once overwhelmingly enthralled—will fiercely pursue us.

Or if the emanational embodiment is abandoned and deserted by the source, then, having until just now lived without an autonomous identity of one's own, one is unprepared to stand alone, and experiences an archetypally rooted desire to kill one's self. This destruction leading toward death need not express itself concretely in murder or suicide, though ever more often it does. As we have noted in earlier chapters, murder can exhibit itself, for example, as searing persecution of the disloyal and of those who are thought to have subverted them; suicide may be experienced as a freezing of our life in apathy. Suicide can also be suffered as people fantasize their involvement in deformation as a substitute for the emanation missing in their life: the wife becomes dearly committed to the abusive husband; the teenager is ready to become a suicide bomber or to be killed at the order of the leader.

There are only two exceptions that prevent this turn into deformation. Sometimes in our personal or political history, human beings have experienced a slow waning or a gradual decay of emanational ties. Then the shock and its consequences may not be as profound. As change moves ever more rapidly, yet still quite unexpectedly for most people, this kind of transition becomes less common. The only other escape from deformation requires a conscious and conscientious movement into Act II of the drama of transformation at the moment that we break with emanation in any of its forms.

THE PARTIAL JUSTICE OF THE WAY OF LIFE
OF FRAGMENTS (INCOHERENCE)

What is justice in the partial way of life of incoherence? In the best of cases in the service of incoherence, namely in democratic liberalism, justice is what needs to be done, developed, and redeveloped within regulated procedures for adversarial competition, paying attention to what needs to be done to keep the least fortunate and the least free from rebelling against the social contract. The social contract represents the legitimated subjectivity of the most powerful that legislatively and executively carries out the objectified regulated procedures for adversarial competition. But there exists no shared sense of substantive justice or compassion since people in the service of a way of life of fragments cannot know the ultimate meaning and purpose of anything.

Our sense of loss is always alive in incoherence though it is not repressed. If we will not free ourselves to listen to ourselves, it will fester in the shadows of our life and become our enemy. Continuous creation can also be distorted into deformation. Since incoherence as a life of fragments is such a vulnerable life, deformation looms as a threat more than ever before. Incoherence is not a modern discovery. But even when incoherence was dominant in the past, it did not, as it does now, affect every aspect of life.

Incoherence is also exacting its cost in the great majority of our relationships. When I first discovered incoherence as an archetypal relationship, I stated as a matter of fact that incoherence exists in any relationship when one of the five faces of capacity our unconscious, our consciousness, our creativity, our linking with others, and our use of just means or one of the five issues of performance collaboration and conflict, continuity and change, and the achieving of justice is missing. How many of us are now unconscious of our unconscious and what archetypal forces possess us? And how many are conscious of the manifest costs to our lives? Do we feel entitled to be creative or only conformist within our established relationships? Are we free to link with others with whom our power and wealth—or the lack of them—does not already link us? Do we have adequate and just means to contribute to our relationships? Is there continuity in our lives? Does change move within the pattern of the relationships available to us? Do our relationships allow collaboration and free us to conflict within them? Is justice achieved thanks to our repertory of relationships? If these faces of our being are not entirely missing, how badly damaged are they?

When incoherence enters any relationship, the control issue becomes the power of the one as against the power of the other, because unilateral power has taken the place of shared capacity. Incoherence is not the absence of relationships, but indeed an archetypal link in which we and the other stand facing each other in the same place and at the same time, unable to agree on how to share crucial aspects of performance and of capacity. Power thus becomes all the more precious precisely when it has become most precarious, most feared, and mutually most misunderstood. And other than incoherence, how many of the other eight archetypal relationships are we in fact free to practice in a democratic liberal society with respect to ourselves, other people, and the problems of our lives? As incoherence dominates, how many relationships that we remain free to practice become instruments to make or manipulate that incoherence?

But even the best of cases cannot overcome the intrinsic limitations of partial justice, however large our defense mechanisiums, however great our competence, however street-wise we are, however expensive a lawyer we can afford. Why *intrinsic* limitations? The most important reason for the intrinsically biased and incomplete nature of justice in the service of incoherence is that incoherence, however overarching as a way of life, is only a *fragment* of the core drama of life.

I want to show how the perspective of transformation fundamentally changes our understanding of justice in our discussions between public and private, between subjective and objective. Let's look at two cases of the biased and incomplete—of partial justice—that we do not normally discuss or act on under the heading of justice.

In the service of incoherence, we need very much to protect our personal privacy. We don't want our partial being, our need for a public persona that can compete successfully with others, undermined by any invasion of our privacy. But look at the price we pay for such a fragmentation of the personal and political faces of our being. Until quite recently, and in many ways even now, we have legally allowed the powerful to protect their private right to own property to exploit workers, to own their wives, and to keep us from acting politically to create more justice in what we can and need to do together.

Or consider the fragmentation called objective and subjective. Compassion, love, beauty, the sacred, and indeed our conception of justice are all called subjective, not objective, and are hence therefore relegated to the private, nonpolitical realm, except for moments when we can discover what is called intersubjectivity.

Instead of analyzing particular cases of partial justice in the service of a way of life of fragments and discovering in what way they are biased and incomplete, I put before you much more frightening matters. Often, when justice is only partial—not in every case, but in many significant cases—it puts the already less powerful (or powerless) on one of the five stations to destructive death. And it puts the more powerful into alliance with the forces of deformation to make sure that they have power enough to keep the discontented in the stations on the road to deformation. These stations are the lesser as inferior, as invisible, as worthy only of becoming like the powerful through assimilation, as exiled when they become disloyal to the powerful, and as moved toward extermination when the powerful consider them to be a dangerous threat or the outsiders are unwilling to be absorbed into the system through the manipulation of cooption. We shall further discuss these five stages on the road to the abyss below when we consider the injustice of deformation as a way of life.

The basic cause of this alliance between incoherence and deformation as ways of life is this: though we may be rich and powerful in the service of incoherence (the way of life of fragments), we are still only fragments of being clutching fragments of life in the service of a fragment of the core drama of life. That makes us feel fragile and anxious even when we are powerful. So, since transformation as a way of life is not currently available to us, we may ally ourselves with a still fiercer fragment of the core drama—the way of life of deformation.

Look at what we do with the poor even as the rich grow richer. The top 1 percent of the rich now have as much income as all of the 40 percent at the bottom and in the face of this wealth, what are the wealthy and powerful prepared to do? Let me read to you from an article that appeared in *The New York Times* (6 July 1990). The article quotes the views of President Bush's Domestic Policy Council—a Cabinet-level advisory body. This Council looked at various possible incremental changes. It considered such options as "large-scale community intervention in high-poverty areas," "expanded family-planning services," "expansion of tax credits for the working poor," creation of "new block grants for investment in poor children," the establishment of a national minimum child-support benefit. They were talking about 32 million Americans living below the poverty line.

They decided to do nothing. The White House acknowledged, according to *The New York Times*, that a major new investment in children would have a big payoff for American society in the long run, but it shelved the idea after concluding that "it was not likely to show an immediate reward." Here are two more direct quotes from a White House official: "It was fun to think about these things. But for the time being, we concluded that we don't want to do anything new and that we should just make things work better." "Keep playing with the same toys but let's paint them a little shinier."

PARTIAL JUSTICE IN THE BEST DRAMA OF INCOHERENCE— DEMOCRATIC LIBERALISM

What is justice in the service of incoherence when it is practiced in the best of its stories, that of democratic liberalism? I have already offered reasons in earlier portions of this volume why democratic liberalism is, by far, the best of all the second-best choices that have hitherto been practiced. The drama of democratic liberalism is in progress in Eastern Europe and parts of Southern Europe and Latin America. Yet most of the people of the world are still governed by authoritarian liberal (or simply authoritarian) regimes in the service of incoherence and deformation including many of our allies in the war against terrorism such as Saudi

Arabia, Pakistan, Kuwait, and Bahrain. But since I shall be critical enough of the best of cases, it is enough to remember that incoherence can be, and in much of the world is, much worse.

But consider that democratic liberalism is in fact nowhere, even in the United States, the dominant drama in the lives of people in the service of incoherence. Authoritarian liberalism is the order for most people most of every day even where democratic liberalism marks the political regime. No corporations, no bureaucracies, and few families—not even all decision making in the executive and legislative branches of our government—are manifestations of democratic liberalism. This fact, as we shall see, gives the organization of incoherence under democratic liberal governments a far more authoritarian shape than we normally recognize.

Each way of life has a form of justice intrinsic to it. To say this about incoherence sounds very odd. Even in liberal democracies, people seldom discuss justice. If they head the government's Department of Justice, they see its task as the enforcement of law and order. If they have important status in society, they focus discussion and action on particular cases, particular laws, procedures, options, and compromises. Discussion of principles, unless they involve affirmations on public holidays, usually focuses on different ways of justifying or interpreting the basic or constitutional procedures that undergird all other procedures.

There is another reason why people in the service of incoherence seldom discuss justice. The tales told by the powerful naturally emphasize the accomplishments of particular individuals, corporations, and groups, and extrapolate their gains to be those of the nation. Even when the powerful worry about risks and experience losses, they do not discuss the costs of this way of life or who bears the costs, and certainly not its archetypal dynamics. Not to discuss the underside in every sense of that term reflects more than prudence. To live in an emanational relationship to this drama prevents us from analyzing its deepest shaping powers and diminishes our capacity to see as human beings those whom we have succeeded in pushing into the shadows of our stage. These barriers render the justice of incoherence partial—that is, incomplete and biased—even in the best of cases.

The people pushed aside or down—the dissenters, those still struggling at the margins, the suppressed, the repressed, and the defeated—are still free to speak. Whether they are able to speak and be heard, and also to act, depends upon their overcoming a number of major obstacles. The concrete manifestations of characteristic obstacles involve, for those still employed, the risk of being fired (and never hired again) for speaking out, of losing friends who fear the risk of associating with such dissenters—that is, with such likely losers. The words used by the more powerful for hiding these costs speak of the virtues or necessities of loyalty and of sharing in the governing consensus, of being practical, of getting along, of being popular.

To translate free speech into practice within such a society depends upon how powerful an interest group dissenters can organize, such as unions, in favor of their own particular interest, so that they may join in discussing particular cases, particular laws and procedures, and enter into compromise. Any translation of human values and practices intrinsically missing from any archetypal drama into interests within the prevailing drama involves a fundamental loss or meaning. But how else could their case seemingly gain recognition—that is, within these limits of partial justice?

How partial has justice been under these circumstances in a country as rich and democratic as the United States? If there were space, it would be easy to document in detail how the great majority of Americans has long been marginalized or excluded from full participation in political life in its public, social, and economic aspects. I refer to women, African Americans, Latinos/Hispanics, American Indians, Asian Americans (and earlier in this century, other religious and ethnic groups), the poor, and those millions of employed workers who are exploited, who were not until the 1930s allowed to unionize, and whose physical safety on the job remains positively endangered as we saw in Chapter 5 in the section on the archetypal drama of capitalism.

Even the middle class has suffered from stagnant wages since 1979. What hid this loss of income was the growing entrance of working mothers and wives into the workforce. Democratic liberalism, as is characteristic of even the best of dramas in the service of the arrest in Act II, both furthers and contradicts democracy. It frees all to strive for more power, but the more powerful are normally unwilling to enhance the power of the less powerful, especially if the less powerful are not on their side and still lack the power to press for the fulfillment of human needs.

Consider alternatively the greatest possible victory for the currently marginal and defeated—they become the powerful. As long as they become powerful as democratic liberals within incoherence as a way of life, by joining the powerful they must make sure once again that the quest for individual power is rewarded, that is to say, that the most powerful and the wealthiest are indeed treated as the most powerful and the wealthiest.

But if we do not understand the power of archetypal stories—in the service of partial ways of life such as capitalism—to keep us unaware, then we will continue to be caught by them. This is the underlying reason why many Americans are not angry over the phenomenal growth in wealth of the upper 1 percent of families and the skewing of the tax cuts in their favor. Most Americans believe that there is no other way to achieve success except to fantasize that someday they themselves will become the powerful. That puts limits on justice, limits on welfare, and above all, limits on how justice is to be conceived and realized. Let anyone speak even now of the needs of human beings in their uniqueness, in what we can and need to do together now to bring the fullness of our beings into historical reality, and it still does not make sense to most people. Why?

Our explanation has two levels: the pattern of concrete practice, and the archetypal dynamics that it reflects. The making and remaking of fragments within the overarching fragment of incoherence—trying to make each of our own fragments bigger lest it grow smaller—is the story we live. In the worst of cases, these fragments hang together for a time in manifest practice through coercion by the most powerful. In some cases, these bits and pieces are juggled by gambling that usually involves secret rigging on the part of the powerful as the most recent revelations about the accounting practices of Enron, Tyco, World.Com and other corporations have exposed. In the case of democratic liberalism, we compete through agreed-upon procedures that are said to leave (but even in the best of cases often fail to leave) the least fortunate with the minimum necessary for survival.

But what keeps us within this drama even when we suffer its injustices? What moves us to express ourselves in terms of these manifest practices is its underlying archetypal force. This is a fact of utmost practical importance. Fundamental changes in this story—and the incomplete and biased justice intrinsic to it—cannot be brought about solely as changes in who holds power or who gets what within this way of life. Only if we discover its underlying patterning forces can we free ourselves from what holds us chained.

Incoherence as a way of life, even in the best of cases (that is, in liberal democracies), works only as long as our repression of its underlying reality remains powerful enough. Suppression is also used when the State, possessing a monopoly of the use of force, uses allegedly legitimate violence on behalf of individuals who profit from inflicting destruction. Many are the harmful pesticides that have been banned at home and sold abroad; the poisonous wastes that can no longer be dumped at home and are dumped instead in poorer countries abroad; or, in this country, the waste that cannot be disposed of in rich neighborhoods but is dumped in poor areas where the people have little if any means of challenging this kind of exploitation. Many are the communities that have been abandoned, sometimes on a day's notice, by their dominant industry whose own loss becomes a tax deduction and whose new investments give not a moment's thought to the people who, until their abandonment, had devoted most of their lives and community to working for the corporation. Anyone in any private corporation can be fired without being given a reason.

In all countries, everywhere, the majority is exceedingly poor while the rich are free to invest their money abroad—and most of them do so. Community is not a concern; individuals are means to other individuals' ends.

The overarching drama of incoherence and the stories in its service provide the context and the procedures that allow us to function in the face of so many broken, absent, and crippled relationships. But even these dramas cannot help us to agree on substantive foundations of ideas, values, or practices conducive to justice. None of these stories can help us discover and express our full capacity to be ourselves and justly and lovingly connect to others. They cannot, for all of them are fantasies. Fantasy also grasps reality, but in contrast to imagination, gets hold of only a fragment of reality—a fragment which serves to disconnect us from other aspects of reality, indeed serves to cut us off more and more until the structure of our life disintegrates. The seemingly saving grace of incoherence as a way of life (akin to that of emanation as a way of life) is that it offers us the largest possible fragment of the core drama of life and also (akin to emanation) many dramas in its service—and indeed far more and ever more and also (in terms of material power) more powerful dramas than emanation. Therefore, even the poor and deprived and defeated still possess, for a time, the underlying sense that they might catch a new and more promising fragment of life and then succeed in combining it with other fragments.

Though larger and more powerful than most fragments that our purely personal fantasies bring into being, all of the archetypal dramas within this way of life are foreshortened. None may go beyond Act II arrested in the core drama of life. All are organized as defense mechanisms. When political dramas fail, the newly dominant normally resort to what they call legitimate coercion, and the newly dominated resort to what the former call violence. Economic defeat ends in what is called loss, as if it were a game. Personal defeat ends in depression. What all have in common is that they mark a return to overt incoherence.

We are accustomed by now to calling neuroses defense mechanisms, but not so all the other foreshortened dramas and our arrested way of life. We even hesitate to call the national defense effort a defense mechanism lest we undermine its emanational character. But emanation is precisely what is at stake in all of these dramas. All archetypal stories to which we are unconsciously bound and cannot imagine and do not know how to criticize as such constitute sources of emanation. Neuroses possess precisely this same nature. What makes all of these defense mechanisms vulnerable is that, like all fragments based on fantasy, they are generated by and in turn generate irreconcilable tensions—to establish deliberate limits for all involved in the same story (though no story need be arrested there, given the fullness of the larger drama we have denied ourselves), to enhance our own controlling power within this story (because we lack the power of our full capacity), and to mask our anxiety in the face of conflict and change, for our unconscious recognizes the threat of deformation and dissolution.

We engage in such fragmenting fantasies and produce these tensions even at our seemingly productive best and with our largest and most powerful of fragments. This is how and why we produce and consume commodities most people need but cannot afford to buy; that is how we turn even science and art into commodities. That is how and why we organize official jurisdictions and academic disciplines—and the persona and politics of ourselves—whenever we live in the service of incoherence. We prefer mechanisms of aggressive defense, the better to mask our defensiveness. We prefer larger mechanisms to make defensiveness seem only the burden of others and to win in the competition between such individuals and their teams. These are our principal interests as the anxieties and tensions of incoherence fuel our fantasy to build such defense mechanisms that, even at their best, give us more power over, at most, several large fragments for a time, but cut us off from our capacity for transformation.

No wonder the justice of incoherence is incomplete and biased. We live with the trauma of persistent breaking and of absence, and at best with the partial satisfaction of changing fragments. Emanational containers are no mercy even for small children or the sick since, by their very nature, they keep us in dependency. Temporary refuge conscientiously provided for the emotionally or physically wounded, even for the dying, can help to bring us beyond a lamed justice only if they serve to aid us to appreciate and to move ourselves onto the path of transformation. Defense mechanisms in a traumatic world are no mercy, for they keep us from being able to help ourselves or others overcome the root causes of these crises.

JUSTICE IN THE PARTIAL WAY OF LIFE OF DEFORMATION

Evil—or deformation—arises all too readily out of the fragility of emanation and incoherence as ways of life, for they are fragments of the core drama of life. As fragments they require repression of our being, thus raising our insecurity, anxiety, and vulnerability. Deformation is the road to destructive death. The five ways of relating to others who are not in the same service of emanation with us are all modes of deformation. These same five ways often survive and are seen as we respond to our own associates in the service of incoherence when they threaten our power and security.

The powerful relate to the others who are considered a threat in only five ways: render them invisible, treat them as inferior, force the allegedly better ones to assimilate, exile those who are disloyal, and exterminate those considered a threat.

What are we doing to 47 million fellow Americans living without health care and who are on the edges of our plenty when we do nothing for them? We are treating them as *lesser* human beings—one of the five stations on the road to destructive death. Far more members of minority groups live in areas of toxic pollution than do other people. In Louisiana, the cancer rate of people of color consequently is eighteen times higher than that of other people. And politically, we want these people to become invisible. We don't want to hear from them. "No justice, no peace," became their cry after the Los Angeles riots of 1992. President Bush vetoed the bill to help Southeast Los Angeles, thus keeping the marginalized invisible.

"Yes," we say to the poor, "you do have another option: assimilate. Practice the values of incoherence yourself. Take personal initiative to compete." In the face of 7 percent unemployment, President Clinton endorsed the state of Wisconsin's law to deny further welfare to people who can't find a job within two years. Even under these extreme conditions, our slogan is this: Assimilate yourself into the system—or die.

We put people, millions of people, on the road to evil not because we consciously mean to do evil, but because our way of life leads us to seek repression of issues—*and of people*—we do not wish to see, cannot bear to see, and do not know what to do with within our way of life. Hence this partly unconscious and partly conscious alliance with deformation to keep these others repressed and suppressed—unconsciously repressed and consciously suppressed.

Those who most directly serve the powerful curb their capacity to see, to feel, to understand, and to connect anew even more than do the powerful elite. They are indeed trained to curb themselves. It allows them convincingly to say to themselves and to others, "I'm only doing my job. I am not competent to take these other aspects of life into account. My job is solely to be competent in my particular specialty and to treat all who come to me impersonally according to impersonal rules." Certainly such conceptions of jobs, of competence, and of procedures cannot produce a compassionate justice.

And if the poor do rebel, then we use the police to suppress them. Institutionalized rebellion is our way of life—but rebellion against our established institutions is illegitimate. It is intrinsically illegitimate. People in our dominant way of life are raised to believe that if *you* didn't make it, then *you* failed. And if you failed, it's *your* personal fault, your own lack of responsibility. It's your *own* fault. You can't blame the system; you can't blame this way of life. You mustn't rebel against it. In the best cases, we'll supply you with minimum welfare. So do not rebel. It's your own fault. And if *you* can't bear it, repress yourself. Otherwise, if you rebel, we will suppress you and send you into exile, into jail—an excommunication that represses the best of being human in all of its participants.

Finally, the fifth station on the road to destructive death is extermination. A society does not have to line people up and shoot them. No, there are other ways such as denying them access to enough food, medicine, and housing that will lead to death before their time.

THE PERSISTENT FULFILLMENT OF JUSTICE IN THE WAY OF LIFE OF TRANSFORMATION

In the way of life of transformation, *what is justice*? The cosmos of human relationships is renewed and nourished—and exists most justly—by virtue of transformation. The cosmos would not long exist without it. Unjust is any act—by us or by sacred sources—that cuts us off from this process, or arrests us in the course of it, or leaves us in incoherence, or exits us from the core drama into the abyss of deformation. In the good of transformation, justice and love become one, here and now, concretely and in the depths, in the experience that heals and moves us to a fundamentally new and better alternative, better than any other we can now discover.

In transformation, practicing a compassionate justice is not something we do simply out of obligation. Being in transformation is being just. The justice of transformation is its healing realization of understanding and love with respect to these people facing this particular problem here and now. We are being just not because we have found means to put arguments about rights or obligations or ethical ends into practice, and not because god says that we must do this or that, but we are just as we discover—thanks to our journey this time into Act III—what practice can in fact move us toward the fundamentally better.

We do not enshrine this moment of truth about justice into a permanent commandment or rule as in the service of emanation, nor do we exploit it as a more powerful battle station or as a reassuring procedure, as in the service of incoherence. We ask each time anew, "What is justice for this person and her or his neighbors in this situation?" Transformation never offers one single unifying concrete truth about justice; neither is it a succession of opinions about contingent moments. We always ask this: What is missing here or present here to harm us and prevent transformation? Does our practice now contribute to transformation and to the persistence of transformation in this concrete case? That is how we apply the theory of transformation to justice, not as propositions to execute as laws, but as a guide to renewed practice of the experience of transformation.

Such justice is personal, never impersonal or merely procedural. Human beings offer their experience of transformation to human beings who are creating or suffering injustice, and guide them into participating in overcoming injustice. It is personal also in the most immediate sense that there can be no justice if we desert ourselves. If we abandon ourselves, we betray ourselves, and if we do not then sink into apathy, we will crave either for unquestioning emanational dependence on another or else plunge into deformation.

All four faces of our being necessarily interpenetrate one another. The illness that arises from the absence of one or more of them also interpenetrates. The political face of what we can and need to do together also depends on what each can and needs to do together with our own self. If we are not lovingly together with our own self, we cannot enter into fruitful political relations with other human beings or with the sacred.

People differ over time from themselves and from others in the present quality of their consciousness and their relationship to what for many is still their unconscious. People who are otherwise contemporaries thus may not have entered into the same historical period in their personal, political, and sacred relationships. They will therefore differ seriously and indeed conflict in their abilities and their needs. But their intrinsic ability and need to come forth and relate freely, fully, and justly is theirs by virtue of being human, however unique their talents and their expression of their humanity. We bring forth such gifts as we can at this time of need.

Transforming justice respects the historical face of our being. It cannot be put into motion except by starting from where different people are now. We do not respect history if we homogenize it through the same filter, or seek to preserve it in its inherited form, or act as if it had a preordained outcome. Each time we act, we decisively create history anew. We move with people from their earlier way of life into transformation as a way of life, or else, we renew the process of transformation once again in old or new areas of life. Our sense of history and of justice is expressed through this process. The justice of transformation is not solely a matter of arriving in Act III. Justice begins by entering into this drama through its first Act.

What concerns us about justice in the service of transformation are not primarily courts and laws, but how we relate to each other with all four faces of our being freely and fully interconnected with each other. Justice does not raise its head in transformation primarily as a question of crime but of what we can and need to do together to create understanding, just, and loving relationships. Even in the case of a crime, we ask, "What archetype led this criminal to do what he or she did, and how can we help this person get out of this drama so that she or he will not repeat this crime? And what can the criminal do to heal the victims of the crime?" Even criminals who commit murder need to be given the opportunity to redeem their lives through transformation.

Strategies of transformation emphasize creating new and better relationships and stories we can share in *all* aspects of life. What would the fundamentally new and better be like? Imagine a situation in which we would not see the poor and discriminated against as potential threats to our political and economic position or future but as opportunities if our tax money and our joint political action enlarged their opportunities in life. Now we cannot even imagine such a society. Why? Because we feel that our present being, our own position, however better than theirs, is only a fragile fragment of life. We are made anxious by the thought of still more competition by people unlike us.

What would the new and fundamentally better be like? We need first of all to free ourselves to see ourselves and others as human beings, and to care for ourselves and others as human beings—to express our fundamentally new understanding and courage to engage in the experience of transformation by inspiring others, by our example and our helping hand, to share the fullness of life with us and to remove the barriers that stand in the way.

When you have truly and fully become yourself, it isn't power or social status that moves you; it isn't the biased and incomplete interest of a still incomplete and biased self. You feel a deep sense of being fully there, fully present *as you*—but all the more caring because history and politics aren't yet what they need to be for everyone to feel such strength, such freedom, such capacity, such love.

Since the source of sources cannot unilaterally will transformation, and since we can begin to participate in transformation historically only where we are now, its justice can only be created through democratic participation here and now. We are judged not by what we accomplish but by what we help to set into motion toward the fundamentally better—for what we help to nourish. And therefore the Book of Life is not closed when we die. But we are not judged according to the Book of Right or Wrong, but indeed according to the Book of Life.*

---

*This is an appropriate way to end this book because Manfred Halpern died before he was able to complete this work. He did indeed set into motion not only the theory of transformation but became for so many of us, his colleagues and students, family and friends, a living guide of transformation who lived the journey he so lovingly understood and so brilliantly wrote about and taught. He was a rare pure spirit who passed our way and because of it we shall be forever blessed; his Book of Life is not closed and neither is ours. The hope of transformation does indeed spring eternal when we choose to participate with Manfred—whose name means man of peace—and with the deepest source of transformation in bringing about the fundamentally new and better in achieving understanding, love, and justice.

Bibliography

Abalos, David T. *La Comunidad Latina in the United States: Personal and Political Strategies for Transforming Culture.* Westport, CT: Praeger, 1998.
———. *The Latino Family and the Politics of Transformation,* Praeger Series in Transformational Politics and Political Science. Westport, CT: Praeger, 1993.
———. *The Latino Male: A Radical Redefinition.* Boulder, CO: Lynne Rienner, 2002.
———. "The Latino Male and the Politics of Transformation," a paper delivered at the Annual Meeting of the American Political Science Association, September 4, 1998.
———. *Latinos in the United States: The Sacred and the Political.* Notre Dame, IN: University of Notre Dame Press, 1986.
———. "The Personal, Political, Historical and Sacred Grounding of Culture: Some Reflections on the Creation of a Latino Culture in the United States from the Perspective of a Theory of Transformation," a paper delivered at a National Conference on Latinos and Religion in the United States, Princeton University, April 16–19, 1993; and later published in *Old Masks, New Faces: Religion and Latino Identities,* PARAL Studies Series, Vol. 2. New York: Bildner Center for Western Hemisphere Studies, 1995.
———. *Strategies of Transformation toward a Multicultural Society: Fulfilling the Story of Democracy,* Praeger Series in Transformational Politics and Political Science. Westport, CT: Praeger, 1996.
Ajami, Fouad. *The Dream Palace of the Arabs: A Generation's Odyssey.* 1st ed. New York: Pantheon, 1998.
———. *The New Republic,* July 15, 1996.
Alfarabi and (trans.) Muhsin Mahdi. *Philosophy of Plato and Aristotle.* New York: Free Press, 1962.
Alperovitz, Gar. *Atomic Diplomacy: Hiroshima and Potsdam: The Use of the Atomic Bomb and the American Confrontation with Soviet Power.* 2nd (expanded) ed. London: Pluto, 1994.

Altmann, Alexander. *Studies in Religious Philosophy and Mysticism*. London: Routledge & K. Paul, 1969.
Augustine and (ed.) Henry Scowcroft Bettenson. *Concerning the City of God against the Pagans*. Harmondsworth, Middlesex: Penguin, 1972.
Augustine and (ed.) Marcus Dods. *The City of God*. New York: Modern Library, 1950.
Augustine and (ed.) R. S. Pine-Coffin. *Confessions*. Harmondsworth (London): Penguin, 1961.
Avineri, Shlomo. "Marx's Vision of Future Society," *Dissent* (Summer 1973), 323–31.
———. *The Social and Political Thought of Karl Marx*, Cambridge Studies in the History and Theory of Politics. London: Cambridge University Press, 1968.
Baldwin, James. *The Fire Next Time*, New York: Random House, 1963.
Balfour, Katharine Lawrence, and Princeton University Dept. of Politics. "'The Evidence of Things Not Said: Race Consciousness and Political Theory." 1996.
Baudelaire, Charles. *The Painter of Modern Life and Other Essays* translated and edited by Jonathan Mayne, London: Phaidon, 1964.
Beha, James A. "Gods of the Younger Generation: A Study of the Transforming Agent in Aeschylus's *The Eumenides*," Essay in Politics 326, Politics Department, Princeton University, 1970.
Bellah, Robert Neelly. *Habits of the Heart: Individualism and Commitment in American Life*. Berkeley: University of California Press, 1985.
Benjamin, Lois. *The Black Elite: Facing the Color Line in the Twilight of the Twentieth Century*. Chicago: Nelson-Hall, 1991.
Berger, Peter L. *The Other Side of God: A Polarity in World Religions*. 1st ed. Garden City, NY: Anchor, 1981.
Berman, Sheri. *The Social Democratic Moment: Ideas and Politics in the Making of Interwar Europe*. Cambridge, MA: Harvard University Press, 1998.
Bermeo, Nancy Gina, and Philip G. Nord. *Civil Society before Democracy: Lessons from Nineteenth-Century Europe*. Lanham, MD: Rowman & Littlefield, 2000.
Bill, James A. *The Eagle and the Lion: The Tragedy of American-Iranian Relations*. New Haven, CT: Yale University Press, 1988.
———. *George Ball: Behind the Scenes in U.S. Foreign Policy*. New Haven, CT: Yale University Press, 1997.
Blake, William, (eds.) David V. Erdman and Harold Bloom. *The Poetry and Prose of William Blake*. 4th ed. (with revisions). Garden City, NY: Doubleday, 1970.
Botwinick, Aryeh. *Postmodernism and Democratic Theory*. Philadelphia: Temple University Press, 1993.
———. *Skepticism, Belief, and the Modern: Maimonides to Nietzsche, Contestations*. Ithaca, NY: Cornell University Press, 1997.
Brettschneider, Marla. *Cornerstones of Peace: Jewish Identity Politics and Democratic Theory*. New Brunswick, NJ: Rutgers University Press, 1996.
———. *The Narrow Bridge: Jewish Views on Multiculturalism*. New Brunswick, NJ: Rutgers University Press, 1996.
Brockelmann, Carl, Moshe Perlmann, and Joel Carmichael. *History of the Islamic Peoples*. New York: G. P. Putnam's Sons, 1947.

Brown, L. Carl, and Norman Itzkowitz. *Psychological Dimensions of Near Eastern Studies*, Princeton Studies on the Near East. Princeton, NJ: Darwin, 1977.

Brown, Peter Robert Lamont. *Augustine of Hippo: A Biography*. Berkeley: University of California Press, 1967.

———. *The Making of Late Antiquity*, The Carl Newell Jackson Lectures, 1976. Cambridge, MA: Harvard University Press, 1978.

Buber, Martin, and (trans. and ed.) Will Herberg. *The Writings of Martin Buber*, New York: Meridian, 1956.

Friedrich, Carl J., ed. *Revolution*, New York: Atherton, 1966.

Cashmore, Ellis. "Women's Greatest Handicaps: Sex, Medicine, and Men," *The British Journal of Sports Medicine* 33 (April 1999), 76–77.

Cassirer, Ernst. *The Philosophy of the Enlightenment*. Princeton, NJ: Princeton University Press, 1951.

Cohen, Mark R. *Under Crescent and Cross: The Jews in the Middle Ages*. Princeton, NJ: Princeton University Press, 1994.

Cohen-Amalgor, Raphael. "Cultural Pluralism and the Israeli Nation-Building Ideology," *International Journal of Middle East Studies* 27 (1995), 461–84.

Corbin, Henry. *Creative Imagination in the Sufism of Ibn 'Arabi*, Bollingen Series 91. Princeton, NJ: Princeton University Press, 1969.

Crowley, Susan L. "On Mothers and Daughters . . . Celebrating the Age-Old Bonds between Women: A Profile of Cokie Roberts," *AARP Bulletin*, January 1999.

Donne, John, and (ed.) John T. Shawcross. *The Complete Poetry of John Donne*. Garden City, NY: Anchor, 1967.

Dostoyevsky, Fyodor, (ed.) Charles B. Guignon, and (trans.) Constance Black Garnett. *The Grand Inquisitor: With Related Chapters from the Brothers Karamazov*. Indianapolis: Hackett, 1993.

Eckstein, Harry. "A Cultural Theory of Social Change," *American Political Science Review* 82 (September 1988), 789–804.

———. "The Idea of Political Development: From Dignity to Efficiency," *World Politics* 34:4 (July 1982), 484–86.

Edwards, Paul, ed. *The Encyclopedia of Philosophy*. New York: Macmillan, 1967.

Esquivel, Laura. *Like Water for Chocolate: A Novel in Monthly Installments, with Recipes, Romances, and Home Remedies*. 1st ed. New York: Doubleday, 1992.

Euben, Roxanne Leslie. *Enemy in the Mirror: Islamic Fundamentalism and the Limits of Modern Rationalism: A Work of Comparative Political Theory*. Princeton, NJ: Princeton University Press, 1999.

Falk, Richard A., ed., and American Society of International Law. *The Vietnam War and International Law*. Princeton, NJ: Princeton University Press, 1968.

Farabi, *The Philosophy of Plato and Aristotle*, translation and introduction by Muhsin Mahdi, New York: Free Press of Glencoe, 1962

Feld, Edward. *The Spirit of Renewal: Crisis and Response in Jewish Life*. Woodstock, VT: Jewish Lights, 1991.

Findsen, Find. "The Road to Evil in the Holocaust: How Good People Were Enlisted in the Service of Deformation," Junior Paper, Politics Department, Princeton University, 1993.

Forster, E. M. *A Passage to India*. London: E. Arnold, 1967.
Friedrich, Carl J., ed. *Revolution: Yearbook of the American Society for Political and Legal Philosophy*, Nomos 8. New York: Atherton, 1966.
Fromm, Erich. *The Art of Loving*. New York: Perennial Library, 1974.
———. *Beyond the Chains of Illusion: My Encounter with Marx and Freud*. New York: Simon & Schuster, 1962.
Geronimus, Aline T. *Love and Politics: A Penetrating Glimpse into the Obvious*, a Senior Thesis, Politics Department, Princeton University, 1978.
Ghiselin, Brewster, ed. *The Creative Process: A Symposium*. New York: New American Library, 1955.
Gilligan, Carol. *In a Different Voice: Psychological Theory and Women's Development*. Cambridge, MA: Harvard University Press, 1982.
Gregory VI, Pope. *Mirani Vos*, 1832.
Greider, William. *Who Will Tell the People: The Betrayal of American Democracy*. New York: Simon & Schuster, 1992.
Groth, Alexander J. *Revolution and Political Change*, International Library of Politics and Comparative Government. Brookfield, VT: Dartmouth, 1996.
Gutiérrez, Gustavo. *We Drink from Our Own Wells: The Spiritual Journey of a People*. Maryknoll, NY: Orbis, 1984.
Gutmann, Amy, and Dennis F. Thompson. *Ethics and Politics: Cases and Comments*. 2nd ed., The Nelson-Hall Series in Political Science. Chicago: Nelson-Hall, 1990.
Halpern, Cynthia. *Suffering, Politics, Power: A Genealogy in Modern Political Theory*. Albany: State University of New York Press, 2002.
Halpern, Manfred. "A Theory for Transforming the Self: Moving Beyond the Nation-State", in Stephen Brim Woolpert, Christa Daryl Slaton, and Edward W. Schwerin, *Transformational Politics: Theory, Study, and Practice*, State University of New York Press, Albany, 1998, 45-56. .
———. "Choosing Between Ways of Life and Death and Between Forms of Democracy: An Archetypal Analysis," *Alternatives* 12 (1987), 5–35.
———. "On Social Transformation A Dialogue: The Dangers of Living in Archetypal Dramas Which Blind Us to Archetypal Choices and Limit Our Capacity and Freedom to Incremental Changes", *Alternatives*, April, 1987, 266-270.
———. "Four Contrasting Repertories of Human Relationships in Islam: Two Pre-Modern and Two Modern Ways of Dealing with Continuity and Change, Collaboration and Conflict, and the Achieving of Justice", in L. Carl Brown and Norman Itzkowitz, *Psychological Dimensions of Near Eastern Studies*, Princeton Studies on the Near East, Darwin Press, 1977, 17-54.
———. "The Politics of Transformation", *Main Currents in Modern Thought*, Vol. 31, No. 5, (May-June 1975), 131-137, and Vol. 32, no. 1 (September-October 1975), 13-19.
———. "A Redefinition of the Revolutionary Situation," *The Journal of International Affairs* 23:1 (1968).
———. "The Revolution of Modernization," in Roy C. Macrides and Bernard Edgar Brown, eds. *Comparative Politics: Notes and Readings*. Homewood, IL: Dorsey, 1968, 513–14.

———. *The Politics of Social Change in the Middle East and North Africa*. Princeton, NJ: Princeton University Press, 1963.

———. "The Revolution of Modernization in National and International Society," in Friedrich, Carl J., ed. *Revolution*.

Herberg, Will, ed. *The Writings of Martin Buber*. New York: Meridian, 1956.

Hirschman, Albert O. *The Passions and the Interests: Political Arguments for Capitalism before Its Triumph*. Princeton, NJ: Princeton University Press, 1977.

Hobbes, Thomas. *Leviathan; or, the Matter, Forme and Power of a Commonwealth, Ecclesiasticall and Civil*. New York: Collier, 1962.

Hodgson, Marshall G. S. *The Venture of Islam: Conscience and History in a World Civilization*. Chicago: University of Chicago Press, 1974.

Ibn, Khaldun, Franz Rosenthal, and N. J. Dawood. *The Muqaddimah: An Introduction to History*. Bollingen Series. Abridged ed. Princeton, NJ: Princeton University Press, 1967.

Idel, Moshe. *Kabbalah: New Perspectives*. New Haven, CT: Yale University Press, 1988.

James, William. *The Varieties of Religious Experience: A Study in Human Nature; Being the Gifford Lectures on Natural Religion Delivered at Edinburgh in 1901–1902*. New York: Longmans Green, 1902.

Jung, Carl Gustav. *Aion; Researches into the Phenomenology of the Self*. Complete Works 9, ii. 2nd ed. Princeton, NJ: Princeton University Press, 1968.

———. *The Archetypes and the Collective Unconscious*. Complete Works 9, Pt.1 2nd ed. Princeton, NJ: Princeton University Press, 1969.

———. *Psychological Types*. Princeton, N J: Princeton University Press, 1971.

Kafka, Franz, Felice Bauer, (eds.) Erich Heller, Jürgen Born, and (trans.) James Stern and Elizabeth Duckworth. *Letters to Felice*. New York: Penguin, 1978.

Kastein, Josef, and Huntley Paterson. *The Messiah of Ismir: Sabbatai Zevi*. New York: Viking, 1931.

Katzelson, Ira. *Black Men, White Cities: Race, Politics, and Migration in the United States, 1900–1930, and Britain, 1948–1968*. New York: Oxford University Press, 1973.

Kennedy, Paul M. *Preparing for the Twenty-First Century*. 1st ed. New York: Random House, 1993.

Khrushchev, Nikita Sergeevich. *Khrushchev Remembers*. Boston: Little Brown, 1970.

Klitgaard, Robert. "Taking Culture into Account: From 'Let's' to 'How,'" International Conference on Culture and Development in Africa, The World Bank, Washington, DC, April 2–3, 1992.

Korner, Kathy. *Medusa*, a Senior Thesis, Politics Department, Princeton University, May 1977.

Kramer, Peter D. *Listening to Prozac*. New York: Viking, 1993.

Kuhn, Thomas S. *The Structure of Scientific Revolutions*. 3rd ed. Chicago: University of Chicago Press, 1996.

Landers, Ann. *The Reader's Digest*, March 1994, 150.

Lapidus, Ira M. *Muslim Cities in the Later Middle Ages*. Cambridge, MA: Harvard University Press, 1967.

Lauman, Edward O., Anthony Paik, and Raymond C. Rosen. "Sexual Dysfunction in the United States," *Journal of the American Medical Association*, 281:6 (February 1999), 537–44.

Lerner, Michael, and Cornel West. *Jews and Blacks: A Dialogue on Race, Religion, and Culture in America*. New York: Plume, 1996.

Levenson, Joseph Richmond. *Confucian China and Its Modern Fate: A Trilogy*. 1st combined ed. Berkeley: University of California Press, 1965.

Lévy-Bruhl, Lucien, *The "Soul" of the Primitive*. New York: Praeger, 1966.

Lifton, Robert Jay. *The Protean Self: Human Resilience in an Age of Fragmentation*. New York: Basic Books, 1993.

Lindblom, Charles Edward. *The Intelligence of Democracy; Decision Making through Mutual Adjustment*. New York: Free Press, 1965.

Locke, John. *An Essay Concerning Human Understanding*, abridged and edited by Raymond Willburn, London: Dent (New York: Dutton), 1948.

Luther, Martin. "The Enslaved Will," cited in Ernst Cassirer, *The Philosophy of the Enlightenment*.

Machiavelli, Niccolò, and (ed. and trans.) Leslie Joseph Walker. *The Discourses of Niccolò Machiavelli, Rare Masterpieces of Philosophy and Science*. New Haven, CT: Yale University Press, 1950.

Macridis, Roy C., and Bernard Edward Brown. *Comparative Politics: Notes and Readings*. The Dorsey Series in Political Science, 3rd ed. Homewood, IL: Dorsey, 1968.

Mahdi, Muhsin. *Ibn Khaldun's Philosophy of History: A Study in the Philosophic Foundation of the Science of Culture*. Chicago: University of Chicago Press, 1964.

Maimonides, Moses, and (trans.) Shlomo Pines. *The Guide for the Perplexed*. Chicago: University of Chicago Press, 1963.

Masserman, Jules Hymen, and John J. Schwab, eds. *Man for Humanity: On Concordance vs. Discord in Human Behavior*. Springfield, IL: Thomas, 1972.

McNamara, Robert S., and Brian VanDeMark. *In Retrospect: The Tragedy and Lessons of Vietnam*. 1st ed. New York: Times Books, 1995.

Mill, John Stuart, Harriet Hardy Taylor Mill, and (ed.) Alice S. Rossi. *Essays on Sex Equality*. Chicago: University of Chicago Press, 1970.

Miller, Alice. *For Your Own Good: Hidden Cruelty in Child-Rearing and the Roots of Violence*. New York: Farrar Straus Giroux, 1983.

Miller, Norman, and Roderick Aya. *National Liberation; Revolution in the Third World*. New York: Free Press, 1971.

Mitchell, Richard P. *The Society of the Muslim Brothers*, Middle Eastern Monographs 9. London: Oxford University Press, 1969.

Molière. *The Misanthrope*. Studio City, CA: Players Press, 1993.

Morris, James Winston. "Ibn 'Arabi and His Interpreters," *Journal of the American Oriental Society* 106 (1986), 539–51 and 733–56; and 107 (1987), 101–19.

———. "Ibn 'Arabi's 'Esotericism': The Problem of Spiritual Authority," *Studia Islamica* 67 (1988), 37–64.

———. "The Spiritual Ascension: Ibn 'Arabi and the Mi'raj," *Journal of the American Oriental Society* 107 (1987), 629–52; and 108 (1988), 63–77.

———. *The Wisdom of the Throne*. (See Sadr al-Din al-Shirazi)

Morrison, Toni, ed. *Race-ing Justice, En-Gendering Power: Essays on Anita Hill, Clarence Thomas, and the Construction of Social Reality*. 1st ed. New York: Pantheon, 1992.

Mulla Sadra. (See Sadr al-Din al-Shirazi.)

Nasr, Seyyed Hossein. *An Introduction to Islamic Cosmological Doctrines: Conceptions of Nature and Methods Used for Its Study by the Ikhwan Al-Safa, Al-Biruni, and Ibn Si.* Revised ed. London: Thames & Hudson, 1978.

The New Jerusalem Bible. Garden City, NY: Doubleday, 1985.

Niebuhr, Reinhold. *The Nature and Destiny of Man: A Christian Interpretation*, Gifford Lectures; 1939. New York: Scribner, 1964.

Nussbaum, Martha Craven, and Joshua Cohen. *For Love of Country: Debating the Limits of Patriotism.* Boston: Beacon, 1996.

Oberdorfer, Don. *Tet!* 1st ed. Garden City, NY: Doubleday, 1971.

Pagels, Elaine H. *Adam, Eve, and the Serpent.* New York: Random House, 1988.

———. *The Gnostic Gospels.* New York: Vintage, 1989.

———. *The Gnostic Paul: Gnostic Exegesis of the Pauline Letters.* Philadelphia: Trinity Press International, 1992.

———. *The Origin of Satan.* 1st ed. New York: Random House, 1995.

———. "The Orthodox Against the Gnostics: Confrontation and Inferiority in Early Christianity," in Peter L. Berger. *The Other Side of God*, 61–73.

Parrino, Mark W., and (U.S.) Center for Substance Abuse Treatment. *State Methadone Treatment Guidelines, Treatment Improvement Protocol (TIP) Series 1.* Rockville, MD: U.S. Dept. of Health and Human Services Public Health Service Substance Abuse and Mental Health Services Administration Center for Substance Abuse Treatment, 1993.

Parsons, Talcott. *The Social System.* Glencoe, IL: Free Press, 1951.

———. *Societies: Evolutionary and Comparative Perspectives.* Englewood Cliffs, NJ: Prentice-Hall, 1966.

———. *The Structure of Social Action: A Study in Social Theory with Special Reference to a Group of Recent European Writers.* 2nd ed. Glencoe, IL: Free Press, 1949.

Pei, Minxin. *From Reform to Revolution: The Demise of Communism in China and the Soviet Union.* Cambridge, MA: Harvard University Press, 1994.

Perera, Sylvia Brinton. *The Scapegoat Complex: Toward a Mythology of Shadow and Guilt*, Studies in Jungian Psychology by Jungian Analysts 23. Toronto: Inner City, 1986.

Perwin, Cynthia. *The Ego, the Self, and the Structure of Political Authority*, a doctoral dissertation, the Politics Department, Princeton University, May 1973.

Peto, Richard, Imperial Cancer Research Fund (Great Britain), and World Health Organization. *Mortality from Smoking in Developed Countries, 1950–2000: Indirect Estimates from National Vital Statistics*, Oxford Medical Publications. Oxford: Oxford University Press, 1994.

Pifer, Alan. *Bilingual Education and the Hispanic Challenge*, Annual Report of the Carnegie Foundation of New York, 1979.

Plato and (trans. and ed.) Francis Macdonald Cornford. *The Republic of Plato.* New York: Oxford University Press, 1947.

Poje, Gerald V. "Think Globally," *The John Hopkins Magazine*, February 1998, 4.

Pye, Lucian W. "The Concept of Political Development," *The Annals of the American Academy of Social and Political Science*, March 1965, 11–12.

Rensenbrink, John. *The Greens and the Politics of Transformation*. San Pedro, CA: R. & E. Miles, 1992.

Reps, Paul. *Zen Flesh, Zen Bones*. Tokyo: C.E. Tuttle, 1957.

Rhodes, Richard. "The General [Curtis LeMay] and World War III," *The New Yorker*, June 19, 1995, 47.

Rilke, Rainer Maria, and Franz Xaver Kappus. *Briefe an Einen Jungen Dichter*. Leipzig: Insel-verlag, 1929.

Robinson, James McConkey, Marvin W. Meyer, and Institute for Antiquity and Christianity, and (trans.) Coptic Gnostic Library Project. *The Nag Hammadi Library in English*. New York: Harper & Row, 1977.

Rosen, Lawrence. *The Anthropology of Justice: Law as Culture in Islamic Society*, Lewis Henry Morgan Lecture Series, 1985. Cambridge: Cambridge University Press, 1989.

———. *Bargaining for Reality: The Construction of Social Relations in a Muslim Community*. Chicago: University of Chicago Press, 1984.

Rosenau, James N., and Woodrow Wilson School of Public and International Affairs, Center of International Studies. *International Aspects of Civil Strife*. Princeton, NJ: Princeton University Press, 1964.

Rosenberg, Claude N. *Wealthy and Wise: How You and America Can Get the Most out of Your Giving*. 1st ed. Boston: Little Brown, 1994.

Rossi, Alice S. (See Mill, John Stuart.)

Sadr al-Din al-Shirazi, Muhammad ibn Ibrahim (aka Mulla Sadra) and (trans.) James Winston Morris. *The Wisdom of the Throne: An Introduction to the Philosophy of Mulla Sadra*, Princeton Library of Asian Translations. Princeton, NJ: Princeton University Press, 1981.

Scholem, Gershom Gerhard. *Major Trends in Jewish Mysticism*. New York: Schocken, 1995.

———, and (trans.) Ralph Manheim. *On the Kabbalah and Its Symbolism*. 1st Schocken paperback ed. New York: Schocken, 1969.

———. *Sabbatai Sevi: The Mystical Messiah, 1626–1676*. Revised and augmented translation. London: Routledge & K. Paul, 1973.

———. *Sabbatai Sevi: The Mystical Messiah, 1626–1676*, Bollingen Series 93. Princeton, NJ: Princeton University Press, 1973.

———. *Von Der Mystischen Gestalt Der Gottheit: Studien Zu Grundbegriffen Der Kabbala*. Zürich: Rhein-Verlag, 1962.

Sharabi, Hisham. *Neopatriarchy: A Theory of Distorted Change in Arab Society*. New York: Oxford University Press, 1988.

Shelburne, Walter A. *Mythos and Logos in the Thought of Carl Jung: The Theory of the Collective Unconscious in Scientific Perspective*. Albany: State University of New York Press, 1988.

Singerman, Diane. *Avenues of Participation: Family, Politics, and Networks in Urban Quarters of Cairo*, Princeton Studies in Muslim Politics. Princeton, NJ: Princeton University Press, 1995.

Smith, Wilfred Cantwell. *Faith and Belief*. Princeton, NJ: Princeton University Press, 1979.

———. *Islam in Modern History*. Princeton, NJ: Princeton University Press, 1957.

———. *The Meaning and End of Religion: A New Approach to the Religious Traditions of Mankind*. New York: Macmillan, 1963.
Steiner, George. "Our Homeland, the Text," *Salmagundi* 66 (1985), 4–25.
Stevens Arroyo, Antonio M., and Gilbert Cadena. *Old Masks, New Faces: Religion and Latino Identities*, Paral Studies Series 2. New York: Bildner Center for Western Hemisphere Studies, 1995.
Suarez, Oscar. *Protestantism and Authoritarian Politics: The Politics of Repression and the Future of Ecumenical Witness in the Philippines*. Quezon City, Phillipines: New Day, 1999.
Thompson, Kenneth W. *Moral Dimensions of American Foreign Policy*, Ethics in Foreign Policy Series. New Brunswick, NJ: Transaction, 1984.
Tilly, Charles. *Coercion, Capital, and European States: AD 990–1990*. Cambridge, MA: B. Blackwell, 1990.
Tucker, Robert C. *The Soviet Political Mind: Stalinism and Post-Stalin Change*. Rev. ed. New York: Norton, 1971.
Vickers, Geoffrey. *Value Systems and Social Process*. New York: Basic Books, 1968.
Vleminckx, Koen, and Timothy M. Smeeding, eds. *Child Well-Being, Child Poverty and Child Policy in Modern Nations: What Do We Know?* Bristol, UK: Policy Press, 2001.
Welbon, Guy Richard. *The Buddhist Nirvana and Its Western Interpreters*. Chicago: University of Chicago Press, 1968.
West, Cornel. *Beyond Eurocentrism and Multiculturalism*. Monroe, ME: Common Courage, 1993.
———. *Race Matters*. Boston: Beacon, 1993.
Williams, Patricia, J. "A Rare Case of Muleheadedness in Men," in Toni Morrison, ed. *Race-ing Justice*.
Woolpert, Stephen Brim, Christa Daryl Slaton, and Edward W. Schwerin, eds. *Transformational Politics: Theory, Study, and Practice*. Albany: State University of New York Press, 1998.
Wren, Christopher S. "Review of Paul. B. Starres, *Global Habit: The Drug Problem in a Borderless World*," *The New York Times Sunday Book Review*, August 18, 1996.
Wright, Betsy. "Women and the Politics of Compassion," Junior paper, Politics Department, Princeton University, May 1977.
Wuthnow, Robert. *God and Mammon in America*. New York: Free Press, 1994.
Yerushalmi, Yosef Hayim. *Zakhor: Jewish History and Jewish Memory*, The Samuel and Althea Stroum Lectures in Jewish Studies. Seattle: University of Washington Press, 1982.
Young, Iris Marion. *Justice and the Politics of Difference*. Princeton, NJ: Princeton University Press, 1990.

Index

Abalos, David, 88, 204, 237, 266, 288, 306, 307, 309, 313, 322, 335
abstraction, 2, 3, 6, 49, 84, 179, 223, 236, 245, 281, 290, 318, 328, 360
abyss, 35, 37, 53, 63, 170, 173, 175, 176, 178, 179, 191, 231, 259, 352, 374, 375, 380, 383, 389
affirmation, 89, 118, 298, 384
Afghanistan, 203, 220
African-Americans, 148, 304, 305
affinity groups and transformation, 45–46, 228–229.262–263, 280–2281, 321
agnostic, 7, 89, 198, 337
Alfarabi, 12, 30, 293, 370
Algeria, 120, 192
alienation, 53, 188
Allah, 105, 297
anarchy, 56, 123
apocalypse, 380
Arabi, Ibn, 12, 30, 38, 39, 43, 107, 118, 119, 120, 124, 293, 296, 297, 298, 299, 348, 370, 384
Arabia, 43, 107, 118, 119, 296, 297, 384
archetypal analysis, 5–16, 30, 69, 264, 326
archetypal, 5–63, 67, 69–105, 140–153, 160–69, 171, 173, 175–182, 208–210, 223–227, 235–244
archetypal drama of transformation, 7, 17–45, 259–260, 335
archetypal relationships, 76, 84, 121–125, 233, 235, 237–239, 243–247, 249–279, 284, 312, 325, 326, 333, 346, 369, 382

archetypal stories, 5, 7, 8, 9, 21, 25, 26, 28, 30, 37, 48, 50, 55, 57–59, 86–89, 119, 129, 161, 169, 196, 236, 266, 270, 330–332, 385, 387
archetypal ways of life, 9, 262, 326, 328, 333, 339, 369
archetype, 6, 7, 9, 10, 12, 18, 23, 27, 34, 50, 63, 327, 328, 332, 334, 356, 360, 391
Aristotle, 30, 347
assimilate, 19, 65, 118, 131, 144, 175, 181–183, 186–187, 197–198, 237, 266, 293–294, 379, 388–389
assimilation, 186, 187, 188, 198, 296, 303, 306, 315, 382
Assisi, 131
Augustine, St, 70, 112, 113, 114, 115, 131, 138, 177, 178, 344, 364, 377, 378
authority, 19, 22, 26, 39, 52, 53, 67, 83, 110–117, 125, 128, 129, 130, 134, 143, 155, 168, 205, 209–210, 237, 239, 240–241, 362–364, 370, 370
autonomy, 19, 131, 169, 247–251, 254–256, 262, 263, 266, 272, 280, 284, 312, 315, 365, 373, 377
Avicenna, 370
Avineri, Shlomo, 160

bargaining, 120, 123–124, 246–247, 254–255, 312
betrayal, 23, 86, 106, 149, 157, 173, 211, 212, 254, 361, 362, 377

403

Buber, Martin, 135
bureaucracy, 86, 212, 299, 357
Bush, George W.H, .172, 383, 388

capacity and freedom, 9, 12, 17, 33, 39, 49, 74, 92, 359, 360, 373, 378
capitalism, 25, 38, 43, 76, 143, 145, 147, 150–170, 185, 192, 195–196, 204, 206–207, 224, 226, 267, 270, 286, 294, 300, 302, 307, 320, 329, 333, 379, 385
Catholic Church, 111, 138, 213, 237, 249, 341, 343
Catholic, 44, 111, 116, 127–131, 138, 198, 213, 237, 249, 301, 304, 312, 341–343, 364–366, 368, 370, 379
celibacy, 92
census, 149, 304
Charlemagne, 115
Chavez, Cesar, 165
Christ, 12, 26–27, 44, 48, 50–51, 70, 72, 105, 108–109, 111–118, 121, 124, 127–128, 130–133, 138, 140, 167, 178, 186, 197, 207, 213, 216, 223, 249, 290–291, 294–297, 301, 312, 341–349, 364–379
Christianity, 50, 70, 112, 114, 116, 130–131, 138, 140, 197, 213, 301, 312, 342, 348–349, 364–365, 368, 377–378
collaboration and conflict, 76, 84, 121, 134, 237, 248, 249, 263, 334, 363, 369, 381
compassion, 3, 4, 12, 21, 24, 41, 63, 68, 82, 92, 124, 127, 131, 149, 161, 164, 167, 175, 212, 215, 216, 219, 226, 228, 230, 245, 262, 281, 298, 304, 308, 314, 319, 342, 345, 356, 381, 382, 389, 390
concreteness, 6, 33, 38, 60, 64, 89, 97, 116, 231, 259, 350
conquest, 109, 120, 137, 138, 197, 202, 241, 247, 297, 364, 378
Constantine, 112, 375
Constantinople, 301
continuity and change, 76, 84, 121, 237, 242, 247, 249, 263, 369, 381
core drama of life, 2, 4, 10, 17, 19, 21–24, 34–35, 37–38, 49, 52, 54, 56, 62, 65, 69, 72, 74, 77, 81, 90, 98, 103–108, 110, 116, 127, 134–143, 146, 164, 169–181, 190–191, 197, 209, 211, 218, 223–231, 242, 252, 256–260, 273, 307, 311, 322–329, 332–341, 343, 346–352, 356–363, 375, 382–383, 387–388
Corinthians, 45, 74, 312, 349

cosmos of continuous creation, 11, 17, 49, 50, 52, 62, 68, 79, 104, 106, 189, 279, 333, 338, 342, 343, 350, 354, 360, 379
cosmos of human relationships, 148, 389
counter-tradition of transformation, 59
counter-tradition, 12, 59, 62
culture, 7, 9, 31, 43, 56, 84, 86, 88, 120, 186, 197, 210, 221, 255, 261, 266, 275, 279, 285, 287, 289–309, 314, 318, 335, 343, 357, 358, 379

deconstruct, 4, 6, 339
deepest source of transformation, 362, 392
deepest source, 5, 12, 19, 21, 38–39, 42, 47, 49, 52, 57–68, 80–82, 96–97, 99, 104, 142, 162, 219–220, 236, 259–262, 275, 280, 316, 340, 346–350, 360, 362, 368, 392
deformation, 2, 4, 11, 12, 17, 21, 23, 26–37, 43–44, 50–56, 63, 71–73, 81–109, 126–137, 143–144, 147, 159, 163–4, 287, 290, 299–305, 311, 316, 325, 330, 333–351, 359–361, 365, 370–390
democracy, 11, 25, 27, 54, 69, 72, 76, 86, 89, 147–153, 154–174, 213, 224, 226, 250, 275, 295, 309, 328, 341, 385
democratic liberalism, 26, 65, 141, 143, 147–153, 155, 159, 185, 187, 251, 253, 256, 294, 301, 302, 307, 331, 357, 381, 383, 384, 385, 386
direct exchange, 245–247, 254, 256, 259, 262–266, 279, 284, 286, 369
dominant culture, 43, 86, 186, 266, 293, 295, 300, 302–303, 306–307, 318
Dostoyevsky, Fyodor, 130
dualism, 11, 80, 98, 214

education, 46, 54, 57, 60, 65, 82, 131, 148, 159, 166, 183, 204, 253, 256, 266, 295, 298, 306–309, 318, 320, 365
ein-sof, 132
emanation, 2, 4, 11–12, 18–32, 34, 36–44, 48–59, 61, 63, 68, 70–73, 80, 82, 84–87, 90–91, 95, 103–148, 151, 160–169, 172–97, 200, 204–263, 272–280, 283–307, 311–317, 320, 327, 384, 387–388, 390
empiricism, 327
empowerment, 162, 164, 167, 207, 241
environment, 10, 94, 151, 157, 176, 194, 205, 217, 254, 256, 285, 304, 306, 330
esotericism, 39, 370
ethics, 103, 248, 274, 344, 369

ethnic, 9, 84, 112, 119, 144, 165, 186, 187, 198, 225, 240, 243, 261, 289, 290-305, 307, 309, 385
ethnicity, 84, 243, 289, 290-301, 303, 305, 307, 309
ethnocentrism, 291
eurocentrism, 305
evil, 12, 36, 51, 63, 76, 111, 113, 122, 132, 145-146, 154, 161-163, 171, 174-179, 188, 192-193, 203-238, 241, 258-259, 328, 345-346, 359, 361, 365-366, 372-378, 388-389
exploitation, 159, 183-184, 222-223, 228, 375, 386
exploration, 3, 19, 36, 90, 97, 133, 165, 204, 235, 250, 257, 269, 270, 284, 288, 290, 316, 370, 374
extermination, 174, 183, 197-199, 376-378, 382, 389

fatalism, 123, 298, 369
feminism, 4, 44, 46
five aspects of capacity, 252, 259
five issues of performance, 381
four faces of our being, 1, 2, 4, 6, 37, 39, 49, 82-83, 89-99, 125, 142, 152, 162, 168, 170, 181, 228, 236, 241, 259, 262, 266, 269-270, 287, 306, 332, 335, 347, 351, 360-363, 368, 390-391
four fundamentally different choices, 273, 329, 337, 348, 352, 358
four fundamentally different sacred sources, 337, 352
four ways of life, 2, 4, 69, 72, 97, 101-138, 140, 142, 144, 146, 148, 150, 152, 154, 156, 158, 160-198, 200, 202, 204, 206, 208-228, 230, 231, 235, 270, 275, 288, 290, 300, 325, 358, 360, 368
fragmentation, 132, 163, 300, 382
fundamentalism, 38, 55, 171, 191-194
fundamentalist, 124, 191-194, 203, 259

gnosis, 33
gnostic, 7, 77, 89, 114, 133, 198, 337, 348
god lower case, 7, 18, 29-30, 38-39
god of transformation, 366
gospels, 76, 133, 348
guide, 23, 24, 30, 32, 39, 40-44, 47, 90, 105, 114, 133, 208, 216, 223, 227-229, 244, 260, 266, 293, 308, 321-322, 329, 333, 335, 350, 362-363, 371, 390, 392
guilt, 26, 163, 211, 249, 365

Halpern, Manfred, 69, 170, 193, 212, 222-223, 299, 369, 392
healthcare, 167, 183, 194
hellenism, 107
heresies, 189
hero, 57, 64, 116, 160, 161, 207, 329, 369
hierarchy, 112, 115, 128, 129, 131, 160, 227, 250, 365, 366, 378, 380
Hindenburg, President, 196, 213
Hiroshima, 202-203, 220
Hirschman, Albert O, .145
Hispanics, 385
historical face, 1, 7, 20, 42, 49-50, 52, 59, 63, 79, 87-90, 97-98, 170, 210, 305, 328, 334, 361-362, 372, 391
holocaust, 89, 127, 174-175, 196-200, 295-296, 350, 377
Hussein, Saddam, 172

Iacocca, Lee, 143
Ibn Arabi, 12, 39, 298, 348, 370
idealism, 57, 143
immigrants, 197
immigration, 98
imperialism, 127, 140, 174, 184, 185, 299, 371
incrementalism, 64, 164, 166
inherited culture, 9, 307
injustice, 2, 3, 76, 84, 122, 125, 171, 177, 181, 204, 218, 238, 241, 253, 258, 261, 319, 359-361, 383, 386, 390
inquisition, 130, 177, 378
intellect, 4, 30, 124, 217, 223, 254, 278, 314, 315, 327
interconnect, 2, 4, 10, 12, 44, 45, 46, 75, 79, 82, 83, 89, 91-98, 136, 144, 154, 165, 168, 228, 238, 270, 288, 331, 339, 348, 353, 354, 356, 363, 391
intimacy, 278, 285, 319, 321
Iran, 172, 193, 194, 237, 240, 299
Iran-Contra, 240
Iraq, 107, 109, 172, 202, 296, 299, 327, 376
Islam, 21, 30, 44, 50, 105, 115-133, 180, 192-194, 247, 249, 293, 297-299, 349, 369, 370, 371, 377
isolation, 56, 74, 95, 200, 242-244, 253-256, 261, 265, 279, 284, 286, 369, 379

Jesus, 12, 44-45, 107, 112, 114-115, 189, 197, 213, 292, 313, 348-349, 362, 377

Jews, 43–44, 105–11, 116–119, 127–133, 138, 189, 197–199, 212, 214, 216, 248, 290, 297, 300, 308, 313, 341–343, 366–368, 371, 376–378
Jordan, 109, 200
journey of transformation, 5, 6, 90, 124, 127, 135, 143, 169, 221, 338, 356, 367, 368, 372
Judaic, 107
Judaism, 21, 50, 296, 349, 367
Jung, C.G, .6, 7, 32, 60, 98, 178, 219, 223, 270, 328
justice in four ways of life, 359–392

kabba, 12, 39, 60, 118, 132, 133, 292, 293, 296, 313, 367, 368, 370, 371, 372, 376
Kafka, Franz, 282
Koran, 39, 116, 118, 119, 124, 194, 296, 313, 342, 366, 377
kristallnacht, 214

Lao-tse, 12, 132
Latina, 288, 306, 309, 315
Latino, 57, 88, 95, 290, 300, 303, 304, 306, 307, 309, 313, 335, 356, 385
laws, 37, 63, 119, 144, 150, 153–157, 165, 169, 172, 180, 184, 194, 209, 248, 292, 305, 312, 333, 347, 355, 384, 385, 390, 391
legitimacy, 112, 123, 129, 138, 147, 169, 209, 236, 250, 256, 326, 364
lobbyists, 149, 153, 157, 250
lord of deformation, 127, 170, 190
lord of emanation, 127, 135, 161, 189, 360–363
lord of incoherence, 146, 161
lord of nothing, 193
love and justice, 34, 47, 67, 69, 75, 169, 215, 228, 277, 349, 350, 356
loyalty, 21, 89, 105, 112, 115, 135, 156, 160, 187, 195, 217, 239, 244, 285, 342, 361, 364, 369, 380, 384

male-dominated, 314, 320
manipulation, 55, 122, 163, 209, 239, 240, 247, 284, 314, 347, 357, 383
marginalization, 184
materialism, 29
messiah, 69, 112, 118, 133, 293, 294, 368, 376
Mexican, 300, 306
Mexico, 296, 306
militarization, 300
minorities, 148, 225, 345
modernity, 192, 345, 371

modernization, 187, 212, 221–223, 237
Molière, 255
monotheism, 189, 340, 341, 344
morality, 8, 160, 196, 205, 239, 272
Morris, James Winston, 39, 133, 348, 370
Muhammad, 39, 43–44, 105, 107, 110, 111, 118–120, 124, 297–298, 341, 343, 362, 366, 375
multicultural, 4, 266, 291, 303, 305–309
Muslim, 12, 39, 48, 60, 109, 111, 115–133, 171, 180, 182, 192–194, 243, 290, 293–299, 301, 304, 313, 341, 343, 366, 369, 370, 371, 376, 377, 378
Muslim society, 119, 121, 123, 243
mutilation, 286, 313
mysticism, 21, 60, 132, 349
mystification, 342

NAACP, 305
Napoleon, 202
narcissism, 243
nationalism, 25, 26, 56, 71, 116, 161, 195, 296, 299, 371
nation-state, 26, 45, 85, 86, 88, 91, 103, 144, 161, 186, 192, 205, 224, 226, 254, 267, 292–295, 299, 302, 345
neo-Islamic, 192, 193
neopatriarchy, 299
Nidal, Abu, 200
Niebuhr, Reinhold, 178
Nietzsche, 354
nine archetypal relationships, 76, 121, 235–267, 325
Noah, 111, 342

orthodoxy, 130
orthopraxis, 124

Pagels, Elaine, 77, 113, 114, 130, 133, 213, 342, 348, 364
Palestine, 107, 109, 128, 130, 200, 295, 368, 376
paradigm, 3, 51, 163, 224, 244, 251
partial lords, 97, 99
partial self, 144, 157, 346, 350
partial ways of life, 82, 84, 209, 385
paternalistic, 306
patriarchy, 63, 143, 299, 301, 312
patriotism, 308
personal face, 1, 20, 47, 50, 63, 65, 79, 80, 81, 86, 88, 90, 93, 95, 97, 98, 105, 109, 111, 125, 170, 210, 212, 218, 226, 306, 328, 331, 332, 350, 357, 361

pilgrims, 84
plurality, 264, 297
political act, 44, 361, 391
political face, 1, 20, 79, 81, 84, 87, 88, 92, 95, 98, 170, 210, 230, 272, 279, 303, 306, 312, 321, 328, 361, 372, 382, 390
politics of uncritical loyalty, 361
politics, 10, 25, 45, 47, 48, 61, 64, 68, 82, 84, 86, 95, 106, 110, 142, 143, 146, 154, 170, 183, 184, 193, 196, 205, 216, 221–223, 228, 231, 237, 243, 274, 281, 299–300, 305, 308–309, 313, 345, 349, 355–356, 361, 387, 391
possessive love, 40
postmodernism, 354
poststructuralism, 354
prejudice, 148, 182, 245, 305
priesthood, 120
primacy, 222
Protestant, 113, 116, 130, 134, 138, 249, 301, 341, 342, 349, 365, 379
pseudo-emanation, 37, 49, 172, 173, 177, 193, 194, 207, 210, 240, 258, 283
psyche, 93, 184, 207

rationalism, 193
rebellion, 20–35, 44, 51–57, 72, 73, 97, 106, 115, 119, 123, 137–170, 172–173, 184–187, 190, 204–205, 209, 225, 252, 254, 255, 257, 260, 264, 283, 287, 292, 302, 314, 344, 346, 364, 365, 373, 389
rebirth, 114, 368
redemption, 180, 377
re-formation, 26, 69, 70, 71, 72, 73, 106, 115, 118, 138, 172, 188, 226, 255, 261, 284, 367
regain, 58, 60, 125, 376
reification, 318
relationship of autonomy, 247–251, 254, 262, 272
relationship of buffering, 122–124, 244–247, 254, 256, 261, 265, 279, 284, 369
relationship of deformation, 239, 240, 242, 258, 259, 263
relationship of direct exchange, 245–247, 254, 262
relationship of emanation, 18, 122, 238–241, 246, 254, 259, 260, 275, 329, 344
relationship of incoherence, 243, 245, 252–258, 260, 272, 273, 280, 315, 329, 357
relationship of isolation, 242–244
relationship of subjection, 241–242, 261
relationship of transformation, 259–263, 264, 280, 335

religion, 3, 42, 51, 70, 80, 88–89, 98, 112, 129, 138–140, 148, 160, 181, 193, 205, 243, 248, 261, 290, 295, 299, 301, 307–308, 337, 370, 371, 375
renew, 1, 2, 4, 10, 17, 32, 38, 40, 43–44, 68, 71, 73, 75, 109, 118, 142, 145–146, 152, 161, 166, 190, 198, 218, 239, 246, 264, 277, 280, 293, 297, 305, 328, 359, 363, 371, 374–375, 389, 390–391
repentance, 20, 344
repertory, 9, 235, 246, 252, 260, 264, 265, 266, 267, 272, 279, 280, 284, 326, 369, 381
repression, 4, 11, 20–22, 26, 37, 41, 49, 63–64, 76, 88, 97, 168, 209–210, 214, 225, 229, 349, 361–362, 365, 373, 386, 388–389
revolution, 12, 25, 41, 42, 72, 200, 212, 223–224, 226, 236, 237, 259, 261, 298, 355
rituals, 26, 118, 134, 244, 284, 289, 292, 294, 296, 298, 303, 361, 369
romantic love, 8, 26, 50, 54, 76, 161–162, 277–288

sacred face, 1, 7, 11, 13, 20, 26, 29, 38, 40, 55, 65, 68, 75, 76, 79, 87–90, 97–98, 146, 165, 170, 210, 218, 227, 270, 273, 306, 328–339, 347, 350, 353, 356, 361, 368
sacred stories, 61
Sadat, Anwar, 42
Satan, 63, 130, 147, 178–179, 189, 193, 196, 213–214, 258, 342, 346
Scholem, Gershom Gerhard, 132–133, 293, 367–368, 372
separation, 139, 146, 163, 219, 252, 319
shame, 26, 125, 163, 209, 285, 286, 362, 373
Shiite, 172, 299, 343
Socrates, 12, 35, 80, 174, 349
soul, 26, 51, 58, 61, 64, 85, 114, 132, 135, 160, 278, 342, 348, 365, 373, 378, 379
spiritual, 10, 39, 59, 89, 94, 126, 253, 370
Stalinism, 195
stereotype, 244, 290, 301, 332, 371, 377
story of capitalism, 150–170, 333
story of democracy, 309
strategies of transformation, 266, 309, 391
subjection, 123, 124, 190, 209, 241–248, 250, 253, 254, 256, 259, 261, 263–265, 279, 284, 312, 317, 329, 341, 369
submission, 122, 126, 172, 329, 344
subversion, 188, 314, 371
Sufis, 133, 298, 343, 348, 370, 371

suicide, 23, 25, 163, 173, 184, 189, 211, 254, 283, 318, 345, 380
Sunni, 30, 124, 299
supernatural, 10, 97
suppression, 21, 22, 41, 49, 76, 131, 138, 168, 208, 209, 225, 229, 362, 365, 386
surrender, 119, 121, 183, 202, 287, 298, 340, 347
symbol, 18, 23, 34, 51, 53, 55, 58, 60, 63, 68, 71, 79, 116, 132, 133, 146, 147, 173, 178, 179, 192, 193, 254, 256, 279, 283, 285, 293, 304, 306, 319, 339, 346, 367, 370
sympathy, 45, 153, 163
synchronicity, 66
systems, 6, 23, 29, 54, 66, 355, 356

taboo, 20, 51
talent, 44, 65, 90, 121, 161, 282, 330, 391
Talmud, 30, 117, 343
temptation, 9, 40, 74, 128, 152, 257
terrorism and deformation, 170, 200, 201, 220, 383
testament, 45, 113, 377
theology, 38, 44, 213, 312, 365, 370, 379
theory of transformation, 1, 3, 12, 64, 69, 74, 88, 105, 131, 171, 176, 236, 237, 257, 269, 307, 309, 325, 349–358, 365, 390, 392
tolerance, 131, 148, 192, 256, 302, 306, 361, 377
totalitarianism, 148, 192, 193, 195, 196, 198, 199, 200, 213
traditional, 2, 42, 130, 192, 239, 312, 320
tragedy, 170, 178, 193, 274, 374
transforming love, 76, 277–288, 316–317
tyranny, 123, 147, 223

uncritical loyalty, 361
undifferentiated, 340, 347

victim, 31, 170, 184, 212, 215, 350, 391
violence, 11, 53, 61, 67, 77, 95, 98, 131, 158, 166, 170, 175, 178, 184, 192, 204, 207, 208, 209, 214, 222, 228, 242, 295, 318, 359, 375, 380, 386, 387
virgin, 64, 243, 312, 379
virtue, 2, 5, 7, 10, 19, 90, 93, 129, 134, 359, 370, 371, 384, 389, 390

war and deformation, 198, 201–205, 292–295, 297–299, 305, 319, 377
way of life of deformation, 171–220, 383, 388
way of life of emanation, 103–136, 192, 290, 295, 373
way of life of incoherence, 137–170, 193, 300, 381
way of life of transformation, 221–231, 389
wealth, 41, 42, 54, 56, 142, 151, 157, 158, 207, 220, 224, 376, 381, 383, 385
westernization, 187, 221
wholeness, 4, 5, 8, 9, 11, 29, 60, 75, 81, 82, 89, 96, 98, 136, 145, 149, 150, 161, 162, 168, 191, 195, 208, 262, 266, 273, 277, 280, 281, 285, 301, 317, 325, 335, 347, 348, 361, 375
wisdom, 31, 40, 51, 87, 113, 120, 125, 135, 227, 262, 312, 313, 318, 349, 360, 370
wounded self, 282

Yahweh, 199, 342, 377